Artist Listing

About a Girl

Words and Music by Kurt Cobain

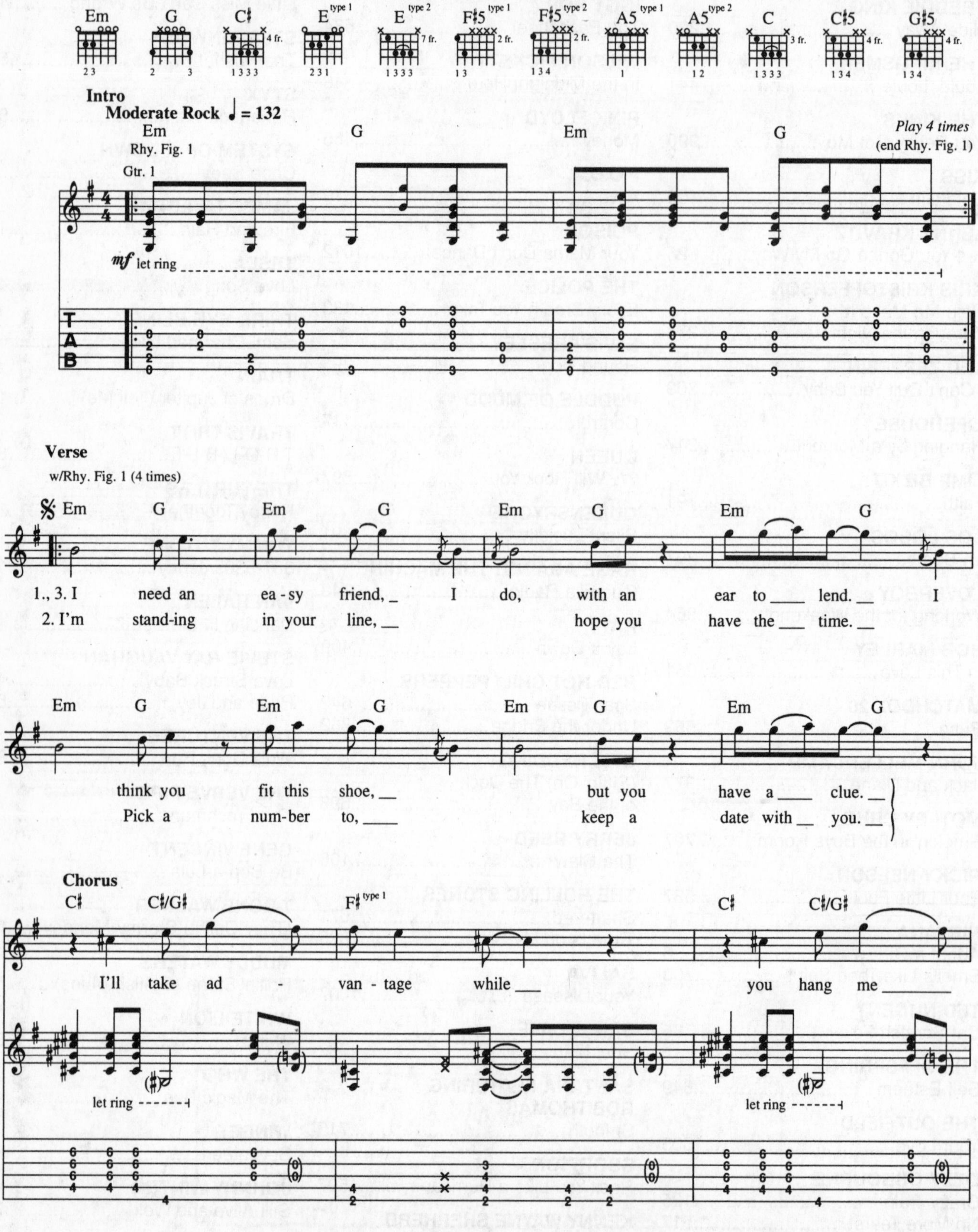

Em G C♯ E type 1 E type 2 F♯5 type 1 F♯5 type 2 A5 type 1 A5 type 2 C C♯5 G♯5

Intro

Moderate Rock ♩ = 132

Em G Em G

Rhy. Fig. 1

Gtr. 1

Play 4 times

(end Rhy. Fig. 1)

mf let ring

Verse

w/Rhy. Fig. 1 (4 times)

Em G Em G Em G Em G

1., 3. I need an ea - sy friend, I do, with an ear to lend. I

2. I'm stand-ing in your line, hope you have the time.

Em G Em G Em G Em G

think you fit this shoe, but you have a clue.

Pick a num-ber to, keep a date with you.

F♯5 type 1
To Coda 𝄌 E type 1
A5 type 1
C
out to dry, ___ but I can't see you ev - ery night ___ (for)
w/Rhy. Fig. 1 (2 times)
substitute w/Rhy. Fill 1 (2nd time)
Em G Em G Em G Em G
free.
Guitar Solo
(Em) (G) (Em) (G) (Em) (G)
let ring
(Em) (G) (Em) (G) (Em) (G)
let ring
let ring
Rhy. Fill 1
Gtr. 1
Em G
let ring

(Em)
(G)
(Em)
(G)
C♯5
G♯5
F♯5type 2
C♯5
G♯5
F♯5type 2
A.H.
(8va)
A.H.
E5
A5type 2
C5
Em
G
Em
G

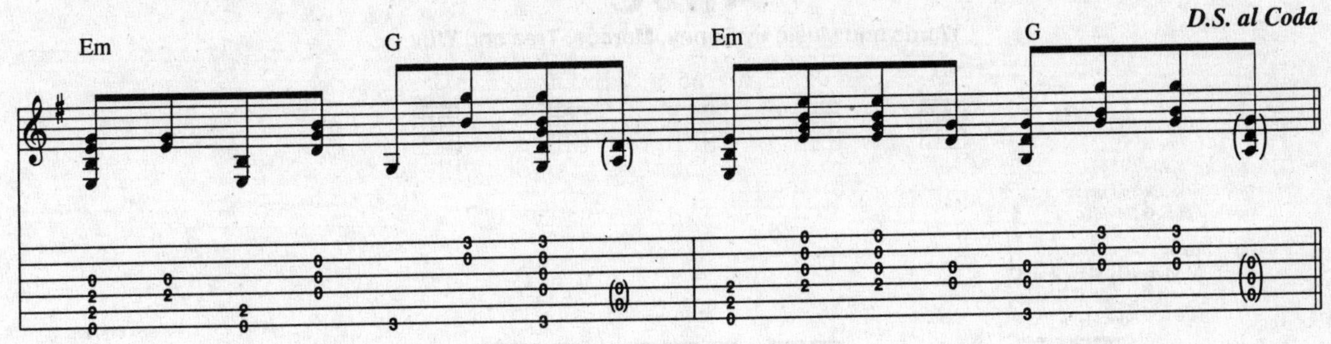
D.S. al Coda
Em
G
Em
G

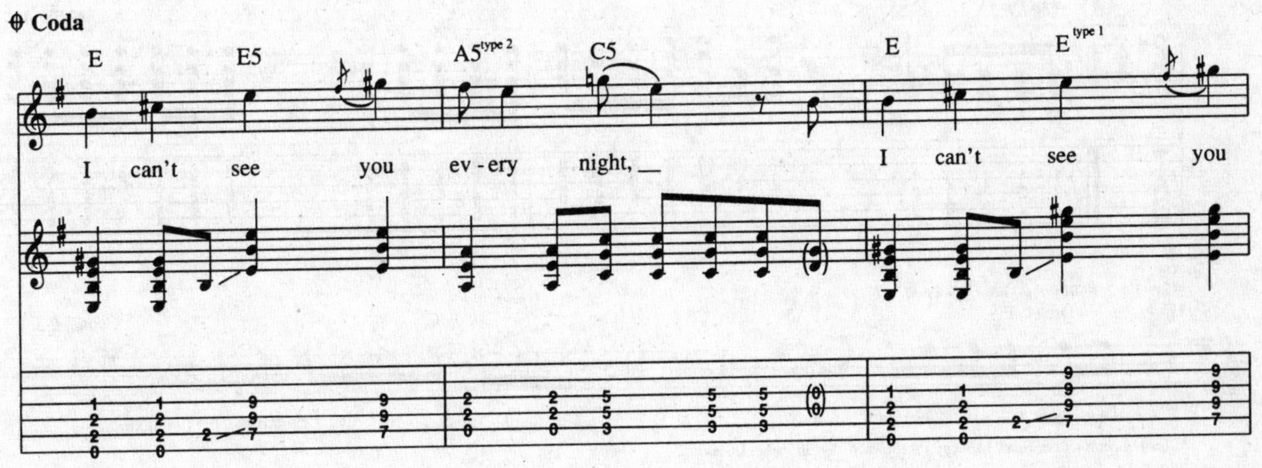
Coda
E
E5
A5type 2
C5
E
Etype 1
I can't see you ev - ery night,
I can't see you

A5type 2
C5
ev - 'ry night
(for)

w/Rhy. Fig. 1
Em G Em G
w/Rhy. Fig. 1
Em G Em G
play 3 times
E
free.

Alive

Words and Music by Sonny, Marcos, Traa and Wuv

Chorus
C5
D5
E5
Rhy. Fig. 3
(cont. in notation)
I, I feel so a - live for the ver - y first time.
Rhy. Fig. 3A
G5
D5
G5
I can't de - ny you. I feel so a - live.
End Rhy. Figs. 3 & 3A
Gtrs. 1 & 2
Gtrs. 1 & 2: w/ Rhy. Figs. 3 & 3A
C
Csus2/4
D5
E5
Esus2
I, I feel so a - live for the ver - y first time.
(I feel so a - live
To Coda 1
To Coda 2
G5
D5
G5
for the ver - y first time.)
And I think I can fly.
*w/ echo set for quarter-note regeneration w/ 3 repeats
Verse
Gtrs. 1 & 2: w/ Rhy. Figs. 1 & 1A (3 times)
E
Dsus4 E
A5
C5
Csus2
C
Csus2 G5
2. Sun - shine up - on my face. A new song for me to sing.
(Sun - shine up - on my face.
Tell the world how I feel in - side e - ven though it might cost me ev - 'ry-thing.
Tell the world how I feel in - side...)

E Dsus4 E A5 C5 Csus2 C Csus2 G5
Spoken: Now that I know this, so be-yond, I can't hold this. I could nev-er turn my back a-way.
Gtrs. 1 & 2: w/ Rhy. Figs. 2 & 2A
D.S. al Coda 1
E Dsus4 E A5 C5 Csus2 C G5
Now that I see you, I could nev-er look a-way.
(Now that I see you...)
Coda 1
Bridge
Gtr. 2 tacet
Gtr. 1
2fr
dim.
Riff A
Gtr. 3 (dist.)
End Riff A
let ring
w/ chorus & heavy reverb
Gtr. 1 tacet
Em
Riff B
8va
End Riff B
Gtr. 3: w/ Riff A
Spoken: And now that I know you, I could nev-er turn my back a-way.
1.
And now that I see you, I could nev-er look a-way.
8va
Gtr. 3
Harm.
2.
Gtr. 3: w/ Riff B
D.S. al Coda 2
And now that I see you, I be-lieve no mat-ter what they say.

Coda 2
Gtrs. 1 & 2: w/ Rhy. Figs. 3 & 3A (1st 3 meas.)
C
Csus2/4
D5
E5
Esus2
I, I feel so a - live for the ver - y first time.
(I feel so a - live
Gtr. 3
1.
G5
D5
G5
Rhy. Fill 1
End Rhy. Fill 1
Gtrs. 1 & 2
for the ver - y first time.)
(For the ver - y first time.)
And I think I can fly.
8va
loco
P.S.
2.
G5
D5
Gtrs. 1 & 2: w/ Rhy. Fill 1
G5
N.C.
for the ver - y first time.)
And I think I can fly.
And I think I can fly.
Outro
Gtr. 3 tacet
E5
D5 E5
Rhy. Fig. 4
End Rhy. Fig. 4
Gtr. 1
Gtr. 2
Rhy. Fig. 4A
End Rhy. Fig. 4A
*w/ echo repeats
Gtrs. 1 & 2: w/ Rhy. Figs. 4 & 4A

All Right Now

Words and Music by Paul Rodgers and Andy Fraser

Gtr. 1: w/ Rhy. Fig. 2, 2 1/2 times
A D A5 Dadd4 D A5
"Hey, now, what is this? Now, ba - by, may - be, may - be she's in need of a kiss." I said - a,
"Look, what's your game, ba - by? Are you try'n' to put me in shame?" I said - a,
A D A5 Dadd4 D A5
"Hey, uh-huh, what's your name, ba - by? May - be we can see things the same. Now don't you
"Slow, don't go so fast. Don't you think that love can last?" She said,
Gtr. 1: w/ Rhy. Fill 1, 2nd time
Gtr. 1: w/ Rhy. Fill 3, 3rd time
Gtr. 1: w/ Rhy. Fill 2, 2nd & 3rd times
A D A5 Dadd4 D A5
wait or hes - i - tate. Let's move be - fore they raise the park - ing rate." Ow!
"Love? Lord a - bove. Oo. Now you're try'n' to trick me in love."
Gtr. 1
Chorus
A5 G5 D A5
All right now. Ba - by, it's all right now.
Gtrs. 1 & 2
Rhy. Fig. 3
End Rhy. Fig. 3
simile on repeat
To Coda 1
To Coda 2
A5 G5 D A5
All right now. Ba - by, it's all right now, woh.
(cont. in slash, 3rd time)
Rhy. Fill 1
Gtr. 1
steady gliss.
Rhy. Fill 2
Gtr. 1
Rhy. Fill 3
Gtr. 1
T
A
B

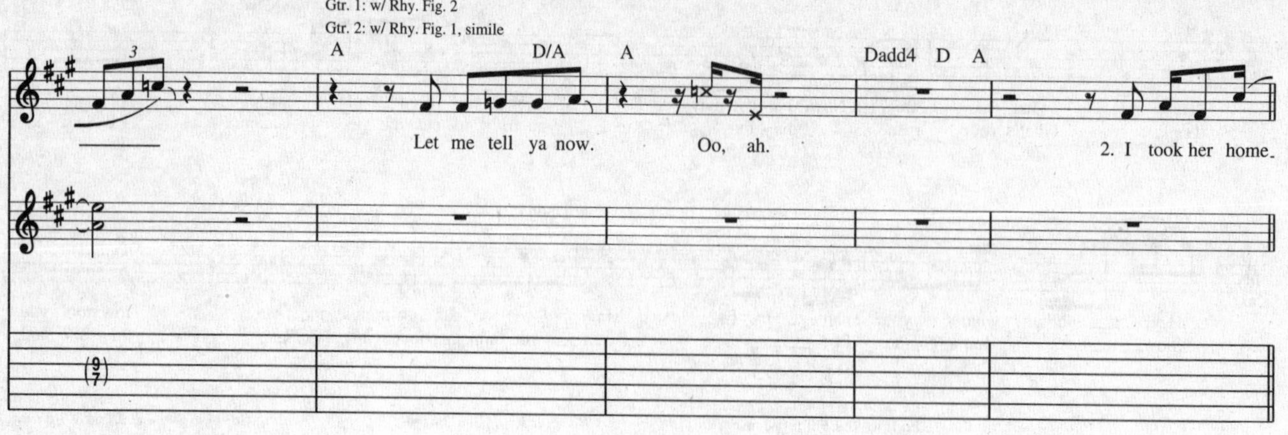
Gtr. 1: w/ Rhy. Fig. 2
Gtr. 2: w/ Rhy. Fig. 1, simile
A
D/A
A
Dadd4 D A
Let me tell ya now.
Oo, ah.
2. I took her home.

Coda 1
D
A5
Guitar Solo
Gtrs. 1 & 2
right now.
Yeah, it's all right now.
Mmm,
Gtr. 3 (dist.)
(cont. in slash)

Gtrs. 1 & 2 tacet
N.C.

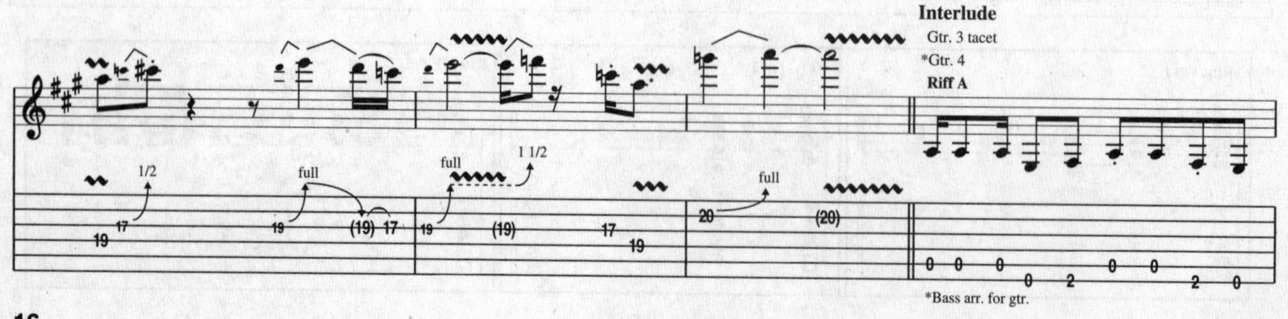
Interlude
Gtr. 3 tacet
*Gtr. 4
Riff A
*Bass arr. for gtr.

Guitar Solo
Gtr. 4: w/ Riff A
Gtr. 4: w/ Riff A, 16 times
Rhy. Fig. 4
End Rhy. Fig. 4
*Gtr. 5
End Riff A
Gtr. 3
let ring
*Piano arr. for gtr.
Gtr. 5: w/ Rhy. Fig. 4, 15 times
full
1/2
8va

Bridge

Gtr. 2: w/ Rhy. Fig. 1, 2 times, simile

Gtr. 3 tacet

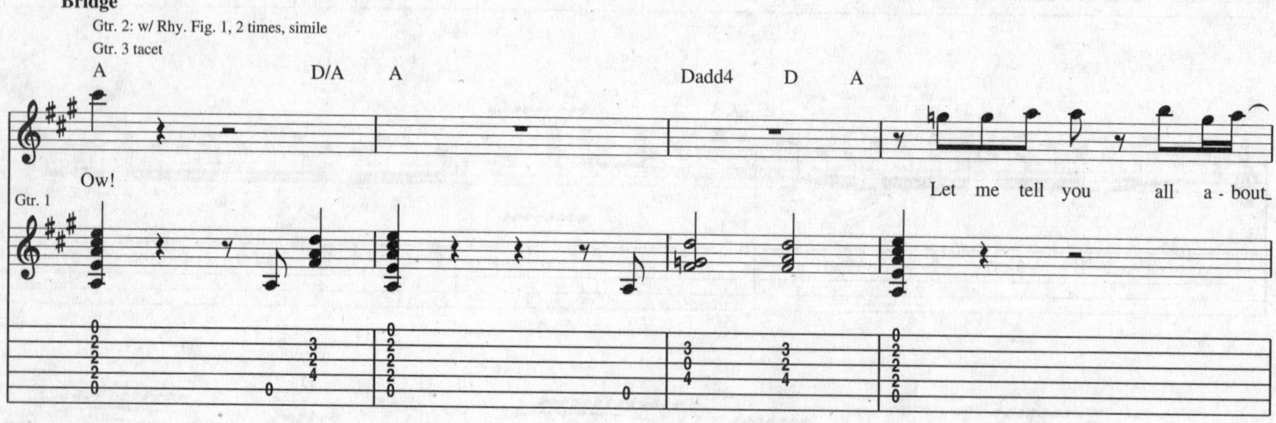

D.S. al Coda 2

(2nd lyrics)

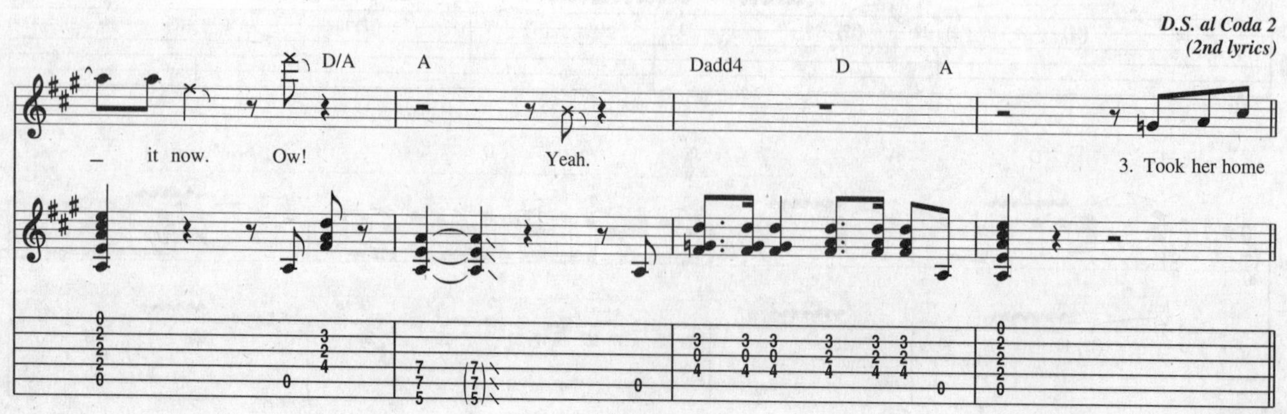

Coda 2
Outro-Chorus
Gtrs. 1 & 2: w/ Rhy. Fig. 3, 3 1/2 times
Bkgd. Voc.: w/ Voc. Fig. 1, 6 times
A5
A5
G5
D
A5
Gtrs. 1 & 2
All right now. Ba - by, it's all right.
G5
D
A5
Yeah. All right now. Ba - by, ba - by, ba - by, it's all
Gtr. 1: w/ Rhy. Fill 4
G5
D
A5
right. All, all right now. Yeah, it's all right, it's all right, it's all
Gtrs. 1 & 2: w/ Rhy. Fig. 3, 1st 2 meas.
G5
D IV
A5
Gtrs. 1 & 2
right, yeah, huh. All right now. Ba - by, it's all right now.
Gtrs. 1 & 2: w/ Rhy. Fig. 3, 1 1/2 times
Gtr. 1: w/ Rhy. Fill 5
G5
D
A5
Yeah. We're so hap - py to - geth - er. Ow! It's all right, it's all right, it's all right. Ev-'ry-thing's all right.
G5
D IV
A5
Gtrs. 1 & 2
Yeah. Woo!
Rhy. Fill 4
(G5)
D
3
7fr
Gtr. 1
Rhy. Fill 5
(G5)
Gtr. 1
Voc. Fig. 1
Bkgd. voc.
(All right now. Ba - by, it's all right now.)

Androgyny

Words and Music by Duke Erikson, Shirley Ann Manson, Steve Marker and Butch Vig

Asus2
Dm
F
G/F
Out of the tree, go pick a plum.
Why can't we all just get a - long?
F
D
Gtrs. 1 & 2 tacet
E5
Chorus
Em
Oh.
Boys in the girls' room,
(Boys.
Gtr. 1
Riff B
End Riff B
Gtr. 4 (elec.)
Riff C
w/ dist.
Gtr. 2
Riff B1
End Riff B1
Gtr. 5 (elec.)
Riff C1
w/ dist.
G6
Cmaj7
Em
girls in the men's room,
Girls.
You free your mind in your an - drog - y - ny.
End Riff C
End Riff C1

Gtrs. 4 & 5: w/ Riffs C & C1 (1st 3 meas.)
G6
Cmaj7
Fmaj7
Boys in the par - lor, they're get - tin' hard - er. I'll free your mind and your an - drog - y - ny.
Boys. Girls.)
2. No
Gtr. 1
15 (15) 13
Gtr. 2
7 (7) 5
Verse
Gtrs. 1 & 2: w/ Riffs A & A1 (3 times)
Asus2 Dm F G/F
sweet - er a taste that you could find than fruit hang - in' ripe up - on the vine. There's
nev - er been an oys - ter so di - vine, a riv - er deep that nev - er runs dry.
Gtr. 3: w/ Riff A2
(What-cha need? What-cha need? What-cha need? What-cha need? What-cha need? What-cha need? What-cha
need? What-cha need? What-cha need? What-cha need? What-cha need? What-cha need? What-cha need? What-cha need?)
The
birds and the bees, they hum a - long. Like treas - ure, they twin - kle in the sun.

Asus2
Dm
F
G/F
Get on board and have some fun, take what you need to turn you on.
Gtrs. 1 & 2: w/ Riffs B & B1
F
D
Oh.
Chorus
Gtrs. 4 & 5: w/ Riffs C & C1 (2 times)
Em
G6
Boys in the girls' room, girls in the men's room,
(Boys. Girls.
Cmaj7
Em
G6
You free your mind in your an - drog - y - ny. Boys in the par - lor,
Boys.
Cmaj7
Fmaj7
they're get - tin' hard - er. I'll free your mind, I'll free your mind, I'll free your mind, I'll free your…
Girls.)
Bridge
E♭
Fm
A♭
C♭
Be - hind closed doors and un - der stars, it does - n't mat - ter where you are.
(Boys, girls,
* Gtr. 6
mp
w/ fingers
* Kybd. arr. for gtr.
E♭
Fm
A♭
C♭
B7
Col - lect - in' jewels that catch your eyes, don't let a soul - mate pass you by.
boys, girls.)

Chorus
Gtrs. 4 & 5: w/ Riffs C & C1 (1 3/4 times)
Gtr. 6 tacet
Em G6 Cmaj7
Boys in the girls' room, girls in the men's room. You free your mind in your an -
Em G6 Cmaj7
drog - y - ny. Boys in the par - lor, they're get - tin' hard - er.
Gtrs. 4 & 5: w/ Riffs C & C1 (2 times)
Fmaj7 G6 Cmaj7
I'll free your mind, I'll free your mind. Boys in the girls' room, girls in the men's room.
Fmaj7 Em G6
You free your mind in your an - drog - y - ny. Boys in the par - lor,
Cmaj7 Fmaj7
they're get - tin' hard - er. I'll free your mind, I'll free your mind, I'll free your mind, I'll free your…
Outro
G5 C Fsus2 G5
(Boys, girls, boys, girls.)
Gtr. 1
Gtr. 6

Are You Gonna Go My Way

Words by Lenny Kravitz
Music by Lenny Kravitz and Craig Ross

G
So that's why you got to try.
So tell me why we got to die
Gtr. 2
Gtr. 1
*T = Thumb on 6th str.
2nd time, Gtr. 2: w/Fill 1
You got to breathe and have some fun.
and kill each oth - er one by one.
Fill 1
Gtr. 2

Gtr. 1: w/Riff B (2 times)
Gtr. 2 tacet
E
Though I'm not paid, I play this game. And I won't stop un - til I'm
We've got to hug and rub - a - dub. We got to dance and be in
done.
love.
Chorus
G6
**A/F♯
Spoken: But what I really want to know is...
*Gtrs. 1 & 2
*Two gtrs. arranged for one.
**bass plays F♯
E
D
E
G
E
Are you gon - na go my way?
1.
Interlude
Gtr. 1: w/Riff A1 (4 times)
Gtr. 2 tacet
Gtr. 2: w/Riff A2 (3 times)
G6
A/F♯
E
And I got to, got to know, yeah.

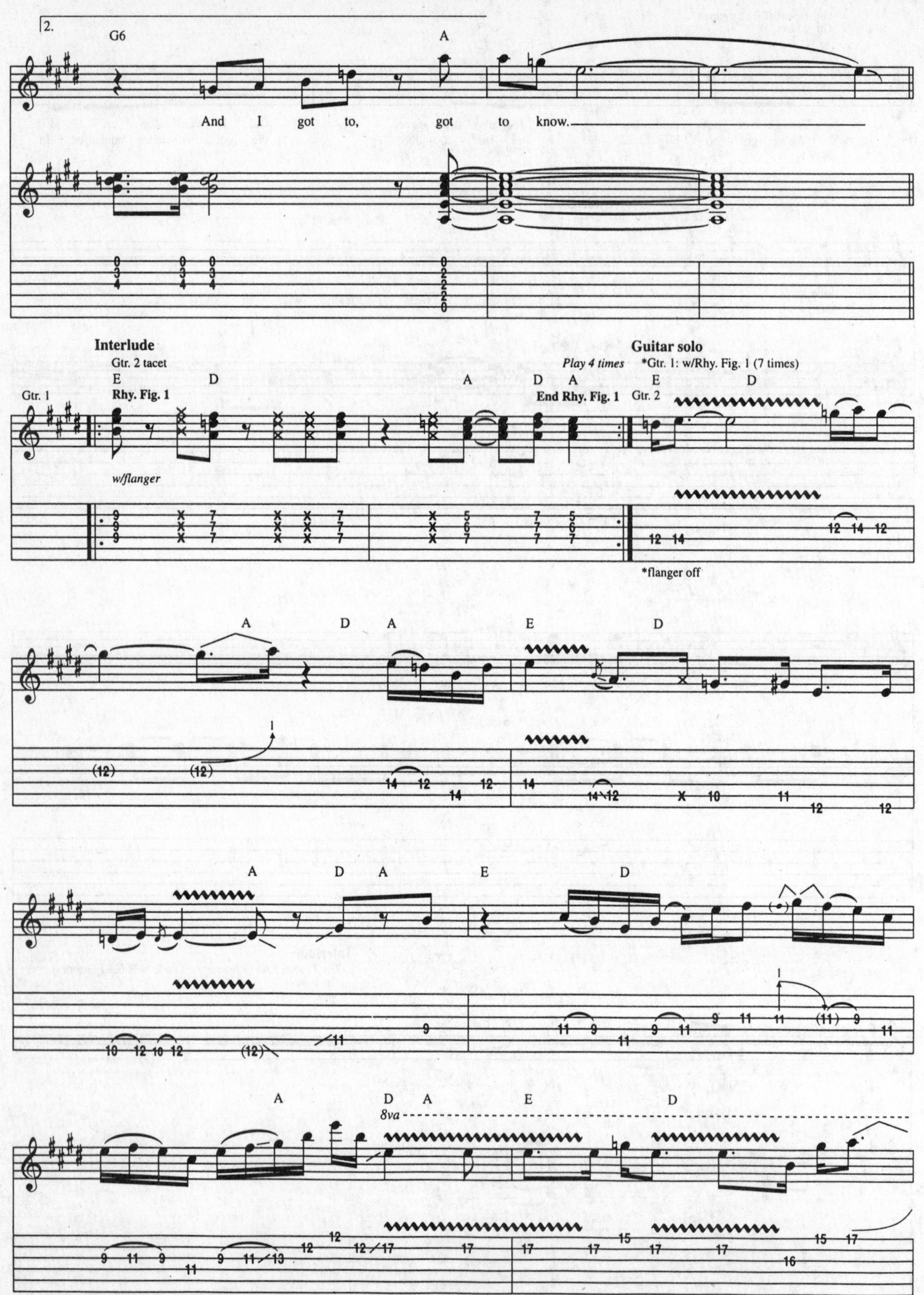
2.
G6
A
And I got to, got to know.
Interlude
Gtr. 2 tacet
E
D
A
D
A
Rhy. Fig. 1
End Rhy. Fig. 1
Gtr. 1
Play 4 times
w/flanger
Guitar solo
*Gtr. 1: w/Rhy. Fig. 1 (7 times)
Gtr. 2
*flanger off
8va

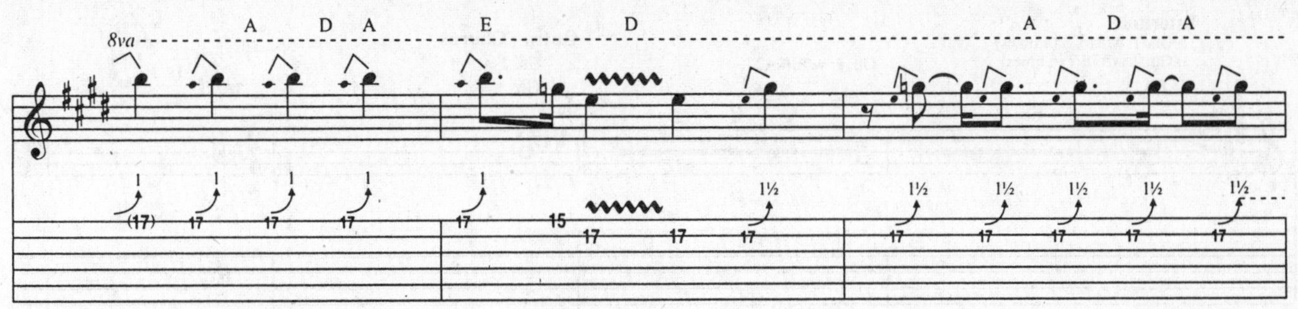
8va
A D A E D A D A

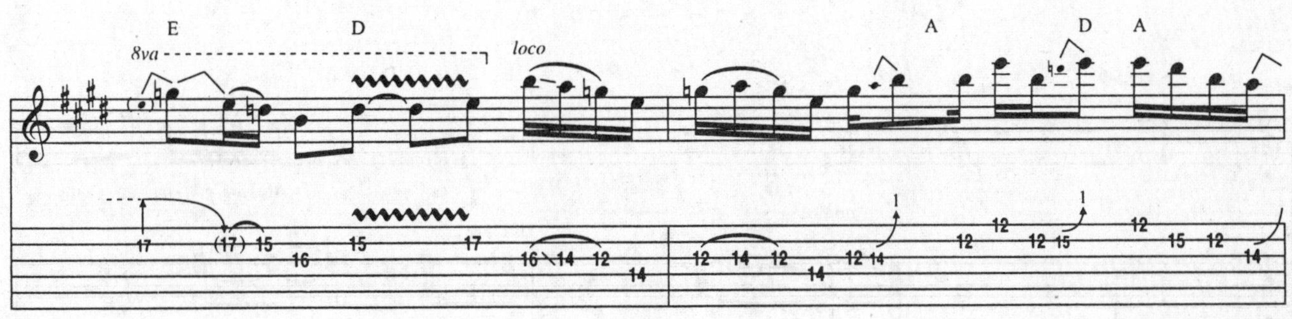
E D A D A
8va
loco

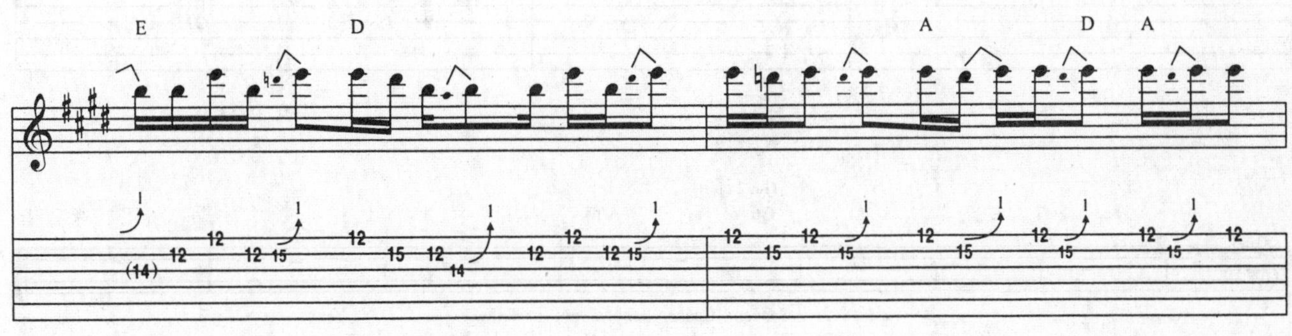
E D A D A

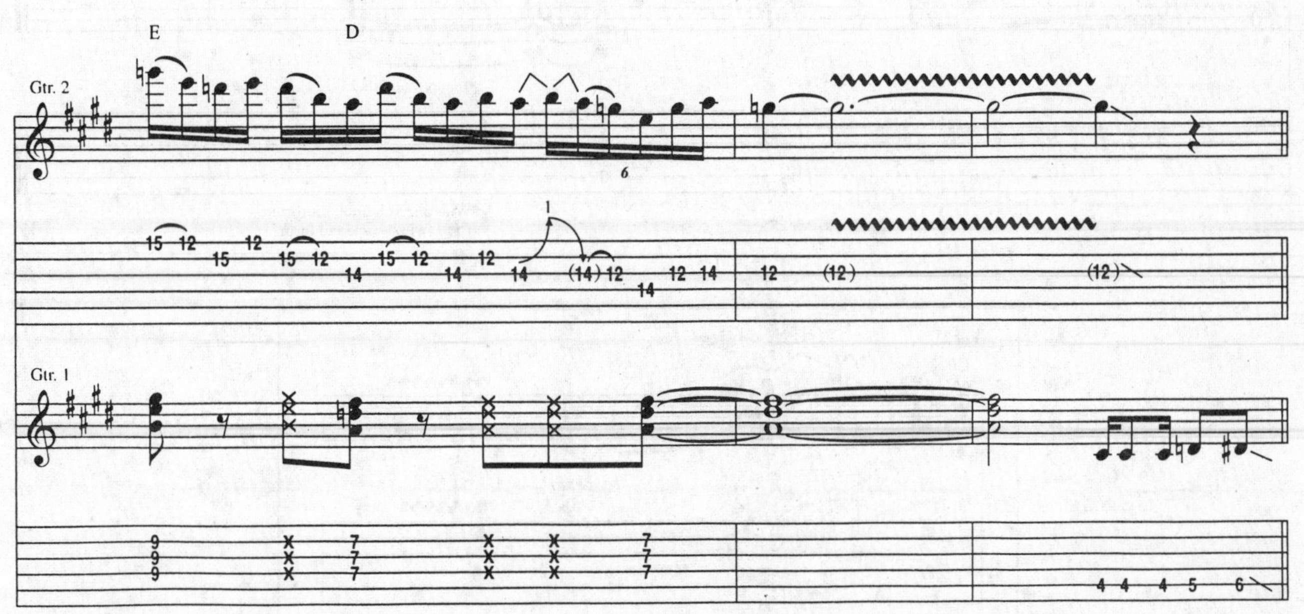
E D
Gtr. 2
Gtr. 1

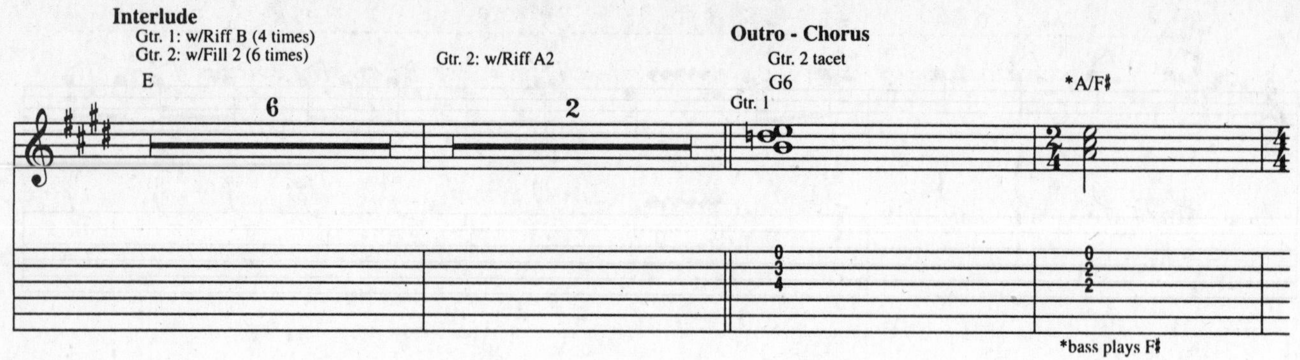
Interlude
Gtr. 1: w/Riff B (4 times)
Gtr. 2: w/Fill 2 (6 times)
E
6
Gtr. 2: w/Riff A2
2
Outro - Chorus
Gtr. 2 tacet
G6
Gtr. 1
*A/F♯
*bass plays F♯

G6
A/F♯
E D E
Are you gon - na go my
Gtrs. 1 & 2

G E
way?
Gtr. 2 tacet
G6
A/F♯
Spoken: 'Cause, baby, I got to know.
Yeah.
Gtr. 1
*toggle switch
*With one vol. knob set to zero, flick switch back and forth.

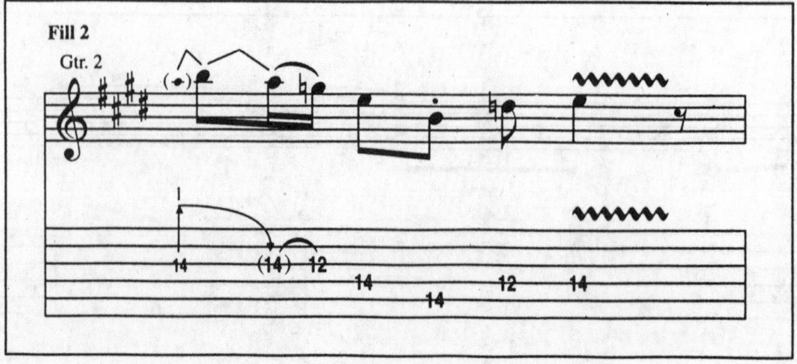
Fill 2
Gtr. 2

Barracuda

Words and Music by Roger Fisher, Nancy Wilson, Ann Wilson and Michael Derosier

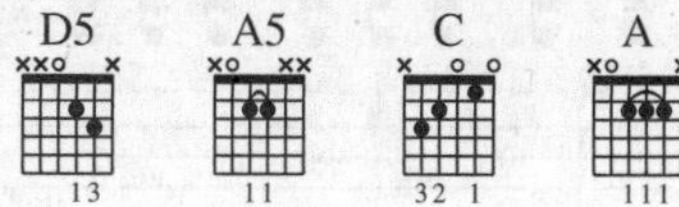

Intro

Moderately fast Rock ♩ = 132

E5 F#5 G5

Gtr. 1 (elec.)

8va

-1/2 -1/2

loco

f

Harm.

w/ bar

slight P.M.

-1/2 -1/2

T
A
B

2 0 2 0 2 0 2 0 2 0 2 0 2 0 2 0 2 0 2 0 2 0 2 0 2 0 2 0 2 0 2 0 2 0 2 0 2 0 2 0 2 0 2 0 4 2 5 3

(X X)

12 12

5 5 5 (5 5 5) (5 5 5)

12

E5 F#5 G5 G6 N.C.

Gtr. 2 (elec.) w/ dist. *f*

slight P.M.

Harm.

w/ bar

Gtr. 1 *divisi*

2 0 2 0 2 0 2 0 2 0 2 0 2 0 2 0 2 0 2 0 2 0 2 0 2 0 2 0 2 0 2 0 2 0 2 0 2 0 2 0 2 0 2 0 4 2 5 3

0 0 0 0 5 5 3

12 12 (12 12)

-1/2 -1 1/2

E5 F#5 G5

Gtr. 2

-1/2 -1/2 -1/2 -1/2 -1/2

slight P.M.

Harm.

3 3

w/ bar

-1/2 -1/2 -1/2 -1/2 -1/2

2 0 2 0 2 0 2 0 2 0 2 0 2 0 2 0 2 0 2 0 2 0 2 0 2 0 2 0 2 0 2 0 2 0 2 0 2 0 2 0 2 0 2 0 4 2 5 3

12

(12) (12) (12) (12) (12)

Gtr. 1

slight P.M.

Harm.

2 0 2 0 2 0 2 0 2 0 2 0 2 0 2 0 2 0 2 0 2 0 2 0 2 0 2 0 2 0 2 0 2 0 2 0 2 0 2 0 2 0 2 0 4 2 5 3

12 12 12

12

E5
F#5
G5
G6
slight P.M.
Harm.
w/ bar
Verse
1. So this ain't the end, I saw you a - gain
2. Back o - ver time we were all try - ing
to - day.
for free,
I had to turn my heart a - way.
you met the por - poise and me.
C5
C5/B
C5/A

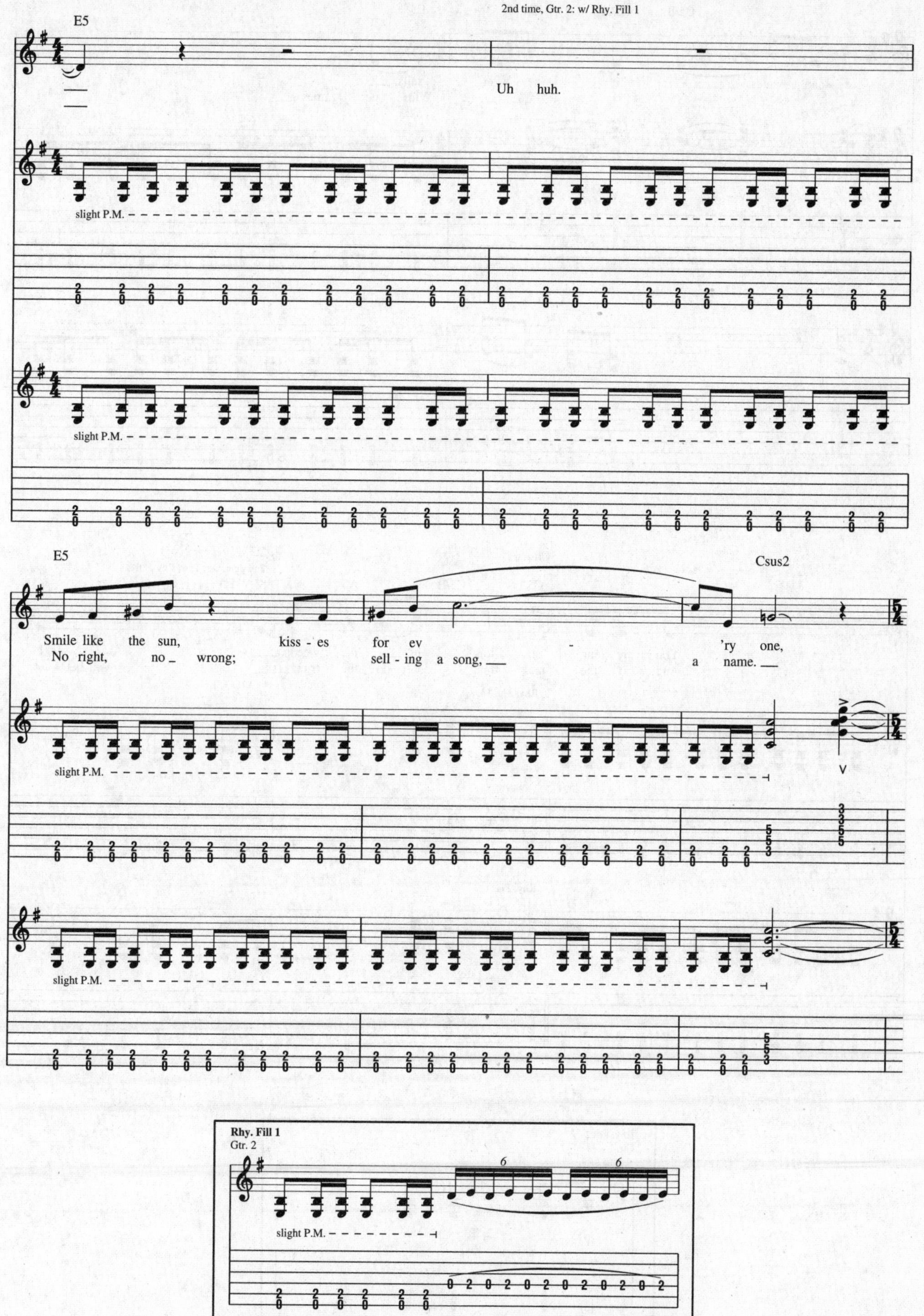
E5
2nd time, Gtr. 2: w/ Rhy. Fill 1
Uh huh.
slight P.M.
slight P.M.
E5
Csus2
Smile like the sun, kiss - es for ev - 'ry one,
No right, no wrong; sell - ing a song, a name.
slight P.M.
slight P.M.
Rhy. Fill 1
Gtr. 2
slight P.M.

C5/B
C5/A
G5
E5
and tales, it nev - er fails.
Whis - per games.

Chorus

2nd time, Gtr. 1: w/ Rhy. Fill 2
C5
C5/B
A5
E5
You ly - ing so low in the weeds. I
And if the real thing don't do the trick you bet - ter
Rhy. Fig. 1A
Rhy. Fig. 1

Rhy. Fill 2
Gtr. 1

C
Am
E5
D5
Rhy. Fig. 2
Gtr. 3 (acous.)
mp
bet you gon - na am - bush me.
You'd have me down, down, down,
make up some - thing quick.
You gon - na burn, burn, burn,
To Coda
Gtr. 3 tacet
N.C.
A5
End Rhy. Fig. 2
down on my knees,
now would - n't you, bar - ra - cu -
burn, burn it to the wick.
End Rhy. Fig. 1A
End Rhy. Fig. 1

E5
F#5 G5
da?
Oh.
slight P.M.
Harm.
w/ bar
E5
F#5 G5
G6
D.S. al Coda
slight P. M.
-1/2
-1 1/2

Coda
Gtr. 3 tacet
N.C.
E5
G5 A5 D5 E5
Ooh, bar - ra - cu - da.
Oh, yeah.
Gtrs. 1 & 2
Rhy. Fig. 3
slight P.M.
End Rhy. Fig. 3
Bridge
C
A
Rhy. Fig. 4A
End Rhy. Fig. 4A
Gtr. 3
"Sell me, sell you," the por-poise said. Dive down, deep down, save my head. You,
Gtr. 1
Riff A
End Riff A
Gtr. 2
Rhy. Fig. 4
End Rhy. Fig. 4

Gtrs. 1 & 2: w/ Rhy. Fig. 3
Gtr. 3 tacet
E5
G5 A5 D5 E5
G5 A5 D5 E5 C
Gtr. 1: w/ Riff A
Gtrs. 2 & 3: w/ Rhy. Fig. 4 & 4A
I think that you had the blues too. All that night
A
and all the next swam with - out look - ing back, made for the west - ern
E5
F#5 G5 A5
pools.
Sil - ly, sil - ly fools.
Gtrs. 1 & 2
Rhy. Fig. 5
End Rhy. Fig. 5
slight P.M.
Guitar Solo
Gtrs. 2 & 3: w/ Rhy. Fig. 4 & 4A
Gtr. 1
w/ chorus
Gtr. 2: w/ Rhy. Fig. 5 (2 times)
steady gliss.
w/ bar

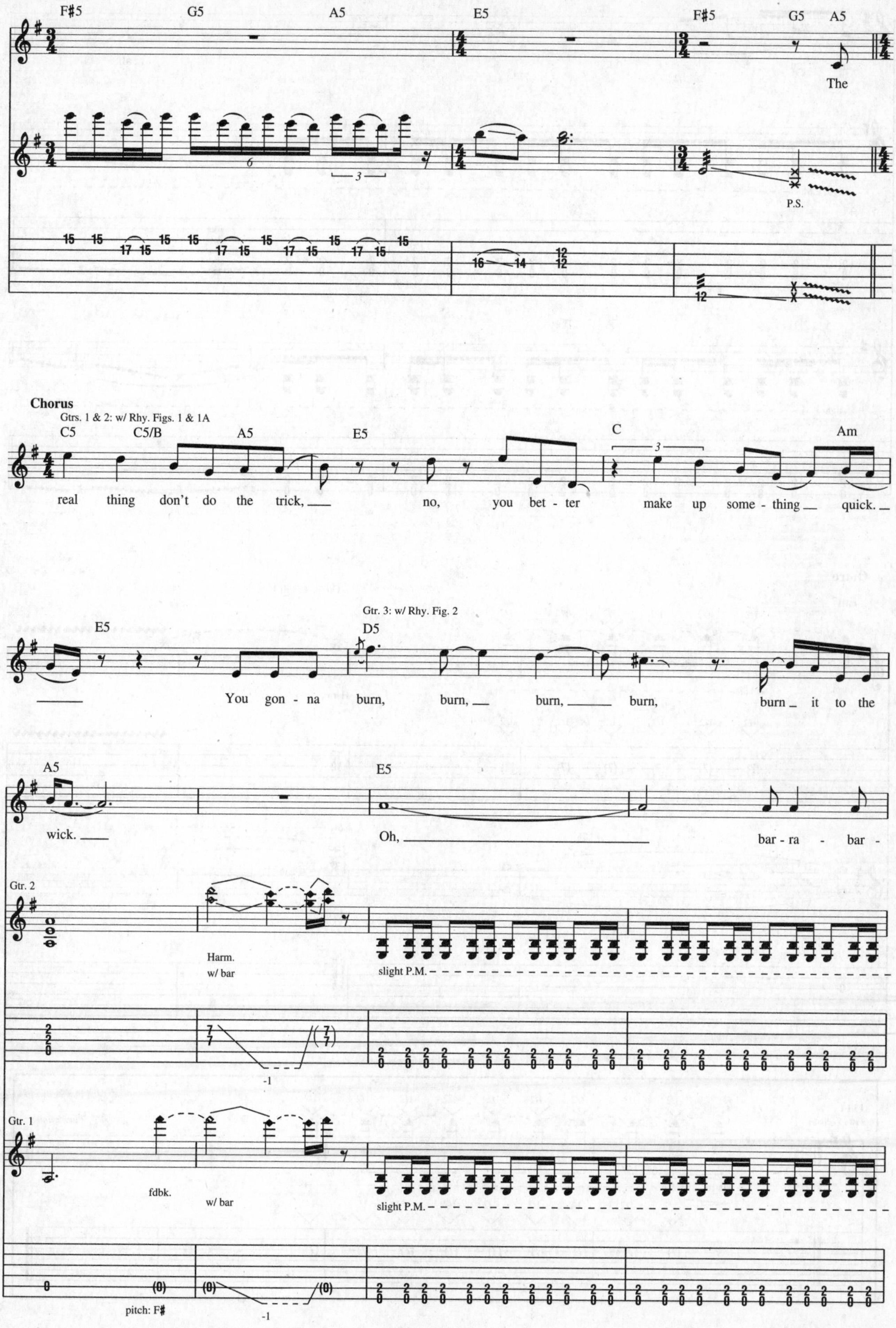

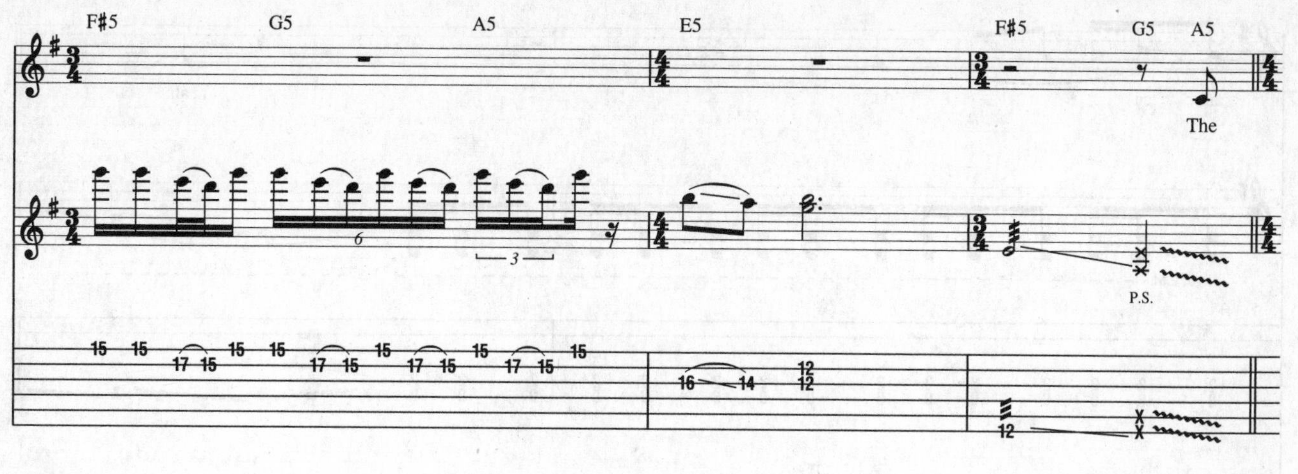

Gtr. 3: w/ Rhy. Fig. 2

E5 D5

You gon - na burn, burn, burn, burn, burn it to the

A5 E5

wick. Oh, bar - ra - bar -

Gtr. 2

Harm.

w/ bar

-1

slight P.M.

Gtr. 1

fdbk.

w/ bar

pitch: F#

-1

slight P.M.

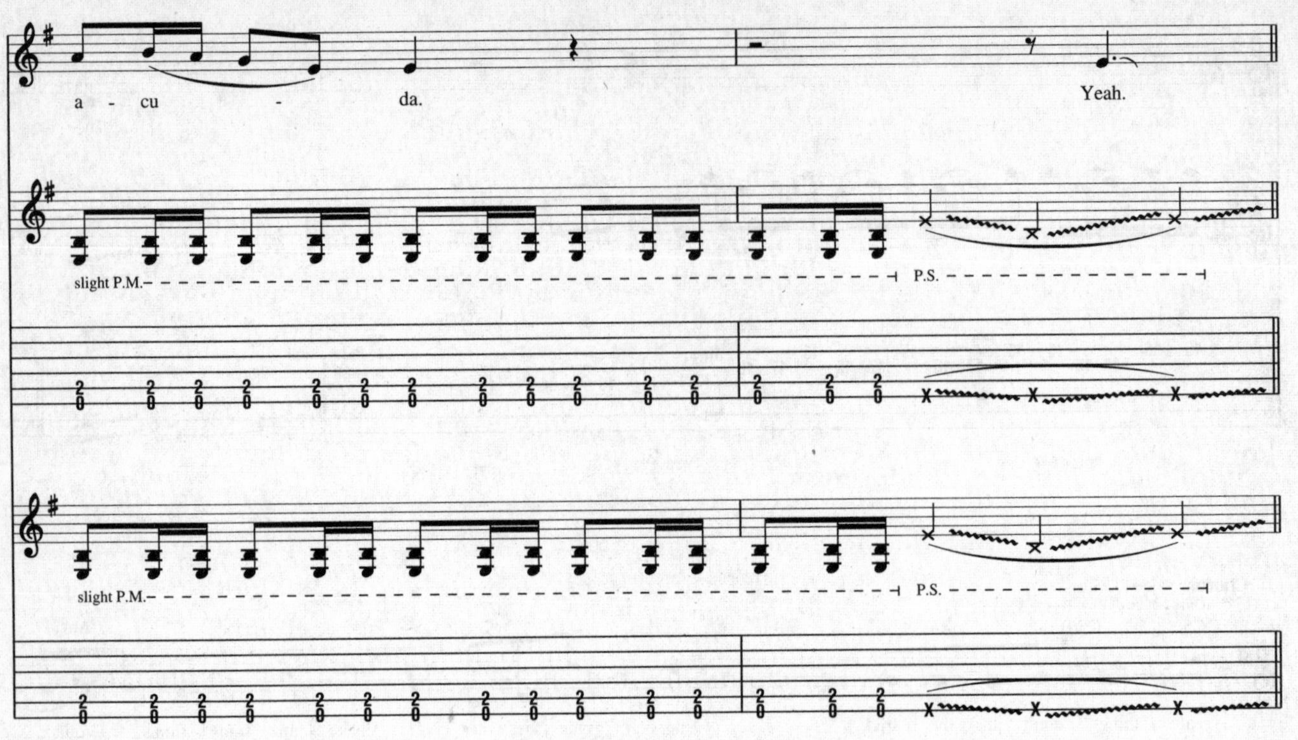
a - cu - da.
Yeah.
slight P.M.
P.S.
slight P.M.
P.S.

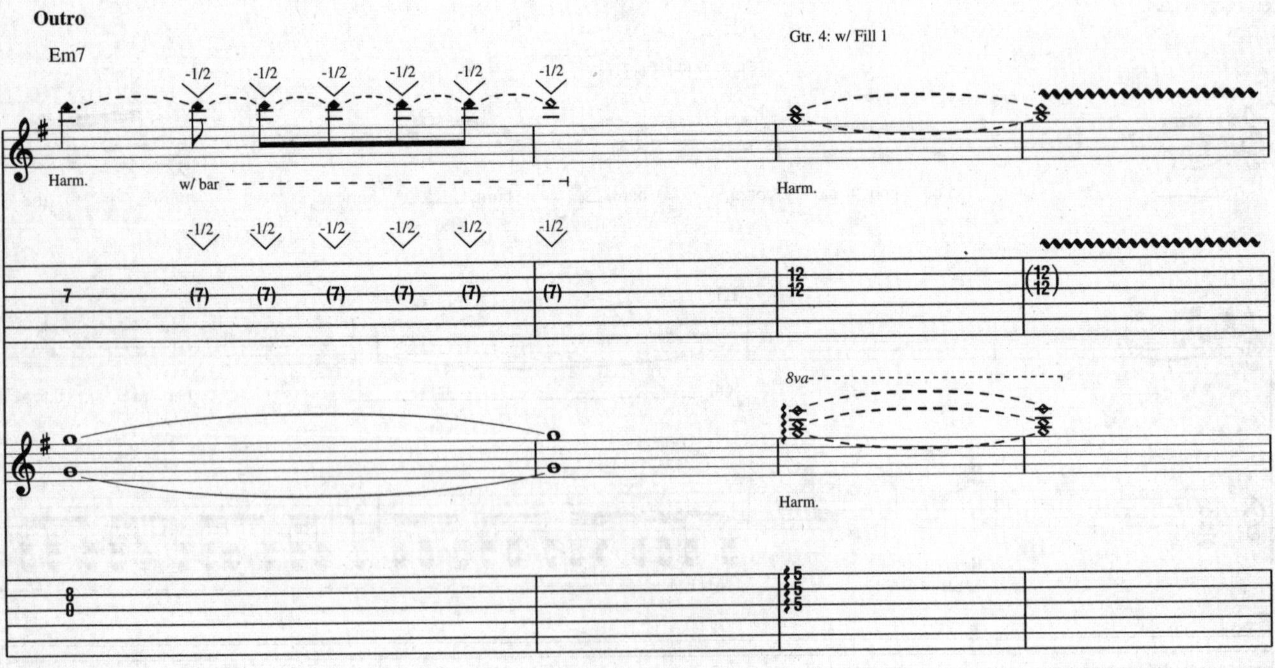
Outro
Em7
Gtr. 4: w/ Fill 1
-1/2
Harm.
w/ bar
Harm.
8va
Harm.

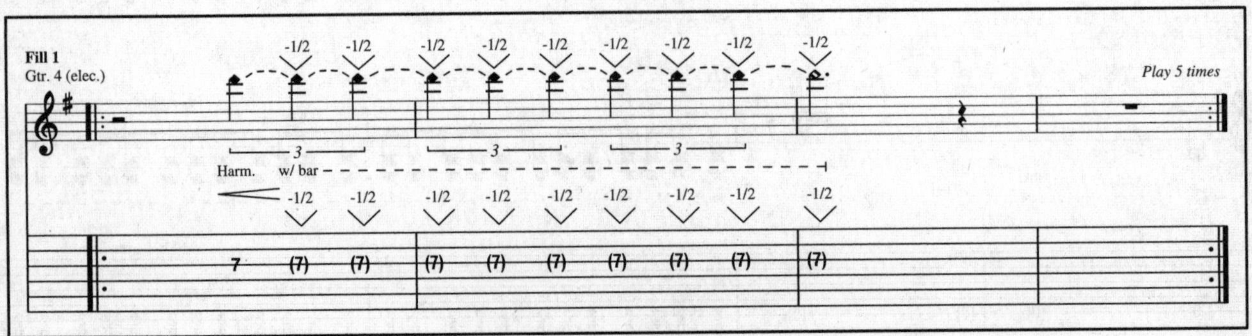
Fill 1
Gtr. 4 (elec.)
Play 5 times
-1/2
Harm.
w/ bar

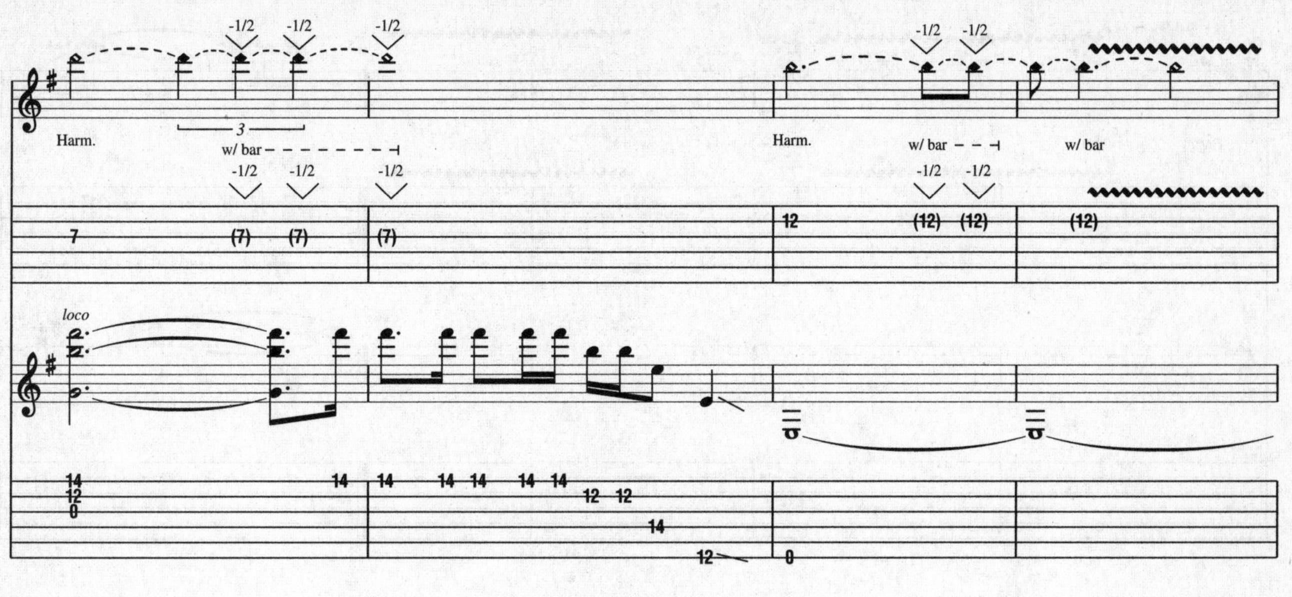
-1/2
-1/2
-1/2
Harm.
w/ bar
loco

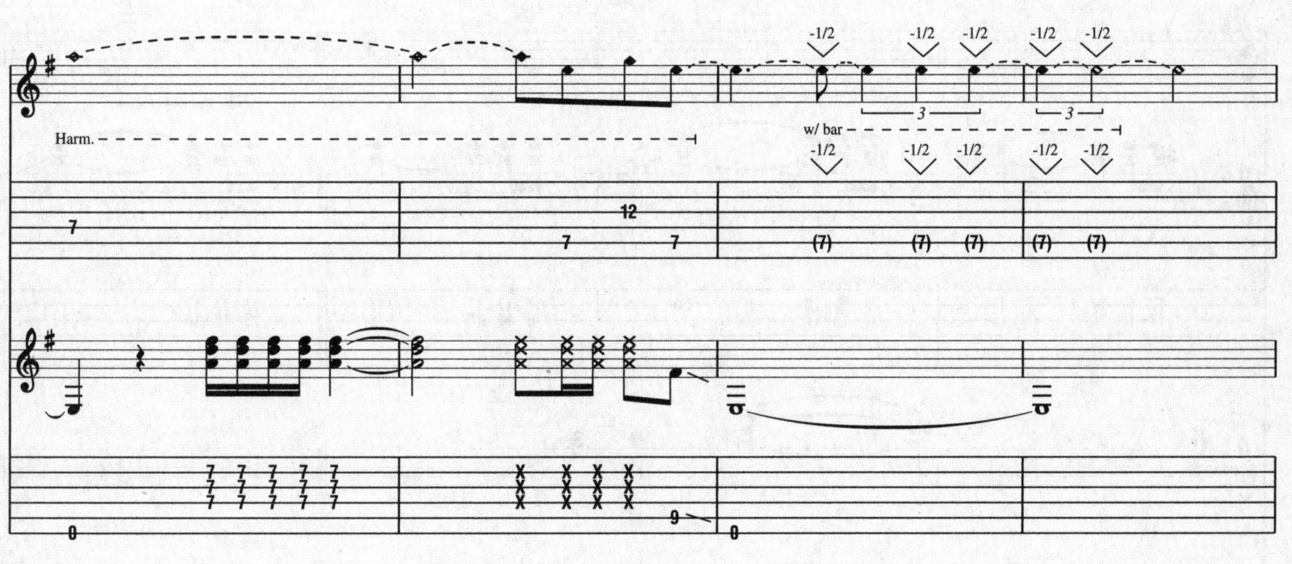
-1/2
Harm.
w/ bar

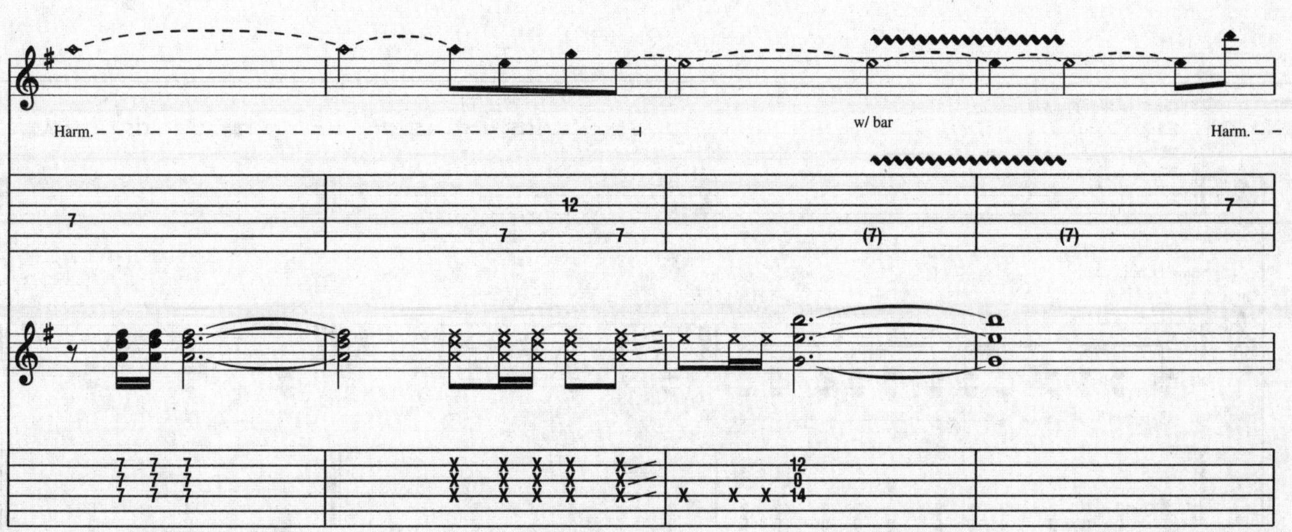
Harm.
w/ bar

Gtr. 1 tacet
Gtr. 2
Harm.
w/ bar
Harm.
w/ bar
Gtr. 1
1.
2.
Ooh,
Harm.
Gtr. 2: w/ Rhy. Fig. 5 (5 times)
E5
1.-4.
F♯5
G5
A5
5.
F♯5
G5
A5
oh.
* Sing 1st time
Gtr. 1
slight P.M.

Be-Bop-a-Lula

Words and Music by Tex Davis and Gene Vincent

A
E
End Rhy. Fig. 1
- e - 's my ba - by doll, my ba - by doll, my ba - by doll. 1.Well,
mp
Verse
E
she's the girl in the red blue jeans, ah, she's the queen of
Gtr. 2 tacet
all the teens. Ah, she's the wom - an that I know,
Chorus
A
Voc. Fig. 1
End Voc. Fig. 1
ah, she's the wom-an that loves me so, say. Be-Bop-a-Lu-la,
(Ah, ha.)
Gtr. 2

E
E7
E6
E
she's my ba - by. Be - Bop - a - Lu - la, I don't mean may - be.
let ring
15
12
14
12
12
14
12
12
14
13
15
14
12
12
12
14
12
14
14
12
12
B7
A
A6/E
A
E
Be - Bop - a - Lu - la, she - e - 's my ba - by doll, my ba - by doll, my ba - by
let ring
15
12
14
12
12
12
12
14
14
12
12
Guitar Solo
E
doll, let's rock.
mf
12
12
14
12
12
14
12
15
12
14
12
15
12
14
12
15
12
14
12
15
12
14
12
14
12
14
12
12
12
14
12
A
1/2
12
14
(14)
12
14
12
12
13
12
11
11
12
12
* Played as even eighth notes.

E
1/2
1/2
1/2
B7
A
E
let ring
Verse
E
E
12fr
2. Well, now she's the wom - an that's got that beat,
oh, she's the wom - an with the fly - in' feet.
Ah, she's the wom-an that walks a -

E
Bkgd. Voc.: w/ Voc. Fig. 1
round _ the _ store, _ she's the wom-an that yells more, _ more, _ more, _ more. _

Chorus
A
E
Be - Bop - a - Lu - la, she's my _ ba - by. Be - Bop - a - Lu - la, I
w/ pick & fingers
let ring
1/4

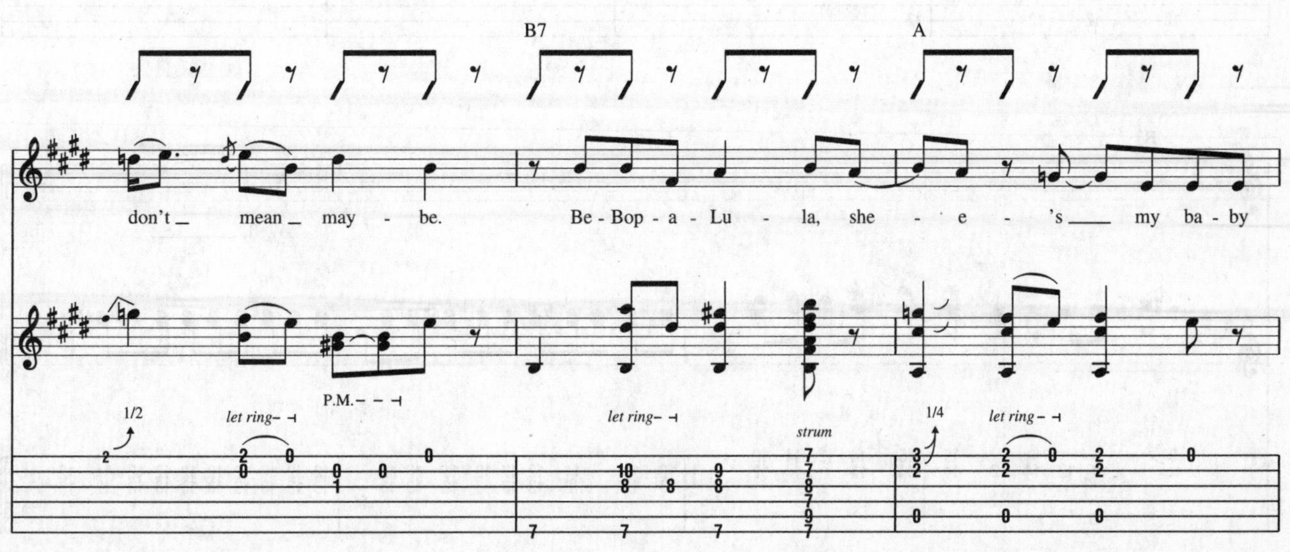
B7
A
don't _ mean _ may - be. Be - Bop - a - Lu - la, she - e - 's ___ my ba - by
P.M.
let ring
strum
1/2
1/4

E
doll, my ba - by doll, my ba by doll, let's rock a - gain now.

Guitar Solo

Gtr. 1: w/ Rhy. Fig. 1
E
w/ bar
let ring
-1/4

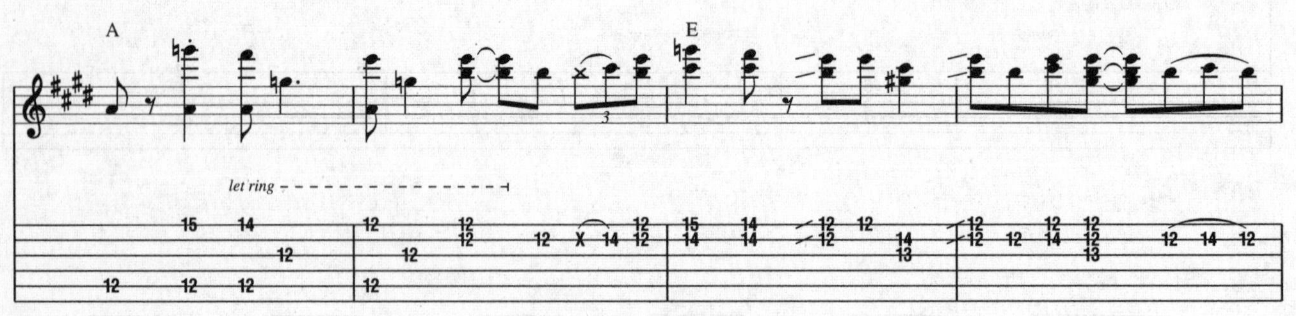
A
E
let ring

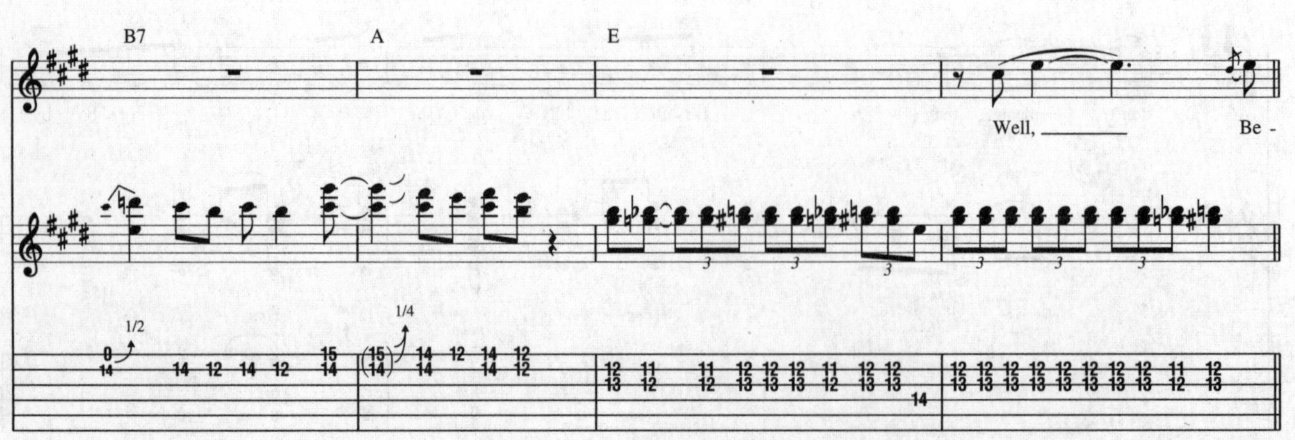
B7
A
E
Well, Be -
1/2
1/4

Chorus

Gtr. 1: w/ Rhy. Fig. 1 (1st 10 meas.)
E
Bop - a - Lu - la, she's my ba - by. Be - Bop - a - Lu - la, I
A
don't mean may - be. Be - Bop - a - Lu - la, she's my ba - by.
let ring
E
B7
Be - Bop - a - Lu - la, I don't mean may - be. Be - Bop - a - Lu - la, she -
let ring
let ④ ring
A
E
Gtr. 1
- e - 's my ba - by doll, my ba - by doll, my ba - by doll.
1/4
let ring

Best of My Love

Words and Music by John David Souther, Don Henley and Glenn Frey

Gtr. 1: w/ Rhy. Fill 1
C
dreams. Think - in' a - bout all the things that we said and
17
12
12
12

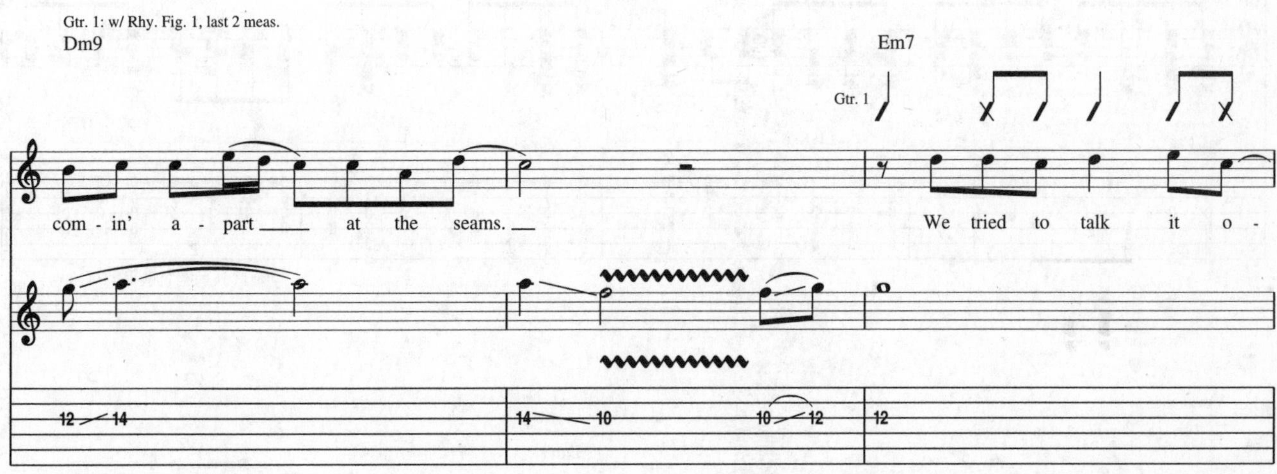
Gtr. 1: w/ Rhy. Fig. 1, last 2 meas.
Dm9
Em7
Gtr. 1
com - in' a - part at the seams. We tried to talk it o -
12 14
14 10 10 12
12

Dm7
Em7
F/G
(cont. in notation)
- ver but the words come out too rough. I

Rhy. Fill 1
Gtr. 1
let ring

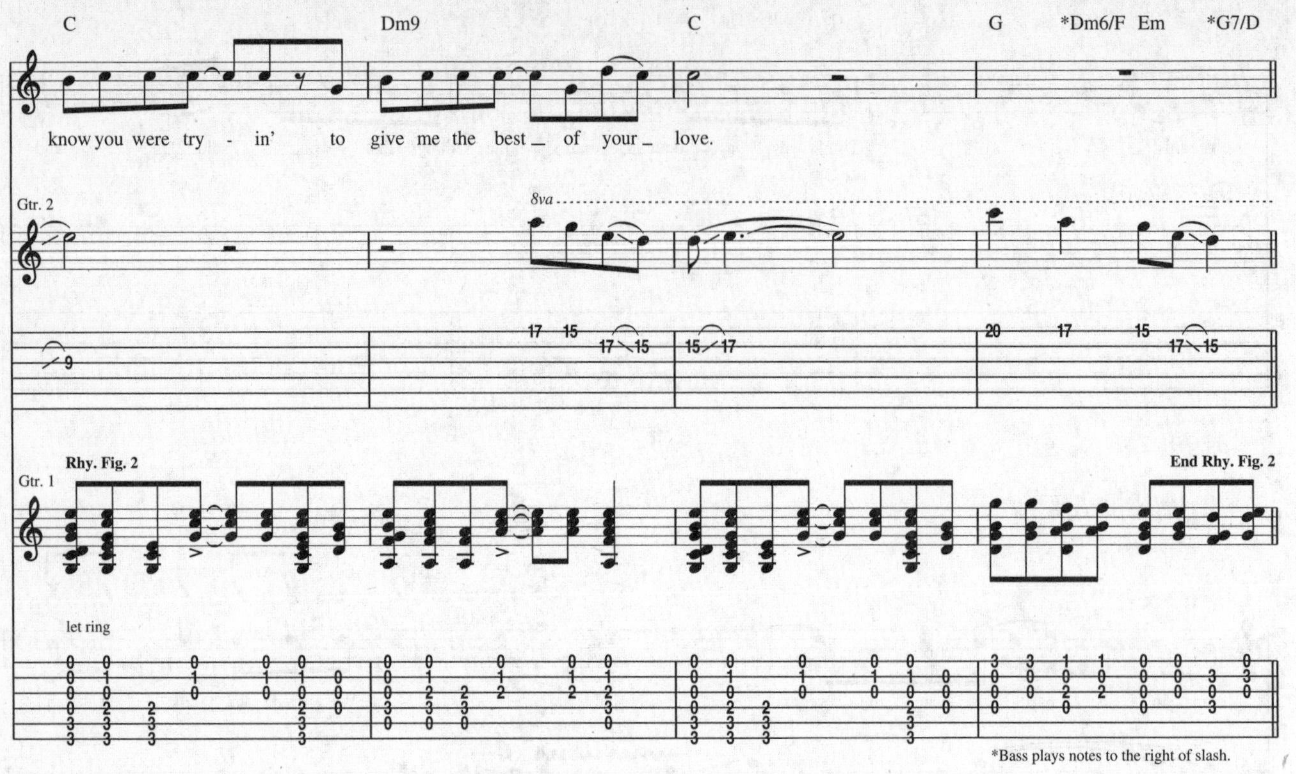
C Dm9 C G *Dm6/F Em *G7/D
know you were try - in' to give me the best _ of your _ love.
Gtr. 2
8va
Rhy. Fig. 2
Gtr. 1
End Rhy. Fig. 2
let ring
*Bass plays notes to the right of slash.

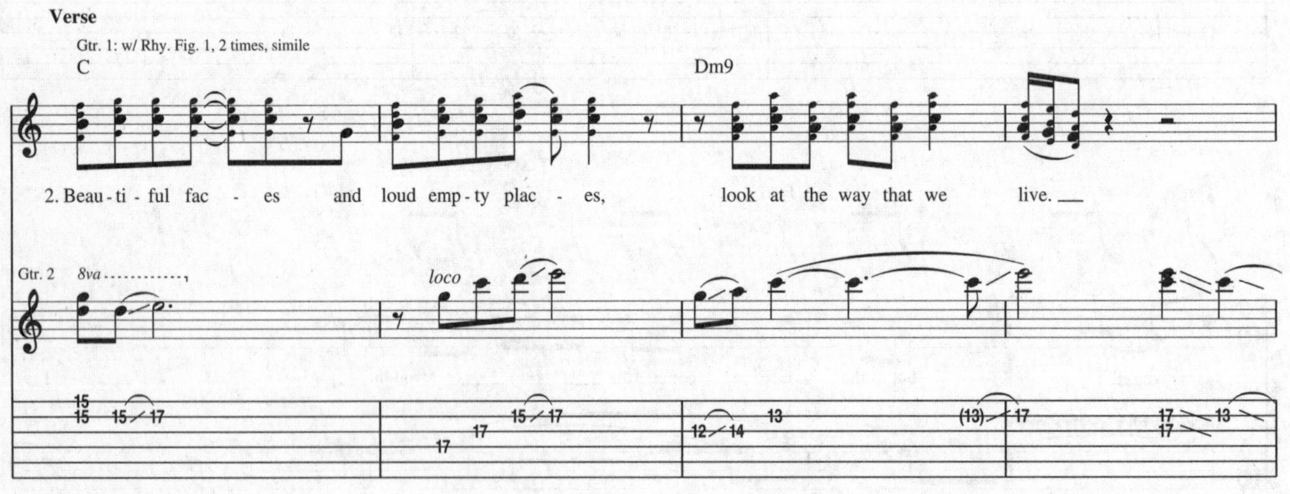
Verse
Gtr. 1: w/ Rhy. Fig. 1, 2 times, simile
C Dm9
2. Beau - ti - ful fac - es and loud emp - ty plac - es, look at the way that we live. __
Gtr. 2 8va
loco

C Dm9
Wast-in' our time _ on cheap talk and wine _ left us so lit - tle to give. __ That

Em7
Rhy. Fig. 3
Gtr. 1
Em7
same old crowd was like a cold, dark cloud that we could nev - er rise a - bove.
(Oo. Oo.
Dm7
End Rhy. Fig. 3
Gtr. 1: w/ Rhy. Fill 2
G7
Gtr. 1: w/ Rhy. Fig. 2
C
Dm9
But here in my heart, I give you the best of my
)
C
G
Dm6/F
Em
G7/D
Chorus
C
Rhy. Fig. 4
Gtr. 1
love.
Whoa,
sweet dar - lin',
(You get the best of my
Rhy. Fill 2
Gtr. 1
let ring

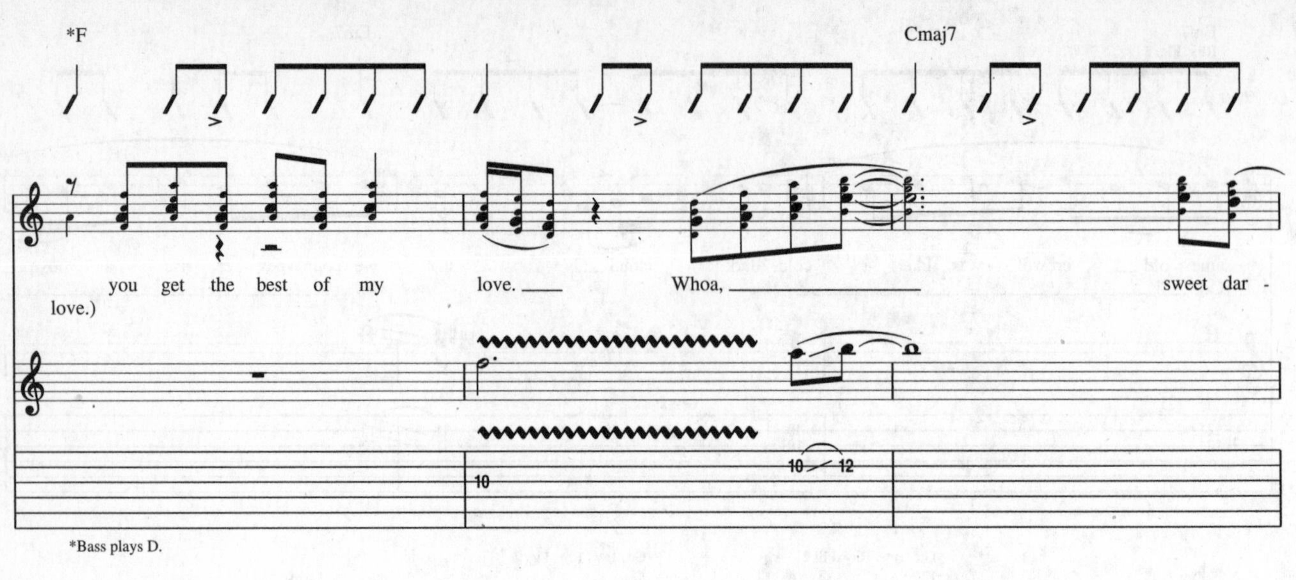
*F
Cmaj7
you get the best of my love.
Whoa,
sweet dar -
love.)
10
10
12
*Bass plays D.

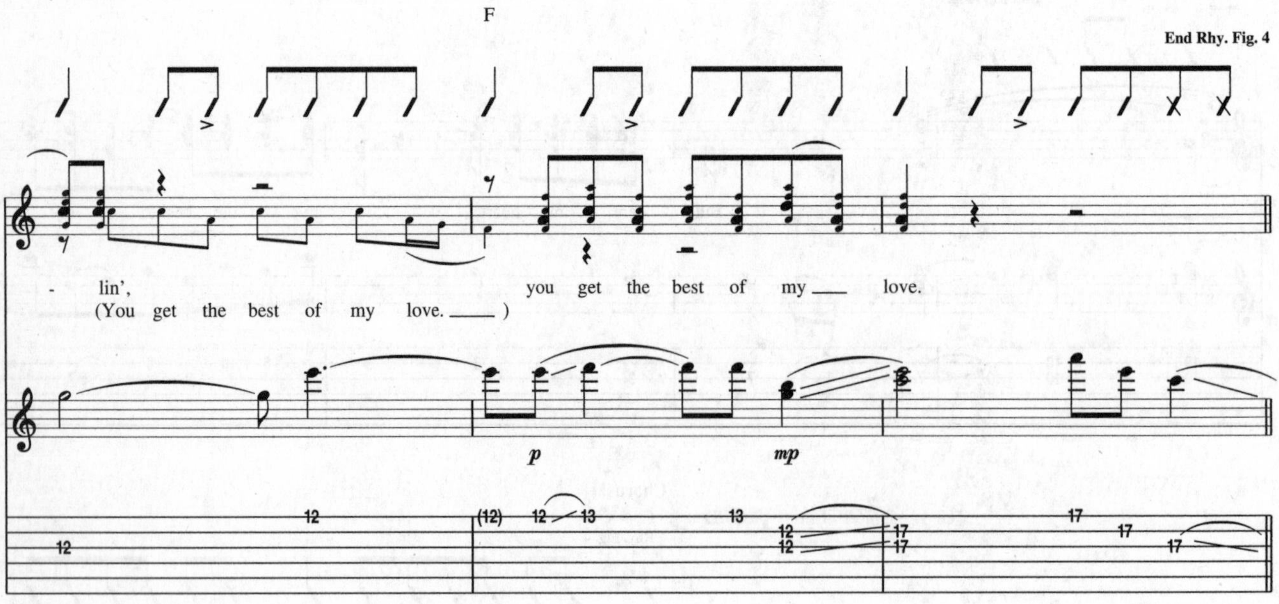
F
End Rhy. Fig. 4
- lin',
(You get the best of my love.)
you get the best of my love.
p
mp

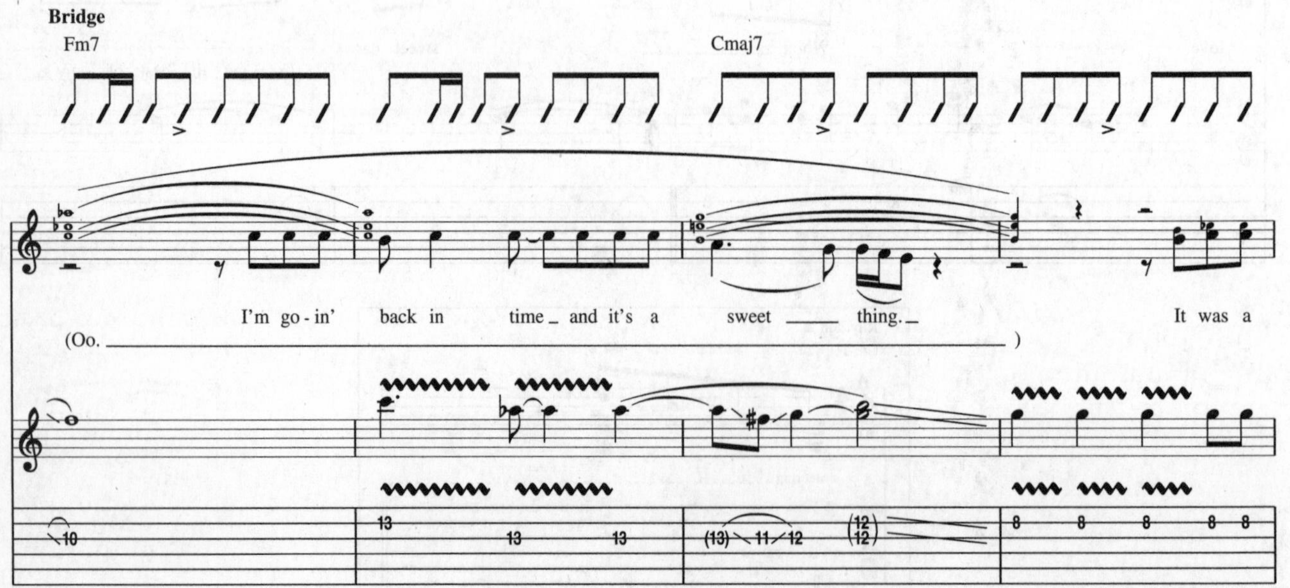
Bridge
Fm7
Cmaj7
I'm go - in' back in time and it's a sweet thing.
It was a
(Oo.)

Fm7
Dm7
G7
qui - et night, and I would be al - right if I could go on sleep - ing 3. But
*Fret higher note w/o slide
Verse
Gtr. 1: w/ Rhy. Fig. 1, 2 times, simile
C
Dm9
ev - 'ry morn - ing I wake up and wor - ry what's gon - na hap - pen to - day.
C
Dm9
You see it your way and I'll see it mine, but we both see it slip - pin' a - way.
Gtr. 1: w/ Rhy. Fig. 3, simile
Em7
Dm7
Em7
You know we al - ways had each oth - er, ba - by.
I guess that was - n't e - nough.
(Oo.
Oo.

*Refers to downstemmed notes only.

F
w/ Voc. Fig. 1A
Cmaj7
you get the best of my love.
Whoa,
sweet dar - lin',
(Oh, oh.)
F
w/ Voc. Fig. 1
C
Begin Fade
you get the best of my love.
Whoa,
sweet dar - lin',
(You get the best of my love.
F
w/ Voc. Fig. 1
Cmaj7
you get the best of my love.
Whoa,
sweet dar - lin',
)
(Oo.
F
w/ Voc. Fig. 1A
Fade Out
you get the best of my love.
Whoa,
sweet dar - lin'...
)

Blackbird

Words and Music by John Lennon and Paul McCartney

1.
D7sus4 G C G/B A7 D7sus4 G
ment to a - rise.

2.
D7sus4 G
ment to be free.
Bridge
Fadd2 Em Dm(add4) C
Black bird fly,

B♭6 C Fadd2 Em Dm(add4) C
black bird fly

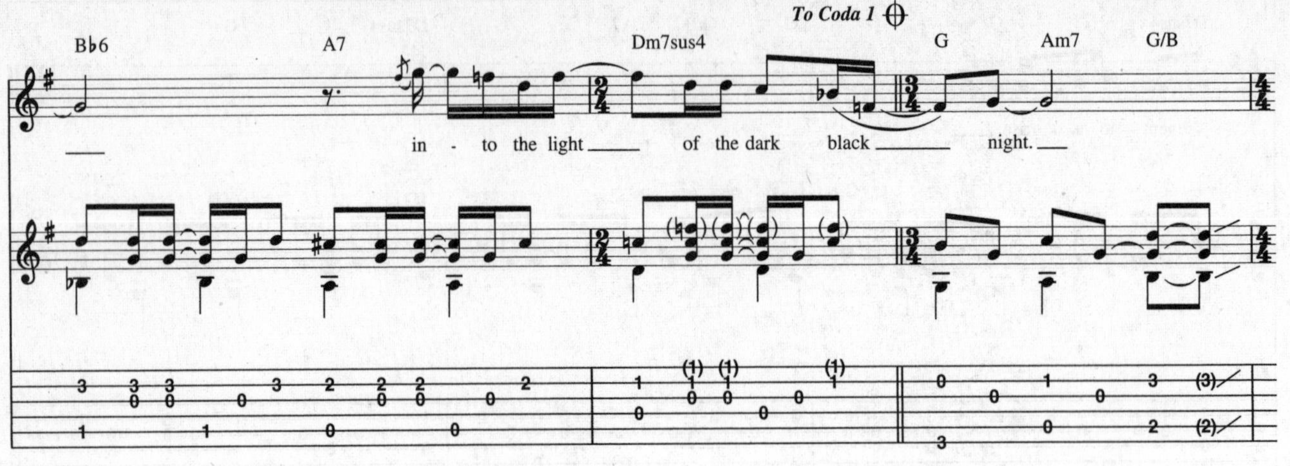
To Coda 1
B♭6
A7
Dm7sus4
G
Am7
G/B
in - to the light of the dark black night.

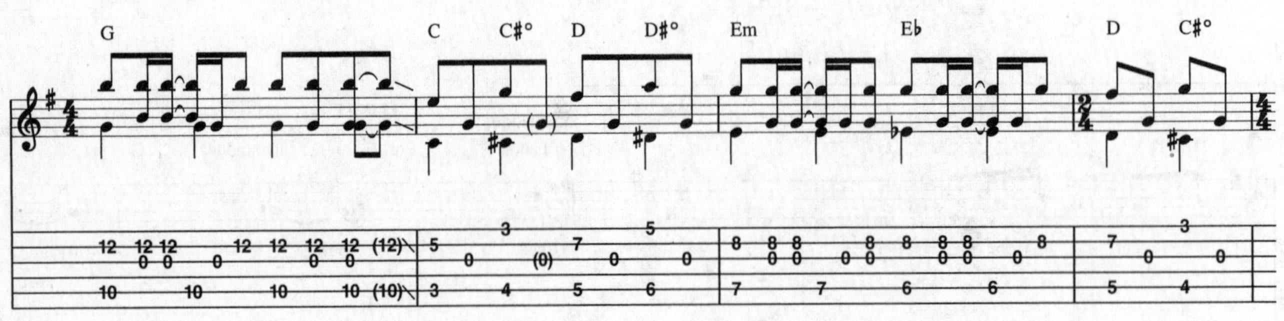
G
C
C#°
D
D#°
Em
E♭
D
C#°

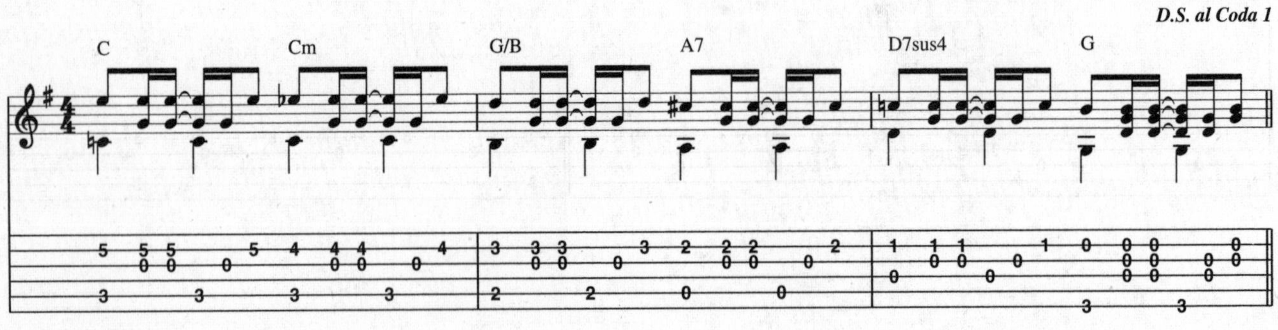
D.S. al Coda 1
C
Cm
G/B
A7
D7sus4
G

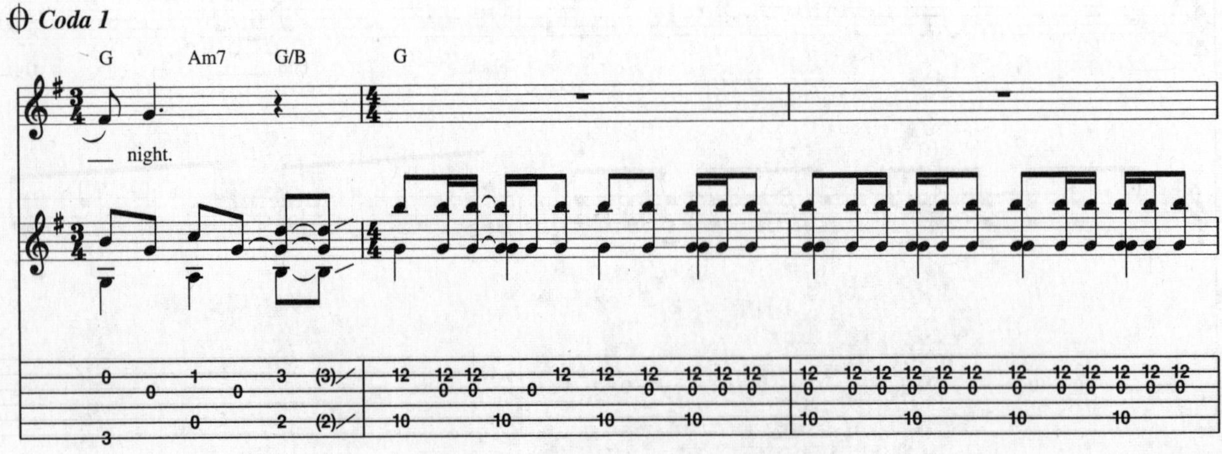
Coda 1
G
Am7
G/B
G
night.

D.S. al Coda 2
Am7
G/B
C
G/B
A7
D7sus4
Coda 2
G/B
A7
D7sus4
G
you were on - ly wait - ing for this mo - ment to a - rise.
C
G/B
A7
D7sus4
G
You were on - ly wait-ing for this mo - ment to a - rise.
C
G/B
A7
D7sus4
rit.
G
You were on - ly wait - ing for this mo - ment to a - rise.
rit.

Blue on Black

Words and Music by Tia Sillers, Mark Selby and Kenny Wayne Shepherd

Chorus
Gtr. 1: w/ Rhy. Fig. 1, 2 times, simile
Gtr. 4: w/ Fill 1, 3rd time
D5 Csus2 D5 Csus2 D5 N. C. Cadd9 G/B G
blue on black, tears on a riv - er, push on a shove, it don't mean much.
* Gtr. 3 (elec.)
Riff A1
End Riff A1
mf
w/ dist & tremolo effect
P.M.
let ring
1/4
* Two gtrs. arr. for one.
Gtr. 3: w/ Riff A1
Jok - er on Jack, match on a fire, cold on ice, a dead man's touch.
Whis - per on a scream does - n't change a thing,
1., 3. don't
2., 4. does - n't
bring you
Gtr. 1
Gtr. 3
Fill 1
Gtr. 4

To Coda 1
To Coda 2
To Coda 3
A5
G
back.
Blue on
Gtr. 1: w/ Rhy. Fig. 1, 2 times, simile
Gtr. 3: w/ Riff A1, 2 times, simile
D5
Csus2
D5
Csus2
D5
N. C.
Cadd9
G/B
G
black.
Oh,
yeah.
Blue on
Gtr. 4 (elec.)
w/ dist. & *harmonizer
full
* Set to harmonize one octave above.
black.
P.M.
full

Verse
Gtr. 1: w/ Rhy. Fig. 1, 8 times, simile
Gtr. 3: w/ Riff A1, 8 times, simile
D5 Csus2 D5 Csus2 D5 N. C. Cadd9 G/B G D5 Csus2 D5 Csus2 D5 N. C. Cadd9 G/B G
2. Blind, oh, now I see.
P.M.
harmonizer off
D5 Csus2 D5 Csus2 D5 N. C. Cadd9 G/B G D5 Csus2 D5 Csus2 D5 N. C.
Truth, lies, and in be - tween.
Cadd9 G/B G D5 Csus2 D5 Csus2 D5 N. C. Cadd9 G/B G
Wrong can't be un -
D5 Csus2 D5 Csus2 D5 N. C. Cadd9 G/B G D5 Csus2 D5 Csus2 D5 N. C.
done. Oh, slipped

D.S. al Coda 1
Cadd9
G/B
G
D5
Csus2
D5
Csus2
D5
N. C.
Cadd9
G/B
G
from
the tip of
your
tongue.
Hey,
P.M.
Coda 1
Gtr. 1: w/ Rhy. Fig. 1, 2 times, simile
Gtr. 3: w/ Riff A1, 2 times, simile
black.
Oh,
blue on
Gtr. 4
w/ harmonizer
full
1/4
black.
Oh,
yeah.
Guitar Solo
Gtr. 1: w/ Rhy. Fig.1, 6 times, simile
Gtr. 3: w/ Riff A1, 6 times, simile
rake
full

D5 Csus2 D5 Csus2 D5 N. C. Cadd9 G/B G
full
1/4
D5 Csus2 D5 Csus2 D5 N. C. Cadd9 G/B G
15ma
loco
P.M.
P.H.
D5 Csus2 D5 Csus2 D5 N. C. Cadd9 G/B G
D5 Csus2 D5 Csus2 D5 N. C. Cadd9 G/B G
P.M.
D5 Csus2 D5 Csus2 D5 N. C. Cadd9 G/B G

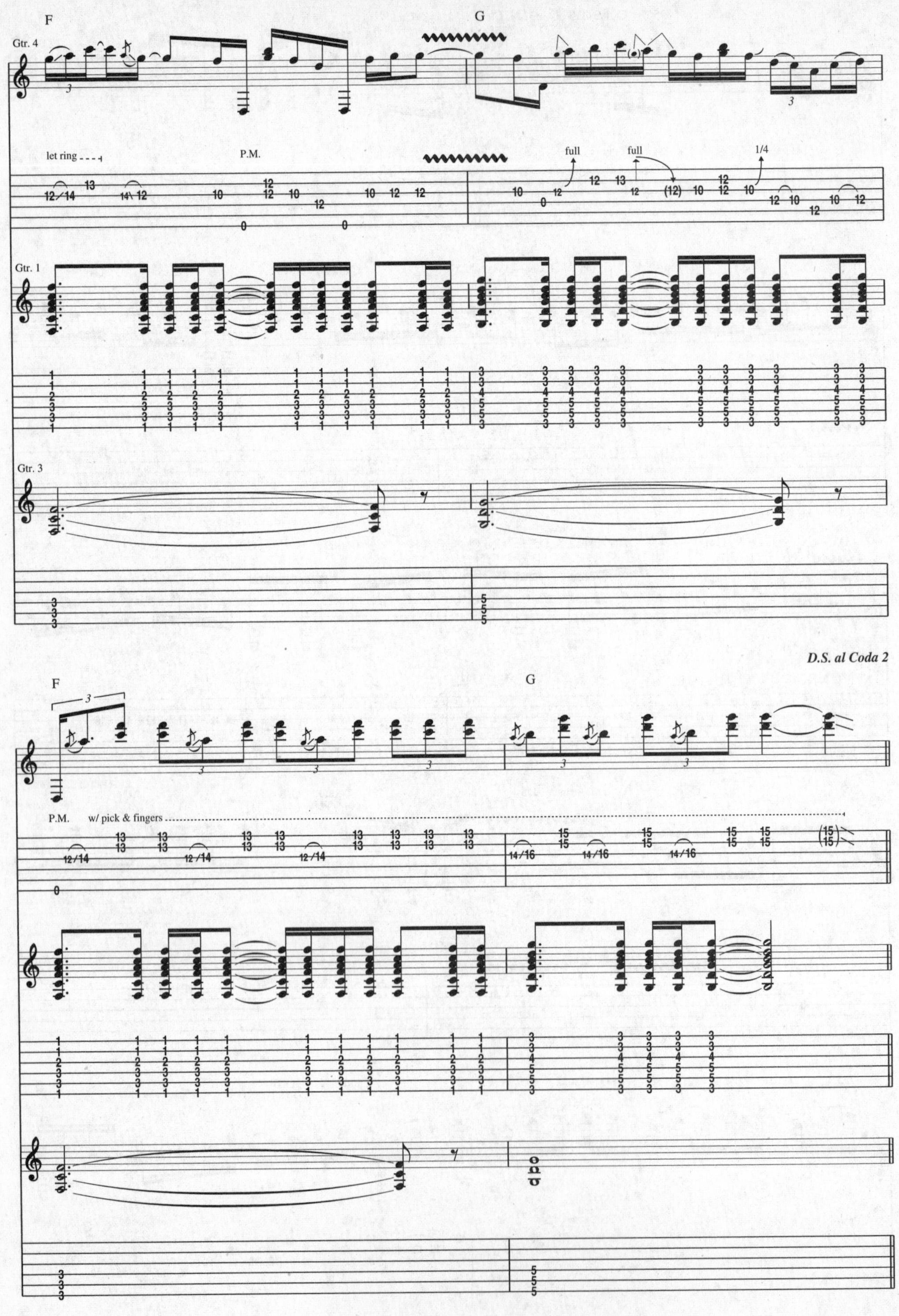
F
G
Gtr. 4
let ring
P.M.
full
full
1/4
Gtr. 1
Gtr. 3
D.S. al Coda 2
F
G
P.M.
w/ pick & fingers

Coda 2
Gtr. 1: w/ Rhy. Fig. 1, 2 times, simile
Gtr. 3: w/ Riff A1, 2 times, simile
D5
Csus2
D5
Csus2
D5
N. C.
Cadd9
G/B
G
black.
Oh,
yeah.
Blue on
* Gtr. 4
w/ Leslie effect
full
*harmonizer off
D.S. al Coda 3
black.
Hey,
Coda 3
Gtr. 1: w/ Rhy. Fig.1, 3 times, simile
Gtr. 3: w/ Riff A1, 3 times, simile
black.
Oh,
blue on
w/ harmonizer
*Leslie effect off
Oh,
P.M.

D5
Csus2
D5
Csus2
D5
N. C.
Cadd9
G/B
G
black.
Oh,
blue on
full
full
full
full
P.M.
D5
Csus2
D5
Csus2
D5
N. C.
Cadd9
G/B
black.
Gtr. 4
full
P.M.
P.M.
Gtr. 1
Gtr. 3
P.M.
let ring

Boot Scootin' Boogie

Words and Music by Ronnie Dunn

A
hon - ky tonk near the coun - ty line. The joint starts jump - in' ev - 'ry
quit - tin' time, I hit the door run - nin'. I fire up my pick - up truck
shot at that red - head yon - der look - in' at me. The dance floor's hop - pin' and it's
4th time only
E
B
night when the sun goes down. They got whis - key, wom - en,
and let the hors - es run. I go fly - in' down that high way -
Fiddle Solo
hot - ter than the Fourth of Ju - ly. I see out - laws, in - laws,
4th time only

3rd time, omit these 2 measures

mu - sic and smoke. It's where all the cow - boy folk go to
to that hide - a - way stuck out in the woods to do the boot scoot - in'
crooks and straights, all out mak - in' it shake, do - in' the

4th time only

1. ,3. 2. ,4.

Gtr. 1 as in 1st verse

Chorus

E A

boo - gie. 2. I've Yeah, heel to toe, do - sa do,
4. The

2nd ending (1st chorus)
Gtr. 2 (Slide)

Gtr. 1

1/2

4th time

4th ending (2nd chorus)

E A

come on ba - by, let's go boot scoot-in'! Whoa, Cad - il - lac, Black-jack,

1st chorus

2nd chorus

E

ba - by meet me out back. We're gon-na boo-gie. Oh,

1st chorus

2nd chorus

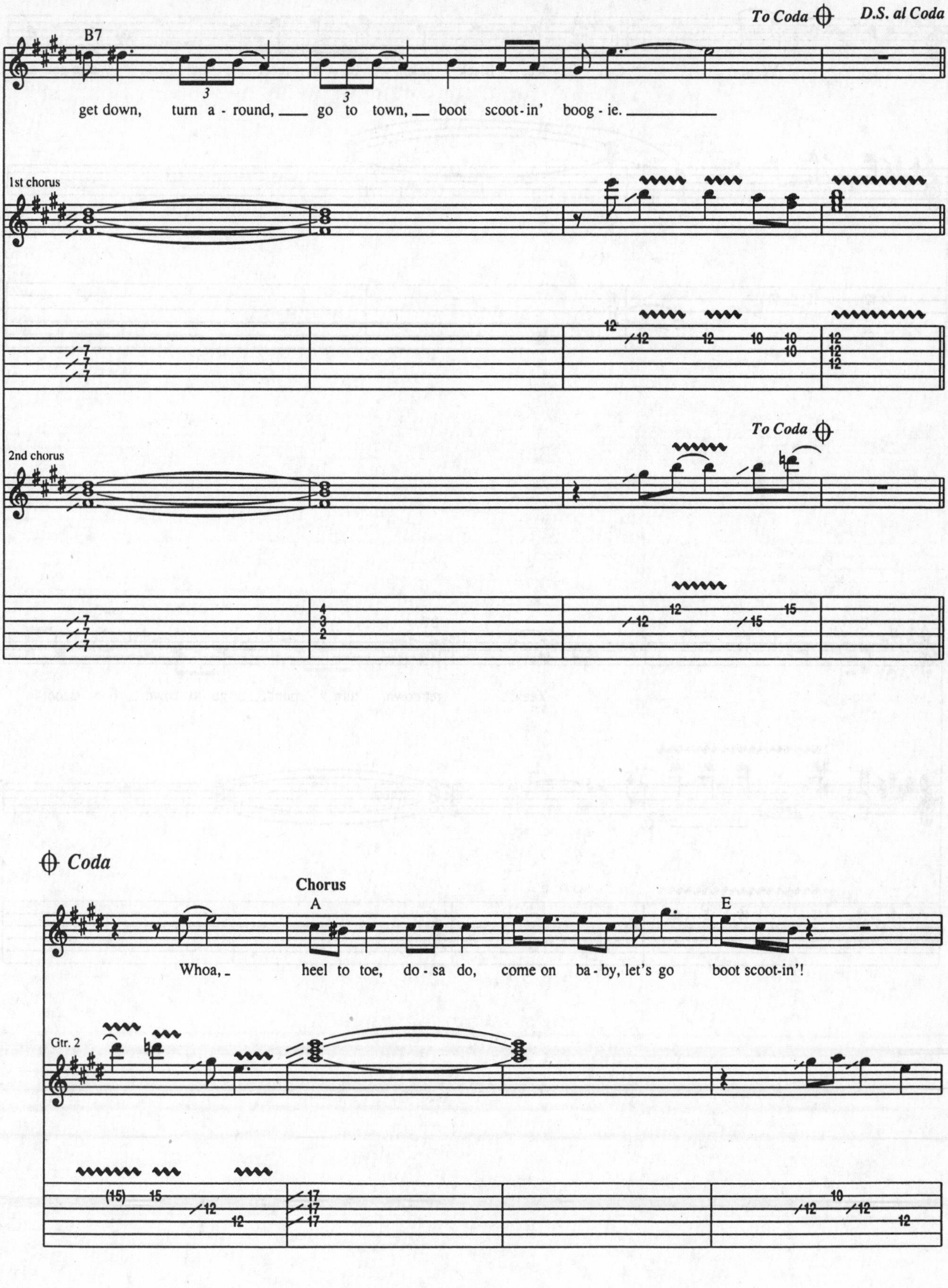

To Coda ⊕ D.S. al Coda

B7

get down, turn a - round, go to town, boot scoot-in' boog - ie.

1st chorus

2nd chorus

To Coda ⊕

A
Yeah, _ Cad - il - lac, Black - jack, ba - by meet me out back. We're gon-na
12
12
10
12
12
17
17
17

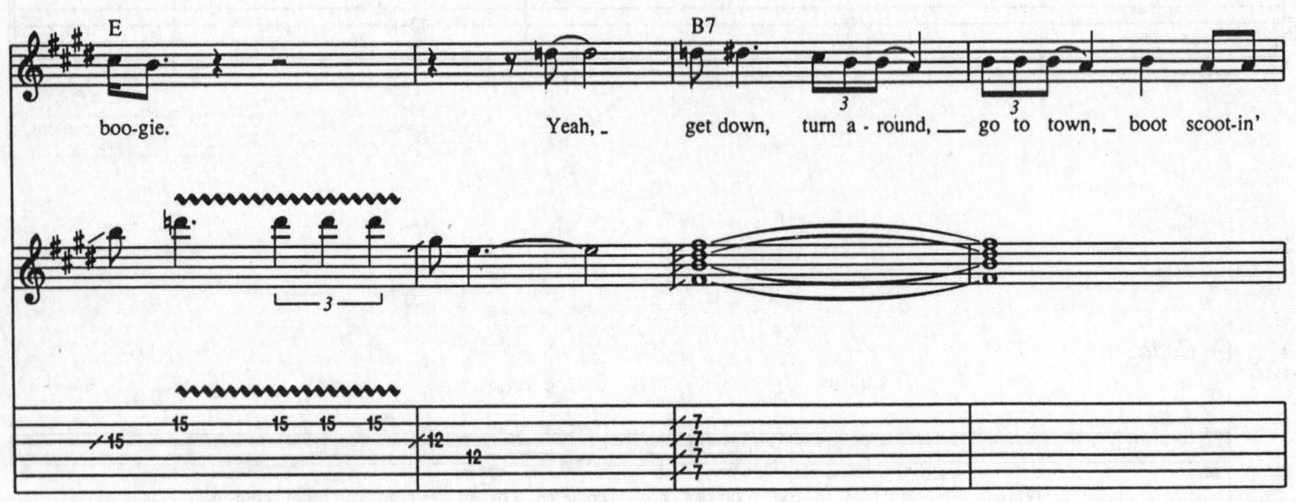
E
B7
boo-gie. Yeah, _ get down, turn a - round, _ go to town, _ boot scoot-in'
3
3
3
15
15
15
15
15
12
12
7
7
7
7

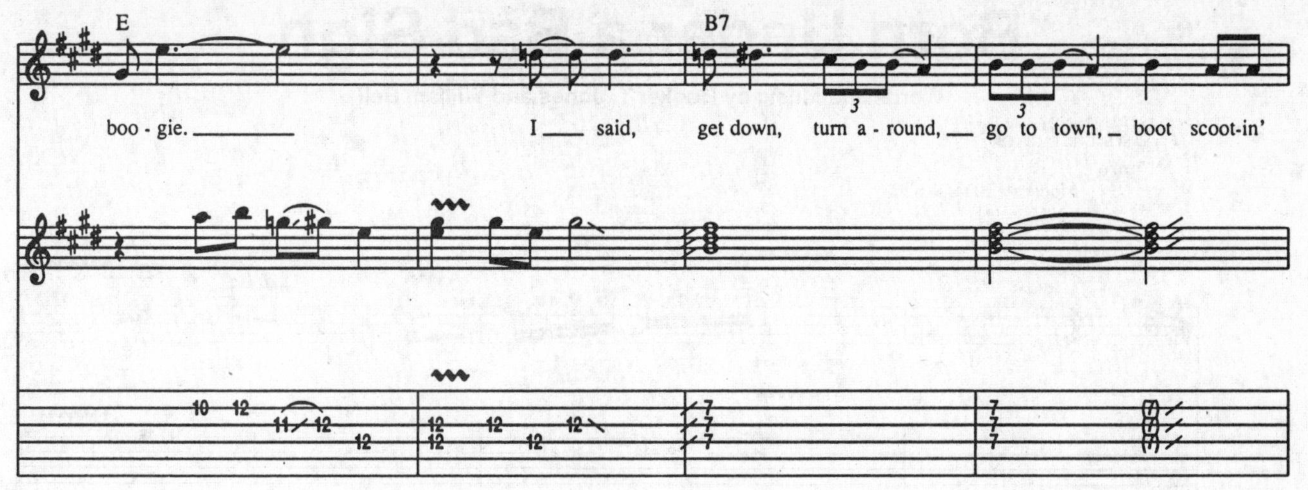
E
B7
boo - gie.
I said, get down, turn a - round, go to town, boot scoot-in'

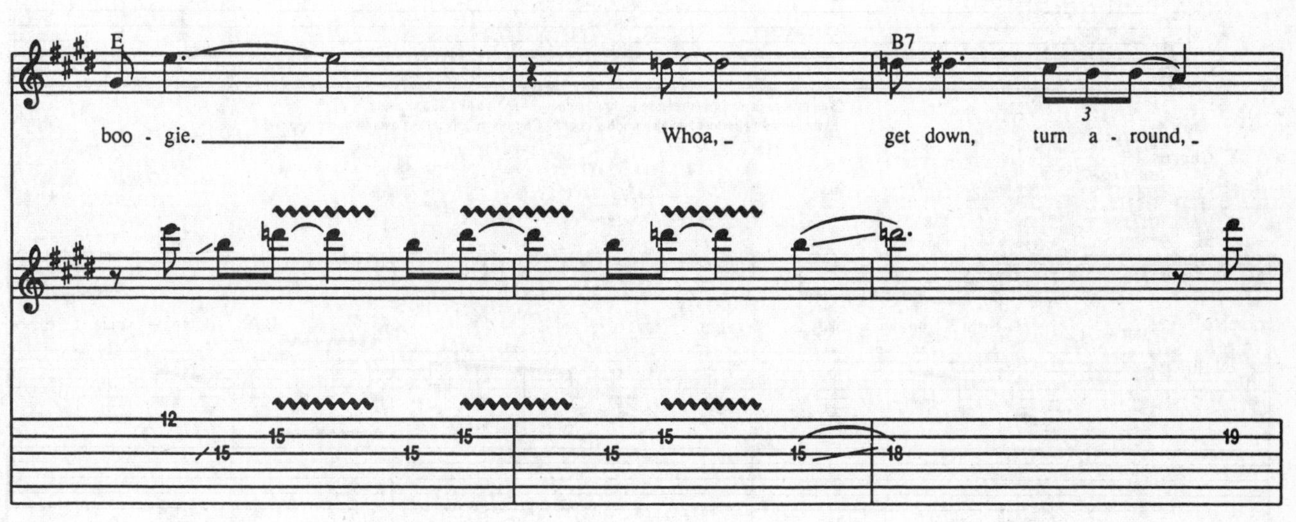
E
B7
boo - gie.
Whoa, get down, turn a - round,

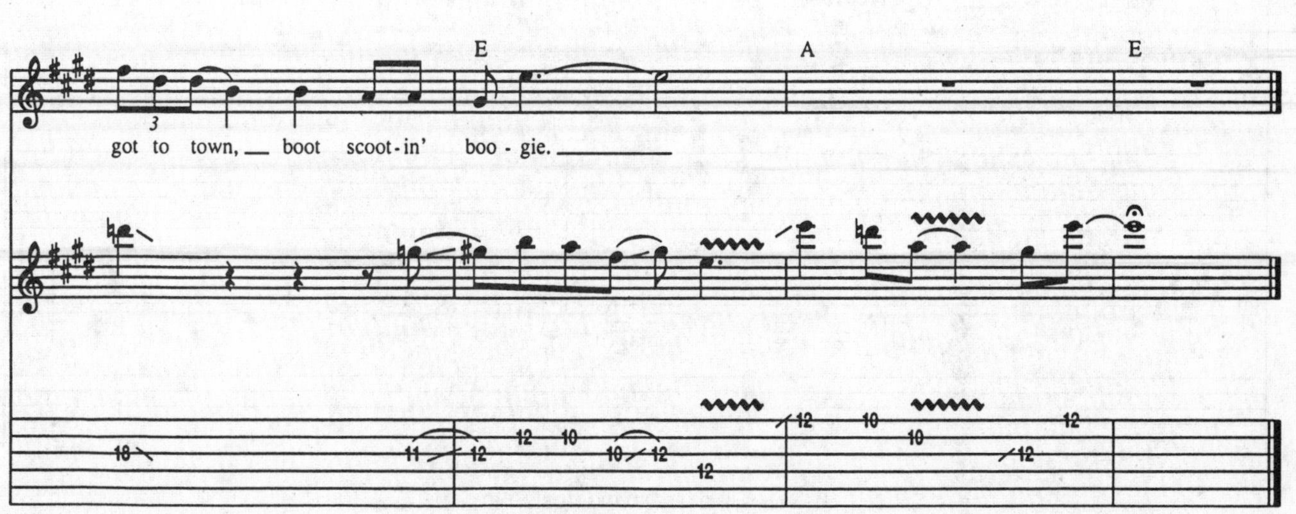
E
A
E
got to town, boot scoot - in' boo - gie.

Born Under a Bad Sign

Words and Music by Booker T. Jones and William Bell

Gtr. 1: D–G–D–G–B–E tuning, down 1 1/2 steps:
(low to high) B–E–B–E–G♯–C♯

Intro
Moderate Blues ♩ = 92
N.C.
C♯7
* (E7)
Gtr. 1 (dist.) (Albert King)
(Bass)
mf w/ thumb
Gtr. 2 (clean) (Steve Cropper)
mf

* Symbols in parentheses represent chord names respective to detuned guitar.
Symbols above reflect actual sounding chords. Chord symbols reflect overall harmony.

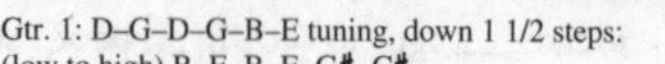

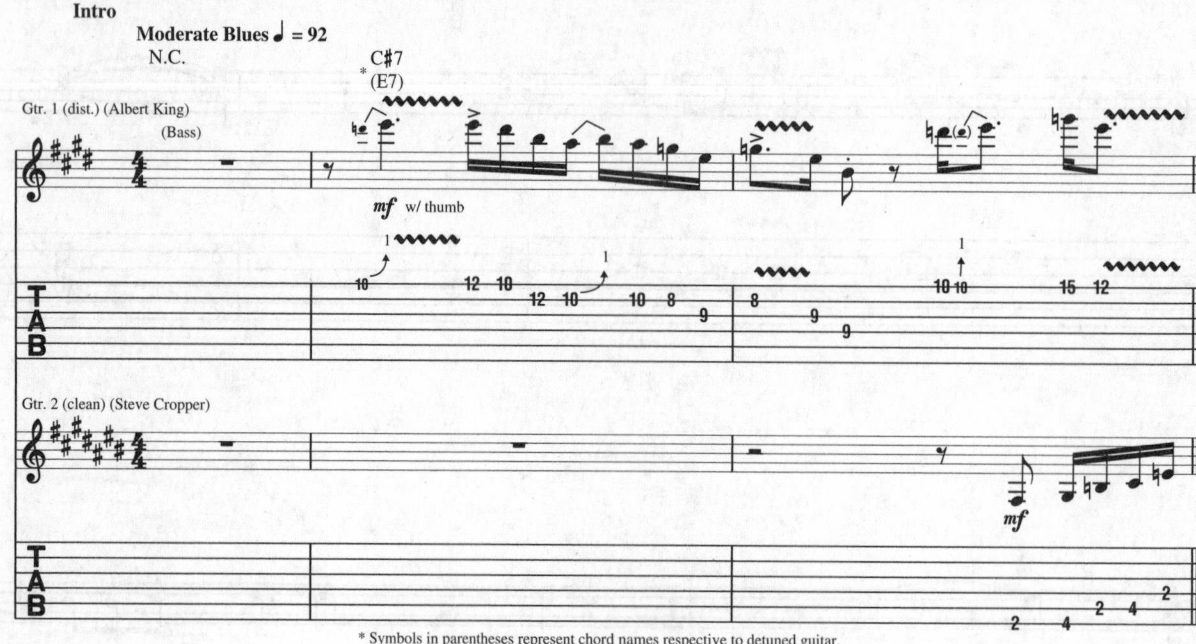

Chorus
Gtr. 1 tacet
C♯7
(E7)
Born _ un-der a bad _ sign.
Been down _ since I be -
Gtr. 2
Riff A

G♯7
(B7)
gan to crawl. _____
If it was-n't for bad luck, _
Gtr. 1
Gtr. 2

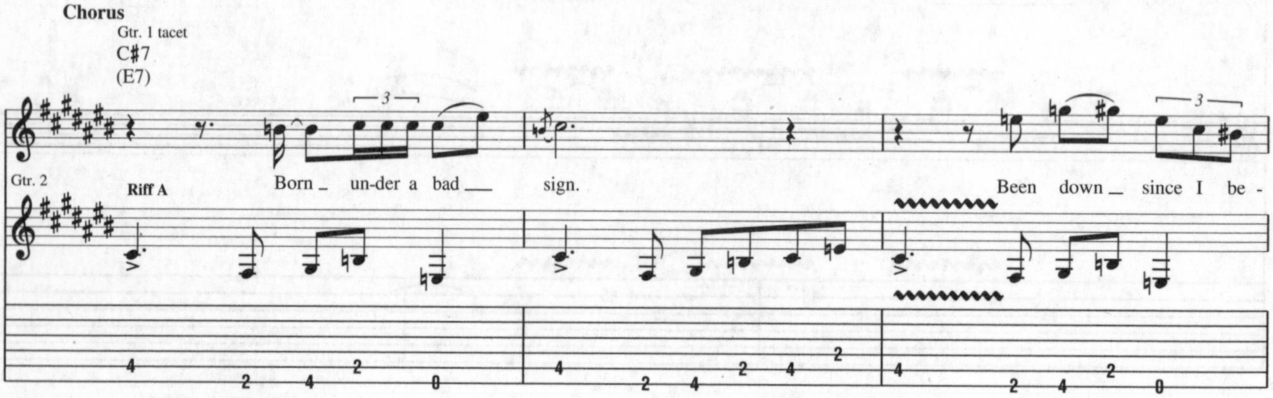

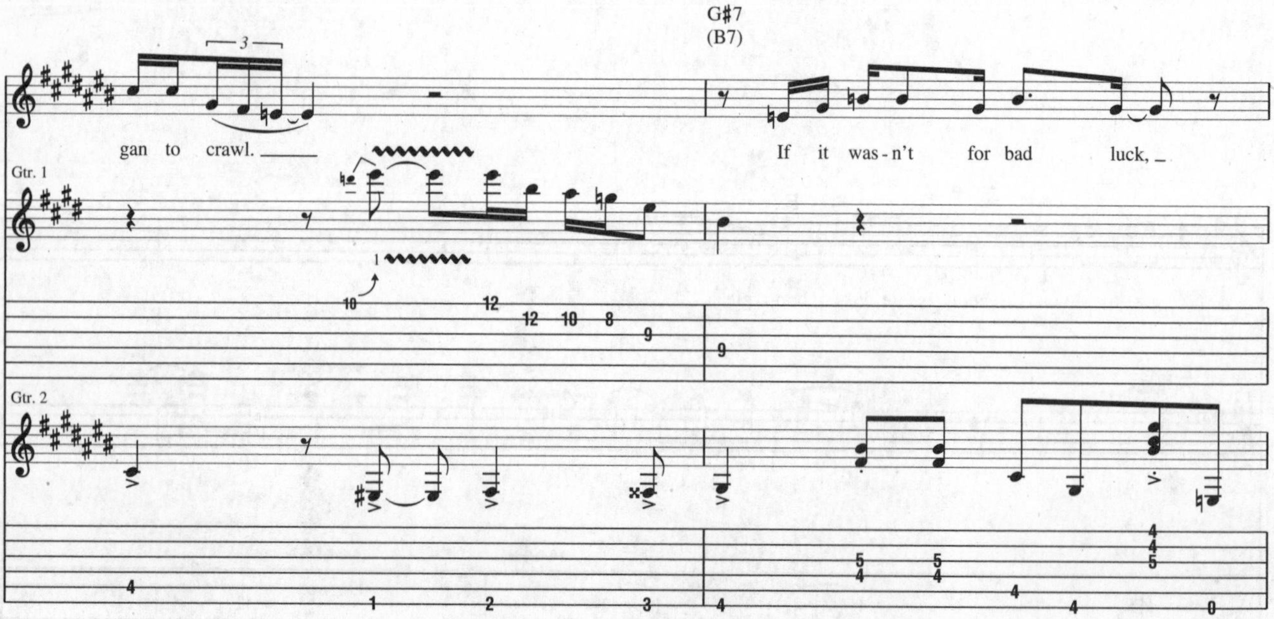

F#7
(A7)
C#7
(E7)
you know I would-n't have no luck at all.
Verse
C#7
(E7)
1. Hard_ luck and trou-ble
been my on - ly friend.
grad. bend
End Riff A
Riff B

I been on my own ever since I was ten.
End Riff B
Chorus
Gtr. 2: w/ Riff A
C#7
(E7)
Born under a bad sign.
Been down since I began to
Gtr. 1
crawl.
G#7
(B7)
If it wasn't for bad luck,
F#7
(A7)
you know I wouldn't have no luck at
C#7
(E7)
all.
Verse
Gtr. 1 tacet
Gtr. 2: w/ Riff B
C#7
(E7)
2. I can't read,

I did-n't learn how to write.
My whole life has been
Chorus
Gtr. 2: w/ Riff A
C#7
(E7)
one big fight.
Born un-der a bad sign.
I been down since I be-gan to crawl.
Gtr. 1
G#7
(B7)
F#7
(A7)
If it was-n't for bad luck,
I say, I would-n't have no luck
C#7
(E7)
at all,
Spoken: n' that ain't no lie.

Guitar Solo
C#7
(E7)
Ow!
Gtr. 1
8va
grad. release
Gtr. 2
Bridge
G#7
(B7)
A7
(C7)
G7
(A#7)
You know if it was-n't for bad luck,
F#7
(A7)
F7
(G#7)
I would-n't have no kind of luck.
If it was-n't for real bad luck,
loco

F#7
(A7)
C#7
(E7)
I would-n't have no luck at all.
P.M.
Verse
Gtr. 1 tacet
Gtr. 2: w/ Riff B
C#7
(E7)
3. You know, wine and wom-en is all I crave.
A big leg wom-an gon-na car-ry me to my grave.
Chorus
Gtr. 2: w/ Riff A
C#7
(E7)
Born un-der a bad sign.
I been down since I be-gan to crawl.
Gtr. 1
G#7
(B7)
F#7
(A7)
If it was-n't for bad luck,
I tell you, I would-n't have no luck at
P.M.

C#7
(E7)
Outro
all.
Yeah, I'm a bad luck boy!
Gtr. 1
Gtr. 2
Been hav-in' bad luck all of my days, yeah.
Begin fade
8va
Fade out

Cat Scratch Fever

Words and Music by Ted Nugent

A5
B5/A
C5/A
N.C.
8va
full
1/2
Verse
Gtr. 2 tacet
G
D
1. Well, I don't
know where they come from, but they sure do come.
I hope they com - in' for me.
time that I got it I was just ten years old,
I got it from some kit-ty next door.
Gtr. 1
Rhy. Fig. 1
let ring

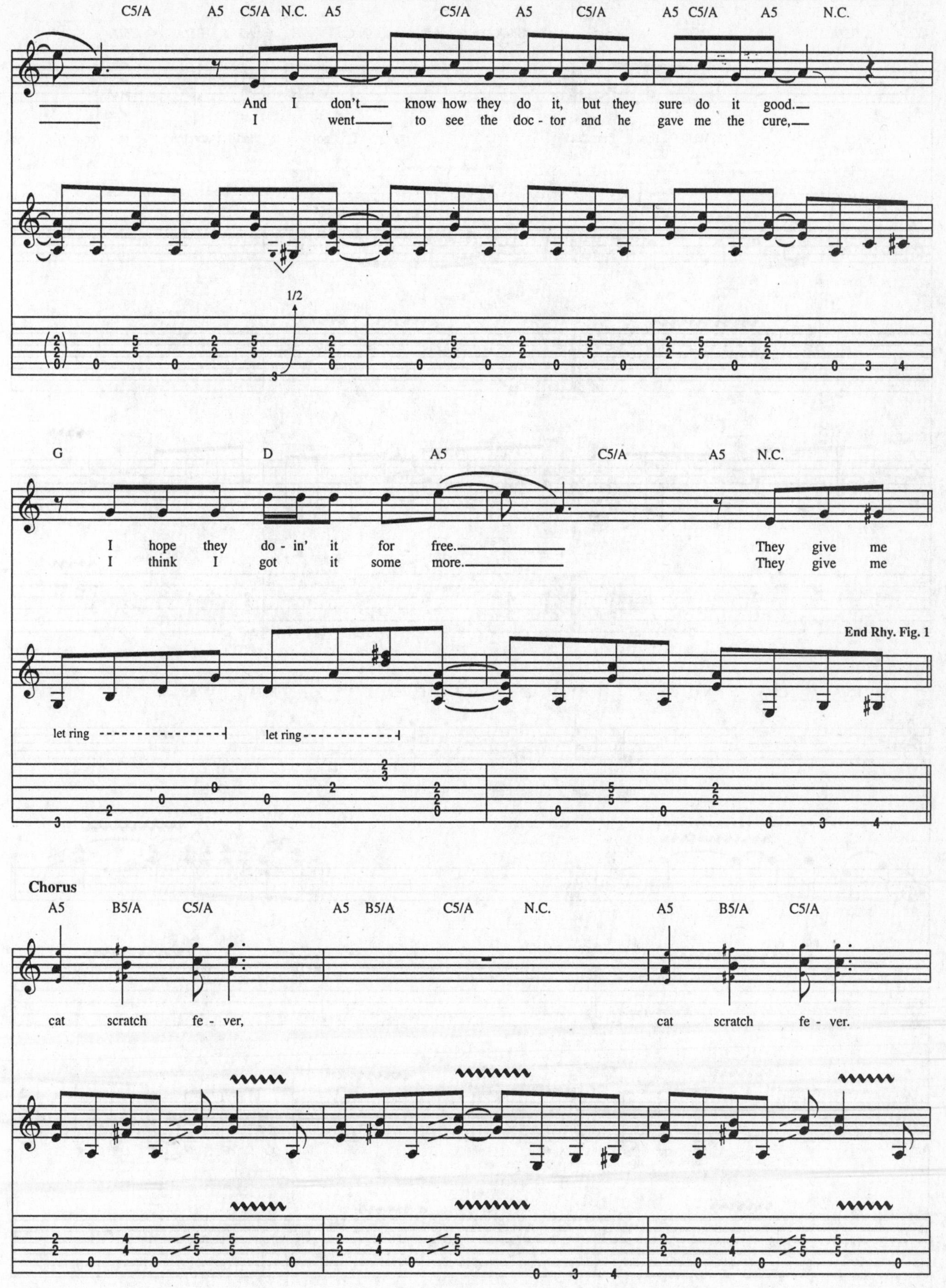
C5/A A5 C5/A N.C. A5 C5/A A5 C5/A A5 C5/A A5 N.C.
And I don't know how they do it, but they sure do it good.
I went to see the doc - tor and he gave me the cure,
1/2
G D A5 C5/A A5 N.C.
I hope they do - in' it for free.
I think I got it some more.
They give me
They give me
End Rhy. Fig. 1
let ring
let ring
Chorus
A5 B5/A C5/A A5 B5/A C5/A N.C. A5 B5/A C5/A
cat scratch fe - ver,
cat scratch fe - ver.

1.
2.
B5/A A5 N.C. A5 B5/A A5 N.C. A5 B5/A C5/A
2. Well, the first— I got a bad scratch fe - ver,
8va
Gtr. 2
full
full
full
Gtr. 1
1/2
A5 B5/A C5/A N.C. A5 B5/A C5/A B5/A A5 E♭5
the cat scratch fe - ver.
8va
8va
full full
full full

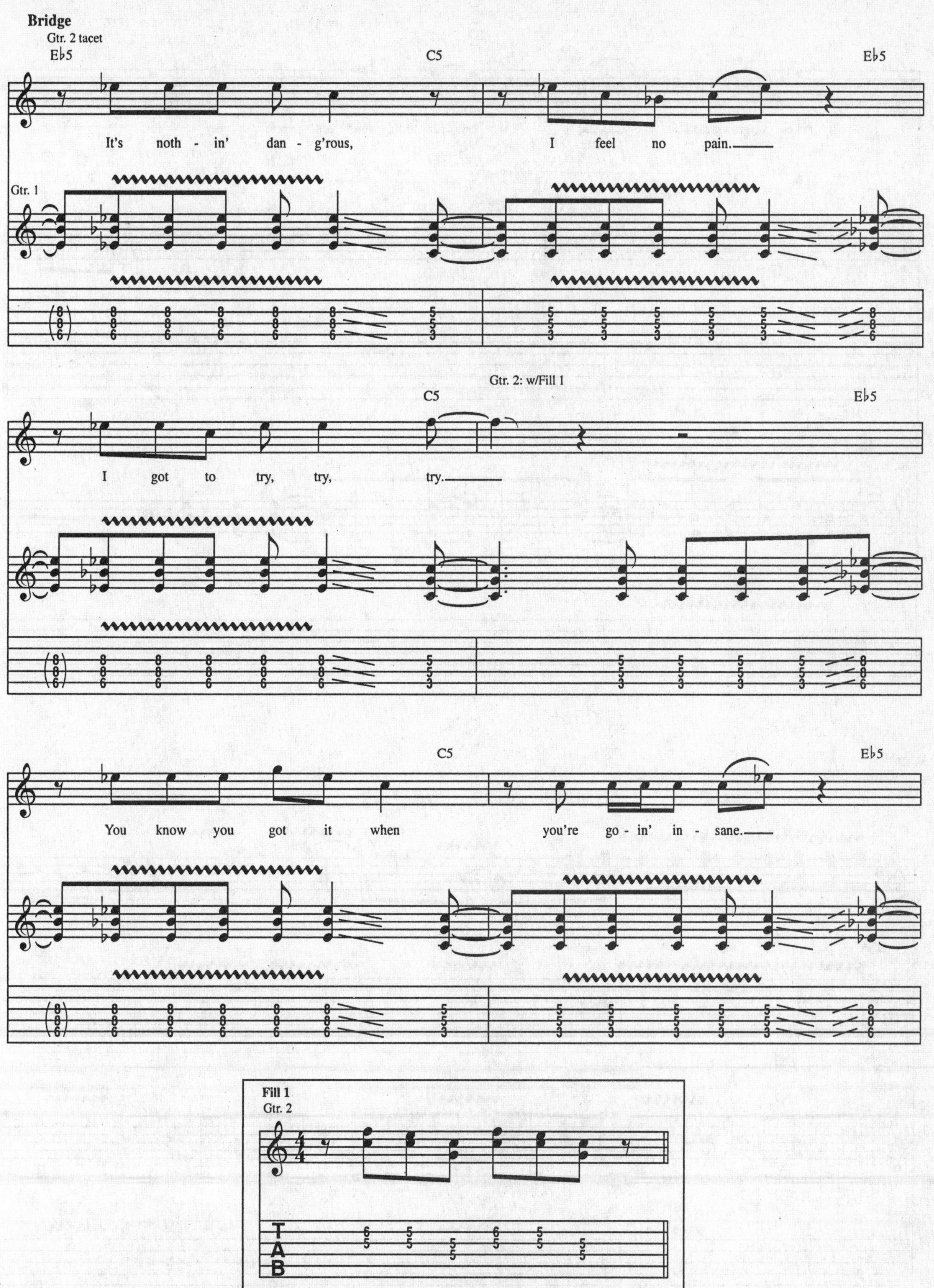
Bridge
Gtr. 2 tacet
E♭5
C5
E♭5
It's noth - in' dan - g'rous, I feel no pain.
Gtr. 1
Gtr. 2: w/Fill 1
C5
E♭5
I got to try, try, try.
C5
E♭5
You know you got it when you're go - in' in - sane.
Fill 1
Gtr. 2
TAB

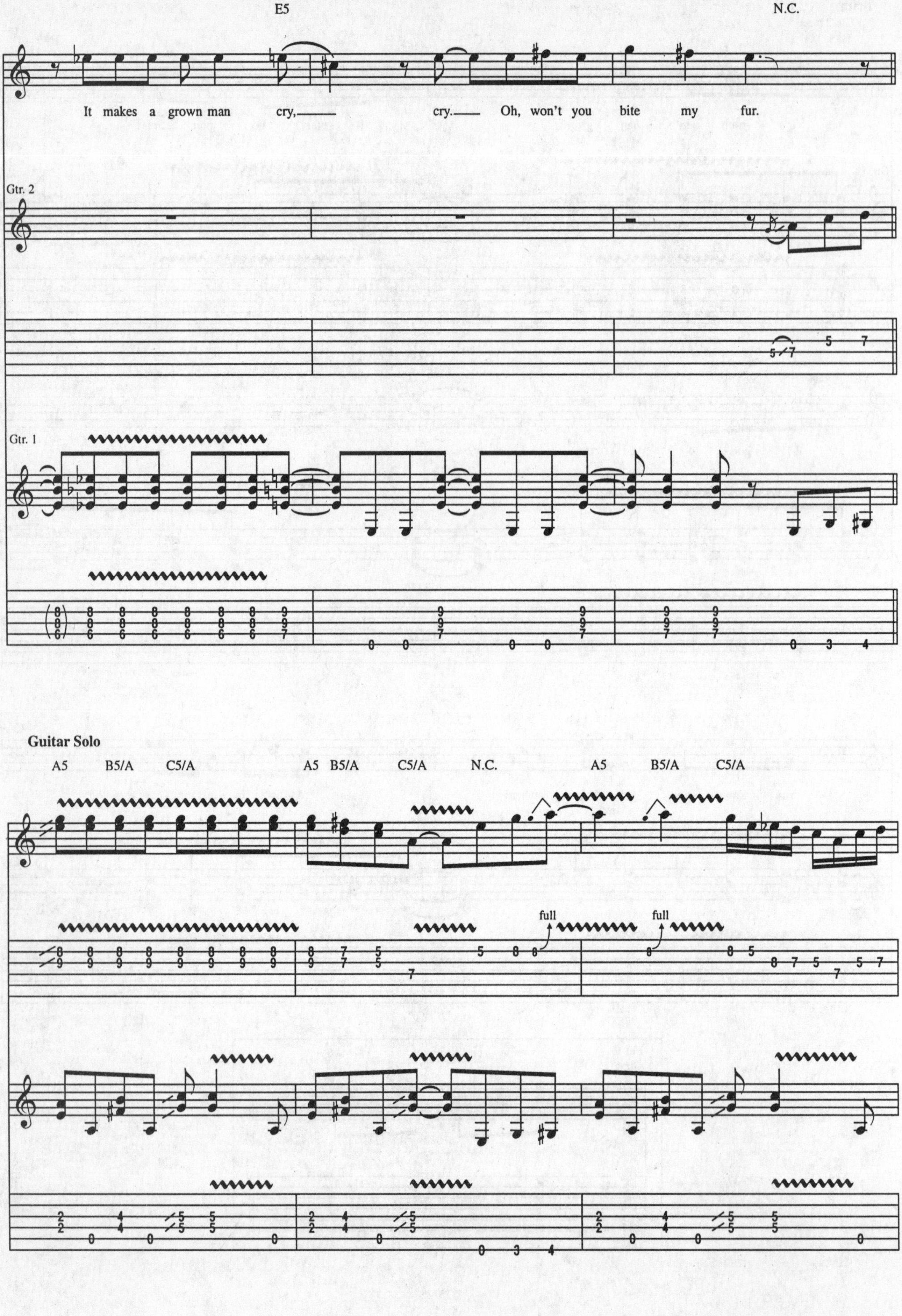

It makes a grown man cry,___ cry.___ Oh, won't you bite my fur.

Gtr. 2

Gtr. 1

B5/A
A5
N.C.
A5
B5/A
C5/A
A5
B5/A
C5/A
N.C.
1/2
full
full
full
grad. release
full
A5
B5/A
C5/A
B5/A
A5
D5
full
full
E5
C5
D5
N.C.
8va
hold bend
hold bend
full
full
full
full
full

A5
B5/A
C5/A
A5 B5/A
C5/A
N.C.
A5
B5/A
C5/A
8va
full
full
full
full
full
full
full
grad. release
1/2
Verse
Gtr. 1: w/Rhy. Fig. 1
B5/A
A5
N.C.
A5
C5/A
A5
C5/A
A5 C5/A
A5
N.C.
3. Well, I make a pus - sy purr with a stroke of my hand.
8va
full
full
1/2
G
D
A5
C5/A
A5
C5/A N.C. A5
C5/A
A5
C5/A
They know they get - tin' it from me.
And they know just where to go when they
Gtr. 2
8va
full
full

A5 C5/A A5 N.C. G D A5 C5/A A5 N.C.
need their lov- in' man.
They know I'm do- in' it for free.
I give 'em
8va
full full
Chorus
Gtr. 2 tacet
A5 B5/A C5/A A5 B5/A C5/A N.C. A5 B5/A C5/A
cat scratch fe - ver,
cat scratch fe - ver.
Gtr. 1
B5/A A5 N.C. A5 B5/A C5/A A5 B5/A C5/A N.C.
They got it bad scratch fe - ver,
a
Gtr. 2
8va
full
Gtr. 1

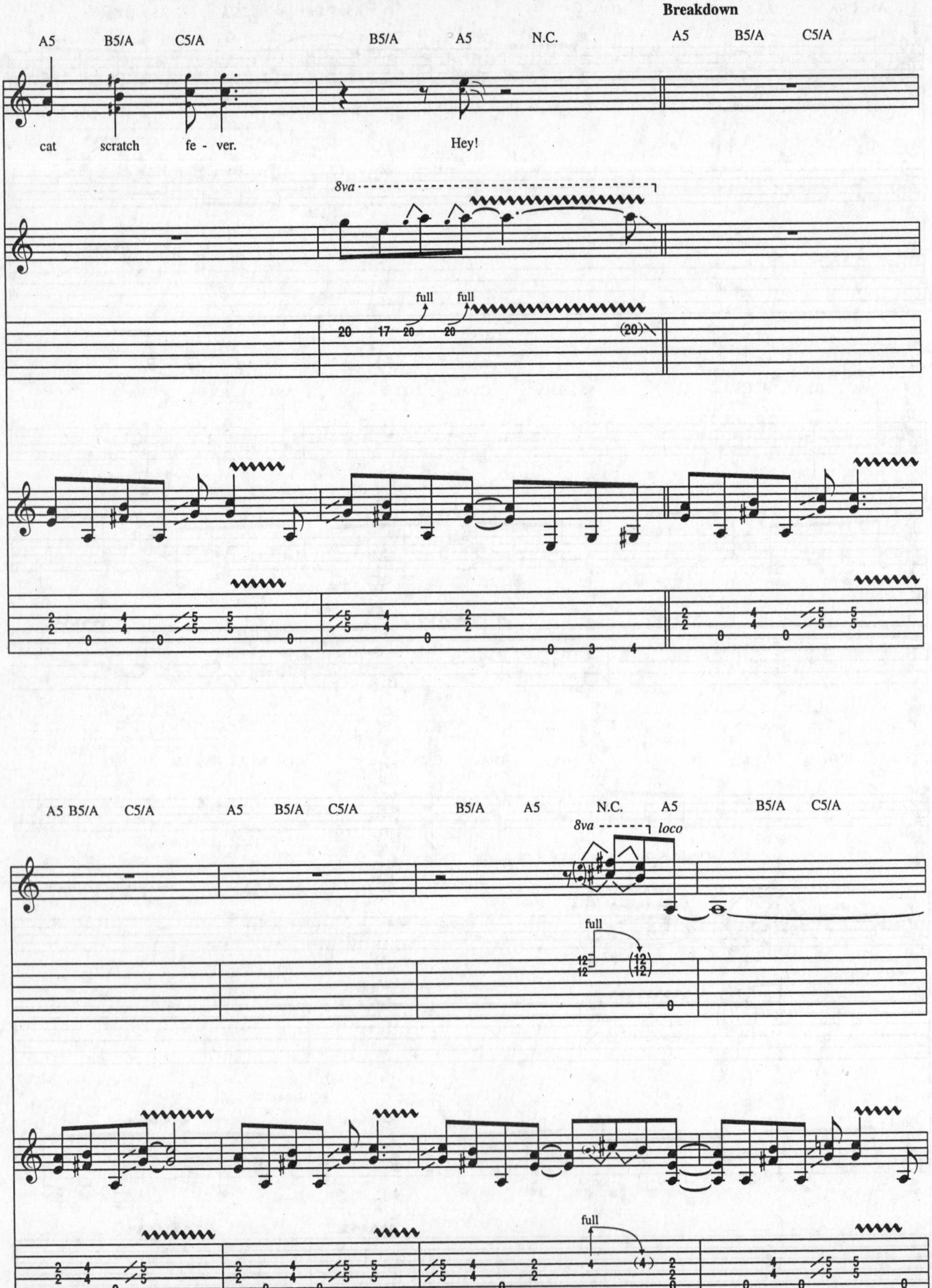

Breakdown

A5 B5/A C5/A B5/A A5 N.C. A5 B5/A C5/A

cat scratch fe - ver. Hey!

8va

full full

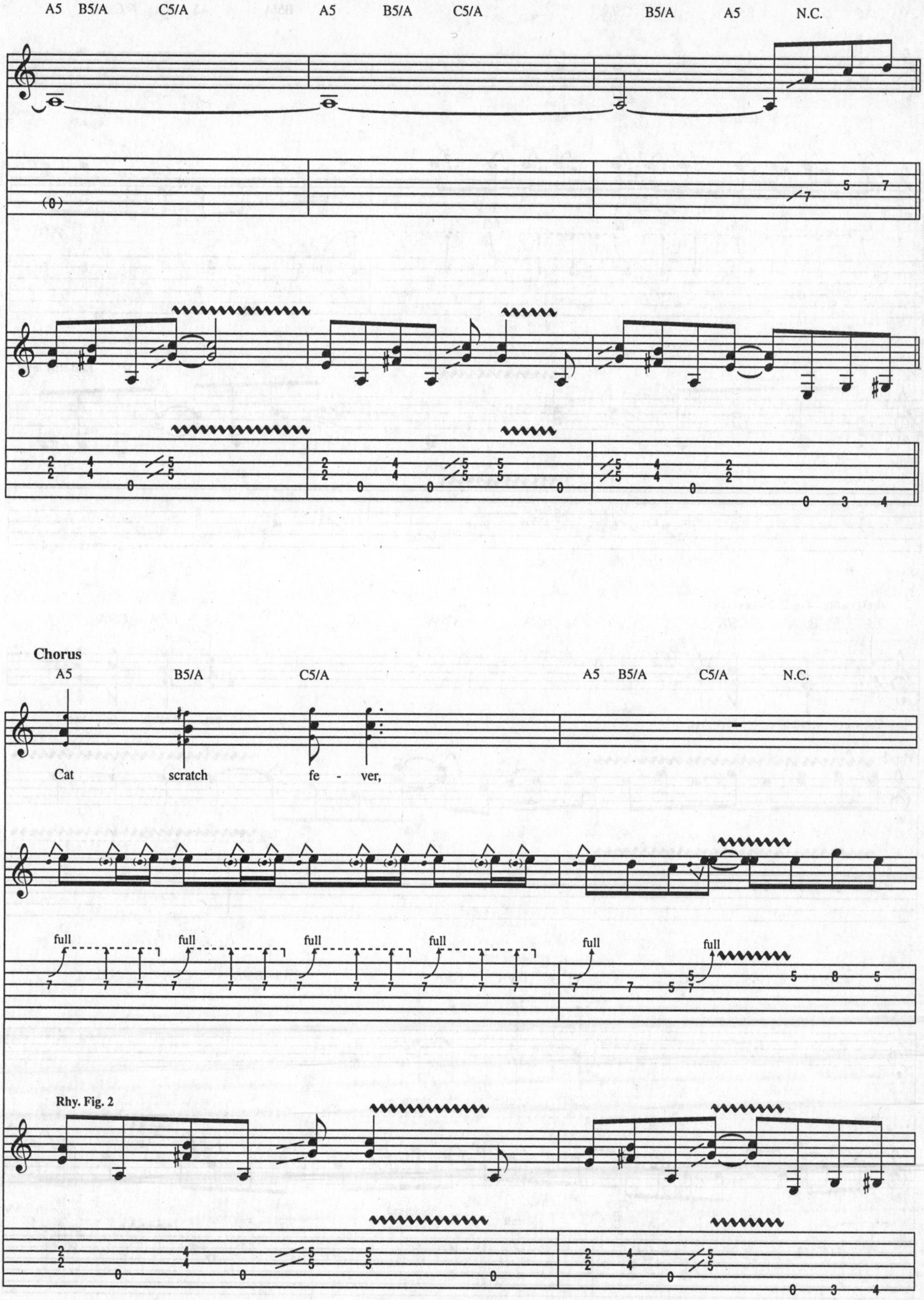

Chorus

A5 B5/A C5/A A5 B5/A C5/A N.C.

Cat scratch fe - ver,

full full full full full full

Rhy. Fig. 2

A5
B5/A
C5/A
B5/A
A5
N.C.
cat
scratch
fe - ver.
full
full
full
full
End Rhy. Fig. 2
Gtr. 1: w/Rhy. Fig. 2, 2 times
A5
B5/A
C5/A
A5
B5/A
C5/A
N.C.
A5
B5/A
C5/A
Cat
scratch
fe - ver,
cat
scratch
fe - ver.
Gtr. 2
8va
full
full
B5/A
A5
N.C.
A5
B5/A
C5/A
A5
B5/A
C5/A
N.C.
Cat
scratch
fe - ver,
8va
full
full
full
hold bend
full
full
full

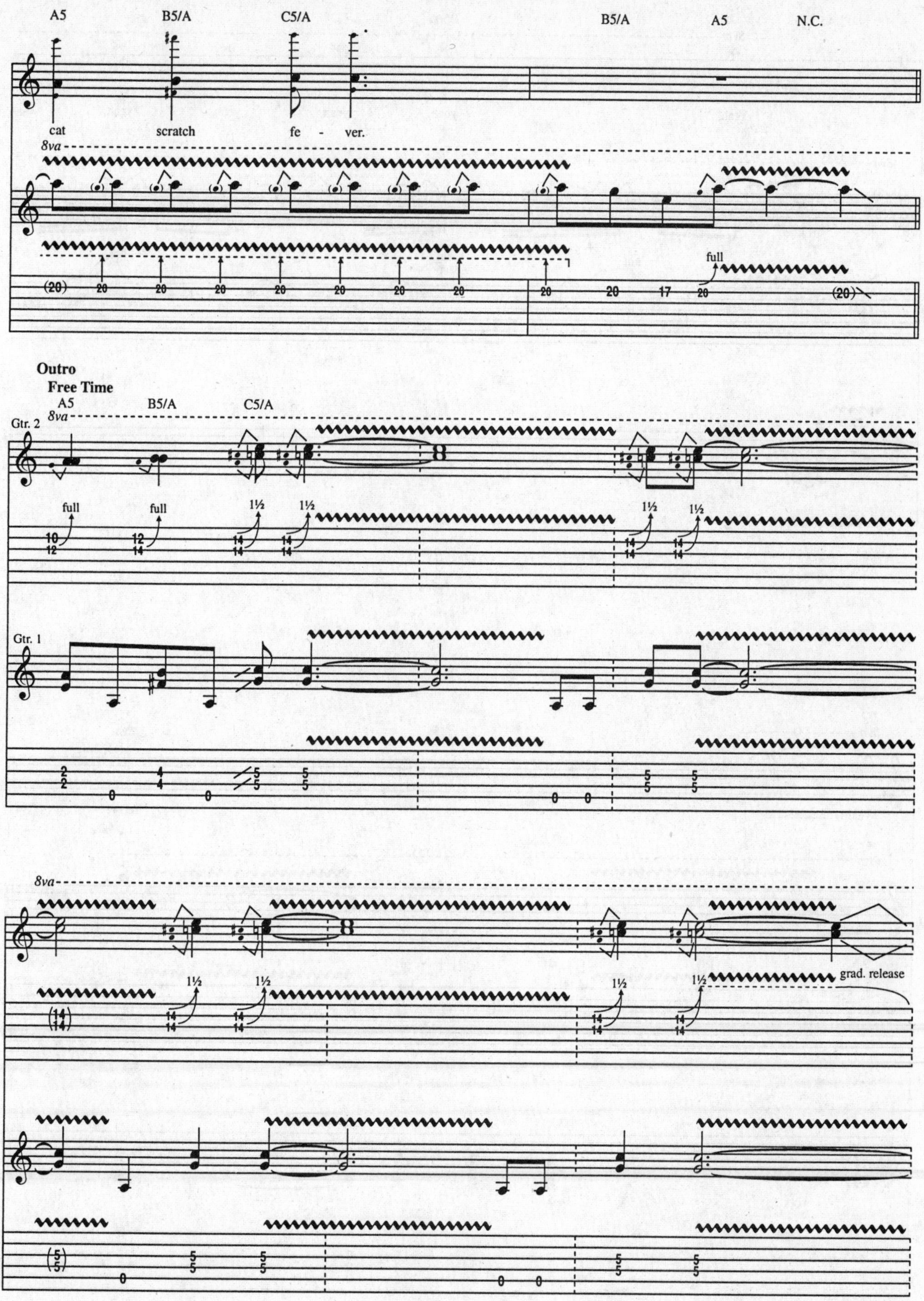
A5
B5/A
C5/A
B5/A
A5
N.C.
cat
scratch
fe - ver.
8va
full
Outro
Free Time
A5
B5/A
C5/A
8va
Gtr. 2
full
full
1½
1½
1½
1½
Gtr. 1
8va
1½
1½
1½
1½
grad. release

A5
B5/A
8va
Yeah,
yeah,
yeah,
yeah,
yeah,
full
yeah!
Yeow!

Chop Suey!

Words and Music by Daron Malakian and Serj Tankian

* Doubled throughout

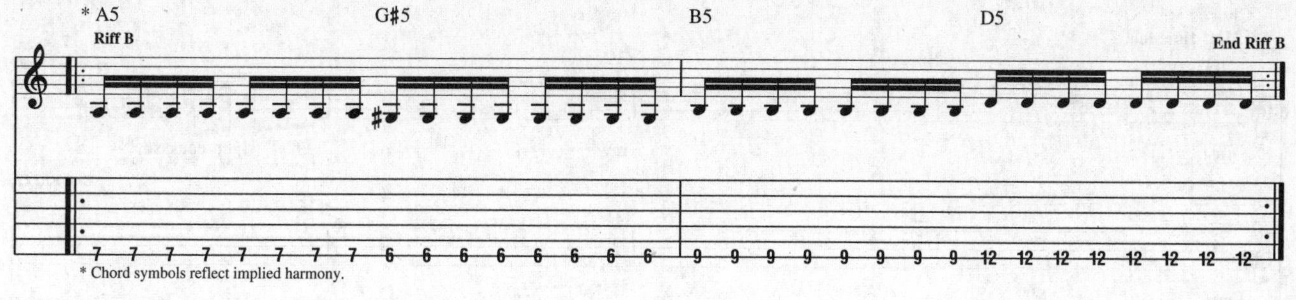

* Chord symbols reflect implied harmony.

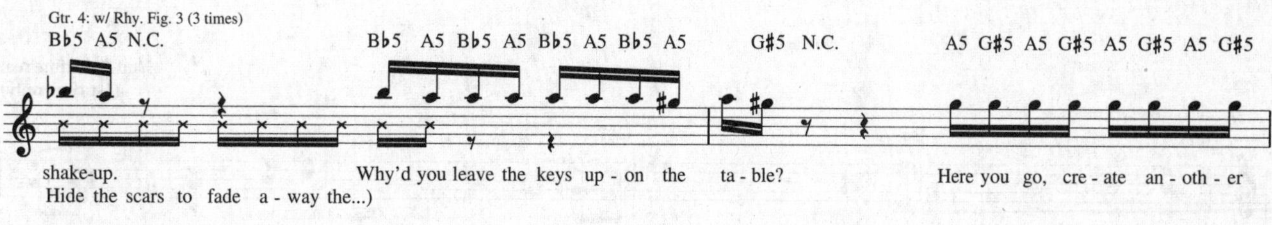

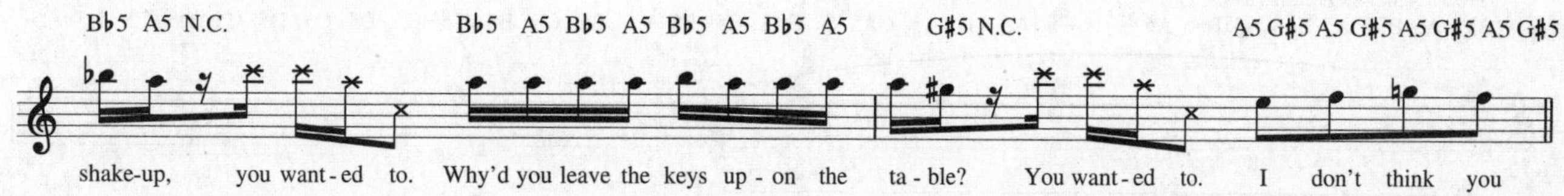

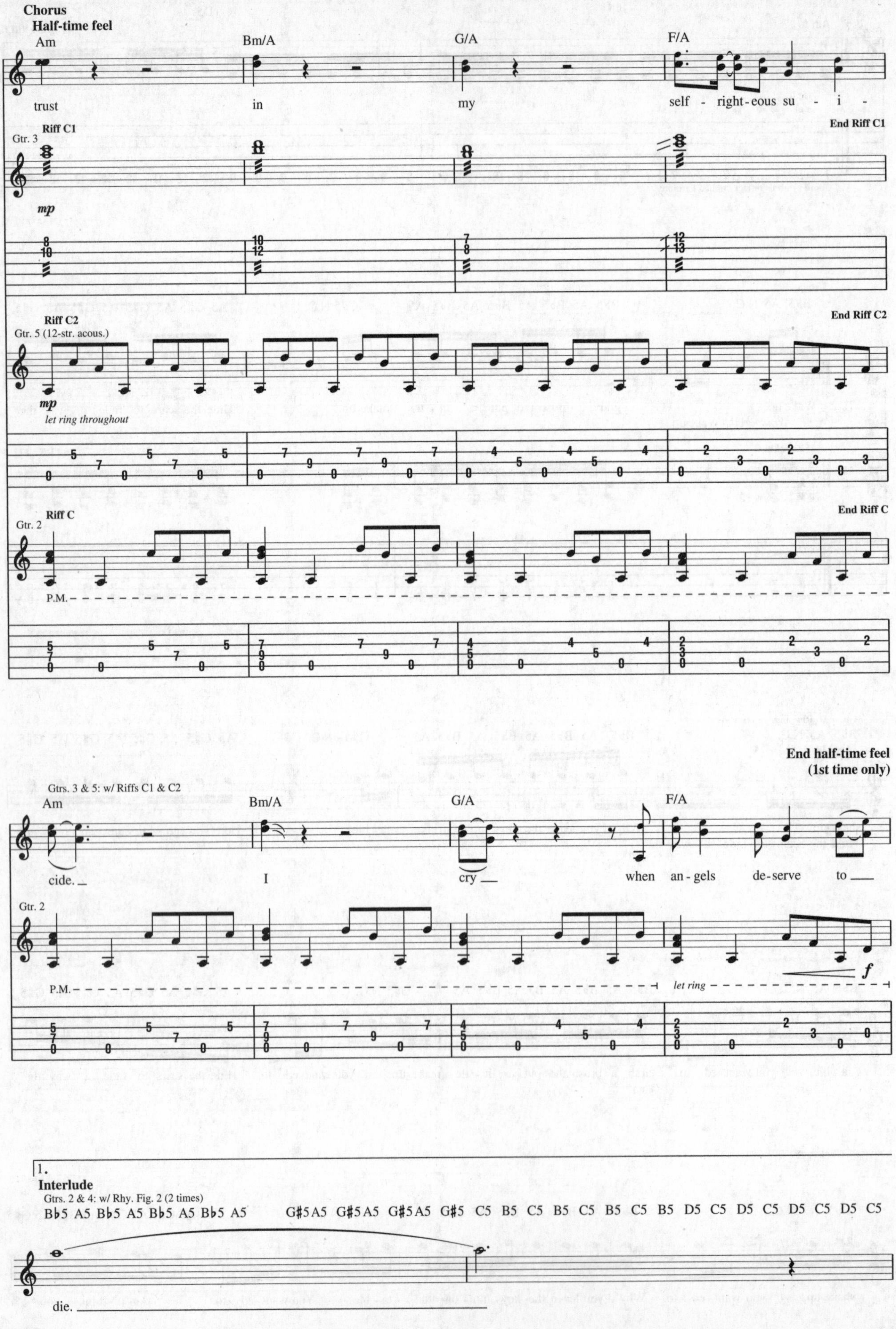

Chorus
Half-time feel

Am Bm/A G/A F/A

trust in my self - right-eous su - i -

Riff C1
Gtr. 3
End Riff C1
mp

Riff C2
Gtr. 5 (12-str. acous.)
End Riff C2
mp
let ring throughout

Riff C
Gtr. 2
End Riff C
P.M.

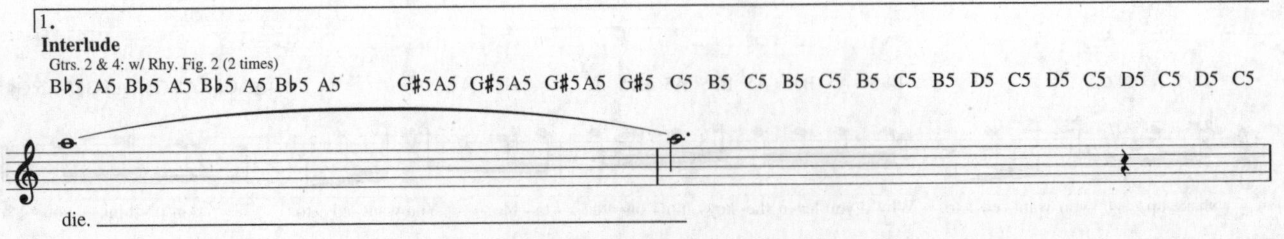

Bb5 A5 Bb5 A5 Bb5 A5 Bb5 A5 G#5 A5 G#5 A5 G#5 A5 G#5 C5 B5 C5 B5 C5 B5 C5 B5 D5 C5 D5 C5 D5 C5 D5 C5
Bb5 A5 Bb5 A5 Bb5 A5 Bb5 A5 Bb5 A5 Bb5 A5 Bb5 A5 Bb5 A5
2.
Gtr. 3: w/ Riff A (1 3/4 times)
Gtr. 5: w/ Riff C2 (1 1/4 times)
Am
Rah!
die
Gtrs. 2 & 4
P.M.
Bm/A
G/A
F/A
Am
in my self - right - eous su - i - cide.
P.M.
let ring
Bm/A
G/A
F
I cry when an - gels deserve to die.
Gtr. 2
Gtr. 3
Gtr. 2
divisi
let ring
Gtr. 5

Bridge
Double-time feel
Gtrs. 2, 3 & 5 tacet
Gtr. 4: w/ Rhy. Fig. 2 (2 times)
2nd time, End double-time feel
Bb5 A5 Bb5 A5 Bb5 A5 Bb5 A5 G#5 A5 G#5 A5 G#5 A5 G#5 C5 B5 C5 B5 C5 B5 C5 B5 D5 C5 D5 C5 D5 C5 D5 C5
Fa - ther! Fa - ther!
(Fa - ther! Fa - ther!
Gtr. 4
P.M.
Fa - ther! Fa - ther!
Fa - ther! Fa - ther!)
Gtr. 4: w/ Riff B (2 times)
A5 G#5 B5 D5 A5 G#5 B5 D5
Fa - ther in - to your hands, I com - mend my spir - it. Fa - ther in - to your hands, why have you for -
Half-time feel
Gtr. 5: w/ Riff C2 (5 3/4 times)
A5 F5 C5 F5
Rhy. Fig. 4
End Rhy. Fig. 4
Gtr. 2
sak - en me in your eyes? For - sak - en me in your thoughts? For -
Gtr. 3
Riff D
End Riff D
Gtr. 4
Rhy. Fig. 4A
End Rhy. Fig. 4A

Gtrs. 2 & 4: w/ Rhy. Figs. 4 & 4A (4 3/4 times)
Gtr. 3: w/ Riff D

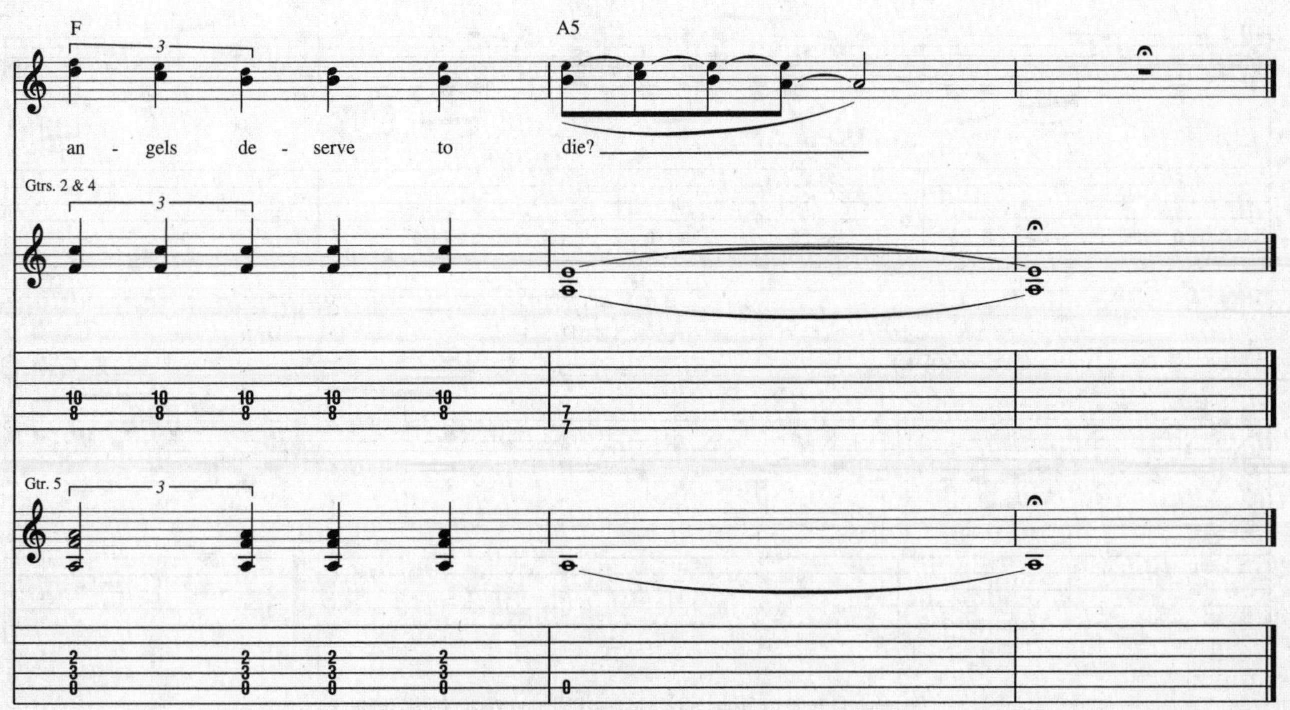

The Claw

By Jerry Reed

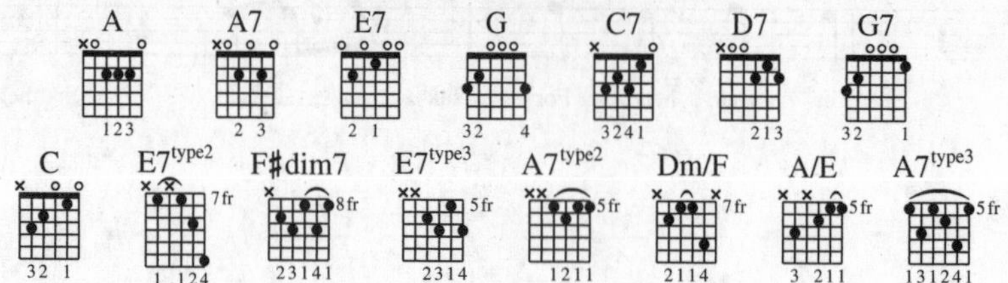

Tune Down 1 Full Step:
① = D ④ = C
② = A ⑤ = G
③ = F ⑥ = D

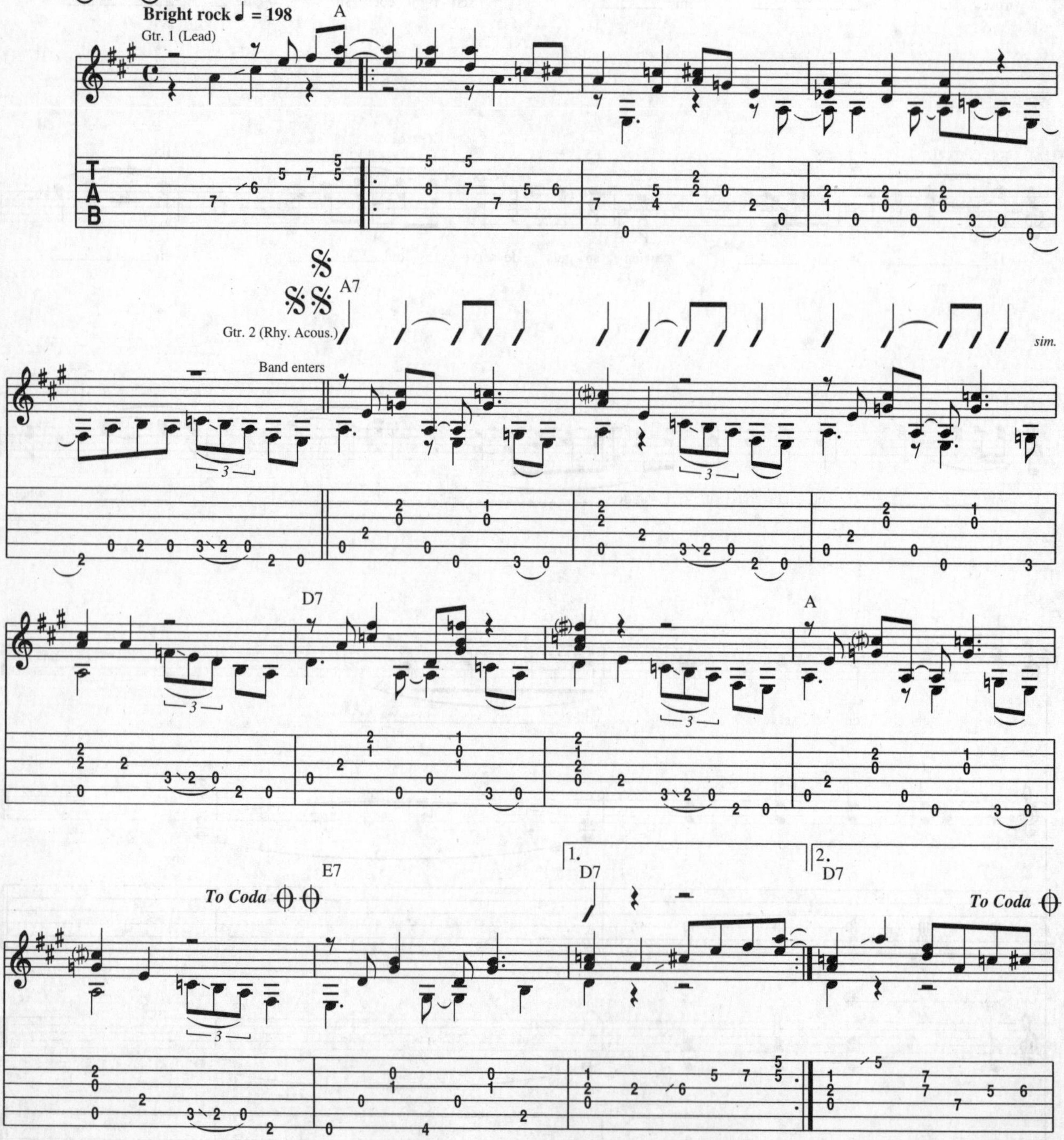

Bright rock ♩ = 198

Gtr. 1 (Lead)

A

Gtr. 2 (Rhy. Acous.)

A7

sim.

Band enters

D7

A

To Coda 𝄌𝄌

E7

1. D7

2. D7

To Coda 𝄌

A7
A7 E7
A
D7 A
D
A
D.S. al Coda
take 2nd ending
Coda
A
E7
A
D7
sim.

A7
E7

D.S. al Coda
take 1st ending and
repeat, al Coda
D7
A
E7

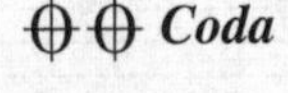
Coda

E7
D7
N.C.

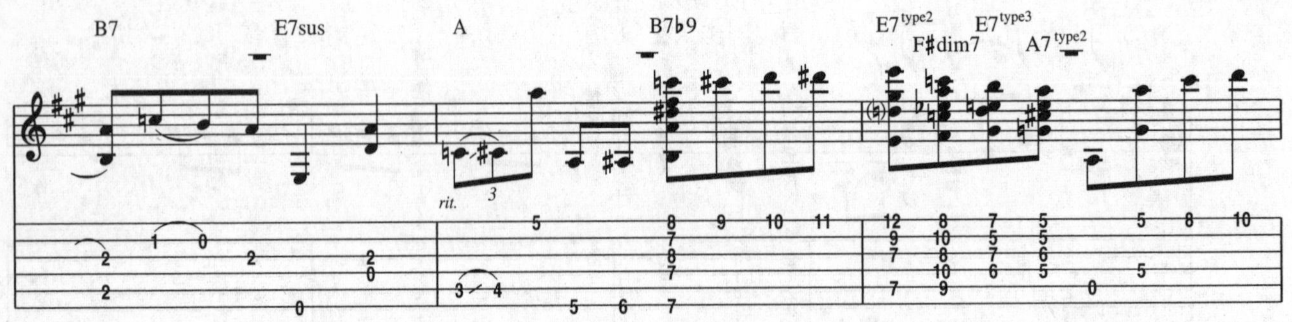
B7
E7sus
A
B7♭9
E7 type2
F♯dim7
E7 type3
A7 type2
rit.

F♯dim7
Dm/F
A/E
A
A7 type3
a tempo

Cold Gin

Words and Music by Ace Frehley

*Chord symbols reflect combined tonality.

Verse
Gtr. 2: w/Rhy. Fill 1, 2nd time
A G6/A A G6/A Dmaj9/A G6/A Dmaj9/A G6/A A
heat - er's broke and I'm, ah, so tired.
time to leave and get an - oth - er quart.
Rhy. Fig. 2
End Rhy. Fig. 2
Gtr. 1
Gtr. 2
Rhy. Fig. 2A
End Rhy. Fig. 2A
Gtrs. 1 & 2: w/Rhy. Figs. 2 & 2A, 2½ times
G6/A A G6/A Dmaj9/A G6/A Dmaj9/A G6/A A
need some fuel to build a fire.
round the cor - ner at the liq - uor store.
The
they had the
Gtr. 2: w/Rhy. Fill 1, 2nd time
G6/A A G6/A Dmaj9/A G6/A
girl next door, her lights are out, yeah.
cheap - est stuff. Is it all I need
Dmaj9/A G6/A A G6/A
The land - lord's gone, I'm down and out.
to get me back on my feet a - gain?
Gtrs. 1 & 2: w/Rhy. Figs. 1 & 1A
Gtr. 2: w/Rhy. Fill 2, 2nd time
A G6/A Dmaj9/A G6/A Dmaj9/A G6/A A G6/A Dmaj9/A G6/A Dmaj9/A G6/A A
Oo, it's
Rhy. Fill 1
Gtr. 2
Rhy. Fill 2
Gtr. 2

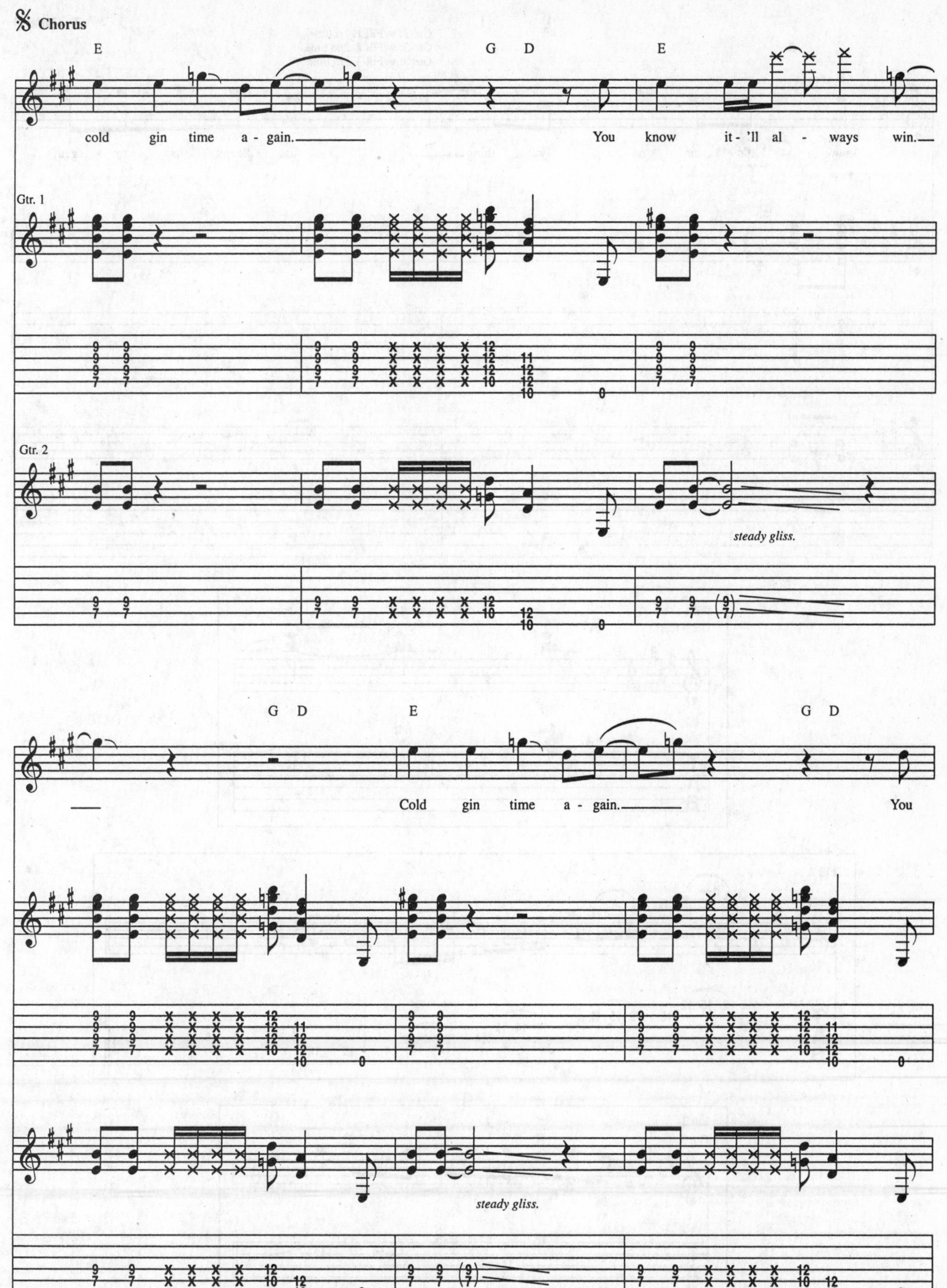
Chorus
E
G D
E
cold gin time a - gain.
You know it - 'll al - ways win.
Gtr. 1
Gtr. 2
steady gliss.
G D
E
G D
Cold gin time a - gain.
You
steady gliss.

To Coda

Gtr. 3: w/Fill 1, 1st time
Gtr. 3: w/Fill 2, 2nd time
Gtr. 3: w/Fill 3, 3rd time
E
know it's the on - ly thing that keeps us to - geth -

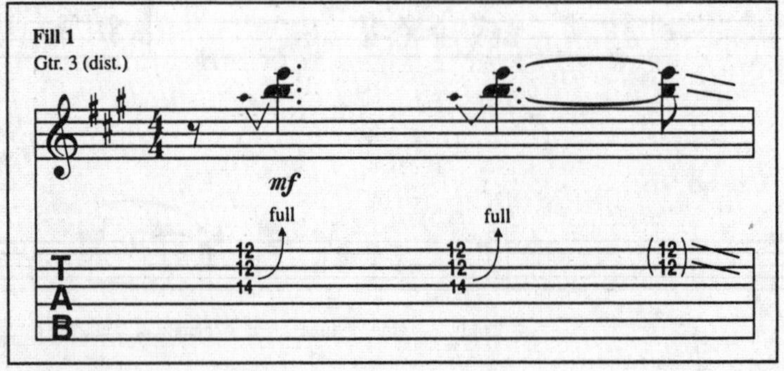
Fill 1
Gtr. 3 (dist.)
mf
full
full

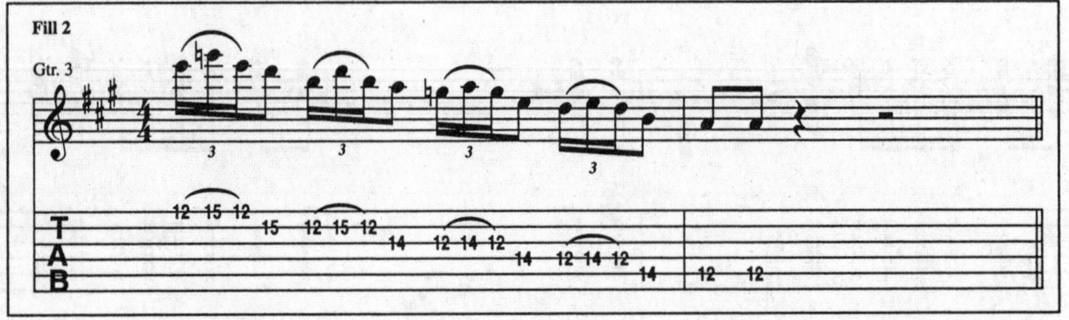
Fill 2
Gtr. 3

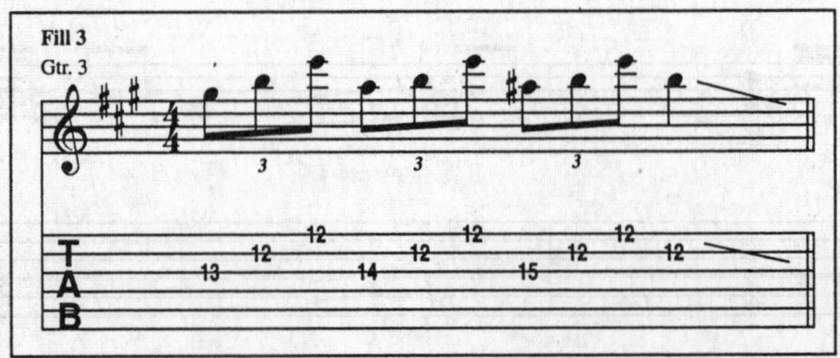
Fill 3
Gtr. 3

Interlude
Gtr. 1: w/Rhy. Fig. 1, 2 times
A G6/A Dmaj9/A G6/A Dmaj9/A G6/A A N.C. A G6/A Dmaj9/A G6/A Dmaj9/A G6/A A N.C.
er.
Ow!
Gtr. 2
A G6/A Dmaj9/A G6/A Dmaj9/A G6/A A N.C. A G6/A Dmaj9/A G6/A Dmaj9/A G6/A A
1.
2. It's
2.
Dmaj9/A G6/A
G5
Gtr. 1
Gtr. 2
fdbk.
pitch: G

Instrumental

2.
N.C.
E
N.C.
play 3 times
E5
D5/E
A/E
Interlude
Gtr. 1: w/Rhy. Fig. 1
A5
G5/A
D/A
G5/A
D/A
G5/A
A5
G5/A
D/A
G5/A
D/A
G5/A
A5
D.S. al Coda
Whoa, yeah!
Oo,
it's
Gtr. 2
Coda
Outro
A
G6/A
Dmaj9/A
G6/A
Dmaj9/A
G6/A
A
N.C.
er.
Ow!

A
G6/A
Dmaj9/A
G6/A
Dmaj9/A
G6/A
A
G6/A
Dmaj9/A
G6/A
Dmaj9/A
G6/A
A
G6/A
Dmaj9/A
G6/A
Dmaj9/A
G6/A
A

Control

Words and Music by Brad Stewart and Wesley Reid Scantlin

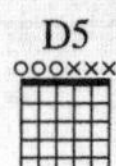

Drop D tuning, down 1/2 step:
(low to high) D♭-A♭-D♭-G♭-B♭-E♭

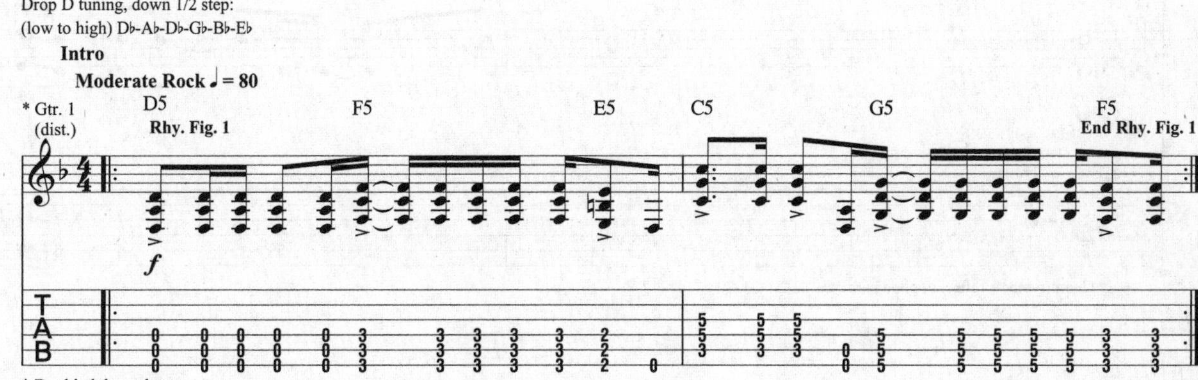

* Doubled throughout

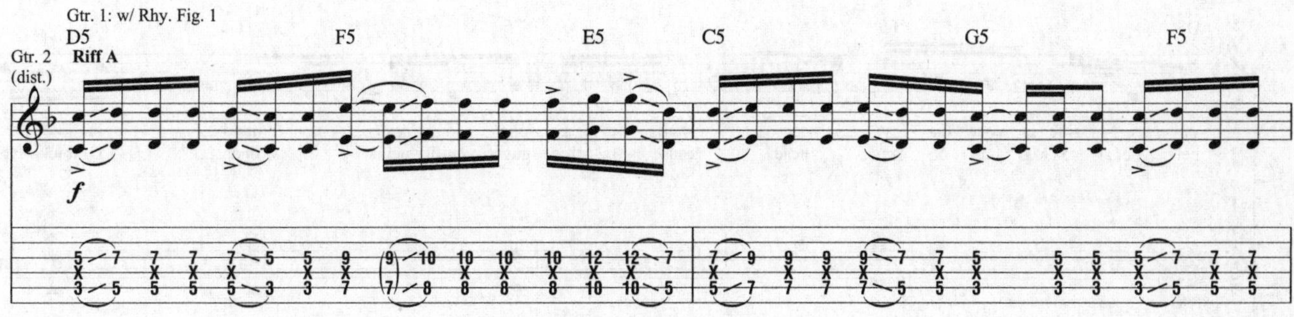

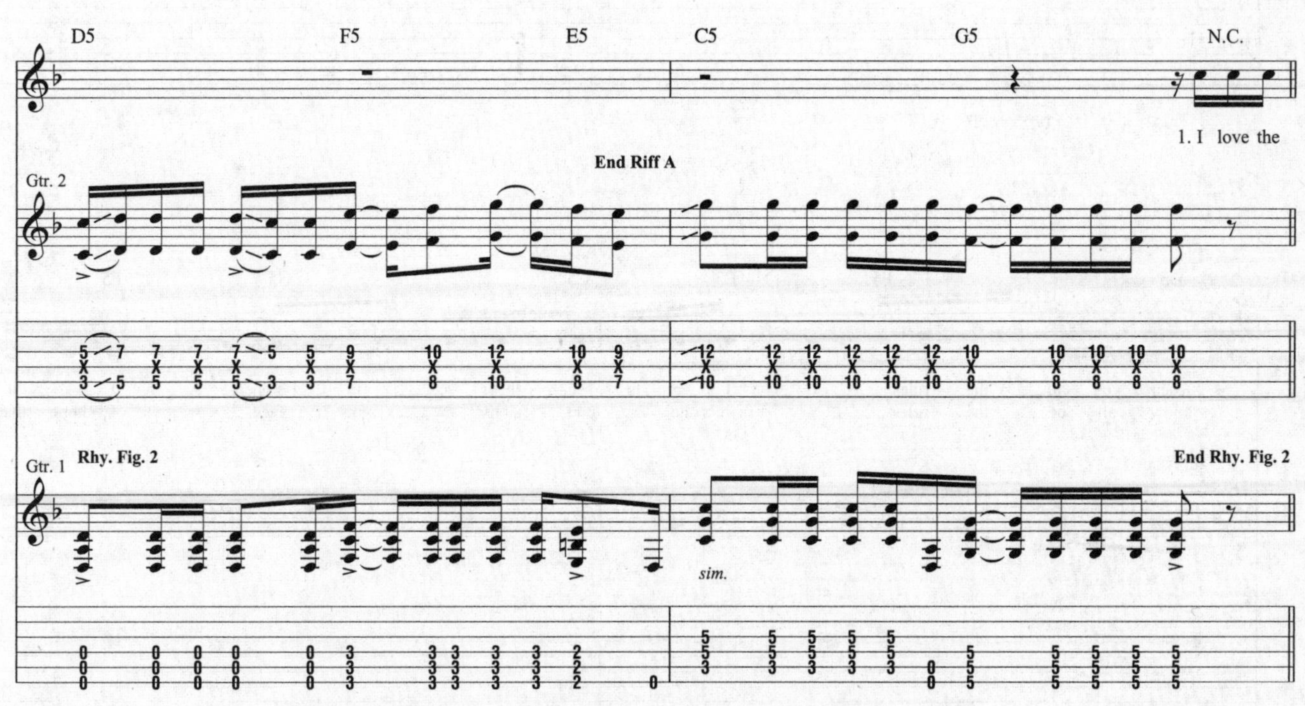

Verse

* Chord symbols reflect implied harmony.

* Set delay for eighth-note regeneration with 3 repeats.

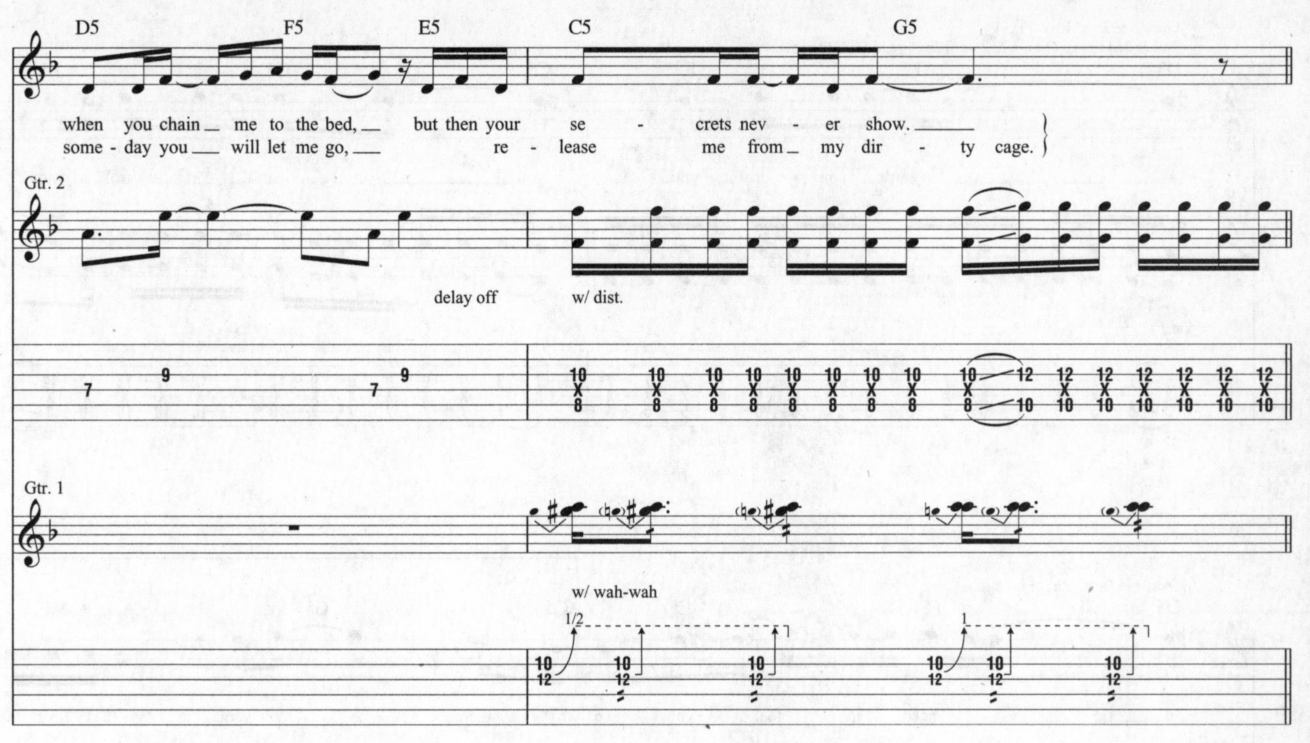
D5
F5
E5
C5
G5
when you chain me to the bed, but then your se - crets nev - er show.
some - day you will let me go, re - lease me from my dir - ty cage.
Gtr. 2
delay off
w/ dist.
Gtr. 1
w/ wah-wah
1/2
1

Chorus
D5
F5
E5
C5
G5
F5
I need to feel you, you need to feel me.
Gtrs. 1 & 2

D5
F5
E5
C5
G5
F5
I can't con - trol you, you're not the one for me, no!

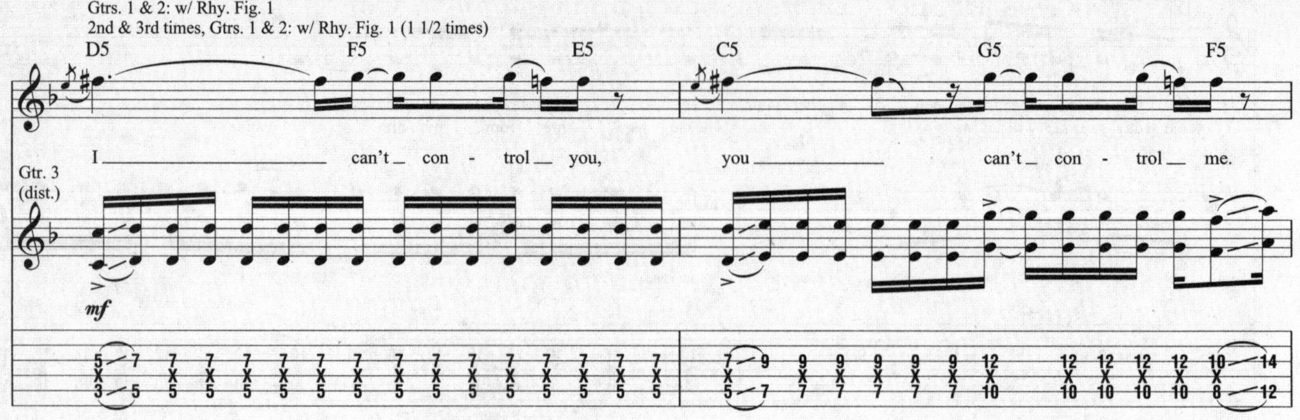

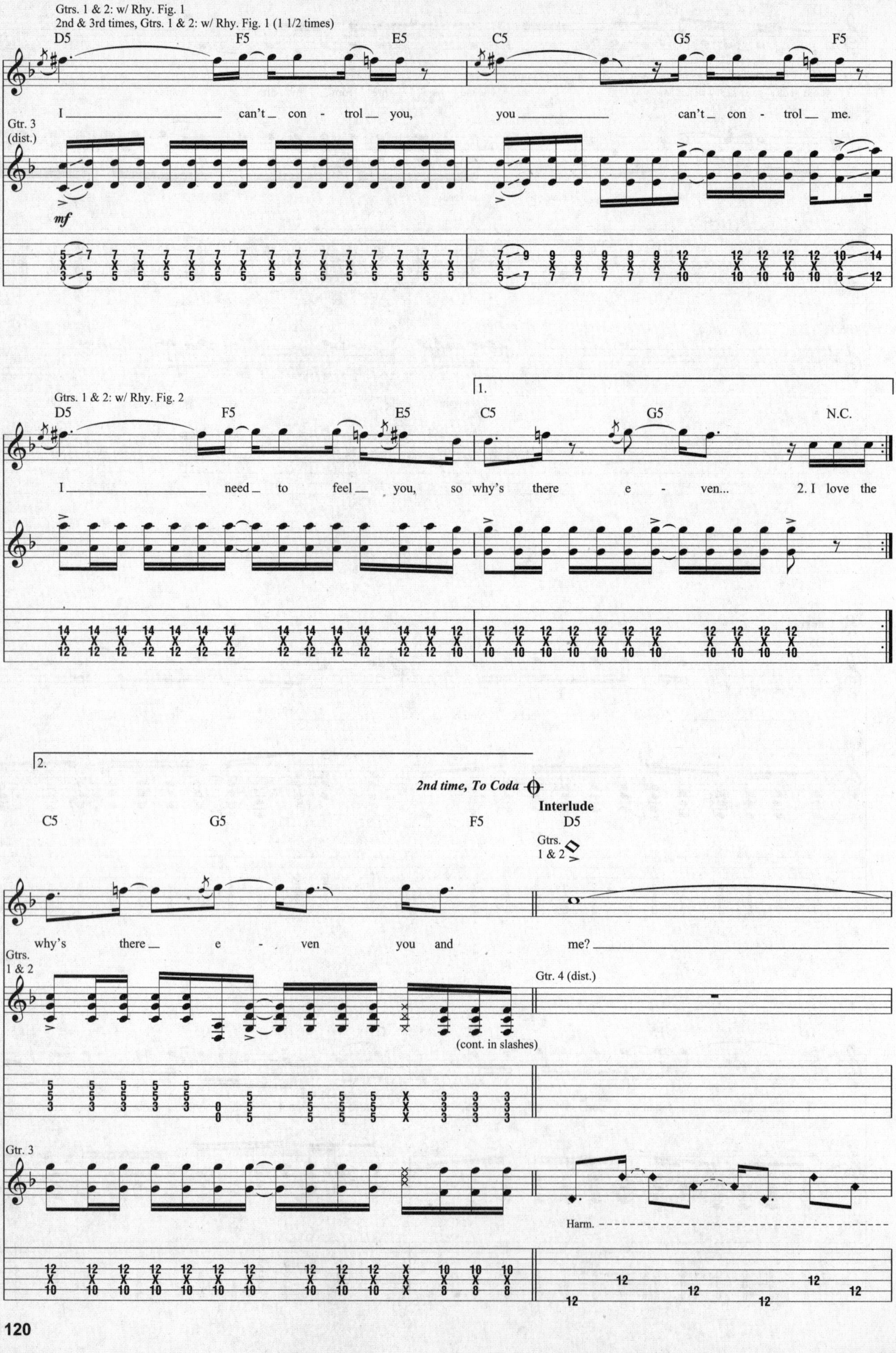

2.

2nd time, To Coda

Interlude

C5 G5 F5 D5

Gtrs. 1 & 2

why's there _ e - ven you and me? ___

Gtrs. 1 & 2

Gtr. 4 (dist.)

(cont. in slashes)

Gtr. 3

Harm.

fdbk.

mf

Harm.

pitch: G

Bridge

Gtrs. 3 & 4 tacet

C5 D5 C5 D5 F5

(cont. in notation)

I love the way you look at me, I love the

Rhy. Fig. 3

Gtr. 1

End Rhy. Fig. 3

grad. bend

1/4

1

mf

w/ clean tone

Rhy. Fig. 3A

Gtr. 2

End Rhy. Fig. 3A

Harm.

mf

w/ clean tone

P.M.

Gtr. 1: w/ Rhy. Fig. 3 (3 times)
Gtr. 2: w/ Rhy. Fig. 3A (7 times)
C5 D5 C5 D5 F5 C5 D5 C5 D5 F5
way you smack my ass. I love the dir - ty things you do.

*Gtr. 1: w fdbk.
* Gtr. 1: w/ Rhy. Fig. 3 (3 times)
C5 D5 C5 D5 F5 C5 D5 C5 D5 F5
I have con - trol of you. I love the way you look at me, I love the
*pitch: G
* f, w/ dist.

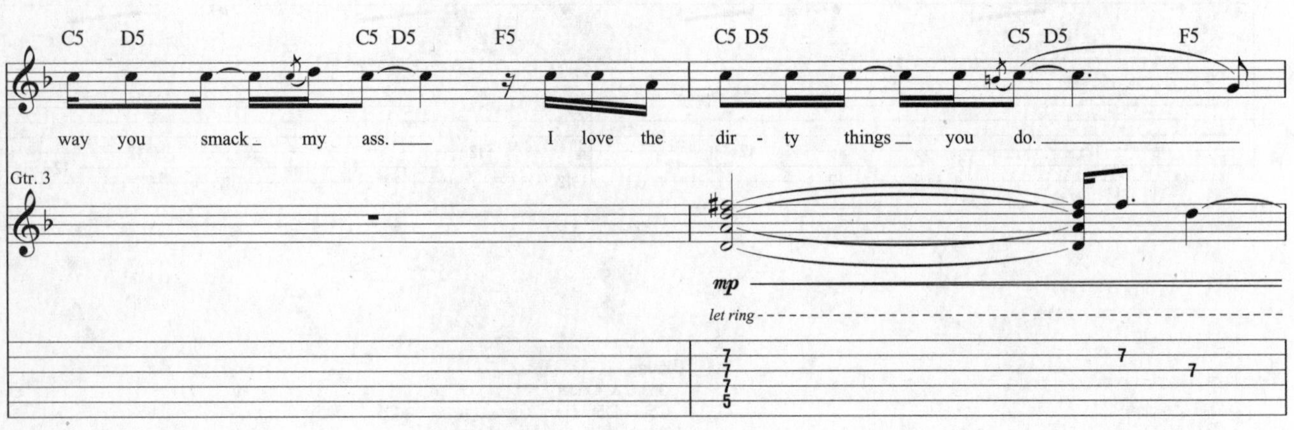
C5 D5 C5 D5 F5 C5 D5 C5 D5 F5
way you smack my ass. I love the dir - ty things you do.
Gtr. 3
mp
let ring

Gtr. 3 tacet
C5 D5 C5 D5 F5 C5 D5 C5 D5 F5
I have con - trol of you. I love the way you look at me, I love the
Gtr. 3
let ring
mf
1/4
1/2
Gtr. 1
Gtrs. 1 & 2
f
w/ dist.
Harm.
f
w/ dist.

C5 D5
C5 D5
F5
C5 D5
C5 D5
F5
way you smack_ my ass.
I love the dir - ty things_ you do.
sim.
C5 D5
C5 D5
F5
C5 D5
C5 D5
F5
I have_ con - trol of you.
I love the way you look at me,
I love the
C5 D5
C5 D5
F5
C5 D5
C5 D5
F5
way you smack_ my ass.
I love the dir - ty things_ you do.
D.S. al Coda
(take 2nd ending)
C5 D5
C5 D5
F5
I have_ con - trol of you!
Coda
Outro
Gtrs. 1 & 2: w/ Rhy. Fig. 1 (3 1/2 times)
Gtr. 3: w/ Riff A
D5
F5
E5
me?
Riff B
Gtr. 4
8va
* w/ chorus, phase & delay
* Set delay for eighth-note regeneration with multiple repeats.

C5
G5
F5
D5
F5
E5
C5
G5
F5
You're not the one for me, no.
(You're not the one for me, no.)
End Riff B
8va
Gtr. 4
Gtr. 3
Gtr. 3: w/ Riff A
Gtr. 4: w/ Riff B
D5
F5
E5
C5
G5
F5
D5
F5
E5
You're not the one for me, no.
C5
G5
F5
You're not the one for me, no.
8va
Gtr. 4
w/ echo repeats
Gtr. 3
Gtrs. 1 & 2
P.M.

Crazy Train

Words and Music by Ozzy Osbourne, Randy Rhoads and Bob Daisley

E/A
D/A
A
E/A
D/A
A
May - be it's not too late to
per - son con - di - tioned to rule and con - trol. The
Cra - zy, I just can - not bear. I'm
E/A
D/A
A
D/F#E/G#
D5
A
learn how to love, and for - get how to hate.
me - di - a sells it, and you live the role.
liv - ing with some - thing that just is - n't fair.
Gtr. 1
P.M.
1/2
Chorus
Gtr. 1: w/ Fill 2, 3rd time
F#5
D5
F#5
D5
Men - tal wounds not heal - ing, life's a bit - ter shame.
Men - tal wounds still scream - ing, driv - ing me in - sane. I'm
Men - tal wounds not heal - ing, who and what's to blame?
8va
loco
Harm.
w/ bar
-1/2
Fill 2
Gtr. 1
15ma
let ring
Harm.
w/ bar
-1/2
Fill 3
Gtr. 1
full

Gtr. 1: w/ Fill 3, 3rd time, see previous page   Gtr. 1: w/ Fill 1, 2nd time

A5   E5   N.C.(F#5)

go - ing off ___ the rails ___ on a cra - zy train. ___

full

A5   E

I'm go - ing off ___ the rails ___ on a cra - zy train. __

P.M.

To Coda

F#5   A5   E5   F#5   D5

15ma   loco   15ma   loco

*Harm.   *Harm.

*Located between 1st and 2nd frets.

1.
Interlude
E
A
E/A
D/A
A
Let's go!
P.M.
1/2
2.
2. I've
Bridge
F#5
A5
E5
D5
I know that things are go - ing wrong for me.
8va
loco
*fdbk.
pitch: D#
*Microphonic fdbk., not caused by string vibration.
E
You've got - ta lis - ten to my words, yeah,

Guitar Solo
F#5
E5
D5
C#5
yeah!
Gtr. 2 (dist.)
hold bend
full
Gtr. 1
B5
A5
G#5
F#5
1/2
full
hold bend
full
full
8va
E5
D5
C#5
B5
A5
G#5
rake
full
full

F#5
8va
-1/2
w/ bar
-1/2
full
E5
5:4
D5
C#5
B5
A5
G#5
F#5
full
full
E5
D5
C#5

D.S. al Coda
B5
A5
G#5
E5
loco
full
full

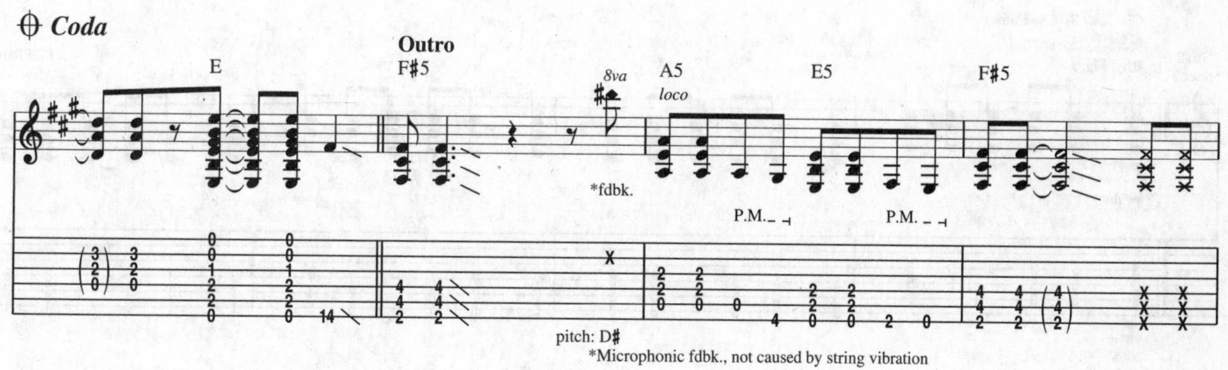

Coda
Outro
E
F#5
8va
A5
loco
E5
F#5
*fdbk.
P.M.
P.M.
pitch: D#
*Microphonic fdbk., not caused by string vibration

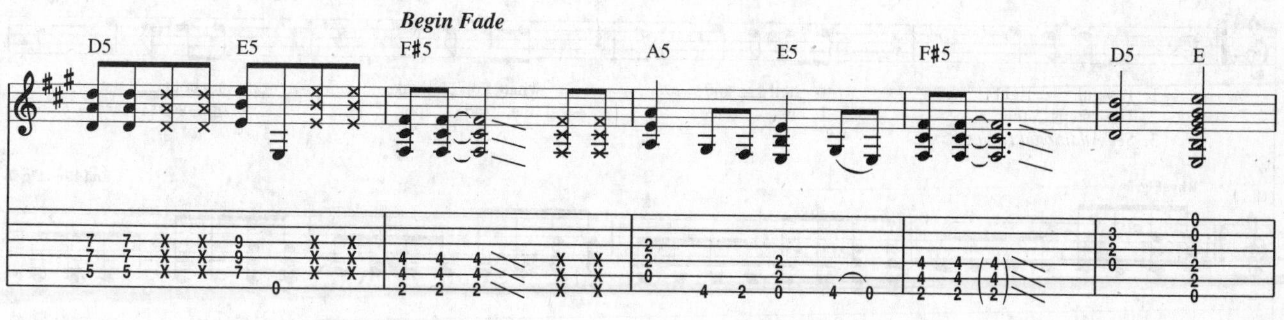

Begin Fade
D5
E5
F#5
A5
E5
F#5
D5
E

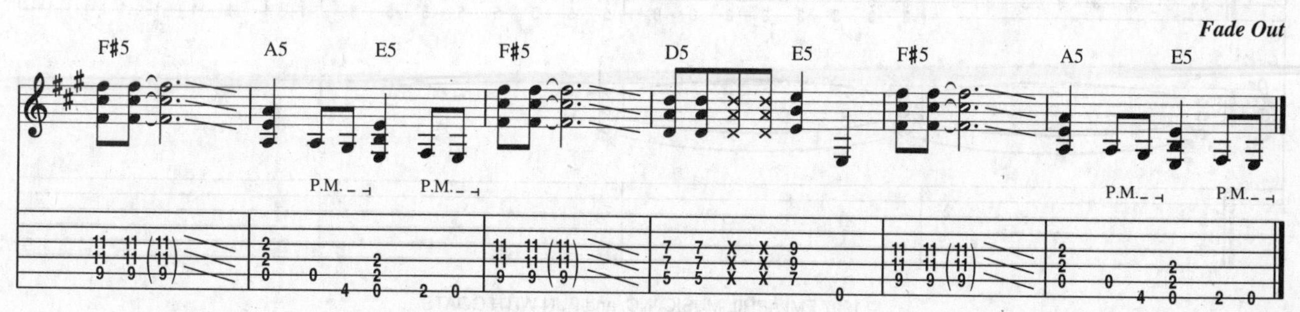

Fade Out
F#5
A5
E5
F#5
D5
E5
F#5
A5
E5
P.M.
P.M.
P.M.
P.M.

Dammit

Words and Music by Scott Raynor, Mark Hoppus and Tom DeLonge

Gtr. 1: w/ Rhy. Fig. 2
C5
G5
A5
F5
I won't try to ar - gue or hold it a - gainst you.
The tim - ing and struc - ture. Did you hear? He f**ked her.
Gtrs. 1 & 2: w/ Rhy. Fig. 1, 2 times
C5
G5
A5
I know that you're leav - in', you must have
A day late, a buck short. I'm writ - ing
F5
C5
G5
your rea - sons. The sea - son is call - in',
the re - port on los - ing and fail - in'.
1.
Interlude
Gtr. 1: w/ Riff A, 2 times
Gtr. 2: w/ Rhy. Fig. 1, 2 times
A5
F5
C5
7
your pic - tures are fall - in' down.
When I move I'm flail - ing
2.
Chorus
Half-Time Feel
C5
G5
now. And it's happened once a - gain, I'll turn to a
back. And it'll hap-pen once a - gain, you'll turn to a
Gtr. 1
Gtr. 2
Rhy. Fig. 3
End Rhy. Fig. 3

End Half-Time Feel
Gtr. 2: w/ Rhy. Fig. 3, 3 times
A5
F5
friend, some - one that un - der - stands, sees
friend, some - one that un - der - stands and sees
Gtr. 1

Half-Time Feel
C5
through the mas - ter plan. But ev - 'ry - bod - y's
through the mas - ter plan. But ev - 'ry - bod - y's

G5
A5
gone, and I've been here for too long to
gone, and you've been there for too long to

To Coda 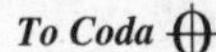

End Half-Time Feel

F5 G5

face this on___ my___ own. Well, I guess this is grow - ing
face this on___ your___ own. Well, I guess this is grow - ing

(cont. in slash, 2nd time)

Gtr. 1: w/ Riff A, 2 times
Gtr. 2: w/ Rhy. Fig. 1, 2 times

C5 G5 A5 F5

up. Well, I guess this is grow - ing

D.S. al Coda
(take 2nd ending)

C5 G5 A5 F5

up.

Coda

Interlude

C Dsus4

Rhy. Fig. 4

Gtr. 1

mp

up.

Gtr. 3
(acous.) Riff B

mp

let ring throughout

Gtr. 2

Additional Lyrics

3. And maybe I'll see you at a movie sneak preview.
You'll show up and walk by on the arm of that guy.
And I'll smile and you'll wave, we'll pretend it's okay.
The charade, it won't last. When he's gone I won't come back.

Dancing in the Street

Words and Music by Marvin Gaye, Ivy Hunter and William Stevenson

D5
C5
Sum - mer's here, and the time is right for danc - in' in the street.
P.H.
P.M.
pitch: F
F
F#

Chorus
D5 D5
Rhy. Fig. 2
Gtr. 2
They're danc - in' in Chi - ca - go,
(They'll be danc - in'.
down in
P.M.
P.H.
pitch: G
G
G

End Rhy. Fig. 2
Rhy. Fig. 3
New Or - leans,
Danc - in' in the streets.
up in New York Cit - y.
Danc - in' in the streets.)
Riff B
P.M.

Post-Chorus
G5
G5
End Rhy. Fig. 3
Rhy. Fig. 4
All we need is mu - sic, sweet mu - sic. There'll be
(Sweet, sweet, sweet, sweet mu - sic.
End Riff B
Riff C
End Riff C
P.M.
D5
mu - sic ev - 'ry - where. There'll be swing-in', sway - in',
Sweet mu - sic ev - 'ry - where. Ooh,
F♯
End Rhy. Fig. 4
rec - ords play - in', danc - in' a in the street. Oh,
ooh.)
P.M.
P.H.
pitch: F E

Bridge
F#
Bm
It does-n't mat-ter what you wear, just as long as you are there. So come on,
(Ah. Ah.
Gtr. 3
P.M.
P.H.
Gtr. 2
let ring
E
A5
ev-'ry guy grab a girl, ev-'ry-where 'round the world. There'll be
Ah.)
pitch: G#
w/ bar
-1 1/2
slack

Interlude
Gtr. 2: w/ Rhy. Fig. 2
Gtr. 3: w/ Riff A (2 times)
D5
danc - in'. They're danc - in' in the street.
2. It's just an
(Ooh,
Verse
Gtr. 2: w/ Rhy. Fig. 2 (2 times)
Gtr. 3: w/ Riff A (4 times)
D5
in - vi - ta - tion, 'cross the na - tion, a chance for the folks to meet.
ooh.)
There'll be laugh - in', sing - in', mu - sic swing - in',
Chorus
Gtr. 2: w/ Rhy. Fig. 2
Gtr. 3: w/ Riff A (2 times)
danc - in' a in the street. Phil - a - del - phia, P. A.,
(Danc - in' in the streets.
Bal - ti - more and D. C., now. Can't for - get the Mo - tor Cit -
Danc - in' in the streets.
Gtr. 2: w/ Rhy. Fig. 3
Gtr. 3: w/ Riff B
Post-Chorus
Gtr. 2: w/ Rhy. Fig. 4
Gtr. 3: w/ Riff C (2 times)
G5
y. All we need is mu - sic, sweet mu -
Danc - in' in the streets.) (Sweet, sweet,
D5
- sic. There'll be mu - sic ev - 'ry - where. There'll be
sweet, sweet mu - sic. Sweet mu - sic ev - 'ry - where. Ooh,
Gtr. 3: w/ Riff A (2 times)
F#
swing-in', sway - in', rec - ords play - in', danc - in' a in the street. Oh,
ooh.)

Bridge
F#
Bm
It does-n't mat-ter what you wear, just as long as you are there. Come on,
(Ah.
Ah.
Gtr. 3
Riff D
P.M.
Gtr. 2
let ring
E5
A5
ev-'ry guy grab your girl, ev-'ry-where 'round the world.
Ah.)
End Riff D
8va
loco
w/ bar
-1 1/2

Interlude
Gtr. 2 tacet
Gtr. 3: w/ Riff A (2 times)
D5
Ah!
Ha, ha, ha!
Ah,
yeah! Ow!
Gtr. 4 (dist.)
w/ bar
Guitar Solo
Gtr. 3: w/ Riff A
D5
Gtr. 2
G5
8va
loco
w/ bar
* Harm.
* Harmonic located between 3rd & 4th frets.
** Vib. w/ bar
Gtr. 3: w/ Riff C
D5
P.S.
† Tap w/ edge of pick.
†† Tap w/ edge of pick a few inches past fretboard.
* † Tap w/ edge of pick.
Gtr. 3: w/ Riff A
G5

Gtr. 3: w/ Riff C
F#
1/2
1/2
1

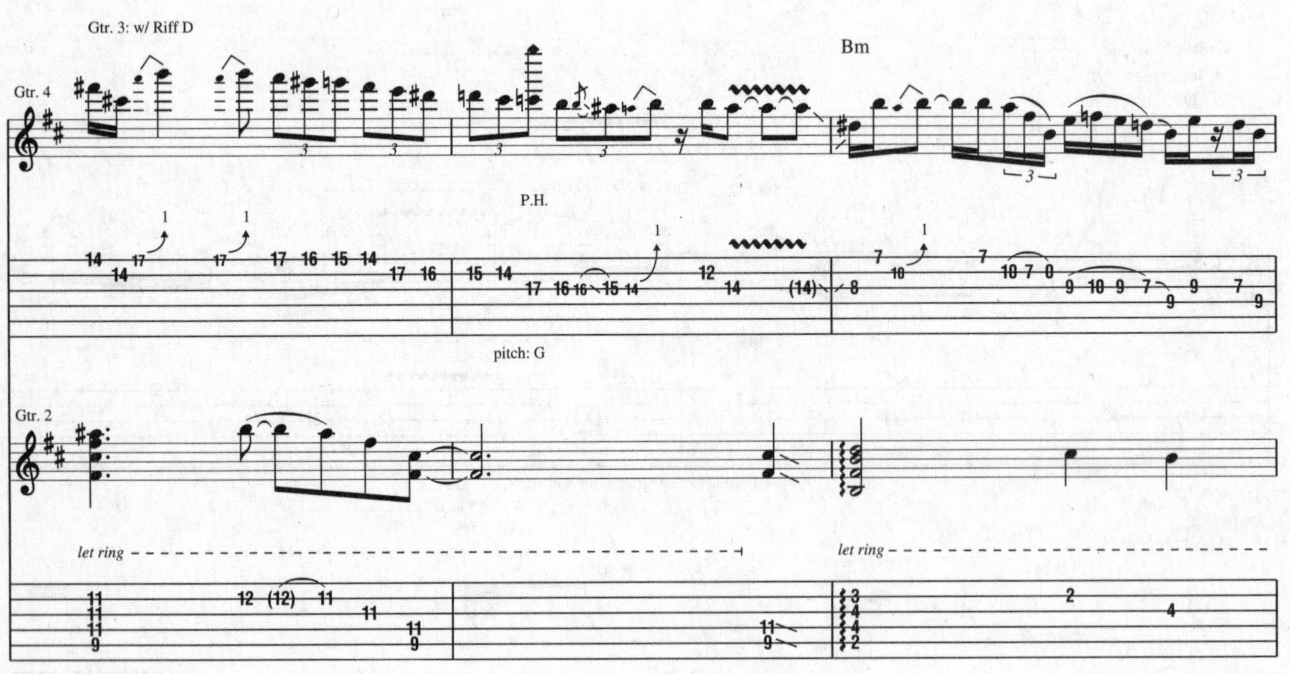

Gtr. 3: w/ Riff D
Bm
Gtr. 4
P.H.
pitch: G
Gtr. 2
let ring
let ring

E
8va
let ring
let ring

A5

8va

loco

P.S.

let ring

w/ bar

-2 1/2

slack

Outro-Chorus

Gtr. 2: w/ Rhy. Fig. 2 (till fade)
Gtr. 3: w/ Riff A (till fade)
Gtr. 4 tacet

D5

Danc - in'. They're danc - in' in the street. (Danc-in' in the streets.) Way down in L. A. ev - er - y day they're danc - in' in the street. Danc-in' in the streets. Danc - in' in the streets.

Begin fade

San Fran-cis - co way, Danc-in' in the streets. they do it ev - er - y day, now. Danc-in' in the streets.

(Ooh, ooh.

Fade out

A-cross the o - cean blue, Danc-in' in the streets. me and you danc-in' in the street. Danc-in' in the streets.)

Ooh, ooh.)

Don't Treat Me Bad

Words and Music by Bill Leverty, Carl Snare, Michael Foster and Cosby Ellis

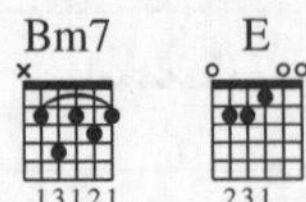

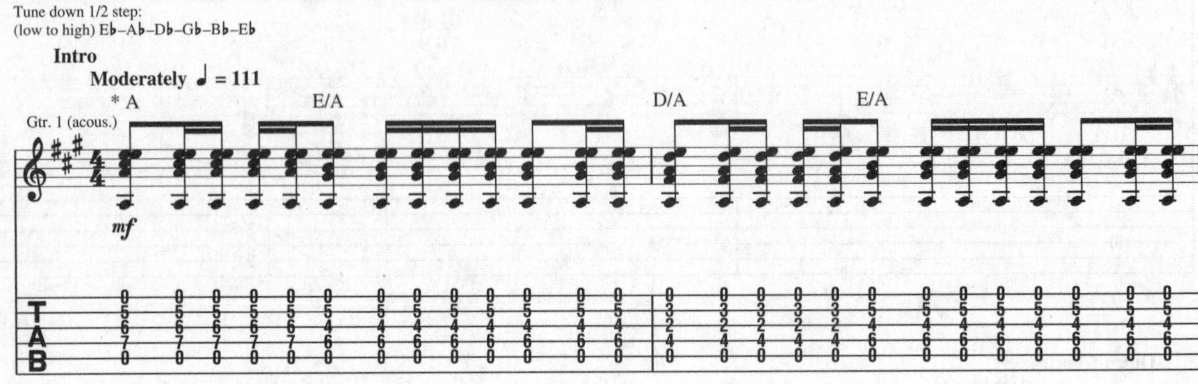

* Chord symbols reflect basic harmony.

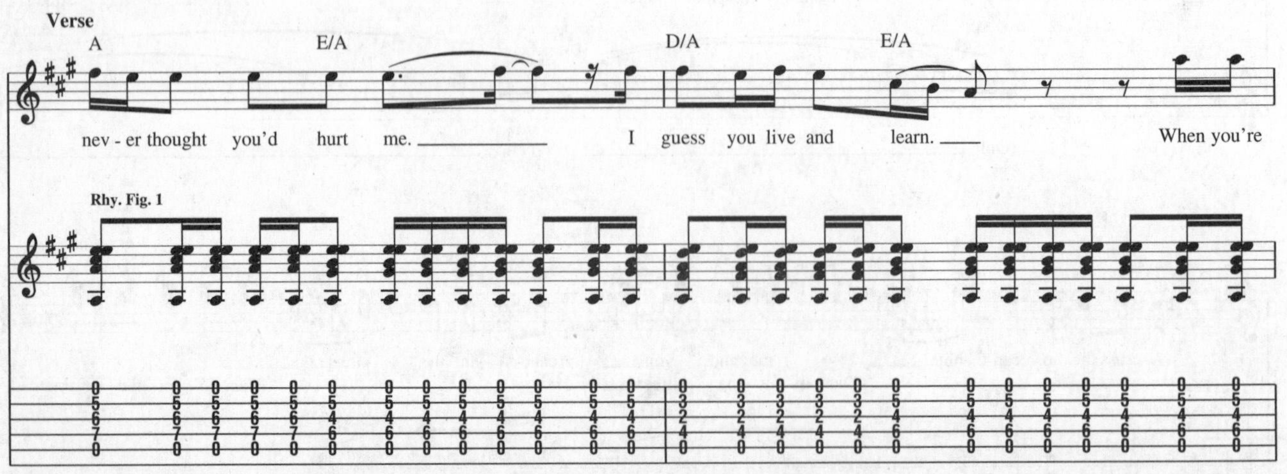

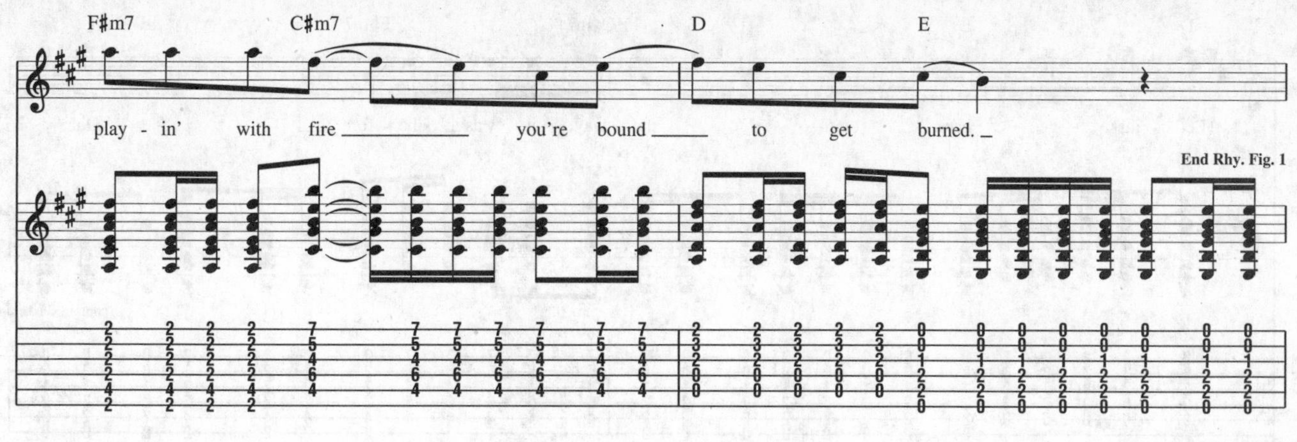
F#m7 C#m7 D E
play - in' with fire you're bound to get burned.
End Rhy. Fig. 1

Gtr. 1: w/ Rhy. Fig. 1
A E/A D/A E/A
I've been mis - treat - ed, I've been used be - fore. I get

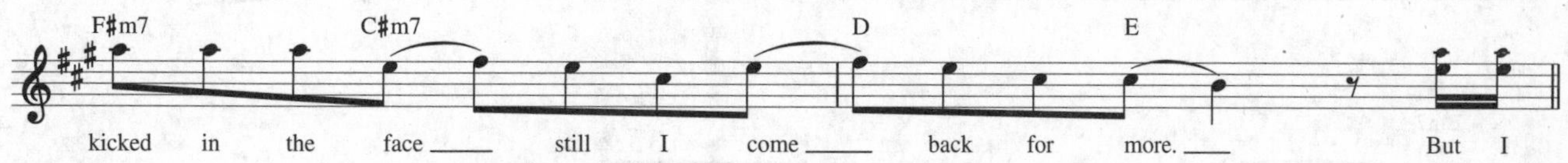
F#m7 C#m7 D E
kicked in the face still I come back for more. But I

Pre-Chorus
D E C#m7 F#m7 E
won't cry no more 'cause the tears are all in vain. We can
Gtr. 1

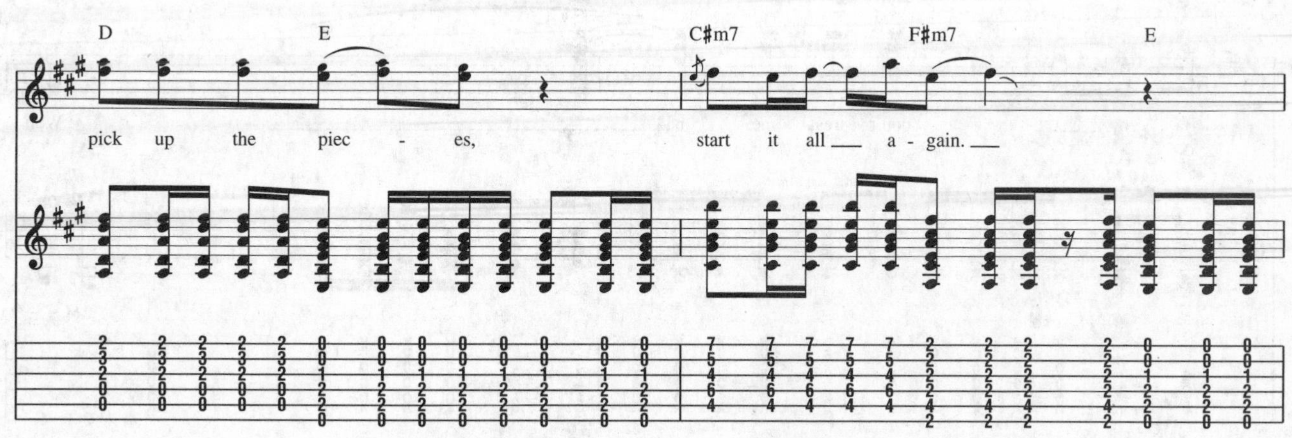
D E C#m7 F#m7 E
pick up the piec - es, start it all a - gain.

D
E
C#m7
F#m7
E
Let's just get back to the way it was be - fore.
Oh,
Gtr. 1
(cont. in slashes)
Gtr. 2 (elec.)
Rhy. Fig. 2
P.S.
w/ dist.
Bm7
E
girl, I can't take an - y - more.
Gtr. 2
End Rhy. Fig. 2
P.M.
Chorus
Gtr. 1 tacet
2nd time, Gtrs. 1 & 3 tacet
A5
Bm7
D5
E5
Ba - by, don't treat me bad.
Well
Rhy. Fig. 3
P.M.

A5
Bm7
D5
E5
Voc. Fig. 1
End Voc. Fig. 1
this could be the best thing that you'll ev - er have.
(Whoa.)
let ring
let ring
Ba - by, don't treat me bad. You can
P.M.
A5
Bm7
E5
A5
A/C♯
D5
A/C♯
do an - y - thing but, ba - by don't treat me bad.
End Rhy. Fig. 3
Rhy. Fig. 4
P.M.
To Coda
B5
D5
E5
Esus4
E
Whoa, don't treat me bad.
2. Oo, I
End Rhy. Fig. 4

Verse
A E/A D/A E/A
gave ev - 'ry - thing, but you threw it all a - way. I can't
Gtr. 2
w/ bar
Rhy. Fig. 5
*Gtrs. 1 & 3
mf w/ chorus
*Gtr. 3 (elec.)
Gtr. 2 tacet
F#7(no3rd) C#m7 D E
Gtrs. 1 & 3: w/ Rhy. Fig. 5
A E/A
take an - y - more of these games that you play. Well I've been through heart-ache, and
(Oo.)
Gtrs. 1 & 3
End Rhy. Fig. 5
D/A E/A F#7(no3rd) C#m7 D E
I've been through pain. And it's hard to be - lieve you still treat me this way. But I
Pre-Chorus
D E C#m7 F#m7 E
won't cry no more 'cause the tears are all in vain. We can
Gtrs. 1 & 3

D.S. al Coda

* P.M. - 5th string.

F#m7
C#m7
D
E
8va
1/2
A
'Cause
girl,
I can't take an - y - more.
Bm7
E5
Esus4
Oo,
loco
steady gliss.
P.S.

Interlude

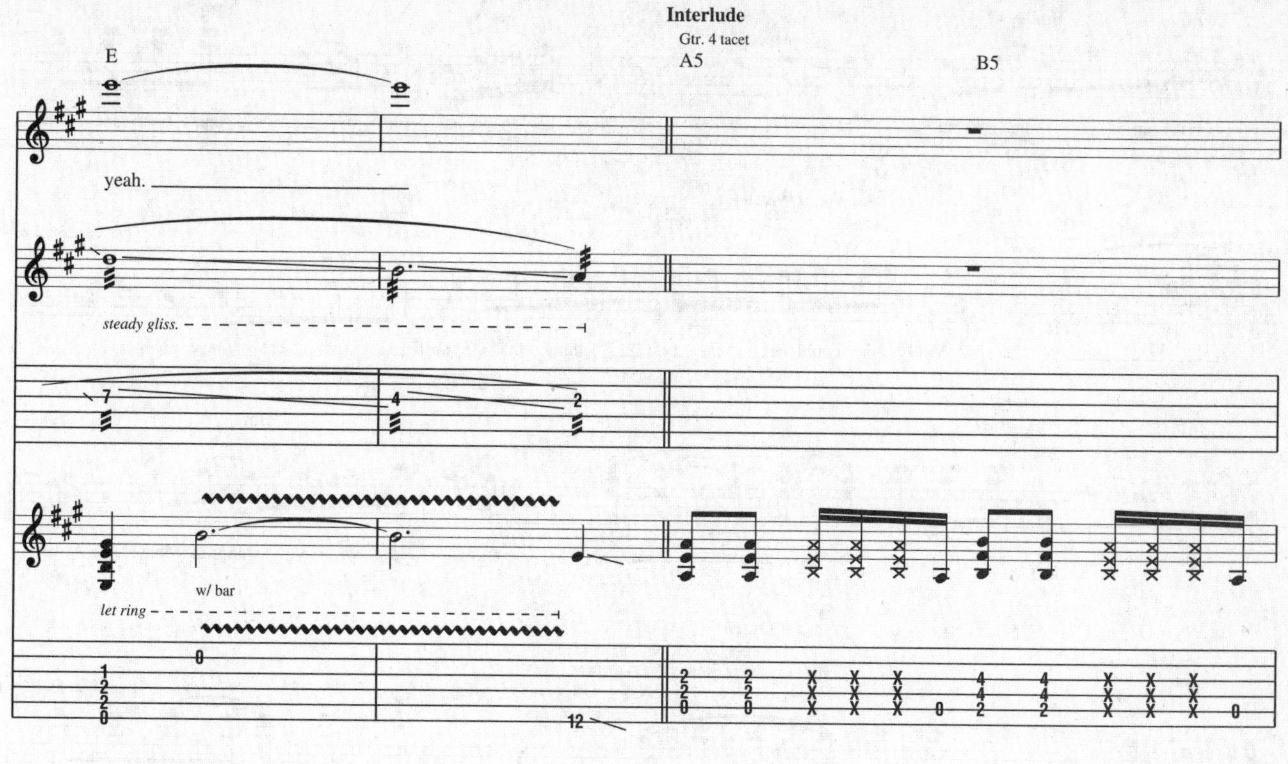

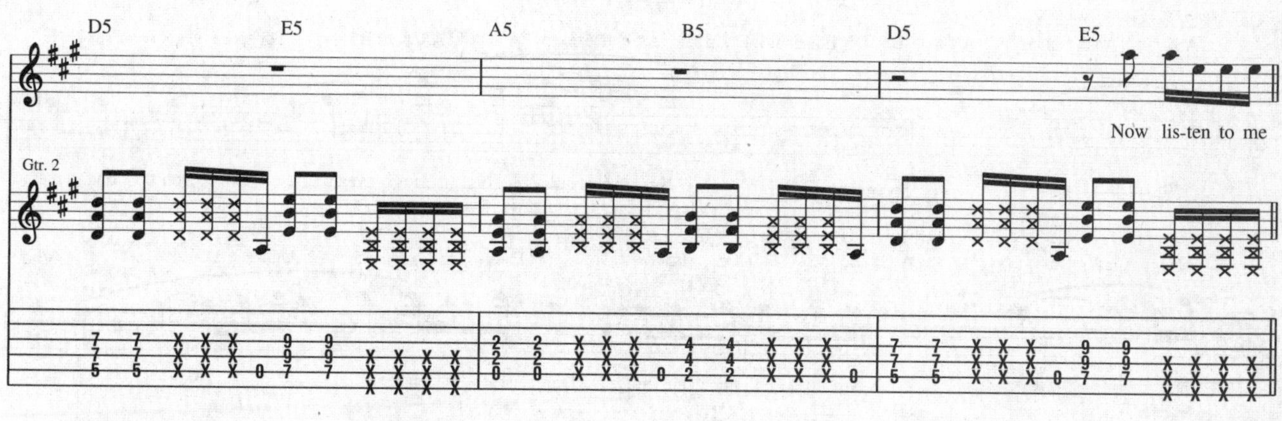

Chorus

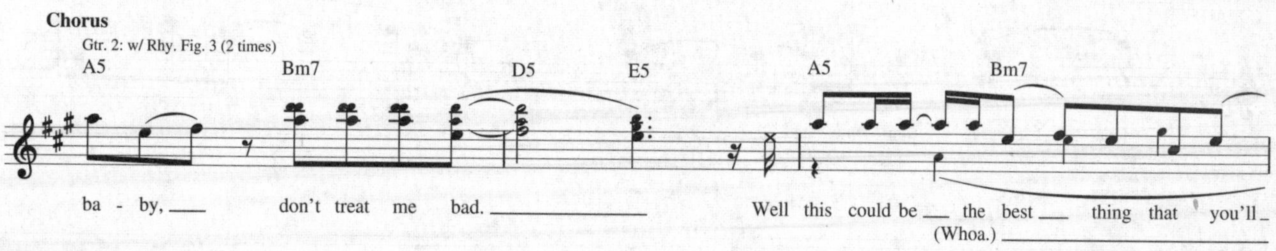

A5 Bm7 E5 A5 Bm7
do an - y - thing but, ba - by. Now lis - ten to me Ba - by, don't treat me bad.
Bkgd. Voc.: w/ Voc. Fig. 1
D5 E5 A5 Bm7 D5 E5
Well this could be the best thing that you'll ev - er have.
A5 Bm7 D5 E5 A5 Bm7 E5
Ba - by, don't treat me bad. You can do an - y - thing, but, ba -
Outro
Bkgd. Voc.: w/ Voc. Fig. 1 (2 times)
Gtr. 2: w/ Rhy. Fig. 4 (6 times)
A5 A/C# D5 A/C# B5 D5 E5 Esus4 E
- by, don't treat me bad. Don't treat me
A5 A/C# D5 A/C# B5 D5 E5 Esus4 E A5 A/C# D5 A/C# B5 D5 E5 Esus4 E
bad. No, yeah. Don't treat me
A5 A/C# D5 A/C# B5 D5 E5 Esus4 E A5 A/C# D5 A/C#
bad. No, no, no, no, no, no. Don't treat me bad.
B5 D5 E5 Esus4 E A5 A/C# D5 A/C# B5 D5 E5 Esus4 E
Don't treat me bad. Ah.
A5 D5 E5 D5 E5 A5 A
Gtr. 2

Double Vision

Words and Music by Mick Jones and Lou Gramm

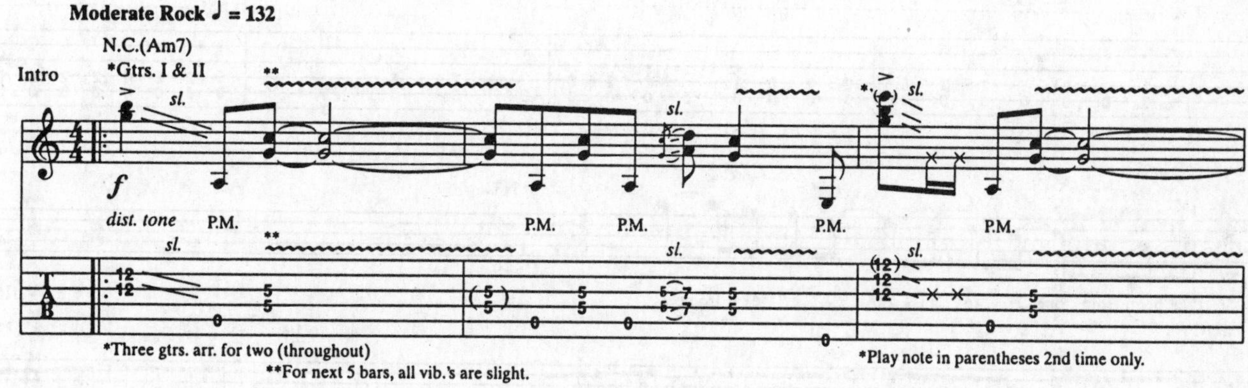

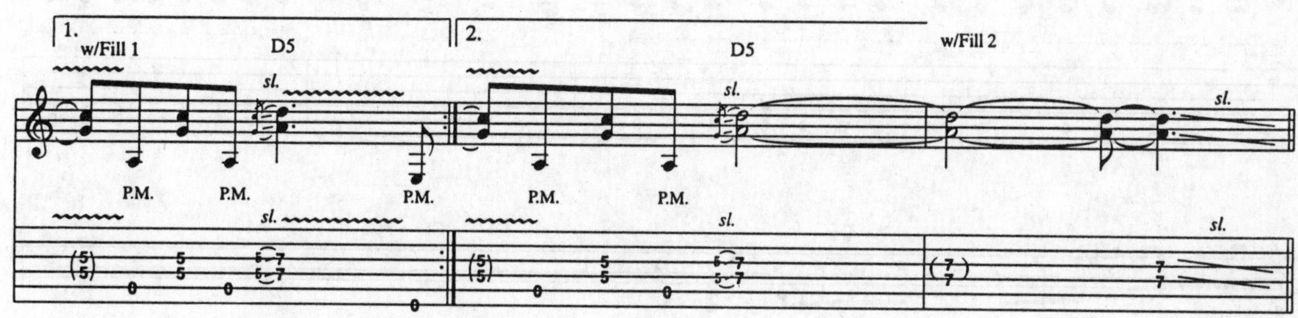

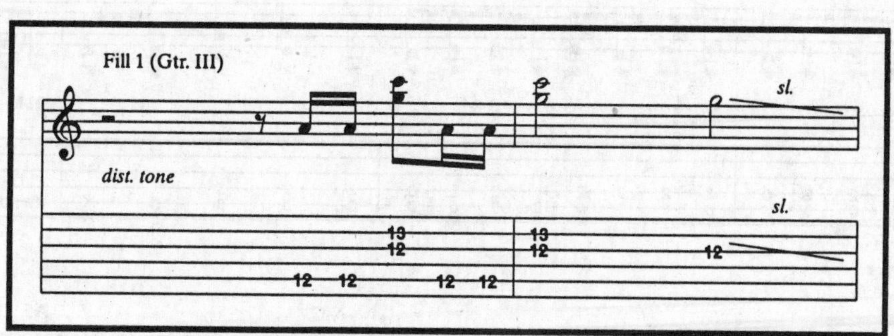

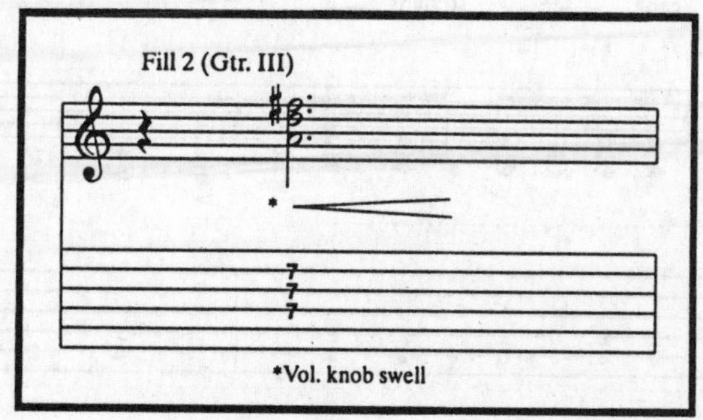

1st Verse
A5
D5 C5 G5 A5
Feel - in' down and dirt - y, feel - in' kind - a mean.
Rhy. Fig. 1
P.M.
N.C.
A5
I've been from one to an - oth - er ex - treme.
It's
1/4
time I had a good time. Ain't got time to wait.
D5 C5 G5 A5
I
N.C.
A5
wan - na stick a - round till I can't see straight.
(end Rhy. Fig. 1)

Chorus

Dm

Am

Fill my eyes with that dou - ble vi - sion.

Rhy. Fig. 2 (Gtr. IV)

clean tone
let ring

Rhy Fig. 3 (Gtrs. I & II)

*P.M. P.M.

*For next 11 bars, all P.M.'s are slight.

Dm

No dis - guise for that dou - ble vi -

P.M. P.M. P.M. P.M. P.M. P.M.

Am

F

C

sion.

Ooh.

When it gets

(end Rhy. Fig. 2) Rhy. Fig. 2A

(end Rhy. Fig. 3)

Rhy. Fig. 3A

sl.

P.M. P.M. P.M. P.M.

sl.

Dm

Fmaj7(no3rd) C

Dm

N.C.

3

through— to— me, it's al - ways new— to— me. My dou-ble vi - sion gets the

(Gtr. IV out)

(end Rhy. Fig. 2A)

sl.

sl.

(end Rhy. Fig. 3A)

sl.

P.M. P.M. P.M. P.M. P.M.

sl.

sl.

sl.

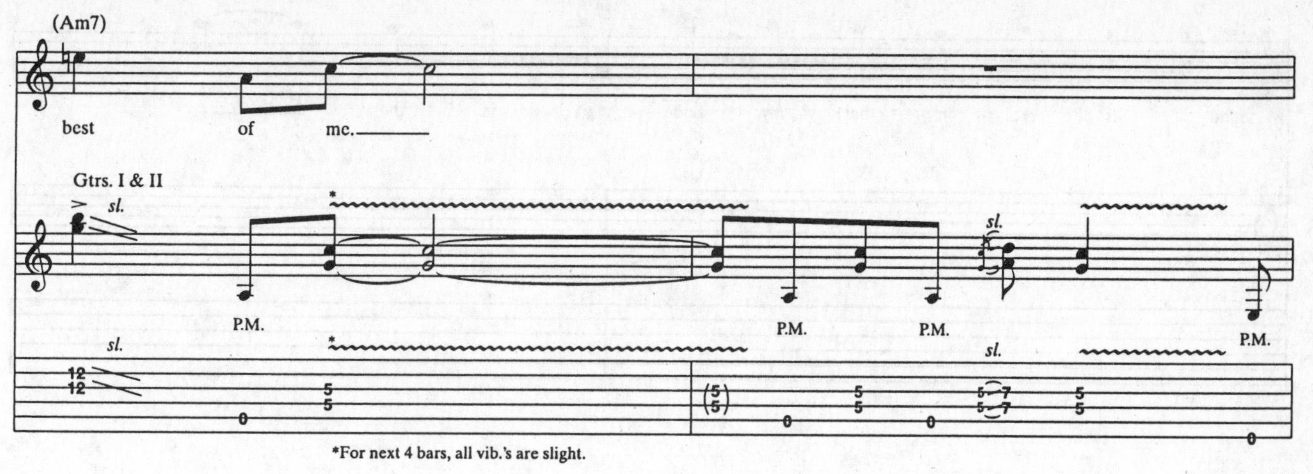
(Am7)
best of me.
Gtrs. I & II
sl.
P.M.
*
*For next 4 bars, all vib.'s are slight.

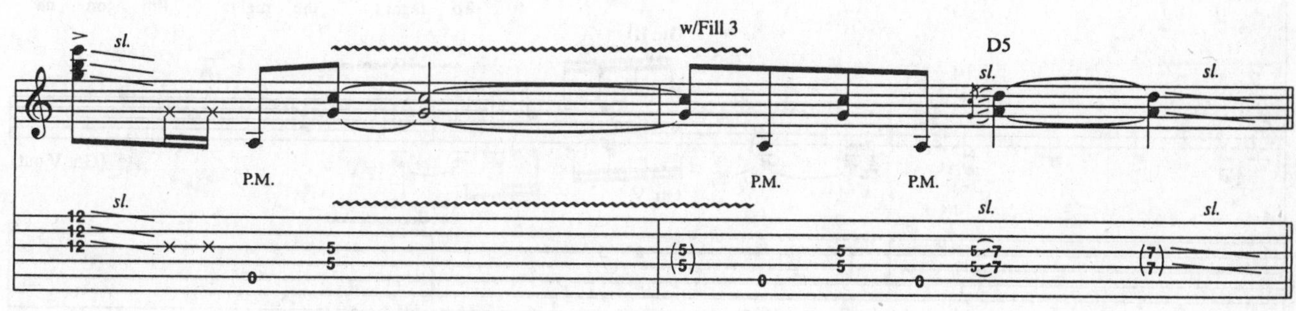
sl.
w/Fill 3
D5
P.M.

2nd Verse
w/Rhy. Fig. 1
A5
D5 C5 G5 A5
Nev - er do more than I, I real - ly need. My
Gtr. III

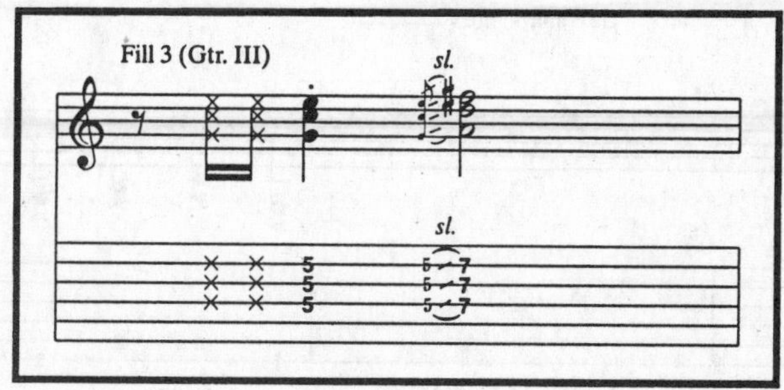
Fill 3 (Gtr. III)
sl.

mind is rac - in', but my bod - y's in the lead.
N.C.
A5
To - night's the night I'm gon - na
Gtr. III
Gtr. V
1/4
sl.
(Gtr. V out)
D5 C5 G5 A5
push it to the lim - it.
I'll live
all of my years in a sin - gle min - ute.
N.C.
Am
(Gtr. III out)

Chorus
w/Rhy. Figs. 2 (1st 6 bars only) & 3
Dm
Am
Fill my eyes with that dou - ble vi - sion.
Dm
w/Rhy. Fill 1
Am
Gtr. I substitute Rhy. Fill 2
No dis - guise for that dou - ble vi - sion.
w/Rhy. Figs. 2A & 3A
F
C
Dm
Ooh. When it gets through to me,
Fmaj7(no3rd)
C
Dm
N.C.
it's al - ways new to me. My dou - ble vi - sion al - ways
(Am7)
seems to get the best of me, the best of me.
Gtrs. I & II
Gtr. II
Gtr. I
sl.
P.M.
*Gtr. II to left of slashes.
*For next 8 bars, all vib.'s are slight.
Rhy. Fill 1 (Gtr. IV)
let ring
Rhy. Fill 2 (Gtr. I)

D5
N.C.(Am7)
*w/Fill 1
Yeah,
hey.
sl.
P.M.
*w/slight variations ad lib in 2nd bar
w/Fill 4
N.C.
Outro
w/Rhy. Figs. 2 (1st 6 bars only) and 3
Dm
*Bkgd. Voc. Fig. 1
Am
Ooh,
ooh,
dou - ble vi - sion.
(Ooh,
dou - ble vi - sion.)
*Refers to cue notes only.
w/Bkgd. Voc. Fig. 1 (3 times)
(end Bkgd. Voc. Fig. 1) Dm
w/Rhy. Fill 1
Am
I need
my dou - ble vi - sion.
Fill 4 (Gtr. III)
(Gtr. III out)

w/Rhy. Fig. 2 (1st 6 bars only)
w/Rhy. Fig. 3 (last 4 bars only) (2 times)
Dm
Am
It takes me out of my head.
Tak - in' me out of my head.
(Ooh,
I get my dou - ble vi -
dou - ble vi -
w/Rhy. Fill 1
sion.
sion.)
Gtr. I substitute Rhy. Fill 2
Woh.
*w/Rhy. Figs. 2 (till end) & 3 and Fill 5
w/Bkgd. Voc. Fig. 1 (till end)
See - in'
*w/slight variations ad lib
dou - ble, dou - ble.
Oh.
w/Rhy. Fig. 3 (last 4 bars only) (2 times) and Fill 5
Oh, my dou - ble vi - sion.
Begin fade
w/Fill 5A
Yeah.
Fade out
I get dou - ble vi - sion.
Fill 5 (Gtr. III)
sl.
Fill 5A (Gtr. III)

Drive

Words and Music by Brandon Boyd, Michael Einziger, Alex Katunich, Jose Pasillas II and Chris Kilmore

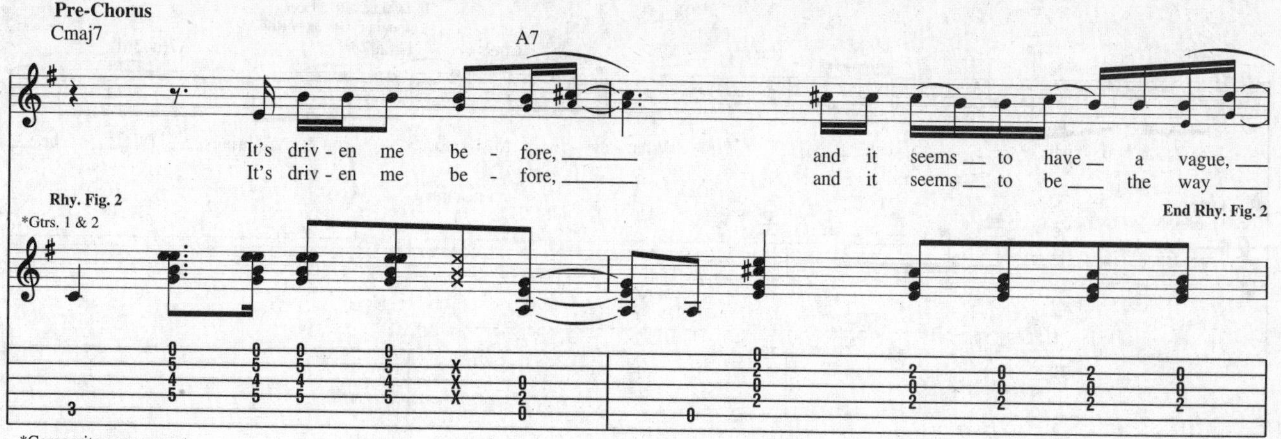

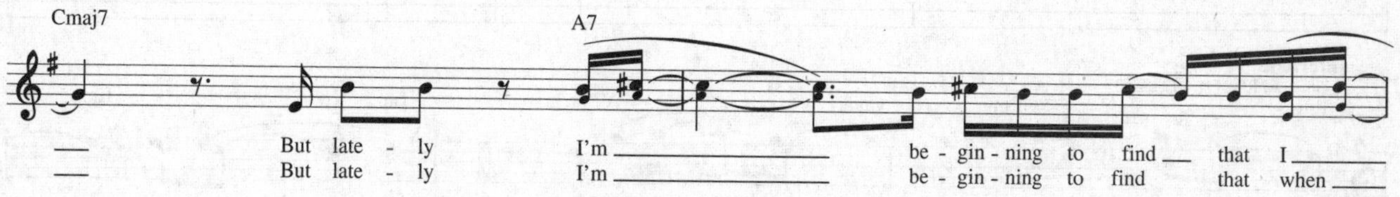

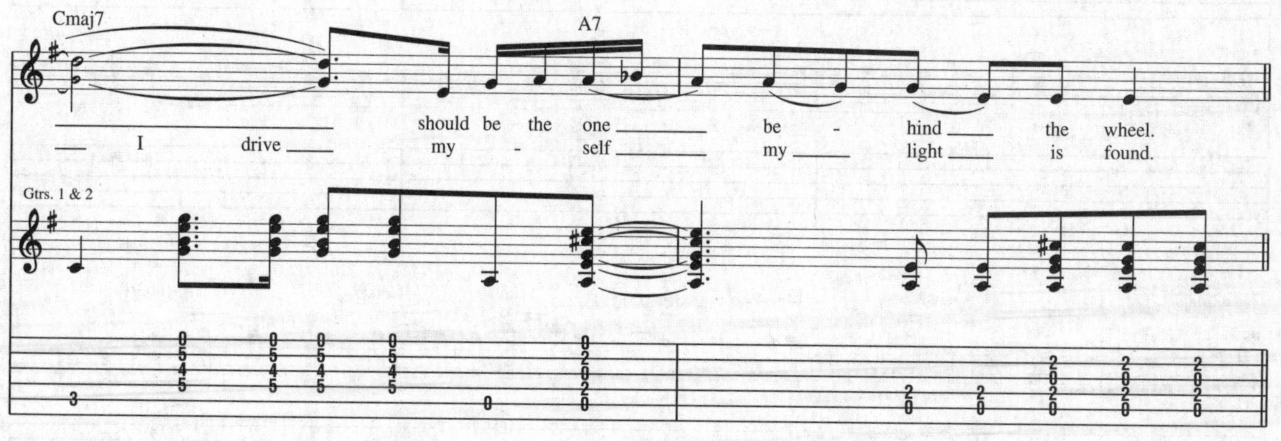

Chorus

Gtrs. 1 & 2: w/ Rhy. Fig. 1 (2 times)

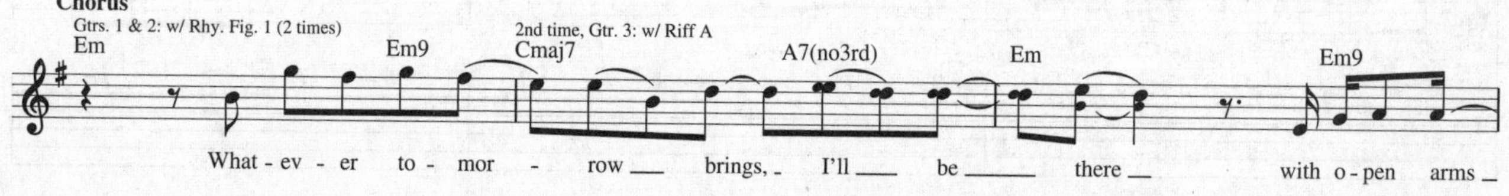

1st time, Gtr. 3 tacet
2nd time, Gtr. 3: w/ Riff A
Cmaj7
A7sus2
Em
Em9
Cmaj7
A7(no3rd)
and o - pen eyes, yeah.
What - ev - er to - mor - row brings, I'll be
Riff A
Gtr. 3 (acous.)
mf
let ring
End Riff A
Gtr. 3: w/ Riff A
Em
Em9
Cmaj7
A7sus2
Cmaj7
A7sus2
there, I'll be there.
there.
Gtr. 4 (elec.)
mf
w/ dist., Leslie effect, & slide
Interlude
Gtr. 1: w/ Rhy. Fig. 1 (2 times)
Gtr. 4
Em
Em9
Cmaj7
A7(no3rd)
Em
Em9
Gtr. 2
Cmaj7
A7sus2
Em
Em9
Cmaj7
A7(no3rd)

Pre-Chorus
Gtr. 1: w/ Rhy. Fig. 2
Em
Em9
Cmaj7
A7sus2
Cmaj7
A7
Would you choose
a, water over wine?
Cmaj7
A7
Hold the wheel and drive.
Gtrs. 1 & 2
Gtr. 4 tacet
N.C.
Chorus
Gtrs. 1 & 2: w/ Rhy. Fig. 1 (2 times)
Em
Em9
Cmaj7
A7(no3rd)
What-ev-er to-mor-row brings, I'll be
Gtr. 3
Riff C
End Riff C
let ring

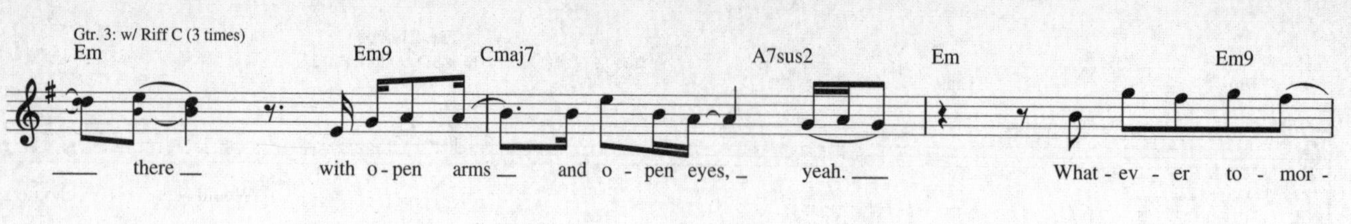
Gtr. 3: w/ Riff C (3 times)
Em Em9 Cmaj7 A7sus2 Em Em9
there with o-pen arms and o-pen eyes, yeah. What-ev-er to-mor-

Cmaj7 A7(no3rd) Em Em9 Cmaj7 A7sus2
-row brings, I'll be there, I'll be there.

Outro
Gtrs. 1 & 2: w/ Rhy. Fig. 1 (2 times)
Gtr. 3: w/ Riff C (3 times)
Em Em9 Cmaj7 A7(no3rd) Em Em9
Do, do, do, do, do, do do, do, do, do. No, no,
*Gtr. 5
Riff D
End Riff D
mf
*Synth. arr. for gtr.

Gtr. 5 tacet
Cmaj7 A7sus2
Gtr. 5: w/ Riff D
Em Em9 Cmaj7 A7(no3rd)
no. Do, do, do, do, do. Do, do, do, do, do, do, do, do, do, do,

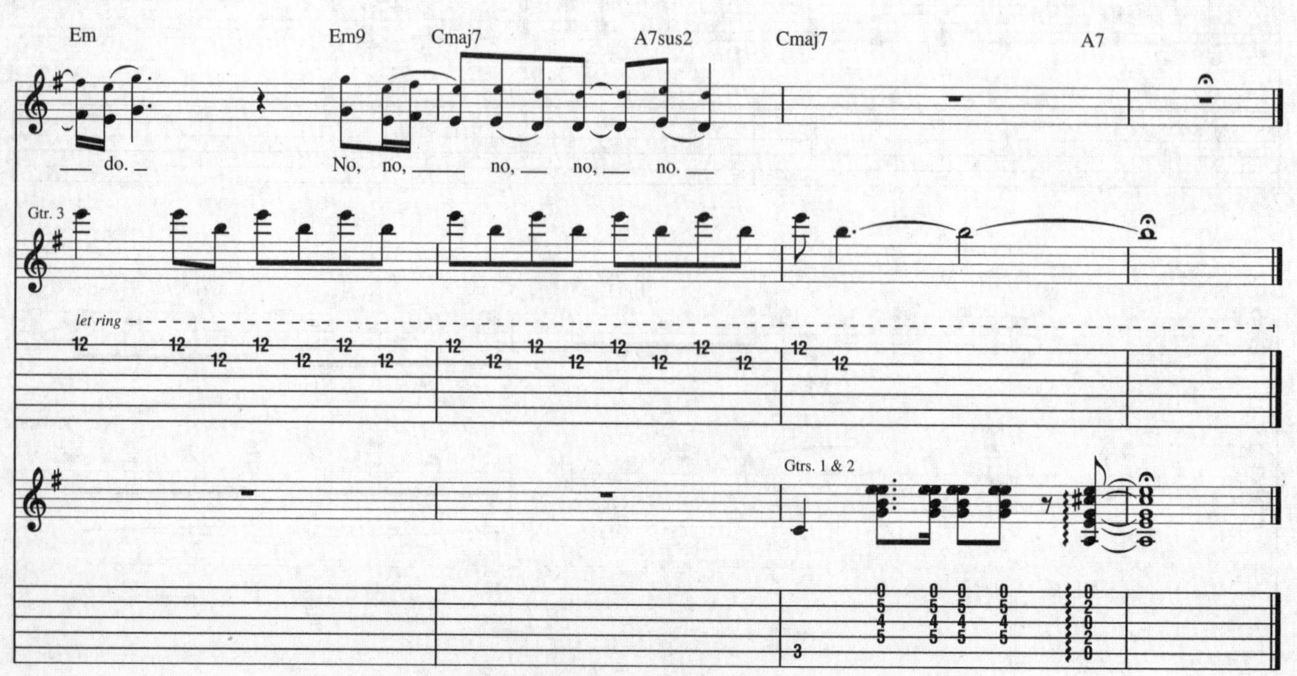
Em Em9 Cmaj7 A7sus2 Cmaj7 A7
do. No, no, no, no, no.
Gtr. 3
let ring
Gtrs. 1 & 2

Drops of Jupiter

(Tell Me)

Words and Music by Pat Monahan, Jimmy Stafford, Rob Hotchkiss, Charlie Colin and Scott Underwood

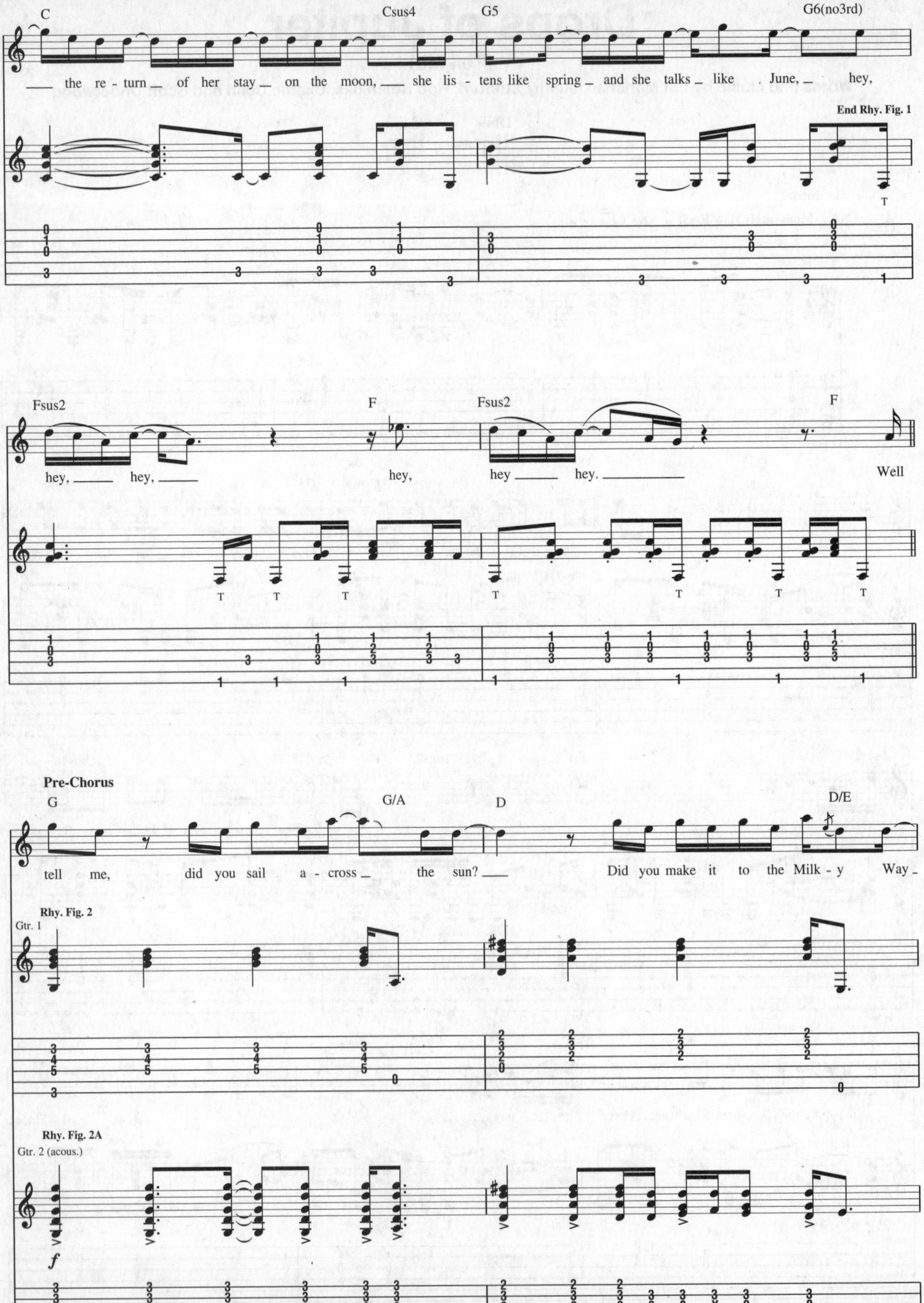

Pre-Chorus

G G/A D D/E

tell me, did you sail a - cross the sun? Did you make it to the Milk - y Way

Rhy. Fig. 2

Gtr. 1

Rhy. Fig. 2A

Gtr. 2 (acous.)

f

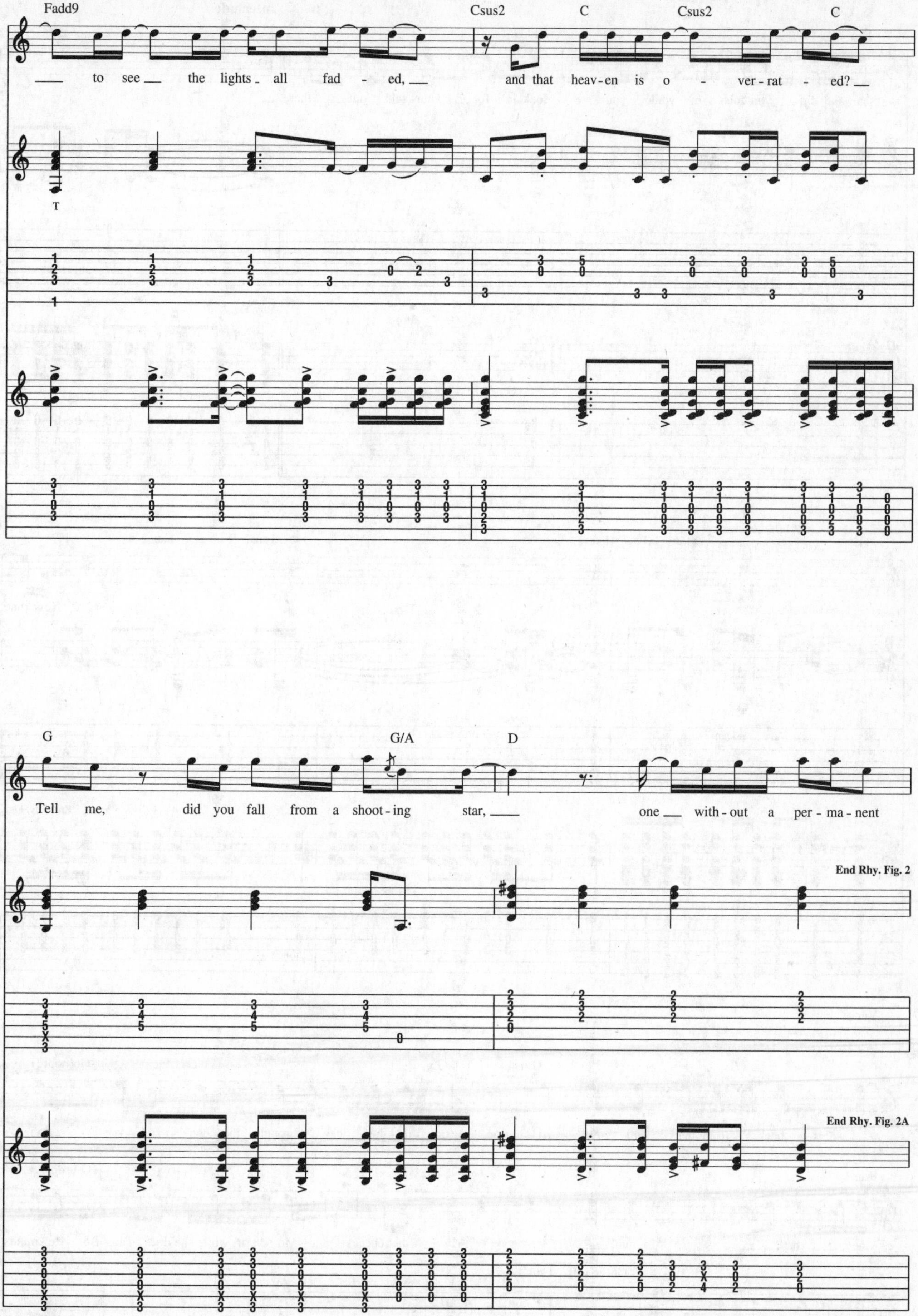

G G/A D

Tell me, did you fall from a shoot - ing star, one with - out a per - ma - nent

End Rhy. Fig. 2

End Rhy. Fig. 2A

Interlude
Dm
Fadd9
C
Csus4
scar, and did you miss me while you were look-in' for your-self out there?
Rhy. Fig. 3
G5
G6(no3rd)
Fsus2
F
Fsus2 F
Fsus2
F
2. Now that
End Rhy. Fig. 3
Verse
Gtr. 1: w/ Rhy. Fig. 1
Gtr. 2: w/ Rhy. Fig. 3 (2 1/2 times)
C
Csus4
G5
G6(no3rd)
she's back from that soul va - ca - tion, trac - in' her way through the con - stel - la - tion,
Fsus2
F
Fsus2
F
C
Csus4
hey, hey, mm. She checks out Mo - zart while she does Tae - Bo. Re - minds
G5
G6(no3rd)
Fsus2
F
F6
me that there's room to grow, hey, hey, hey, yeah. Now that

C
Csus4
G5
G6(no3rd)
she's back in the at - mos - phere, I'm a - fraid that she might think of me as
Fsus2
F
Fsus2
F
Fsus2
plain ol' Jane. Told a sto - ry 'bout a man who was too a - fraid to fly, so he nev - er did land. But
Gtr. 1
Gtr. 2
Pre-Chorus
Gtrs. 1 & 2: w/ Rhy. Figs. 2 & 2A
G
G/A
D
D/E
Fsus2
tell me, did the wind sweep you off your feet? Did you fin-'ly get the chance to dance a - long the light of day,
Rhy. Fig. 4
Gtr. 3 (slight dist.)
f let ring throughout
Csus2
C
Csus2
C
G
G/A
D
and head back to the Milk - y Way? And tell me, did Ve - nus blow your mind? Was it ev-'ry-thing you want - ed to find?
End Rhy. Fig. 4

Chorus
Dm
Fsus2
Csus2 C Csus2 C
and did you miss me while you were look-in' for your-self out there?
Gtr. 3
Rhy. Fig. 5A
Gtr. 1
Rhy. Fig. 5
G5 G6 G5 G6
Fsus2
F
Fsus2
F
Can you im-ag-ine no
End Rhy. Fig. 5A
End Rhy. Fig. 5
Gtrs. 1 & 3: w/ Rhy. Figs. 5 & 5A
Csus2 C Csus2 C
G5 G6 G5 G6
love, pride, deep - fried chick-en, your best friend al - ways stick-in'
Fsus2
F
Fsus2
F
up for you e-ven when I know you're wrong? Can you im-ag-ine no

Csus2
C
Csus2
C
G5
G6
G5
G6
G5
first dance, freeze - dried ro - mance, five hour phone con - ver - sa - tion, the
Gtr. 3
Gtr. 1
B♭
C/B♭
B♭
F
best soy lat - te that you ev - er had and me? But
Pre-Chorus
Gtr. 2: w/ Rhy. Fig. 2A, 1st 4 meas.
Gtr. 3 tacet
G
G/A
D
D/E
tell me, did the wind sweep you off your feet? Did you fin - 'ly get the chance to dance

F
Csus2
C
Csus2
C
a - long the light of day,
and head back t'ward the Milk - y Way? And
T
Gtrs. 1 & 2: w/ Rhy. Fig. 2 & 2A
Gtr. 3: w/ Rhy. Fig. 4
G
G/A
D
D/E
tell me, did you sail a - cross the sun?
Did you make it to the Milk - y Way
Fsus2
Csus2
C
Csus2
C
to see the lights all fad - ed,
and that heav - en is o - ver - rat - ed? And
G
G/A
D
tell me, did you fall from a shoot - ing star,
one with - out a per - ma - nent
Dm9
Fsus2
Gtr. 2
scar, and did you miss me while you were look - in' for your - self?
Gtr. 3
Gtr. 1
T
Outro-Chorus
Gtrs. 1 & 3: w/ Rhy. Fig. 5 & 5A (2 times)
Gtr. 2 tacet
Csus2
C
Csus2
C
G5
G6
G5
G6
(Na, na, na, na, na, na, na, na, na, na, na, na,

Fsus2 F Fsus2 F Csus2 C Csus2 C
And did you fin-'ly get the chance to dance a-long the light of day?
na, na. Na, na, na, na, na, na,
G5 G6 G5 G6 Fsus2 F Fsus2 F
And did you fall from a shoot-ing star, fall from a shoot-ing star?
na, na, na, na, na, na, na, na.
Csus2 C Csus2 C G5 G6 G5 G6 G5
And are you
Na, na, na, na, na, na, na, na, na, na, na, na,
Gtr. 3
Gtr. 1
B♭ C/B♭ B♭ F
lone-ly look-in' for your-self out there?
na, na.)

867-5309/Jenny

Words and Music by Alex Call and James Keller

2nd time, Gtr. 3: w/ Rhy. Fill 1
D5
A5
B5
F#5
You give me some-thing I can hold on to.
You don't know me, but you make me so hap - py.
Gtr. 4 (slight dist.)
Riff B
End Riff B
mf
Gtr. 1: w/ Riff A (4 times)
Gtr. 4 tacet
2nd time, Gtr. 3: w/ Rhy. Fig. 1 (3 1/2 times)
I know you'll think I'm like the oth - ers be - fore,
I tried to call you be - fore, but I lost my nerve.
I tried
1st time, Gtr. 4: w/ Riff B
F#
who saw your name and num - ber on the wall.
my i - mag - i - na - tion, but I was dis - turbed.
Pre-Chorus
E
D5open
A
Rhy. Fill 2A
End Rhy. Fill 2A
Rhy. Fig. 2
Gtr. 3
Jen - ny, I've got your num - ber.
Gtr. 2
Rhy. Fill 2
End Rhy. Fill 2
Riff C
P.M.
I need to make you mine.
Jen - ny, don't change your num - ber.
End Rhy. Fig. 2
End Riff C

Chorus
Gtrs. 2 & 3: w/ Rhy. Fig. 1 (3 1/2 times)
2nd & 3rd times, Gtr. 1: w/ Riff A (4 times)
F#5 D5 A5 B5 F#5 D5 A5 B5 F#5
Eight Six Sev - en Five Three "O" Nine.
(Eight Six Sev - en Five Three "O" Nine.

To Coda
2nd & 3rd times, Gtr. 4: w/ Riff B
Gtrs. 2 & 3: w/ Rhy. Fill 2
D5 A5 B5 F#5 D5 A5 B5
Eight Six Sev - en Five Three "O" Nine.
Eight Six Sev - en Five Three "O" Nine.)

Bridge
C#m
E type2
F#m
Gtr. 3
I got it. I got it. I got your
(I got it.)
Gtr. 2
let ring

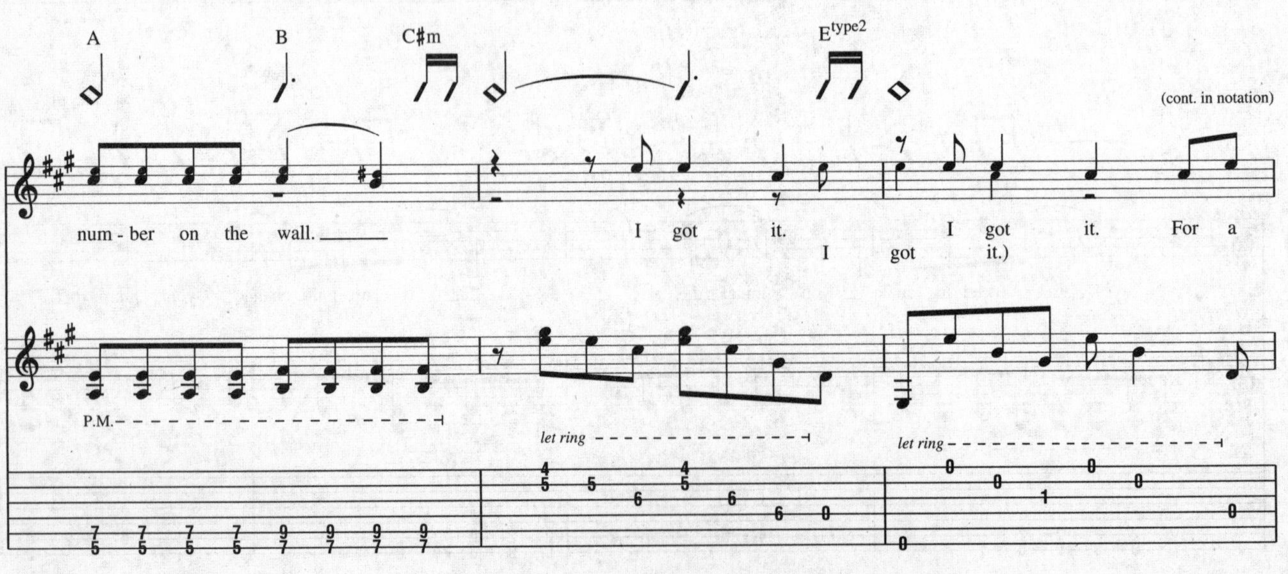

A B C#m E type2
(cont. in notation)
num - ber on the wall. I got it. I got it. For a
I got it.)
P.M.
let ring

Interlude
Gtr. 1: w/ Riff A (4 times)
Gtrs. 2 & 3 tacet
F♯5
A5
B5
F♯m7 Dsus2 A
Badd4
F♯m7 Dsus2 A
good time, for a good time call. . .
Gtrs. 2 & 3
P.M.

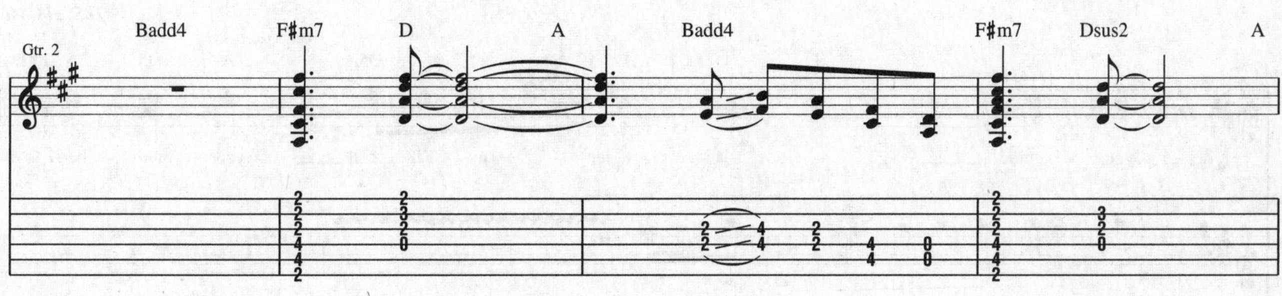
Badd4
F♯m7
D
A
Badd4
F♯m7
Dsus2
A
Gtr. 2

Guitar Solo
Gtr. 1: w/ Riff A (4 times)
Gtrs. 2 & 3: w/ Rhy. Fig. 1 (3 1/2 times)
Gtr. 3: w/ Rhy. Fill 1
Badd4
F♯5
F♯5
D5
A5
B5
F♯5
D5
A5
Gtr. 5 (dist.)
mf
w/ chorus
Gtr. 2

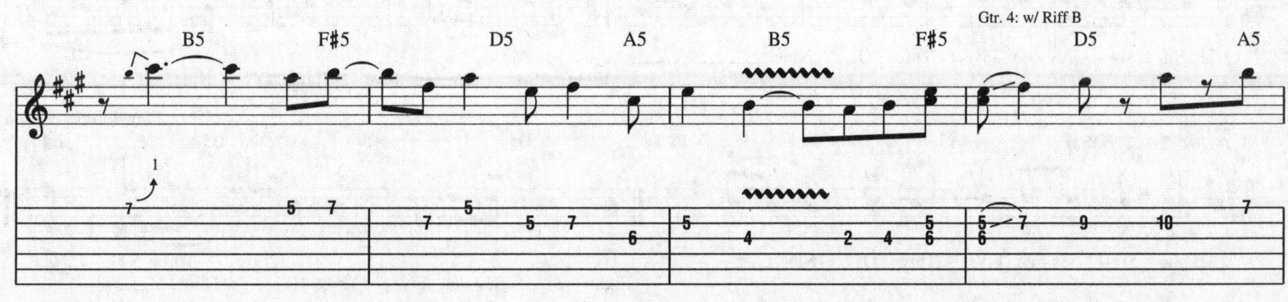
Gtr. 4: w/ Riff B
B5
F♯5
D5
A5
B5
F♯5
D5
A5

Pre-Chorus
Gtr. 1 tacet
Gtr. 2: w/ Riff C
Gtr. 3: w/ Rhy. Fig. 2
Gtrs. 2 & 3: w/ Rhy. Fills 2 & 2A
B5 E D5 A D5 A E A
Hey! Jen - ny, don't change your num - ber. I need to make
8va
D.S. al Coda
Gtr. 5 tacet
D5 E D5 A D5 A F#5
you mine. Jen - ny, I'll call your num - ber.
8va
Coda
Outro-Chorus
Gtr. 1: w/ Riff A (till fade)
Gtr. 2: w/ Riff D (till fade)
Gtr. 3: w/ Rhy. Fig. 1 (till fade)
F#5 D5 A5 B5 F#5 D5 A5 B5 F#5
Jen-ny, Jen-ny, who can I turn to?
(Eight Six Sev-en Five Three "O" Nine.
For the
Gtr. 4: w/ Riff B
D5 A5 B5 F#5 D5 A5 B5 F#5
price of a dime I can al-ways turn to you.
Eight Six Sev-en Five Three "O" Nine.
D5 A5 B5 F#5 D5 A5 B5 F#5
Eight Six Sev-en Five Three "O" Nine.
Eight Six Sev-en Five Three "O" Nine.
Play 4 times & fade
D5 A5 B5 F#5 D5 A5 B5 F#5
Eight Six Sev-en Five Three "O" Nine.
Eight Six Sev-en Five Three "O"
Five Three "O" Nine.
Nine.)

Every Breath You Take

Written and Composed by G.M. Sumner

Badd9
Esus2
aches
with ev-'ry step you take.
3., 4. Ev-'ry move you
P.M.
Verse
Gtr. 1: w/ Rhy. Fig. 1
Aadd9
F♯m9
Dsus2
make.
Ev-'ry vow you break.
Ev-'ry smile you fake.
Ev-'ry claim you stake,
To Coda
Bridge
Gtr. 1: w/ Rhy. Fig. 2
Esus2
F♯m9
Gtr. 2
F
F
G
w/ dist.
I'll be watch-ing you.
Since you've gone I've been lost with-out a trace,
I dream at night I can on - ly see your face.
I look a-round, but it's you I can't re-place,
I feel so cold and I long for your em-brace.
I keep cry-ing, ba - by, ba - by, please.
Interlude
Gtr. 2 tacet
Aadd9
F♯m9
Ooh.
Ooh.
Ooh.
Ooh.
Gtr. 1
P.M.

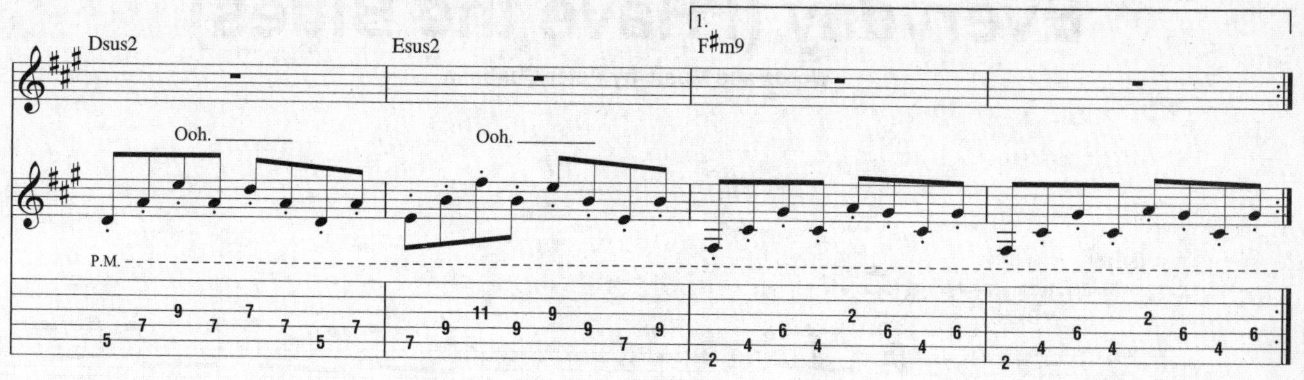
1.
Dsus2
Esus2
F#m9
Ooh.
Ooh.
P.M.

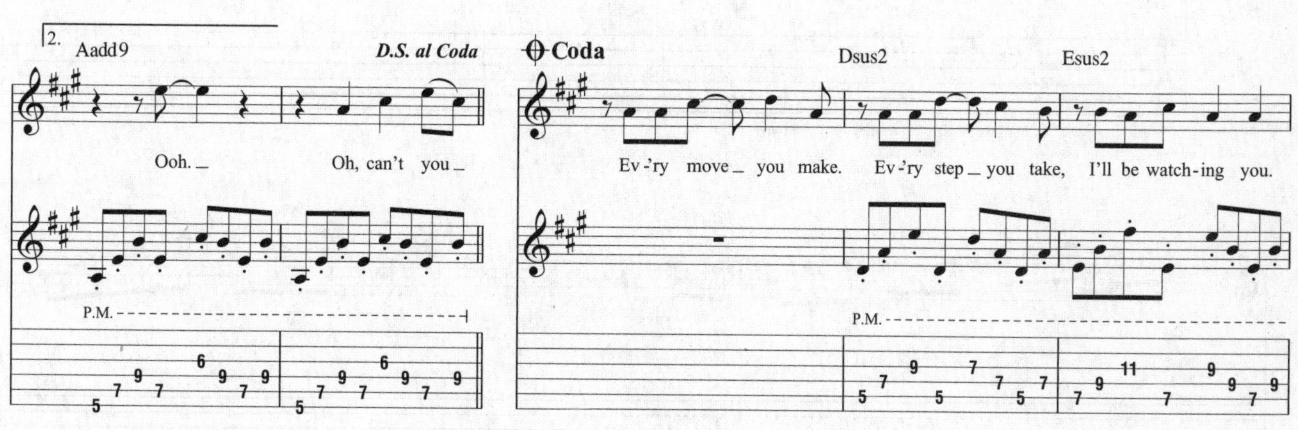
2.
Aadd9
D.S. al Coda
Coda
Dsus2
Esus2
Ooh.
Oh, can't you
Ev-'ry move you make. Ev-'ry step you take, I'll be watch-ing you.
P.M.

F#m9
I'll be watch - ing

Outro
Voc.: w/ ad Lib (till fade)
Aadd9
F#m9
Dsus2
Play 8 Times & Fade
you.
I'll be watch - ing
1., 5. (Ev-'ry breath you take. Ev-'ry move you make. Ev-'ry bond you break. Ev-'ry step you take.)
2., 4., 6., 8. (Ev-'ry sin - gle day. Ev-'ry word you say. Ev-'ry game you play. Ev-'ry night you...)
3., 7. (Ev-'ry move you make. Ev-'ry vow you break. Ev-'ry smile you fake. Ev-'ry claim you stake.)
P.M.

Everyday (I Have the Blues)

Words and Music by Peter Chatman

ev - 'ry day I have the blues.
Oh,
full
full
Eb7
Bb7
ev - 'ry day,
ev - 'ry day I have the blues.
full
1/2
F7
Eb7
When you see me wor-ry, babe,
yeah, it's you I
Bb7
Verse
Bb7
hate to lose.
2. Well, no - bod-y loves me,
1/2

no - bod - y seems to care.
Oh,
full
1/2
Eb7
Bb7
no - bod - y loves me,
no - bod - y seems to care.
full
F7
Eb7
Well, wor-ries and trou-ble, dar-ling,
babe, you know I've had
1/2
Bb7
my share.
Oh, look out!
Guitar Solo
Bb7
1/2
full
* Played behind the beat.

full
Eb7
w/ Voc. ad Lib
Bb7
1/2
1/4
F7
Eb7
Bb7
3. Ev - 'ry
Verse
Gtr. 1 tacet
Bb7
day, ev - 'ry day, ev - 'ry day, ev - 'ry day, ev -
Eb7
Bb7
ry day, ev - 'ry day I have the blues.
Gtr. 1
full
F7
Eb7
When you see me wor-ry-in', babe, babe, it's you I
1/2

Verse
Bb7
hate to lose.
4. Oh, no one loves me, no - bod-y seems to
1/2
care.
Whoa, no-bod-y loves me, no - bod-y seems to
Eb7
D7
Eb7sus4
care.
Hey, now, wor - ries and trou - ble, dar - lin',
F7
Eb7
Bb N.C.
Bb9
babe, you know I've had my share.
full

Faith

Words and Music by George Michael

Drop D tuning, down 1 1/2 steps:
(low to high) B–F♯–B–E–G♯–C♯

twice a be - fore I give my heart a - way. And I know
C
D
all the games you play, 'cause I play them too. Oh, but I
Pre-Chorus
C
D
C
need some - time off from that e - mo - tion. Time to
fore this riv - er be - comes an o - cean. Be - fore you
pick my heart up off the floor.
w/ slight dist.
let ring throughout
D
C
D
When that love comes down with - out de - vo - tion. Well, it

Chorus
A
D5 C5/D
D5 N.C.
takes a strong - man, ba - by, but I'm a - show - in' you that door. I got - ta have faith. Got - ta have
w/ dist.
P.M.
1/4
To Coda
D5 C5/D
N.C.
faith. Got - ta have faith. Got - ta have faith. 2. Ba -
Verse
Double-time feel
D5
G5/D
D
by, I know you're ask - ing me to stay. Say please, please,
Rhy. Fig. 1
1/2
* Two gtrs. arr. for one.
C5
C
please a go a - way 'cause you're giv - in' me the blues. Ba -
End Rhy. Fig. 1

Gr. 1: w/ Rhy. Fig. 1
D5
D
N.C.
D5
G5/D
D
N.C.
by,
a you re - mind me,
all them words _ you say.
Can't _ help but

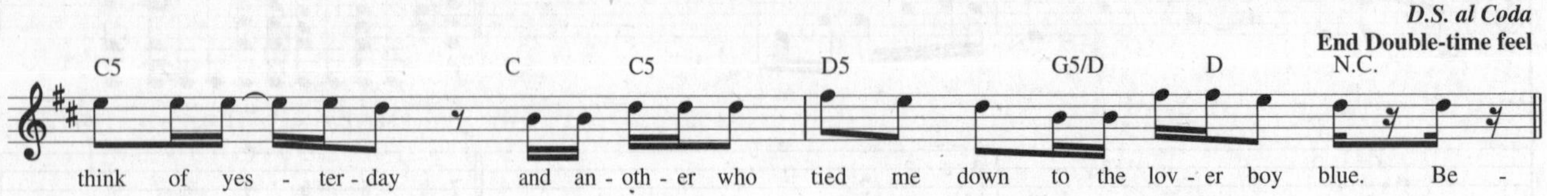
D.S. al Coda
End Double-time feel
C5
C
C5
D5
G5/D
D
N.C.
think of yes - ter - day
and an - oth - er who
tied me down to the lov - er boy blue.
Be -

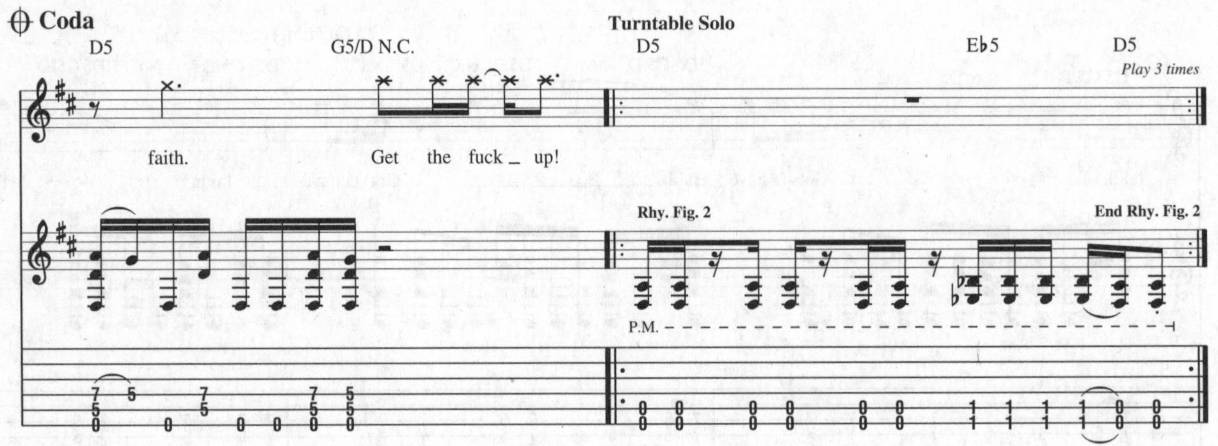
Coda
Turntable Solo
D5
G5/D N.C.
D5
E♭5
D5
Play 3 times
faith.
Get the fuck _ up!
Rhy. Fig. 2
End Rhy. Fig. 2
P.M.

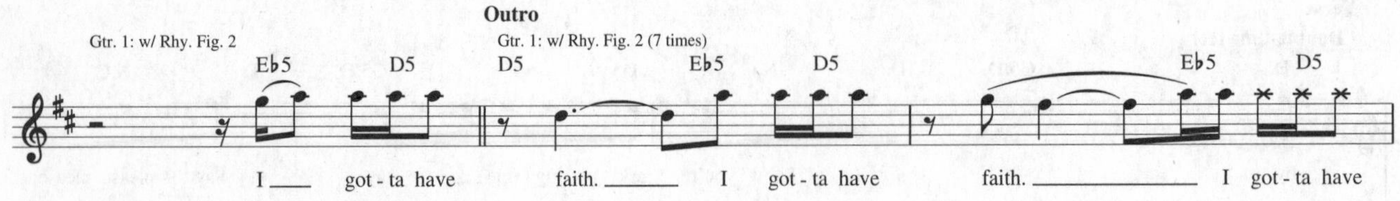
Outro
Gtr. 1: w/ Rhy. Fig. 2
Gtr. 1: w/ Rhy. Fig. 2 (7 times)
E♭5
D5
D5
E♭5
D5
E♭5
D5
I ___ got - ta have
faith. ___ I got - ta have
faith. ___ I got - ta have

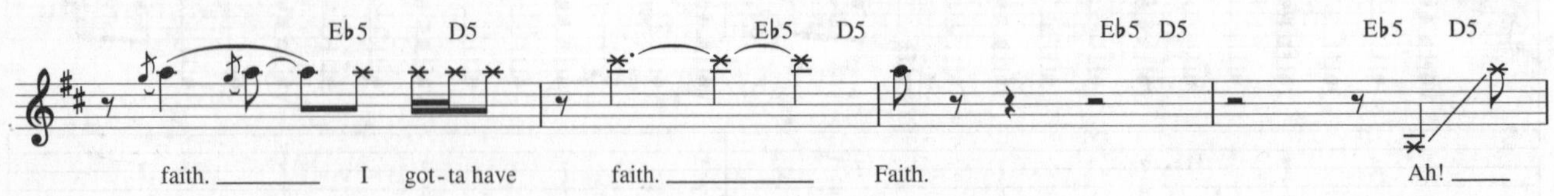
E♭5
D5
E♭5
D5
E♭5
D5
E♭5
D5
faith. ___ I got - ta have
faith. ___
Faith.
Ah! ___

E♭5
D5
Gtr. 1 tacet
Faith.
Wah! ___
Voc. ad lib
Gtr. 1
P.M.

Fast Car

Words and Music by Tracy Chapman

3.
Verse
Gtr. 1: w/ Rhy. Fig. 1, 4 times
F#m
(Em)
Eadd4
(Dadd4)
Dmaj7
(Cmaj7)
A5
(G5)
F#5
(Em)
Eadd4
(Dadd4)
4. You got a fast car, but is it fast e - nough - so we can fly a - way?

Dmaj7
(Cmaj7)
A5
(G5)
F#m
(Em)
Eadd4
(Dadd4)
We got - ta make a de - ci - sion: Leave to - night or live and die this way.

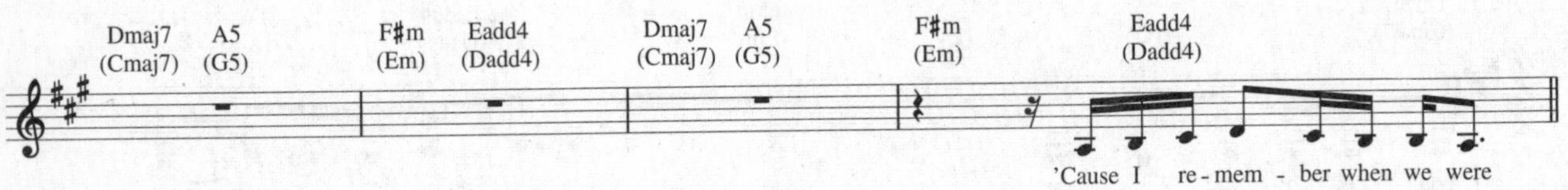
Dmaj7
(Cmaj7)
A5
(G5)
F#m
(Em)
Eadd4
(Dadd4)
Dmaj7
(Cmaj7)
A5
(G5)
F#m
(Em)
Eadd4
(Dadd4)
'Cause I re - mem - ber when we were

Chorus
D
(C)
A
(G)
driv - ing, driv - ing in your car, the speed so fast I felt like I was drunk.
Gtr. 1
mf
simile on repeats

F#m
(Em)
E
(D)
Cit - y lights lay out be - fore us and your arm felt nice wrapped 'round my shoul - der. And

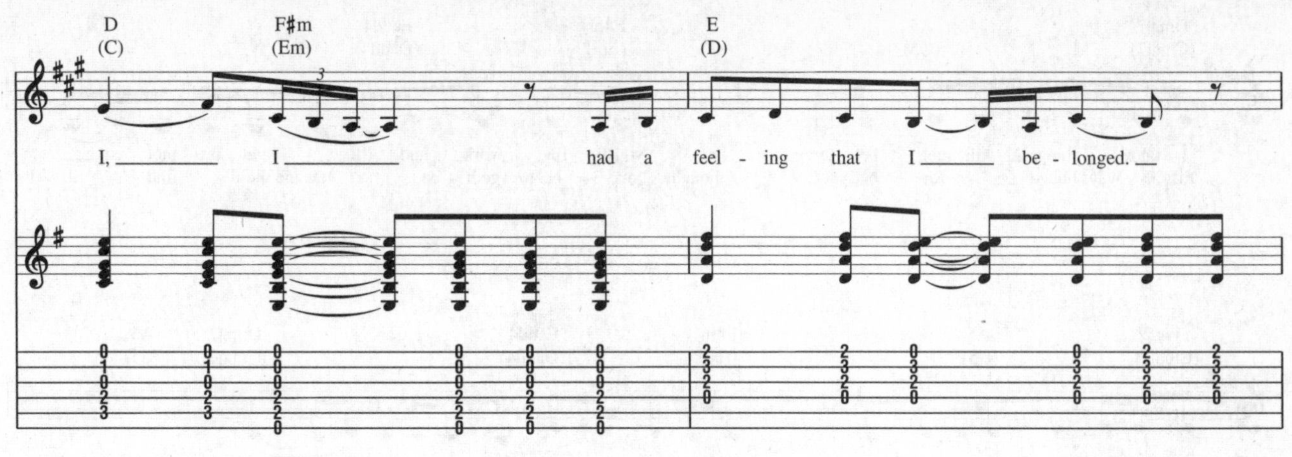

Interlude

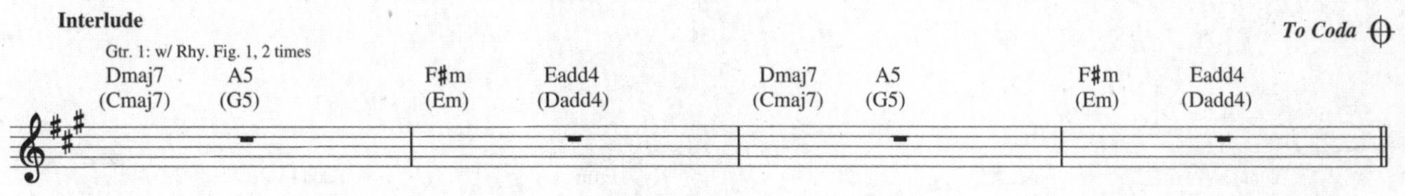

Verse

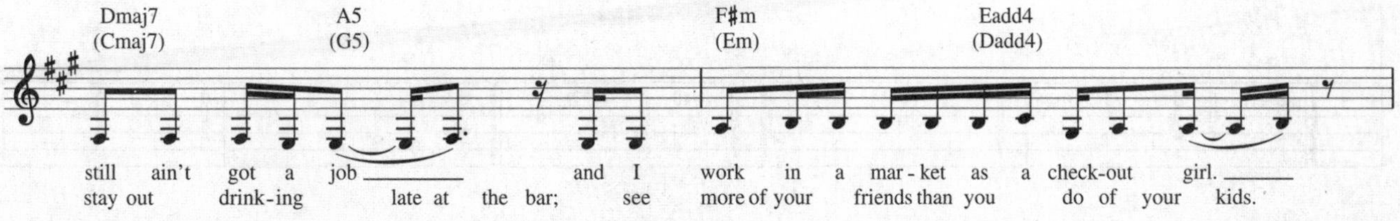

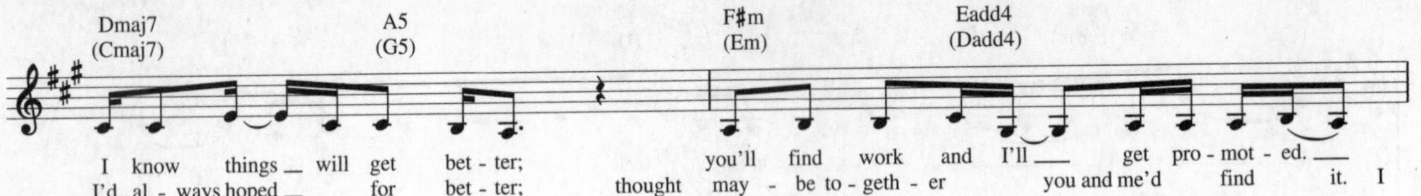

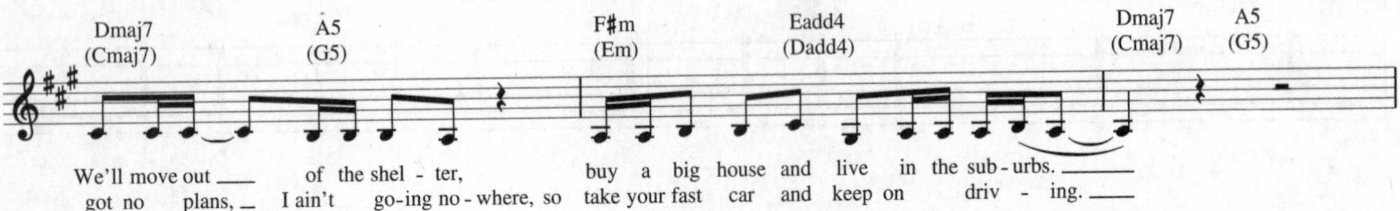

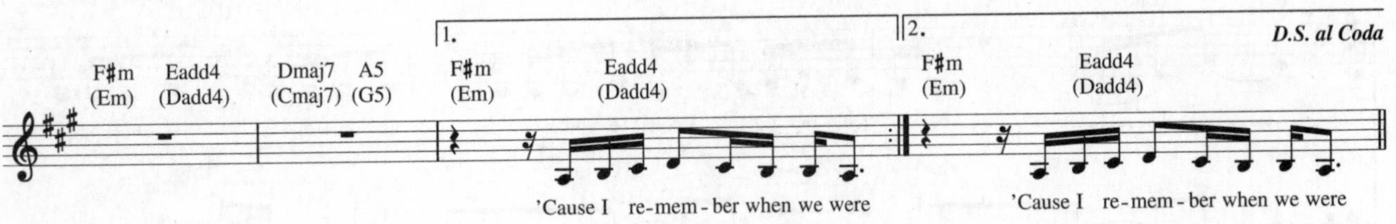

Coda

Verse

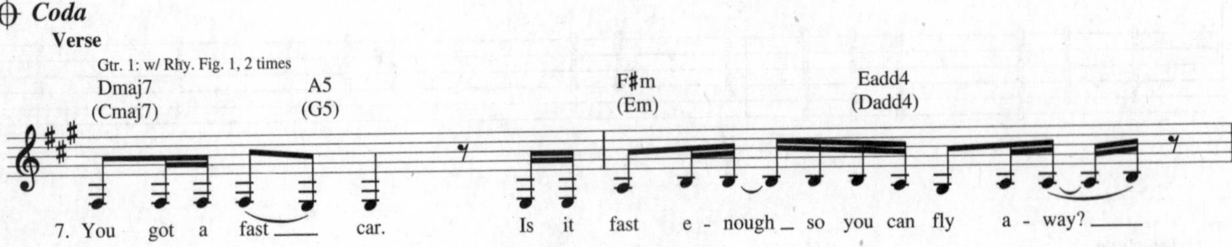

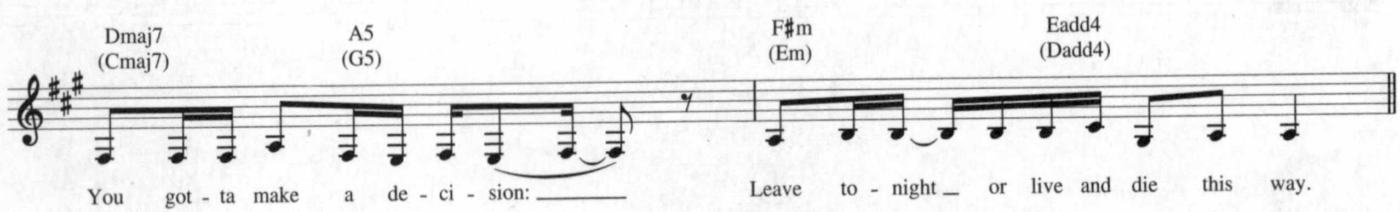

Outro

Fire and Rain

Words and Music by James Taylor

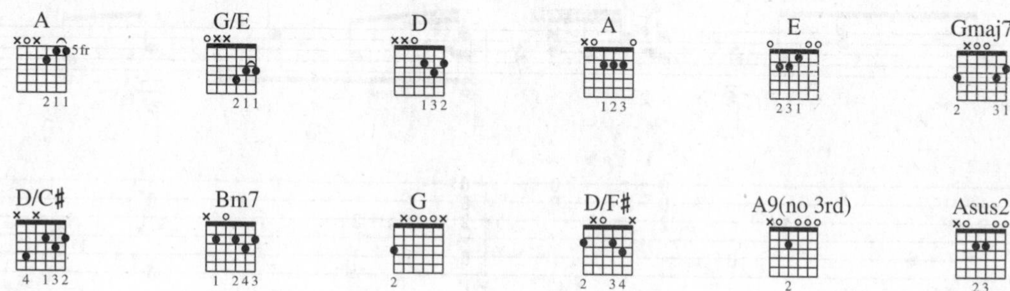

Capo III

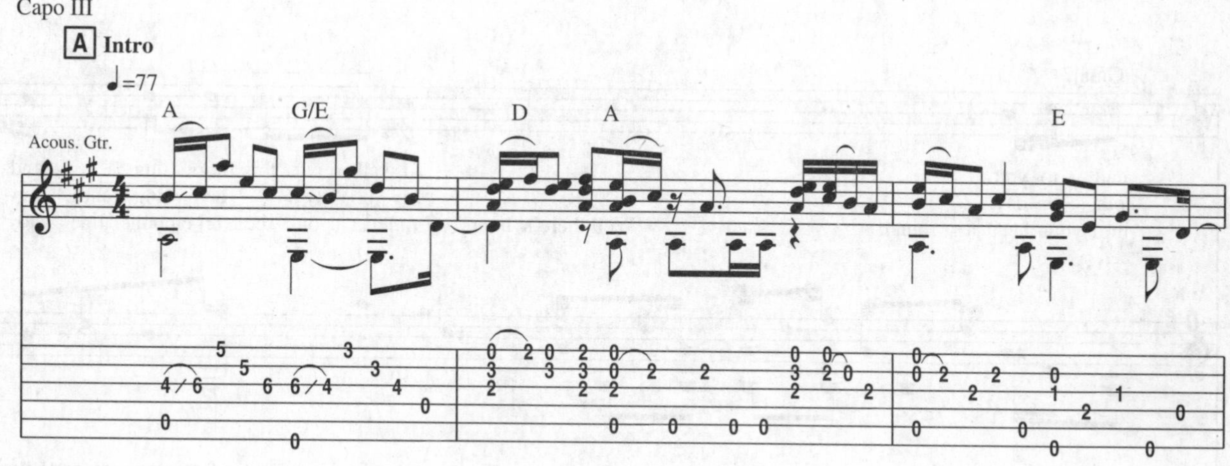

D
A
E
— you were gone. Su - zanne, the plans they made — put an
me make a stand. You've just got to see me through an -
back turned towards the sun. Lord knows when the cold wind blows, it - 'll
2nd time

Gmaj7
A
G/E
end to you. I walked out this morn - ing and I
oth - er day. My bo - dy's ach - ing and my
turn your head a - round. Well there's hours of time — on the tel-e-phone line to

D
A
E
wrote down this song. — I just can't re-mem - ber who to send —
time is at hand. — I won't make it an - y
talk a-bout things to come, — sweet dreams and fly-ing ma - chines in

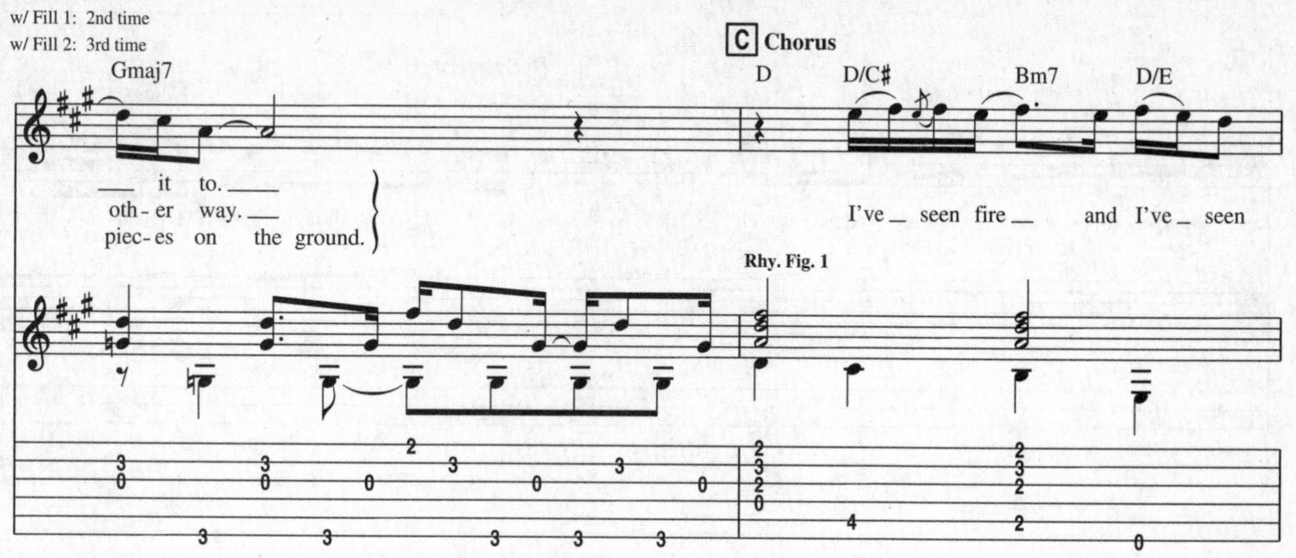
w/ Fill 1: 2nd time
w/ Fill 2: 3rd time
C Chorus
Gmaj7
D
D/C#
Bm7
D/E
it to.
oth - er way.
piec - es on the ground.
I've seen fire and I've seen
Rhy. Fig. 1
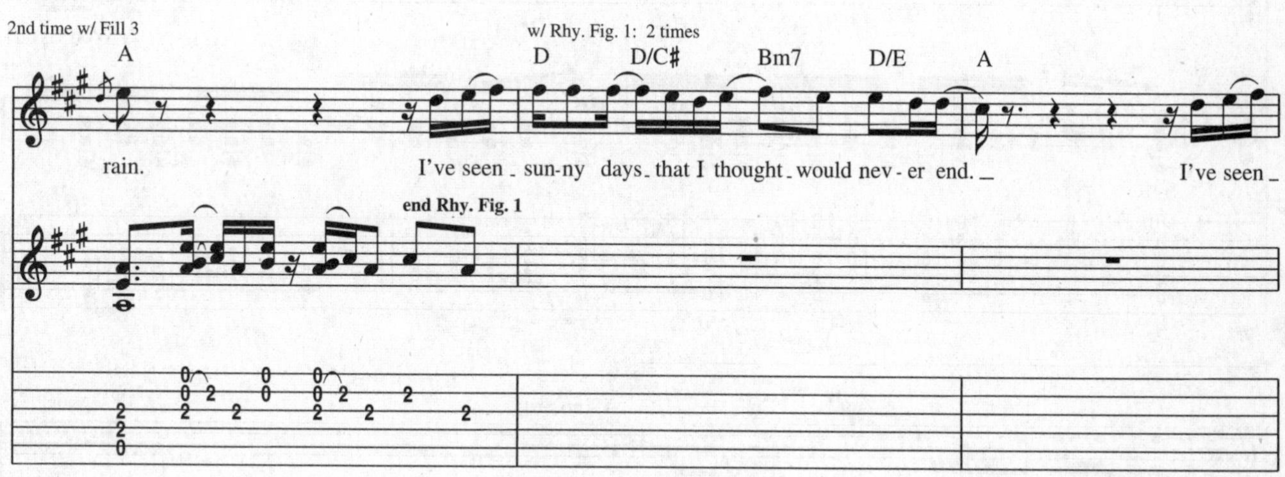
2nd time w/ Fill 3
w/ Rhy. Fig. 1: 2 times
A
D
D/C#
Bm7
D/E
A
rain.
I've seen sun-ny days that I thought would nev - er end.
I've seen
end Rhy. Fig. 1

Fill 1

Fill 2

Fill 3

To Coda
1.
D
D/C#
Bm7
D/E
A
G
D/F#
E7sus4
Em7
lone - ly times when I could not find a friend,
but I al - ways thought that I'd see you a - gain.
A9(no 3rd)
Asus2
2. Won't you
2.
G
D/F#
E7sus4
Em7
A9(no 3rd)
Asus2
al - ways thought that I'd see you a - gain.
Coda
D.S. al Coda
3. Been
G
D/F#
E7sus4
Em7
al-ways thought that I'd see you ba - by,

D Outro
A9(no 3rd)
Asus2
one more time again, now.
Thought I'd see

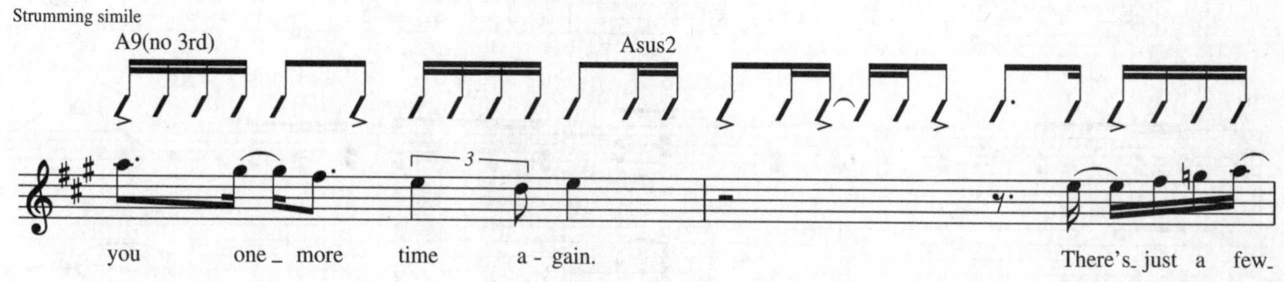
Strumming simile
A9(no 3rd)
Asus2
you one more time again.
There's just a few

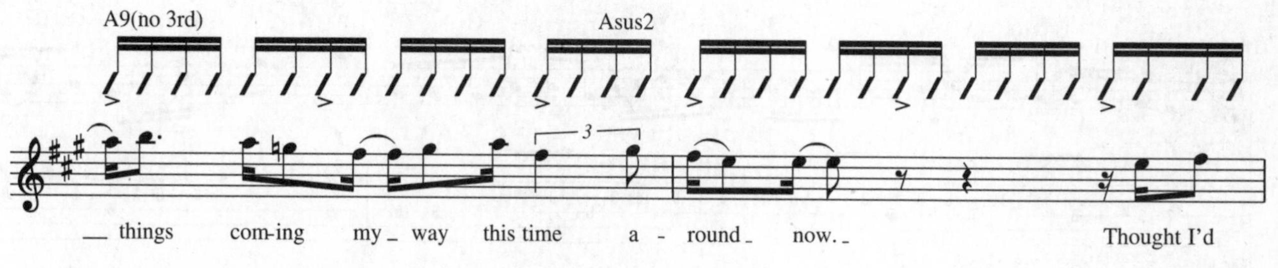
A9(no 3rd)
Asus2
things coming my way this time around now.
Thought I'd

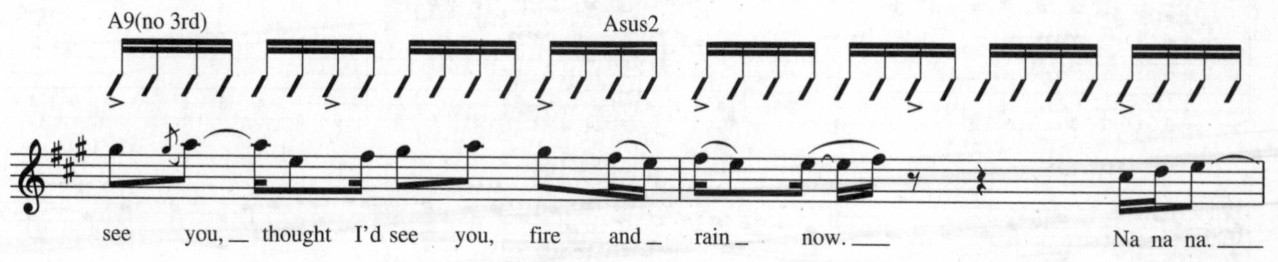
A9(no 3rd)
Asus2
see you, thought I'd see you, fire and rain now.
Na na na.

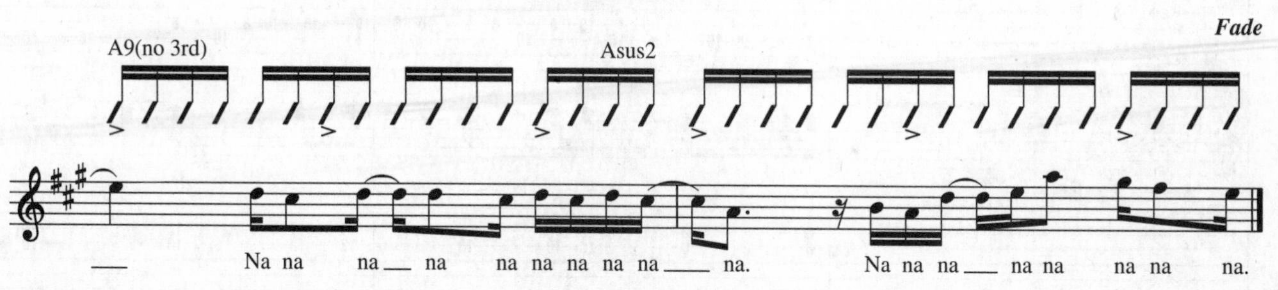
Fade
A9(no 3rd)
Asus2
Na na na na na na na na na na.
Na na na na na na na na.

Frankenstein

By Edgar Winter

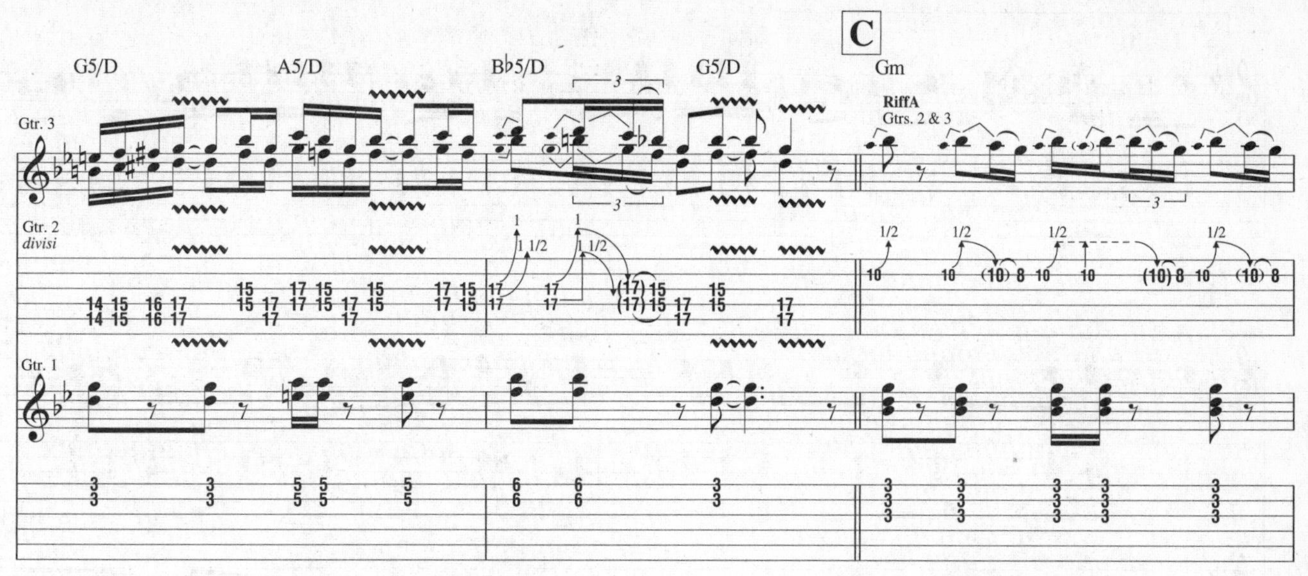

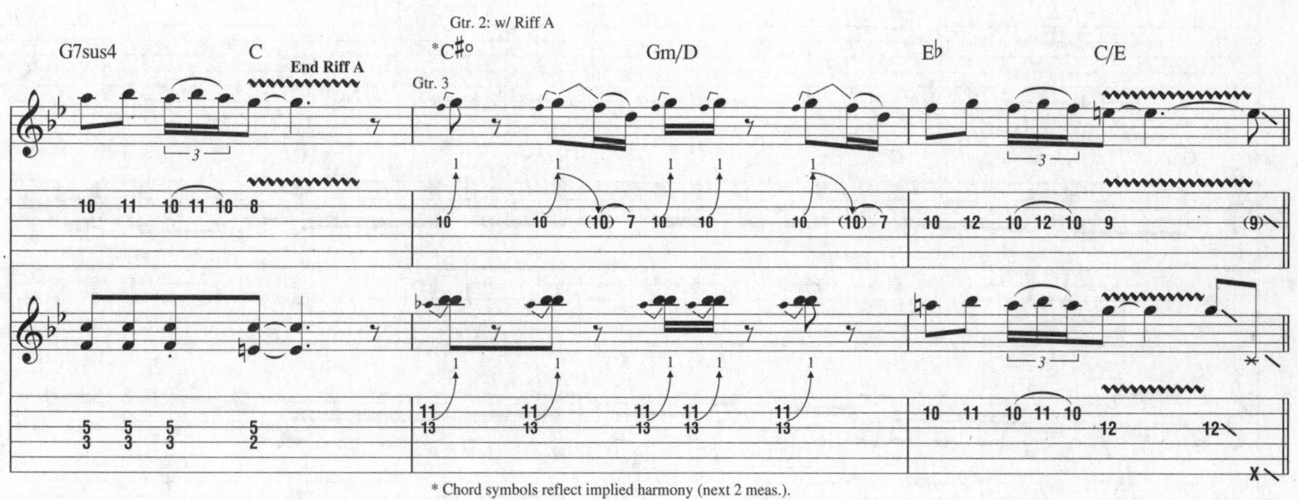

* Chord symbols reflect implied harmony (next 2 meas.).

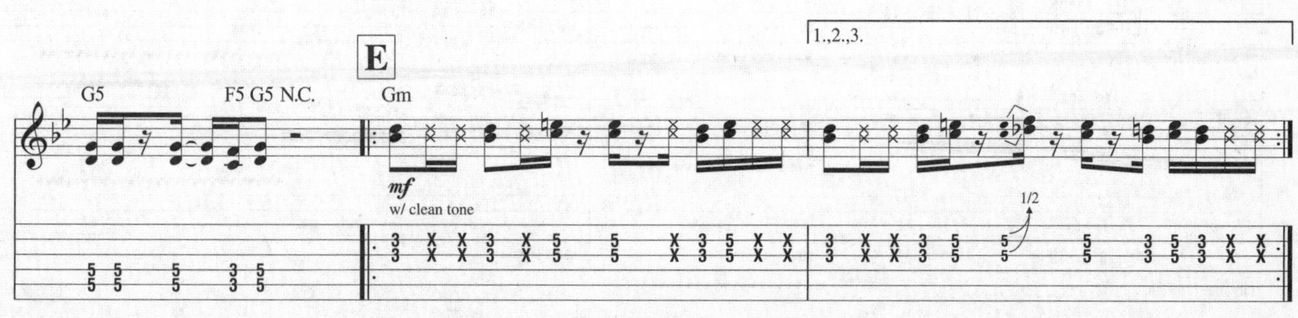

4.
Gm9
1/2
F
Gtr. 1
Gm
C
Gm7
C9
Gtr. 2
G
Gtr. 2 tacet
Rhy. Fig 1
End Rhy. Fig. 1
*Gtr. 6
**Gtr. 4
Gtr. 5 (clean)
divisi
** Sax. arr. for gtr.
Gtr. 1
*Organ arr. for gtr.

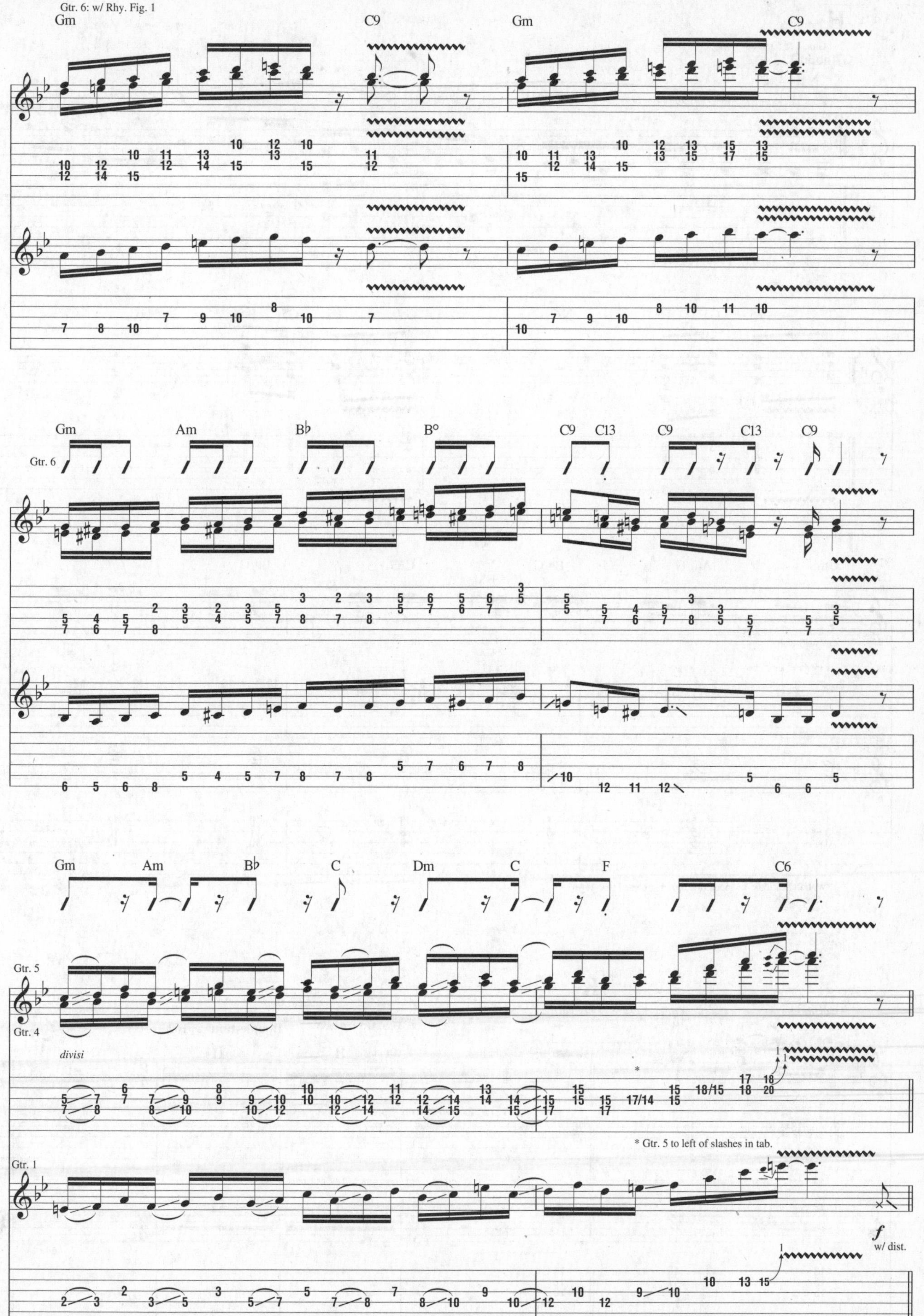
Gtr. 6: w/ Rhy. Fig. 1
Gm
C9
Gm
C9
Gm
Am
B♭
B°
C9
C13
C9
C13
C9
Gtr. 6
Gm
Am
B♭
C
Dm
C
F
C6
Gtr. 5
Gtr. 4
divisi
* Gtr. 5 to left of slashes in tab.
Gtr. 1
f
w/ dist.

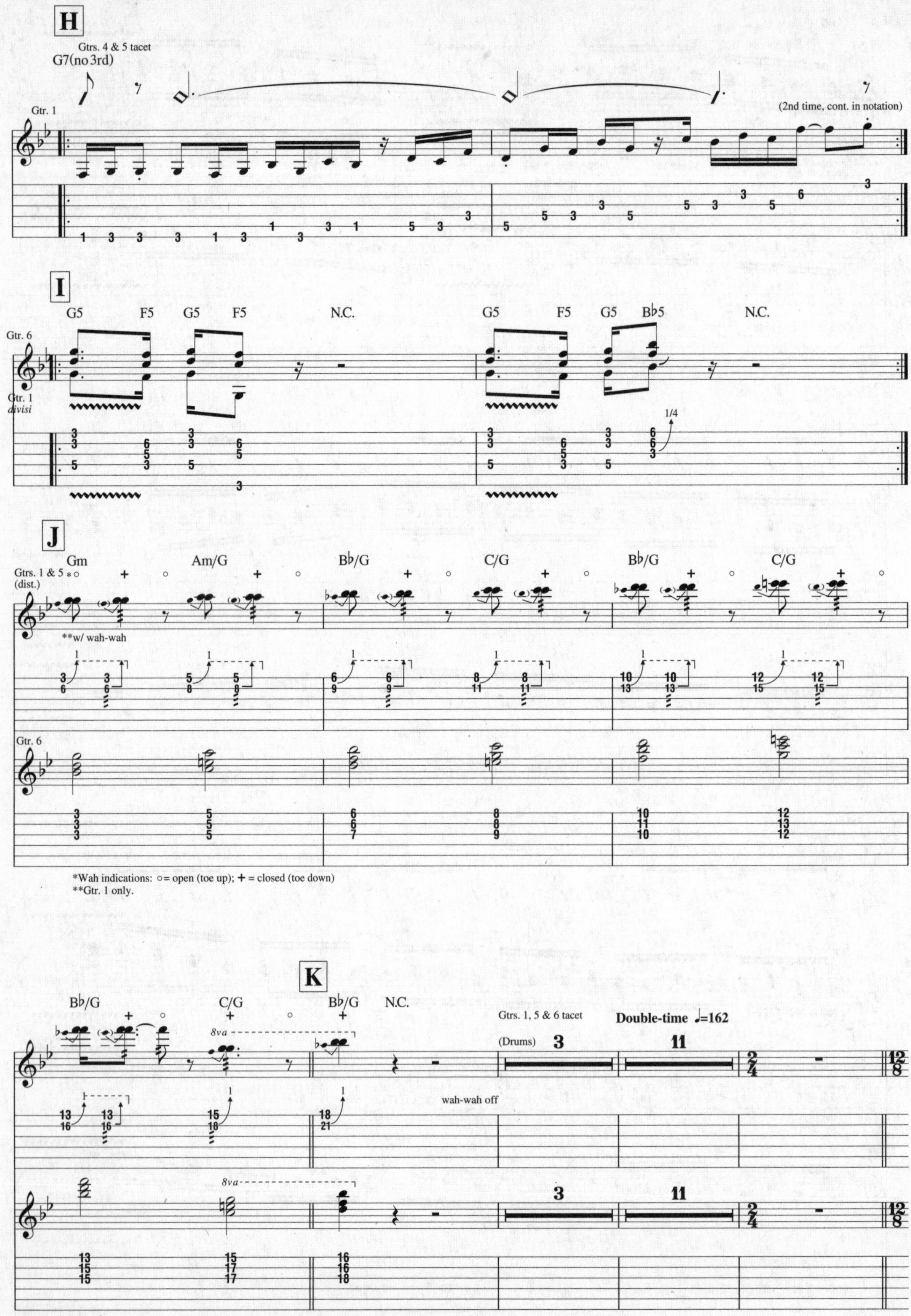

H

Gtrs. 4 & 5 tacet

G7(no 3rd)

Gtr. 1

(2nd time, cont. in notation)

I

G5 F5 G5 F5 N.C. G5 F5 G5 B♭5 N.C.

Gtr. 6

Gtr. 1 *divisi*

J

Gm Am/G B♭/G C/G B♭/G C/G

Gtrs. 1 & 5 (dist.)

**w/ wah-wah

Gtr. 6

*Wah indications: ○ = open (toe up); + = closed (toe down)
**Gtr. 1 only.

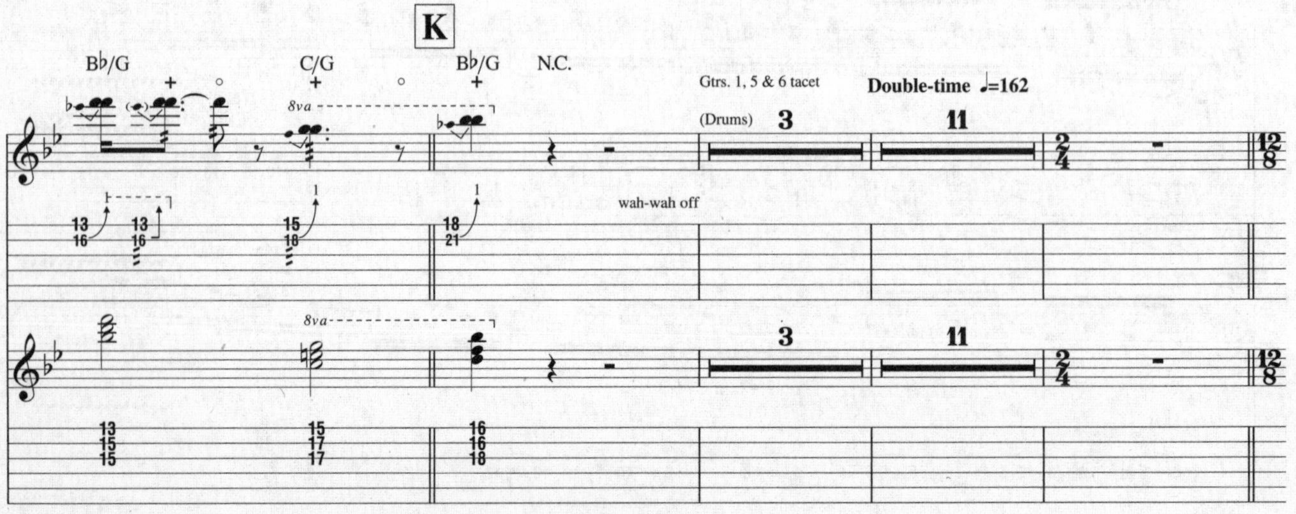

L
A tempo (♩. = 96)
Gtr. 1
N.C.
G5
N.C.
G5
N.C.
G5
B♭5
N.C.
G5
F5
Play 3 times
1/4

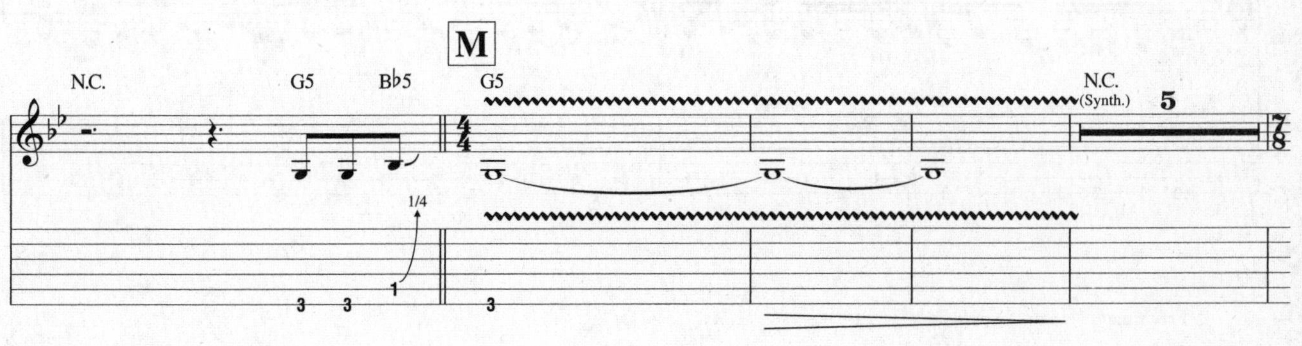
M
N.C.
G5
B♭5
G5
N.C.
(Synth.)
5
1/4

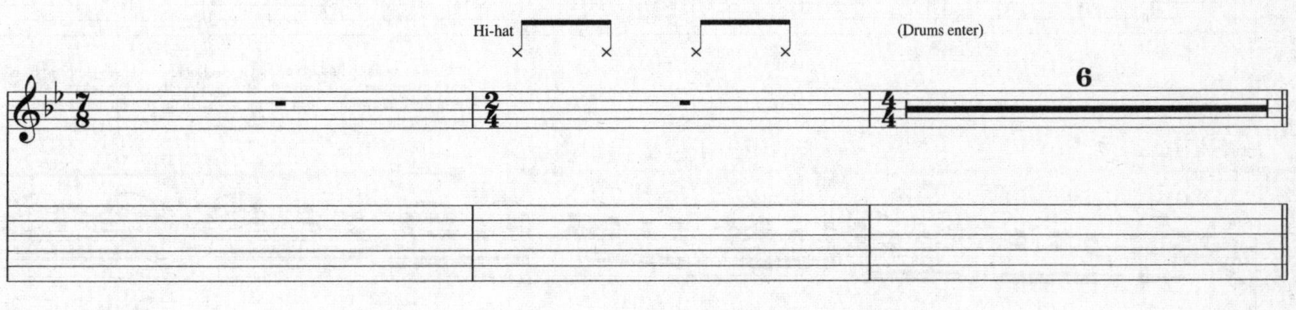
Hi-hat
(Drums enter)
6

N
G5
F5 G5
B♭5
G5
Gtr. 1
F5 G5
N.C.
G5
F5 G5
B♭5
Gtr. 2
divisi

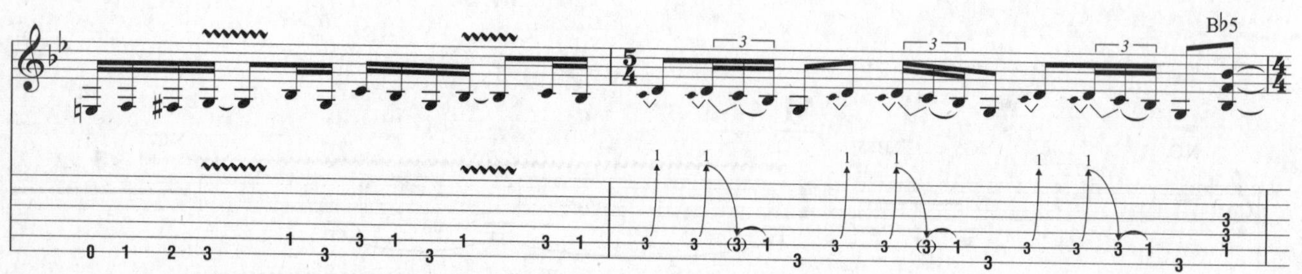

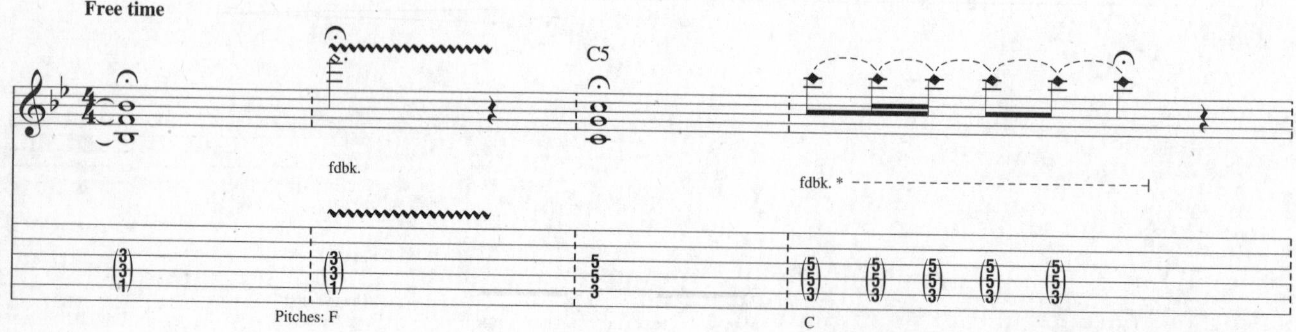

* Using a guitar with Les Paul style electronics, set lead volume to 0 and rhythm volume to 10. Strike the strings while the pickup selector switch is in the lead position, then flip the switch in the rhythm indicated to simulate the re-attack.

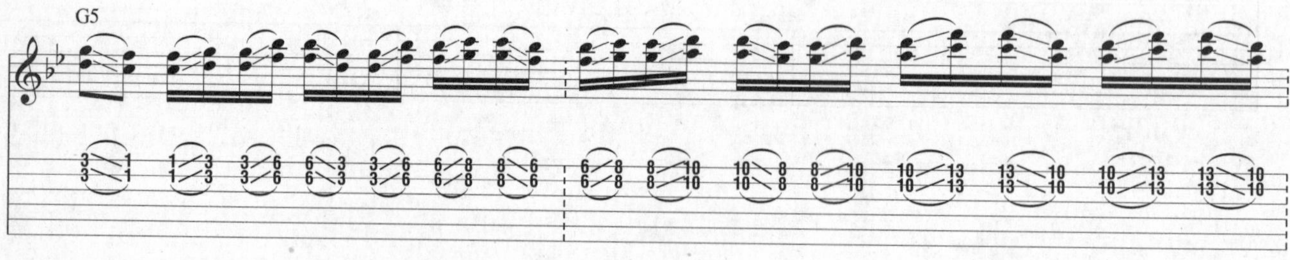

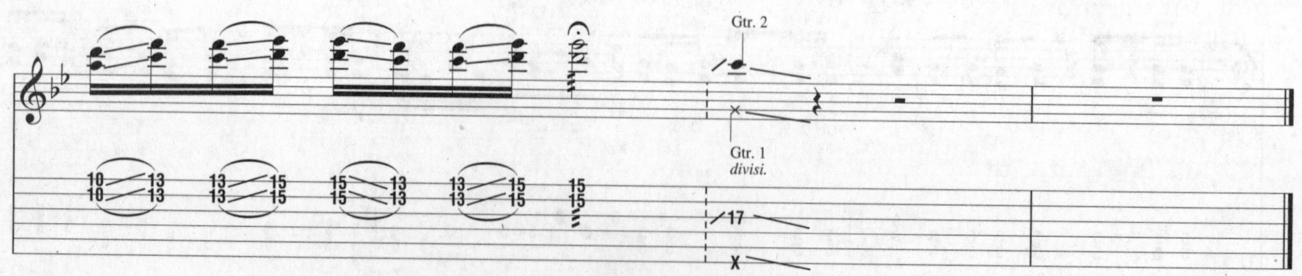

Freeway Jam

By Max Middleton

*③ is sounded sympathetically.

G
F/G
G
w/ bar
Gtr. 2: w/ Riff A (1 1/2 times)
End Riff A
Gtr. 1
1/2
-1
Gtr. 2
-1 1/2

E
Gtr. 2 tacet
F/G
F7sus2
D/G
*15ma
Gtr. 1
* P.H.
*Applies to harmonic pitches only.
F/G
F7sus2
15ma
loco
Amaj7
P.H.
slight P.H.
Gadd9/A
F/G
B♭7
A♭7
G7
slight P.H.
w/ bar
** T
**T = Thumb on ⑥
F
G
F/G
G
F/G
G
F/G

*Applies to harmonic pitch only.

G
Gtr. 2: w/ Riff A (1st 7 meas. only)
G F/G G F/G G F/G
Gtr. 1
w/ bar
G F/G
w/ bar
G F/G G F/G G F/G
Gtrs. 1 & 2
slight P.H.
w/ bar
H
Gtr. 2 tacet
G F/G
Gtr. 1
F7sus2
slight P.H.
D/G F/G F7sus2 Amaj7
w/ bar

Gadd9/A
F/G
B♭7
A♭7
G7sus4
G7
1/4
1/2
Begin fade
let ring
Segue into "Diamond Dust"
Gtr. 1 tacet
Fade out

The Freshmen

Words and Music by Brian Vander Ark

Gtr. 1: w/ Riff B
Esus2
(Dsus2)
A
(G)
guilt strick - en, sob - bing with my head on the floor.

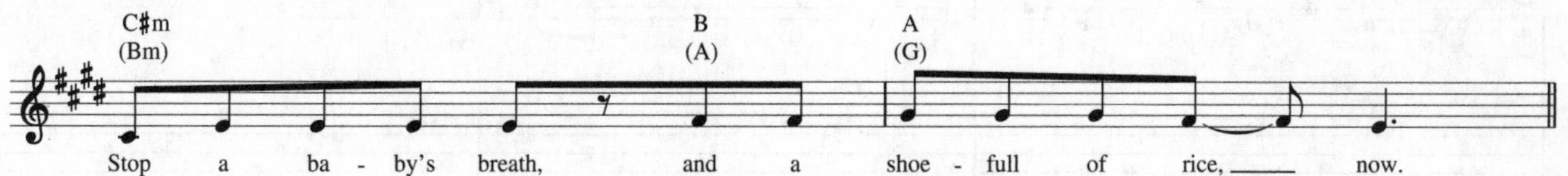
C♯m
(Bm)
B
(A)
A
(G)
Stop a ba - by's breath, and a shoe - full of rice, now.

Pre-Chorus
C♯m B A C♯m B A
(Bm) (A) (G) (Bm) (A) (G)
I can't be held re - spon - si - ble, 'cause she was touch - ing her face.
Gtr. 1
Riff C
End Riff C

Gtr. 1: w/ Riff C
C♯m B A C♯m B A
(Bm) (A) (G) (Bm) (A) (G)
I won't be held re - spon - si - ble. She fell in love in the first place.

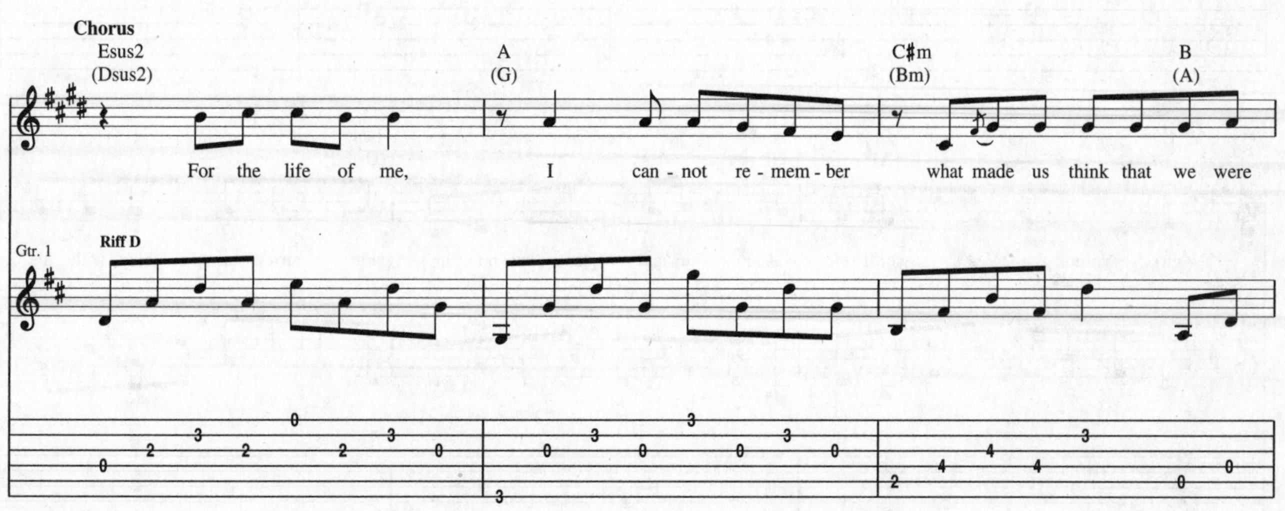
Chorus
Esus2 A C♯m B
(Dsus2) (G) (Bm) (A)
For the life of me, I can - not re - mem - ber what made us think that we were
Gtr. 1
Riff D

A
(G)
E
(D)
A
(G)
wise and we'd nev - er com - pro - mise. For the life of me, I can - not be - lieve we'd
End Riff D
Interlude
Gtr. 2: w/ Riff A
C#m
(Bm)
B
(A)
A
(G)
Esus2
(Dsus2)
A
(G)
ev - er die for these sins. We were mere - ly fresh - men.
Verse
C#m
(Bm)
B
(A)
A
(G)
Esus2
(Dsus2)
A
(G)
2. My best friend took a week's va - ca - tion to for - get her. His
C#m
(Bm)
B
(A)
A
(G)
Esus2
(Dsus2)
girl took a week's worth of val - ium and slept. And now he's guilt strick - en, sob - bing with his

A
(G)
C#m
(Bm)
B
(A)
A
(G)
head on the floor. Thinks __ a - bout her now and how he nev - er real - ly wept. He says,
Pre-Chorus
C#m
(Bm)
B
(A)
A
(G)
can't be held re-spon - si - ble, __ 'cause she was touch-ing her face.
Gtr. 3
(dist.)*
Riff E
mf
sim.
let ring throughout
Gtr. 1
* vol. swells
I won't be held re-spon - si - ble. __ She fell in love __ in the first place.
End Riff E
(cont. in slash)

Chorus
Gtr. 1: w/ Riff D, 2 times, simile
E5
A5
C#7(no3rd)
B
E
open
open
Rhy. Fig. 1
Gtr. 3
For the life of me, I can - not re - mem - ber what made us think that we were
A5
End Rhy. Fig. 1
E5
A5
wise and we'd nev - er com - pro - mise. For the life of me, I can - not be - lieve we'd
C#5
B
E
A(♭5)
open
open
(cont. in notation)
ev - er die for these sins. We were mere - ly fresh - men.
Bridge
Gtr. 3 tacet
G#m
(F#m)
A
(G)
E
(D)
B
(A)
G#m
(F#m)
A
(G)
Hey, yeah.
Gtr. 3
sim.
* Gtrs. 1 & 4 (dist.)
mf
let ring throughout
* composite arrangement

E
(D)
B
(A)
G♯m
(F♯m)
A
(G)
E
(D)
B
(A)
Hey, yeah.
Hey, yeah.
G♯m
(F♯m)
A
(G)
E
(D)
Bsus2
(Asus2)
Verse
Gtr. 3 tacet
Esus2
(Dsus2)
A
(G)
C♯m
(Bm)
B
(A)
3. We tried to wash our hands of all of this. We nev - er talk of a lack in re -
Gtrs. 1 & 4

A
(G)
Esus2
(Dsus2)
A
(G)
la - tion - ships, and how we're guilt strick - en, sob - bing with our heads on the floor. We
Pre-Chorus
Gtr. 3: w/ Riff E
C♯m
(Bm)
B
(A)
A
(G)
C♯m
(Bm)
B
(A)
fell through the ice when we tried not to slip. We'd say,
Riff F
A
(G)
C♯m
(Bm)
B
(A)
A
(G)
can't be held re - spon - si - ble, 'cause she was touch - ing her face.
End Riff F
Gtr. 3: w/ Riff F
C♯m
(Bm)
B
(A)
A
(G)
C♯m
(Bm)
B
(A)
And I won't be held re - spon - si - ble. She fell in
Chorus
Gtr. 1 tacet
Gtr. 3: w/ Rhy. Fig. 1, 3 1/2 times, simile
Gtr. 4: w/ Riff D, 3 1/2 times, simile
A
(G)
Esus2
(Dsus2)
A
(G)
love in the first place. For the life of me, I can - not re - mem - ber
Gtr. 1: w/ Riff D, 2 1/2 times, simile
C♯m
(Bm)
B
(A)
A
(G)
Esus2
(Dsus2)
what made us think that we were wise and we'd nev - er com - pro - mise. For the life of me,

A (G) C#m (Bm) B (A) A (G)
I can - not be - lieve we'd ev - er die for these sins. We were mere - ly fresh - men.
Esus2 (Dsus2) A (G) C#m (Bm) B (A)
For the life of me, I can - not re - mem - ber what made us think that we were
A (G) Esus2 (Dsus2) A (G)
wise and we'd nev - er com - pro - mise. For the life of me, I can - not be - lieve we'd
Outro
Gtr. 2: w/ Riff A, 2 times
C#m (Bm) B (A) A (G) Esus2 (Dsus2)
ev - er die for these sins. We were mere - ly fresh - men. We
Gtr. 4
Gtrs. 1 & 4
A (G) C#m (Bm) B (A) A (G)
were mere - ly fresh - men. We were on - ly fresh - men.
E5
Asus2
Gtr. 3

Fun, Fun, Fun

Words and Music by Brian Wilson and Mike Love

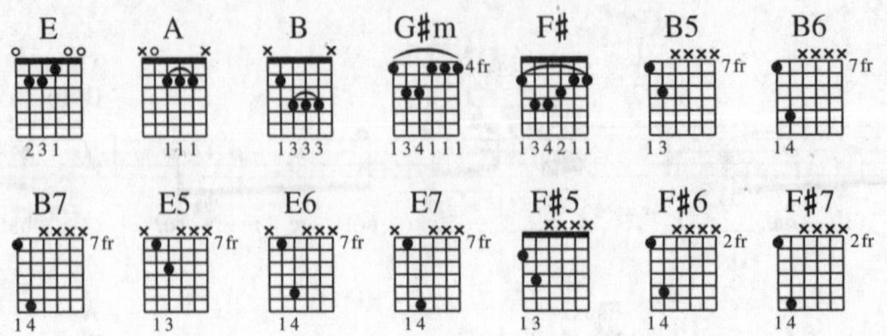

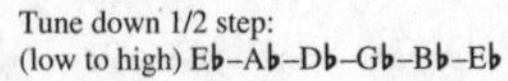

Intro

Moderately fast ♩ = 168

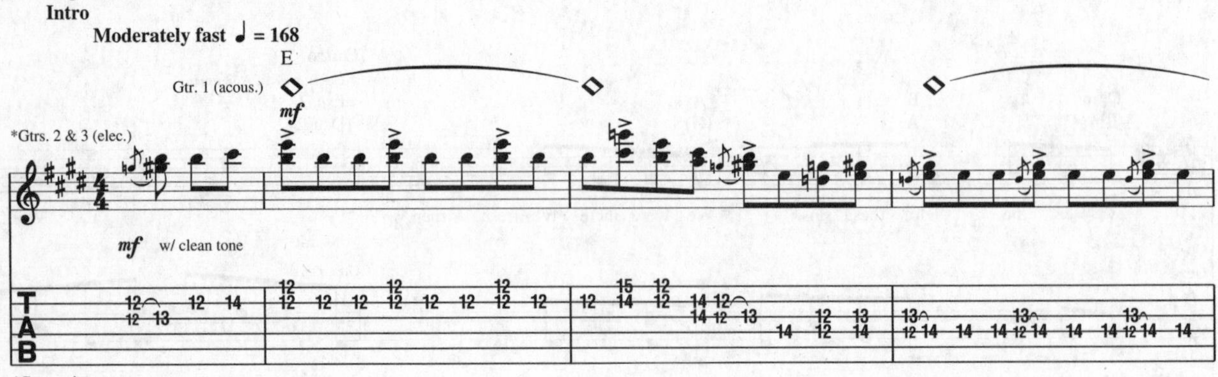

*Composite arrangement

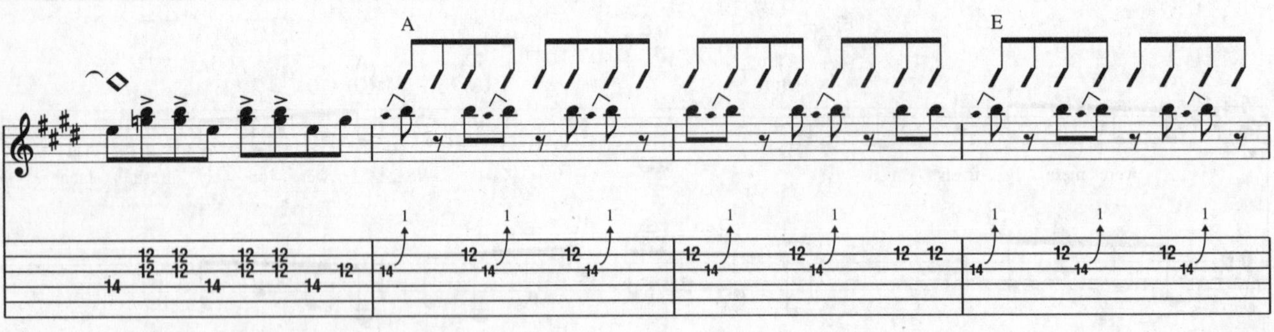

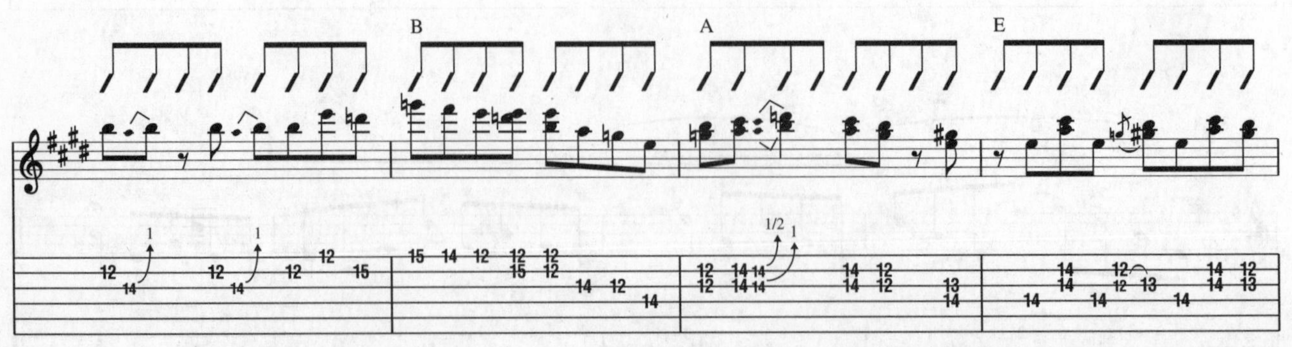

Verse
Gtrs. 2 & 3 tacet
B
E
Rhy. Fig. 1
1. Well, she got her dad - dy's car and she cruised through the ham - burg - er stand, now.
Rhy. Fig. 1A
Gtr. 4 (elec.)
mf w/ clean tone
P.M.
A
E
Seems she for - got all a - bout the li - brar - y like she told her old man, now.
B
And with the
E
A
ra - di - o blast - in' goes cruis - in' just as fast as she can, now.

E
G♯m
A
B
End Rhy. Fig. 1
Rhy. Fig. 2
And she'll have fun, fun, fun till her dad - dy takes the T - Bird a - way.
(Fun, fun, fun till her dad - dy takes the T - Bird a - way.)
(Fun, fun, fun till her dad - dy takes the T - Bird.
End Rhy. Fig. 1A
Rhy. Fig. 2A
P.M.
Verse
Gtrs. 1 & 4: w/ Rhy. Figs. 1 & 1A
2nd time, Bkgd. Voc.: w/ Voc. Fig. 1
2nd time, Gtr. 2 tacet
E
A
G♯m
B
End Rhy. Fig. 2
E
2. Well, the girls can't stand her 'cause she
3. See additional lyrics
Fun, fun, fun till her dad - dy takes the T - Bird a - way.)
End Rhy. Fig. 2A
P.M.
A
walks, looks and drives like an ace, now. She makes the
(You walk like an ace, now, you walk like an ace.
Voc. Fig. 1
(Oo. You...

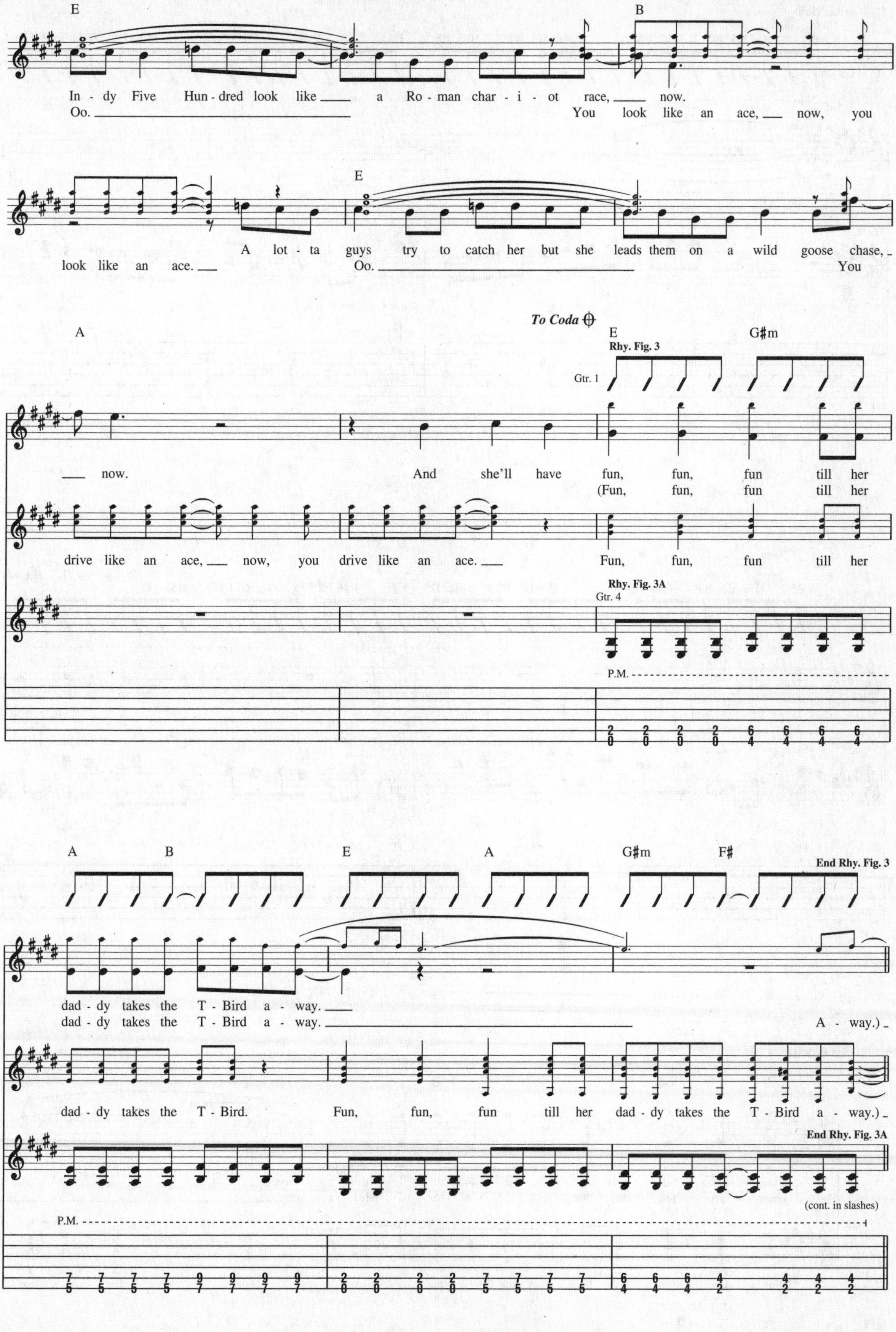

E B

In - dy Five Hun - dred look like ___ a Ro - man char - i - ot race, ___ now.
Oo. ___ You look like an ace, ___ now, you

E

A lot - ta guys try to catch her but she leads them on a wild goose chase, ___
look like an ace. ___ Oo. ___ You

To Coda ⊕

A E G♯m

Rhy. Fig. 3

Gtr. 1

___ now. And she'll have fun, fun, fun till her
(Fun, fun, fun till her
drive like an ace, ___ now, you drive like an ace. ___ Fun, fun, fun till her

Rhy. Fig. 3A

Gtr. 4

P.M.

Guitar Solo

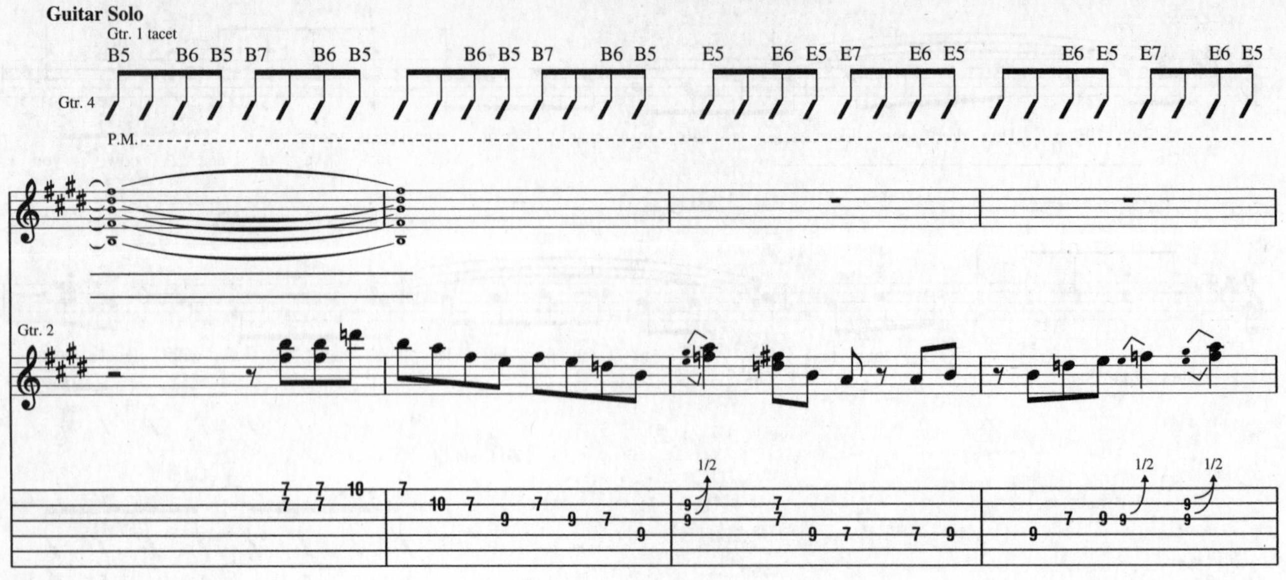
Gtr. 1 tacet
B5 B6 B5 B7 B6 B5 B6 B5 B7 B6 B5 E5 E6 E5 E7 E6 E5 E6 E5 E7 E6 E5
Gtr. 4
P.M.
Gtr. 2
1/2
1/2
1/2

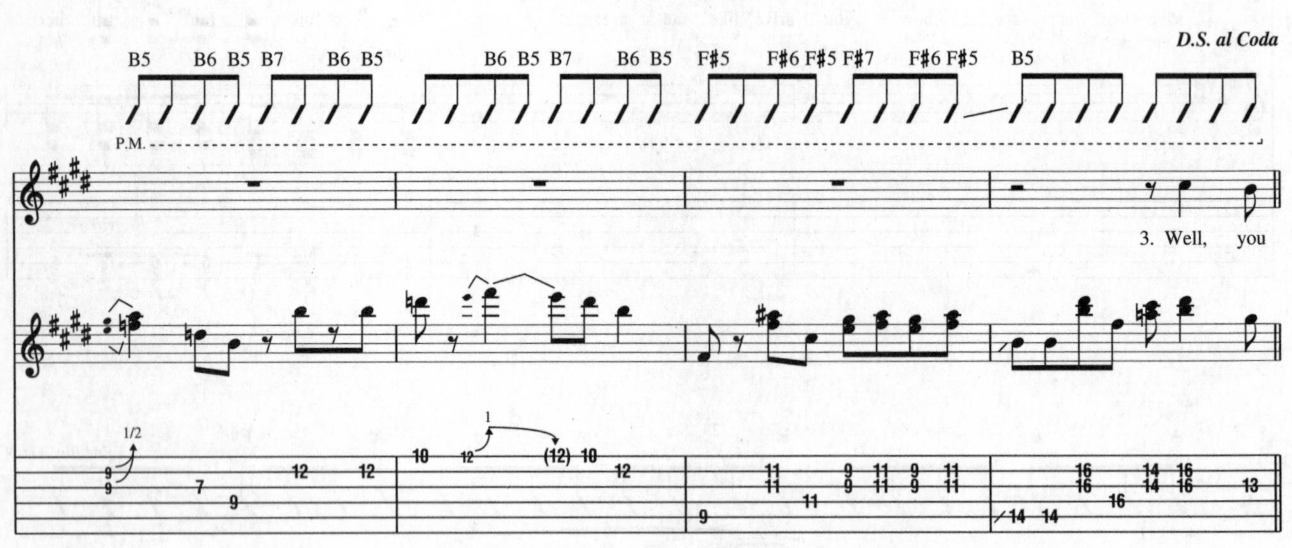
D.S. al Coda
B5 B6 B5 B7 B6 B5 B6 B5 B7 B6 B5 F#5 F#6 F#5 F#7 F#6 F#5 B5
P.M.
3. Well, you
1/2
1

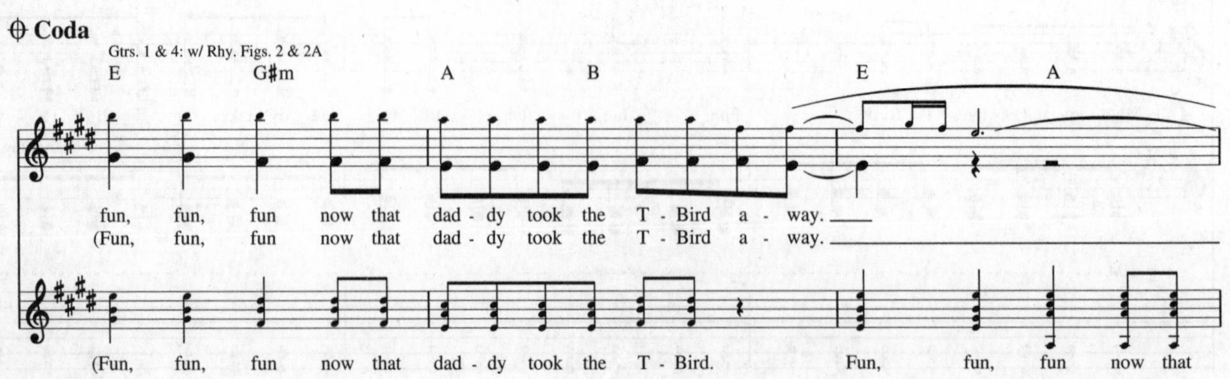
Coda
Gtrs. 1 & 4: w/ Rhy. Figs. 2 & 2A
E G#m A B E A
fun, fun, fun now that dad - dy took the T - Bird a - way.
(Fun, fun, fun now that dad - dy took the T - Bird a - way.
(Fun, fun, fun now that dad - dy took the T - Bird. Fun, fun, fun now that

Additional Lyrics

Well, you knew all along
That your dad was gettin' wise to you, now.
(You shouldn't have lied, now, you shouldn't have lied.)
And since he took your set of keys
You've been thinkin' that your fun is all through, now.
(You shouldn't have lied, now, you shouldn't have lied.)
But you can come along with me
'Cause we got a lotta things to do now.
(You shouldn't have lied, now, you shouldn't have lied.)
And we'll...

Galloping on the Guitar

By Chet Atkins

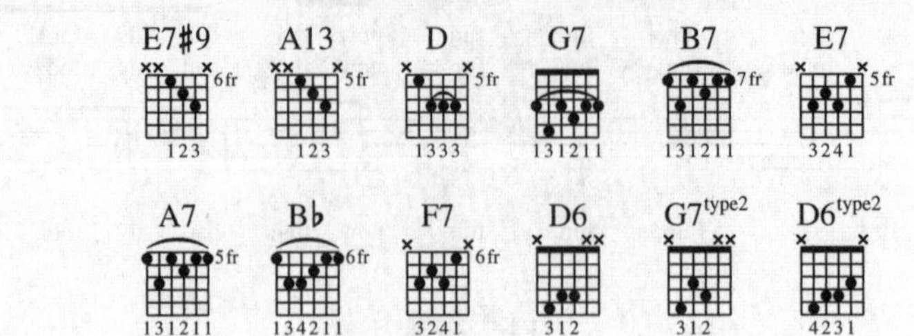

Gtr. 3: Capo II

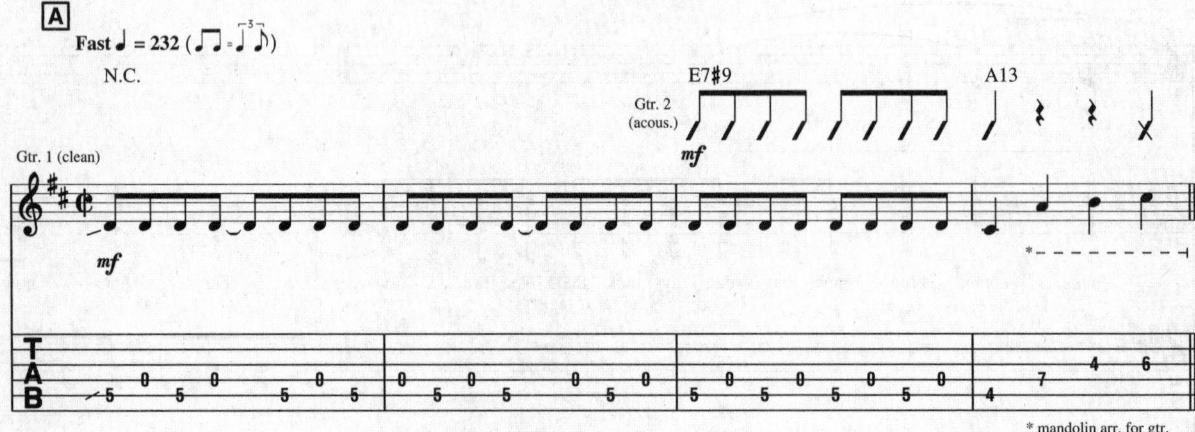

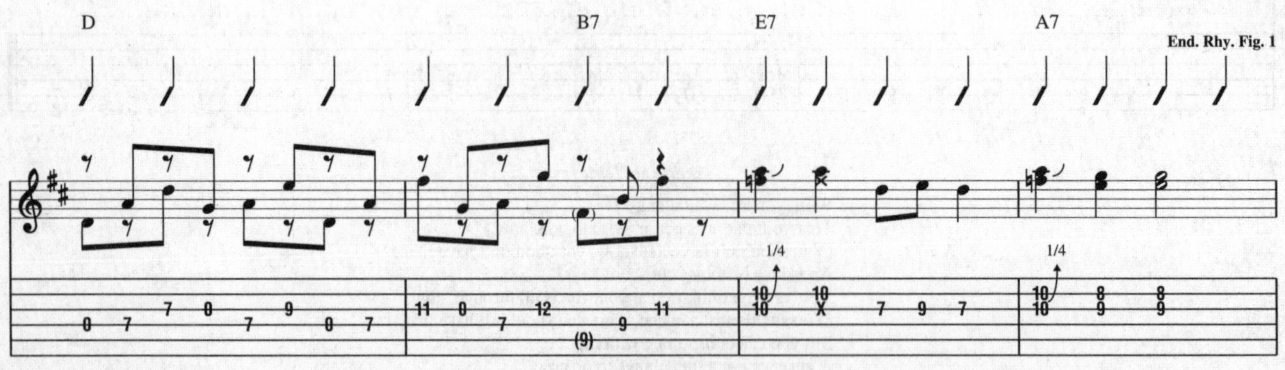

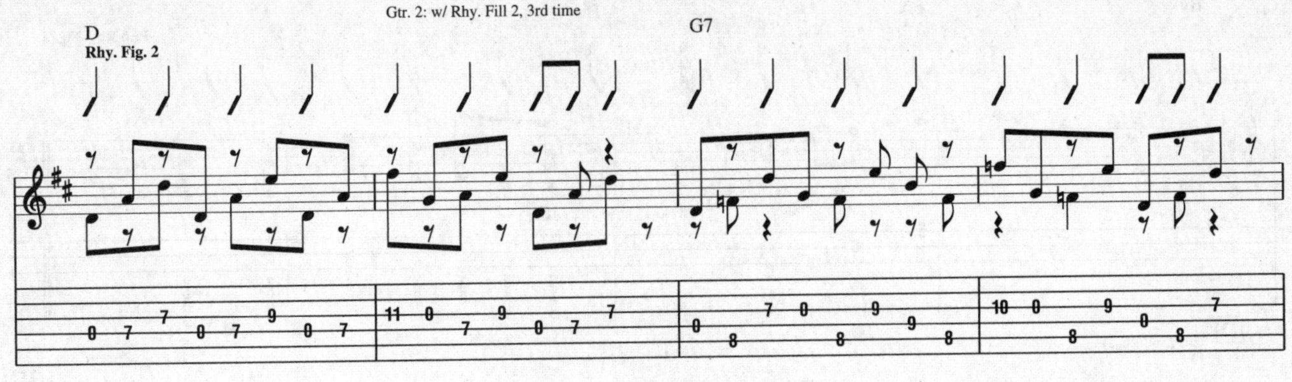
Gtr. 2: w/ Rhy. Fill 2, 3rd time
D
Rhy. Fig. 2
G7

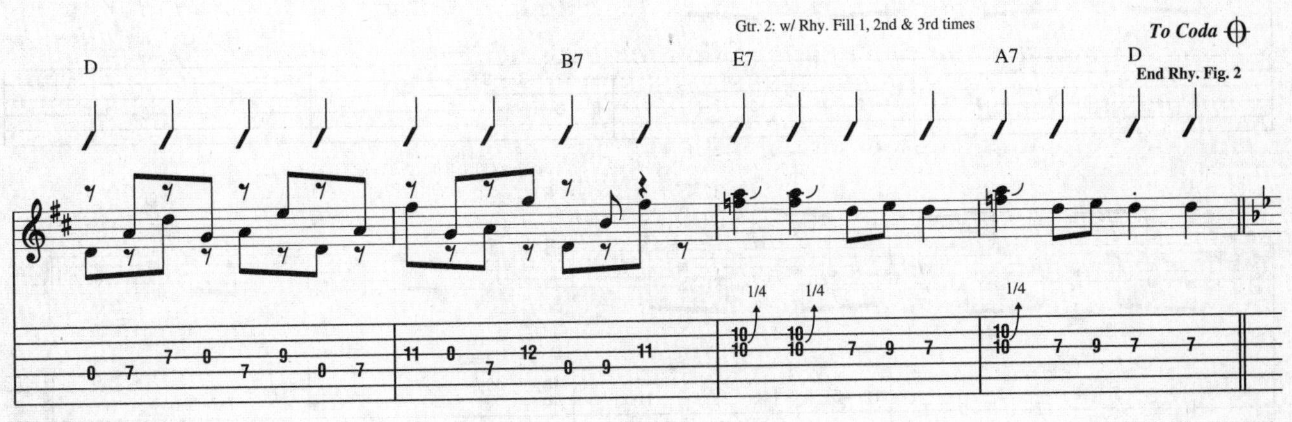
Gtr. 2: w/ Rhy. Fill 1, 2nd & 3rd times
To Coda
D
B7
E7
A7
D
End Rhy. Fig. 2
1/4
1/4
1/4

C
B♭
Rhy. Fig. 3
F7
B♭
F7

Rhy. Fill 1
E7
A7
D
Gtr. 2
Rhy. Fill 2
Gtr. 2
steady gliss.

B♭
F7
B♭
A7
End Rhy. Fig. 3
D
Gtr. 2: w/ Rhy. Fig. 2, simile
D
G7
Gtr. 2: w/ Rhy. Fill 1, 2nd time
D
B7
E7
A7
D
E
Gtr. 2: w/ Rhy. Fig. 1, 1 3/4 times
Gtr. 1 tacet
D
G7
Gtr. 3
D
B7
E7
A7
D
G7

Gtr. 2: w/ Rhy. Fill 1
D
B7
E7
A7
D
F Mandolin Solo
Gtr. 3 tacet
Gtr. 2
B♭
F7
B♭
F7
B♭
F7
B♭
A7
Gtr. 1
G
D
sim.
G7
D.S. al Coda
D
B7
E7
A7
D
1/2
1/2
w/ bar

Coda
H
Gtr. 2: w/ Rhy. Fig. 3
B♭
F7
B♭
F7
B♭
F7
B♭
A7
I
D6
Gtr. 2
D
5fr
D6
w/ bar
w/ bar
G7type2
E7
B7
A7
D6 type2
1/4
1/4
1/4

Green Onions

Written by Al Jackson, Jr., Lewis Steinberg, Booker T. Jones and Steve Cropper

C Organ Solo
Riff A
End Rhy. Fig. 2
let ring
P.M.
Bb Db Eb F5 Ab Bb F5 Ab Bb F5 Ab5 Bb5
F5 Ab5 Bb5 F5 Ab5 Bb5 F5 Ab5 Bb5 Db5 Eb5
Bb5 Db5 Eb5 F5 Ab5 Bb5 F5 Ab5 Bb5 C5 Eb5 F5

Bb5
Db5
Eb5
F5
Ab5
Bb5
F5
Ab5
Bb5
End Riff A
P.M.
Gtr. 2: w/ Riff A
Gtr. 1
C5

D Guitar Solo

C
Eb
F
Bb
Db
Eb
F5
Ab
Bb
F5
Ab
Bb
reverb off
E Organ Solo
Gtr. 2: w/ Riff A (2 times)
F5
Ab5
Bb5
F5
Ab5
Bb5
F5
Ab5
Bb5
F5
Ab5
Bb5
Gtr. 1
Db5
Eb5
Bb5
Db5
Eb5
F5
Ab5
Bb5
F5
Ab5
Bb5
C5
Eb5
F5
Bb5
Db5
Eb5
F5
Ab5
Bb5
F5
Ab5
Bb5
F5
Ab5
Bb5

F5 Ab5 Bb5 F5 Ab5 Bb5 F5 Ab5 Bb5
Db5 Eb5 Bb5 Db5 Eb5 F5 Ab5 Bb5 F5 Ab5 Bb5
C5 Eb5 F5 Bb5 Db5 Eb5 F5 Ab5 Bb5 F5 Ab5 Bb5
F Outro
Gtr. 1: w/ Rhy. Fig. 1 (5 times)
Gtr. 2
F5 Ab Bb F5 Ab Bb F5 Ab Bb F5 Ab Bb F5 Ab Bb
Begin fade
F5 Ab Bb F5 Ab Bb F5 Ab Bb F5 Ab Bb F5 Ab Bb
Fade out

Guerrilla Radio

Written and Arranged by Rage Against The Machine

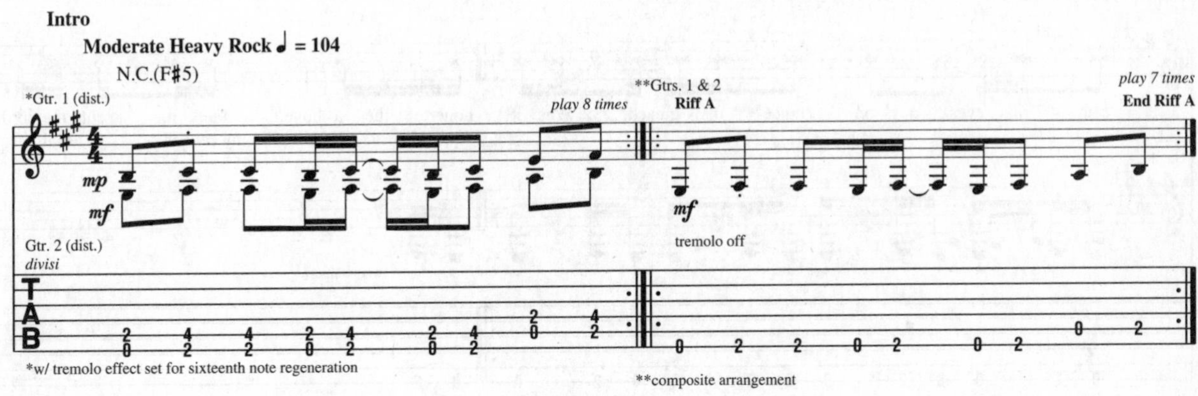

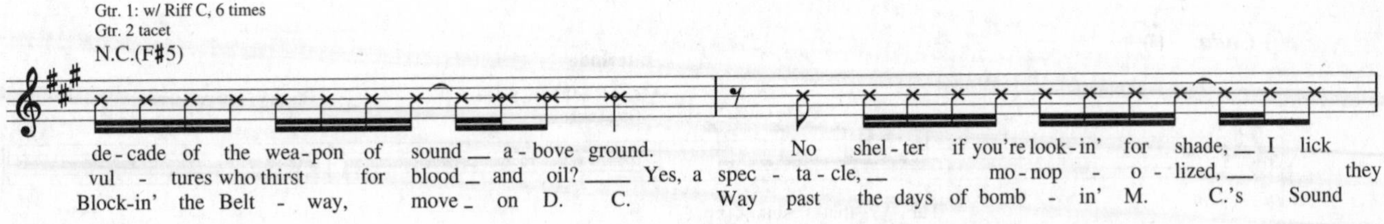

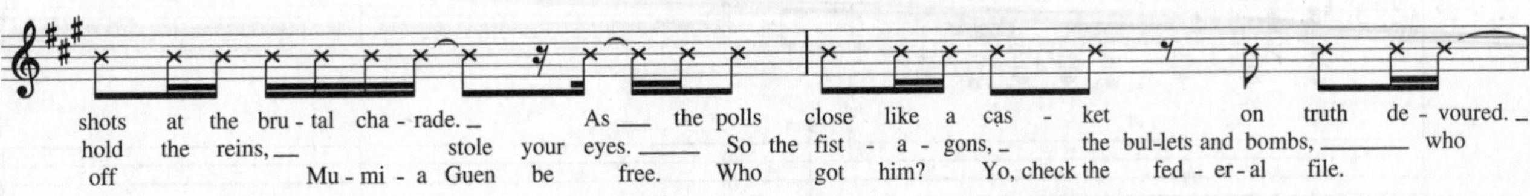

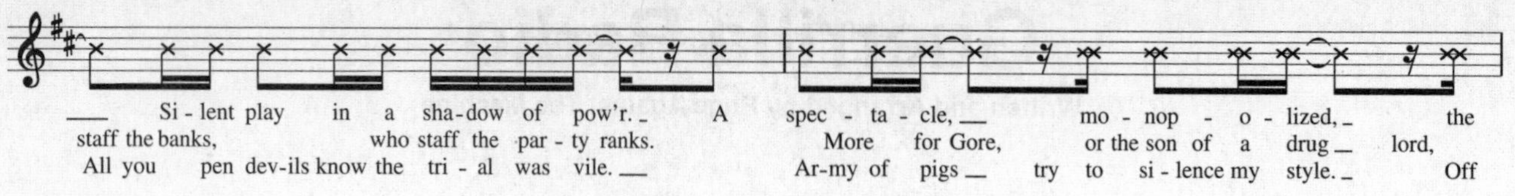

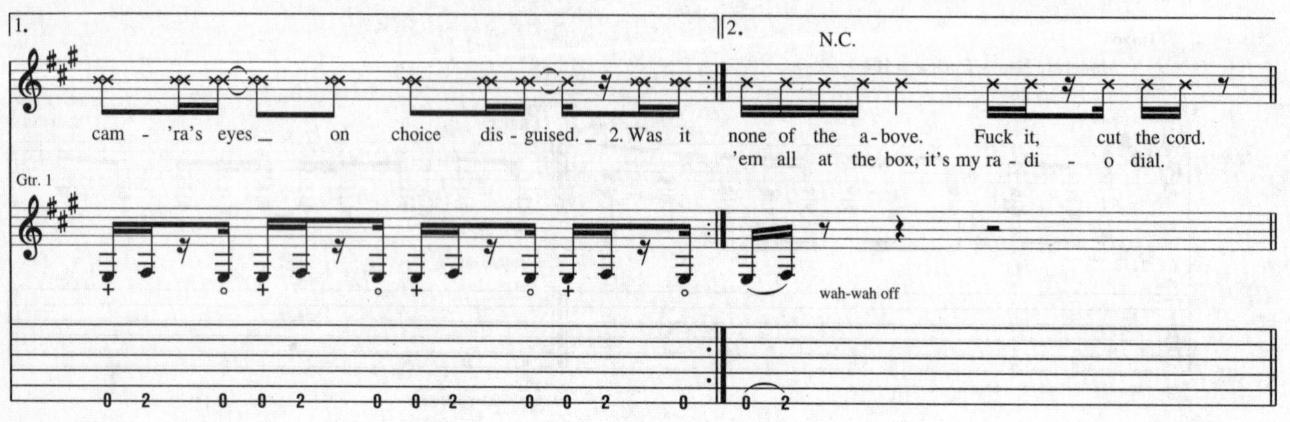

Chorus

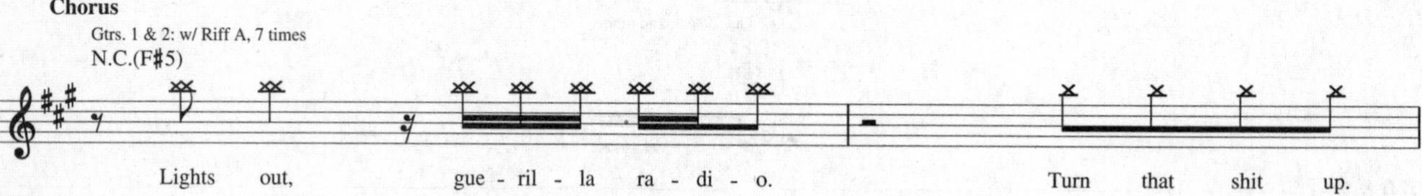

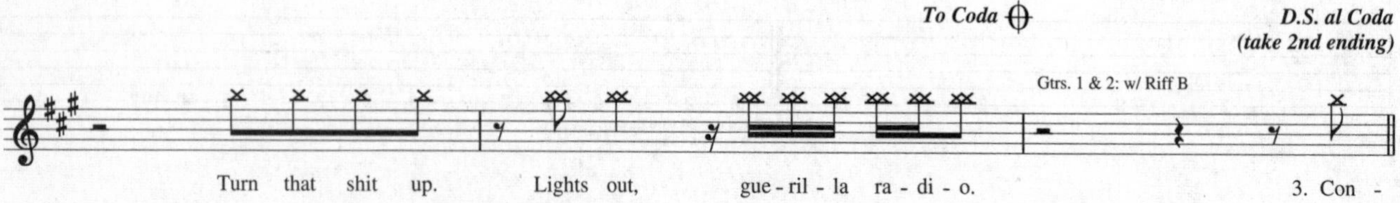

Coda

Interlude

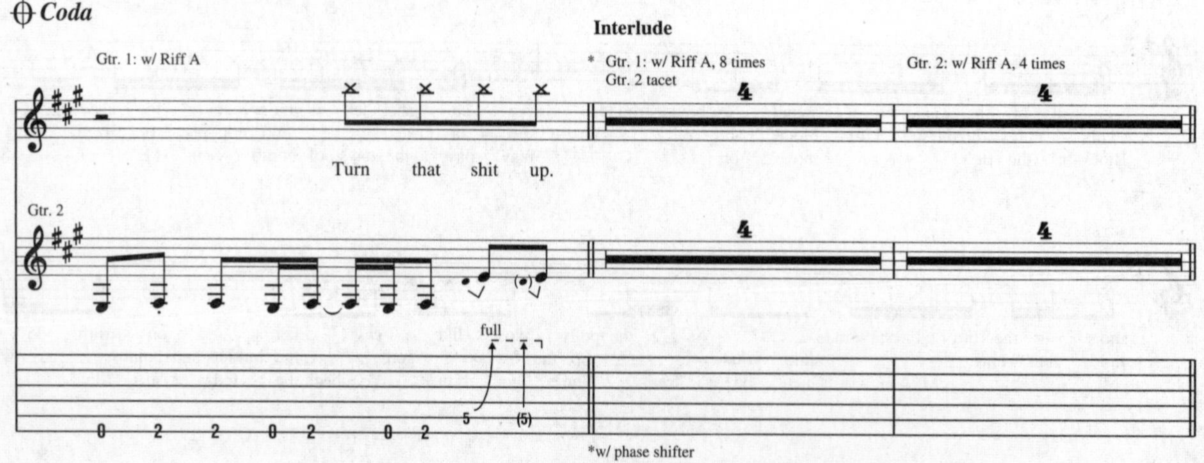

Guitar Solo

Gtr. 1
N.C.(F#5)
f
Gtr. 3 (dist.)
divisi
*w/ Digitech Whammy Pedal & talk box
*set for two octaves above

** B5
A5
B5
N.C.
Gtr. 3
1 1/2
Gtr. 1
P.S.
steady gliss.
*Using a guitar with Les Paul style electronics, set lead volume to 0 and rhythm volume to 10.
Strike the strings while the pickup selector swtich is the lead position, then flip the switch to the rhythm position to simulate the attack. Flip switch in specified rhythm.
**Chord symbols reflect basic tonality.

*Gtr. 2: w/ Riff B
B5
A5
B5
B5
A5
B5
N.C.
B5
B♭m
A♭m
Gm
Whispered: It
1 1/2
full
*w/ wah-wah

Outro

Gtrs. 1 & 3 tacet
N.C.(F#5)
N.C.
Gtr. 2 tacet
has to start some-where. It has to start some-time. What bet - ter place than here? What
Gtr. 2
wah-wah off
bet-ter time than now?
(F#5)
All hell can't stop us now.
Gtrs. 1 & 2
Riff D
End Riff D
Gtrs. 1 & 2: w/ Riff D, 2 times
All hell can't stop us now. All hell can't stop us now.
All hell can't stop us now.
Gtrs. 1 & 2
Riff E
End Riff E
Gtrs. 1 & 2: w/ Riff E, 2 times
All hell can't stop us now. All hell can't stop us now.

Hanging by a Moment

Words and Music by Jason Wade

Drop D tuning, tune down 1/2 step:
low to high (D♭-A♭-D♭-G♭-B♭-E♭)

Intro

Moderate Rock ♩ = 124

*D

Gtr. 1 (clean)

Riff A

mf *let ring throughout*

*Chord symbols reflect implied harmony.

I'm clos - er to where I start - ed, oh,
End Riff A1

chas - ing af - ter you. I'm fall - ing e - ven
Harm.

Chorus
Bm A D Bm A D
more in love with you, let-ting go of all I've held on to. I'm stand-ing here un -
Gr. 2 (clean)
mf
Gtr. 1

Interlude

Verse

I'll take your in - vi - ta - tion.
8va
loco
Harm.
let ring

D5
You take all of me, now. I'm fall - ing e - ven
w/ dist.

Chorus
B5 A5 D5 B5 A5 *D5/F♯
more in love with you, let - ting go of all I've held on to.
Riff C
Gtr. 1
w/ dist.
Rhy. Fig. 1
Gtr. 2

*Bass plays F♯.

B5
A5
D5
I'm stay - ing here un - til you make me move.
I'm hang - ing by a

B5
A5
D5
mo - ment here with you.
I'm liv - ing for that
End Riff C
End Rhy. Fig. 1

Gtr. 1: w/ Riff C
Gtr. 2: w/ Rhy. Fig. 1 (1st 7 meas.)
2nd time, Gtr. 2: w/ Rhy. Fig. 1
B5 A5 D5 B5 A5 D5/F♯
on - ly thing I know. I'm run - ning and not quite sure where to go.
B5 A5 D5
And I don't know what I'm div - ing in - to, just hang - ing by a
1st time, Gtr. 2: w/ Fill 1
To Coda
B5 A5 D5
mo - ment here with you.
There's noth - ing else to lose,
Just hang - ing by a
Bridge
G5 D5
there's noth - ing else to find.
Gtrs. 1 & 2
1/2
G5
There's noth - ing in the world that can change my
Fill 1
Gtr. 2

B5
mind.
There is noth - ing
1/2

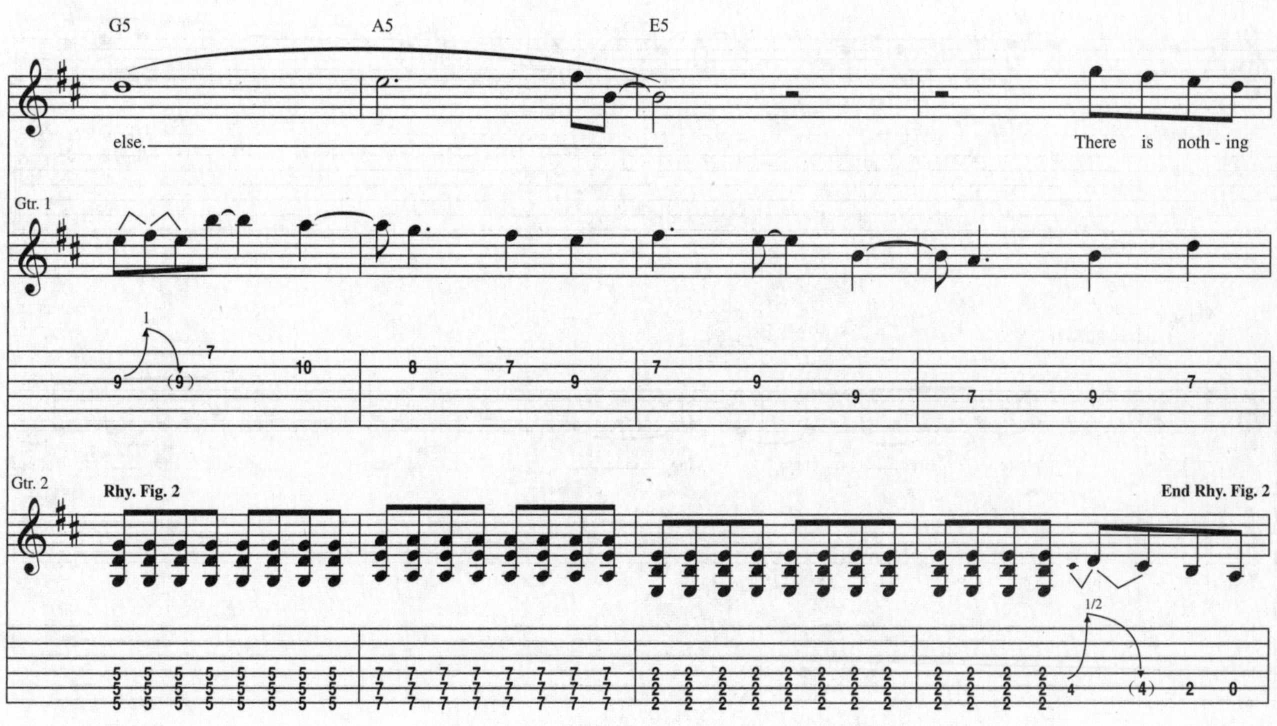
G5
A5
E5
else.
There is noth - ing
Gtr. 1
Gtr. 2
Rhy. Fig. 2
End Rhy. Fig. 2
1/2

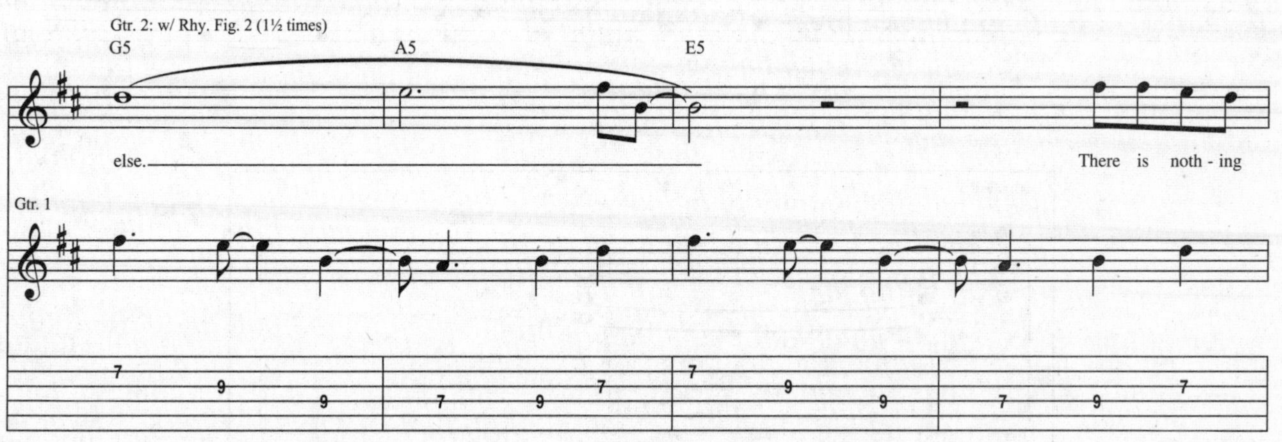
Gtr. 2: w/ Rhy. Fig. 2 (1½ times)
G5
A5
E5
else.
There is noth - ing
Gtr. 1

Gtr. 2: w/ Rhy. Fill 1
G5
A5
Em
else.
7
9
8
7
9
7
9

Interlude
*Gtr. 1: w/ Riff A
Gtr. 2
D
w/ clean tone
let ring
3
0
2
3
0
3
3
0
2
3
3 2 0
*w/ clean tone

Verse
Gtr. 1: w/ Riff A1
D
Gtr. 2 tacet
3. Des - p'rate for chang - ing, starv - ing for truth.
Gtr. 2
3

I'm clos - er to where I start - ed, oh,

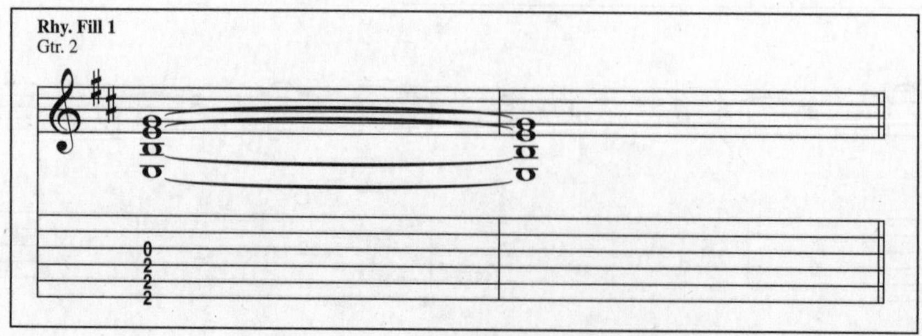
Rhy. Fill 1
Gtr. 2
0
2
2
2

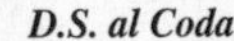
D.S. al Coda

chas - ing
af - ter
you.
I'm fall - ing e - ven
Gtr. 1
let ring
Harm.

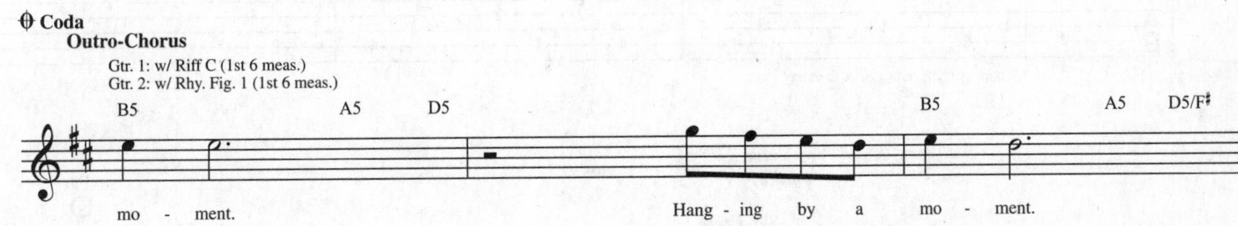
Coda
Outro-Chorus
Gtr. 1: w/ Riff C (1st 6 meas.)
Gtr. 2: w/ Rhy. Fig. 1 (1st 6 meas.)
B5
A5
D5
B5
A5
D5/F♯
mo - ment.
Hang - ing by a mo - ment.

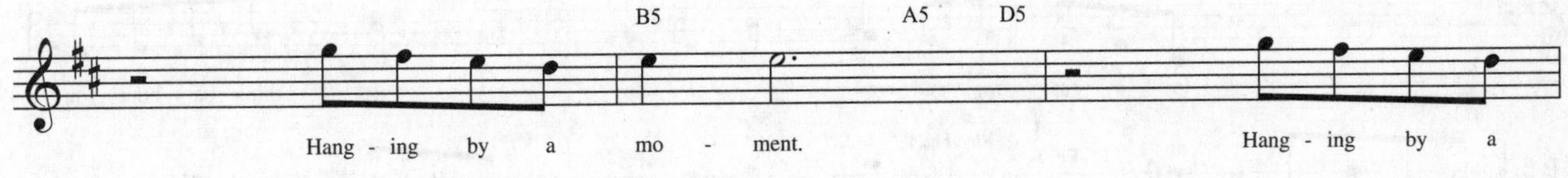
B5
A5
D5
Hang - ing by a mo - ment.
Hang - ing by a

B5
A5
D5
mo - ment here with you.
Gtr. 1
Gtr. 2

Happy Together

Words and Music by Garry Bonner and Alan Gordon

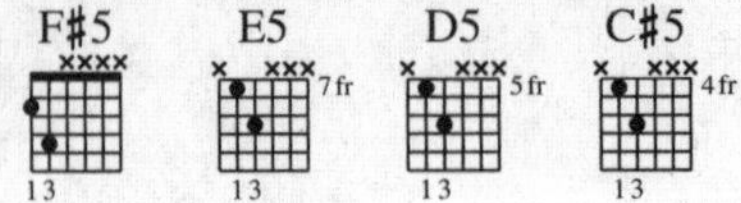

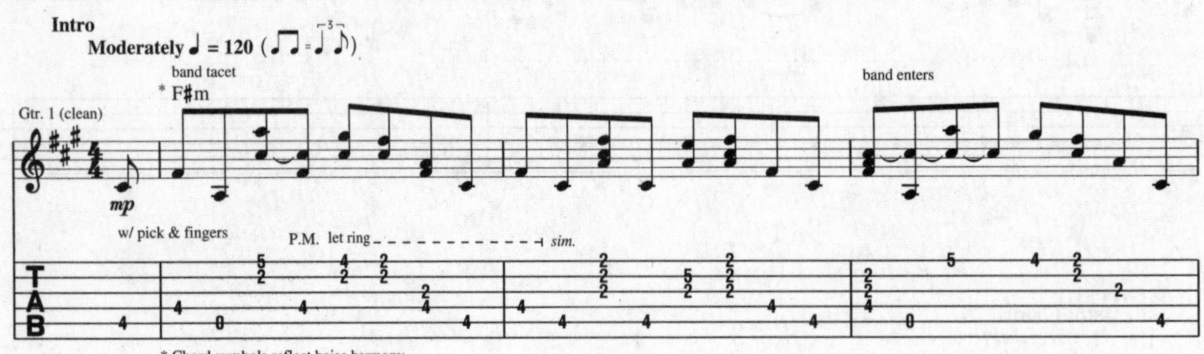

* Chord symbols reflect baisc harmony.

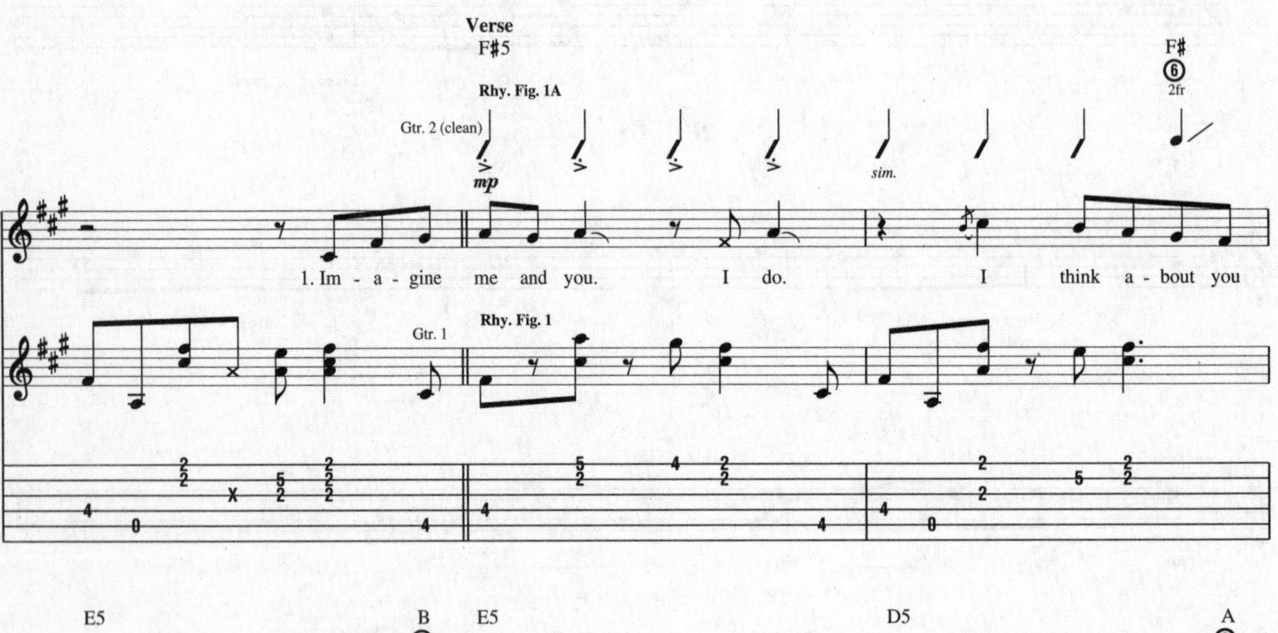

D5
E
C♯5 G♯
G♯
C♯5 G♯
C♯5 G♯
C♯
A
open
4fr
open
End Rhy. Fig. 1A
tight. So hap - py to - geth - er.
2. If I should
End Rhy. Fig. 1
Gtrs. 1 & 2: w/ Rhy. Figs. 1 & 1A, simile
F♯5
E5
call you up, in - vest a dime and you say you be - long to me and ease my
(Call you up. Ease my
D5
C♯5
mind. Im - a - gine how the world could be so ver - y fine. So hap - py to - geth - er.
mind. Ver - y fine.)
Chorus
F♯
C♯m7
Voc. Fig. 1
I can't see me lov - ing no - bod - y but
(Ah.
* Gtrs. 1 & 2
Rhy. Fill 1
End Rhy. Fill 1
Rhy. Fig. 2
simile on repeat
* composite arrangement
F♯
A
Bkgd. Voc.: w/ Voc. Fig. 1, simile
F♯
End Voc. Fig. 1
you for all my life.
When you're with me,

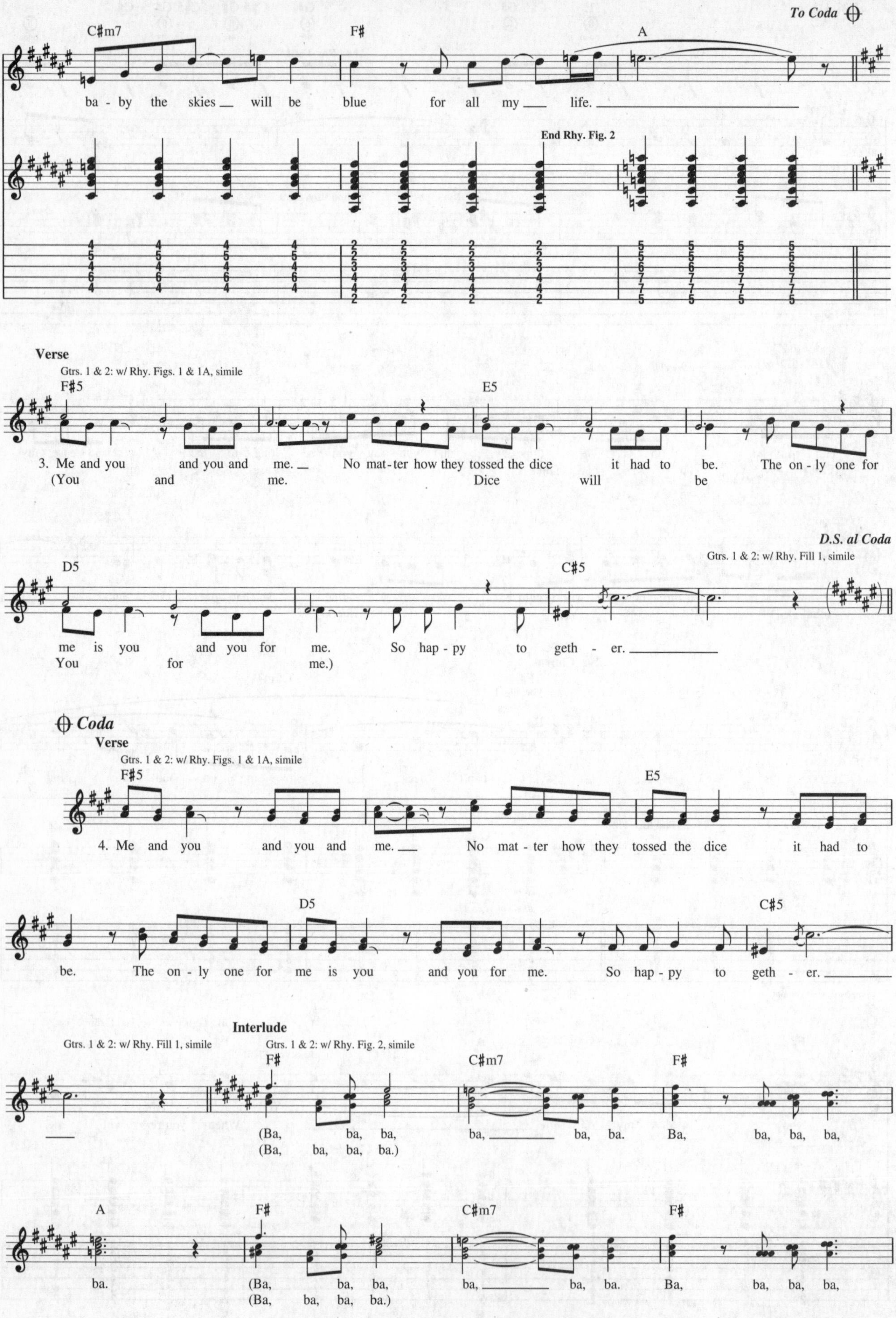

To Coda ⊕

C#m7 F# A

ba - by the skies will be blue for all my life.

End Rhy. Fig. 2

Verse

Gtrs. 1 & 2: w/ Rhy. Figs. 1 & 1A, simile

F#5 E5

3. Me and you and you and me. No mat-ter how they tossed the dice it had to be. The on - ly one for
(You and me. Dice will be

D.S. al Coda

Gtrs. 1 & 2: w/ Rhy. Fill 1, simile

D5 C#5

me is you and you for me. So hap - py to geth - er.
You for me.)

⊕ ***Coda***

Verse

Gtrs. 1 & 2: w/ Rhy. Figs. 1 & 1A, simile

F#5 E5

4. Me and you and you and me. No mat - ter how they tossed the dice it had to

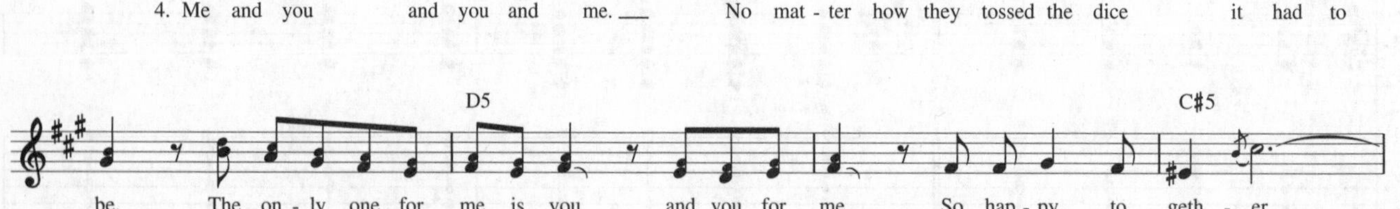

Interlude

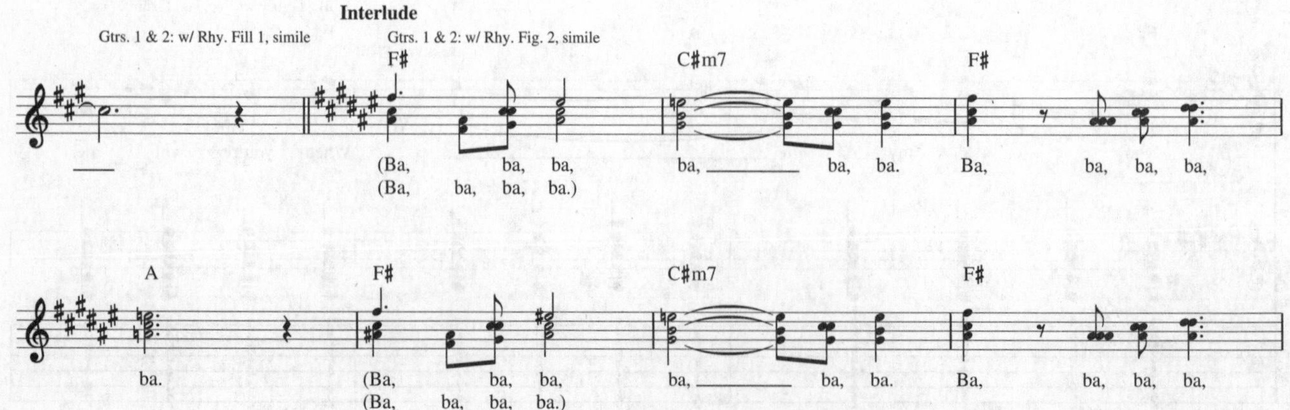

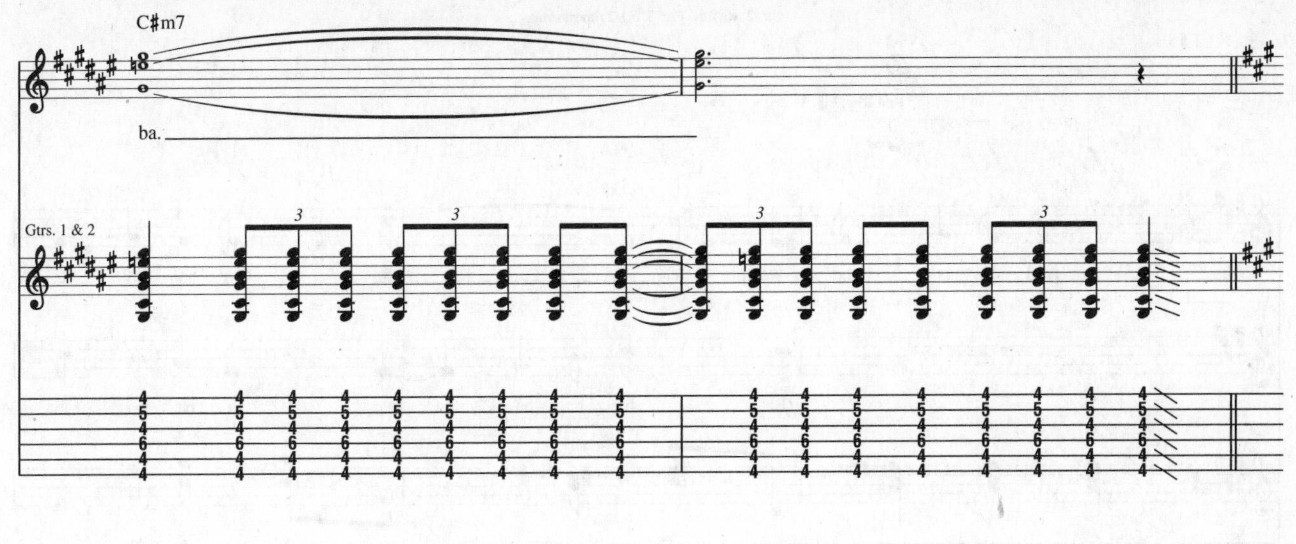
C♯m7
ba.
Gtrs. 1 & 2

Verse

Gtrs. 1 & 2: w/ Rhy. Figs. 1 & 1A, 1st 6 meas., simile
F♯5
E5
5. Me and you and you and me. No mat - ter how they tossed the dice it had to
(Ah.
Ah.

D5
be. The on - ly one for me is you and you for me. So hap - py to -
Ah.

Outro

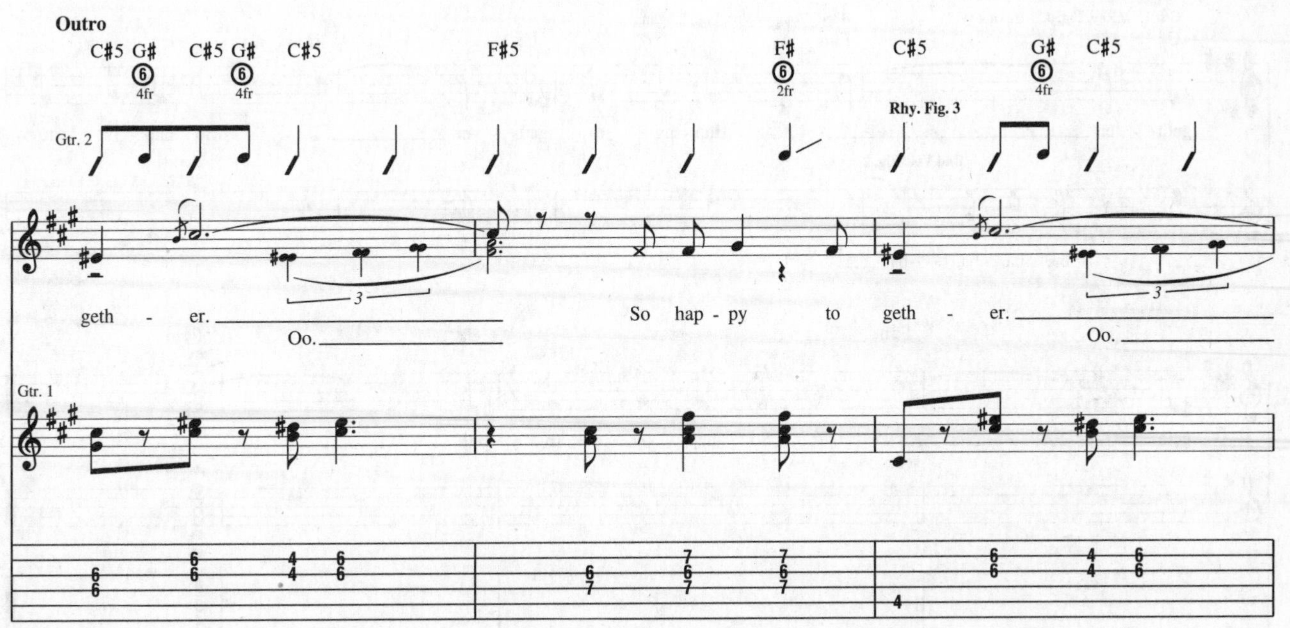
C♯5 G♯ C♯5 G♯ C♯5 F♯5 F♯ C♯5 G♯ C♯5
4fr
4fr
2fr
4fr
Rhy. Fig. 3
Gtr. 2
geth - er. So hap - py to geth - er.
Oo.
Oo.
Gtr. 1

Gtr. 2: w/ Rhy. Fig. 3, 6 1/2 times, simile
F#5
F#
2fr
End Rhy. Fig. 3
C#5
F#5
And how is the weath - er?
So hap - py to -
(Ba, ba, ba, ba, ba,
ba, ba, ba, ba,
Gtr. 1
C#5
F#5
C#
F#m
geth - er.
We're hap - py to geth - er.
So hap - py to -
ba, ba, ba, ba.
Ba, ba, ba, ba,
ba, ba, ba, ba.
Voc. Fig. 2
Ba, ba, ba, ba,
Rhy. Fig. 4
End Rhy. Fig. 4
Gtr. 1: w/ Rhy. Fig. 4, 3 1/2 times
Bkgd. Voc.: w/ Voc. Fig. 2, 3 times
C#
F#m
C#
F#m
geth - er.
Hap - py to geth - er.
So hap - py to -
End Voc. Fig. 2
ba, ba, ba, ba.
C#
F#m
C#
F#m
geth - er.
So hap - py to - geth - er.
Gtrs. 1 & 2

Heart and Soul

Words and Music by Mike Chapman and Nicky Chinn

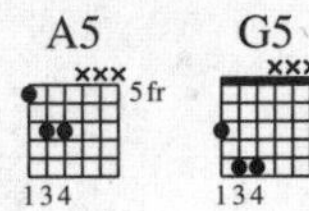

Verse
A6
G6
1. Two o-clock this morn - ing if she should come a-call - ing I would-n't dream of turn-ing her a-way.
2. And if it got hot and hec - tic I know she'd be e-lec - tric. I'd let her take her chan - ces with me.
3., 4. See additional lyrics
Rhy. Fig. 2
Rhy. Fig. 2A
dist. off
End Rhy. Fig. 2
End Rhy. Fig. 2A
G
1., 3.
Gmaj7
2., 4.
You see
She gets what she wants
She got what she want - ed
Gtrs. 1 & 2
* w/ dist.
* Gtr. 2

Chorus
Gtr. 1 tacet
G5
A5
G5
'cause she's heart and soul.
She's hot and cold.
* Gtrs. 2 & 3 (dist.)
Rhy. Fig. 3
p
f
* Composite arrangement
A5
G5
A5
She's got it all.
Hot lov - ing ev - 'ry
End Rhy. Fig. 3
Gtrs. 1 & 2: w/ Rhy. Figs. 1 & 1A
Gtr. 3 tacet
A6
G6
A6
G6
night.
Whoa.
Whoa.
A6
G6
To Coda
D
D.S. al Coda
(take repeat)
Coda
D
Interlude
N.C.
Whispered: Ah.
Gtrs. 2 & 3
P.M.
w/ dist.
P.M.

(E)
(A)
(E)
Ah.
Ah.
Gtr. 2
P.M.
Gtr. 3
P.M.

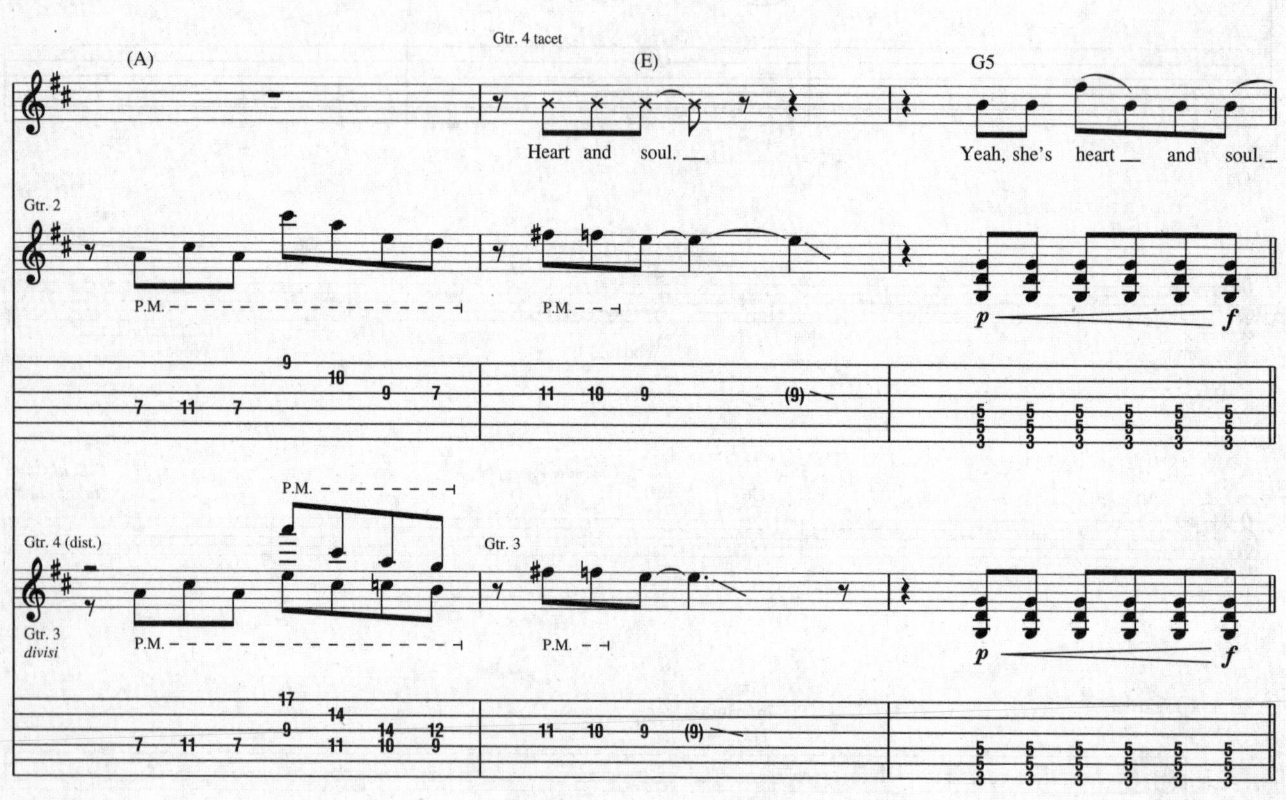
(A)
Gtr. 4 tacet
(E)
G5
Heart and soul.
Yeah, she's heart and soul.
Gtr. 2
P.M.
Gtr. 4 (dist.)
Gtr. 3
Gtr. 3
divisi
P.M.

Chorus

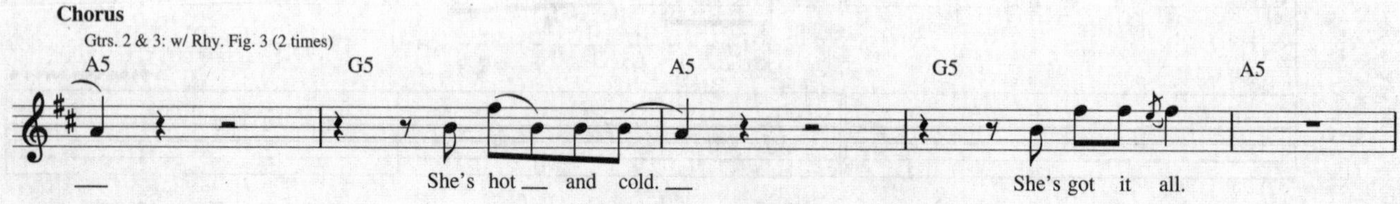
Gtrs. 2 & 3: w/ Rhy. Fig. 3 (2 times)
A5
G5
A5
G5
A5
She's hot and cold.
She's got it all.

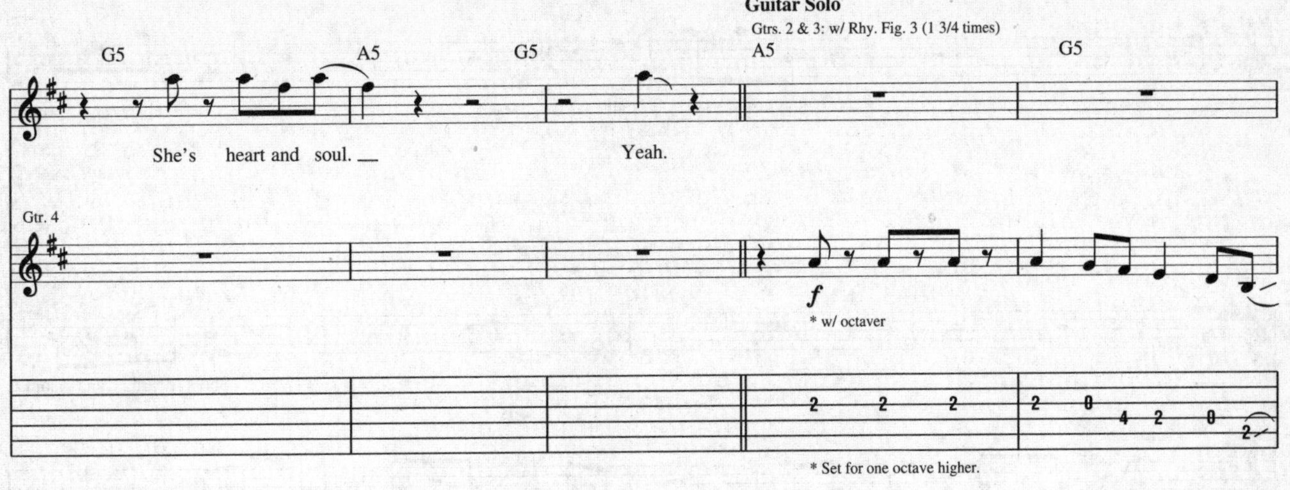
Guitar Solo
Gtrs. 2 & 3: w/ Rhy. Fig. 3 (1 3/4 times)
G5
A5
G5
A5
G5
She's heart and soul.
Yeah.
Gtr. 4
f
* w/ octaver
* Set for one octave higher.

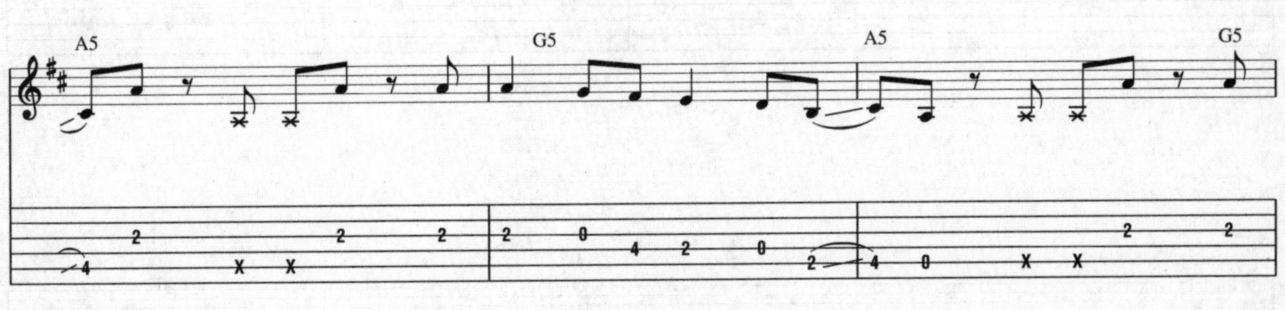
A5
G5
A5
G5

G5
A5
A5 G5
Gtrs. 2 & 3
She's got lov - ing ev - 'ry
Gtr. 4

Outro
Gtrs. 1 & 2: w/ Rhy. Figs. 2 & 2A (till fade)
Gtrs. 3 & 4 tacet
A6
G6
A6
G6
night.
Whoa.
Whoa.

A6
G6
A6
G6
She's got it all.
She's heart and soul.

A6
G6
A6
G6
She's heart and soul.
Gtr. 4
octaver off

A6
G6
A6
G6
She's heart and soul.

Begin fade
A6
G6
A6
G6
She's heart and soul.

Additional Lyrics

3. Well, can't you see her standing there?
See how she looks, see how she cares.
I let her steal the night away from me.

4. Nine o'clock this morning
She left without a warning.
I let her take advantage of me.

Heat of the Moment

Words and Music by Geoffrey Downes and John Wetton

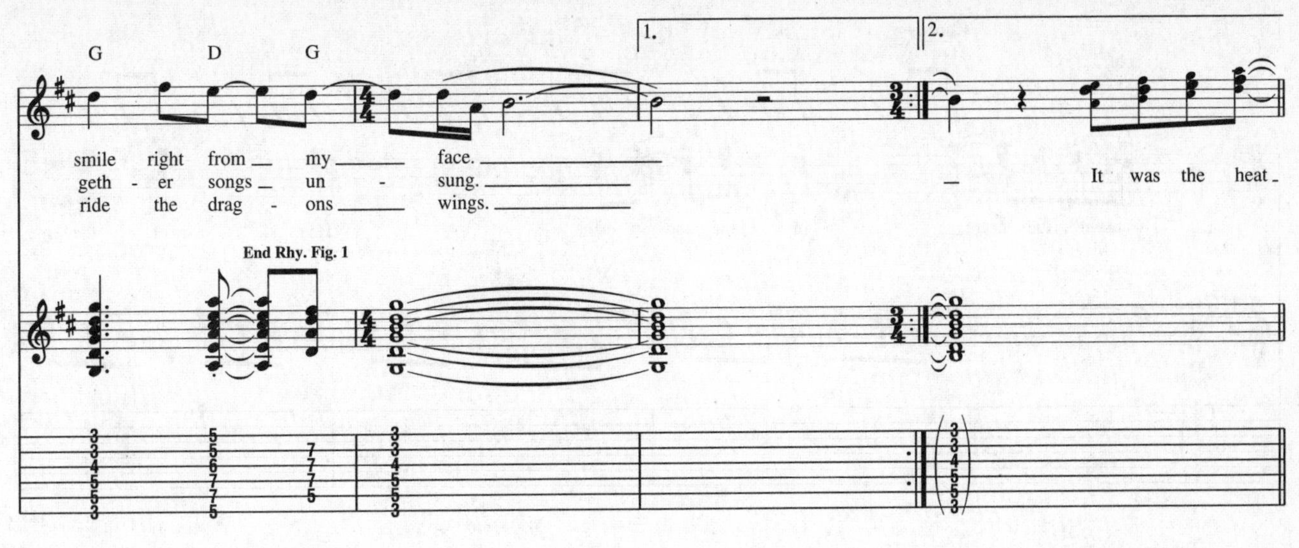
G D G
1.
2.
smile right from my face.
geth - er songs un - sung.
ride the drag - ons wings.
It was the heat
End Rhy. Fig. 1

Chorus
D A G A D A Bm G
Gtr. 2 (acous.)
mf
of the mo - ment tell - in' you what my heart meant. The
Gtr. 1

D A Bm Em Asus4 A
heat of the mo - ment showed in your eyes.
(Eyes.)

3.
Chorus
D A G A D A
Gtr. 2
'Cause it's the heat of the mo - ment. Heat of the mo -
Gtr. 1
Bm G D A Bm Em Asus4 A7/G
- ment. The heat of the mo - ment showed in your eyes.
(Eyes.
full
Gtr. 2 tacet
* F#m7 Em7
Interlude
B7sus4
)
Gtr. 1
full
* Chord symbols reflect overall tonality.
Bm B7sus4 Bm B7sus4

Bm
B7sus4
G
P.M.
Verse
Gtr. 1: w/ Rhy. Fig. 1
A
Bm
G
A
D
4. And when your looks are gone and you're a - lone,
how man - y nights you
sit be - side the phone?
What were the things you want - ed for your -
self?
Teen - age am - bi - tions you re - mem - ber
Chorus
Gtr. 2
well.
It was the heat of the mo - ment
Gtr. 1
Em
tell - in' you what your heart meant.
The heat of the mo - ment showed in your eyes.

Asus4
A
D
A
G
A
It was the heat of the mo - ment.
8va
loco

D
A
Bm
G
D
A
Bm
Em
Voc. Fig. 1
End Voc. Fig. 1
Heat of the mo - ment. Heat of the mo - ment showed in your eyes.

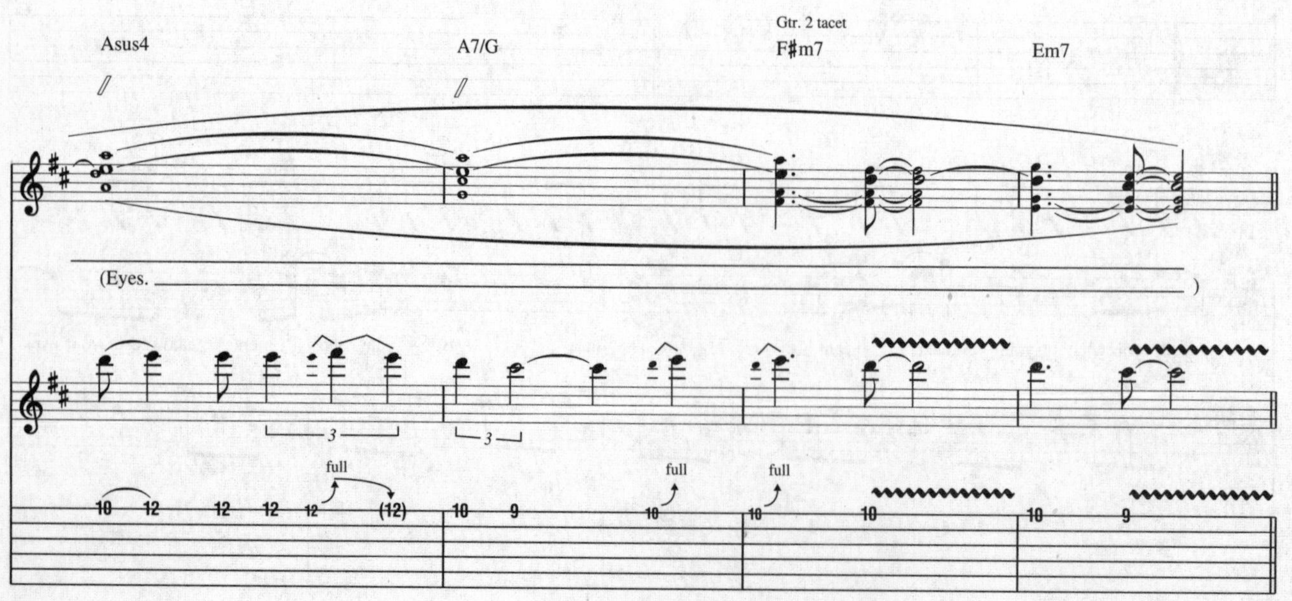
Asus4
A7/G
Gtr. 2 tacet
F♯m7
Em7
(Eyes.)
full
full
full

Outro-Guitar Solo
N.C.
D
A
G
Bm
Em
Asus4
* Played behind the beat.
hold bend
full
w/ Voc. Fig. 1, 3 times
8va
Begin Fade
Fade Out

Help Me Make It Through the Night

Words and Music by Kris Kristofferson

* Symbols in parentheses represent chord names respective to Gtrs. 2 & 3. Symbols above reflect actual sounding chords.

* composite arrangement

F
(G)
Dm
(Em)
fall.
Lay - ing soft up - on my
G7
(A7)
G7sus4
(A7sus4)
G7
(A7)
G7sus4
(A7sus4)
G7
(A7)
skin,
like the shad - ows on the wall.
C
(D)
Csus4
(Dsus4)
C
(D)
2. Come and lay down by my
End Riff A
Riff B
End Riff B
End Rhy. Fig. 1
Rhy. Fig. 2
End Rhy. Fig. 2

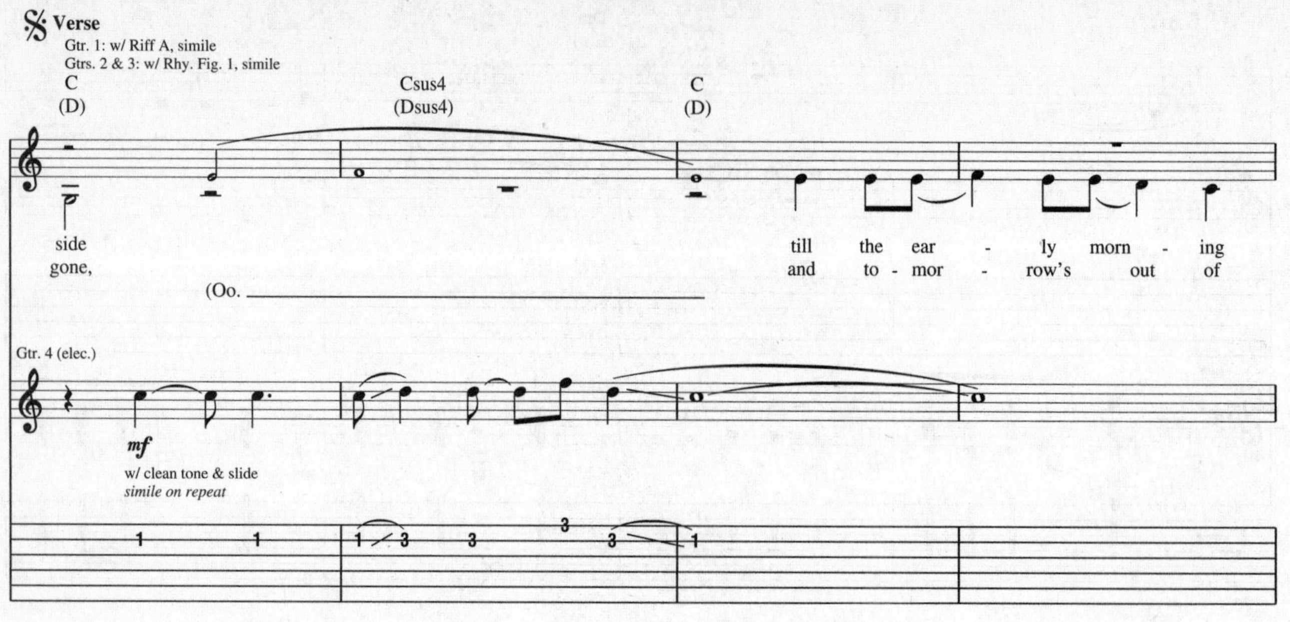
Verse
Gtr. 1: w/ Riff A, simile
Gtrs. 2 & 3: w/ Rhy. Fig. 1, simile
C
(D)
Csus4
(Dsus4)
C
(D)
side till the ear - ly morn - ing
gone, and to - mor - row's out of
(Oo.
Gtr. 4 (elec.)
mf
w/ clean tone & slide
simile on repeat

F
(G)
Dm
(Em)
light. All I'm tak - ing is your
sight. And it's sad to be a -
Oo.

G7
(A7)
G7sus4
(A7sus4)
G7
(A7)
G7sus4
(A7sus4)
G7
(A7)
time.
lone.
Oo.
Help me make it through the night.
Help me make it through the night.

To Coda
Gtr. 1: w/ Riff B
C
(D)
Csus4
(Dsus4)
C
(D)
I don't care who's right or wrong.
Gtr. 4
* Gtrs. 2 & 3
* composite arrangement
Bridge
Gtrs. 1, 2 & 4 tacet
F
(G)
F6
(G6)
F
(G)
F6
(G6)
F
(G)
I don't try to un - der -
(Oo.
Gtr. 3
C
(D)
Dm/C
(Em/D)
C
(D)
stand.
Oo.
Let the dev - il take to - mor -
D
(E)
Dadd9
(Eadd9)
D
(E)
Dadd9
(Eadd9)
D
(E)
- row.
Oo.
Lord, to - night I need a
Oo.

G7
(A7)
G7sus4
(A7sus4)
G7
(A7)
G7sus4
(A7sus4)
G7
(A7)
D.S. al Coda
friend.
Oo.)
3. Yes - ter - day is dead and

Coda
Outro
2nd time, Begin Fade
w/ ld. voc. ad lib, 2nd time
Gtrs. 2 & 3: w/ Rhy. Fig. 2
Gtrs. 2 & 3: w/ Rhy. Fig. 1, simile
C
(D)
C
(D)
Csus4
(Dsus4)
C
(D)
Mm, mm, mm, mm, mm, mm.
(Oo.
Mm, mm,
Gtr. 1
Gtr. 4
w/o slide

2nd time, Fade Out
F
(G)
Dm
(Em)
mm, mm, mm.
Oo.
Lord, it's good to be a - lone.
w/ slide

G7 (A7) G7sus4 (A7sus4) G7 (A7) G7sus4 (A7sus4) G7 (A7)

Oo.

Help me make it through the night.
Help me make it through the night.

w/o slide

C (D) Csus4 (Dsus4)

Gtrs. 2 & 3: w/ Rhy. Fig. 2

C (D)

Mm, mm, mm, mm,

w/o slide

Help Me Rhonda

Words and Music by Brian Wilson and Mike Love

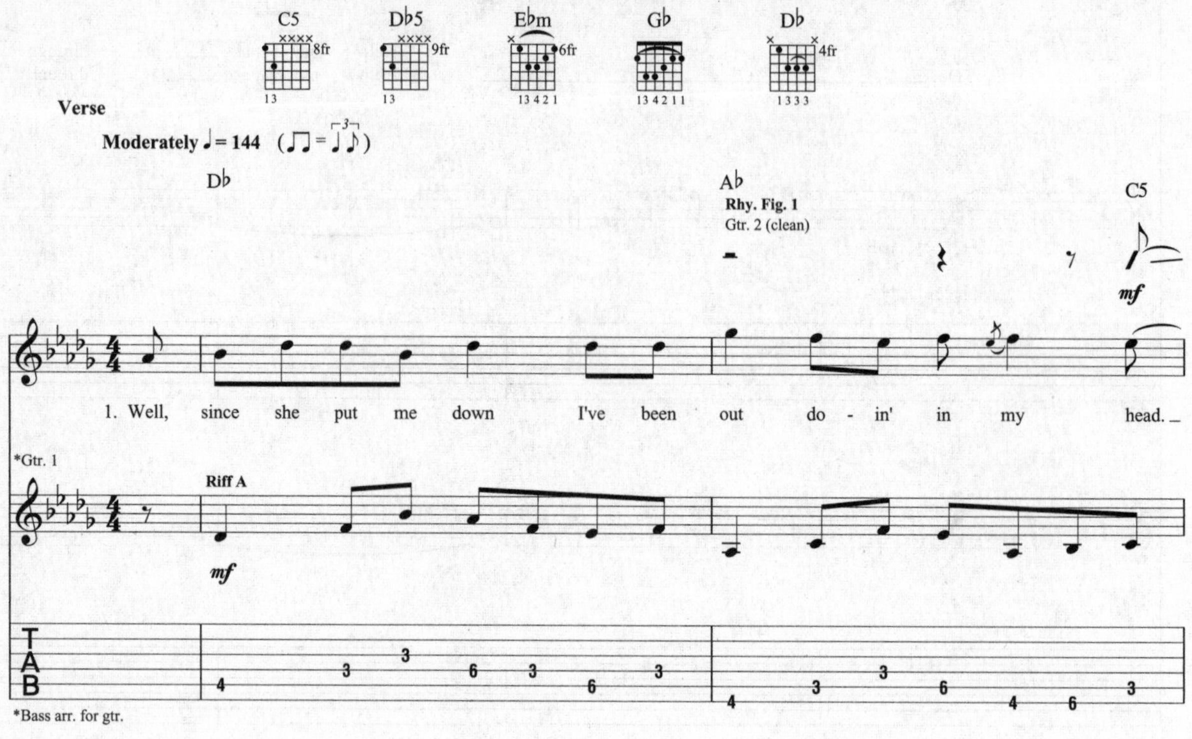

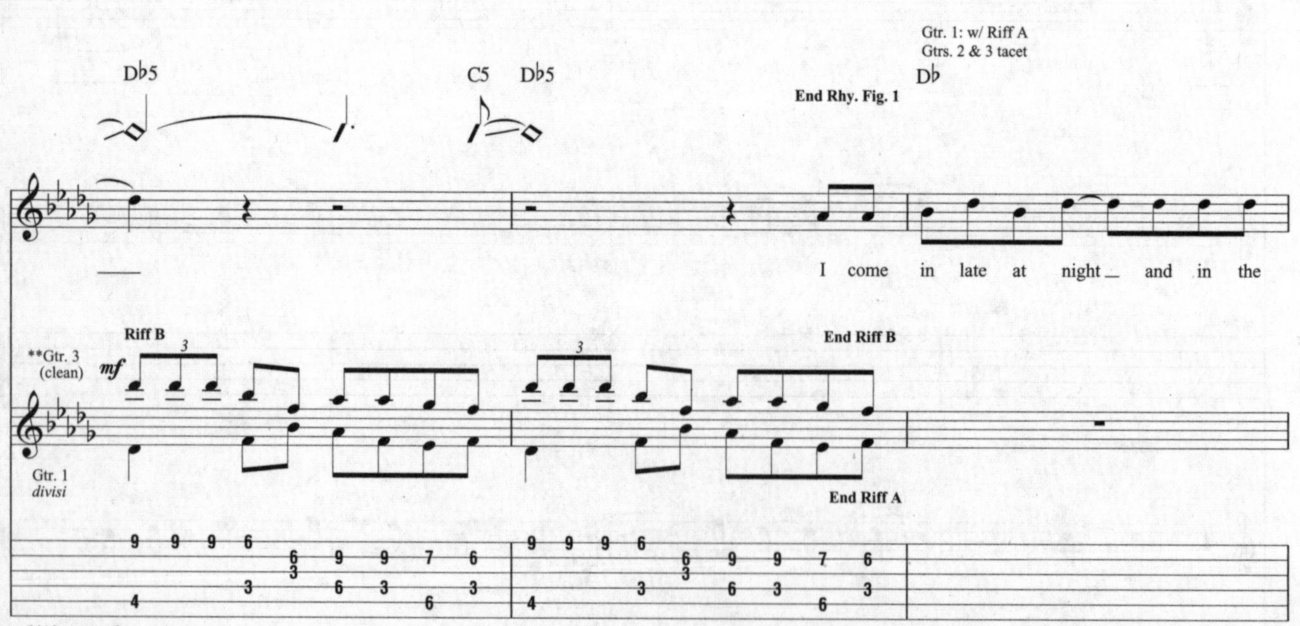

Gtr. 2: w/ Rhy. Fig. 1
Gtr. 3: w/ Riff B
A♭
C5
D♭5
C5
D♭5
morn - in' I just lay in bed.
Well,

Pre-Chorus
B♭m
G♭
E♭7
Rhon - da, you look so fine,
and I know it would - n't take much time
for you to
Rhon - da, you caught my eye,
and I could give you lots of rea - sons why
you got - ta
(Oo,
look so fine.
(Oo,
caught my eye.
Gtr. 2

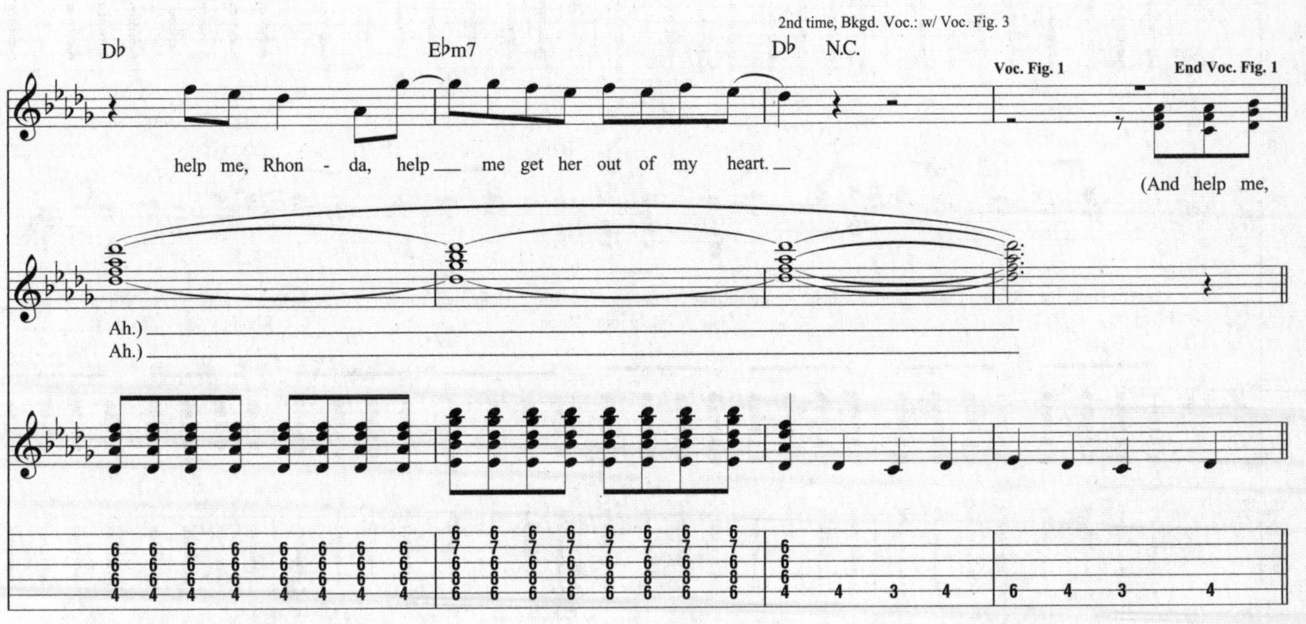
2nd time, Bkgd. Voc.: w/ Voc. Fig. 3
D♭
E♭m7
D♭
N.C.
Voc. Fig. 1
End Voc. Fig. 1
help me, Rhon - da, help me get her out of my heart.
(And help me,
Ah.)
Ah.)

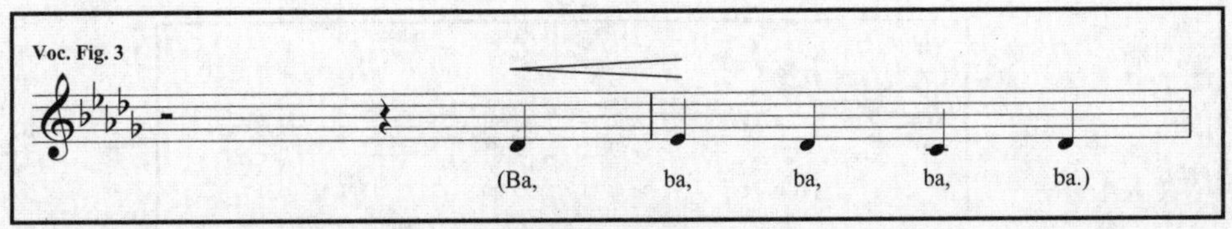
Voc. Fig. 3
(Ba, ba, ba, ba, ba.)

𝄋𝄋 Chorus

Ab | Db | Dbsus4 Db | Bkgd. Voc.: w/ Voc. Fig. 2 | Dbsus4 Db

Help me, Rhon - da, help, ___ help me, Rhon - da. Help me, Rhon - da, help, ___ help me, Rhon - da.

Rhon - da, Rhon - da. Help me, Rhon - da, Rhon - da. Help me,

Ab | Db | Bkgd. Voc.: w/ Voc. Fig. 2

Help me, Rhon - da, help, ___ help me, Rhon - da. Help me, Rhon - da, help, ___ help me, Rhon - da.

Rhon - da, Rhon - da. Help me, Rhon - da, Rhon - da. Help me,

Gb | Bbm | Bkgd. Voc.: w/ Voc. Fig. 2 | Db

Help me, Rhon - da, help, ___ help me, Rhon - da. Help me, Rhon - da, help, ___ help me, Rhon - da.

Rhon - da, Rhon - da. Help me, Rhon - da, Rhon - da.)

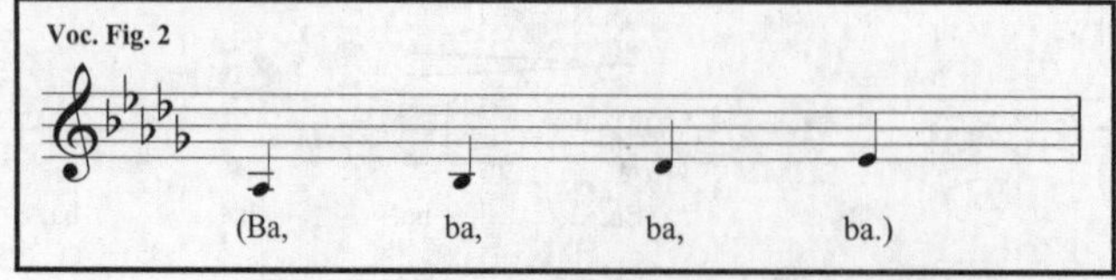

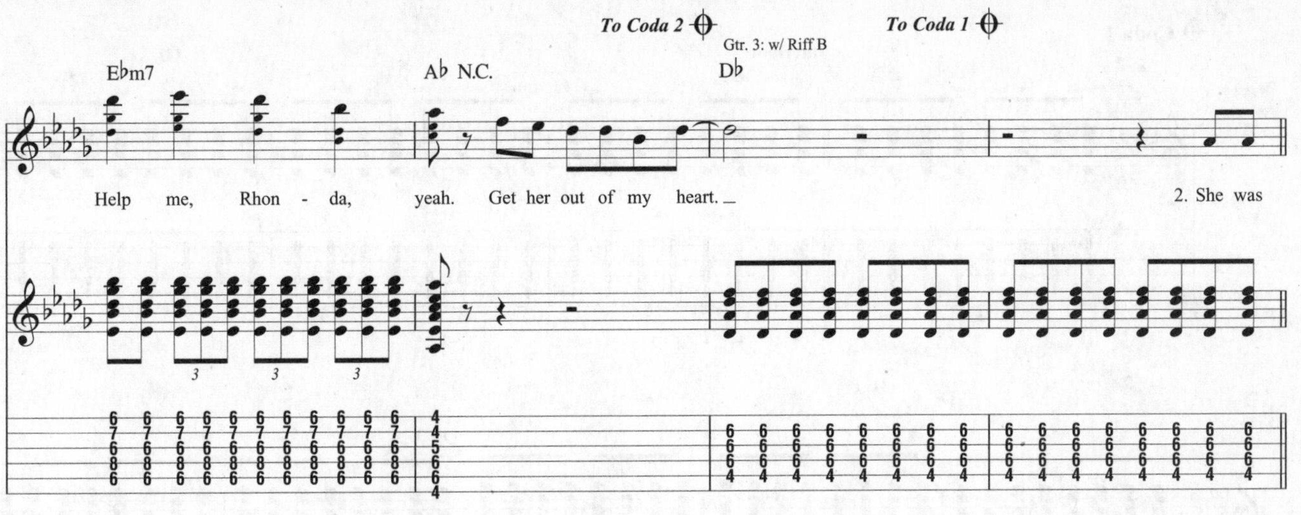
To Coda 2
To Coda 1
Gtr. 3: w/ Riff B
E♭m7
A♭ N.C.
D♭
Help me, Rhon - da, yeah. Get her out of my heart.
2. She was

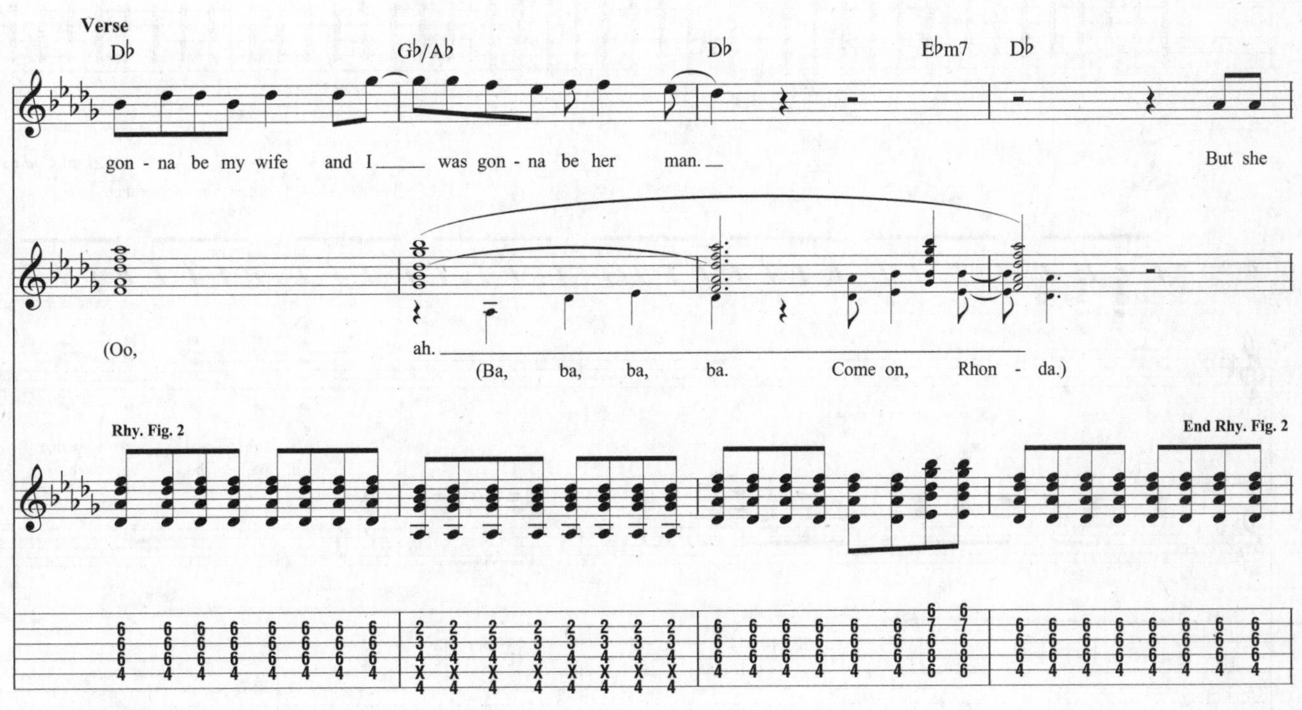
Verse
D♭
G♭/A♭
D♭
E♭m7
D♭
gon - na be my wife and I was gon - na be her man.
But she
(Oo,
ah.
(Ba, ba, ba, ba. Come on, Rhon - da.)
Rhy. Fig. 2
End Rhy. Fig. 2

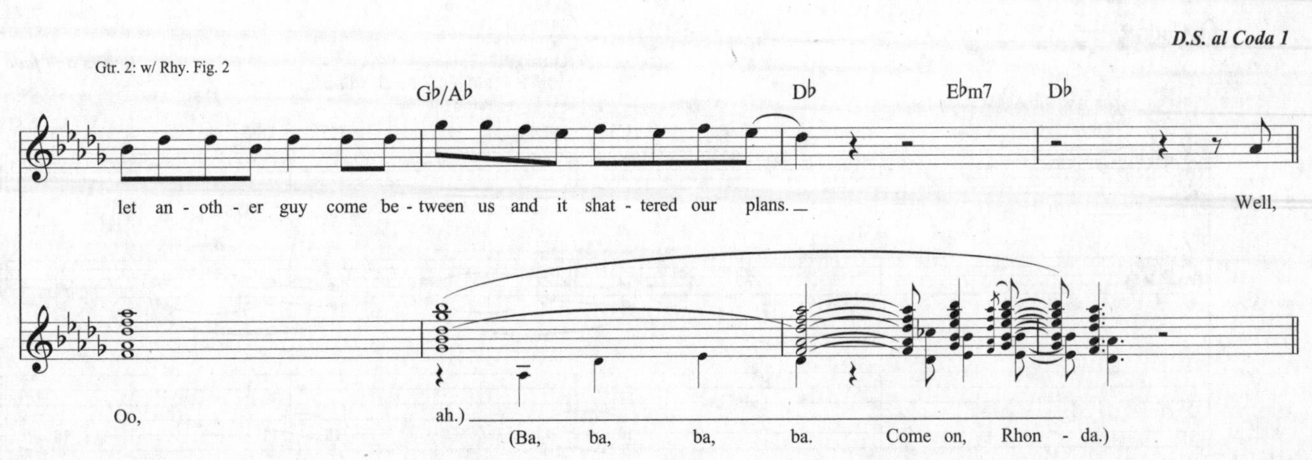
D.S. al Coda 1
Gtr. 2: w/ Rhy. Fig. 2
G♭/A♭
D♭
E♭m7
D♭
let an - oth - er guy come be - tween us and it shat - tered our plans.
Well,
Oo,
ah.)
(Ba, ba, ba, ba. Come on, Rhon - da.)

Coda 1

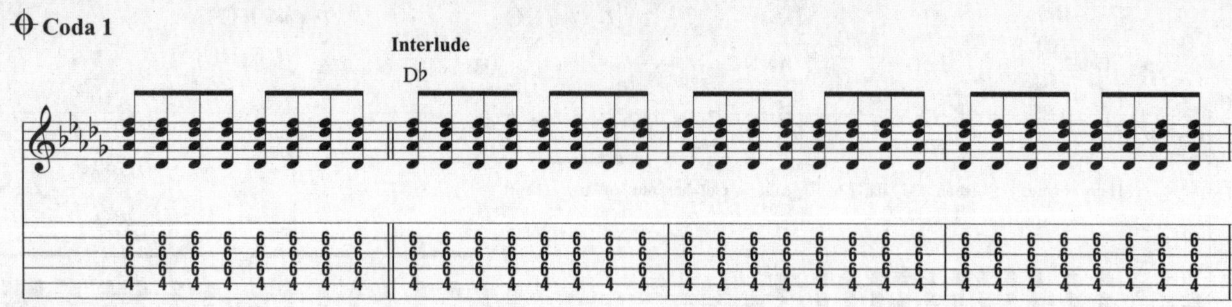

Interlude
D♭

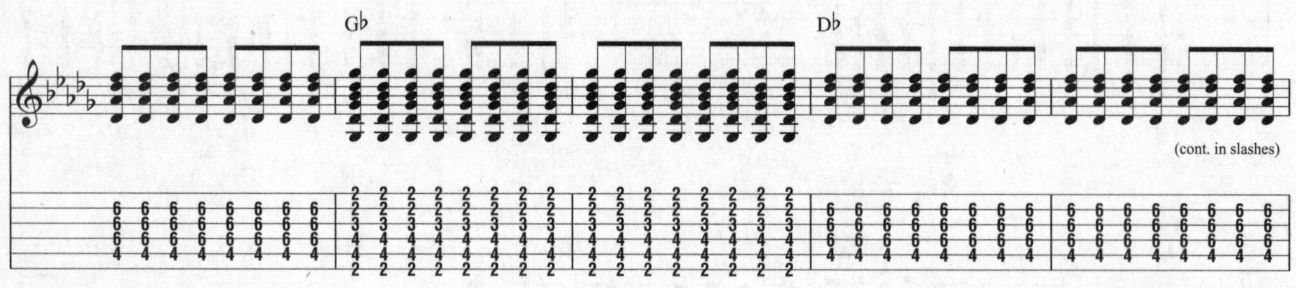

G♭
D♭
(cont. in slashes)

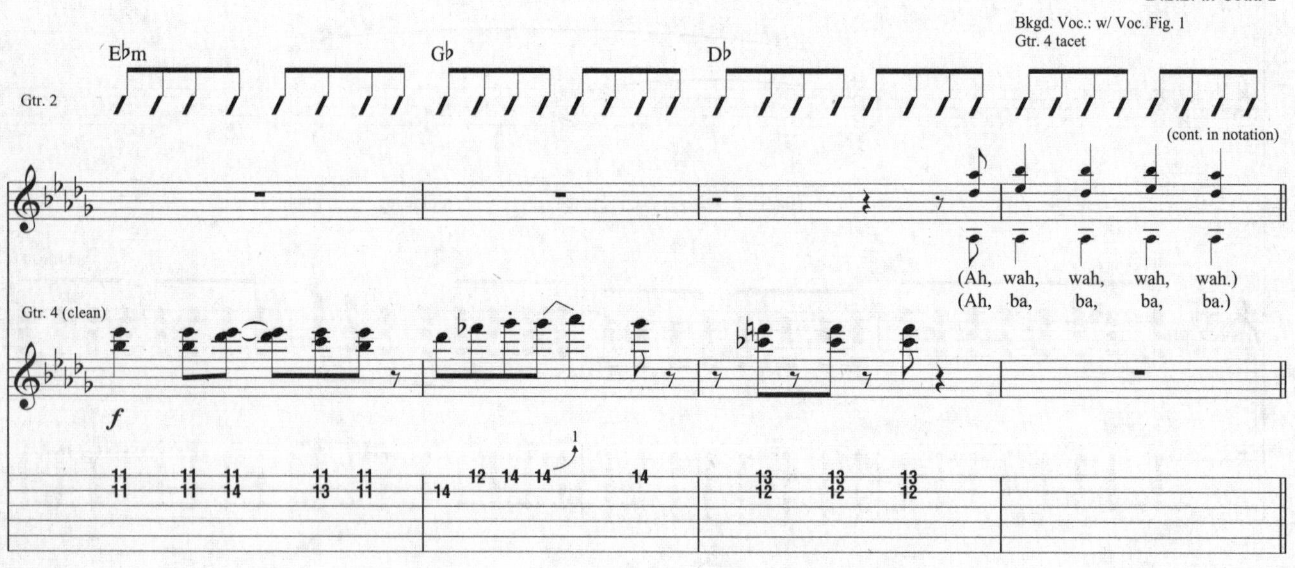

D.S.S. al Coda 2
Bkgd. Voc.: w/ Voc. Fig. 1
Gtr. 4 tacet
E♭m
G♭
D♭
Gtr. 2
(cont. in notation)
(Ah, wah, wah, wah, wah.)
(Ah, ba, ba, ba, ba.)
Gtr. 4 (clean)
f

Coda 2

Outro
Repeat and fade
Gtr. 1: w/ Riff A (last 2 meas.) (till fade)
Gtr. 3: w/ Riff B (till fade)
Gtr. 1: w/ Riff A (last 2 meas.)
D♭
C5
D♭5
C5
D♭5
C5

Here Comes the Sun

Words and Music by George Harrison

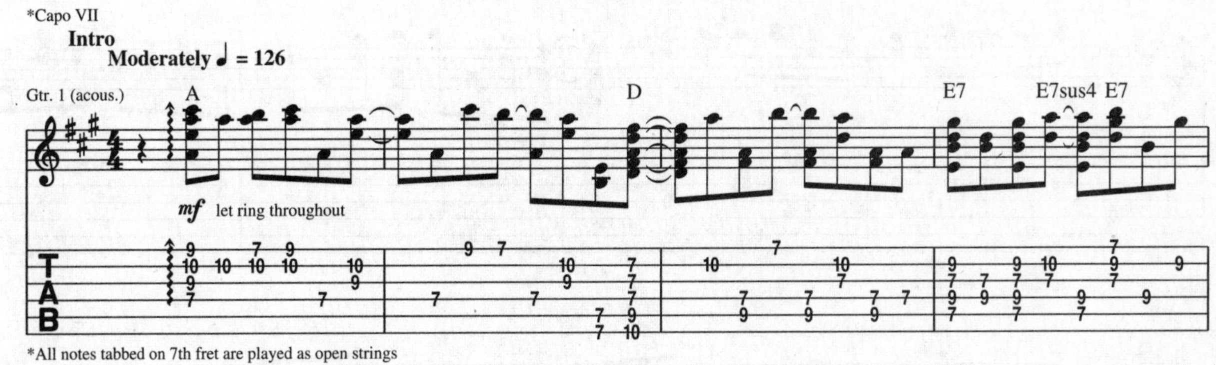

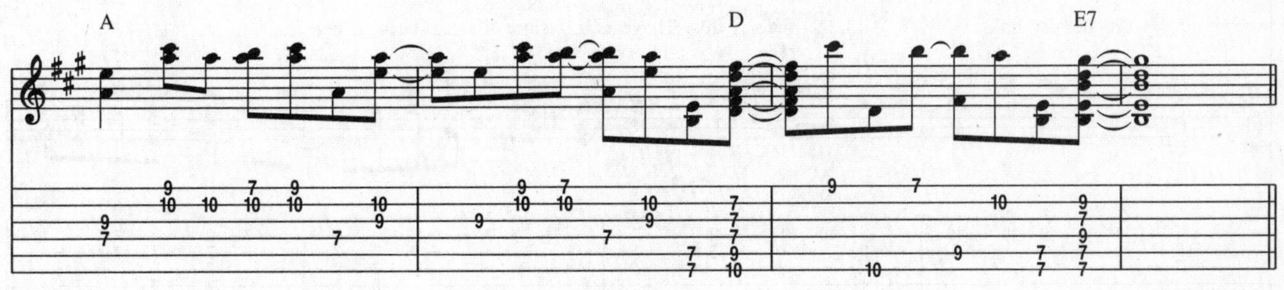

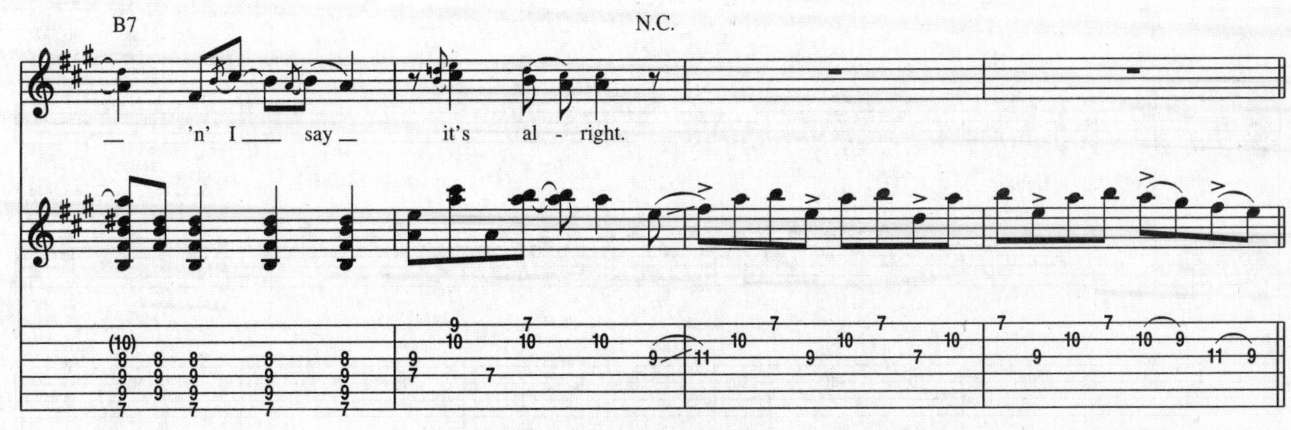

Verse
A
D
E7
E7sus4 E7
1. Lit - tle dar - lin', it's been a long, cold, lone - ly win - ter.
A
D
E7
E7sus4
Lit - tle dar - lin', it feels like years since it's been here.
Chorus
A
D
B7
Here comes the sun, doo 'n' doo doo. Here comes the sun 'n' I say
A
N.C.
A
E7
E7sus4 E7
it's al - right.

Verse
A
D
E7
E7sus4
E7
2. Lit-tle dar-lin', the smiles re-turn-ing to their fac-es.
Lit-tle dar-lin', it seems like years since it's been here.
Chorus
B7
Here comes the sun. (Doo 'n' doo doo.) Here comes the sun 'n' I say
N.C.
To Coda
N.C. (E)
it's al-right.

Bridge
(C)
(G)
(D/F#)
(D)
A
E7
N.C. (E)
Sun, sun, sun, here it comes.
1., 2., 3.
4.
E7sus4
E
Verse
D
3. Lit-tle dar-lin', I feel that ice is slow-ly melt-ing.

D.S. al Coda
A
D
E7
E7sus4
Lit - tle dar - lin', it seems like years since it's been clear.
Coda
B7
Here comes the sun. (Doo 'n' doo doo.) Here comes the sun.
N.C.
It's al - right.
It's al - right.
(C)
(G)
(D/F♯)
(D)
rit.

Hide Away

Words and Music by Freddie King and Sonny Thompson

* Chord symbols reflect overall tonality.

A7
E7
P.M.
B7
A7
E7
let ring
C
B7
E7
A7
E7
B7
E7
tr

D
E7
P.M.
A7
P.M.
E7
P.M.
B7
A7
B7
E
E7
w/ pick & middle finger

A7
w/ pick & middle finger
P.M.
B7
w/ pick & middle finger
P.M.
A7
E7
B7
let ring
P.M.
F
E7
P.M.
A7
E7
P.M.

B7
A7
E7
B7
P.M.
G
E7
P.M.
P.M.
A7
P.M.
E7
P.M.
P.M.
B7
A7
E7
straight ♪'s

Hound Dog

Words and Music by Jerry Leiber and Mike Stoller

G7
F7
N.C.
nev - er caught a rab - bit an' you ain't no friend of mine.
1. Well, they said you was high
End Rhy. Fig. 1
Verse
Gtr. 1: w/ Rhy. Fig. 1, simile
C5
classed. Well, that was just a lie. Yeah, they said you was high
F
F7
C5
class. Well, that was just a lie. Yeah, you ain't
G7
F7
To Coda 1
N.C.
nev - er caught a rab - bit an' you ain't no friend of mine.
Chorus
Gtr. 1: w/ Rhy. Fig. 1, 1st 11 meas., simile
C5
You ain't noth - in' but a hound dog ah, cry - in' all the time.
F
F7
C5
You ain't noth - in' but a hound dog ah, cry - in' all the time.
To Coda 2
G7
F7
N.C.
Well, you ain't nev - er caught a rab - bit an' you ain't no friend of mine.

Guitar Solo
* C7
(Ah.
Gtr. 1
mf
* Chord symbols reflect implied tonality.
F7
ah,
1/2
C7
ah.
1/4
G7
Ah,
1/4
D.S. al Coda 1
F7
ah,
C7
ah.)
2. Well, they said you was high

Coda 1
Guitar Solo
* C7
(Ah.
Gtr. 1
mf
1/4
* Chord symbols reflect implied tonality.
F9
C7
ah,
ah,
1/4
G7
F7
C7
D.S. al Coda 2
ah,
ah,
ah.)
3. Well, they said you was high
Coda 2
G5
N.C.
Db6/9 C6/9
nev-er caught a rab-bit; you ain't no friend of mine. Spoken: You ain't noth-in' but a hound dog.
Gtr. 1

I Am a Man of Constant Sorrow

Words and Music by Carter Stanley

B♭5
(G5)
Csus2
(Asus2)
sor - row. I've seen trou - ble all my
F5
(D5)
B♭5
(G5)
days. I bid fare -
F5
(D5)
B♭5
(G5)
well to old Ken - tuck - y, the place where I
1/4
Csus2
(Asus2)
F5
(D5)
was born and raised. The place where
1/4

C5
(A5)
F5
(D5)
he was born and raised.
Rhy. Fig. 1
1/4
Verse
Gtr. 1: w/ Rhy. Fig. 1 (3 11/12 times)
F5
(D5)
B♭5
(G5)
2. For six long years I've been in trou-ble, no pleas-ure here on earth I've found.
3. It's fare thee well, my own true lov-er. I nev-er ex-pect to see you a-gain.
4. You can bur-y me in sun-ny val-ley for man-y years where I may lay.
5. May-be your friends think I'm just a strang-er, my face you nev-er will see no home.
Csus2
(Asus2)
For in this world I'm bound to ram-ble. I have no friends to help me now.
For I'm bound to ride that north-ern rail-road. Per-haps I'll die u-pon this train.
Pray and you may learn to love an-oth-er while I am sleep-ing in my grave.
But there is one prom-ise that is giv-en, I'll meet you on God's gold-en shore.
He has no friends to help him now.
Per-haps he'll die u-pon this train.
While he is sleep-ing in his grave.
He'll meet you on God's gold-en
1., 2., 3.
4.
shore.

I Believe I'll Dust My Broom

Words and Music by Robert Johnson

* Tunings were determined using the original 78s. To play along with the *Robert Johnson - The Complete Recordings* CD set, Capo I.

E7
B7
Girl-friend, the black man you been
A7
E/B
E7/D
A/C♯
Am/C
lov - in',
girl-friend, can get my room.
* Sung behind the beat.
E/B
B9
Verse
E7
2. I'm gon' write a let-ter,
tel - e - phone
ev - 'ry town I know.
A7
I'm gon' write a let-ter,

E7
tel - e - phone ev - 'ry town I know.
B7
A7
If I can't find her in West Hel - 'na,
she must be in East Mon - roe, I know.
E
E7/D
A/C#
Am/C
E/B
B9
Verse
E7
3. I don't want no wom - an
wants ev - 'ry
down - town man she meet.
I don't

A7
E7
want no wom-an
wants ev-'ry down-town man she meet.
B7
A7
She's a no good don - ey,
they should-n't al-low her on the street.
E/B
E7/D
A/C#
Am/C
E/B
B7
Verse
E7
4. I be - lieve,
I be - lieve I'll go
back home.

A7
I be - lieve, I
be - lieve I'll go back home.
E7
You can mis-treat
B7
me here, babe,
A7
but you can't when I go home.
E/B
E7/D
A/C♯
Am/C
E/B
B9
Verse
E7
5. And I'm get-tin' up in the morn-in'.
I be -

A7
lieve I'll dust my broom.
I'm get-tin' up in the morn-in'.
E7
I be-lieve I'll dust my broom.
Girl-friend, the black
B7
A7
man you been lov-in',
girl-friend, can get my room.
E7
A7
B7
Verse
E7
6. I'm gon' call up Chin - ey,
see is my

A7
good girl o - ver there.
I'm gon' call up Chin-a,
see is
my good girl o - ver there.
E7
B7
'F I can't find her on Phil - li - pine's Is - land,
she
A7
E/B
E7/D
A/C#
Am/C
E/B
E7/B
must be in E - thi - o - pi - a some - where.

I Can't Quit You Baby

Written by Willie Dixon

E♭7

— you messed up my hap-py home ba-by.

D♭7

You made ___ me mis - treat ___ my

Gtr. 2

let ring

Gtr. 1

rake

rake

A♭9

A9

A♭9

A9

home - less child. ___

let ring

full

(cont. in slash)

Verse

Ab9
Gtr. 1
Db7
2. Yes, you know I love you, babe.
My love for you I could nev-er hide.
full
let ring
A9
Well,
you know I love you, babe.
My love for you I could nev-er hide.
1/2
(cont. in notation)
Yes, you know

Eb7
Db7
I love you ba-by.
Well, you know you're my de-sire
Gtr. 2
Gtr. 1
full
Ab9
A9
Ab9
A9
full
full
(cont. in slash)
Guitar Solo
Ab9
Gtr. 1
Gtr. 2
full

Db7
Ab9
A9
mp
mf
3
full
let ring
rake
V
Eb7
D7
Ab9 type2
A9 type2
1/4
1/2
* Only lower note is played staccato.

Verse
C
5
3fr.
A♭9 type2
A9 type2
A♭9
3. When _ you hear me moan - in' and groan - in' ba - by,
D♭7
A♭9
A9
you know it hurts me deep down in - side.
full
full
(cont. in notation)
Yes, when you hear me moan - in' and groan - in', ba - by,
Gtr. 2
Gtr. 1
divisi
8:6
full
oh, you know it hurts _ me deep down in - side.
Gtr. 1
A9 type2
(Gtr. 1 cont. in slash)
full

Ab9 type2
Gtr. 1: w/ Rhy. Fill 2
Eb7
Yes, when you hear me hol-ler, ba-by,
Gtr. 2
full
1/2
4:3
Db7
Gtr. 1
Ab9
Ab9 type2
A9 type2
well, you know you're my de-sire.
Gtr. 2
full
Ab9
Ab9 type2
A9 type2
Ab9
full
Rhy. Fill 2
Gtr. 1
rake
(cont. in slash)

I Feel Fine

Words and Music by John Lennon and Paul McCartney

Chorus
D
C
G
I'm in love with her and I feel fine.
End Rhy. Fig. 1

Bridge
G
Bm
C
D
I'm so glad that she's my lit - tle girl.
(Oo, oo.)

G
Bm
Am
D
She's so glad, she's tell - in' all the world
(Oo, oo.)
3.,5. that her ba -

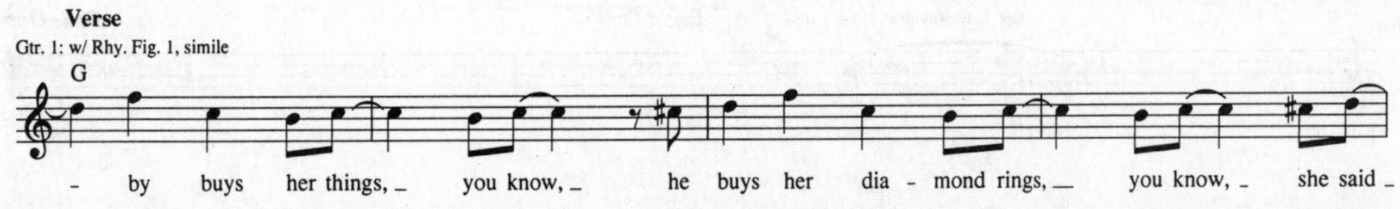
Verse
Gtr. 1: w/ Rhy. Fig. 1, simile
G
- by buys her things, you know, he buys her dia - mond rings, you know, she said

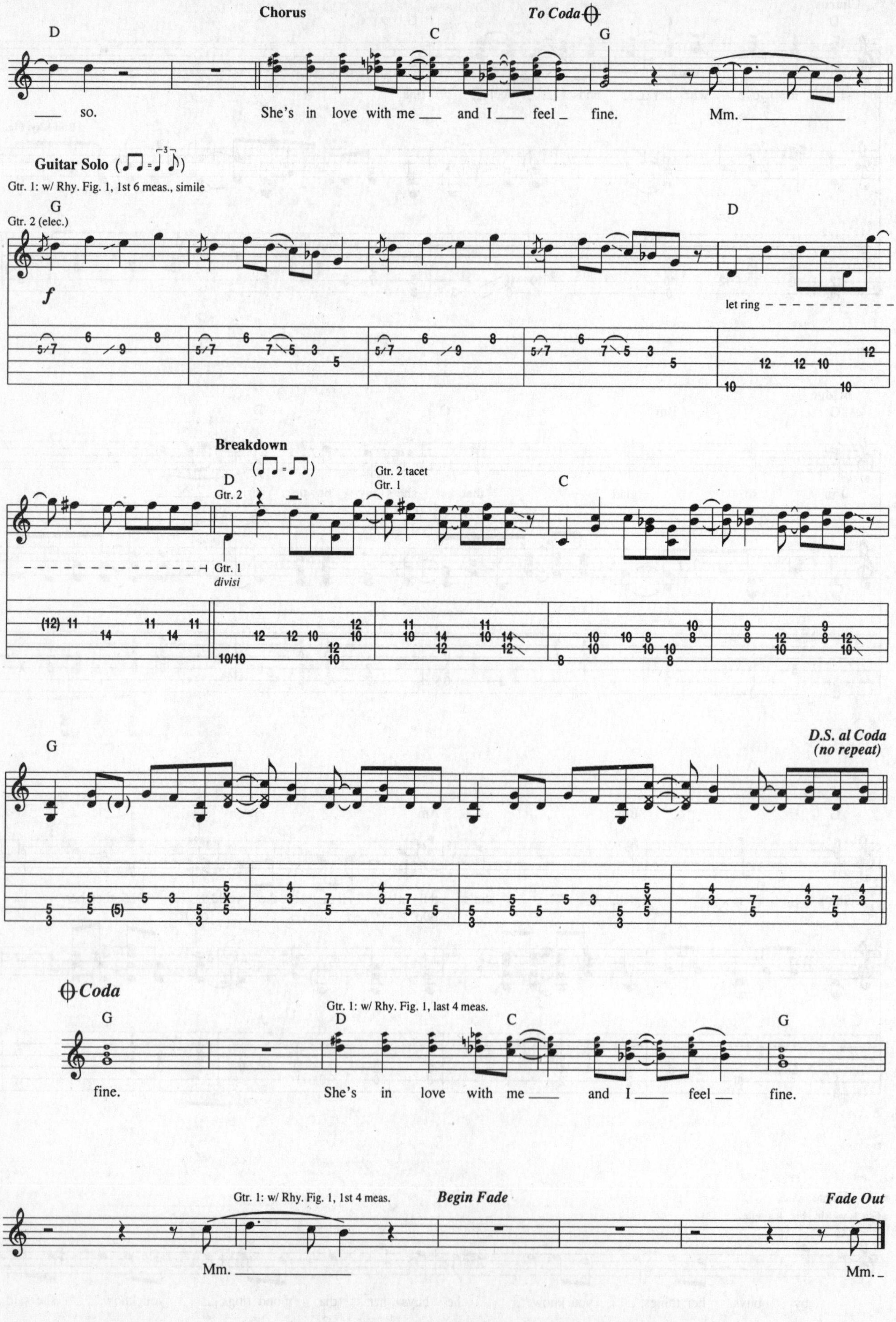

Chorus *To Coda* 𝄌

D C G

so. She's in love with me and I feel fine. Mm.

Guitar Solo (♫ = ♩♪ triplet)

Gtr. 1: w/ Rhy. Fig. 1, 1st 6 meas., simile

G

Gtr. 2 (elec.)

f

D

let ring

Breakdown

(♫ = ♫)

D

Gtr. 2

Gtr. 2 tacet

Gtr. 1

Gtr. 1

divisi

C

G

D.S. al Coda
(no repeat)

𝄌 ***Coda***

G D C G

Gtr. 1: w/ Rhy. Fig. 1, last 4 meas.

fine. She's in love with me and I feel fine.

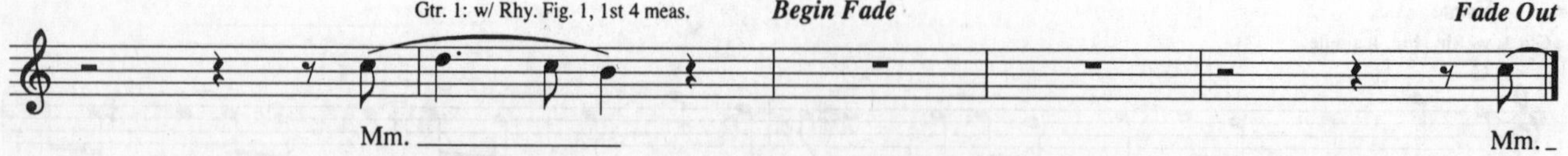

I Got You
(I Feel Good)

Words and Music by James Brown

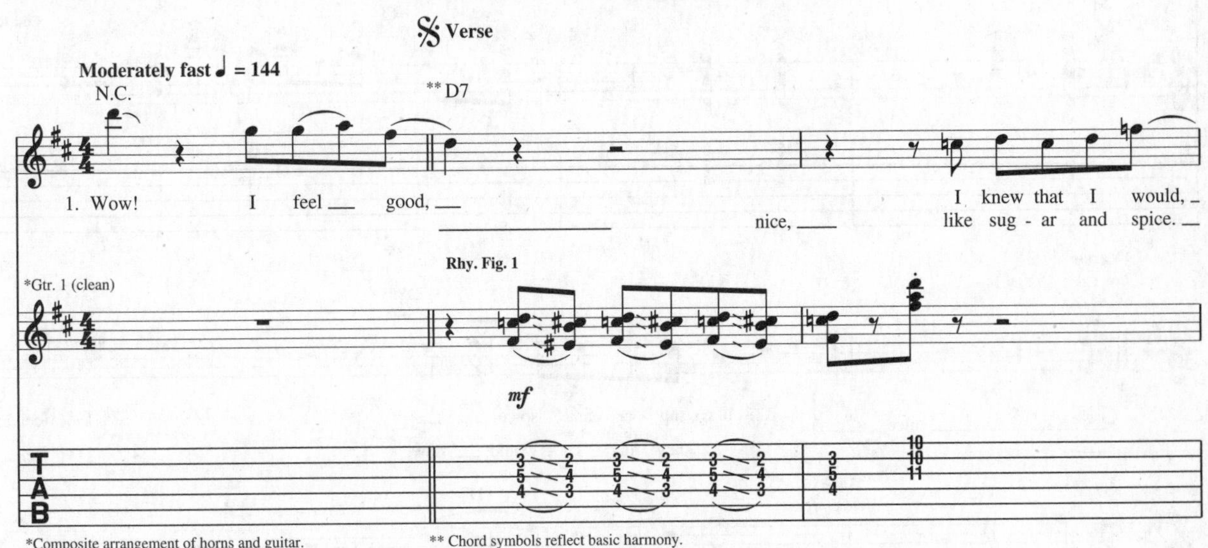

*Composite arrangement of horns and guitar.

** Chord symbols reflect basic harmony.

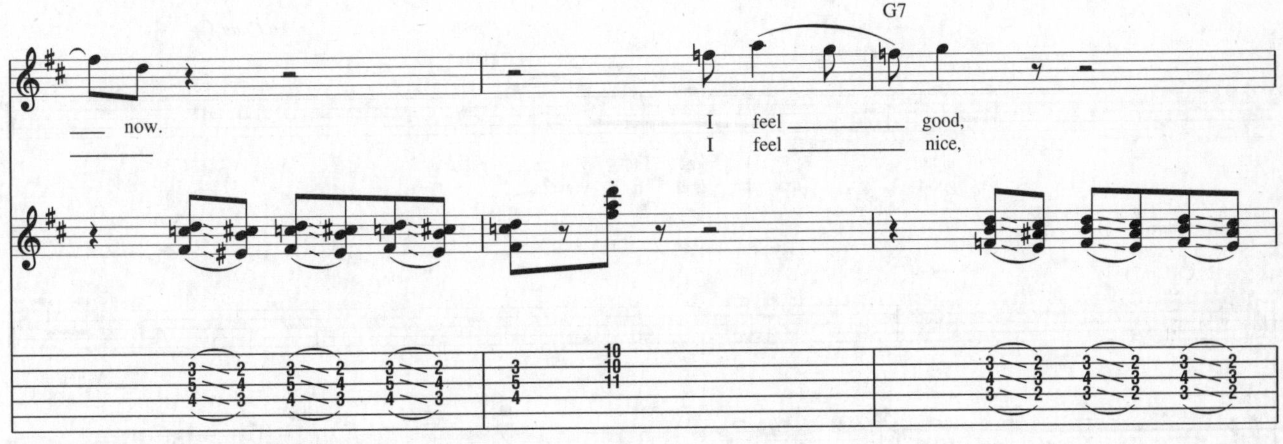

A
G
N.C.(D9)
so good, I got a - you.
so nice that I got a - you.
2. Wow! I feel nice,
5. Wow! I feel good,
End Rhy. Fig. 1
Verse
Gtr. 1: w/ Rhy. Fig. 1
D7
nice,
2., 3. like sug - ar and spice.
5. I knew that I would, now.
I feel
I feel
G7
nice,
good,
like sug - ar and spice.
I knew that I would.
D7
So nice,
So good,
To Coda
A
G
N.C.(D9)
so nice, I got a - you.
so good that I got a - you.
Interlude
Gtr. 1 tacet
N.C.(Dm7)
When I
* Gtr. 2
mf
* Sax arr. for gtr.
Bridge
Gtr. 2 tacet
G
D
hold you in my arms
I know that I can't do no
Gtr. 1
sim.

G
wrong. And when I hold you in my arms my
1.
2.
D.S. al Coda
A
love can't do you no harm. 3. And I feel 4. And I feel
Coda
Gtr. 1: w/ Rhy. Fig. 1 (last meas.) Gtr. 1: w/ Rhy. Fig. 1 (last 4 meas.)
A
G
N.C.(D9)
So good, so good, 'cause I got a you. So good,
A
G
N.C.(D9)
so good, 'cause I got a you.
Gtr. 1
slight rit.
Free time
D9
Hey! Ah, oo.

I Shot the Sheriff

Words and Music by Bob Marley

Gm
Eb
Bb/Eb
Dm7
E
Gm7
6fr
2fr
full
town,
they're try-ing to track me down.
They
Bb/Eb
Dm7
Gm
Bb/Eb
Dm7
say they want to bring me in guil - ty,
for the kil-lin' of the dep - u - ty,
* sung behind the beat.
Gm
Bb
Bb/Eb
A
Dm7
Gm
8fr
7fr
(cont. in notation)
for the life of the dep - u - ty.
But I say,
Gtrs. 1 & 2
N.C.
dim.
(Gtr. 2. cont. in slash)

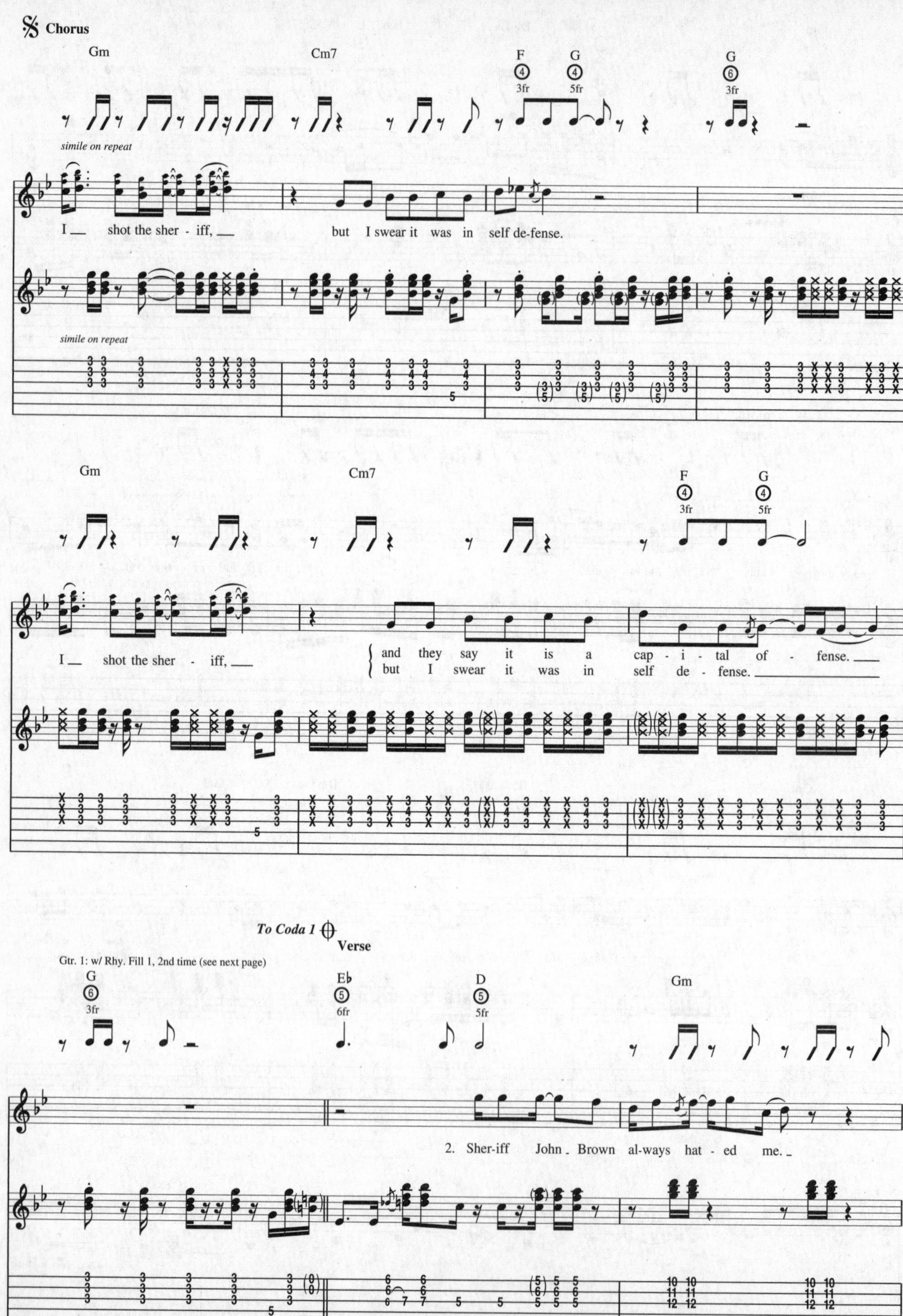

Chorus
Gm
Cm7
F
G
3fr
5fr
simile on repeat
I shot the sher - iff, but I swear it was in self de-fense.
Gm
Cm7
F
G
3fr
5fr
I shot the sher - iff,
and they say it is a cap - i - tal of - fense.
but I swear it was in self de - fense.
To Coda 1
Verse
Gtr. 1: w/ Rhy. Fill 1, 2nd time (see next page)
G
3fr
Eb
6fr
D
5fr
Gm
2. Sher-iff John Brown al-ways hat - ed me.

E♭
B♭/E♭
D
Gm
B♭/E♭
Dm7
For what, I don't know. And ev - 'ry time that I

Gm
B♭/E♭
Dm7
Gm
plant a seed, he said, "Kill it be - fore it grows." He

D.S. al Coda
B♭/E♭
Dm7
Gm
(cont. in notation)
said, "Kill it be - fore it grows." I say,
Gtrs. 1 & 2
let ring
(Gtr. 2. cont. in slash)

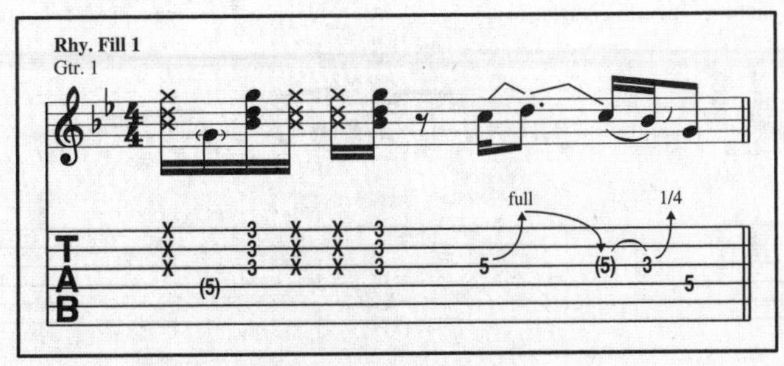

Rhy. Fill 1
Gtr. 1
full
1/4

Coda 1

Verse

Eb
D
Gm
Eb Bb Bb/Eb D A Dm7
3. Free-dom came my_ way_ one day,_ an' I start - ed out of town,.

Gm
Bb/Eb D Dm7 Gm
yeah. All of a sud-den, I_ see sher-iff John_ Brown._

Eb Bb/Eb D Dm7 Gm Eb Bb/Eb D Dm7
aim - in' to shoot me_ down,_ so I shot, I shot him

N.C. Gm
(cont. in notation)
down. An' I say,
(organ)
Gtrs. 1 & 2
1/4
Chorus
Gm
Cm7
Gtr. 2
simile on repeat
I shot the sher - iff,
but I did not / did - n't shoot the
Gtr. 1
(Gtr. 2 cont. in slash)
simile on repeat
F
G
3fr
5fr
Gtr. 2 tacet, 2nd time
D F A G
5fr 3fr 7fr 5fr
Gm
dep - u - ty.
I shot the sher - iff,

To Coda 2
Cm7
F
3fr
G
5fr
G
3fr
(cont. in notation 2nd time)
but I did - n't shoot the / did not shoot no dep - u - ty.
Verse
E♭
6fr
D
5fr
Gm
B♭/E♭
Dm7
(cont. in notation)
4. Re - flex - es got the bet - ter of me, _
and what _ is _ to be,
Gtr. 1
Gtr. 2
1/2
full
Gm
B♭/E♭
Dm7
Gm
must _ be. _
Ev - 'ry day the buck - et goes to the well, _
full
1/4

* S = snap B string

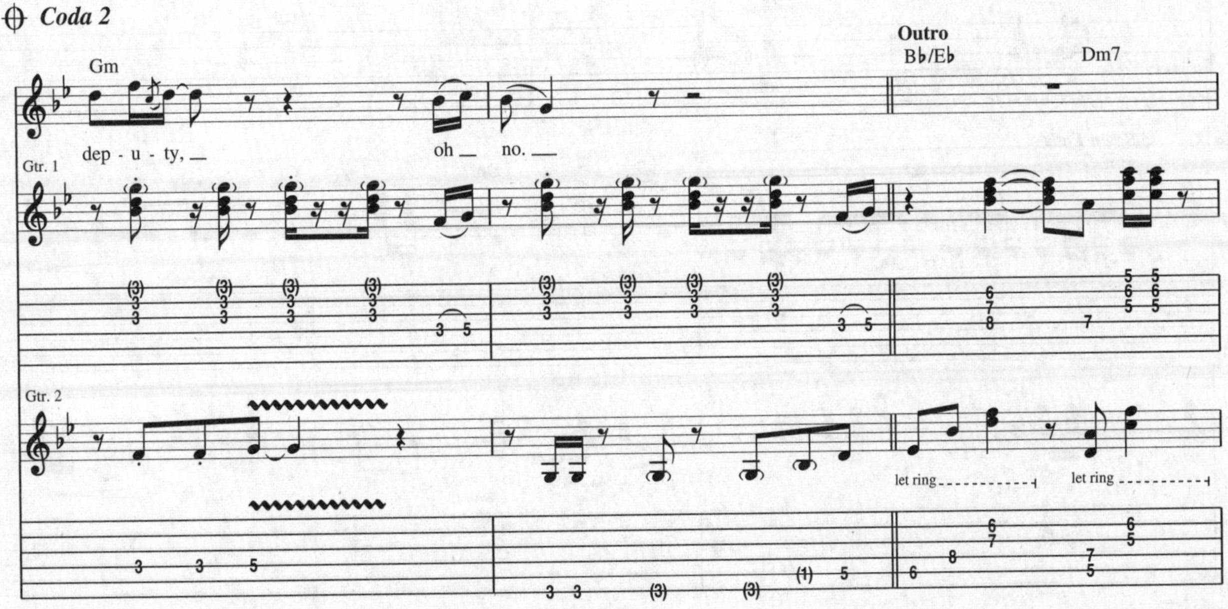

Gm
full
hold bend
B♭
Dm7
Gm
let ring
let ring
B♭/E♭
Dm7
Gm
E♭9
Dm7
let ring
let ring
let ring
Gm
E♭9
Dm7
1/4
Begin Fade
Gm
E♭9
Dm7
Gm
Fade Out
1/4

I Want You to Want Me (Live)

Words and Music by Rick Nielsen

Chorus
Gtr. 2 tacet
*A
A/G#
F#m
want you to want me. I need you to need
Gtr. 1
P.M.
let ring
*Chords symbols represent implied tonality.
E
D
D/C#
me. I'd love you to love me. I'm
15ma
loco
P.H.
A
F#m
beg - gin' you to beg me. I want you to want me. I
full
Harm.
D
D/C#
A
need you to need me. I'd love you to love me. I'll

F♯m7
B7
G5
A
F♯m7
B7
Gtr. 2
shine up the old brown shoes,
put on a brand-new shirt. _
I'll get home ear-ly from work _ if you
full
Pre-Chorus
G
G5
F♯m
A
A5
A6
A5
A6
A5
3fr
open
P.M.
say
that you love _ me.
Did-n't I, did-n't I, did-n't I see you cry -
Rhy. Fig. 1
E5
E6
E5
E6
F♯
F♯m
2fr
P.M.
- in'?
Oh, _
did-n't I, did-n't I, did-n't I see you cry - in'?
A5
A6
A5
A6
A5
E5
E6
E5
E6
Rhy. Fig. 1A
P.M.
Feel-in' all a-lone with-out a friend, you know you feel like dy - in'.
Oh, _

Chorus
Gtr. 2 tacet
F# F#m D A
2fr
P.M.
End Rhy. Fig. 1A
did-n't I, did-n't I, did-n't I see you cry - in'? I want you to want
End Rhy. Fig. 1
full
A/G# F#m E D
me. I need you to need me. I'd love you to love
D/C# A A/G#
me. I'm beg - gin' you to beg me. I'll
F#m7 B5 G5 G6 G5 A5
shine up the old brown shoes, put on a brand - new shirt. I'll
let ring
P.M.
1/2

F#m7 B7 G G5 F#m F#5 G5 G#5

Gtr. 2

(cont. in notation)

get home ear-ly from work _ if you say that you love _ me.

*Gtrs. 1 & 2

let ring

P.M. P.M.

*Composite arrangement

Pre-Chorus

Gtr. 1: w/ Rhy. Fig. 1, 1st 3 meas., simile
Gtr. 2: w/ Rhy. Fig. 1A, 2 times, simile

A5 A6 A5 A6 A5 E5 E6 E5 E6 F#m D

Did-n't I, did-n't I, did-n't I see you cry - in'? Oh, _ did-n't I, did-n't I, did-n't I see you cry -

Gtr. 1: w/ Rhy. Fill 1

Gtr. 1: w/ Rhy. Fig. 1, last 3 meas., simile

A5 A6 A5 A6 A5

- in'? Feel - in' all a - lone with - out a friend, you know you feel like dy -

E5 E6 E5 E6 F#m D

- in'. Oh, _ did - n't I, did - n't I, did - n't I see you cry -

Guitar Solo

Gtr. 2: w/ Rhy. Fig. 1A, simile

A5 A6 A5 A6 A5 E5 E6 E5 E6

- in'? Oh. _

Gtr. 1

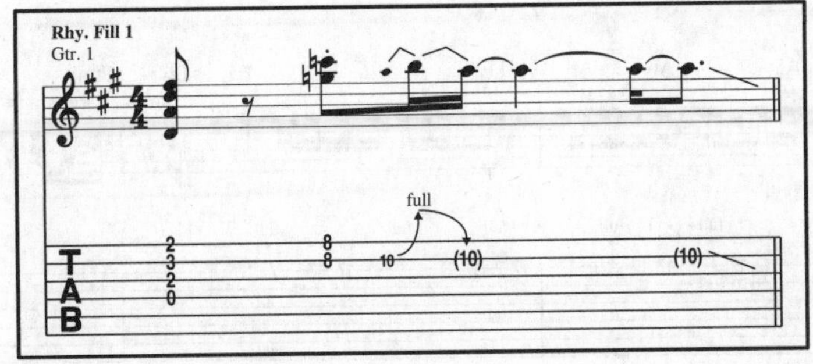

Pre-Chorus

Guitar Solo

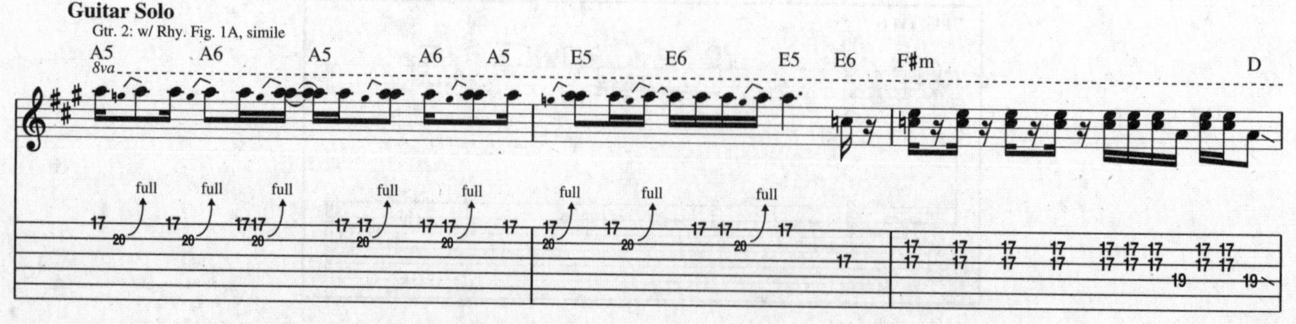

Chorus
Gtr. 2 tacet
A
A/G#
I want you to want me. I
8va
loco
P.M.
full
*Chords implied by bass (next 8 bars).

F#m
E
D
D/C#
need you to need me. I'd love you to love me. I'm
8va
full

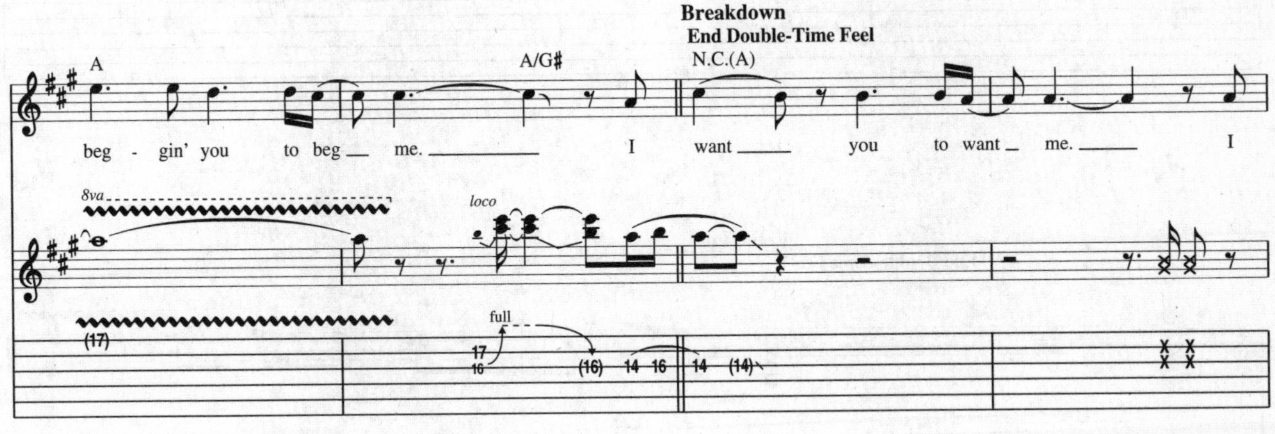
Breakdown
End Double-Time Feel
A
A/G#
N.C.(A)
beg - gin' you to beg me. I want you to want me. I
8va
loco
full

want you to want me. I want you to want
1/2

me.
I
want
you
to want
me.
6
3
6
3
7 5 3 5 3 2 3 2 0 0 2
4 5 3 2 4 2 0 0
2 0
4
0

Outro

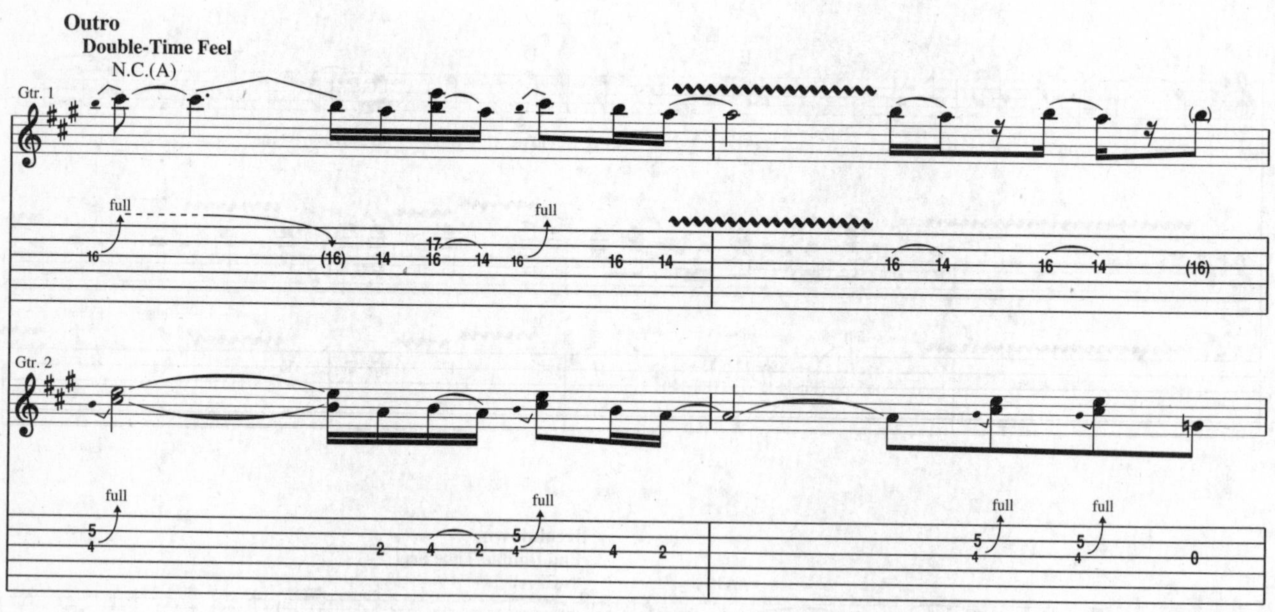
Double-Time Feel
N.C.(A)
Gtr. 1
full
16
(16)
14
17
16
14
full
16
16
14
16
14
16
14
(16)
Gtr. 2
full
5
4
2
4
2
full
5
4
4
2
full
5
4
full
5
4
0

G5
D
End Double-Time Feel
Free Time
A5
let ring
rit.
full
3
3
0
0
X
3
2
3
2
0
2
2
0
3
4
2
4
6
5
7
8
9
(9)
(9)
(9)
let ring
rit.
full
0
0
5
4
(4)
2
4
5
2
2
2
0

I'll Stick Around

Words and Music by David Grohl

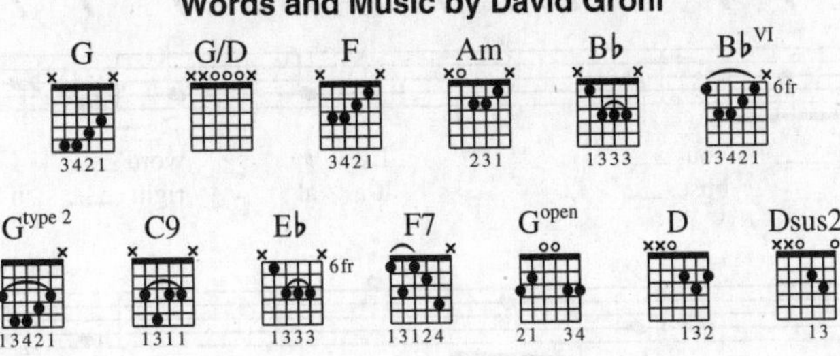

Intro

Aggressive Rock ♩ = 138

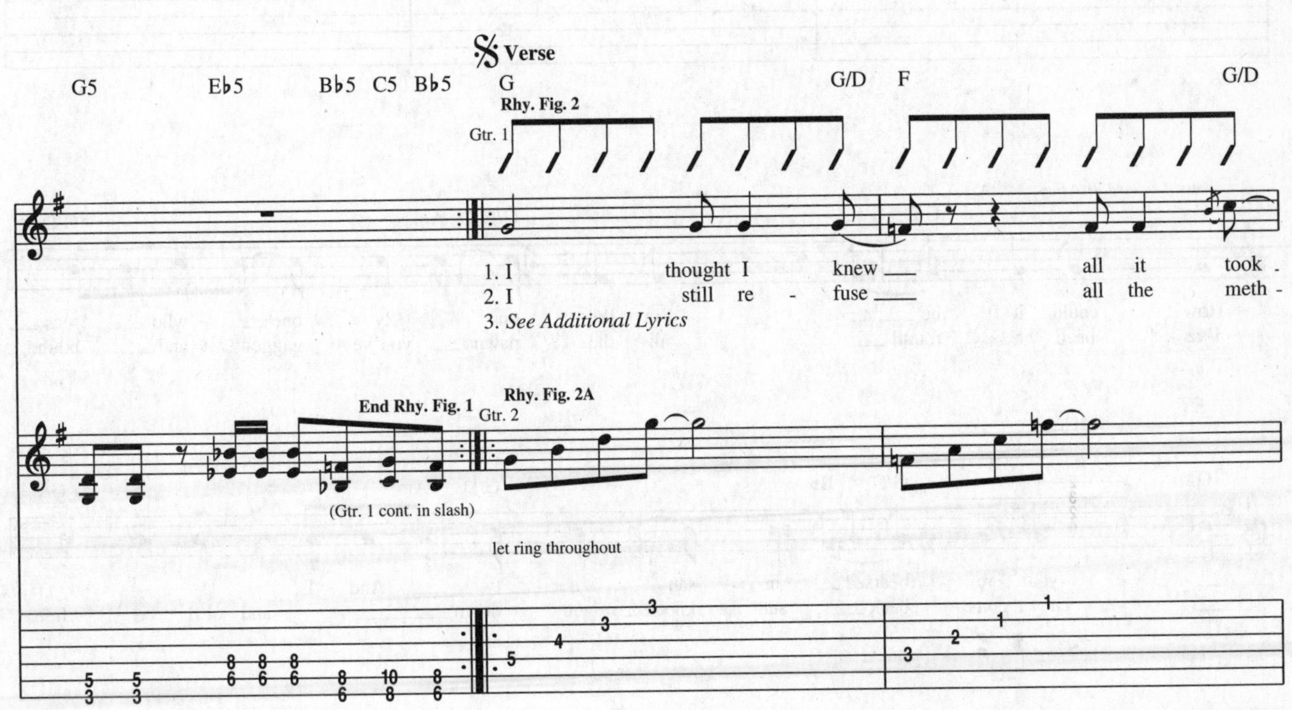

Am G/D G G/D B♭ G/D
to both - er you. Ev - 'ry word I said was true,
- ods you a - buse. It'a al - right if you're con - fused,

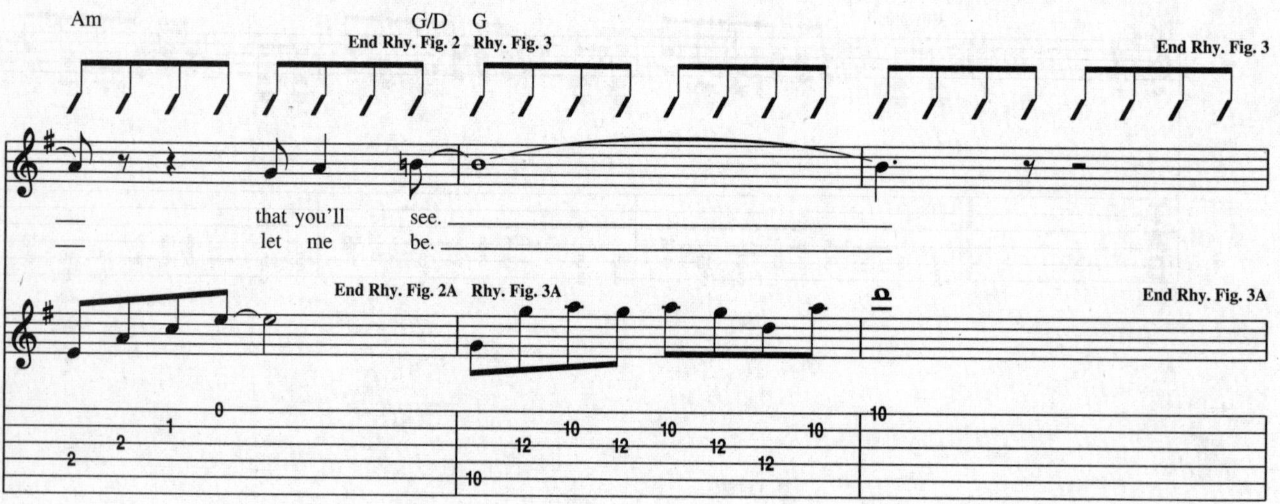

Am G/D G
End Rhy. Fig. 2 Rhy. Fig. 3 End Rhy. Fig. 3
that you'll see.
let me be.
End Rhy. Fig. 2A Rhy. Fig. 3A End Rhy. Fig. 3A

Gtrs. 1 & 2: w/ Rhy. Figs. 2 & 2A
G G/D F G/D Am G/D
How could it be I'm the on - ly one who sees
I've been a - round all the pawns you've gagged and bound.

G G/D B♭ G/D Am G/D
your re - hearsed in - san - i - ty. And I...
They'll come back and knock you down and I'll be free.

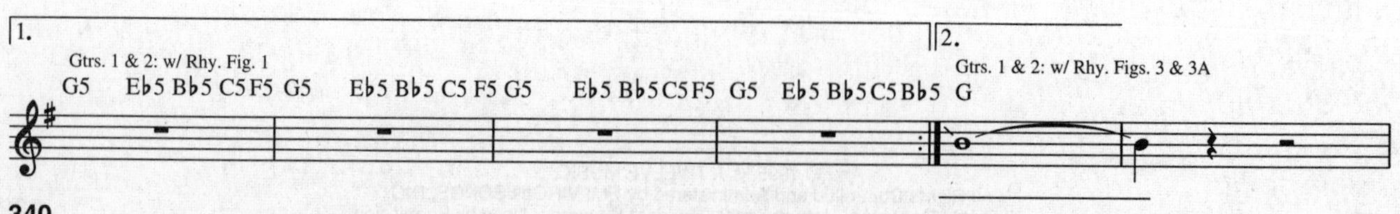

1.
Gtrs. 1 & 2: w/ Rhy. Fig. 1
G5 E♭5 B♭5 C5 F5 G5 E♭5 B♭5 C5 F5 G5 E♭5 B♭5 C5 F5 G5 E♭5 B♭5 C5 B♭5
2.
Gtrs. 1 & 2: w/ Rhy. Figs. 3 & 3A
G

Pre-Chorus
Gtrs. 1 & 2: w/ Rhy. Fill 1, 2nd time
Bb VI
G type 2
C9
A
open
Gtr. 2
I've tak - en all that I've en - dured.
Gtr. 1
let ring
Bb
G
Gtrs. 1 & 2: w/ Rhy. Fill 2
C9
One day it all will fade I'm sure.
Chorus
Gtrs. 1 & 2: w/ Rhy. Fig. 1, 2 times
G5 Eb5 Bb5 C5 F5 G5 Eb5 Bb5 C5 F5 G5 Eb5 Bb5 C5 F5 G5 Eb5 Bb5 C5 Bb5
I don't owe you an - y - thing. I don't owe you an - y - thing.
D.S. (take 2nd ending)
G5 Eb5 Bb5 C5 F5 G5 Eb5 Bb5 C5 F5 G5 Eb5 Bb5 C5 F5 G5 Eb5 Bb5 C5 Bb5
I don't owe you an - y - thing. I don't owe you an - y - thing.
Rhy. Fill 1
Gtrs. 1 & 2
Gtr. 1
Gtr. 2
divisi
* Gtr. 1 tabbed to the left.

Gtrs. 1 & 2: w/ Rhy. Fig. 1

G5 Eb5 Bb5 C5 F5 G5 Eb5 Bb5 C5 F5 G5 Eb5 Bb5 C5 F5 G5 Eb5 Bb5 C5 Bb5

I don't owe you__ an - y - thing.__ I don't owe you__ an - y - thing.__

Bridge

Eb F7 G open

Rhy. Fig. 4

Gtrs. 1 & 2

(___) I'll__ stick a - round.__ I'll__ stick a - round,__ learn__ from all

D Dsus2 D Dsus2

play 4 times

End Rhy. Fig. 4

Gtrs. 1 & 2: w/ Rhy. Fig. 4, 1 1/2 times

Eb F7

__ that come__ from it.___

* slurred last time only.

G D Dsus2 D Dsus2 Eb F7

Hey!___

Outro

Gtrs. 1 & 2: w/ Rhy. Fig. 1

G5 Eb5 Bb5 C5 F5 G5 Eb5 Bb5 C5 F5 G5 Eb5 Bb5 C5 F5 G5 Eb5 Bb5 C5 Bb5 G5

Gtrs. 1 & 2

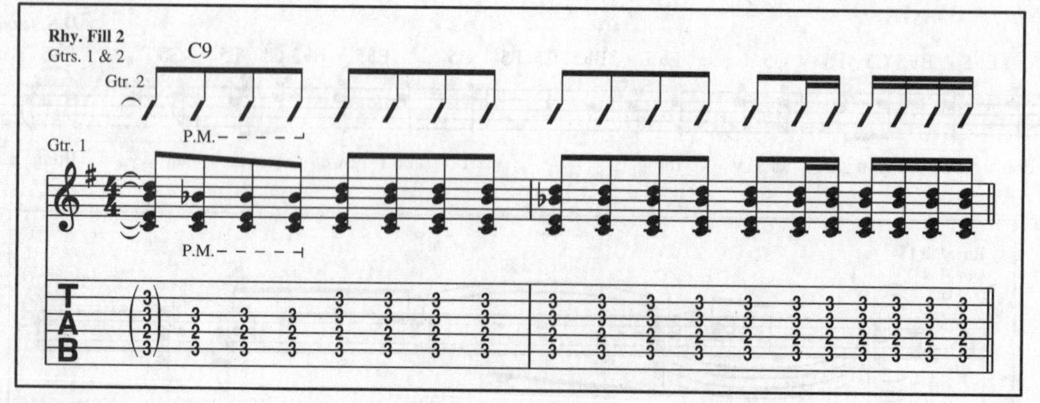

Additional Lyrics

3. I had no hand in your ever desperate plan.
It returns and when it lands words are due.
I should have known we were better off alone.
I look in and I was shown you were too.

In and Out of Love

Words and Music by Jon Bon Jovi

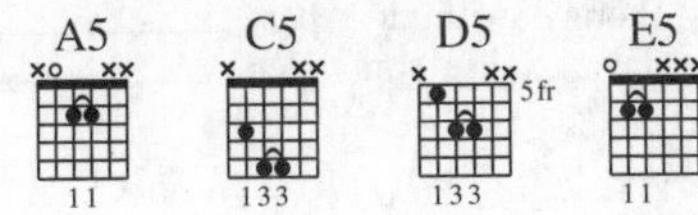

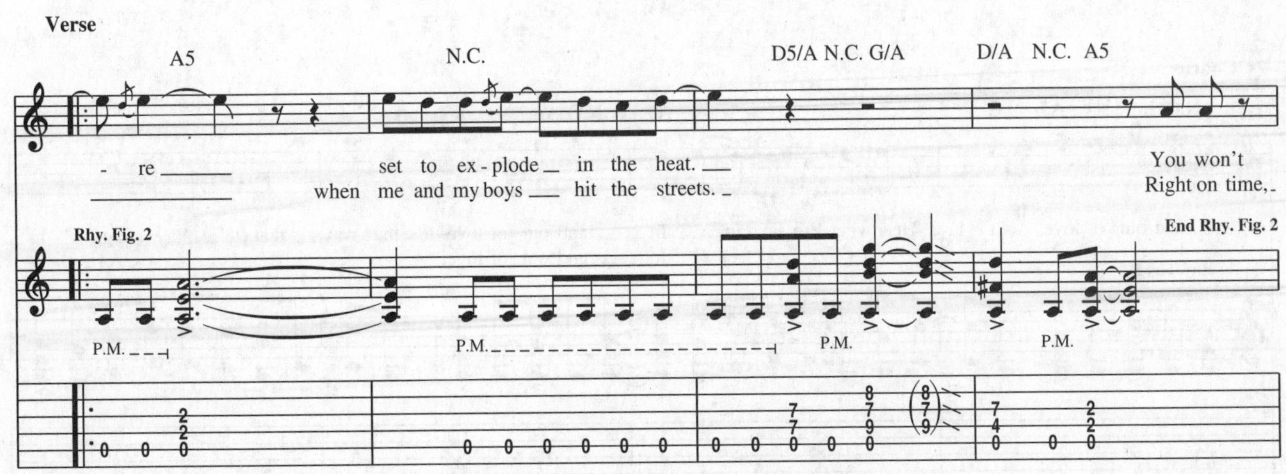

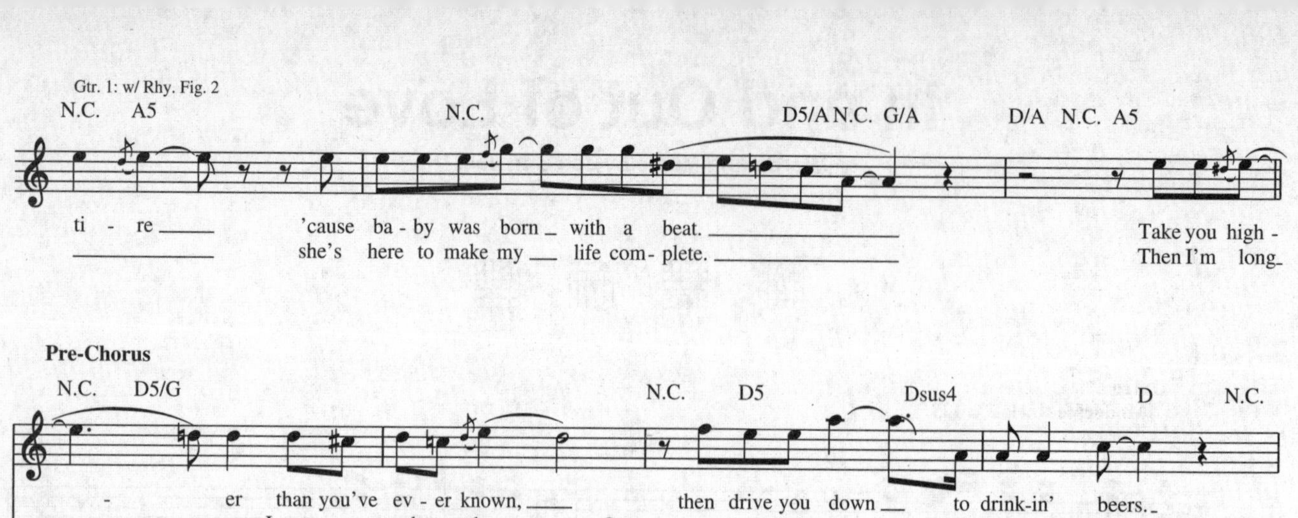
Gtr. 1: w/ Rhy. Fig. 2
N.C. A5 N.C. D5/A N.C. G/A D/A N.C. A5
ti - re 'cause ba - by was born with a beat. Take you high -
she's here to make my life com - plete. Then I'm long

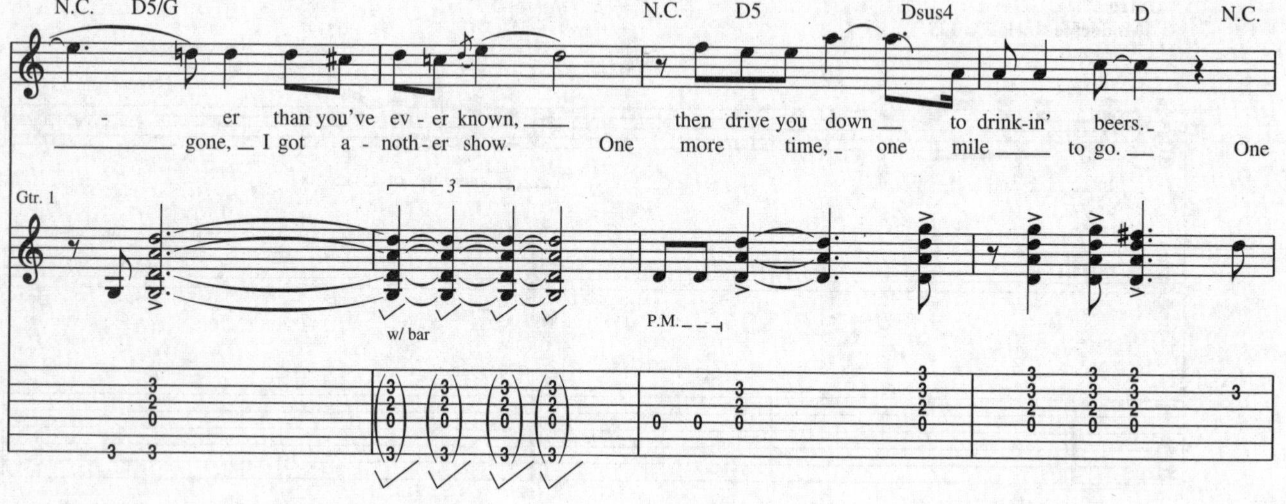
Pre-Chorus
N.C. D5/G N.C. D5 Dsus4 D N.C.
- er than you've ev - er known, then drive you down to drink-in' beers. One
gone, I got a - noth - er show. One more time, one mile to go.
Gtr. 1
w/ bar
P.M.

D5/G N.C. D5/G N.C. D5/G N.C. D5/G N.C. D5/G N.C. D5 N.C. D5 N.C. A5
I pick you up when you've had e - nough. You've been burned, ba - by, les - son's learned. In -
end - less night of fan - ta - sy. It's all she left of her with me.
P.M. P.M. P.M. P.M. P.M. P.M.

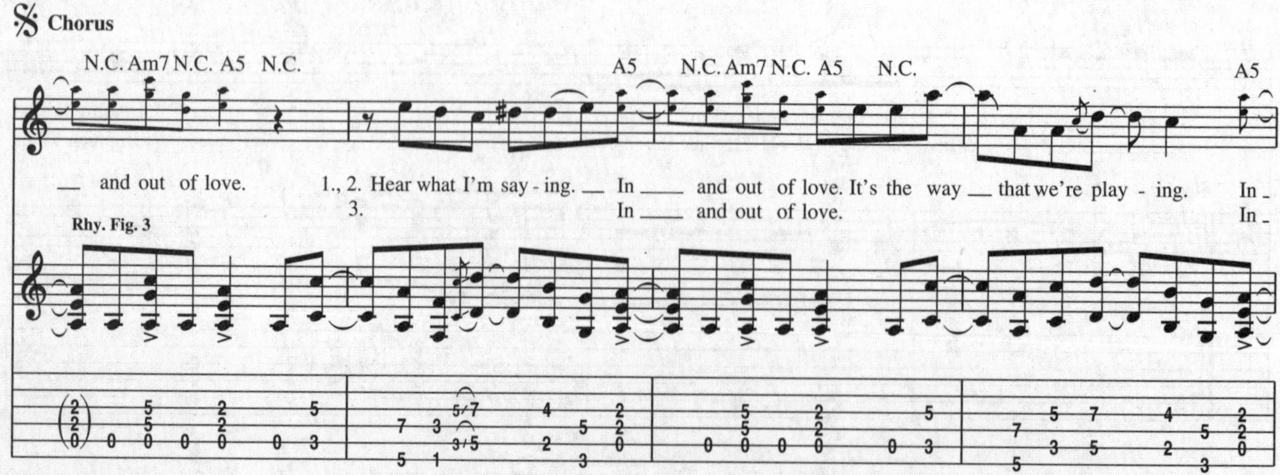
Chorus
N.C. Am7 N.C. A5 N.C. A5 N.C. Am7 N.C. A5 N.C. A5
and out of love. 1., 2. Hear what I'm say - ing. In and out of love. It's the way that we're play - ing. In
3. In and out of love. In -
Rhy. Fig. 3

Gtr. 1: w/ Rhy. Fill 1, 2nd & 3rd times
1.
N.C. Am7 N.C. A5 N.C.
E5
N.C.
A5
and out of love.
and out of love.
1. Too much is nev-er e-nough.
2. When we're to-geth-er. In
3. In
She's gon-na get ya.
8va loco
End Rhy. Fig. 3
let ring
let ring
Harm.
w/ bar
2., 3.
Gtr. 1: w/ Rhy. Fig. 1
N.C. Am7 N.C. A5 N.C.
A5 N.C. Am7 N.C. A5 N.C.
Gtr. 1: w/ Rhy. Fig. 3, 3rd & 4th meas.
N.C. Am7 N.C. A5 N.C.
2. Run-ning wild,
2. and out of love. Love's too
3. and out of love.
Gtr. 1: w/ Rhy. Fig. 3
A5 N.C. Am7 N.C. A5 N.C.
A5 N.C. Am7 N.C. A5 N.C.
A5
much for-ev-er. In and out of love.
In and out of love.
Hear what I'm say-ing. In and out of love. It's the way that we're play-ing. In
In and out of love. You want me to meet your what? In
Gtr. 1: w/ Rhy. Fill 1, 2nd time
To Coda
N.C. Am7 N.C. A5 N.C.
E5
N.C.
A5
and out of love.
and out of love.
Too much is nev-er e-nough.
Your dad-dy is who? In
She's gon-na get ya.
Interlude
Ad-lib laughs, whistles & vocs.
band tacet
band enters
N.C. Am7 N.C. A5
N.C. Am7 N.C. D5
G5 D N.C. A5
N.C. Am7 N.C. A5
N.C. Am7 N.C. D5 N.C.
Gtr. 1
P.M.
* Vib. top 2 notes only.
Rhy. Fill 1
Gtr. 1

1.
G5 D N.C. A5 N.C.
Oh, oh, oh.
2.
A5 G5 D B5 A5
Oh, oh, oh.
Gtr. 1
Gtr. 2 (dist.)
w/ bar
(cont. in slash)
Guitar Solo
G E A5
3 fr open
Rhy. Fig. 4
End Rhy. Fig. 4
P.M.
P.H.
w/ bar
Gtr. 1: w/ Rhy. Fig. 4, 2 1/2 times
N.C. A5
8va
full
hold bend
steady gliss.
C5
D5

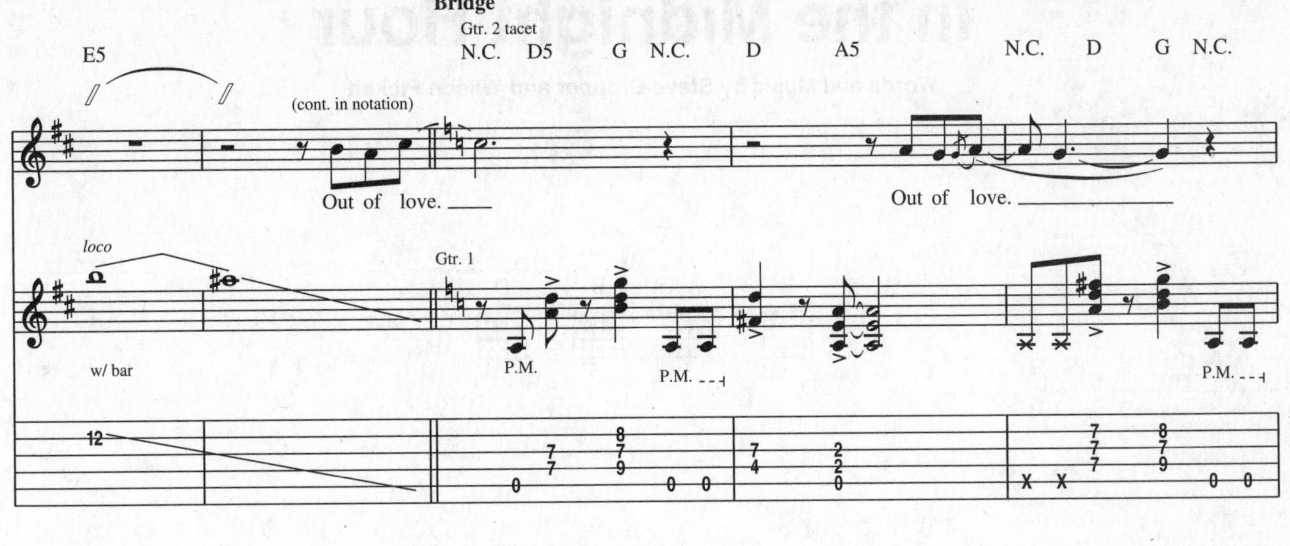
Bridge
Gtr. 2 tacet
E5
N.C. D5 G N.C. D A5 N.C. D G N.C.
(cont. in notation)
Out of love.
Out of love.
loco
Gtr. 1
w/ bar
P.M.
P.M.
P.M.

D5 C5 N.C. D G N.C. D/A A5 N.C. D5 N.C. G N.C. D5 C5 A5
Out of love.
Out of love.
In
w/ bar
Harm.
P.M.
P.M.
P.M.
w/ bar

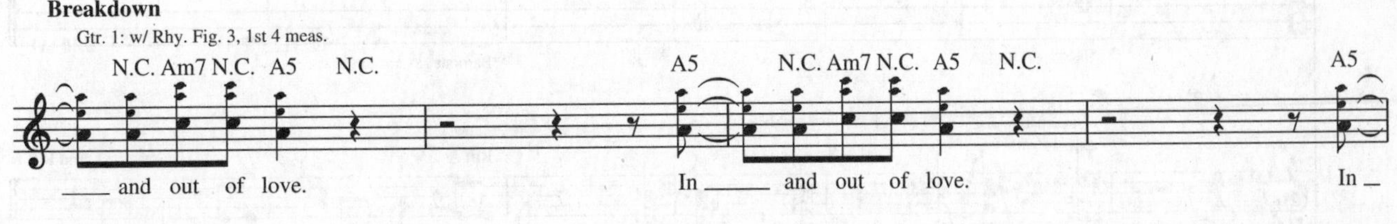
Breakdown
Gtr. 1: w/ Rhy. Fig. 3, 1st 4 meas.
N.C. Am7 N.C. A5 N.C. A5 N.C. Am7 N.C. A5 N.C. A5
and out of love.
In and out of love.
In

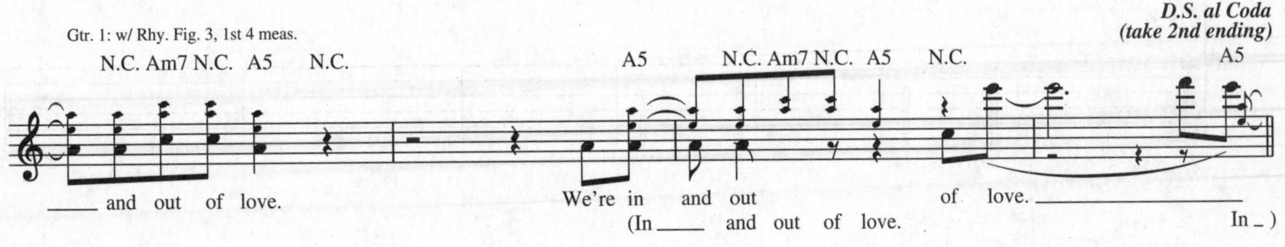
Gtr. 1: w/ Rhy. Fig. 3, 1st 4 meas.
D.S. al Coda
(take 2nd ending)
N.C. Am7 N.C. A5 N.C. A5 N.C. Am7 N.C. A5 N.C. A5
and out of love.
We're in and out of love.
(In and out of love.
In)

Coda
Gtr. 1: w/ Rhy. Fig. 3, 3rd & 4th meas.
Gtr. 1: w/ Rhy. Fig. 3, 1st 4 meas.
Fade Out
N.C. Am7 N.C. A5 N.C. A5 N.C. Am7 N.C. A5 N.C. A5 N.C. Am7 N.C. A5 N.C. A5
and out of love.
In and out of love.
In and out of love.
In
Spoken: Hey, just how old are you anyway?

In the Midnight Hour

Words and Music by Steve Cropper and Wilson Pickett

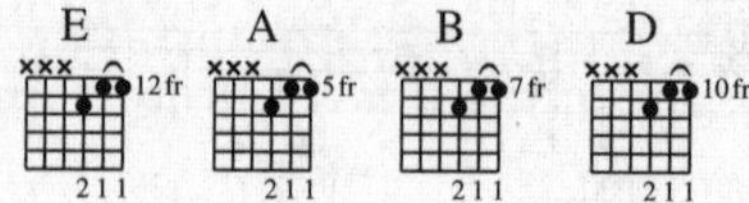

Intro

Moderately ♩ = 112

D B A G

Gtr. 1 tacet

E A E A

Rhy. Fig. 1 **End Rhy. Fig. 1**

Gtr. 3 (clean)

mf

(Drums)

1. I'm gon-na

*Gtr. 1

mf

**Gtr. 4

mf

T	10	7	5	15			
A	10	7	5	12			
	11	8	6	12			
B	12	9	7	12			
				12			
				10		10 11	12 10 11

*Horns arr. for gtr.

**Baritone sax arr. for gtr.

Gtr. 2 (slight dist.)

Riff A **End Riff A**

mf

T	11	8	6	4		
A	12	9	7	5		
	12	9	7	5		
B	10	7	5	3	7	7 7 7 5 5 / 7 7 7 5 5

Verse
Gtrs. 2 & 3: w/ Riff A & Rhy. Fig. 1 (4 times)
2nd time, Gtr. 1 w/ Riff B
2nd time, Gtr. 4 tacet
*E A E A E A E A
wait till the mid-night hour. That's when my love comes tum-bling down. I'm gon-na
wait till the stars come out and see that twin-kle in your eyes. I'm gon-na
Gtr. 4
12 10 11 12 10 11 12 10 11 12 10 11
*Chord symbols reflect overall harmony.

E A E A E A E A
wait till the mid-night hour, when there's no one else a-round. I'm gon-na
wait till the mid-night hour. That's when my love be-gins to shine. You're the
12 10 11 12 10 11 12 10 11 12

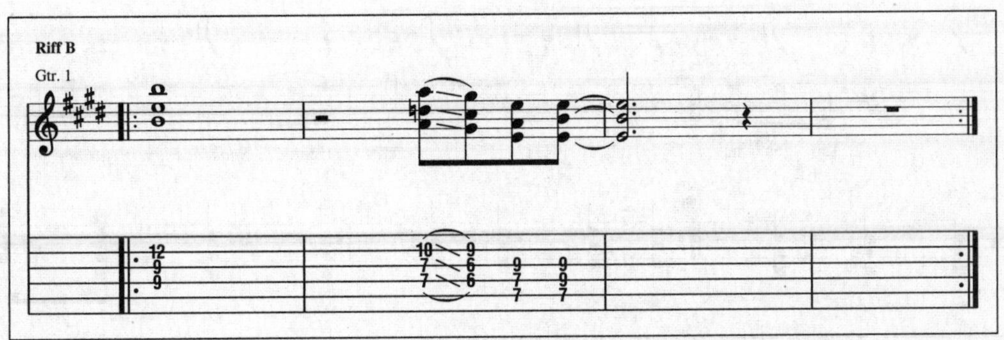
Riff B
Gtr. 1
12 9 9
10 9 7 6 7 6 9 9 7 7 7 7

1st time, Gtr. 4 tacet
B
A
B
A
Gtr. 3
take you, girl, and hold you, and do all the things I told you, in the mid-night hour.
on - ly girl I know that real - ly loves me so, in the mid-night hour.
Gtr. 1
Gtr. 2
Gtrs. 2 & 3: w/ Riff A & Rhy. Fig.1 (1 1/2 times)
E A E A E A
1.
Gtr. 1 tacet
D
Gtr. 3
Yes, I am, whoa, yes, I am.
Spoken: One more thing I just wan-na say right here.
Oh, yeah. In the mid-night hour. Yeah.
Gtr. 1
Gtr. 2
2.
Gtr. 1 tacet
B
D
B
Gtr. 3
2. I'm gon - na All right.
Spoken: Play it for me one time, now.
Gtr. 2

Interlude

E
A
E
A
E
D
B
Gtr. 1
Gtr. 2
E
A
E
A
E
A
B
I'm gon - na
3
Outro
Gtrs. 2 & 3: w/ Riff A & Rhy. Fig. 1 (till end)
E
A
E
A
E
A
E
A
wait
till the mid-night hour.
That's when my
love
comes tum-bl-ing down.
I'm gon - na wait
Riff C
End Riff C
Gtr. 1
Gtr. 4
Riff C1
End Riff C1
divisi

Gtrs. 1 & 4: w/ Riffs C & C1 (till end)
E A E A E A E A
way in the mid-night hour. That's when my love be-gins to shine. Just you and I.
*Gtr. 5
8va
mf
17 16 17 16
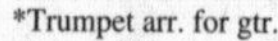
*Trumpet arr. for gtr.

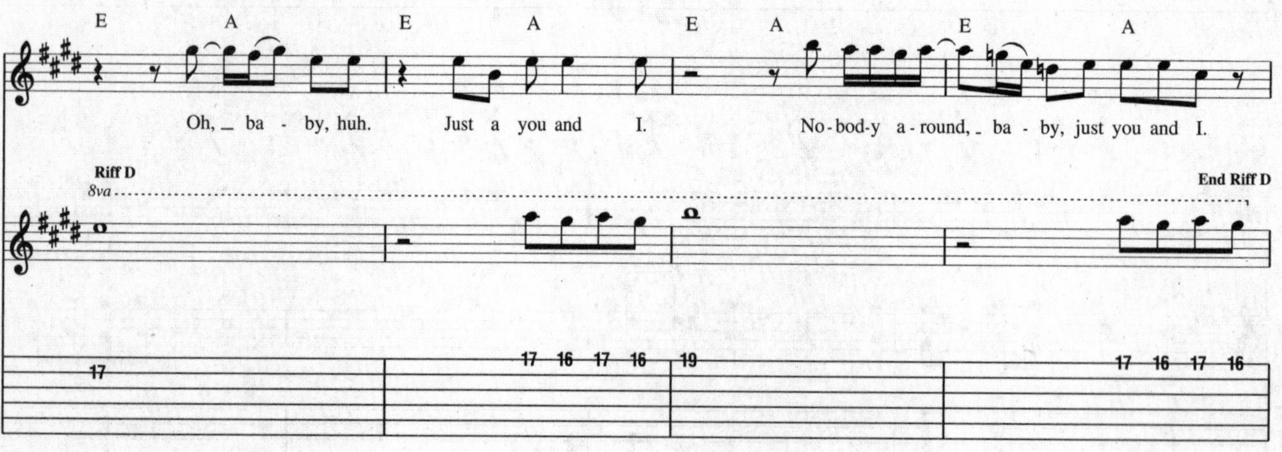
E A E A E A E A
Oh, ba - by, huh. Just a you and I. No-bod-y a-round, ba - by, just you and I.
Riff D
8va
End Riff D
17
17 16 17 16
19
17 16 17 16

Gtr. 5: w/ Riff D (till end)
E A E A E A
All right. You know what? I'm gon - na hold you in my arms,

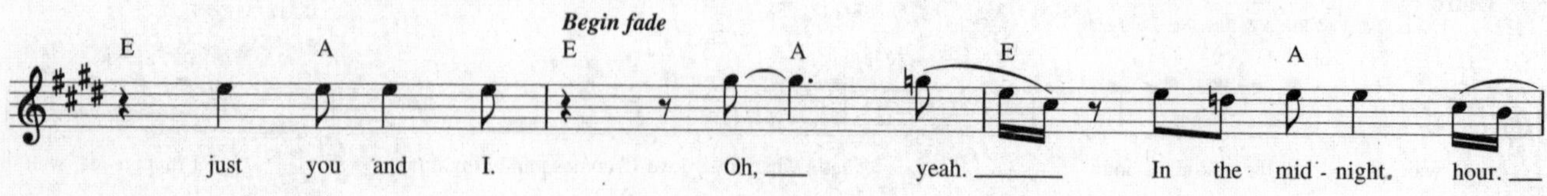
Begin fade
E A E A E A
just you and I. Oh, yeah. In the mid - night. hour.

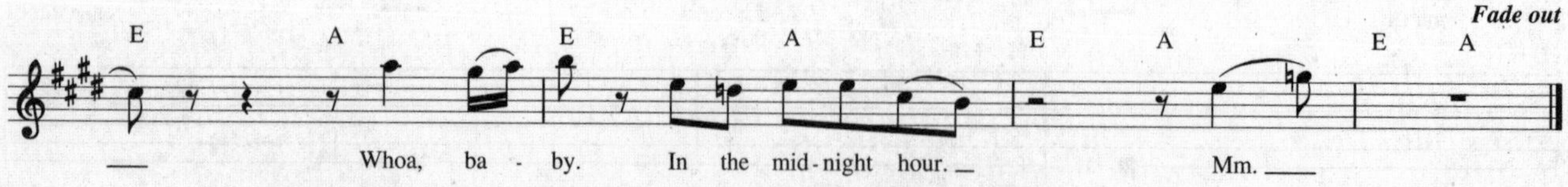
Fade out
E A E A E A E A
Whoa, ba - by. In the mid-night hour. Mm.

Iris

Words and Music by John Rzeznik

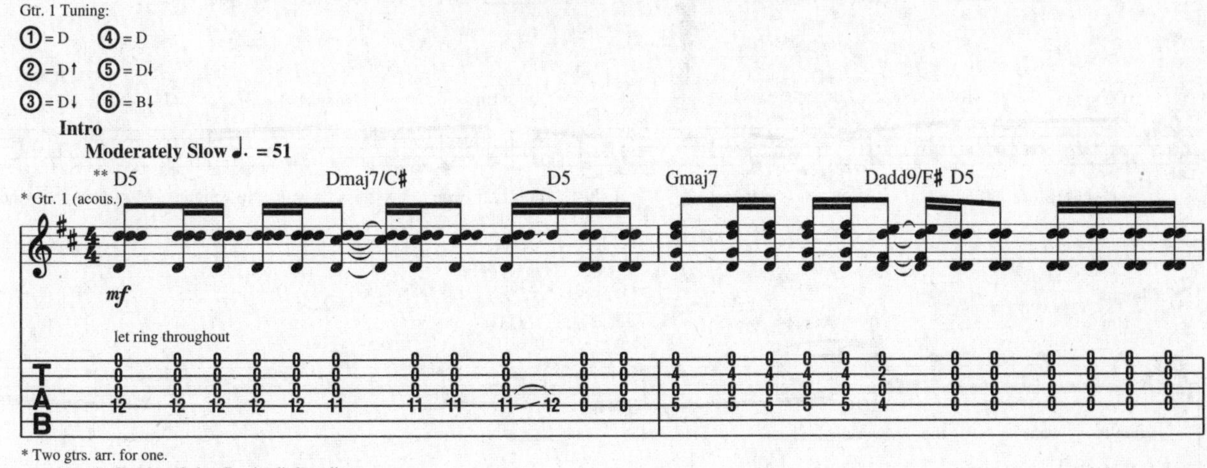

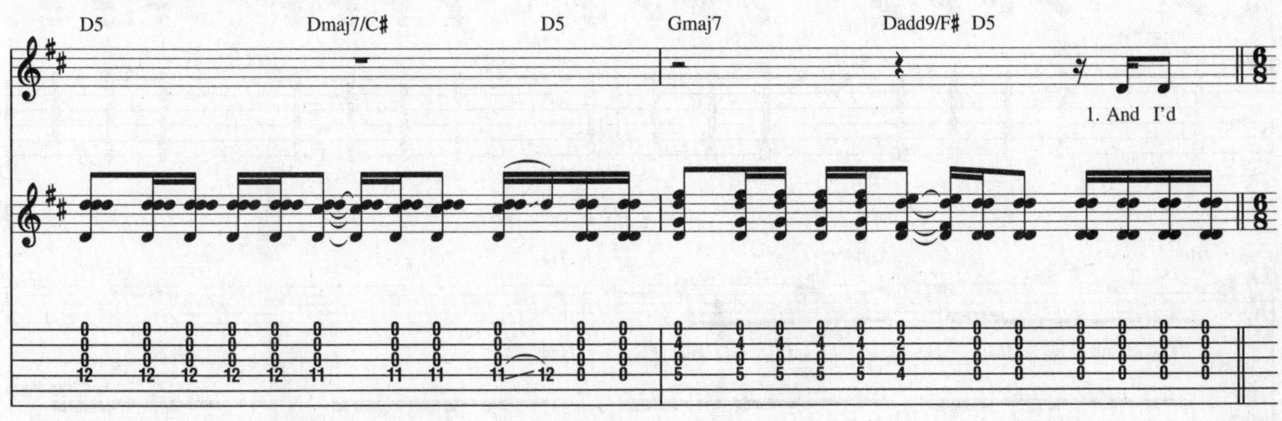

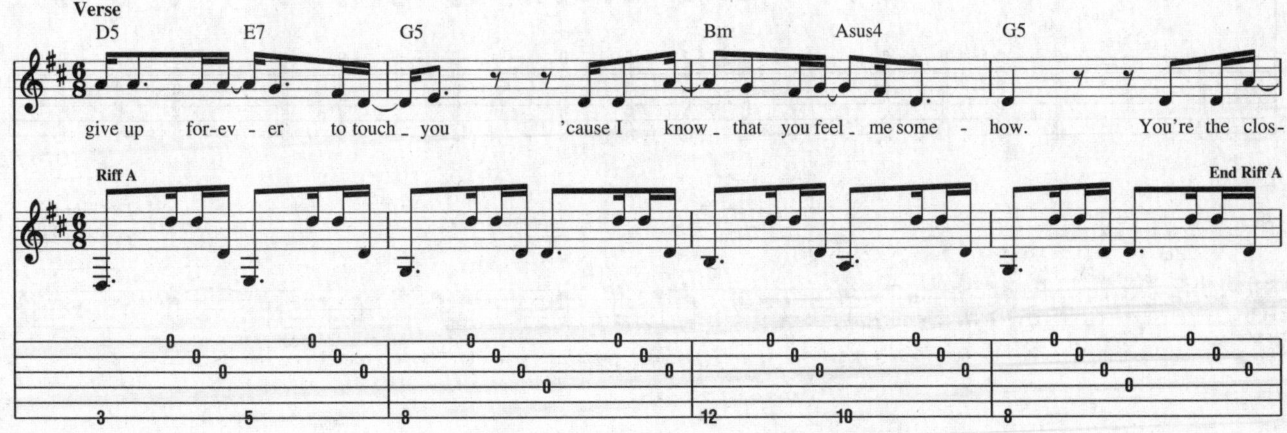

D5
E7
G5
Bm
Asus4
G5
I can taste is this mo-ment, and all I can breathe is your life. Well,

D5
E7
G5
Bm
Asus4
G5
soon-er or lat - er it's o - ver, I just don't wan-na miss you to-night. And I

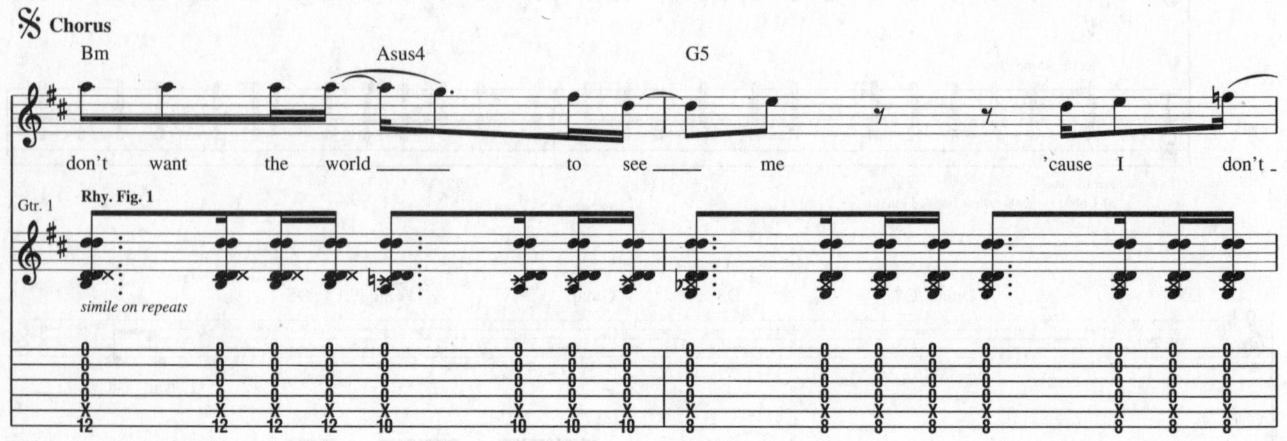
Chorus
Bm
Asus4
G5
don't want the world to see me 'cause I don't
Gtr. 1
Rhy. Fig. 1
simile on repeats

Bm
Asus4
G5
think that they'd un - der - stand. When
End Rhy. Fig. 1

Gtr. 1: w/ Rhy. Fig. 1
To Coda 1
To Coda 2
Bm
Asus4
G5
Bm
Asus4
G5
ev-'ry-thing's made to be bro-ken, I just want you to know who I am.

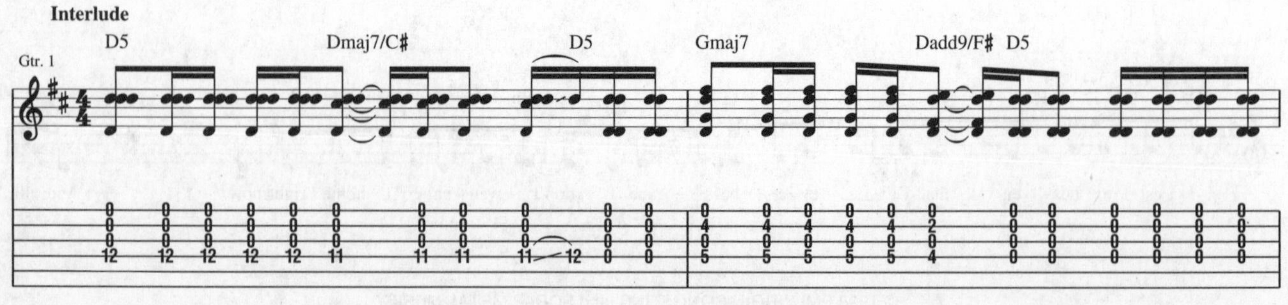
Interlude
D5
Dmaj7/C#
D5
Gmaj7
Dadd9/F#
D5
Gtr. 1

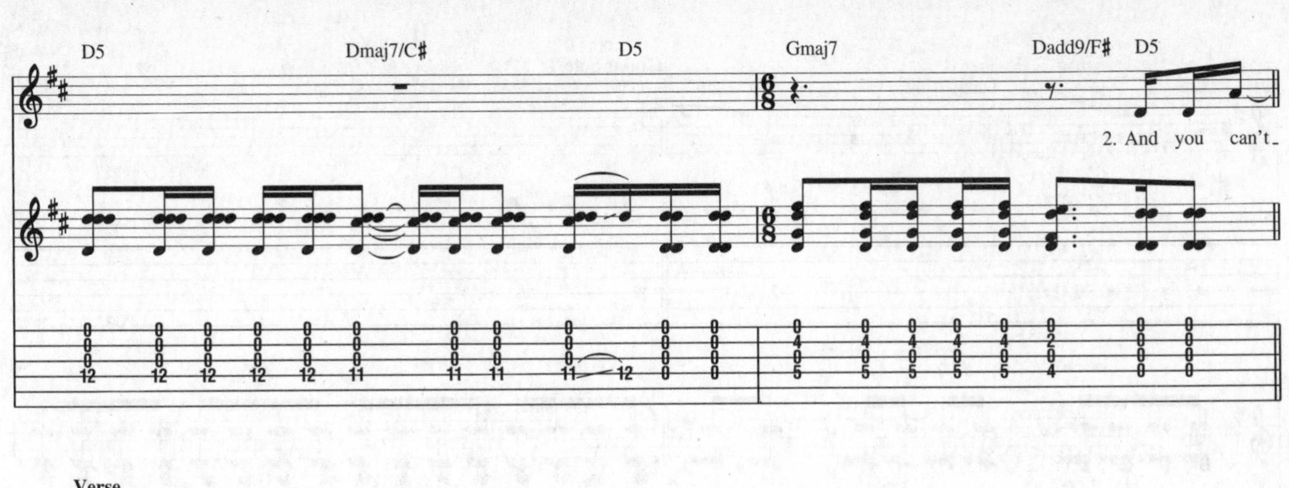

Verse

Gtr. 1: w/ Riff A, 2 times, simile

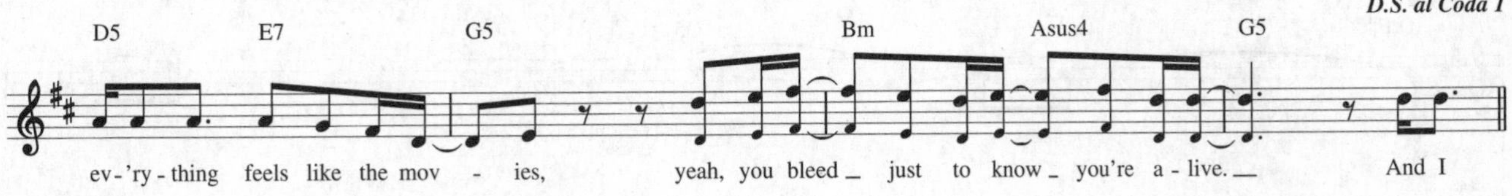

Coda 1

Interlude

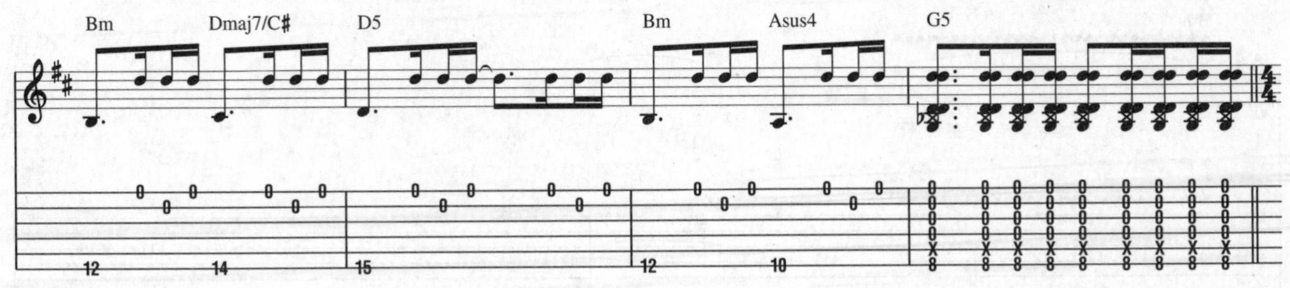

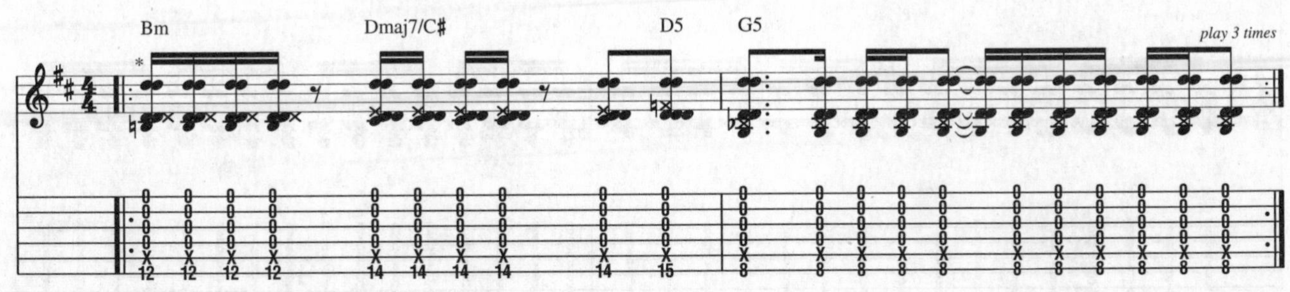

* doubled by elec. w/ dist., simile, next 15 meas.

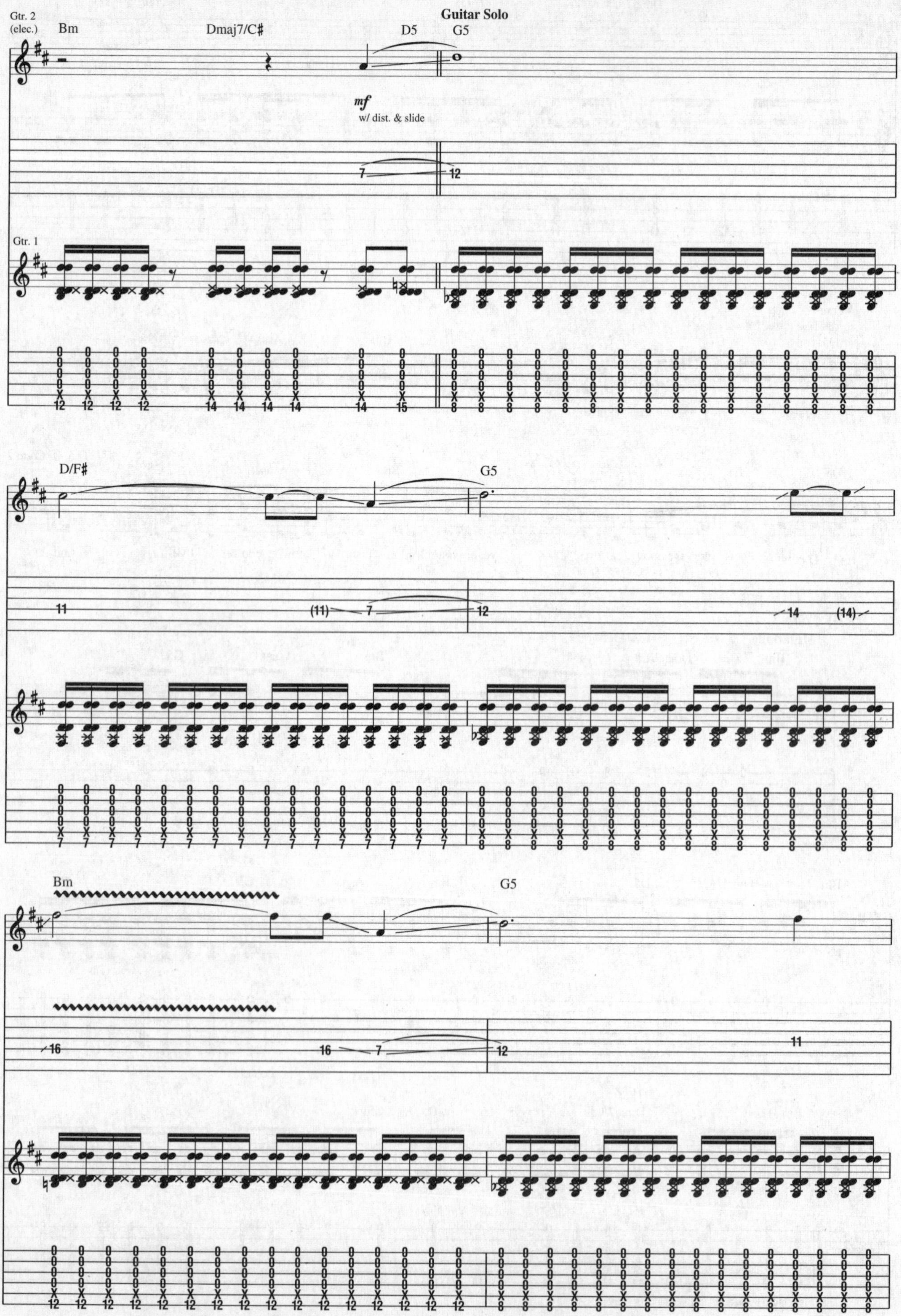
Gtr. 2
(elec.)
Bm
Dmaj7/C#
Guitar Solo
D5
G5
mf
w/ dist. & slide
Gtr. 1
D/F#
G5
Bm
G5

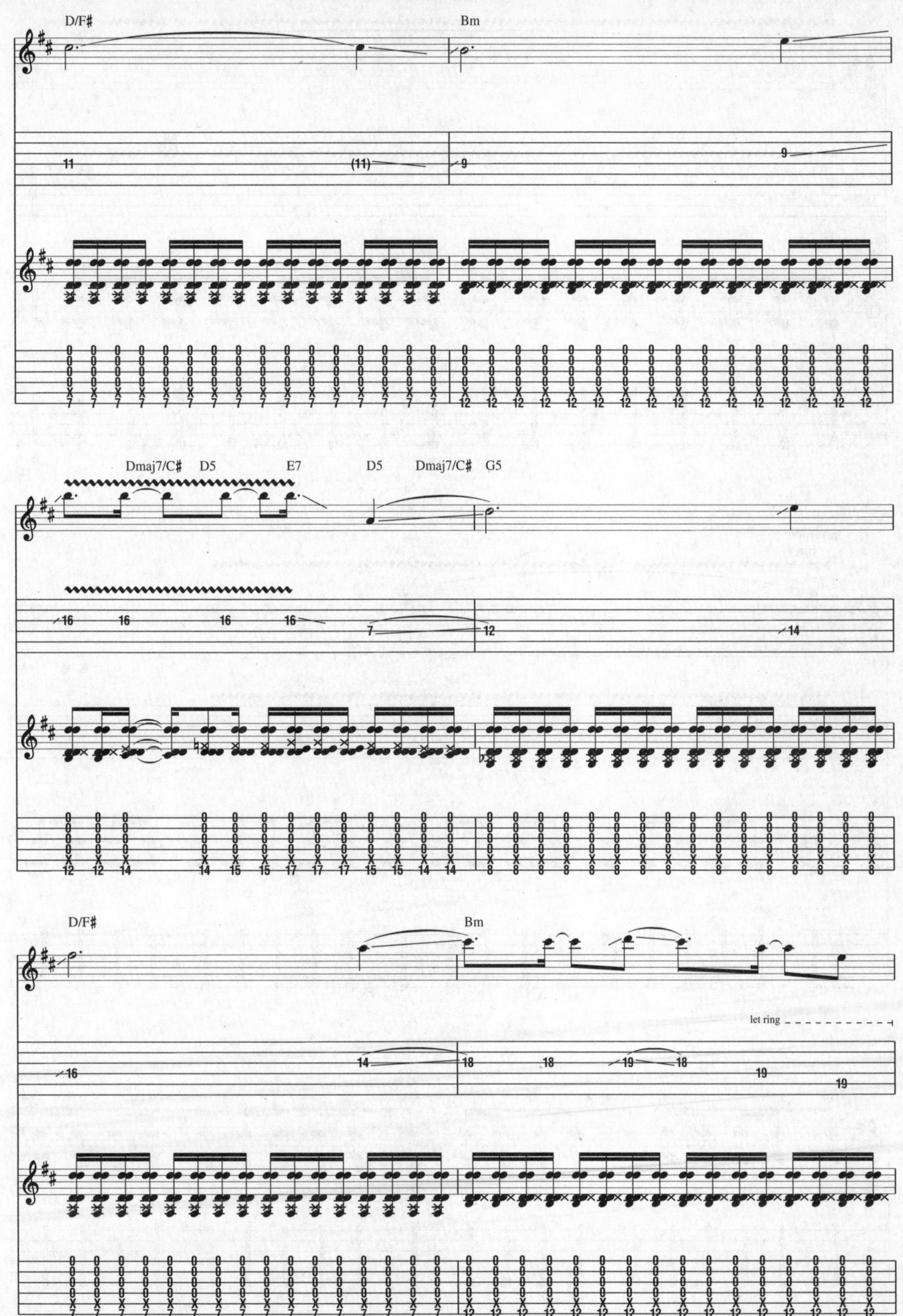
D/F#
Bm
Dmaj7/C#
D5
E7
D5
Dmaj7/C#
G5
D/F#
Bm
let ring

Interlude
Bm
Dmaj7/C#
D5
Gtr. 2 tacet
Gtr. 1
Bm
Asus4
G5

D.S. al Coda 2
Bm
Dmaj7/C#
D5
Asus4
G5
And I
Coda 2
Gtr. 1
And I don't want the world to see me 'cause I don't
think that they'd un - der - stand.
When
ev - 'ry - thing's made to be bro - ken
I just want

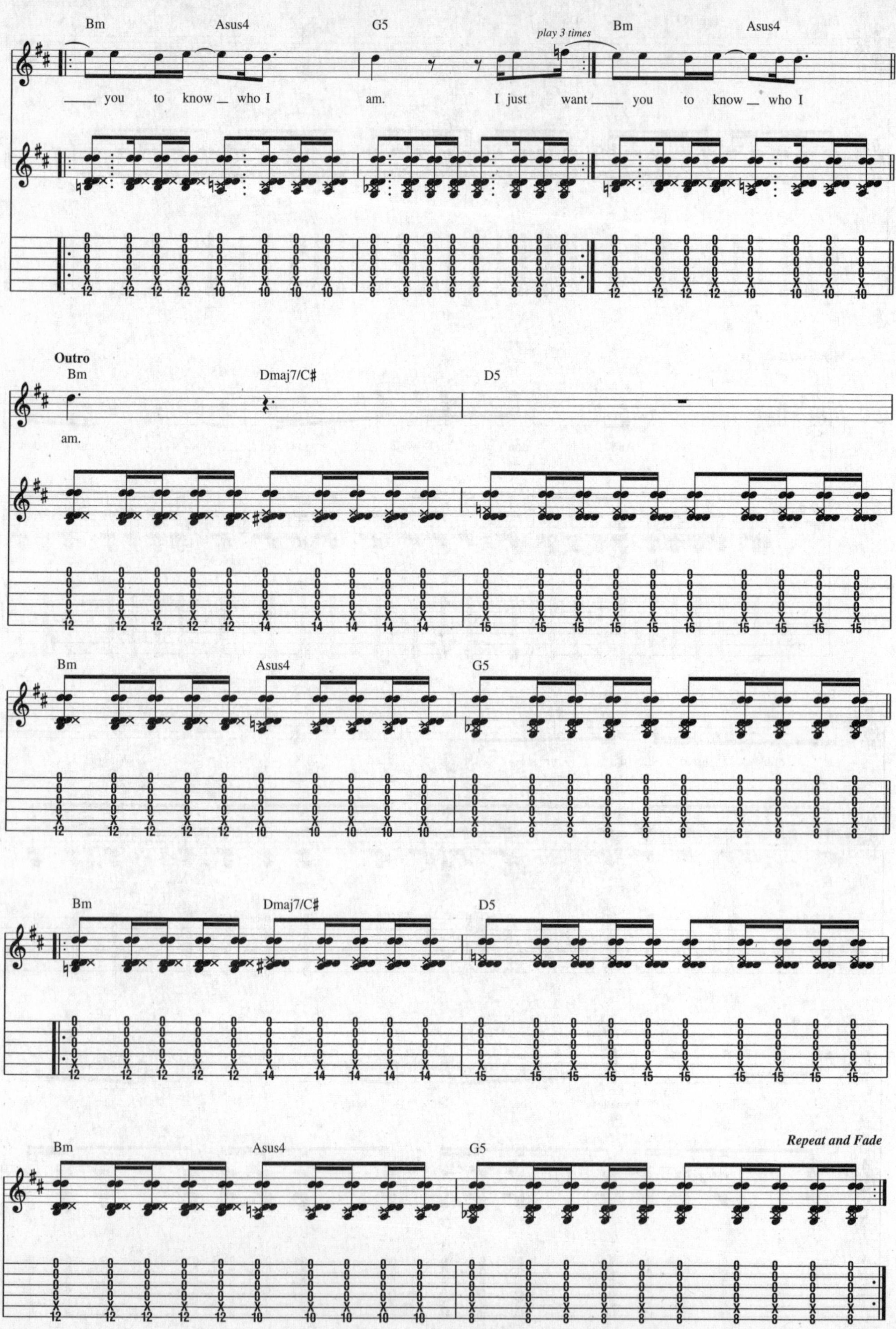
Bm
Asus4
G5
play 3 times
Bm
Asus4
you to know who I
am.
I just want you to know who I
Outro
Bm
Dmaj7/C♯
D5
am.
Bm
Asus4
G5
Bm
Dmaj7/C♯
D5
Bm
Asus4
G5
Repeat and Fade

Is This Love

Words and Music by Bob Marley

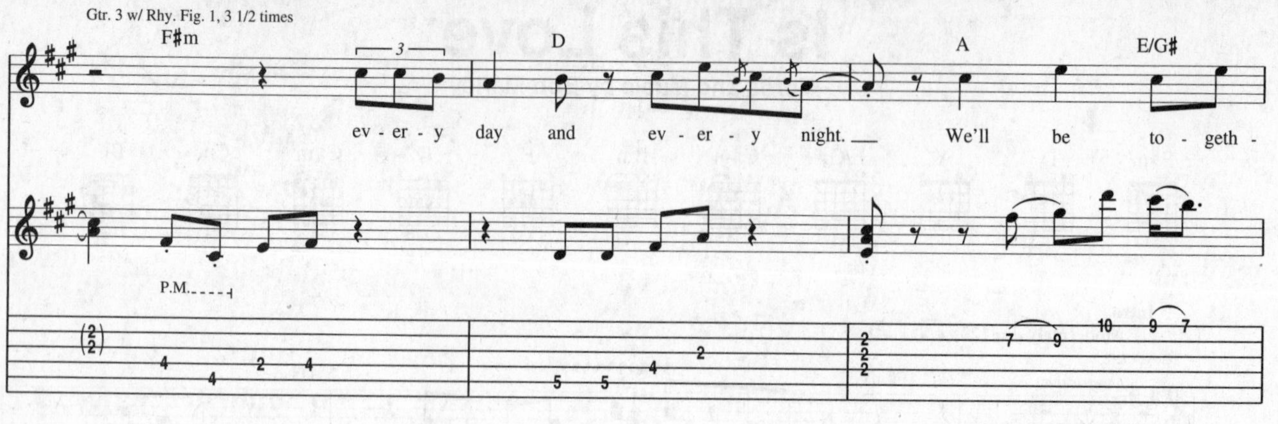
Gtr. 3 w/ Rhy. Fig. 1, 3 1/2 times
F#m
D
A
E/G#
ev - er - y day and ev - er - y night.
We'll be to - geth -
P.M.

F#m
D
er
with the roof right o - ver our heads.
P.M.

A
E/G#
F#m
We'll share the shel - ter
P.M.
P.M.

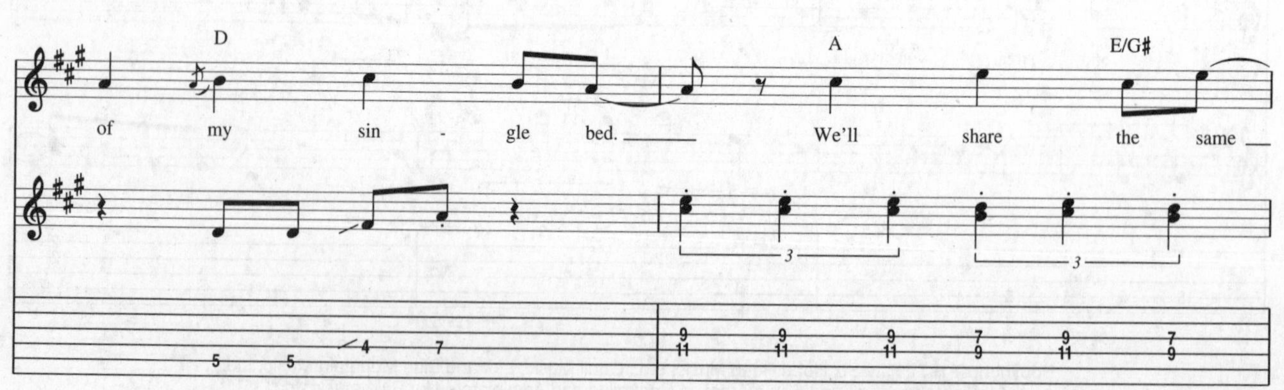
D
A
E/G#
of my sin - gle bed.
We'll share the same

F#m D A

Gtr. 3

— room, yeah, oh, Jah pro - vide our bread. — Is this

Gtr. 1

mf

semi-harm.

P.M.

full 1/4

Gtr. 2

P.M.

pp

P.M.

Chorus

C#m Bm

Rhy. Fig. 2

love, is this love, is this love, is this love that I'm feel - ing?
(Love, love, love, love that I'm feel - ing?)

full full full

Riff A

End Rhy. Fig. 2
Gtr. 3: w/ Rhy. Fig. 2
C♯m
Is this love, is this love, is this love, is this love that I'm
Love, love,)
full
Bm
feel - ing?
Gtrs. 2 & 3 tacet
N.C.(Bm) (C♯m) (D)
Riff B
Gtr. 1
End Riff A
(E)
Bridge
N.C.(D6)
I wan - na know, wan - na know, wan - na know now.
8va
loco
P.M.

(Bm)
(C#m)
(D)
(E)
(C#m)
I've got to know, got
End Riff B
8va
1/2
Gtr. 1 tacet
C#m
Gtr. 3
to know, got to know, now.
I,
(Ah.
)
I'm will-ing and a -
Gtr. 2
Bm
F#m
- ble,
(Ah.
)
so I throw my cards on your ta -
(Ah.
)
Gtr. 1
full
Gtr. 2
(cont. in slash)
Verse
Gtr. 1 tacet
Gtr. 3: w/ Rhy. Fig. 1, 4 1/2 times
Gtr. 3 tacet
E
D
C#m
Cm
Bm
(cont. in notation)
F#m
- ble.
2. I wan-na love ya.
I wan - na
(Ooh.
Gtr. 1
Gtr. 2
1/2

D
A
E/G#
F#m
love and treat, love and treat you right.
(Love and treat you right.)
I wan-na love ya ev-'ry
* Gtrs. 1 & 2
semi-harm.
*composite arrangement
Gtr. 2: w/ Fill 1
Bkgd. Voc. Fig. 1
day and ev-er-y night. We'll be to-geth-er, yeah,
(Ooh.
Gtr. 1
Gtrs. 1 & 2
End Bkgd. Voc. Fig. 1
with the roof right o-ver our heads. We'll share the shel-
ter, yeah oh, yeah, of my sin-gle bed.
(Ooh.)

Gtr. 2: w/ Fill 1
Gtr. 4: w/ Fill 2
A
E/G#
w/ Bkgd. Voc. Fig. 1
F#m
D
We'll share the same room, yeah,
oh, Jah pro - vides the bread.
Gtrs. 1 & 2
Chorus
Gtr. 2: w/ Riff A, simile
Gtr. 3: w/ Rhy. Fig. 2, 2 times
Gtr. 3
C#m
Is this love, is this love, is this love, is this love that I'm
Gtr. 1
Gtr. 2
divisi
P.M.
full
1/2
Bm
feel-ing?
Is this love, is this love, is this love, is this love that I'm
Gtr. 1: w/ Riff B
Gtrs. 2 & 3 tacet
N.C.(Bm) (C#m) (D) (E)
feel - ing?
Whoa.
semi-harm.
Fill 2
Gtr. 4 (clean)
mf
T
A
B

Bridge

N.C.(D6)
(Bm) (C♯m) (D) (E) (C♯m)
Oh yes, I know, yes, I know, yes, I know now.
Gtr. 1 tacet
C♯m
Gtr. 3
Oh, yes I know, yes I know, yes I know now. I, I'm will-ing and a-
(Ah.)
Gtr. 2
Bm
F♯m
-ble, so I throw my cards on your ta-
(Ah.) (Ah.)
Gtr. 1
full
semi harm.
Gtr. 2
(cont. in slash)
Gtr. 3 tacet
E
D^V
C♯m^IV
Cm
Bm^II
Gtr. 2
(cont. in notation)
-ble. 3. See, I wan-na love
Gtr. 1
full

Verse
Gtr. 3: w/Rhy. Fig. 1, til fade
w/ Bkgd. Voc. Fig. 1
F#m
D
A
E/G#
ya. I wan-na love and treat ya, love and treat you right.
Gtr. 1
full
full
full
Gtr. 2
w/ Bkgd. Voc. Fig. 1
I wan-na love ya ev-er-y day and ev-er-y night. We'll be to-geth-
* Gtrs. 1 & 2
semi-harm.
Gtr. 4
Riff C
End Riff C
*composite arrangement
w/ Bkgd. Voc. Fig. 1
Gtr. 4: w/ Riff C, 4 times, simile
er with the roof right o-ver our heads.
semi-harm.

w/ Bkgd. Voc. Fig. 1
A
E/G#
F#m
We'll share the shel - ter
semi-harm.
D
A
E/G#
F#m
of my sin - gle bed. We'll share the same room, yeah,
1/4
1/2
semi-harm.
Begin Fade
D
A
E/G#
Jah pro - vides the bread. We'll share the shel -
full
w/ Bkgd. Voc. Fig. 1
F#m
D
A
E/G#
Fade Out
- ter of my sin - gle bed. We'll share the same
full
full

It's Only Love

Words and Music by Bryan Adams and Jim Vallance

Verse
Gtr. 1: w/ Rhy. Fig. 1 (2 times)
2nd time, Gtr. 2: w/ Fill 1
D
Csus2
Asus4
B♭5
N.C.
feel - in' is ___ end - ed, there ain't no use pre - tend - in'. ___ Don't ya wor -
heart has been bro - ken, hard words have been spo - ken, it ain't eas -
F5
D
Csus2
- ry, well, it's on - ly love. When your world has been ___ shat - tered, ain't
- y, but it's on - ly love. And if your life ain't worth liv - in' and you're
Asus4
B♭5
N.C.
F5
1.
noth - in' else mat - ters. It ain't o - ver, well, it's on - ly love and that's all, yeah. ___
read - y to give in, ___ just re - mem - ber that it's on - ly
Guitar Solo
Gtr. 1: w/ Rhy. Fig. 1
D
Csus2
Asus4
B♭5
N.C.
Gtr. 2
F5
2.
Tina Turner: Yeah. ___ 2. If your love. Oh. ___
P.M.
P.M.
P.M.
Fill 1
Gtr. 2

Guitar Solo

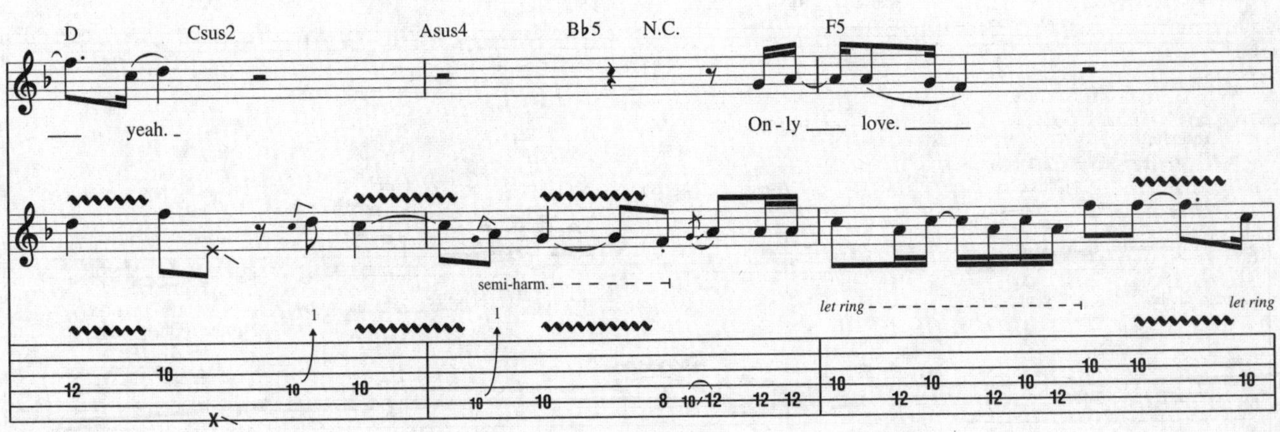

Bridge

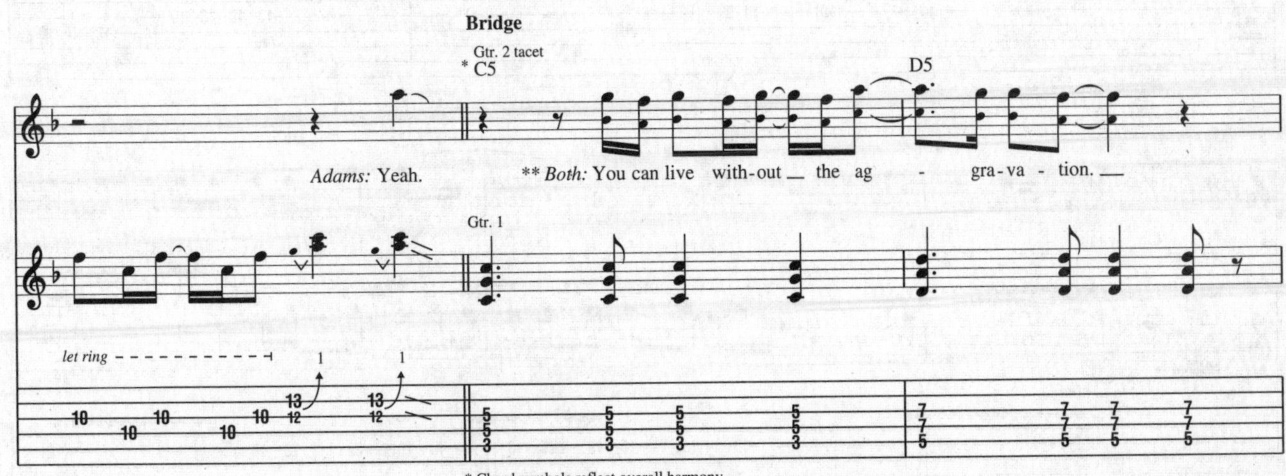

* Chord symbols reflect overall harmony.

** Bryan Adams sings top notes throughout.

B♭
Gm7
C5
Ya got-ta wan - na win, _
ya got-ta wan - na win. _
You keep look-in' back _ in
D5
B♭/C
des - per - a - tion
o - ver _ and o - ver _ and o - ver _ a - gain.
Interlude
Gtr. 1: w/ Rhy. Fig. 1
D
Csus2
Asus4
B♭5
N.C.
F5
Interlude
Gtr. 1: w/ Rhy. Fig. 1 (2 times)
Adams: Yeah, oh, _ yeah. _
It's on - ly love, _ ba - by.
Turner: (Oh, yeah.)
Gtr. 2
Oh, yeah.
Oo, _ ba - by, ba - by, it's on - ly

F5
love, love, love.
3. When your world is
(Love, love, love. …world is)
1
13
12
(12)
10

Verse

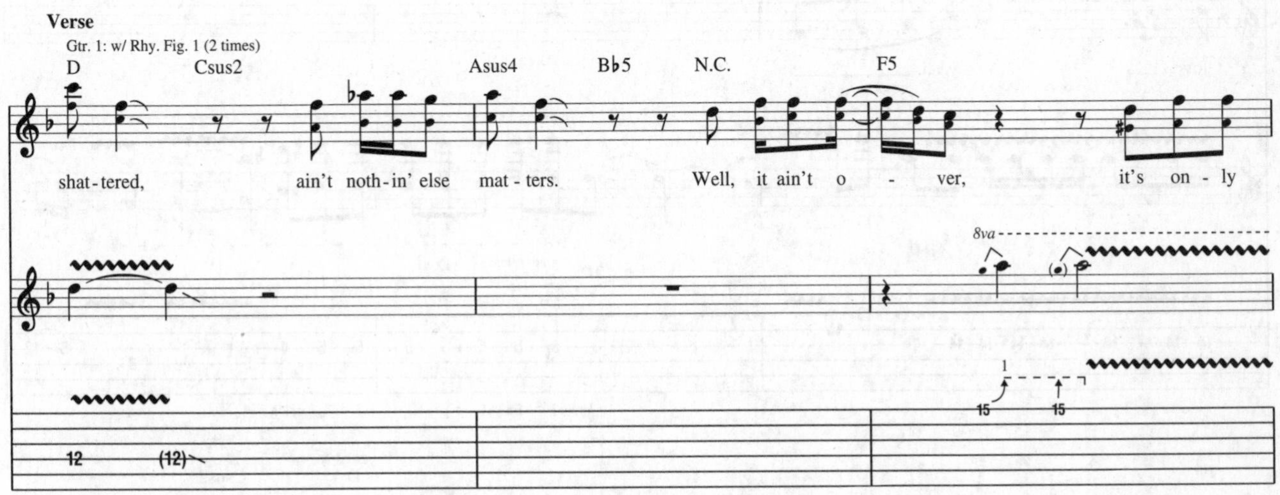
Gtr. 1: w/ Rhy. Fig. 1 (2 times)
D
Csus2
Asus4
B♭5
N.C.
F5
shat-tered, ain't noth-in' else mat-ters. Well, it ain't o - ver, it's on-ly
8va
1
15
12
(12)

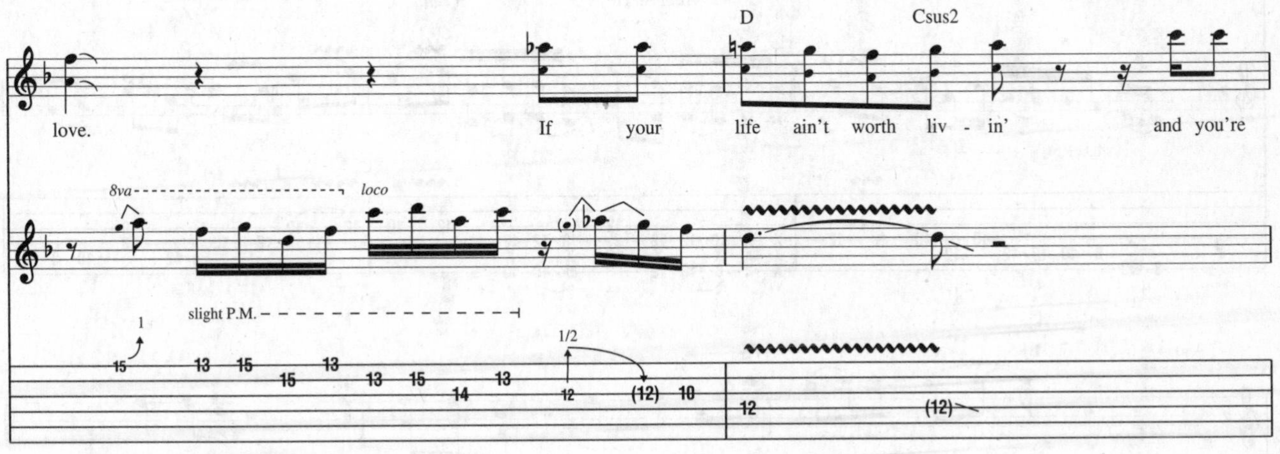
D
Csus2
love. If your life ain't worth liv - in' and you're
8va
loco
slight P.M.
1
1/2
15
13
14
12
(12)
10

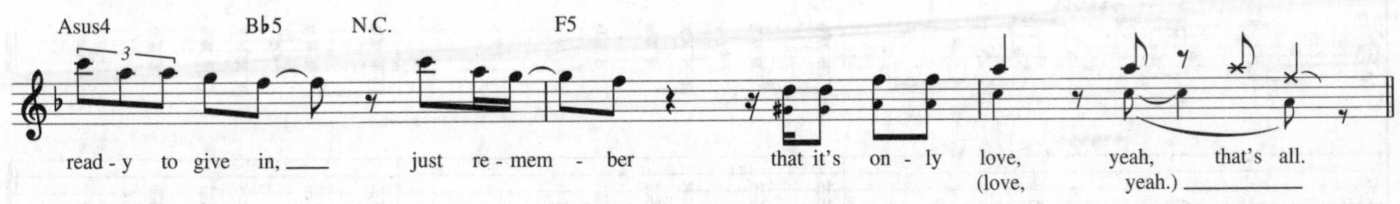
Asus4
B♭5
N.C.
F5
3
read - y to give in, just re - mem - ber that it's on - ly love, yeah, that's all.
(love, yeah.)

Outro-Guitar Solo
Gtr. 1: w/ Rhy. Fig. 1 (3 times)
D
Csus2
Asus4
B♭5
N.C.
F5
Turner: Oh, love, love, yeah.
hold bend
let ring
8va
loco
P.H.
grad. release
pitch: F F♮ E D♯ B A
Adams: Hey. Yeah.
slight P.M.
Yeah, it ain't eas - y, ba - by. It's on - ly love and that's all.

Jack and Diane

Words and Music by John Mellencamp

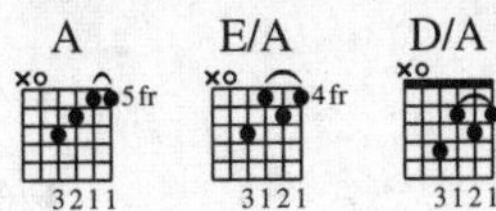

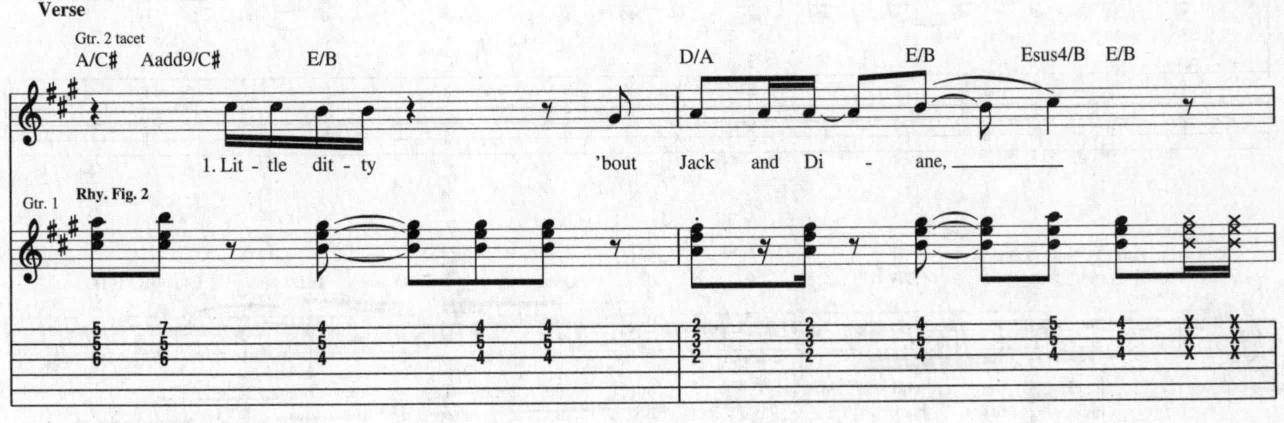

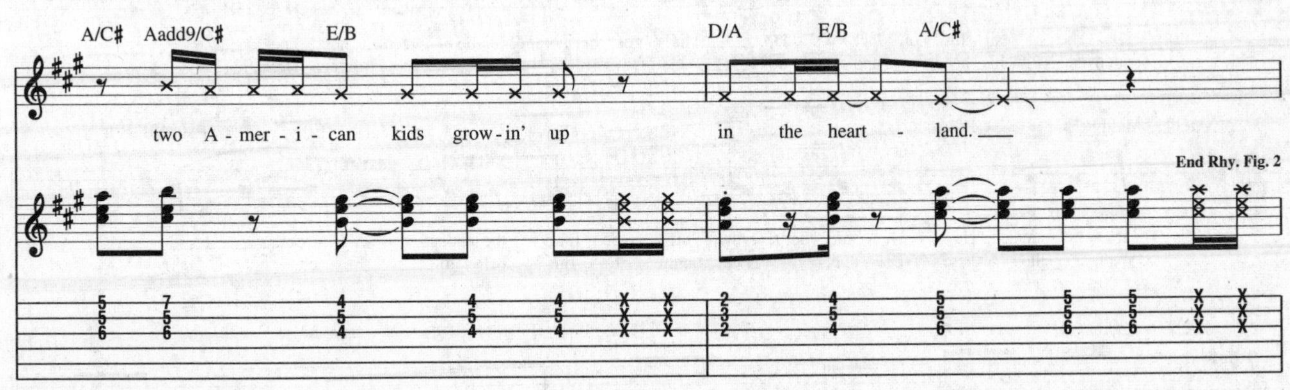

Gtr. 1: w/ Rhy. Fig. 2
A/C♯ Aadd9/C♯ E/B D/A E/B Esus4/B E/B
Jack, he's gon - na be a foot - ball star.
A/C♯ Aadd9/C♯ E/B D/A E/B A/C♯
Di - ane's deb - u - tante back seat of Jack - y's car.
Interlude
A D/A A E/A D/A E/A C♯m/A E/A
Rhy. Fig. 3
Gtr. 1
A D/A A E/A D/A A
End Rhy. Fig. 3
Verse
Gtr. 1: w/ Rhy. Fig. 2 (2 times)
A/C♯ Aadd/C♯ E/B D/A E/B Esus4/B E/B
Snack - in' on a chil - i dog out - side the Tast - ee - Freez;
Jack, he sits back, col - lects his thoughts for the mo - ment,
A/C♯ Aadd9/C♯ E/B D/A E/B A/C♯
Di - ane sit - tin' on Jack - y's lap, he's got his hands be - tween her knees.
scratch - es his head and does his best James Dean.
A/C♯ Aadd9/C♯ E/B D/A E/B Esus4/B E/B
Jack, he say, "Hey, Di - ane let's run off be - hind the shad - y trees.
"Well, then there Di - ane, we ought to run off to the cit - y."
A/C♯ Aadd9/C♯ E/B D/A E/B A/C♯
Drib - ble off those Bob - by Brooks. let me do what I please." Say - in',
Di - ane says, "Ba - by, you ain't miss - in' a thing." But Jack, he say, ah,

Chorus
Gtr. 1: w/ Rhy. Fig. 2 (1st 2 meas., 3 times)
A/C♯ Aadd9/C♯ E/B D/A E/B Esus4/B E/B A/C♯ Aadd9/C♯ E/B
"Oh, yeah, life goes on long af - ter the thrill of
D/A E/B Esus4/B E/B A/C♯ Aadd9/C♯ E/B D/A E/B Esus4/B E/B
liv - in' is gone." Say - in', "Oh, yeah, life goes on
Gtr. 1: w/ Rhy. Fig. 2 (last 2 meas.)
A/C♯ Aadd9/C♯ E/B
long af - ter the thrill of
1.
D/A E/B A/C♯
liv - in' is gone." Now, walk on.
Interlude
Gtrs. 1 & 2: w/ Rhy. Figs. 1 & 1A (2 times)
8
2.
D/A E/B A/C♯
liv - in' is gone.
Gtr. 1 tacet
N.C.
Gtr. 1
Bridge
N.C.
Oh, let it rock, let it roll. Let the Bi - ble belt come and
save my soul. Hold on to six - teen as long as you can.
Chang - es come a - round real soon, make us wom - en and men.
Interlude
(Drums)
4
Chorus
Gtr. 1: w/ Rhy. Fig. 3
4
Gtr. 1: w/ Rhy. Fig. 2 (1st 2 meas., 3 times)
A/C♯ Aadd9/C♯ E/B D/A E/B Esus4/B E/B
Oh, yeah, life goes on

A/C♯ Aadd9/C♯ E/B D/A E/B Esus4/B E/B A/C♯ Aadd9/C♯ E/B
long af - ter the thrill of liv - in' is gone.
Oh, yeah, I say life
Gtr. 1: w/ Rhy. Fig. 2 (last 2 meas.)
D/A E/B Esus4/B E/B A/C♯ Aadd9/C♯ E/B D/A E/B A/C♯
goes on long af - ter the thrill of liv - in' is gone.
Outro
A E/A D/A E/A
A lit - tle dit - ty 'bout Jack and Di - ane.
Gtr. 1
mp
let ring
A E/A D/A A A E/A
Gtr. 2
two A - mer - i - can kids do - in' best they can.
Gtr. 1
let ring
mf
Play 4 times & fade
A E/A A E/A D/A
p mf
p mf

Jump, Jive an' Wail

Words and Music by Louis Prima

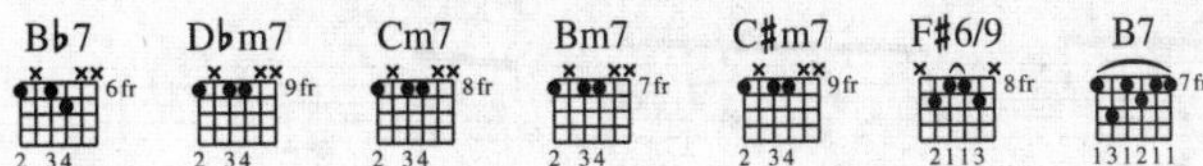

Fast Rockabilly Swing ♩ = 208

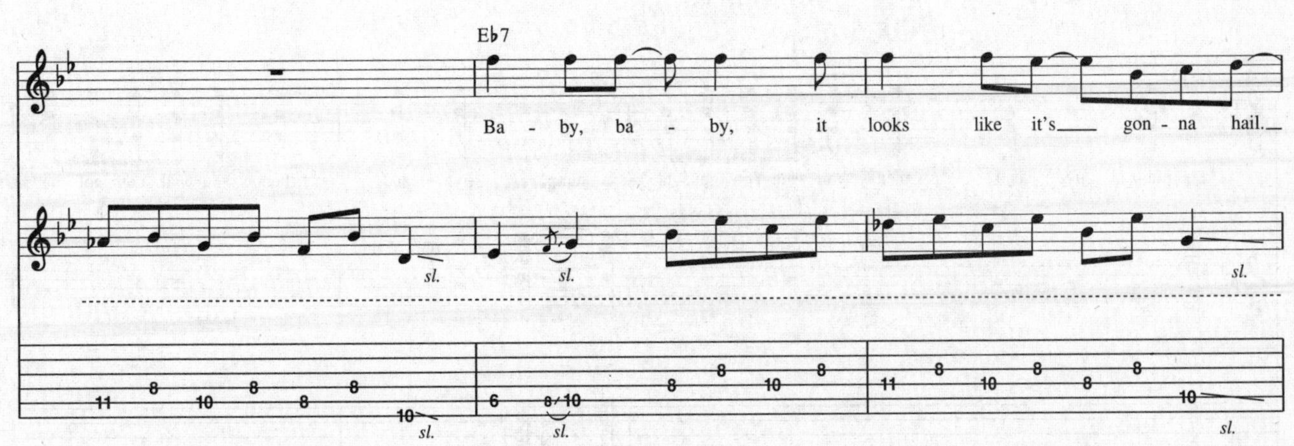

B♭7
Cm7
You bet - ter come in - side; let me
sl.
F7
B♭
teach you how to jive and wail.
Oh, you got - ta
(end Rhy. Fig. 1)
Chorus
w/Rhy. Fig. 1 (1st 8 bars only)
B♭9
jump, jive and then you wail. You got - ta jump, jive and then you wail. You got - ta
*Gtr. II
mf
w/light dist.
*Play w/slight variations ad lib on repeat.
E♭13
jump, jive and then you wail. You got - ta jump, jive and then you wail. You got - ta
*1/2
trem. bar
(Gtr. II out)
*Depress bar before striking chord.

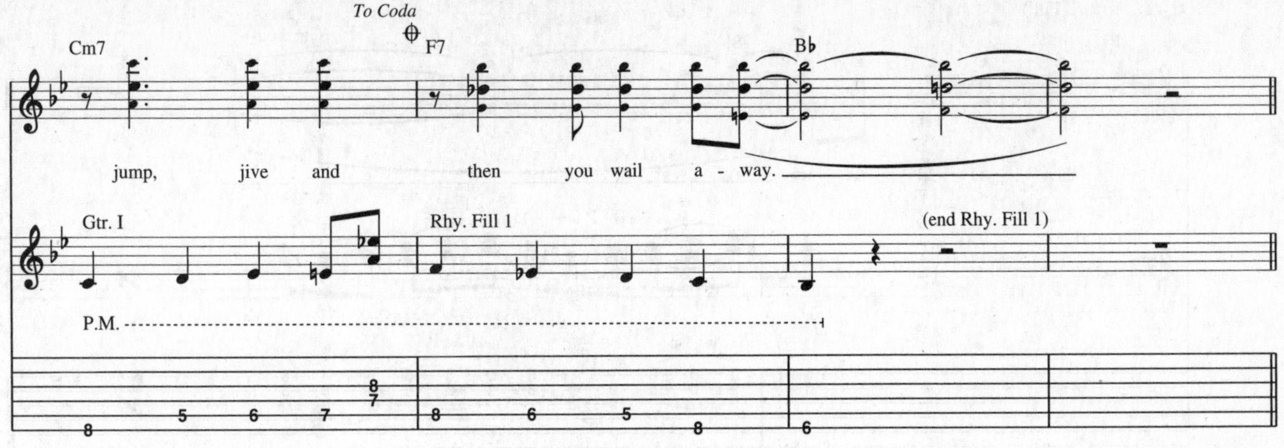
To Coda
Cm7
F7
B♭
jump, jive and then you wail a - way.
Gtr. I
Rhy. Fill 1
(end Rhy. Fill 1)
P.M.
8 5 6 7 8 7 8 6 5 8 6

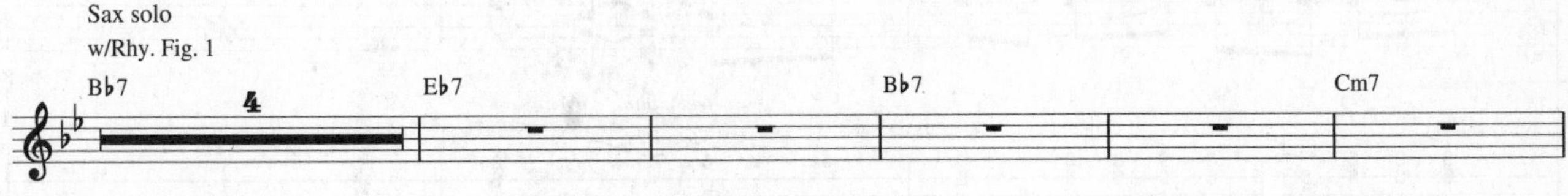
Sax solo
w/Rhy. Fig. 1
B♭7
4
E♭7
B♭7
Cm7

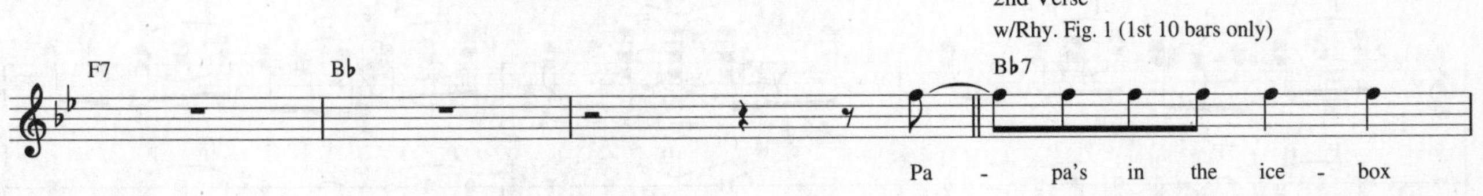
F7
B♭
2nd Verse
w/Rhy. Fig. 1 (1st 10 bars only)
B♭7
Pa - pa's in the ice - box

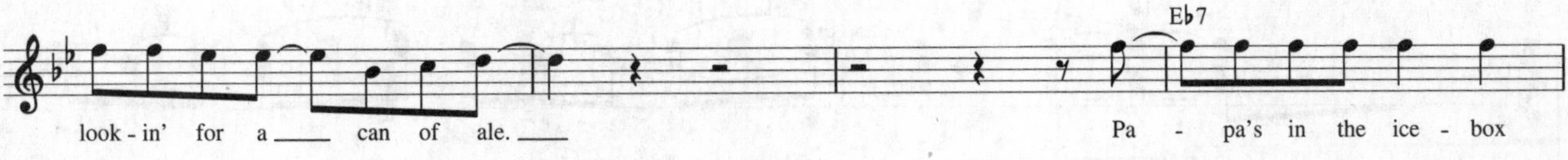
E♭7
look - in' for a can of ale.
Pa - pa's in the ice - box

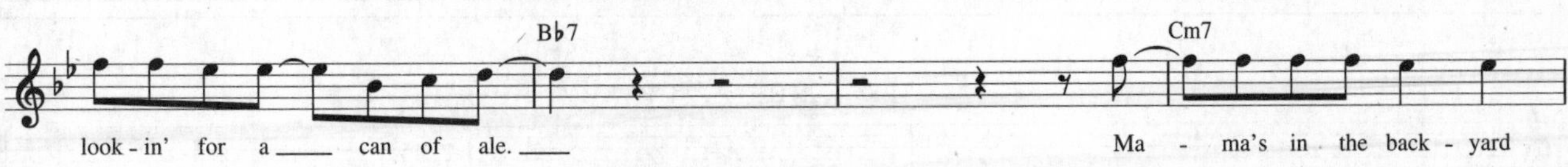
B♭7
Cm7
look - in' for a can of ale.
Ma - ma's in the back - yard

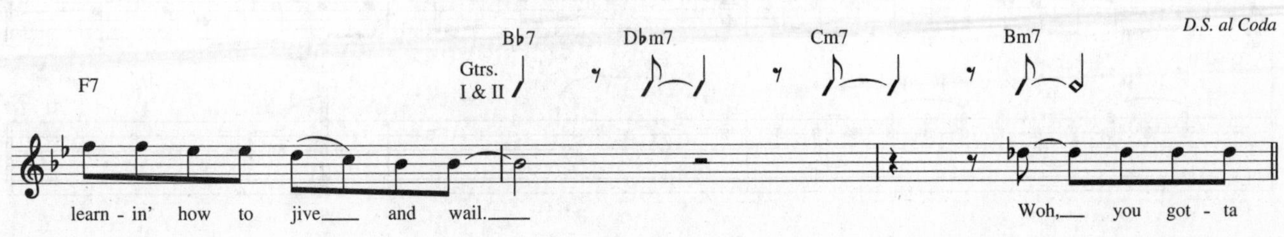
D.S. al Coda
F7
Gtrs. I & II
B♭7
D♭m7
Cm7
Bm7
learn - in' how to jive and wail.
Woh, you got - ta

Coda
w/Rhy. Fill 1
F7
B♭
(Gtr. I out)
then you wail a - way.
Gtr. II
Guitar Solo
B♭7
trem. bar
1/2
E♭7
B♭7
Cm7
F7
B♭
N.C.
Full
1/2
sl.
A

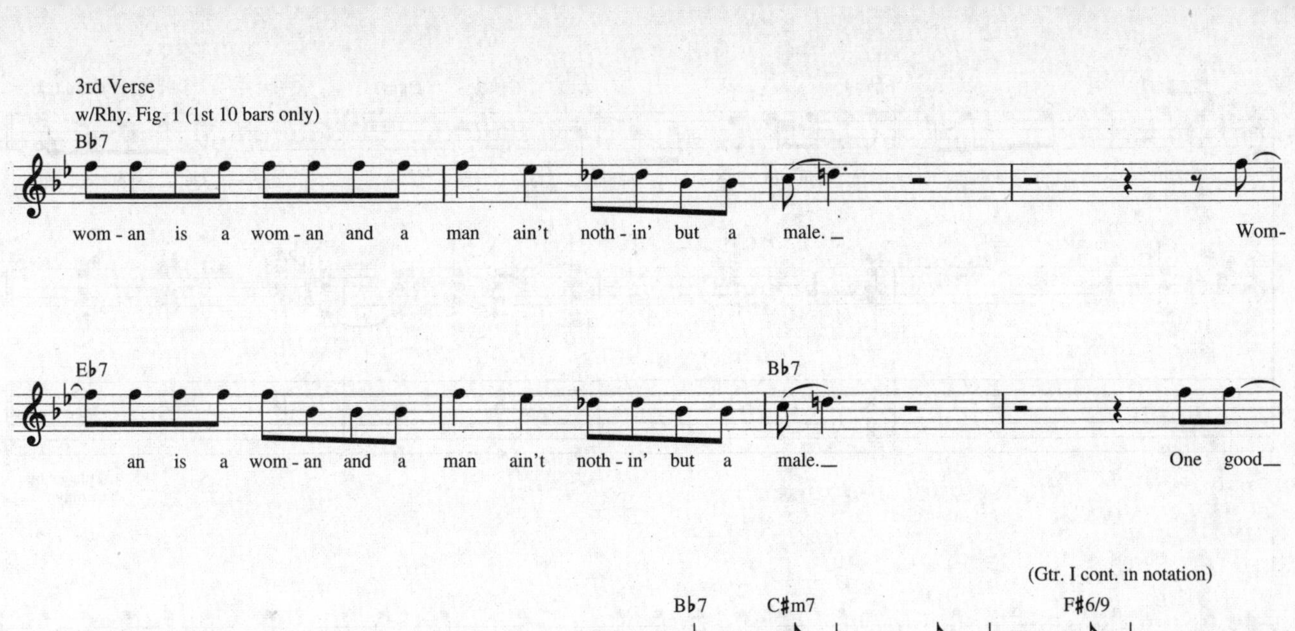
3rd Verse
w/Rhy. Fig. 1 (1st 10 bars only)
B♭7
wom - an is a wom - an and a man ain't noth - in' but a male.
Wom-
E♭7
B♭7
an is a wom - an and a man ain't noth - in' but a male.
One good

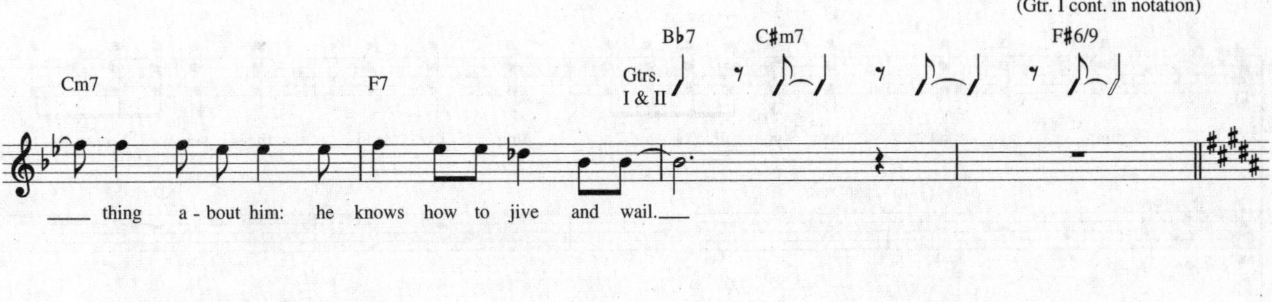
(Gtr. I cont. in notation)
Cm7
F7
Gtrs. I & II
B♭7
C♯m7
F♯6/9
thing a - bout him: he knows how to jive and wail.

4th Verse
B7
Gtr. II
(Gtr. II out)
Jack and Jill went up the hill to get a pail.
Rhy. Fig. 2 (Gtr. I)
sl.
P.M.

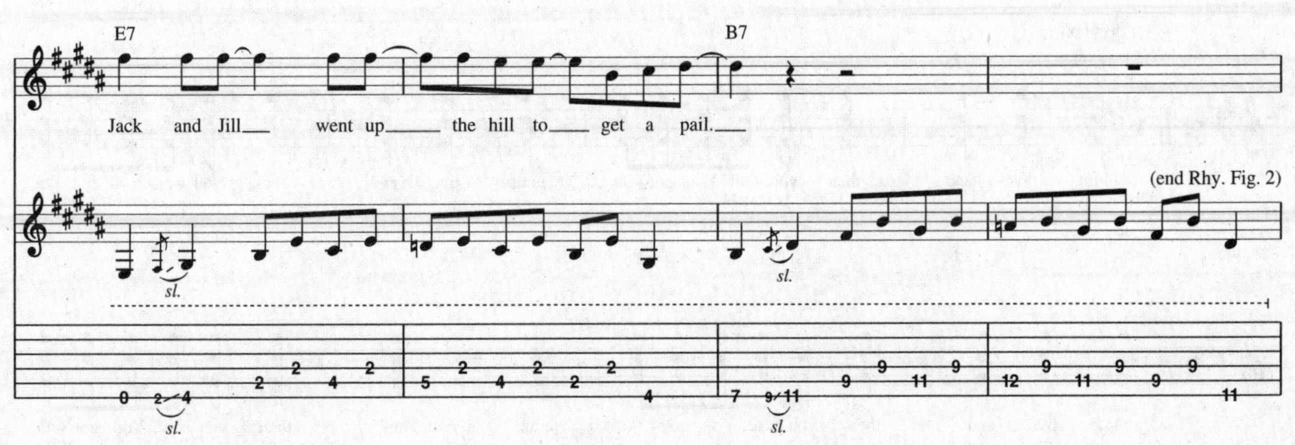
E7
B7
Jack and Jill went up the hill to get a pail.
(end Rhy. Fig. 2)
sl.

C#m7
F#7#9
A13
G#13
C#m7
G7#9
F#9
*F#7#9/C#
Jill stayed up; she wants to learn how to jive and wail.
Oh, you got - ta
*C# played by bass only.
Chorus
Tacet
B7
jump, jive and then you wail. You got - ta jump, jive and then you wail. You got - ta
(Gtr. I out)
jump, jive and then you wail. You got - ta jump, jive and then you wail. You got - ta
jump, jive and then you wail a - way. You got - ta
Chorus/Outro
w/Rhy. Fig. 2
B7
jump, jive and then you wail. You got - ta jump, jive and then you wail. You got - ta
E7
B7
jump, jive and then you wail. You got - ta jump, jive and then you wail. You got - ta

1.
C#m7
F#7
B7
A7
G#7
Dm7
C#m7
G7
F#7
jump, jive and then you wail a - way.
Oh, you got - ta.
Gtr. I
P.M.
2.
Begin fade
N.C.
B
You got - ta jump, jive and...
Jump, jive and...
E
Jump, jive and...
B
Jump, jive and...
Fade out

Killing Floor

Words and Music by Chester Burnett

Gtr 2: Tune down 1 step:
(low to high) D–G–C–F–A–D

Intro

Moderately ♩ = 104

**A♭7
*Gtr. 1 (clean)
f
sim.

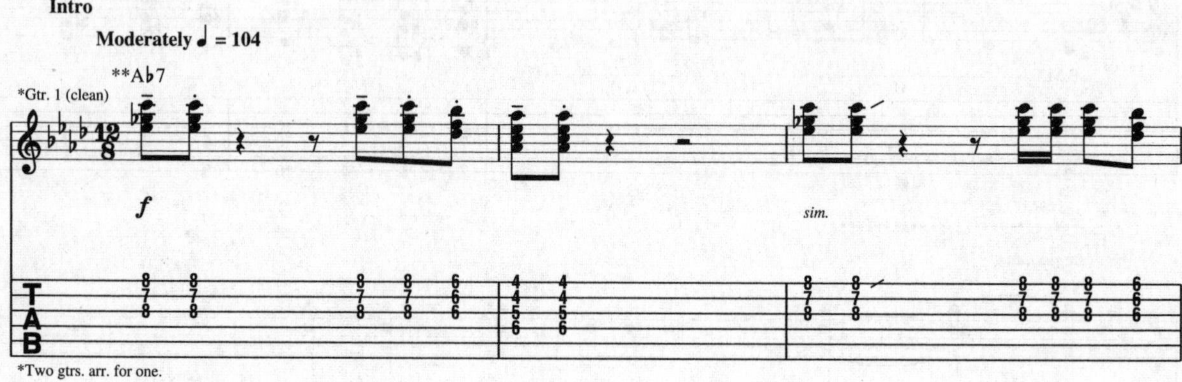

*Two gtrs. arr. for one.
**Chord symbols reflect basic harmony.

Verse

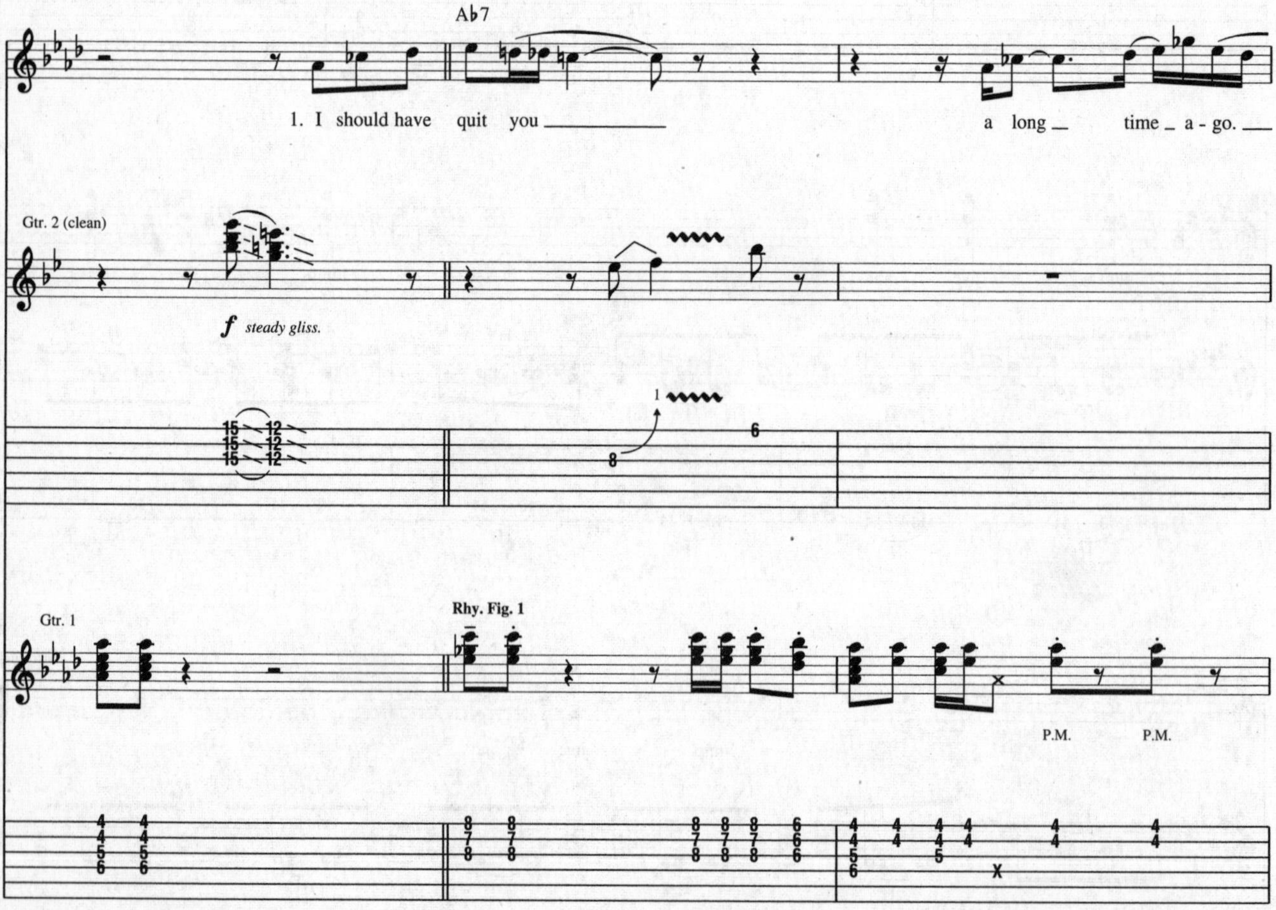

A♭7
1. I should have quit you ___ a long _ time _ a - go. _
Gtr. 2 (clean)
f steady gliss.
Gtr. 1
Rhy. Fig. 1
P.M.
P.M.

D♭7

I should have quit you, ba - by,

sim.

A♭7

a long time a - go.

I should have

Eb9
Db9
Ab7
quit you, ba - by,
and went on to Mex - i - co.
let ring
let ring
Verse
Gtr. 1: w/ Rhy. Fig. 1 (1st 8 meas.)
Ab7
2. If I had a fol - lowed my first mind,
End Rhy. Fig. 1
Db7
if I had a fol - lowed

Ab7
my first mind
I
Eb9
Db9
Ab7
would have been gone, yeah,
my sec - ond time.
Gtr. 2
Gtr. 1
Guitar Solo
Ab7
Yeah.
Rhy. Fig. 2

D♭7
grad. bend
End Rhy. Fig. 2
A♭7
E♭7
D♭7
grad. bend
A♭7

Verse

Gtr. 1: w/ Rhy. Fig. 1

E♭7 A♭7

3. I should have went on __ when my friends come from Mex - i - co and

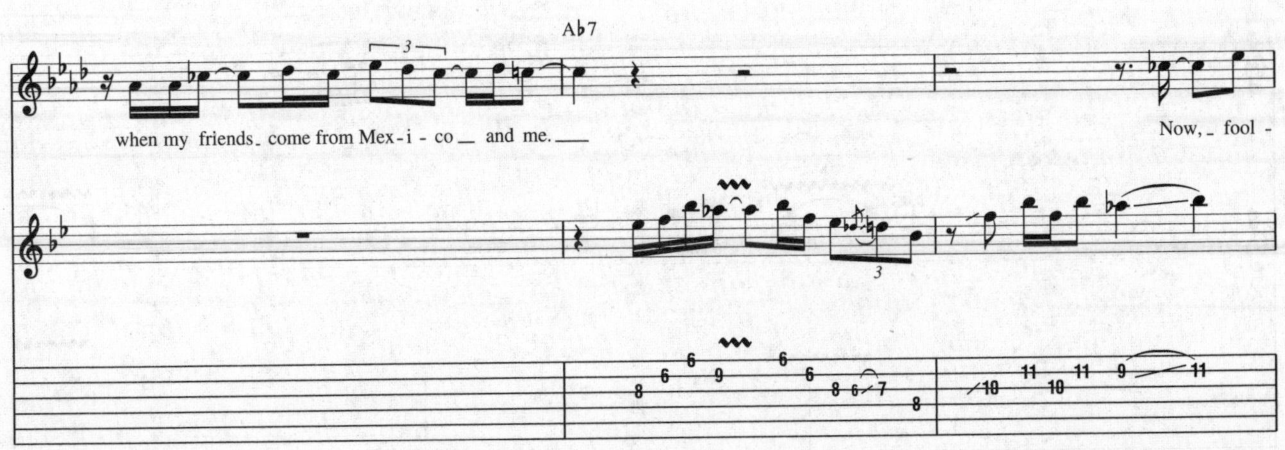

Eb9
Db9
Ab7
ing 'round with you, dar - ling,
you got me on the kill-ing floor.

Verse
Gtr. 1: w/ Rhy. Fig. 1
Eb7
Ab7
4. I know
I should have been gone.

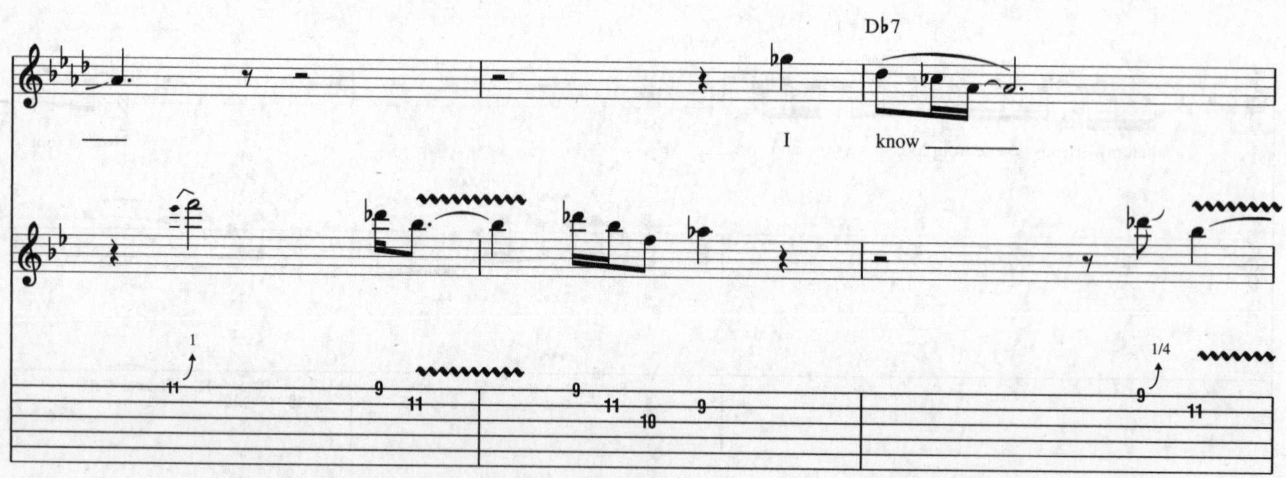
Db7
I know

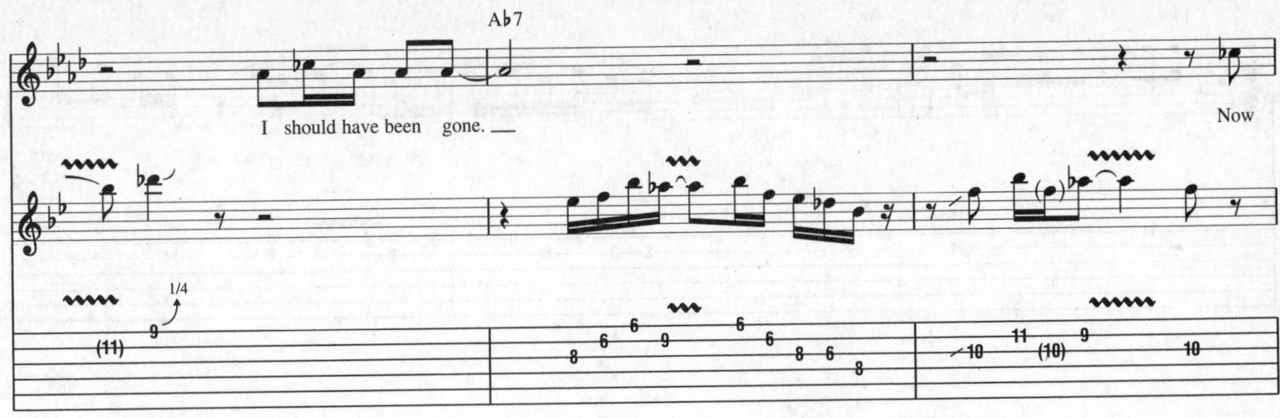

Guitar Solo

Gtr. 2: w/ Rhy. Fig. 1

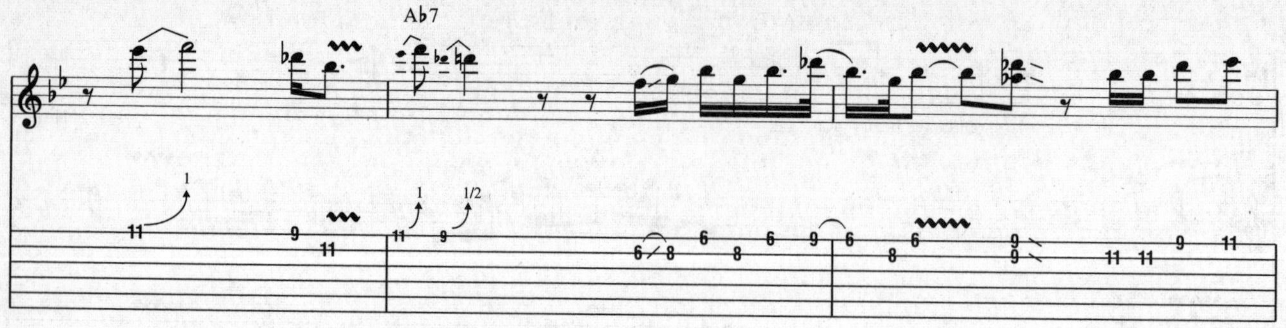

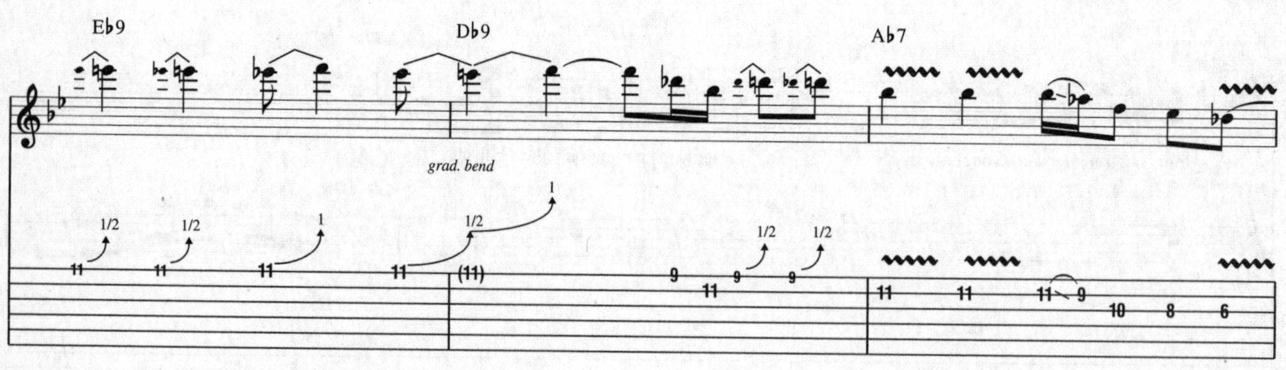

Gtr. 2: w/ Rhy. Fig. 2

Begin fade

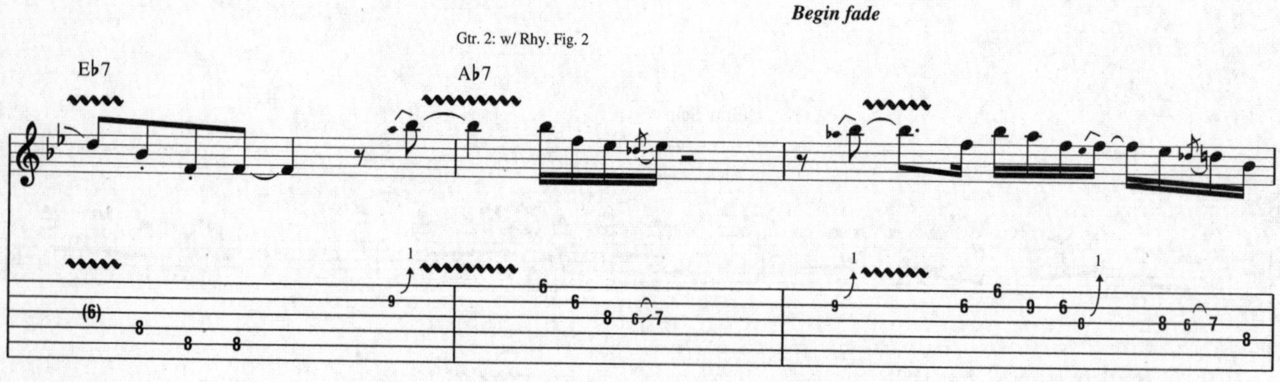

Fade out

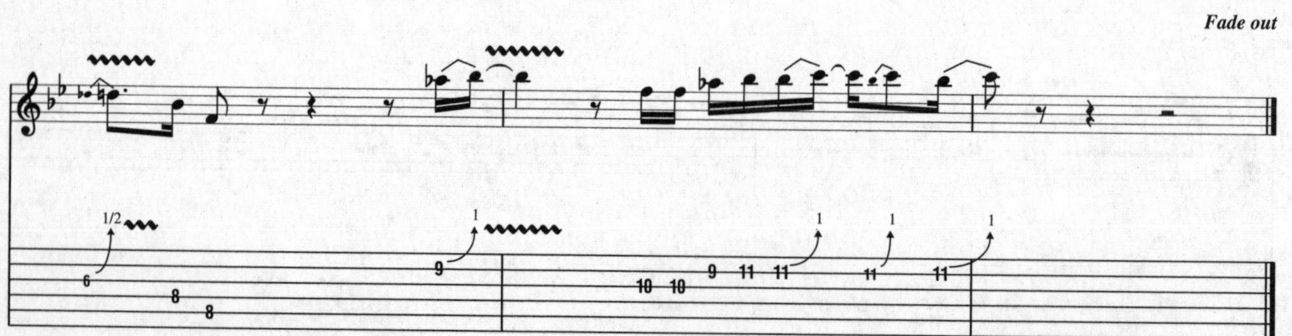

La Bamba

By Ritchie Valens

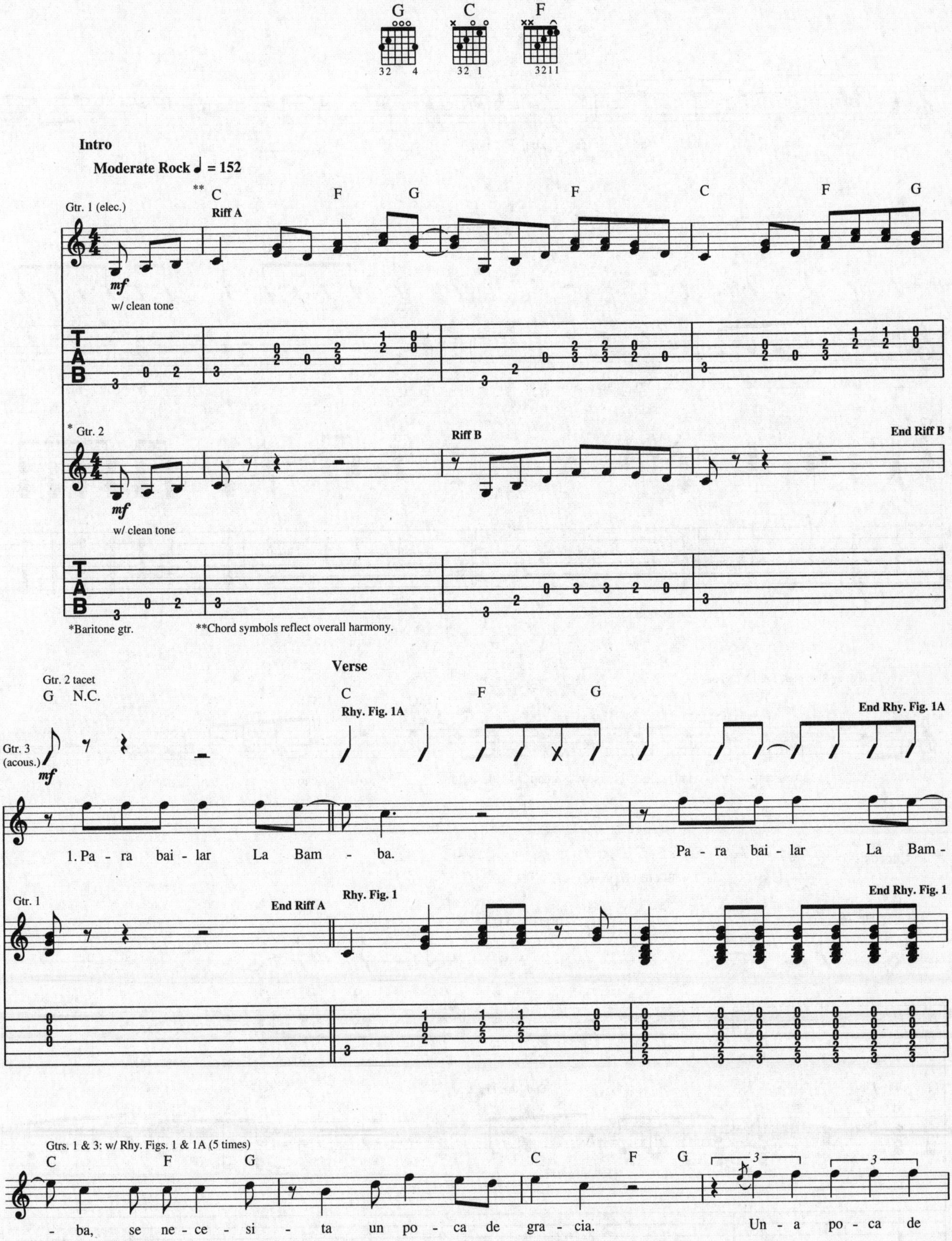

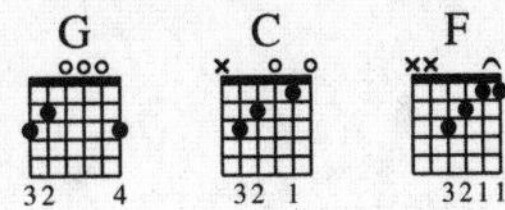

Intro

Moderate Rock ♩ = 152

** C F G F C F G

Gtr. 1 (elec.)

Riff A

mf

w/ clean tone

* Gtr. 2

Riff B

End Riff B

mf

w/ clean tone

*Baritone gtr.

**Chord symbols reflect overall harmony.

Gtr. 2 tacet

G N.C.

Verse

C F G

Rhy. Fig. 1A

End Rhy. Fig. 1A

Gtr. 3 (acous.)

mf

1. Pa - ra bai - lar La Bam - ba. Pa - ra bai - lar La Bam -

Gtr. 1

End Riff A

Rhy. Fig. 1

End Rhy. Fig. 1

Gtrs. 1 & 3: w/ Rhy. Figs. 1 & 1A (5 times)

C F G C F G

- ba, se ne - ce - si - ta un po - ca de gra - cia. Un - a po - ca de

C F G C F G
gra - cia, pa'ra mi pa'ra ti y ar - ri - ba, ar - ri - ba.

C F G
Y ar - ri - ba, ar - ri - ba, por ti se re, por ti se re,

Verse
C F G N.C. C F G
Gtr. 3
por ti se re. 2. Yo no soy mar - i - ne - ro. Yo no soy mar - i -
Gtr. 1

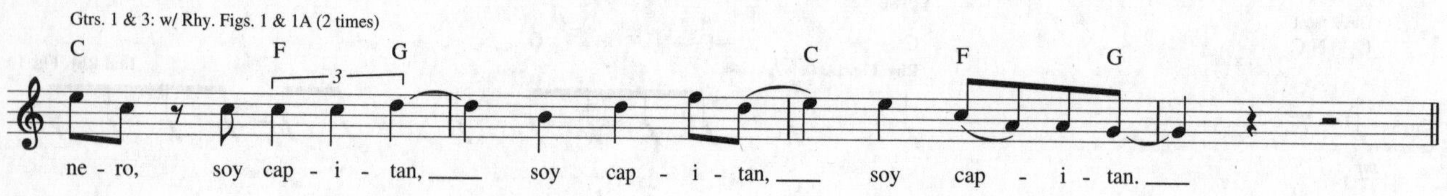
Gtrs. 1 & 3: w/ Rhy. Figs. 1 & 1A (2 times)
C F G C F G
ne - ro, soy cap - i - tan, soy cap - i - tan, soy cap - i - tan.

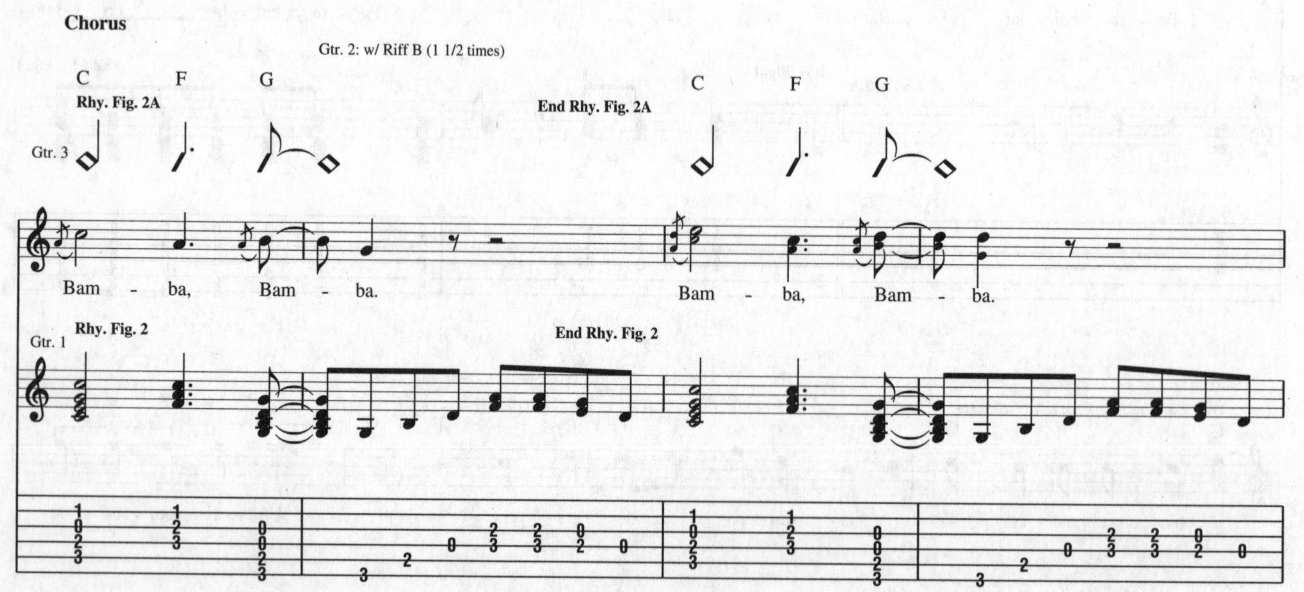
Chorus
Gtr. 2: w/ Riff B (1 1/2 times)
C F G C F G
Rhy. Fig. 2A
End Rhy. Fig. 2A
Gtr. 3
Bam - ba, Bam - ba. Bam - ba, Bam - ba.
Rhy. Fig. 2
End Rhy. Fig. 2
Gtr. 1

C F G C F G N.C.
Rhy. Fill 1
End Rhy. Fill 1
Gtr. 3
Bam - ba, Bam - ba. B-Bam - ba. Hmm. 3. Pa - ra bai - lar La Bam-
Gtr. 1
Gtr. 2
Riff C
End Riff C
Verse
Gtrs. 1 & 3: w/ Rhy. Figs. 1 & 1A (4 times)
Gtr. 2 tacet
C F G C F G
- ba. Pa - ra bai - lar La Bam - ba, si ne - ce - si - ta un po - ca de
C F G C F G
gra - cia. Un - a po - ca de gra - cia, pa'ra mi pa'ra ti y ar - ri - ba ar - ri
Guitar Solo
Gtrs. 1 & 3: w/ Rhy. Figs. 1 & 1A (10 times)
C F G C F G C F G
ba.
Gtr. 4 (elec.)
f w/ clean tone

C
F
G
Interlude
Gtr. 1: w/ Riff A
Gtr. 2: w/ Riff B, 1st meas.
Gtrs. 4 & 5 tacet
Gtr. 2: w/ Riff C
Gtr. 3: w/ Rhy. Fill 1
N.C.
4. Pa - ra bai - lar La Bam -
Gtr. 4
Gtr. 5 (elec.)
divisi
mf
w/ clean tone

*Nylon str. (Mexican Folk instruments are used for this section, arr. here for standard gtrs.)

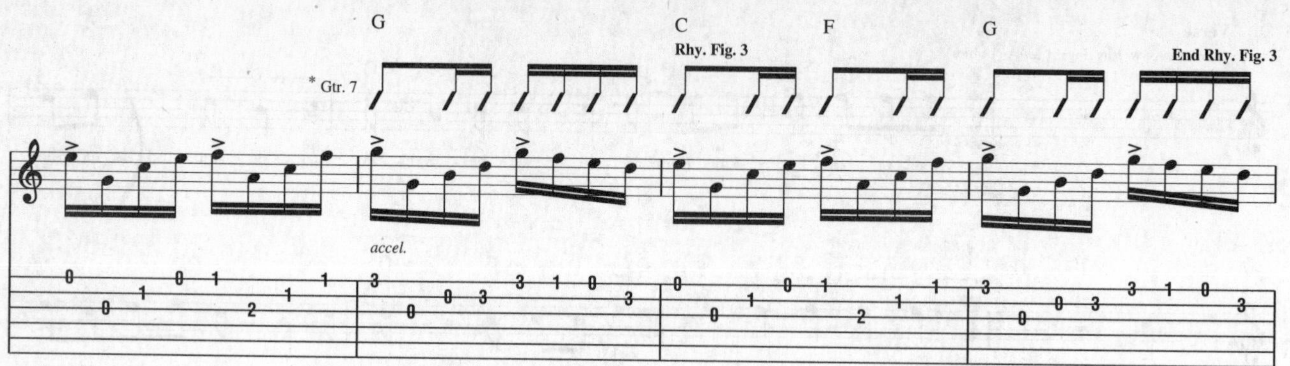

*Nylon str. (Mexican Folk instruments are used for this section, arr. here for standard gtrs.)

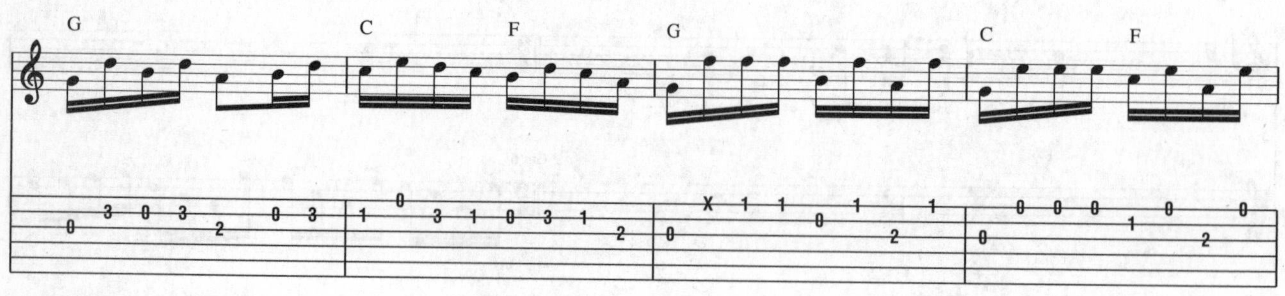

Begin fade
G
C
F
G
C
F
Fade out

Last Resort

Words and Music by Papa Roach

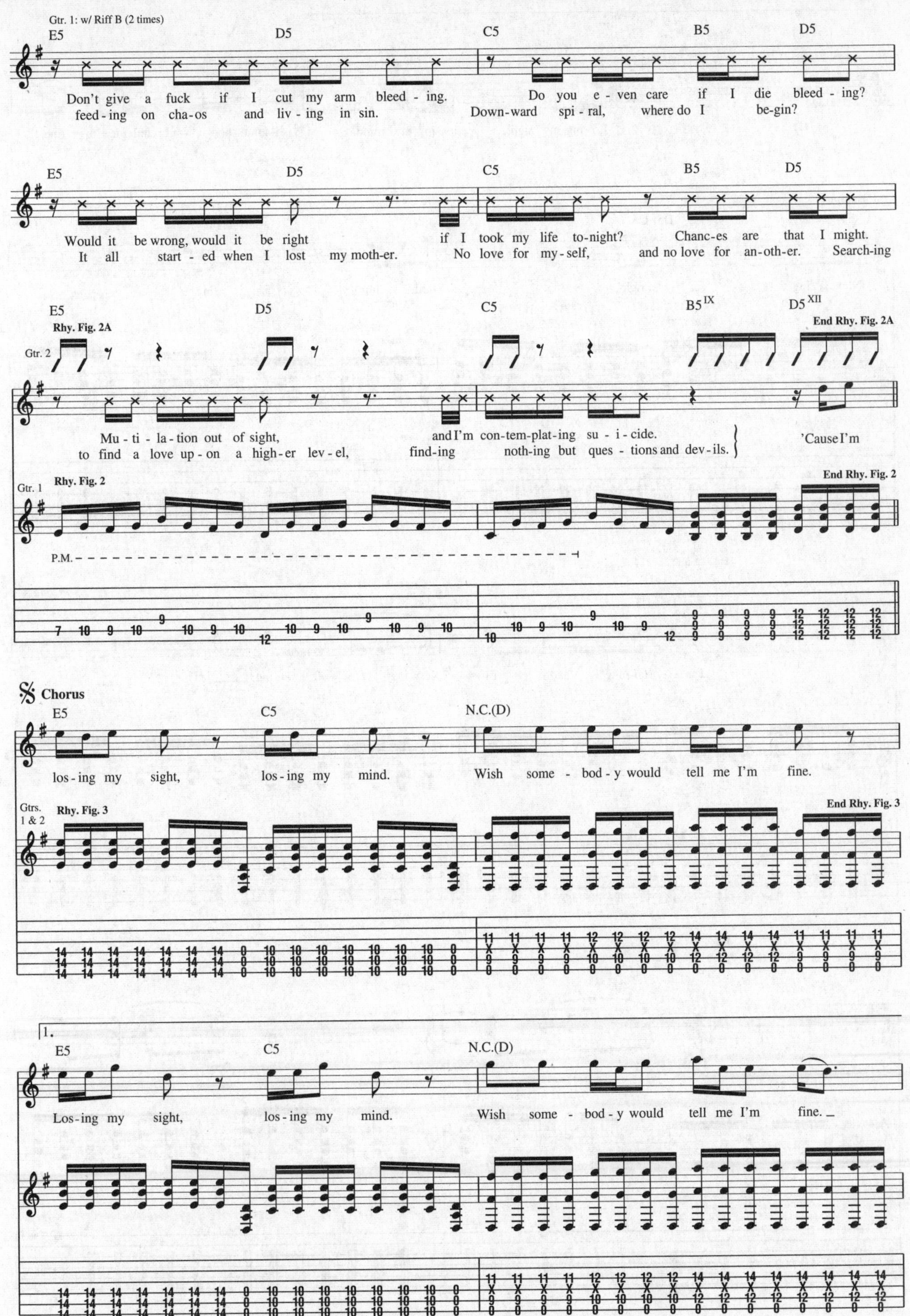

Gtr. 1: w/ Riff B (2 times)
E5
D5
C5
B5
D5
Don't give a fuck if I cut my arm bleed - ing. Do you e - ven care if I die bleed - ing?
feed - ing on cha - os and liv - ing in sin. Down - ward spi - ral, where do I be - gin?
Would it be wrong, would it be right if I took my life to - night? Chanc - es are that I might.
It all start - ed when I lost my moth - er. No love for my - self, and no love for an - oth - er. Search - ing
Rhy. Fig. 2A
Gtr. 2
End Rhy. Fig. 2A
Mu - ti - la - tion out of sight, and I'm con - tem - plat - ing su - i - cide.
to find a love up - on a high - er lev - el, find - ing noth - ing but ques - tions and dev - ils.
'Cause I'm
Gtr. 1
Rhy. Fig. 2
End Rhy. Fig. 2
P.M.
Chorus
N.C.(D)
los - ing my sight, los - ing my mind. Wish some - bod - y would tell me I'm fine.
Gtrs. 1 & 2
Rhy. Fig. 3
End Rhy. Fig. 3
1.
Los - ing my sight, los - ing my mind. Wish some - bod - y would tell me I'm fine.

2.
Gtr. 1: w/ Riff A
Gtr. 2: w/ Rhy. Fig. 1
Gtrs. 1 & 2: w/ Rhy. Fig. 3
E5 D5 C5 B5 D5 E5 C5 N.C.(D)
Los-ing my sight, los-ing my mind. Wish some-bod-y would tell me I'm fine.
Bridge
E5 D5 C5 G5 B5 D5
Noth-ing's al-right, noth-ing is fine.
Gtrs. 1 & 2
E5 D5 C5 D5 G5 B5
To Coda
I'm run-ning and I'm cry-ing.
E5 G5 C5 B5 D5
I'm cry-ing. I'm cry-ing.

E5 G5 C5 B5
I'm cry - ing. I'm cry - ing.
Gtrs. 1 & 2: w/ Rhy. Fig. 1 (4 times)
E5 D5 C5 B5 D5 E5 D5
Whispered: I can't go on liv - ing
C5 B5 D5 E5 D5 C5 B5 D5
this way. Cut my life in - to piec - es, this is my last re - sort.
E5 D5 C5 B5 D5
Suf - fo - ca - tion, no breath - ing. Don't give a fuck if I cut my arm bleed - ing.
Verse
Gtr. 1: w/ Riff A
Gtr. 2: w/ Rhy. Fig. 1
E5 D5 C5 B5 D5
3. Would it be wrong, would it be right if I took my life to - night? Chanc - es are that I might.
D.S. (take 2nd ending) al Coda
Gtrs. 1 & 2: w/ Rhy. Fig. 2
E5 D5 C5 B5 D5
Mu - ti - la - tion out of sight, and I'm con - tem - plat - ing su - i - cide. 'Cause I'm
Coda
E5 C5 N.C.(D) E5 C5
Screamed: I can't go on liv - ing
Gtrs. 1 & 2

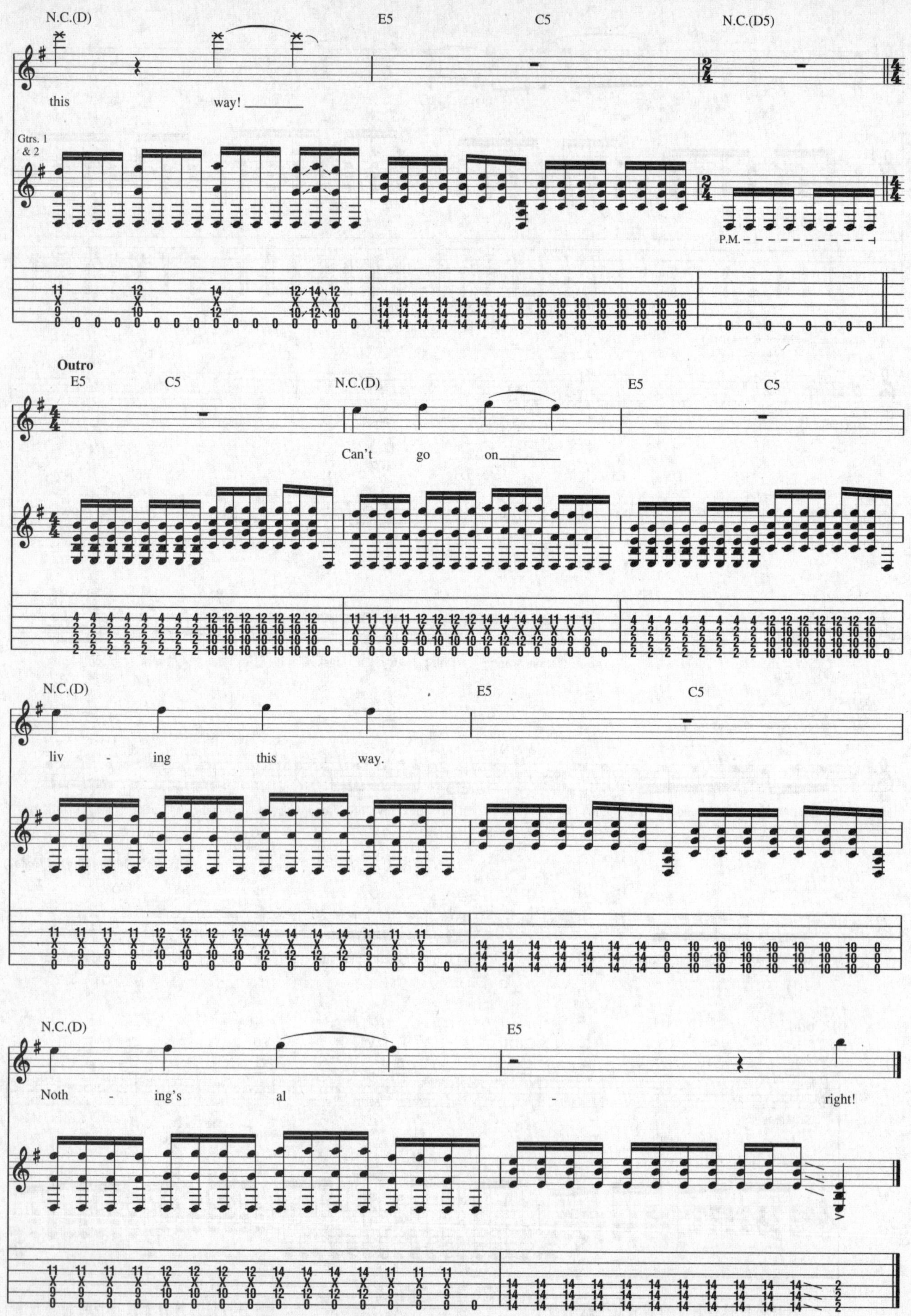
N.C.(D)
E5
C5
N.C.(D5)
this
way!
Gtrs. 1 & 2
P.M.
Outro
E5
C5
N.C.(D)
E5
C5
Can't
go
on
N.C.(D)
E5
C5
liv - ing this way.
N.C.(D)
E5
Noth - ing's al - right!

Lay It Down

Words and Music by Robbin Lantz Crosby, Juan Carlos Croucier, Warren DeMartini and Stephen E. Pearcy

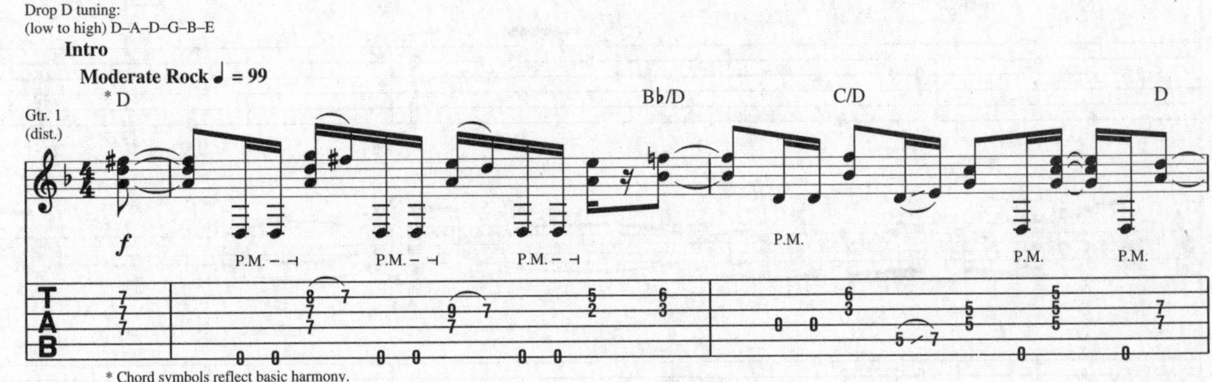

* Chord symbols reflect basic harmony.

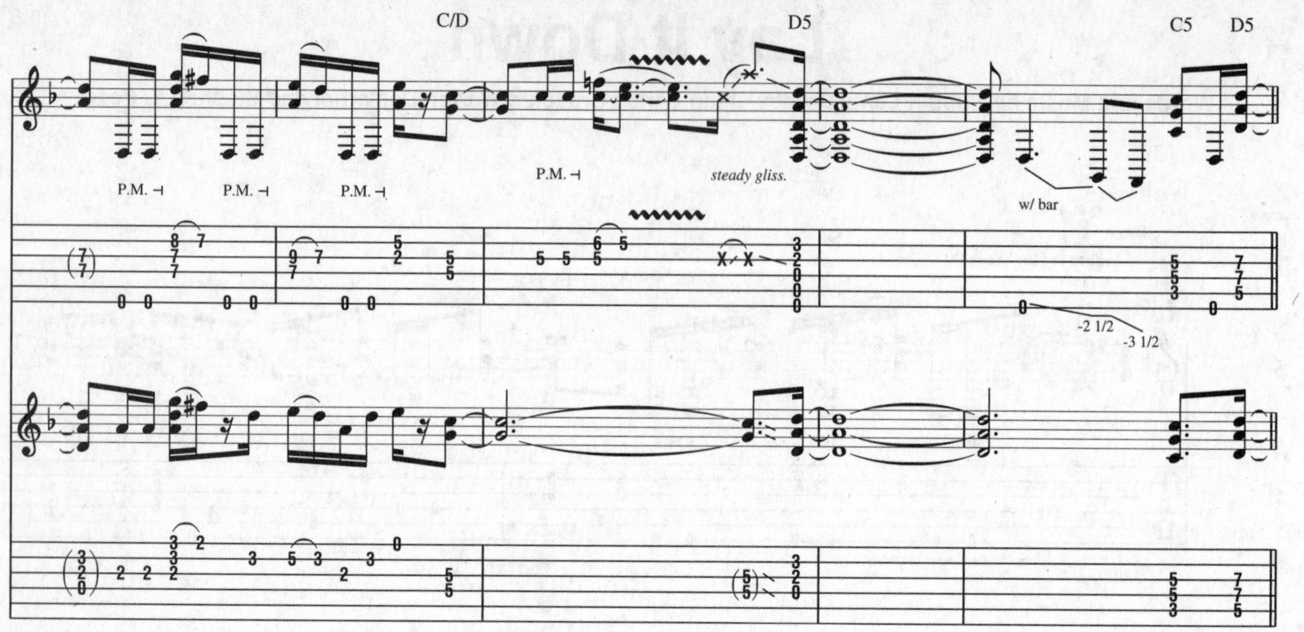

* Lower vol. knob about halfway to produce a slightly distorted tone.

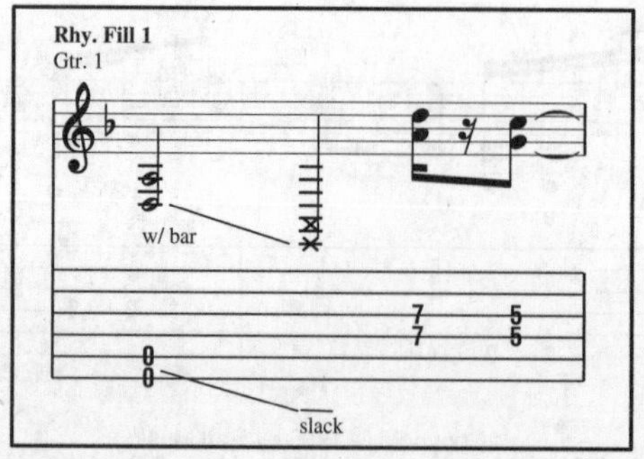

C/D
F5/C
C/D
D5
I know you don't real - ly care to see me.
I know that noth - ing's for free.
P.M.
C5/D
D5
I'm in - to to - tal af - fec - tion,
You take what's good for your pleas - ing,
P.M.

C/D F5/D C/D E5 F5

not be - ing scared if you nev - er please ___ me.
I'll take what's good for this cra - zy eve - ning.

* f

P.M. P.M.

* Turn vol. knob to 10.

Chorus

G5

You know you really want to lay ___ it down right now, _

P.M. P.M. P.M.

C5 D5 E5 F5

and how.

P.M.

G5 D

I know you real - ly want to lay it down, right now.

P.M. P.M. P.M.

Bb/D
C/D
D
Lay it down.
Lay it down.
Rhy. Fig. 1
End Rhy. Fig. 1
P.M.
Rhy. Fig. 1A
End Rhy. Fig. 1A
P.M.

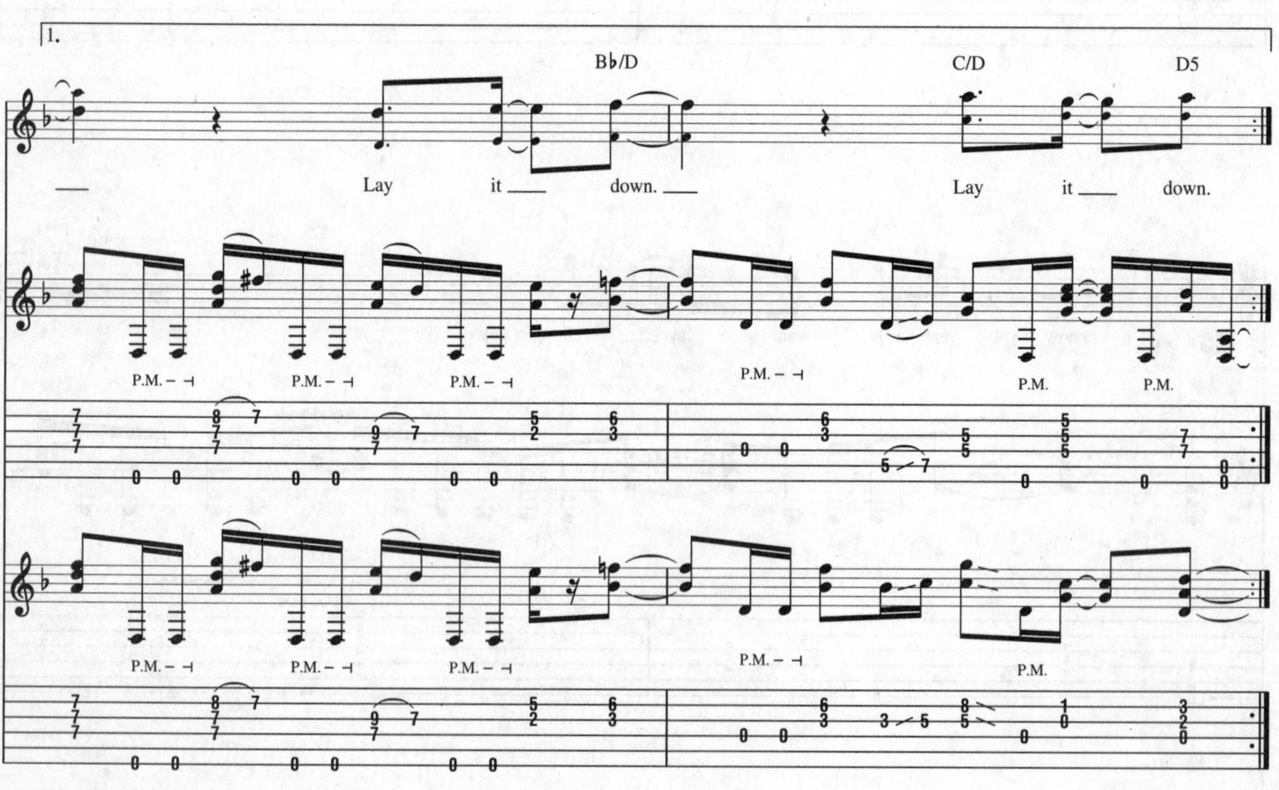
1.
Bb/D
C/D
D5
Lay it down.
Lay it down.
P.M.

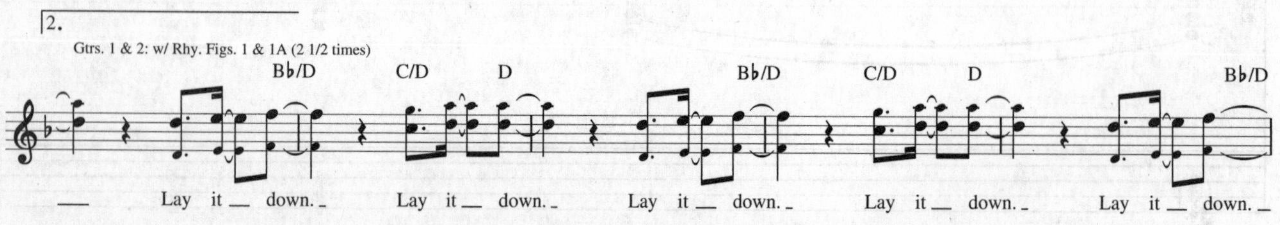
2.
Gtrs. 1 & 2: w/ Rhy. Figs. 1 & 1A (2 1/2 times)
Bb/D
C/D
D
Bb/D
C/D
D
Bb/D
Lay it down.
Lay it down.
Lay it down.
Lay it down.
Lay it down.

Bridge
C/D
A5
B♭5
G5
Lay it down.
Spoken: I know you only want romance.
Gtr. 1
P.M.
mf
Gtr. 2
P.M.
P.M.
* Lower vol. knob halfway.
Gtr. 2 tacet
C/B♭
C/G
B♭
C/B♭
C/G
B♭
I'll give you all that I can
if you give me just one chance
Gtr. 1
f
Guitar Solo
C/B♭
F5
G5
C
A♭/C
to prove my-self
and my love.
Gtr. 1
Gtr. 3
1/2
Gtr. 2
* Gtrs. 1 & 2
P.M.
P.M.
P.M.
* Composite arrangement

Bb5
C
Ab/C
P.M.
1/2
steady gliss.
6

D
Outro-Chorus
Gtrs. 1 & 2: w/ Rhy. Figs. 1 & 1A (3 1/2 times)
B♭/D
C/D
D
B♭/D
Lay it down.
Lay it down.
Lay it down.
tacet on repeat
w/ bar
grad. dive
C/D
D
B♭/D
Lay it down.
Lay it down.
Repeat & fade
Gtrs. 1 & 2: w/ Rhy. Fill 1
C/D
D
B♭/D
N.C.
D
Lay it down.
Lay it down.
Yeah, yeah, yeah.
P.M.
P.M.

Layla

Words and Music by Eric Clapton and Jim Gordon

Verse
C#m7
G#7
C#m7
C
D
1. What will you do when you get lone - ly?
No one wait - ing by your
E
E7
F#m
B
E
A
side.
You've been run - nin',
hid - in' much too long.
F#m
B
E
A
You know it's just your fool - ish pride.
Lay - la,
Chorus
Dm
N.C.(C)
Bb
C
D5
N.C.
Dm
N.C.(C)
Bb
got me on my knees. Lay - la,

C D5 N.C. Dm B♭ C D5 N.C. D5
beg - gin' dar - lin', please. Lay - la,
dar - lin' won't you ease my wor - ried
Dm (C) B♭ C N.C. (A) (C)
mind?
Verse
C♯m7 G♯7 C♯m7 C D
2. Tried to give you con - sol - a - tion,
3. Make the best of the sit - u - a - tion,
your old man had let you
before I fin - ally go in -
E E7 F♯m B E A
down.
sane.
Like a fool, I fall in love with you.
Please don't say we'll nev - er find a way.
*T = Thumb on ⑥

F♯m A E A
You turned my whole world up - side down.
Tell me all my love's in vain.
Lay - la,
Chorus
Dm N.C.(C) B♭ C Dm N.C. Dm N.C.(C) B♭
got me on my knees. Lay - la,
C D5 N.C. Dm N.C.(C) B♭ C D5 N.C. Dm
To Coda
beg - gin' dar - lin', please. Lay - la,
dar - lin', won't you ease my wor - ried
1.
N.C.(C) B♭ C N.C.(A) (C)
mind?

2.
N.C.(C)
B♭
C
D5
Dm
Dsus2
D5
mind?
Lay -

Chorus

Dm
N.C.(C)
B♭
C
D5
N.C.
Dm
N.C.(C)
B♭
la.
got me on my knees. Lay - la,

C
D5
N.C.
D5
(C)
B♭
C
Dm
N.C.
beg - gin' dar - lin, please. Lay - la,
dar - lin', won't you ease my wor - ried

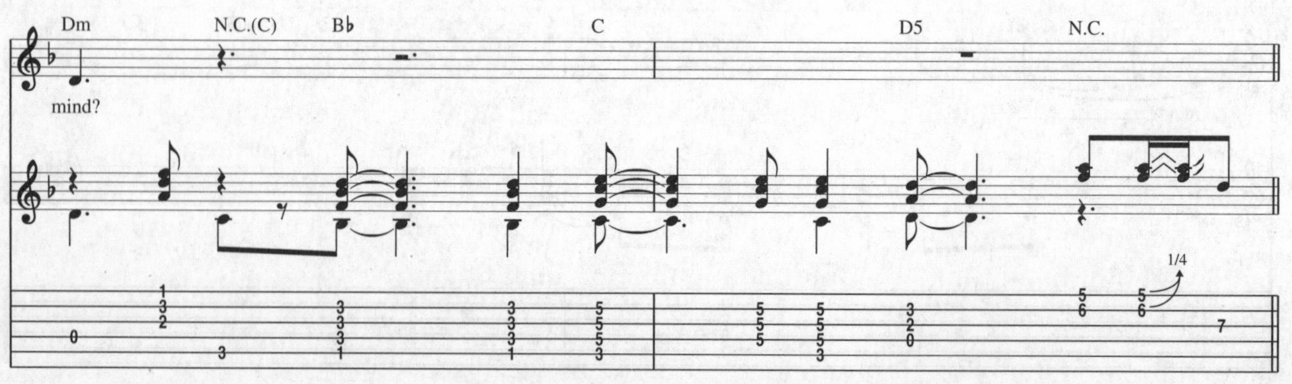
Dm
N.C.(C)
B♭
C
D5
N.C.
mind?
1/4

Guitar Solo

Dm
N.C.(C)
Bb
C
Dm
1/4
1/4
1/4
N.C.(C)
Bb
C
Dm
N.C.(C)
Bb
C
Dm
1/4
N.C.(C)
Bb
C
Dm
N.C.(C)
Bb
C
Dm
N.C.(C)
Bb
C
1/4
1/2
Dm
N.C.(C)
Bb
C
Dm
1/2

D.S. al Coda
N.C.(C) B♭ C Dm N.C.
Lay - la,
1/4
Coda
Dm N.C.(C) B♭ C D Dm N.C.(C) B♭
mind. Lay - la,
C Dm N.C.(C) Dm N.C.(C) B♭ C D5 N.C.
got me on my knees. Lay - la,
beg - gin' dar - lin', please. Lay - la,
D5 Dm (C) B♭ C
rit. poco a poco
dar - lin' won't you ease my wor - ried
Rubato
N.C.(Dm)
mind?
5:4

Little Miss Can't Be Wrong

Words and Music by Spin Doctors

1st Verse
G5 G6 G5 G6 C5 D5 D6 C5 C6
Been a whole lot eas - i - er ___ since the bitch left town.
(Gtr. 2 out)
G5 G6 G5 G6 C5 D5 D6 N.C.
Been a whole lot hap - pi - er ___ with-out her face a - round. _
G5 G6 G5 G6 C5 D5 D6 C5 C6
No - bod - y up - stairs gon - na stomp and shout. _
G5 G6 G5 G6 C5 D5 C
No - bod - y at the back door gon - na throw my ___ laun - dry ___ out.

G5 G6 G5 G6 C5 D5 D6 C5 C6
She hold the shot - gun while you dote - se - doe.
G5 G6 G5 G6 C5 D5 D6 C5 C6
She want one man made of Her - cu - les and Cyr - an - o.
G5 G6 G5 G6 C5 D5 D6 C5 C6
Been a whole lot eas - i - er since the bitch is gone.
G5 G6 G5 G6 C5 D5 D6 C5 C6
Lit - tle miss, lit - tle miss, lit - tle miss can't be wrong.

Chorus
G5 G6 G5 G6 D5 D6 C5 C6 Csus4
Lit - tle miss, lit - tle miss, lit - tle miss can't be wrong.
Rhy. Fig. 2
(end Rhy. Fig. 2)
G5 G6 G5 G6
2nd time substitute Fill 1
D5 D6 N.C.
Ain't no - bod - y gon - na bow no more when you sound your gong.
G5 G6 G5 G6 D5 D6 C5 C6
Lit - tle miss, lit - tle miss, lit - tle miss can't be wrong.
G5 G6 G5 G6 D5 D6 C5
To Coda
What d'ya go 'n' do to get in - to an - oth - er one of these here rock 'n' roll songs?
Fill 1
Gtr. 1
full

Guitar Solo
w/Rhy. Fig. 2 (4 times)
G5 G6 G5 G6 D5 D6 C5 C6 Csus4 G5 G6 G5 G6
Gtr. 2
8va
1/2
1/4
full
2nd Verse
Oth - er peo - ples thoughts, they ain't your hand - me - downs.
(Gtr. 2 out)
N.C.
Would it be so bad to sim - ply turn a - round?

G5 G6 G5 G6 D5 D6 C5 C6
You cook so well, all nice and French._ You do your
G5 G6 G5 G6 D5 D6 C5 C6
brain surg'ry too,__ ma-ma, with a mon-key wrench._
Chorus
G5 G6 G5 G6 C5 D5 D6 C5 C6
Lit-tle miss, lit-tle miss, lit-tle miss can't be wrong._
G5 G6 G5 G6 D5 D6 N.C.
Ain't no-bod-y gon-na bow no more when you sound your gong.___

G5 G6 G5 G6 C5 D5 D6 C5 C6
Lit - tle miss, lit - tle miss, lit - tle miss can't be wrong.
G5 G6 G5 G6 D5 D6 C5 G
What'ya go 'n' do to get in - to an - oth - er one of there here rock 'n' roll songs.
Interlude
G A5 B♭ C G A5
Gtr. 1
Yeah, yeah. Can't be wrong, no, no, no.
Gtr. 2
B♭ C G A5 B♭ C G
Ya can't be wrong. Oh, ya can't be wrong,

A5
B♭
C
G
you can't be wrong, ya can't be wrong.
B♭
C
G
play 3 times
B♭
C
C9
w/Rhy. Fill 1
3rd Verse
G5
G6
G5
G6
C5
D5
D6
C5
C6
I hope them cig - a - rettes are gon - na make you cough.
Gtr. 1
G5
G6
G5
G6
D5
D6
N.C.
I hope you hear this song, and it pissed you off.
Rhy. Fill 1
Gtr. 1
C
C9
T
A
B

G5 G6 G5 G6 C5 D5 D6 C5 C6
I take that back, I hope you're do-in' fine.
And
G5 G6 G5 G6 D5 D6 C5
D. S. al Coda
if I had a dol - lar, I might give you nine - ty - nine.
w/Vocal ad lib (till end)
w/Rhy. Fig. 1 (4 times)
Coda
Gtr. 2
G5 D5 C5 G5
Gtr. 1 substitute Rhy. Fill 2
D5 C5
full
G5 D5 G5 G5
8va
full
full
full
Rhy. Fill 2
Gtr. 1
D B5 C5 C B♭

w/Rhy. Fig. 2 (3 times)
D5
C5
G5
8va
full
w/Fill 2
loco
1/4
1/2
Gtr. 1
C#5
D
Gtr. 2
hold bend
grad. bend
Free time
Csus4
rit.
Fill 2
Gtr. 3 (overdub)
T
A
B

Loco

Words by B. Dez Fafara
Music by Miguel Rascon, Rayna Foss and Mike Cox

Faster ♩ = 134
Gtrs. 3 & 4
N.C.
Riff B
End Riff B
Riff C
1., 3.
C♯5
N.C.
End Riff C
2.
C♯5
N.C.
D5
4.
Verse
1st & 3rd times, Gtr. 4: w/ Riff B (4 times)
2nd time, Gtr. 4: w/ Rhy. Fill 2
3rd time, Gtr. 3: w/ Fill 1
3rd time, Gtr. 1 tacet
N.C.
1., 2., 3. Steam - roll - er roll - in' through my head, said at - tached to lo - co. Pow - er up coal
Gtr. 3
8va
Harm.
let ring
Rhy. Fill 2
Gtr. 4
loco
8va
Harm.
Fill 1
Gtr. 3

through the sys - tem, out to the right. Said, "You're in my light, uh."
loco
Lock down the gen - er - a - tor on, man. Screw down, use the sys - tem, use the main plan.
8va
Harm.
let ring
Full pow - er up to the point man. Don't fuck with me.
8va
loco
(cont. in slashes)
Harm.
let ring
Chorus
C#
Lo - co, lo - co, lo - co,
Gtrs. 3 & 4

C
lo - co.
Mí lo - co,
mí lo - co,
To Coda
B
mí lo - co,
mí lo - co.
1.
Gtrs. 3 & 4: w/ Riff B
N.C.
Gtrs. 3 & 4: w/ Riff C
C♯5 N.C.
Pull!
2.
Gtr. 3: w/ Riff B (2 times)
Gtr. 4: w/ Riff B (1 1/2 times)
B
N.C.
Play 4 times
Gtr. 4
8va
Harm.

Bridge

N.C.

Lock _ down _ here, latch the gen - er - a - tor on.

Gtr. 3

Gtr. 4

Screw _ the sys - tem. Full pow - er, hit the main _ plan. _

A Tempo
Gtr. 2: w/ Riff A (2 times)
Gtrs. 3 & 4 tacet
N.C.
Gtr. 1
mf
1/2
Gtr. 1 tacet
B5
Gtrs. 3 & 4
1/2
Faster ♩ = 134
Gtrs. 3 & 4: w/ Riff B (3 times)
N.C.
Gtr. 1
8va
loco
f
A.H.
D.S. al Coda
Gtrs. 3 & 4: w/ Riff C
C♯5 N.C.
8va
A.H.
fdbk.
Coda
B
N.C.
Spoken: Steamroller rollin' through my head, said attached to loco. Power up coal to the system, out to the right. Said, "You're in my light."
P.M.

Louie, Louie

Words and Music by Richard Berry

* Lyrics omitted at the request of the publisher.

A
D
Em
D
End Rhy. Fig. 2
Gtr. 1: w/Rhy. Fig. 2
Chorus
Gtr. 1: w/Rhy. Fig. 1, 4 times
Guitar Solo
Gtr. 1: w/Rhy. Fig. 1, 8 times
Gtr. 2 (clean)
1/4

A
D
Em
D
A
D
1/4
1/2
Em
D
A
D
Em
D
A
D
Em
D
A
D
1/4
Em
D
A
D
Em
D
Gtr. 1: w/Rhy. Fig. 2, 1st 2 meas.
A
D
Em
D
A
D
Em
D

Verse
Gtr. 1: w/Rhy. Fig. 2, 2 times
Gtr. 2 tacet
A D Em D A D
Em D A D Em D
Outro-Chorus
Gtr. 1: w/Rhy. Fig. 1, 4 times
A D Em D A D Em D
A D Em D A D
Em D A D Em D A D
Gtr. 1
Em D A D Em D A

Love Song

Words and Music by Jeffrey Keith and Frank Hannon

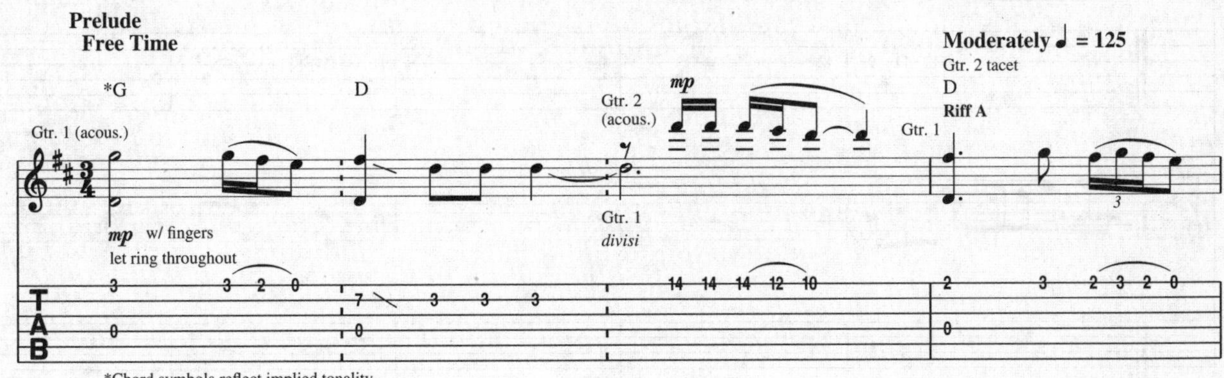

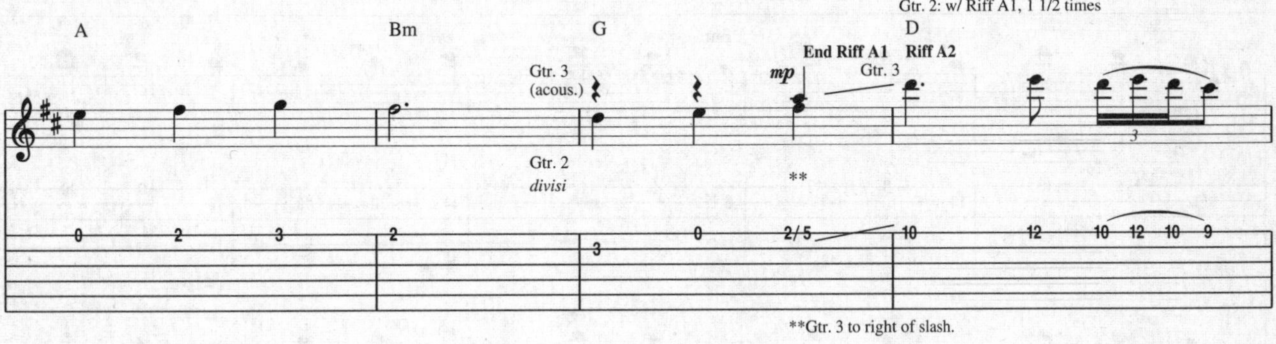

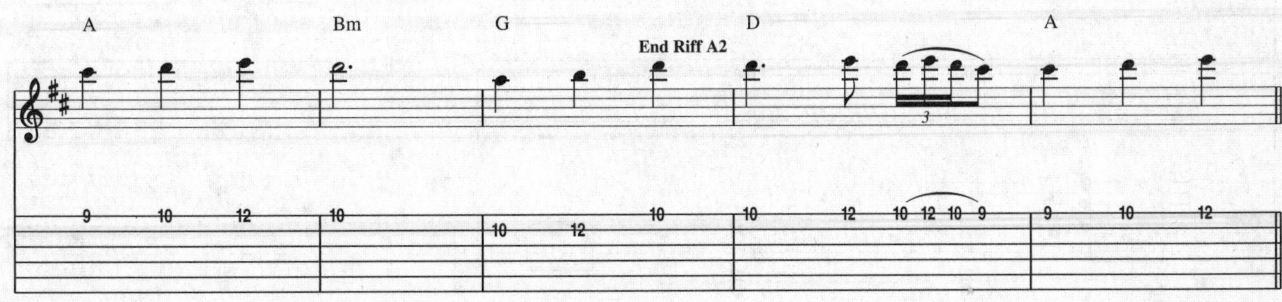

Gtr. 3

Bm A E/G♯ G5 A 1. D/F♯

Gtr. 2

Gtr. 1

G D/F♯ Em D/F♯ G

D/F♯ Em A N.C.

Gtrs. 1, 2 & 3: w/ Riffs A, A1 & A2, 3 1/2 times

2.

D

Harm.

*Let notes ring into next meas.

Intro

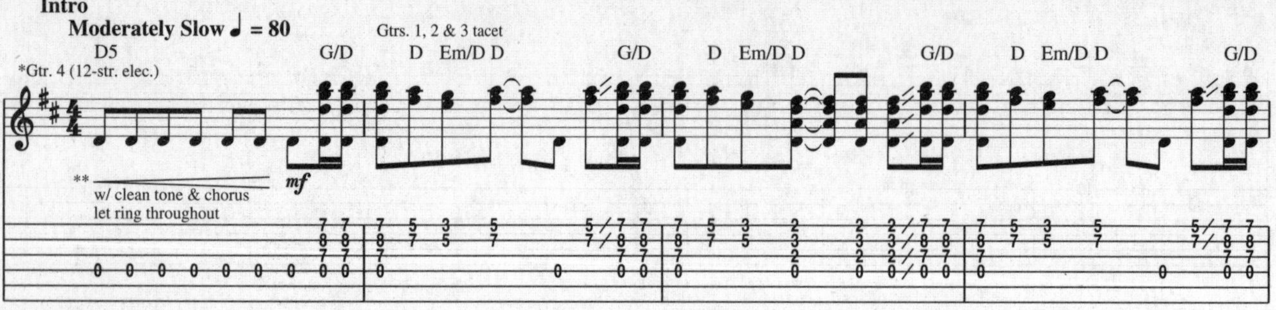

*For next 5 meas. two gtrs. are arr. for one.
**vol. swell

Verse

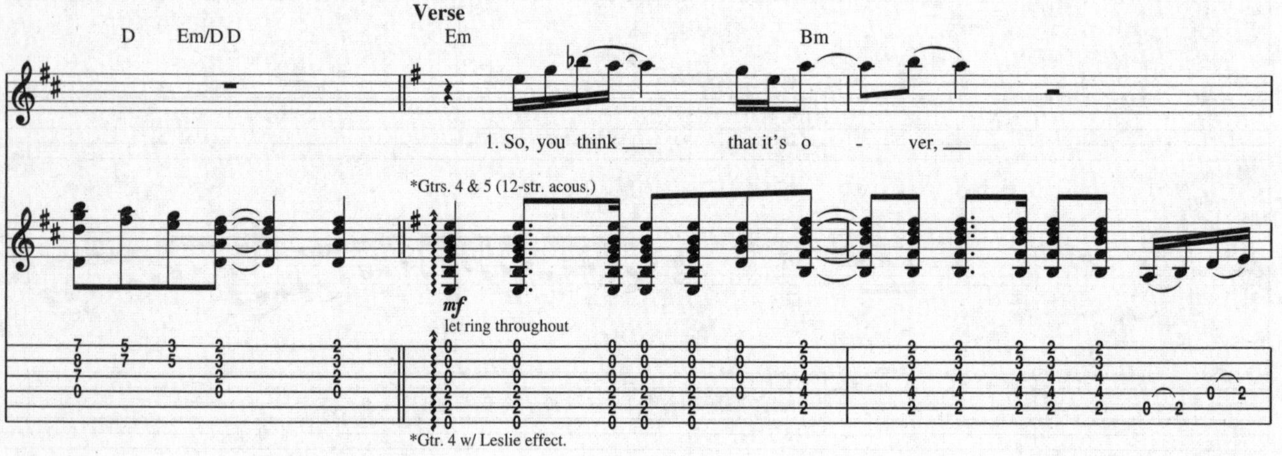

*Gtr. 4 w/ Leslie effect.

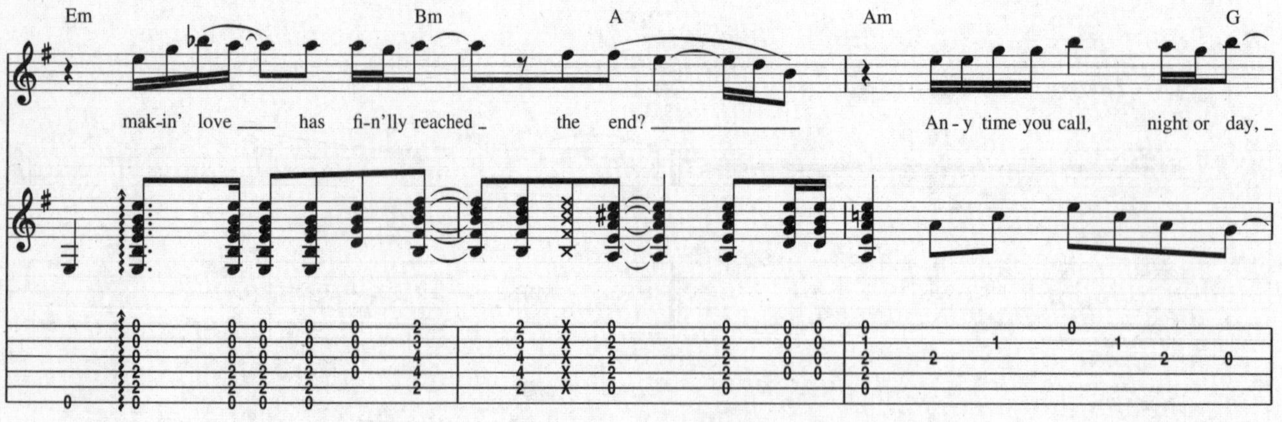

Verse
Em
Bm
Bsus2
Bm
Em
Bm
2. It's gon-na take a lit-tle time.
Time is sure to mend your bro -
A
Am
G
- ken heart.
Don't you e-ven wor - ry, pret - ty dar - lin', 'Cause
Bm
D
G/D
Gtr. 5 tacet
D
Em/D D
G/D
I know you'll find love a - gain.
Gtr. 5
Gtr. 4
Gtr. 4
divisi
w/ chorus
D
Em/DD
Chorus
G5
D/F#
G5
D/F#
Oo, yeah,
Love is all a - round you.
*Gtrs. 1, 4 & 6 (elec.)
mf w/ clean tone & chorus
let ring throughout
**T
T
*composite arrangement
**T=Thumb on 6

G5 D/F♯ G5 D/F♯ Em

Love is knock-in' out-side your door. Wait-in' for you is this

T T

C D Dsus4 D 1. Dsus4 D Dsus2 D 2. E

Gtr. 7 (elec.)

⑥ 12 fr

f w/ dist. (cont. in notation)

love made just for two. Keep an o - pen heart and you'll find love a-gain, I know. you'll find love a-gain, I

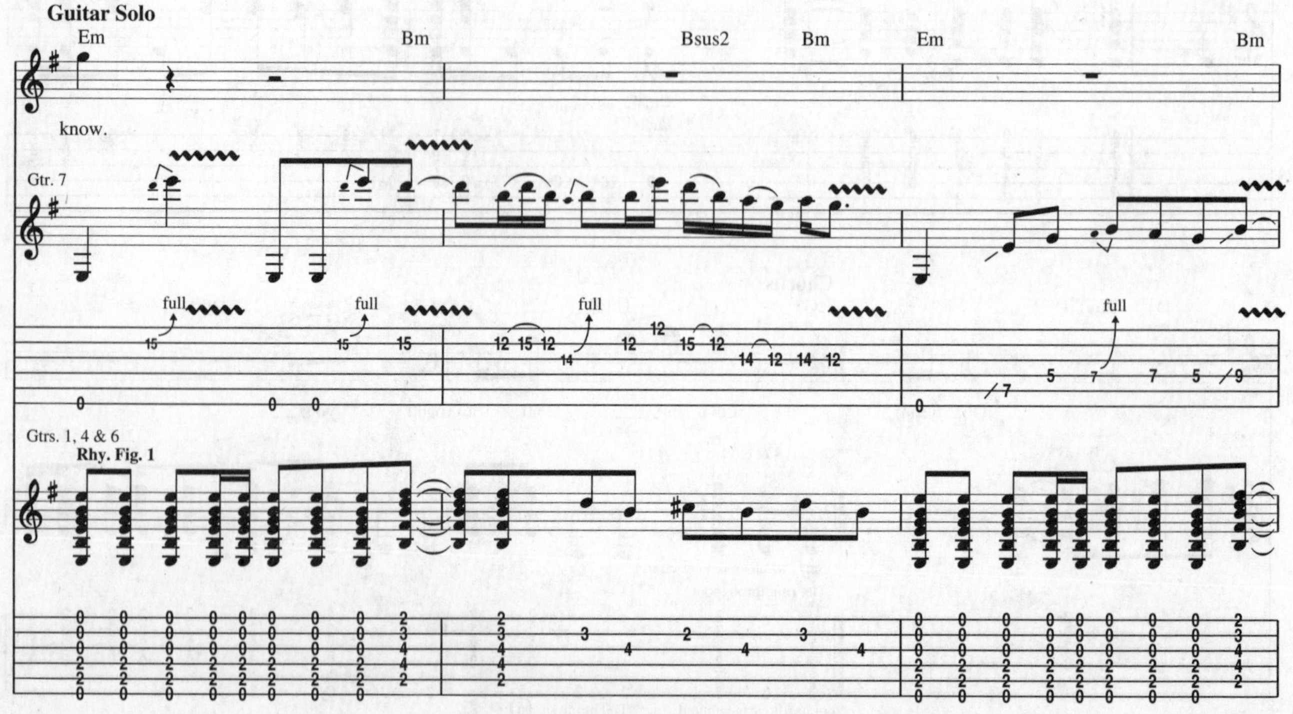

A
Am
G5
hold bend
let ring
full
Bm
D
End Rhy. Fig. 1
Gtrs. 1, 4 & 6: w/ Rhy. Fig. 1
Em
Bm
Bsus2
Bm
Em
Bm
Gtr. 7
A
Am
G5
hold bend
let ring

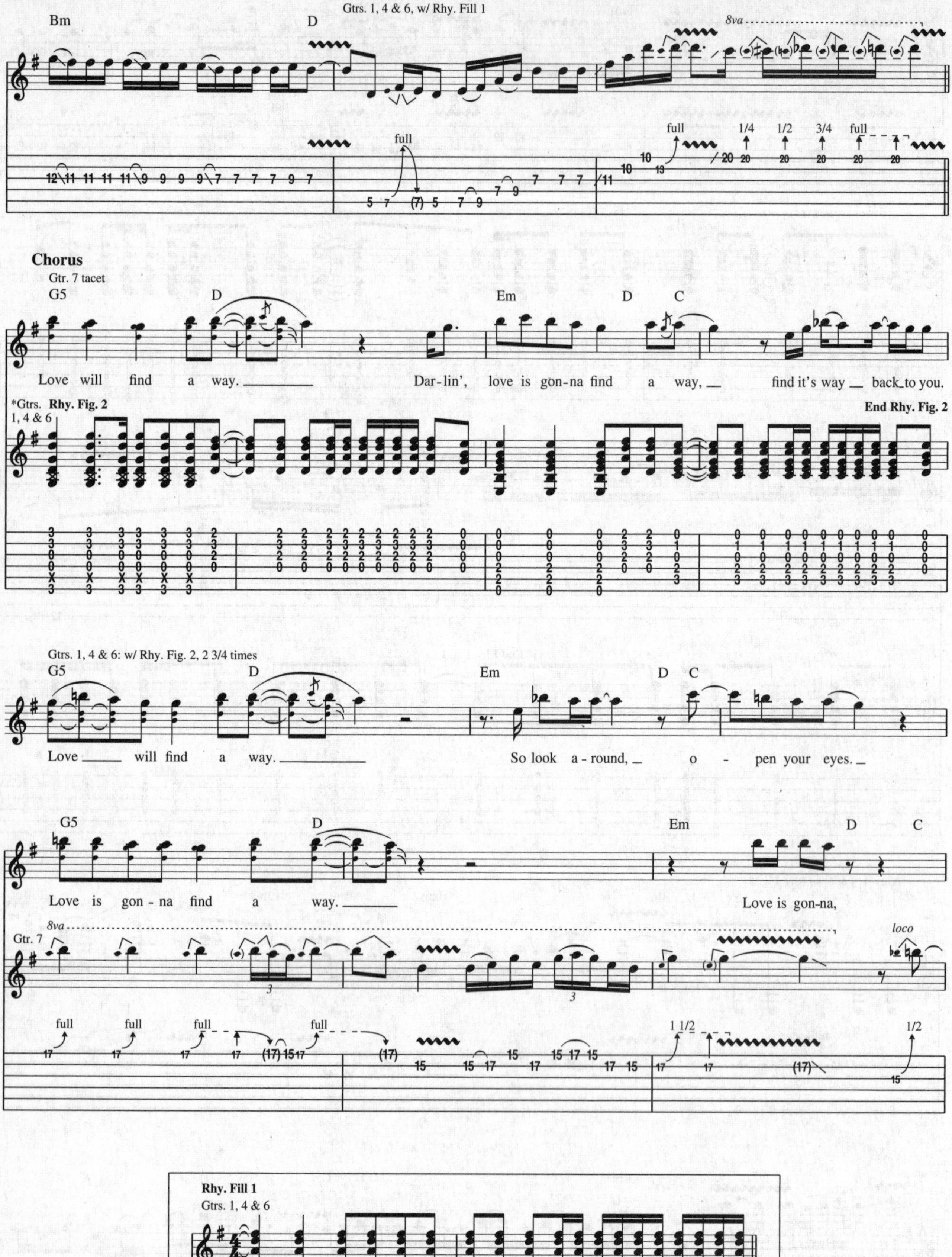

Gtrs. 1, 4 & 6, w/ Rhy. Fill 1

Bm D 8va

full 1/4 1/2 3/4 full

Chorus

Gtr. 7 tacet

G5 D Em D C

Love will find a way. Darlin', love is gon-na find a way, find it's way back to you.

*Gtrs. 1, 4 & 6 **Rhy. Fig. 2** **End Rhy. Fig. 2**

Gtrs. 1, 4 & 6: w/ Rhy. Fig. 2, 2 3/4 times

G5 D Em D C

Love will find a way. So look a-round, o-pen your eyes.

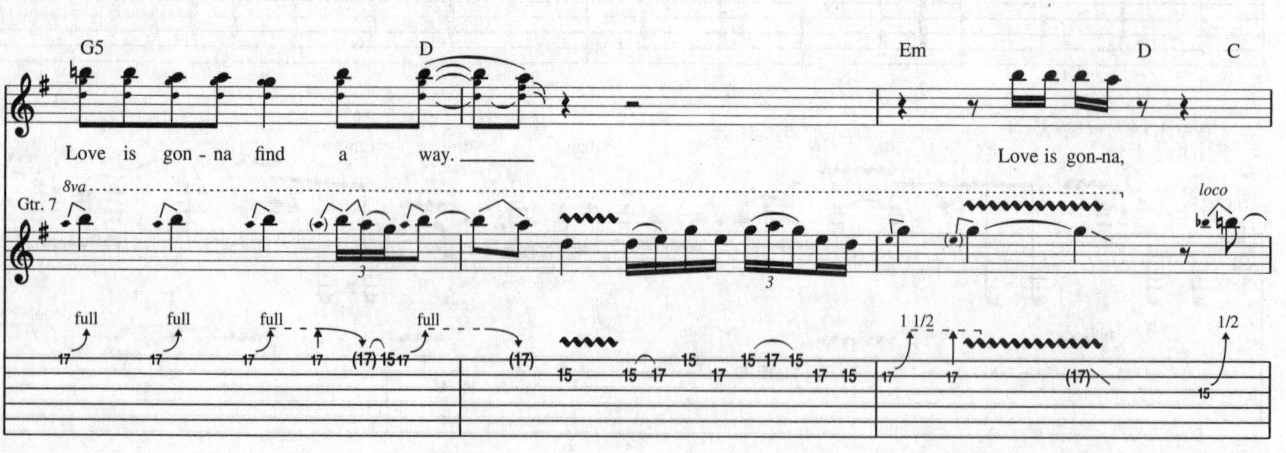

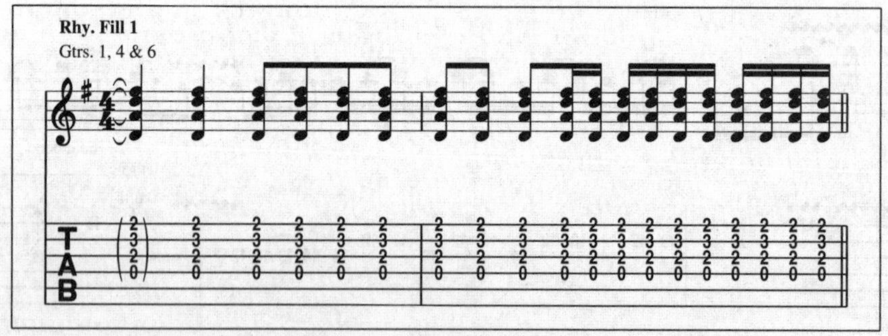

G5
D
love is gon - na find a way.
Love will find a way.
Love is gon-na
P.M.
P.M.
1/4
1/2
full

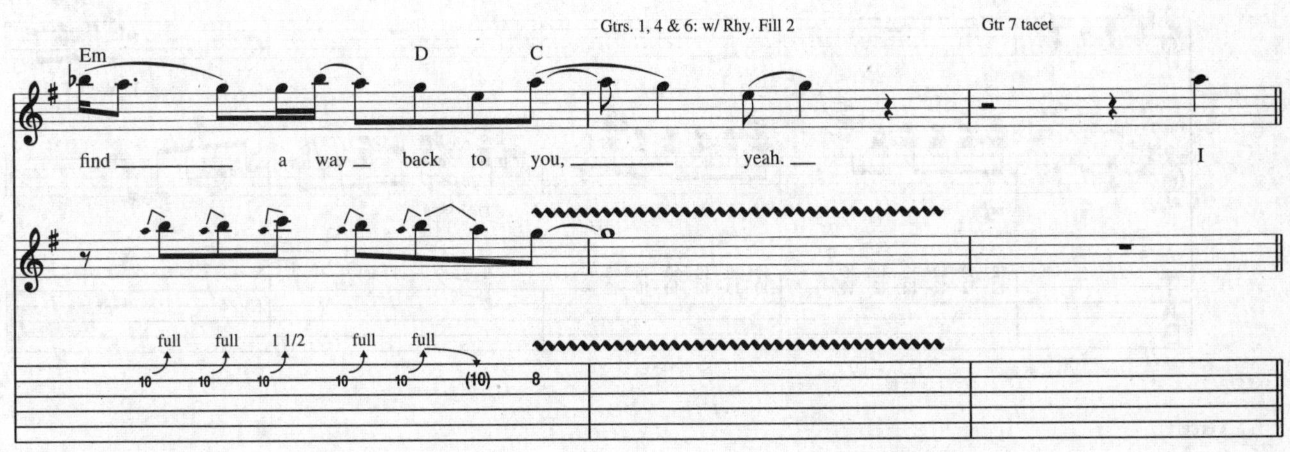
Gtrs. 1, 4 & 6: w/ Rhy. Fill 2
Gtr 7 tacet
Em
D
C
find a way back to you, yeah.
I
full
full
1 1/2
full
full

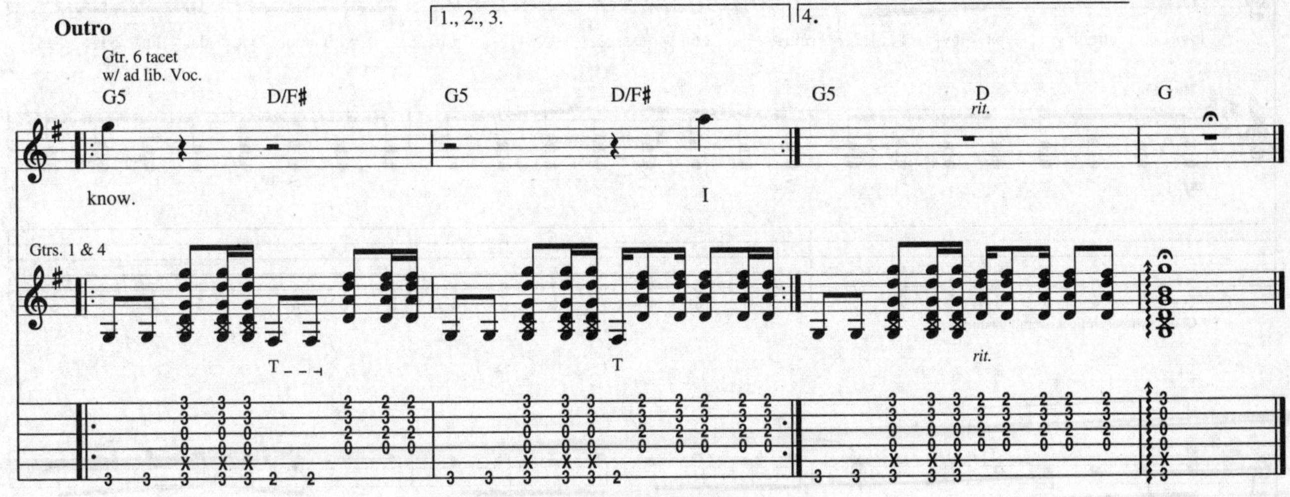
Outro
Gtr. 6 tacet
w/ ad lib. Voc.
G5
D/F#
G5
D/F#
1., 2., 3.
4.
G5
D
rit.
G
know.
I
Gtrs. 1 & 4
T
T
rit.

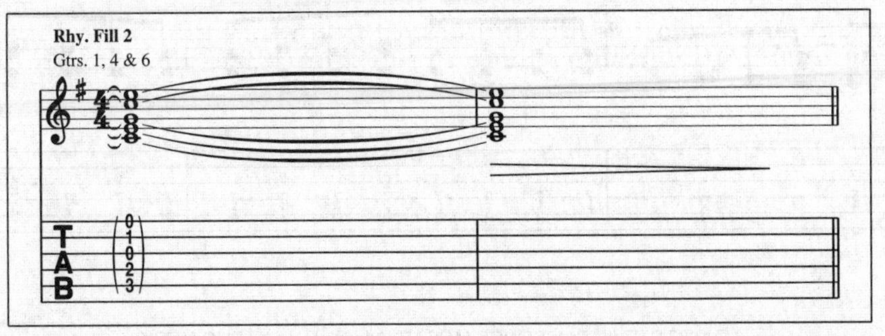
Rhy. Fill 2
Gtrs. 1, 4 & 6
TAB

Love Struck Baby

Written by Stevie Ray Vaughan

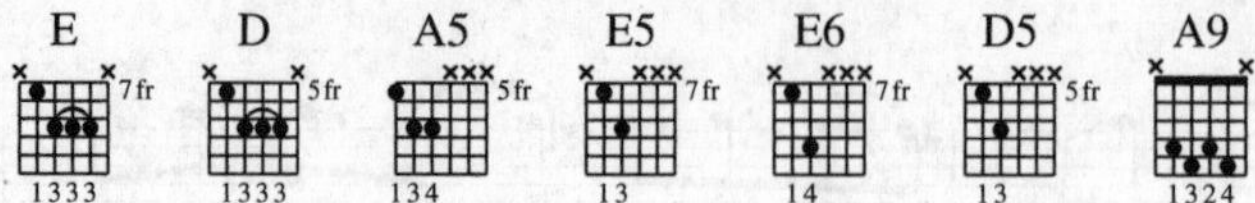

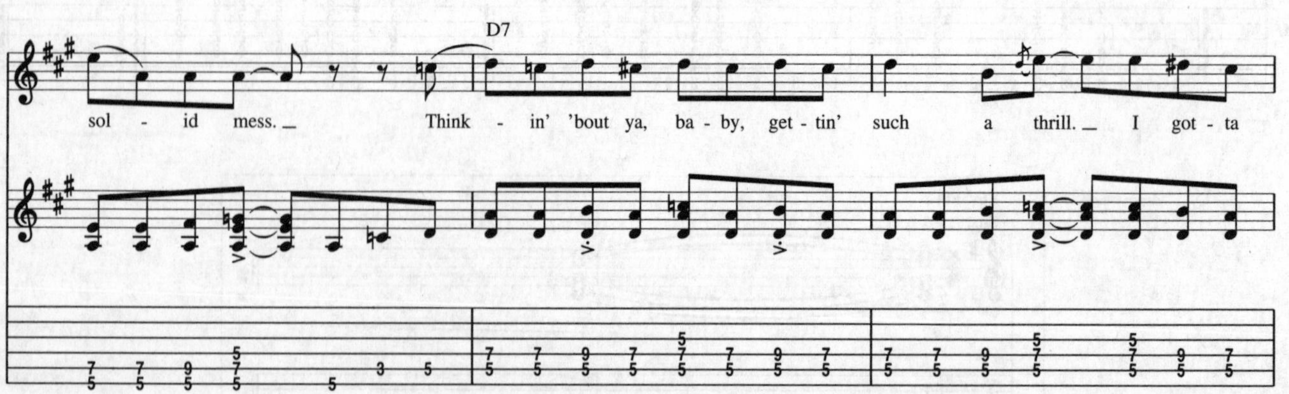

A7
E7
have you ba - by, can't ___ get my fill. ___ I ___ love you, ba - by, an' I
know just what ___ to do.
I ___
End Rhy. Fig. 1
Pre-Chorus
D7
A7
___ still ___ re - mem - ber, let it be said, ___ the way ___ ya make me feel, _ it takes a
- 'ry time _ I see ya make me feel so fine, ___ my heart ___ beat - in' cra - zy,
___ start - ed fly - in' ev - 'ry time we meet. ___ Don't - cha know, ba - by, ya knock
simile on repeats
D7
fool to for - get. ___ Swore a ton o' bricks had hit me in the head. ___ What you
blood is run - nin' wild. Your lov - in' makes me feel ___ like a might - y, might - y man, 'cause you
me off my feet? Your kiss 'll trip me up, they're so dog - gone sweet. Don't - cha

1.
2., 3.
E7
do to me, ba - by, ain't o - ver yet.
Ev - know pret - ty ba - by, am I
know pret - ty ba - by, you can't
Chorus
A7
your man? An' I'm a
be beat? I'm a
love struck ba - by.
(You) got me
I'm a
D7
love struck, ba - by.
You got me love struck ba - by,
You got me, you got
me love struck, an' I know just what to do.
To Coda

Guitar Solo

Gtr. 2: w/ Rhy. Fig. 1, 3 times, simile
A7
Gtr. 1
f
1/2
full
full
grad. bends
1/4
D7
E7
grad. bend

D7
A7
8va
E7
grad. bend
rake
P.M.

A7 8va loco E7

rake

1/4 full 1/4 1/4

D.S. al Coda

A7

The sparks

P.M. P.M. P.M.

1/4 1/2 full 1/2 1/4

Coda

E E6 E5 D5 A5

Gtr. 2

Gtr. 1

f

poco rit.

1/4 1/2 1/2 1/2 1/2

The Magic Bus

Words and Music by Peter Townshend

A A5 C/G G/D Dsus4 D A5 A G D A G/D D
get on the bus that takes _ me to you. (Too much ___ the mag-ic bus._) I'm so ner-vous, I ___ just sit and
A5 A G D A G/D D A5 A G D
Rhy. Fig. 1
End Rhy. Fig. 1
smile. ___ Your house _ is on - ly an-oth-er mile. _ (Too much ___ the mag-ic bus._)
(Too much, ___ the mag-ic bus._)
Rhy. Fig. 1A
End Rhy. Fig. 1A
Verse
Gtr. 2: w/Verse Rhy., simile
A C/G G/D D A5 A G D A
2. Thank you driv-er for get-ting me here. (Too much, ___ the mag-ic bus._) You'll be an in-spec-tor, have _
C/G G/D Dsus4 D A5 A G D A G/D D
___ no fear. ___ (Too much, mag-ic bus._) I don't wan-na cause _ no fuss,
A5 A G D A G/D D A5 A G D
(Too much, mag-ic bus. _) but can I buy your mag-ic bus? (Too much, _ the mag-ic bus._) No. _
Interlude
A N.C. A5 N.C.
Gtr. 2
Gtr. 2 tacet
Gtr. 1
P.S.

D5 A5 A C/G G/D
Verse
A G D A5 A G/D D A
Gtr. 2
3. I don't care how much I pay. (Ride the mag-ic bus.) I wan-na drive my bus to my
Dsus4 D A G D A G/D D
ba-by each day. (Ride the mag-ic bus.)
A G/D A N.C.
Gtr. 2 tacet
I want it, I want it, I want
(I want it, I
Gtr. 1 tacet
it, I want it, you can't have it. I
want it, I want it, I want it, I want it, I want it, I

A5
N.C.
Gtr. 2
want it.
Gtr. 1
want it, I want.)
Lov - er drives six miles ev - e - ry day.
1/4
A C A5
open 3fr
Just to drive to my ba - by.
Lov - er drives six miles each day.
'Cause I drive my ba - by ev -
A7 D/A
Chorus
Gtr. 3: w/Rhy. Fill 1
Dsus4
G/D
- e - ry way.
Oh,
Mag-ic bus.
(Mag-ic bus.)

Gtr. 2: w/Rhy. Fig. 1, simile till end
Gtr. 1: w/Rhy. Fig. 1A, simile till end
w/Voc. Fig. 1, 6 1/2 times
Gtr. 3: w/Rhy. Fill 2, 3 1/2 times
Outro
A G/D D G/D D A
Voc. Fig. 1
play 3 times
*Gtr. 3 tacet
8
5
(Mag-ic bus. _)
*Gtr. 3 gets lost in mix at this point.
I said now I get my
G/D D A G/D D A G/D D A
Voc. Fig. 2
w/Voc. Fig. 2
mag-ic bus. _ Said now I got my mag-ic bus. _
(Too much, _ the mag-ic bus. _)
G/D D A G/D D A G/D D A
w/Voc. Fig. 2
I drive my ba - by ev - e - ry way. Each time I go a dif -
G/D D A G/D D A G/D D A
w/Voc. Fig. 2
w/Voc. Fig. 1, 4 times
ad lib answer vocals
- f'rent way. _ I want _ it, I want it, I want it, I
G/D D A G/D D A G/D D A
want it, I want it, I want it, I want it, I want _ it. Ev - 'ry-day _ you'll
Begin Fade
Gtr. 2: w/Rhy. Fill 3
Fade Out
G/D D A G/D D A G/D D A G/D D
w/Voc. Fig. 2
w/Voc. Fig. 2
see the dust. _ I drive my ba-by in my mag-ic bus. _
Rhy. Fill 1
Gtr. 3
play 4 times
w/dist.
1/4
1/4
Rhy. Fill 2
Gtr. 3
Rhy. Fill 3
Gtr. 2
1/4
1/4

Money

Words and Music by Roger Waters

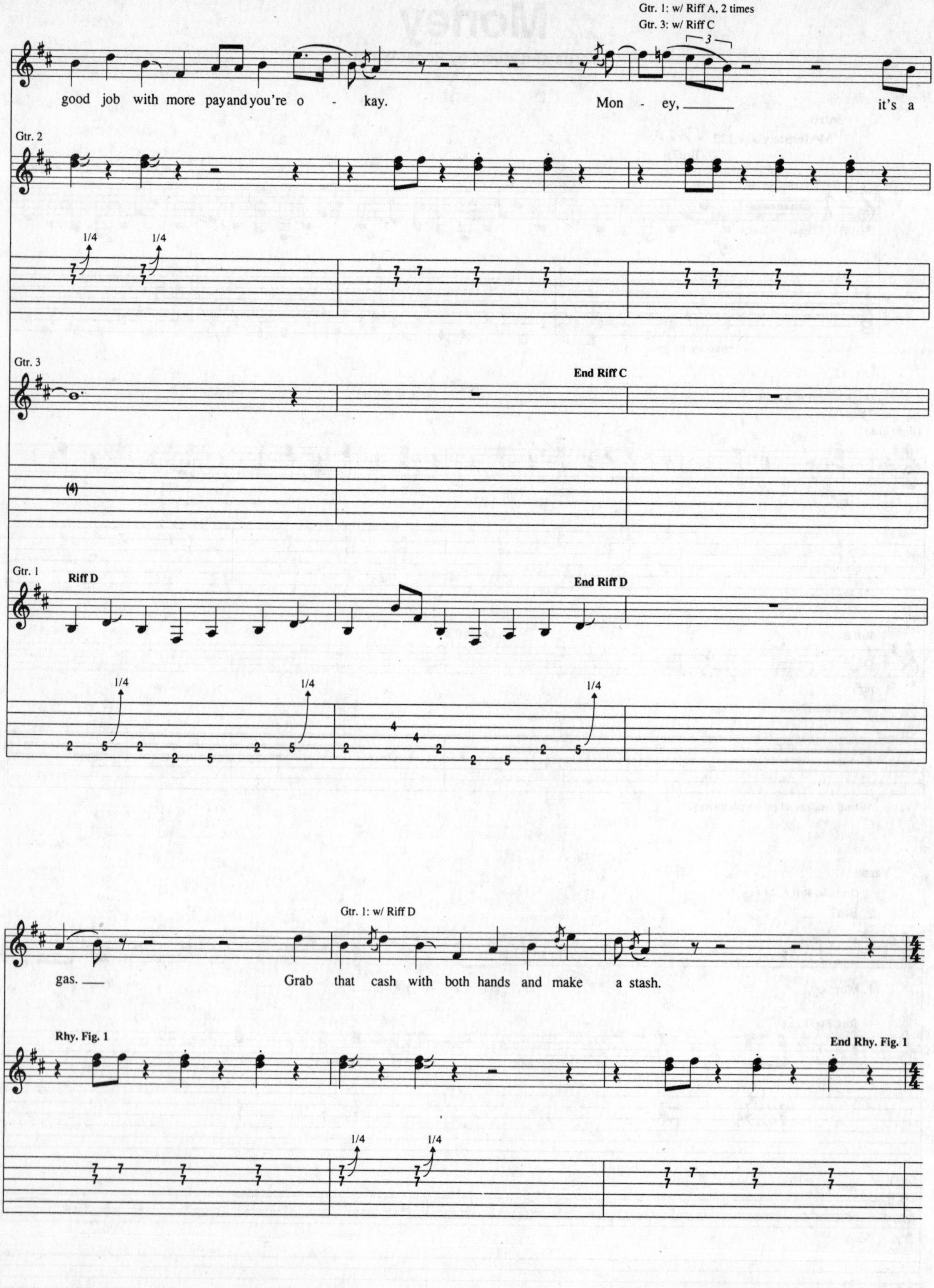

Gtr. 1: w/ Riff A, 2 times
Gtr. 3: w/ Riff C

good job with more pay and you're o - kay. Mon - ey, it's a

Gtr. 2

Gtr. 3
End Riff C

Gtr. 1
Riff D
End Riff D

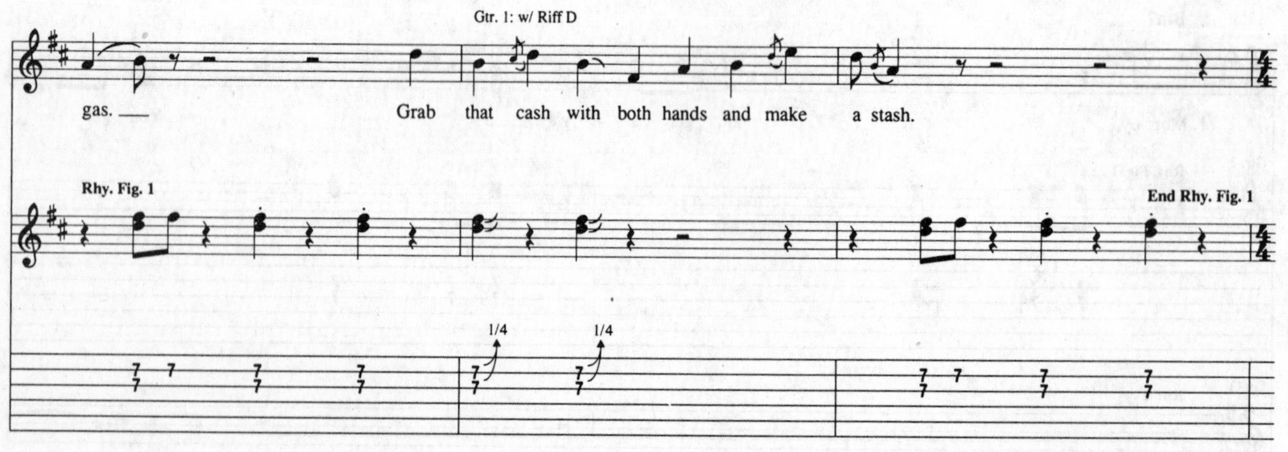

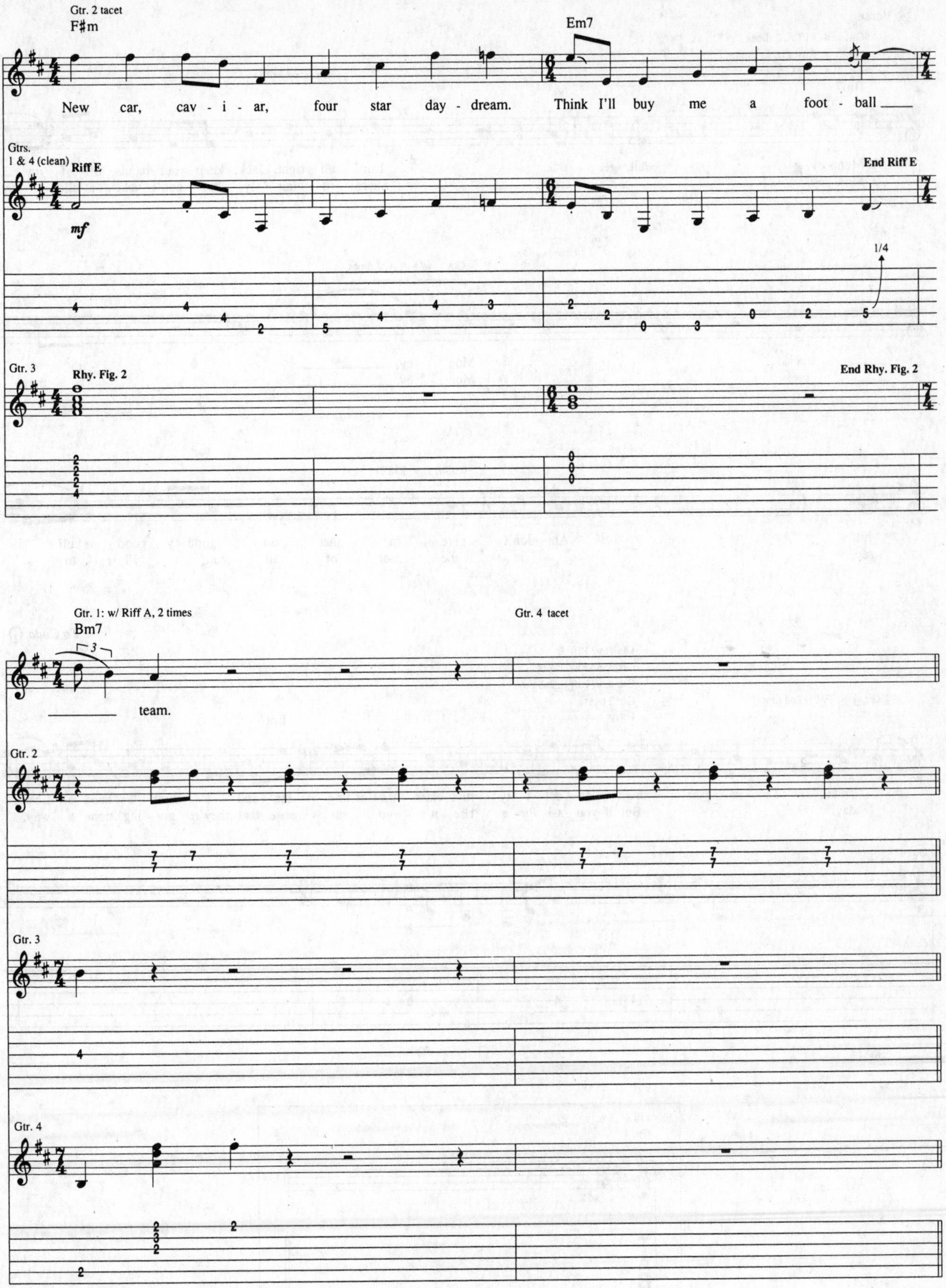

Gtr. 1: w/ Riff A, 2 times

Gtr. 4 tacet

Bm7

team.

Gtr. 2

Gtr. 3

Gtr. 4

Verse
Gtr. 1: w/ Riff A, 2 times
Gtr. 2: w/ Rhy. Fig. 1, simile
Gtr. 3: w/ Riff C, 2 times
Bm7
Gtr. 1: w/ Riff D
2. Mon - ey, well, get back. I'm all right, Jack, keep your hands off of my
3. Mon - ey, it's a crime. Share it fair - ly, but don't take a slice of my
Gtr. 1: w/ Riff A, 2 times
stack. Mon - ey, it's a
pie. Mon - ey, so they
Gtr. 1: w/ Riff D
hit. Ah, don't give me that do good - y good bull -
say, is the root of all e - vil to -
To Coda
Gtr. 4: w/ Fill 1, 2nd time
Gtr. 1: w/ Riff E
Gtr. 3: w/ Rhy. Fig. 2
Gtr. 4: w/ Riff E, 2nd time
Gtr. 2 tacet
F♯m
Em7
- shit I'm in the high fi - del - i - ty first class trav - el - ling set, and I think I need a Lear
- day. But if you ask for a rise it's no sur - prise that they're giv - ing none a - way,
Gtr. 4
Fill 1
Gtr. 4
TAB

Saxophone Solo

Gtr. 1: w/ Riff A, 2 times

Bm7

jet.

Gtr. 4 tacet

Gtr. 1: w/ Riff A, 8 times

Gtr. 3: w/ Riff B, 4 times, simile

Bm7

Gtr. 2

Gtr. 3

Gtr. 4

1/4

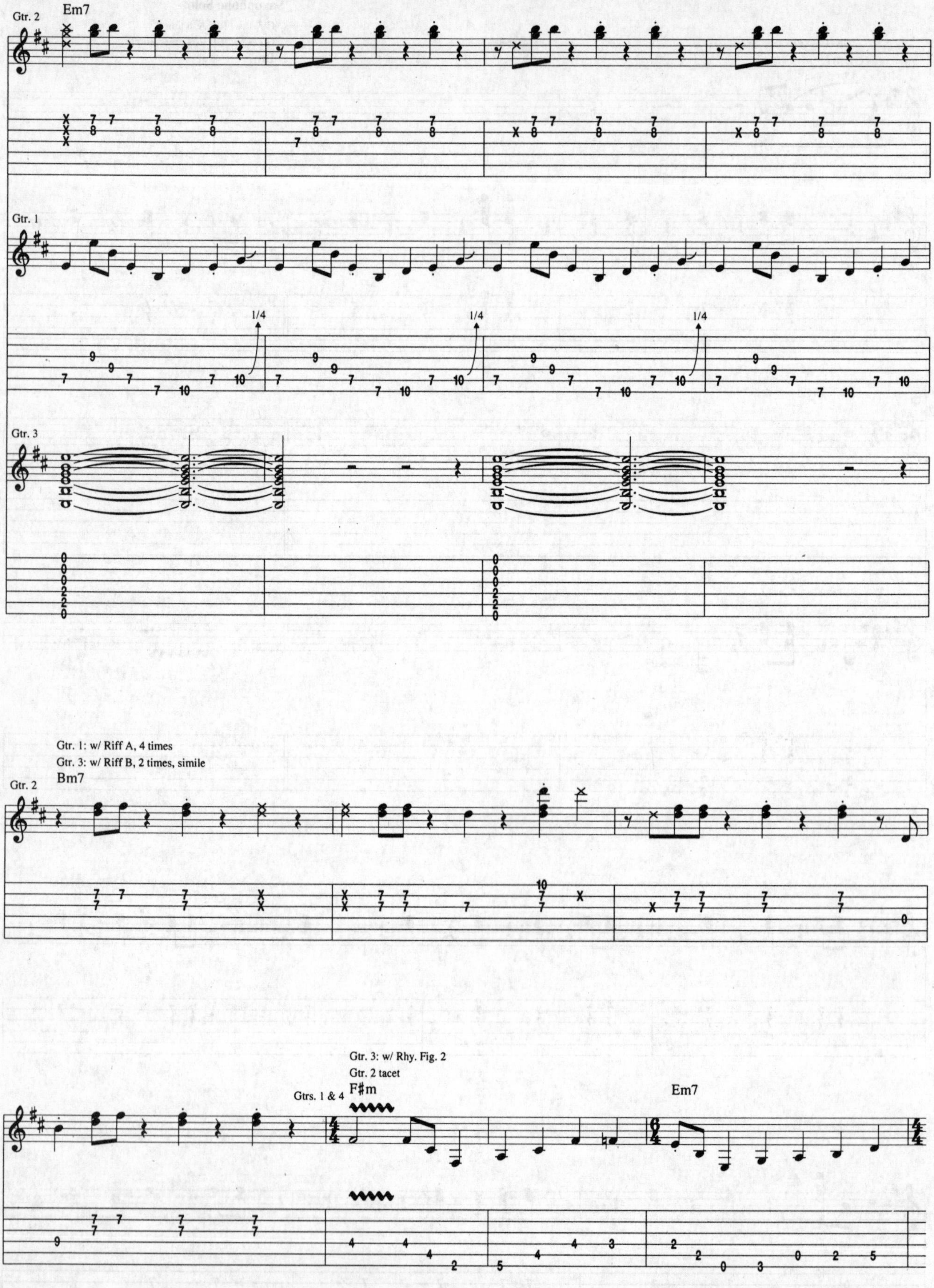

Gtr. 2

Em7

Gtr. 1

1/4 1/4 1/4

Gtr. 3

Gtrs. 1 & 3 tacet
Gtr. 4
B5
f
w/ slight dist.
Gtr. 5
f
w/ slight dist.

Guitar Solo

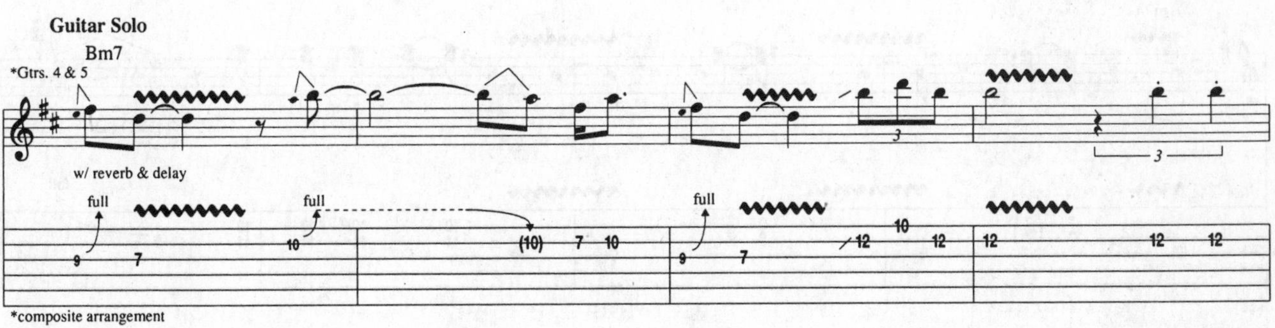
Bm7
*Gtrs. 4 & 5
w/ reverb & delay
full
full
full
*composite arrangement

full
full
full
full

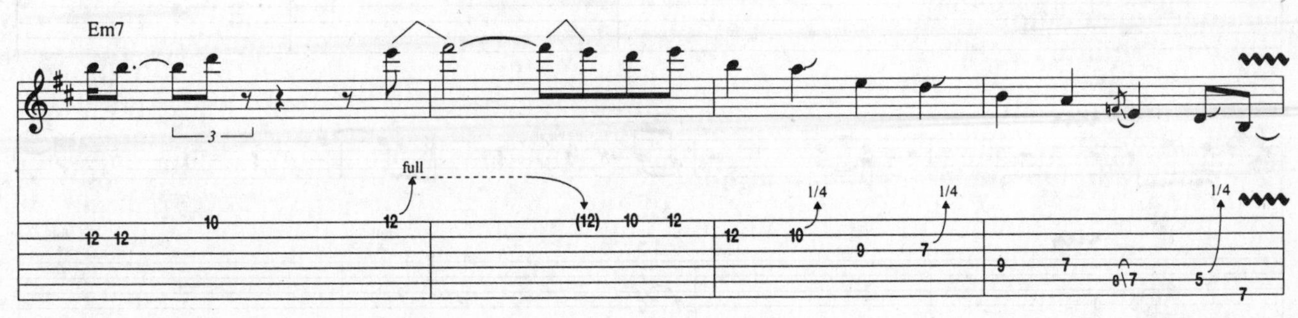
Em7
full
1/4
1/4
1/4

Bm7
full
F#m7
N.C.
Gtr. 4
grad. bend
1/4
Gtr. 5
Gtr. 5 tacet
mf

Em7
full
full
full
full
full
full
full
Bm7
full
full
F#m7
full
full
N.C.
f
Gtr. 5
Bm7
Gtr. 3 tacet
full
full
Gtr. 4
full
1/4
Gtr. 3

Gtr. 5
8va
full
full
full
full
Gtr. 4
Gtr. 2
8va
loco
grad. release
2
1/4
1/4
Rhy. Fig. 3
End Rhy. Fig. 3

Em7
8va
full
2
Gtr. 4: w/ Rhy. Fig. 3, simile
Bm7
8va
Gtr. 5
full
Gtr. 2

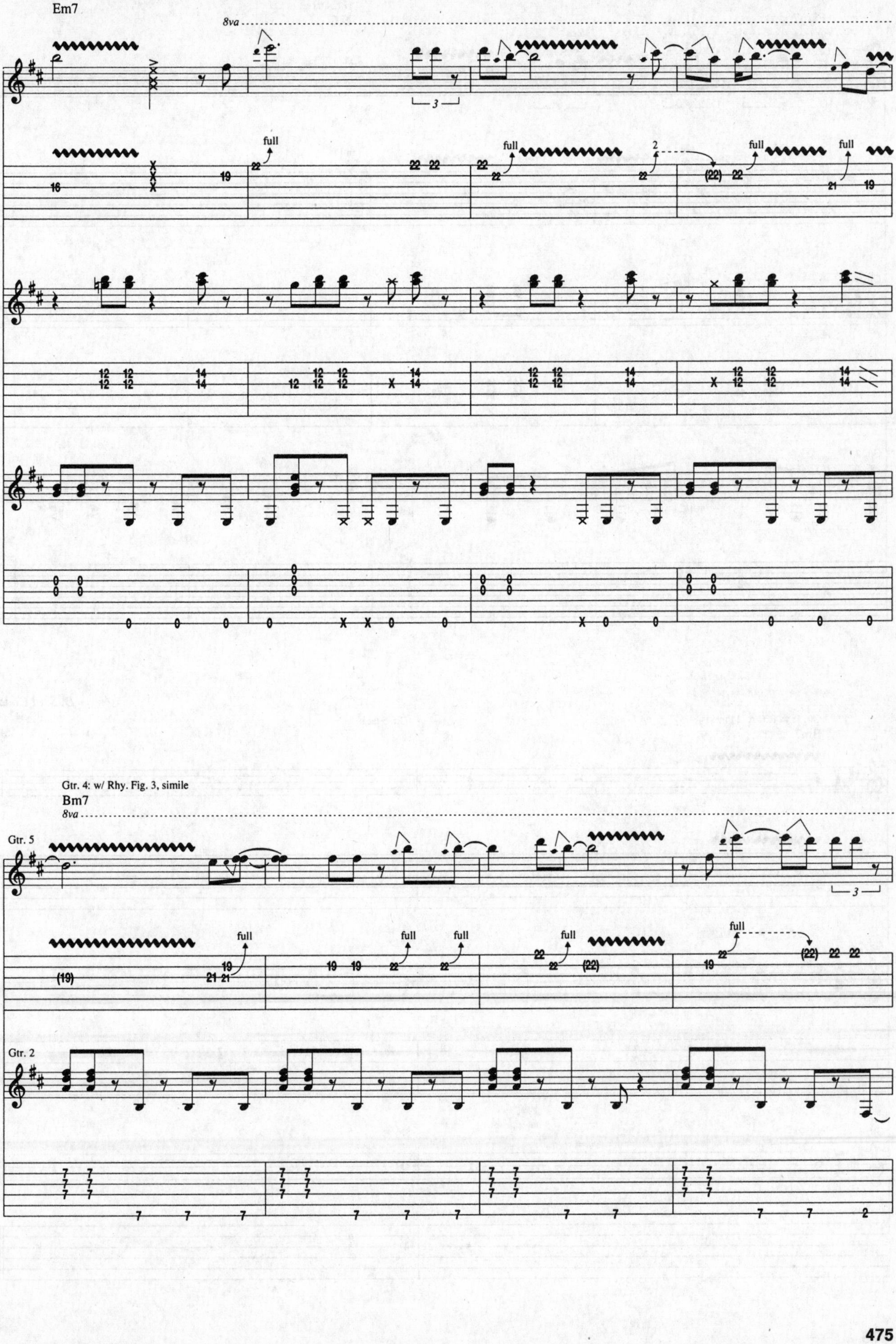

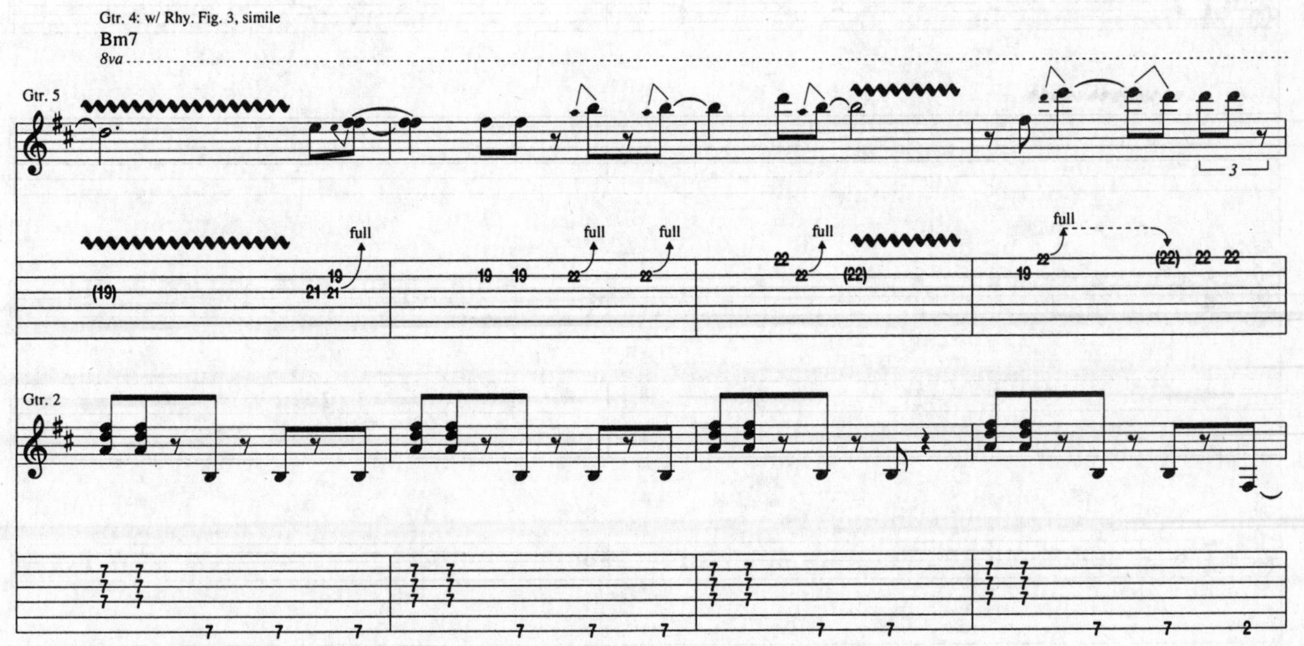

F♯m7
8va
loco
Gtr. 5
full
full
full
Gtr. 4 tacet
N.C.
Gtr. 4
Gtr. 2
D. S. al Coda
Gtr. 1: w/ Riff A, 2 times
Bm7
Gtr. 5
Gtr. 5 tacet
Gtr. 2
Gtr. 3

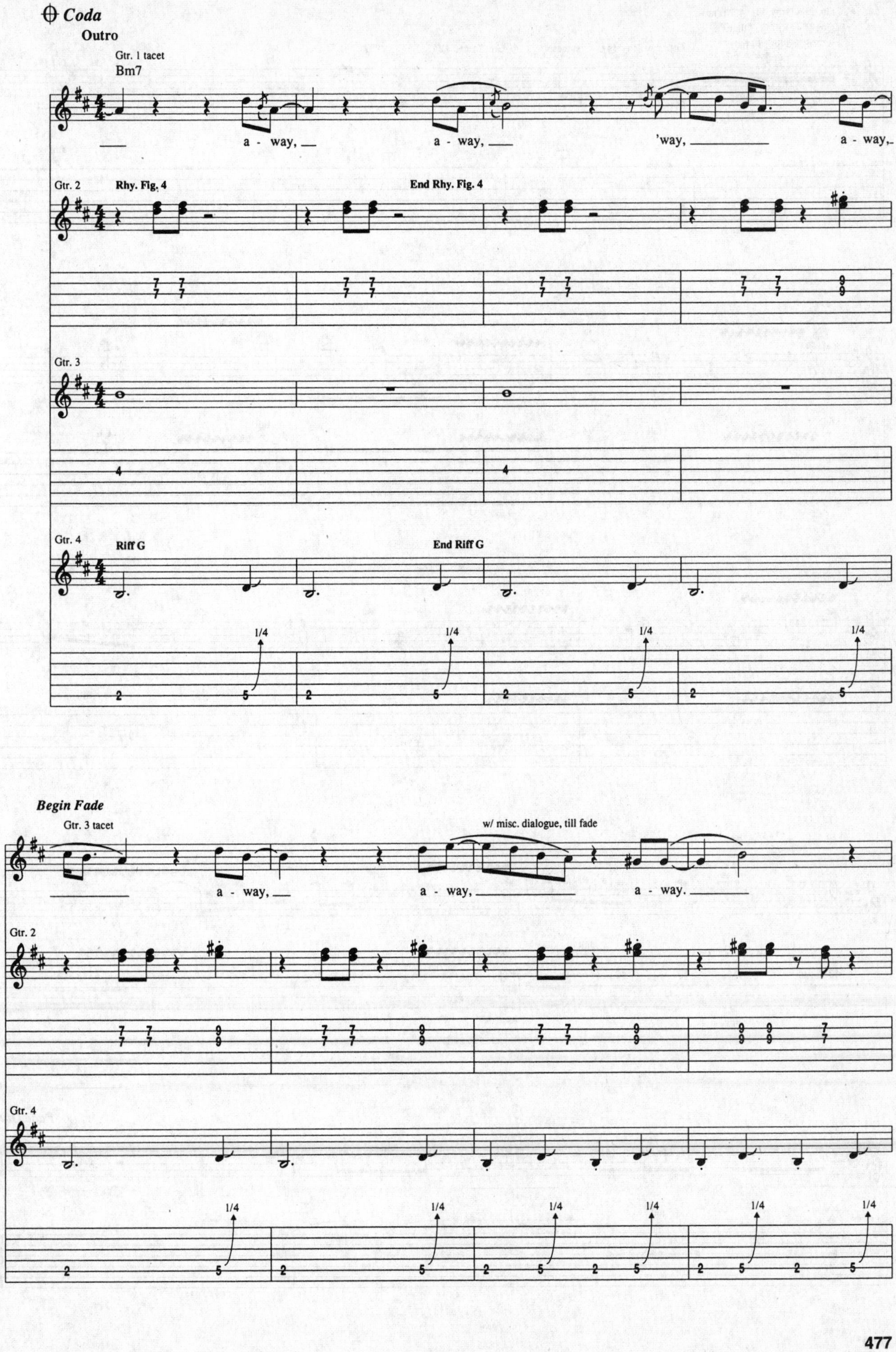

Coda

Outro

Gtr. 1 tacet

Bm7

a - way, a - way, 'way, a - way,

Gtr. 2 — Rhy. Fig. 4 — End Rhy. Fig. 4

Gtr. 3

Gtr. 4 — Riff G — End Riff G

1/4 1/4 1/4 1/4

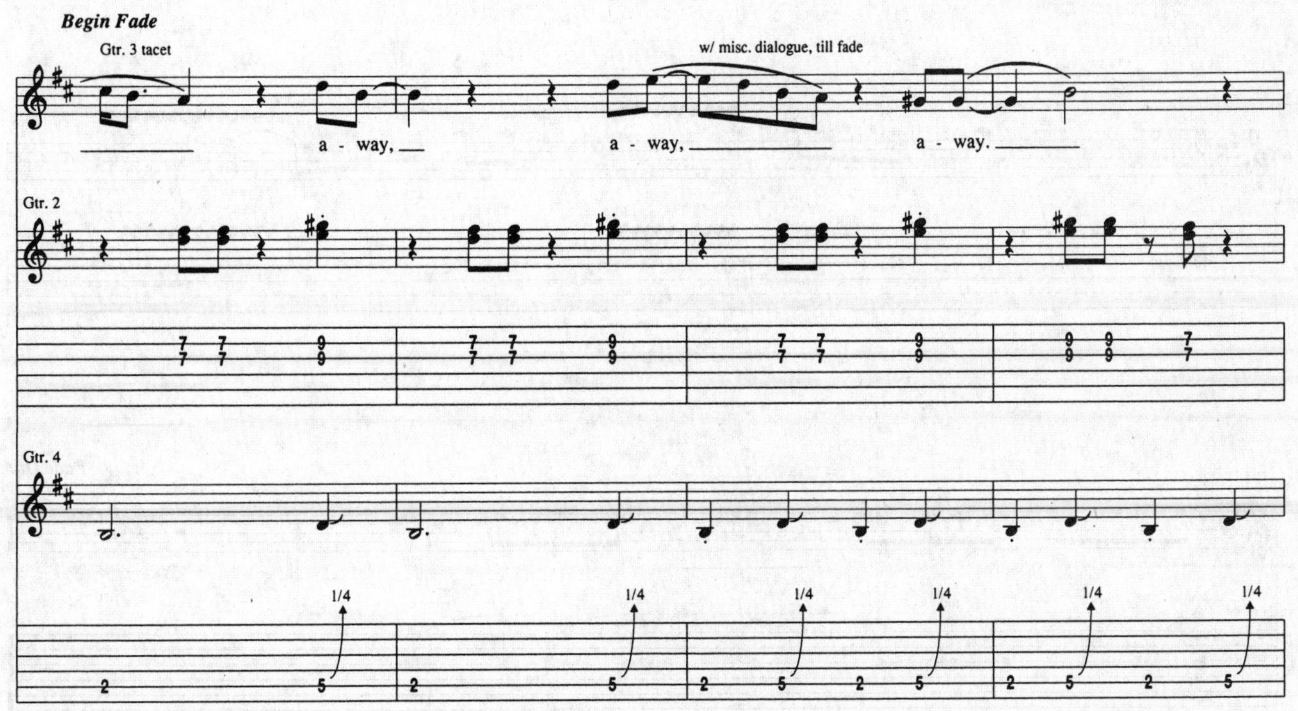

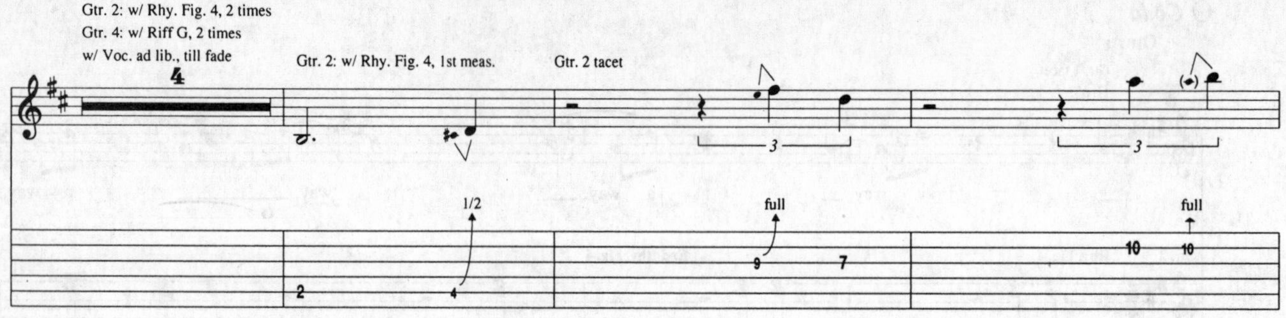
Gtr. 2: w/ Rhy. Fig. 4, 2 times
Gtr. 4: w/ Riff G, 2 times
w/ Voc. ad lib., till fade
Gtr. 2: w/ Rhy. Fig. 4, 1st meas.
Gtr. 2 tacet
1/2
full
full
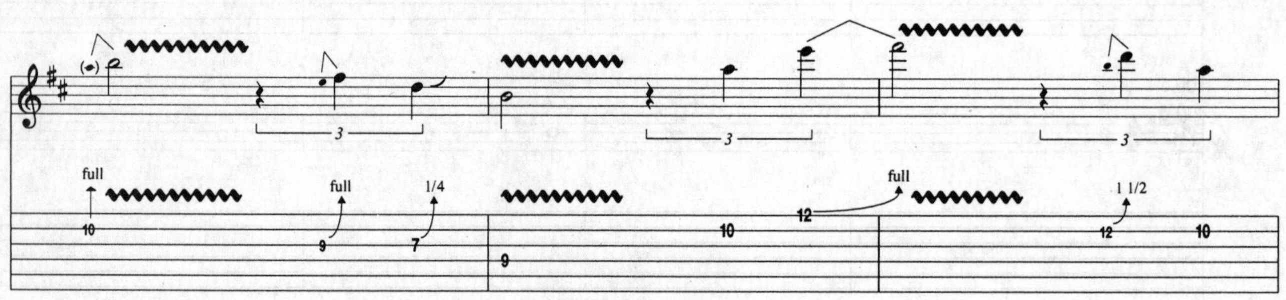
full
full
1/4
full
1 1/2

full
full
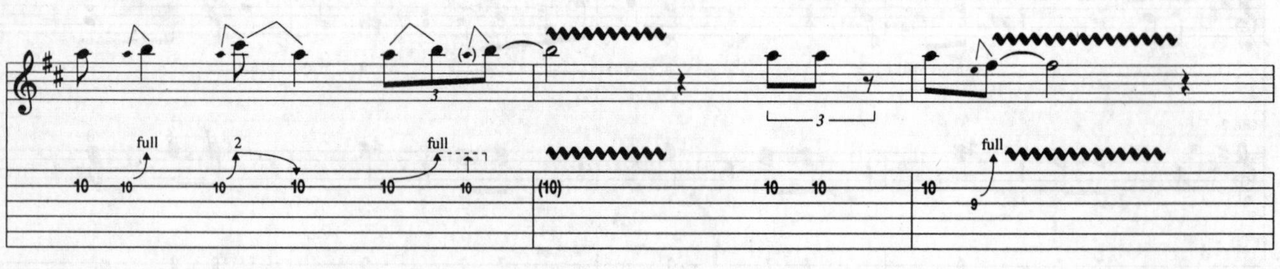
full
2
full
full
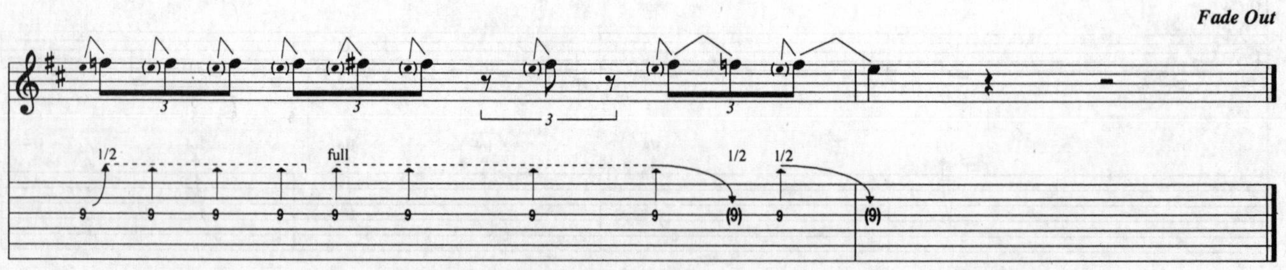
Fade Out
1/2
full
1/2
1/2

Money for Nothing

Words and Music by Mark Knopfler and Sting

B♭5
C5
G5

F5
G5
Verse
G5
Huh!
1. Now, look at them yo - yos, that's the way you do it,

B♭5
C5
G5
you play the gui - tar on the M. T. V.
That ain't work-in', that's the way you do it,

F5
G5
mon-ey for noth-in' and your chicks for free.
Now, that ain't work-in', that's the way you do it,

Bb5
C5
G5
let me tell ya them_ guys ain't dumb._ You may-be get a blis-ter on your lit-tle fin-ger,
8va
loco
Harm.
pitch: D
Chorus
F5
G5
Eb5
Bb5
may-be get a blis-ter on your_ thumb._ We got-ta in-stall mi-cro-wave_ ov-ens,
*Gtrs. 1 & 2 (dist.)
Rhy. Fig. 1
mf
w/ fingers
*Composite arrangement
Eb5
F5
G5
cus-tom kitch-en de-liv-er-ies. We got-ta move these re-frig-er-a-tors,
End Rhy. Fig. 1
C5
D5
E
We got-ta move these col-or T. V.'s. Ow!

Verse

G5 Bb5 C5

2. See the lit - tle fag - got with the ear-ring and the make - up? Yeah bud-dy, that's his own hair.

Gtr. 2

Gtr. 1

G5 F5 G5

That lit - tle fag - got got his own jet air - plane. That lit - tle fag - got, he's a mil - lion - aire.

Chorus
Gtr. 1: w/ Rhy. Fig. 1, simile
E♭5
B♭5
E♭5
F5
We got - ta in - stall mi - cro - wave ov - ens, cus - tom kitch - en de - liv - er - ies.
Gtr. 2
G5
C5
We got - ta move these re - frig - er - a - tors, we got - ta move those col - or T. V.'s.
Gtrs. 1 & 2
Interlude
E
G5
Oo, a - move - a.
Gtr. 2
Gtr. 1
divisi
Gtrs. 1 & 2
*Gtr. 1 to left of slashes in TAB.
B♭5
C5
G5
Huh!
8va
loco
Harm.

Chorus

F5 G5 Eb5 Bb5

(Got-ta in - stall mi-cro-wave ov-ens,

Gtr. 2

Gtr. 1

Eb5 F5 G5

We got - ta move these re-frig-er-a-tors.

cus-tom kitch-en de-liv-er-ies. We got-ta move these re-frig-er-a-tors,

C5 D5 E5

we got-ta move these col-or T. V.'s.)

Look at ya look here.

Verse

G5

3. I should-a learned to play the gui-tar,

I should-a learned to play them drums.

B♭ C5

Look at that

Gtr. 2 tacet
G5
F5
G5
ma-ma, she got it. Stick-in' in the cam-er-a __ man, __ we could have some fun. And
Gtr. 1
Bb5
C5
he's up there. What's that? Ha-wai-ian nois-es? He's bang-in' on the bon-gos like a chim - pan - zee. Oh, that
8va
loco
Harm.
pitch: D
G5
F5
G5
ain't work-in', that's the way you _ do it, get your mon-ey for noth-in', get your chicks for free.
(That's _ the way you do it, mon-ey for noth-in', get your chicks for free.)
Chorus
Eb5
Bb5
Eb5
F5
We got-ta in - stall mi-cro-wave _ ov-ens, cus-tom kitch-en de - liv - er - ies.
Gtrs. 1 & 2

G5
C5
D5
We got-ta move these re-frig-er-a-tors,
we got-ta move thse col-or T. V.'s.
(We got-ta move these re-frig-er-a-tors,)
Interlude
E5
G5
Gtr. 2
Gtr. 1
B♭5
C5
G5
Ow!

Verse

F5 G5 G5

Lis-ten here. 4. Now, that ain't work - ing, that's

1/2

the way you do it, you play the gui - tar on the M. T. V.

B♭5 C5

G5
F5
G5
That ain't _ work-in', that's _ the way you do it, mon-ey for noth-in' and your chicks for free. _

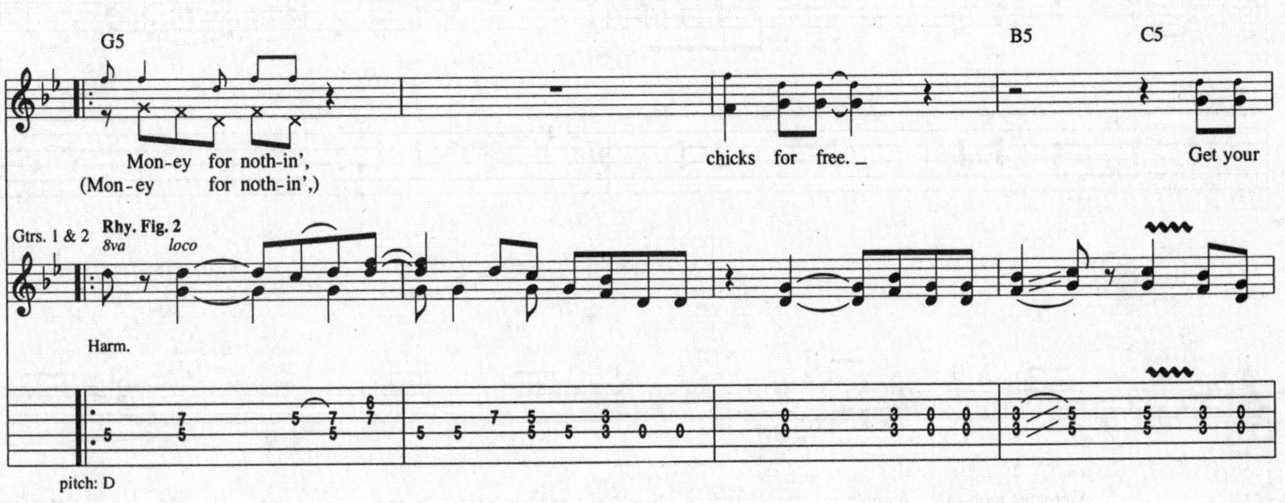
G5
B5
C5
Mon-ey for noth-in', chicks for free. _ Get your
(Mon-ey for noth-in',)
Gtrs. 1 & 2
Rhy. Fig. 2
8va
loco
Harm.
pitch: D

G5
1.
F5
G5
mon-ey for noth-in' and your chicks for free. _____ All that...
8va
loco
End Rhy. Fig. 2
Harm.
pitch: D

2.
F5
G5
All that mon-ey for noth-in', chicks for free.
(Mon-ey for noth - in' and your chicks for free.

B♭5
C5
G5
Mon-ey for noth-in', chicks for free.
Get your mon-ey for noth-in' and your chicks for free.

F5
G5
B♭5
C5
Ow. yeah.
Get your mon-ey for noth-in' and your chicks for free. Get your
Gtr. 1
full
full
full
Gtr. 1
8va
loco
Harm.
pitch: D

G5
F5
G5
What's that?
mon - ey for noth-in' and your chicks for free. _
Look at that, look at that.
Get your
hold bend
full
Gtrs. 1 & 2: w/ Rhy. Fig. 2, 2 1/2 times, simile
w/ Lead Voc. ad lib., 2nd & 3rd times
B♭5
C5
mon-ey for noth-in' and your chicks for free. _ Mon
(I want my, I want my, I want my M. T. V.
*Sing simile on repeats.
1., 2.
ey for noth - in' ___ and your chicks for free. _ Get your
I want my, I want my, I want my M. T. V.
3.
Mon - ey for noth - in' and your chicks for free. _)
That ain't
I want my, I want my, I want my M. T. V.)
Gtr. 2
1/2
Gtr. 1

Outro

G5
B♭5
C5
work-in'.
Gtrs. 1 & 2
8va
loco
Harm.
pitch: D

Gtr. 2
G5
F5
G5
Gtr. 1

Gtr. 2: w/ Rhy. Fig. 2, simile
Gtr. 1
B♭5
C5
full

G5
8va
loco
F5
G5
Harm.
P.M.
full
1/2
pitch: D

Gtr. 1: w/ Rhy. Fig. 2, simile
Gtr. 2
B♭5
C5
full
G5
F5
1/4
Gtr. 2: w/ Rhy. Fig. 2, simile
Gtr. 1
8va loco
Harm.
pitch: D
Begin Fade
8va
loco
Harm. ⅃
D

G5
F5
G5
Mon-ey for noth -
Gtrs. 1 & 2
Gtr. 3
(dist.)
mp
Gtrs. 1 & 2
divisi
full
full
full
full

Gtr. 3 tacet
Bb5
C5
in', ___
chicks for free. ___
Mon-ey for noth -
Gtrs. 1 & 2
8va loco
8va
loco
Harm.
Harm.
pitch: D
F#

Fade Out
G5
F5
G5
in',
chicks for free. ___

More Than Words

Words and Music by Nuno Bettencourt and Gary Cherone

Tune down 1/2 step:
(low to high) Eb–Ab–Db–Gb–Bb–Eb

Intro

Moderately slow ♩ = 96

* Hit muted strings w/ R.H. throughout.

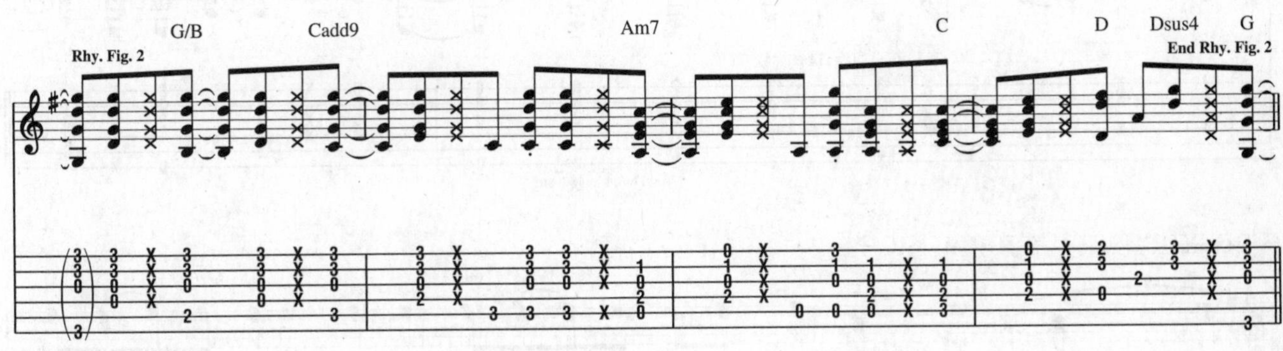

Verse

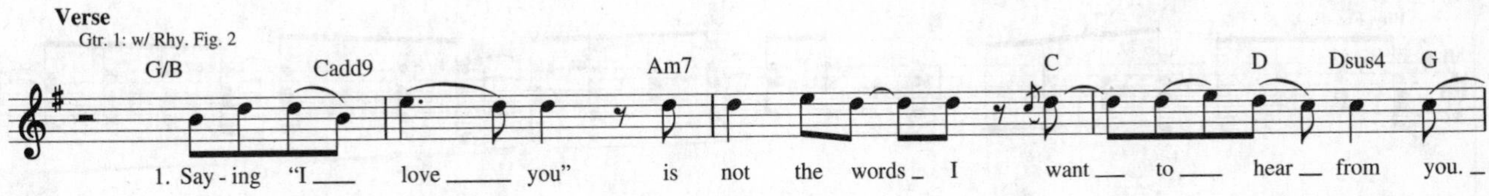

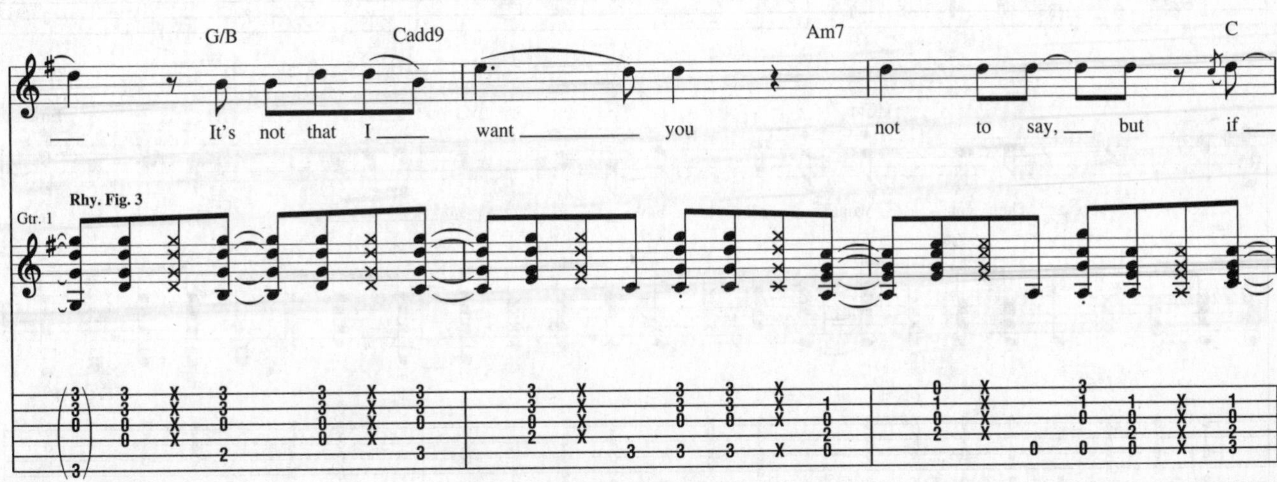

D Dsus4 Em Am7
you on - ly knew how eas - y
End Rhy. Fig. 3
D7 G D/F# Dadd2/F# Em Am7
it would be to show me how you feel. More than words
* T = Thumb on 6th str.
Chorus
D7 G7 G7/B C
is all you have to do to make it real.
Rhy. Fig. 4
Cm G Em7
Then you would - n't have to say that you love

Am7
D7
G
me,
'cause I'd al - read - y know.
What
End Rhy. Fig. 4
Dadd2/F#
Em
Bm
C
would you do if my heart was torn in two?
Rhy. Fig. 5
G/B
Am7
D7
More than words to show you feel that your love
G
for me is real.
What would you say

Dadd2/F#
Em
Bm
C
if I took those words a - way? Then you could-

G/B
Am7
D7
-n't make things new just by say - ing "I love you."
(You.
End Rhy. Fig. 5

Interlude

Gtr. 1: w/ Rhy. Fig. 1
G
G/B
Cadd9
Am7
C
D
Dsus4
G
La, dee, da, la, dee, da, dee, dai, dai, da. More than words.
La, dee, da.)

G/B
Cadd9
Am7
D7
La, dee, da, dai, da.
Gtr. 1
* Hit body of gtr.

Verse

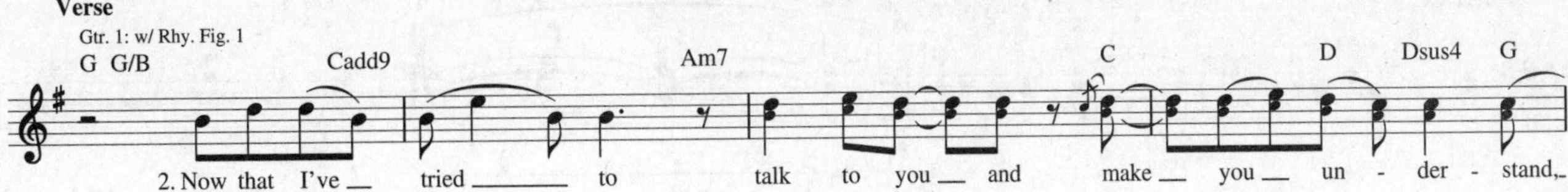

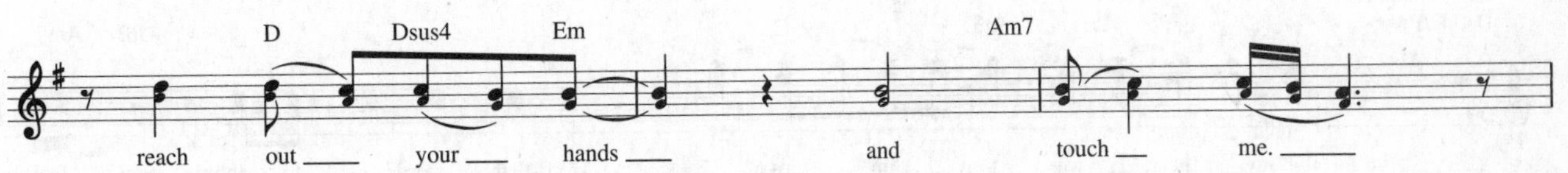

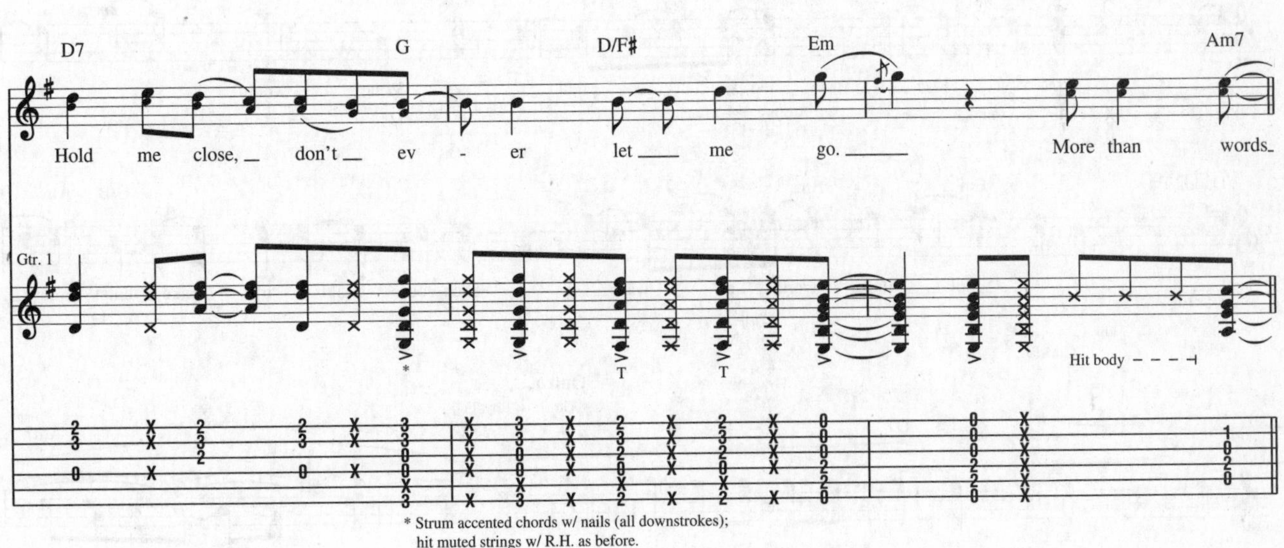

Chorus

Am7 D D7♭9/A G
I'd already know.
What would you do
Gtr. 1
Gtr. 1: w/ Rhy. Fig. 5
Dadd2/F♯ Em Bm C G/B Am7
if my heart was torn in two?
More than words to show you feel
D7 G
that your love for me is real.
What would you say
Dadd2/F♯ Em Bm C G/B Am7
if I took those words away?
Then you could-n't make things new
Outro
Gtr. 1: w/ Rhy. Fig. 1
D7 G G/B Cadd9 Am7
just by say-ing "I love you."
La, dee, da, dai, dai,
Gtr. 1: w/ Rhy. Fig. 2
C D Dsus4 G G/B Cadd9
dee, dai, dai, da.
More than words.
Am7 C D Dsus4 G
La, dee, da, dai, dai, dee, dai, dai, da.
More than words.

G/B
Cadd9
Am7
La, dee, dai, dai, dai, dee, dai, dai, da.
(La, dee, dai, dai, da. La,
Gtr. 1
* strum
* As before
C
D
Dsus4
G
G/B
Cadd9
Am7
More than words.
da, da, da, da.
La, da, da, dai, da.
La, da, da, dai, da.
strum
Hit body
C
D
G
More than words.
La, da, da, da, da, da.)
Dadd2/F#
Dm(add2)/F
Esus4
rit.
Oo, oo, oo, oo, oo, oo,
rit.

Slower
Am7
rit.
oo.
Free time
D
accel.
N.C.
More than
A tempo
G
words.
8va
Harm.
Bend neck
Csus2
G/B
Gm/B♭
Freely
Am7
G

Mustang Sally

Words and Music by Bonny Rice

*Chord in parenthesis is for Gtr. 4

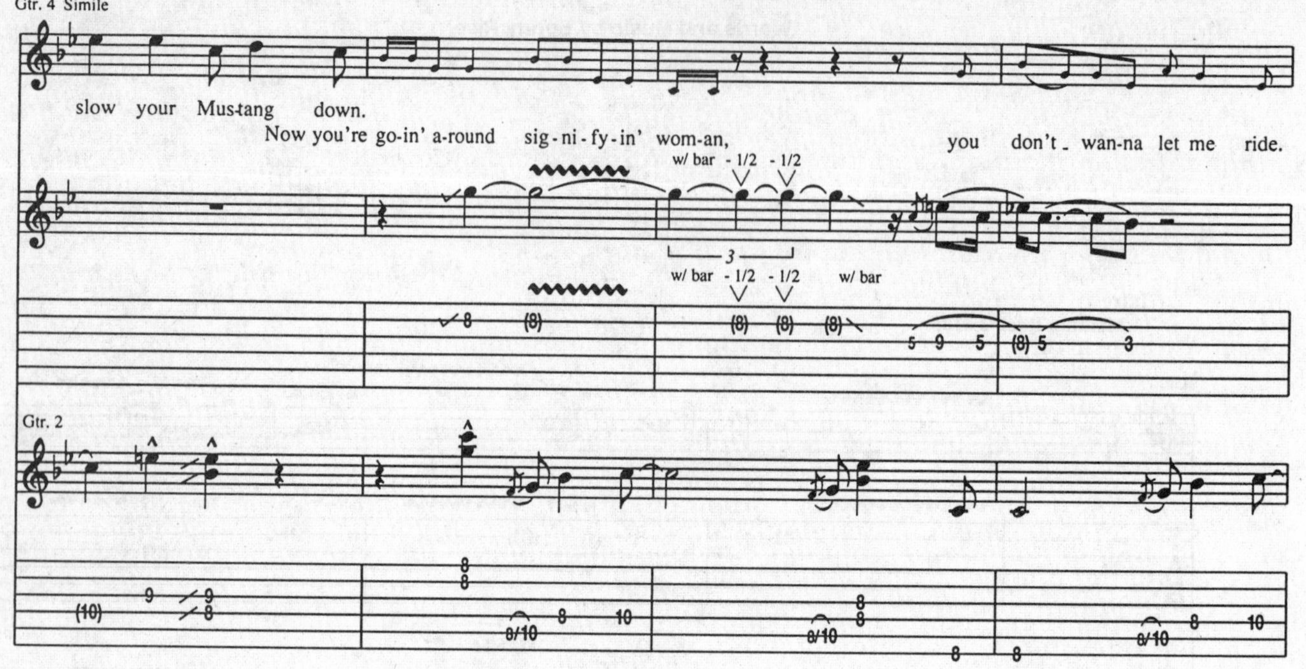
Gtr. 1: w/ Fill 12, 2nd time
Gtr. 2: Substitute Fill 2, 2nd time
Gtr. 4 Simile
Gtr. 1: w/ Fill 12, 2nd time
slow your Mus-tang down.
Now you're go-in' a-round sig - ni - fy - in' wom-an,
you don't _ wan-na let me ride.
w/ bar - 1/2 - 1/2
w/ bar
Gtr. 2

Fill 11
Gtr. 1
w/ bar

Fill 2
Gtr. 2

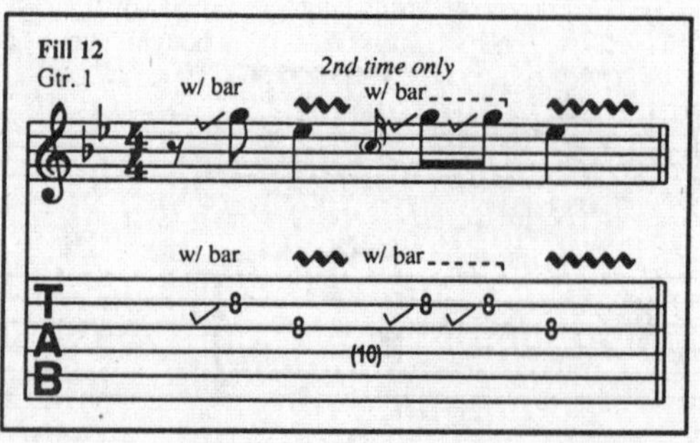
Fill 12
Gtr. 1
w/ bar
2nd time only
w/ bar

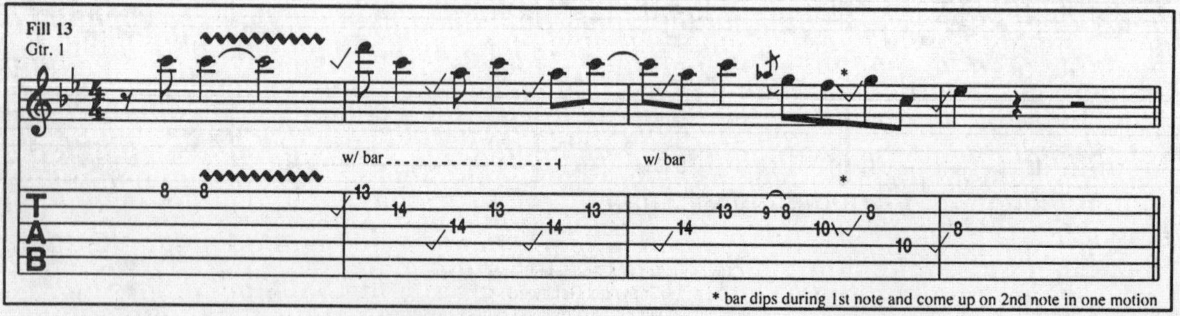
Fill 13
Gtr. 1
w/ bar
* bar dips during 1st note and come up on 2nd note in one motion

Gtr. 1: w/ Fill 13, 2nd time
Gtr. 2: Substitute Fill 3, 2nd time
F7(F5)
Mus-tang
Sal-ly,
ba - by,
I guess you bet-ter
8va
full

Gtr. 2: substitute Fill 4, 2nd time
Gtr. 1: w/ Fill 14, 2nd time
C7(C5)
slow your Mus-tang down.
Spoken: I hope you will.
2nd time: Yes, you will now.
* w/bar
** w/bar ** w/bar
1/4
* Pull off and simultaneously dip slightly with vibrato bar
** Hammer and simultaneously dip with vibrato bar

Fill 3
Gtr. 2
TAB

Gtr. 2: w/ fill 5, 2nd time

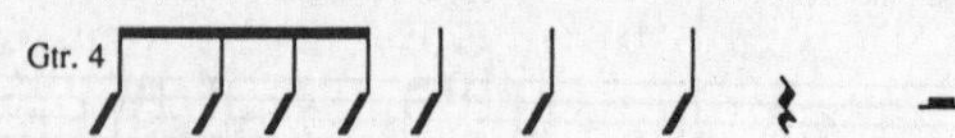

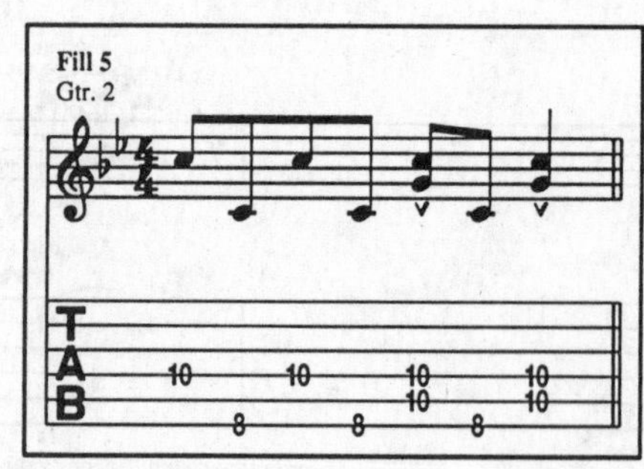

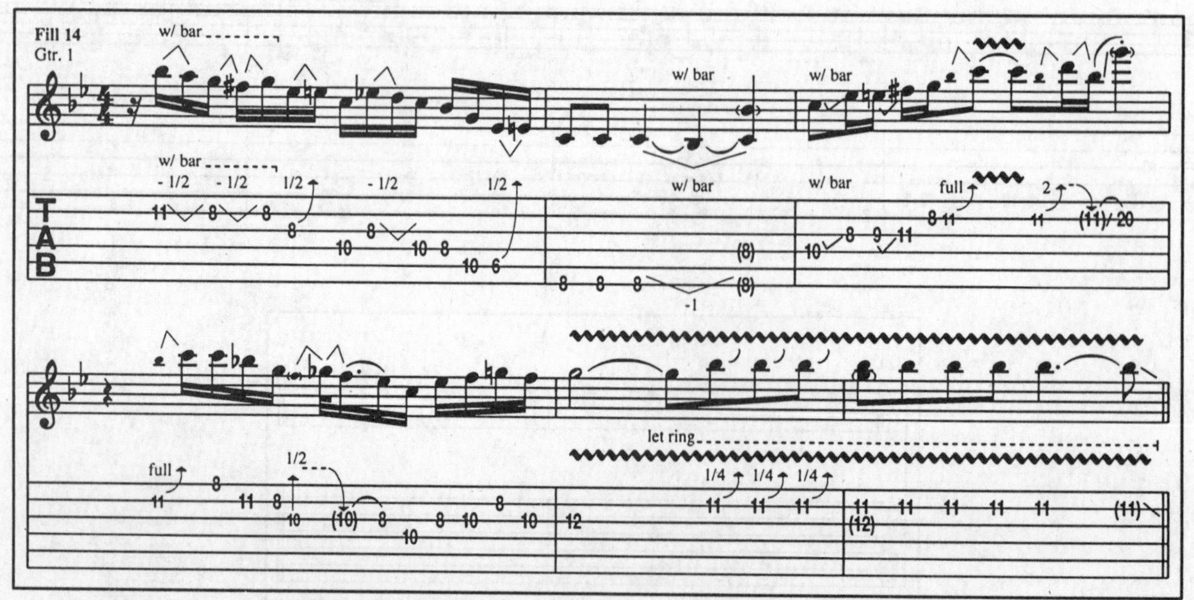

Gtr. 1: w/ Fill 15, 2nd time
C7(C5)
B♭/C
C7
put your big feet on the ground.
big fat feet on the ground.
Oh yes, I will.
Oh yah, Sal-ly, well.
sweep
Gtr. 4: Simile
C7(C5)
Gtr. 2: Rhy. Fig. 1, 7 times
Gtr. 2: w/ Fill 16, 2nd time
All you wan-na do is ride a-round Sal-ly.
Backups: (Ride Sal-ly, ride..
Rhy. Fig. 1
End Rhy. Fig. 1
Fill 15
Gtr. 1
w/ bar
w/ bar
-1/2

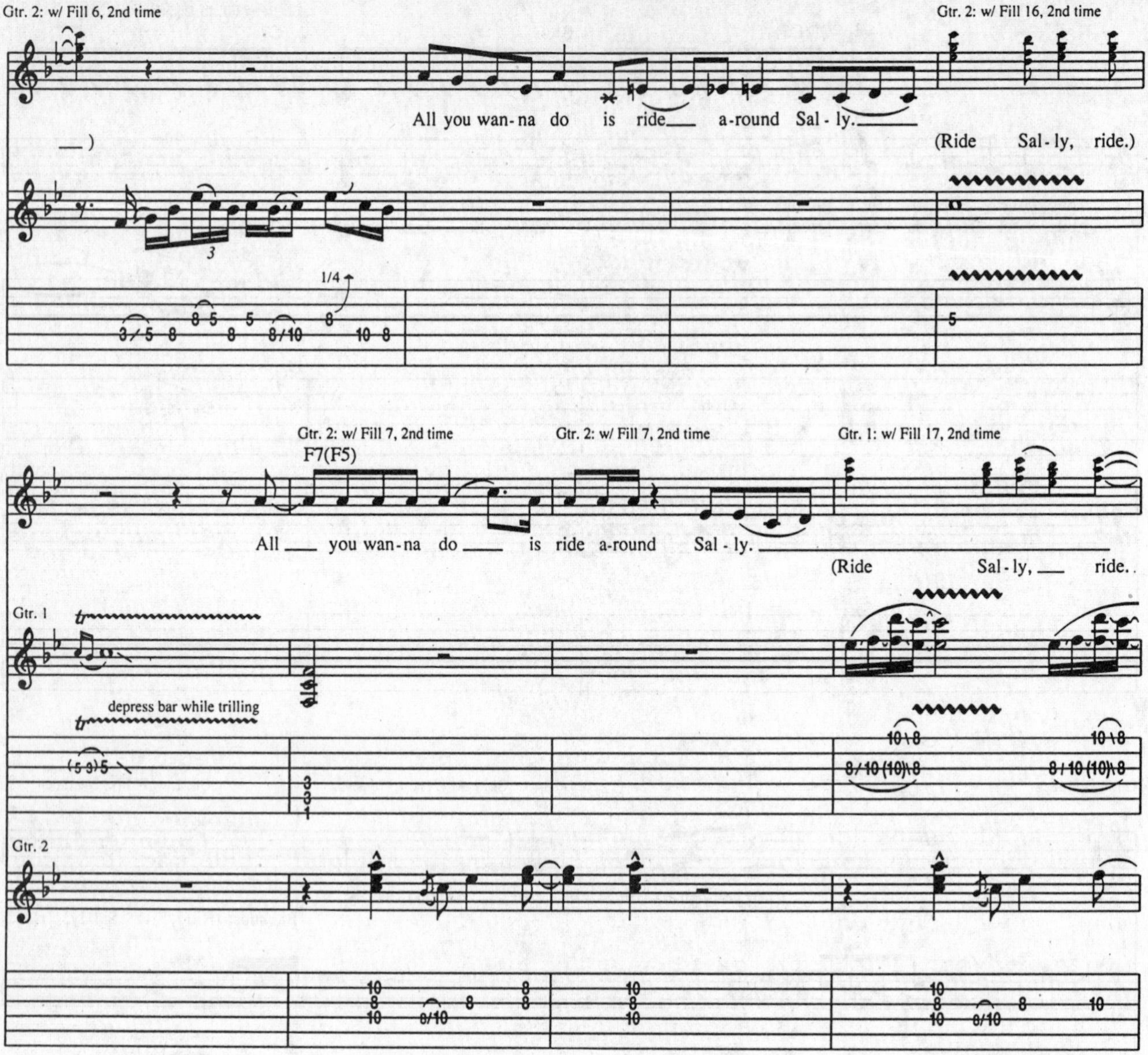

Gtr. 2: w/ Fill 6, 2nd time

Gtr. 2: w/ Fill 16, 2nd time

All you wan-na do is ride___ a-round Sal-ly.___ (Ride Sal-ly, ride.)

___)

1/4

Gtr. 2: w/ Fill 7, 2nd time

F7(F5)

Gtr. 2: w/ Fill 7, 2nd time

Gtr. 1: w/ Fill 17, 2nd time

All ___ you wan-na do ___ is ride a-round Sal-ly. ___ (Ride Sal-ly, ___ ride..

Gtr. 1

depress bar while trilling

Gtr. 2

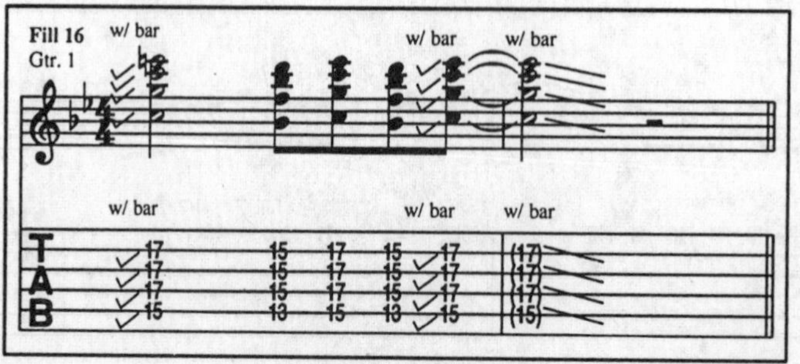

Gtr. 2: w/ Rhy. Fig. 1, 4 times
Gtr. 1: w/ Fill 16, 2nd time
C7(C5)
All you wan-na do is ride a-round Sal-ly.
(Ride Sal - ly, ride.)
w/bar
1/2
Gtr. 2: w/ Fill 8, 2nd time
Gtr. 1: w/ Fill 18, 2nd time
Gtr. 2: w/ Fill 1
G7(G5)
(F5) N.C.
Gtr. 4
One of these a ear - ly morn - in',
you gon-na be a wip-in' your weep-in'
Gtr. 1
w/ bar
Fill 7
Gtr. 2
Fill 1
Gtr. 2
Fill 17
Gtr. 1
w/ bar

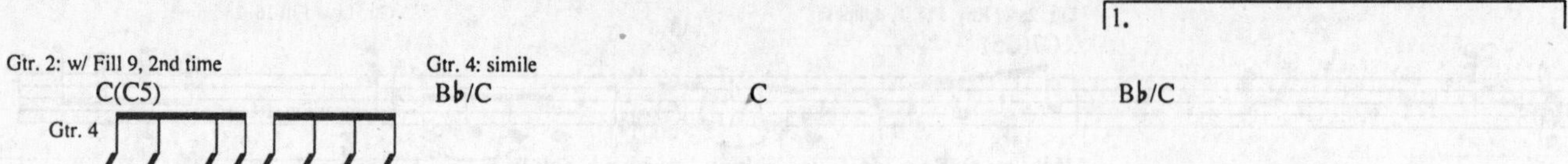
Gtr. 2: w/ Fill 9, 2nd time
Gtr. 4: simile
1.
C(C5)
B♭/C
C
B♭/C
Gtr. 4

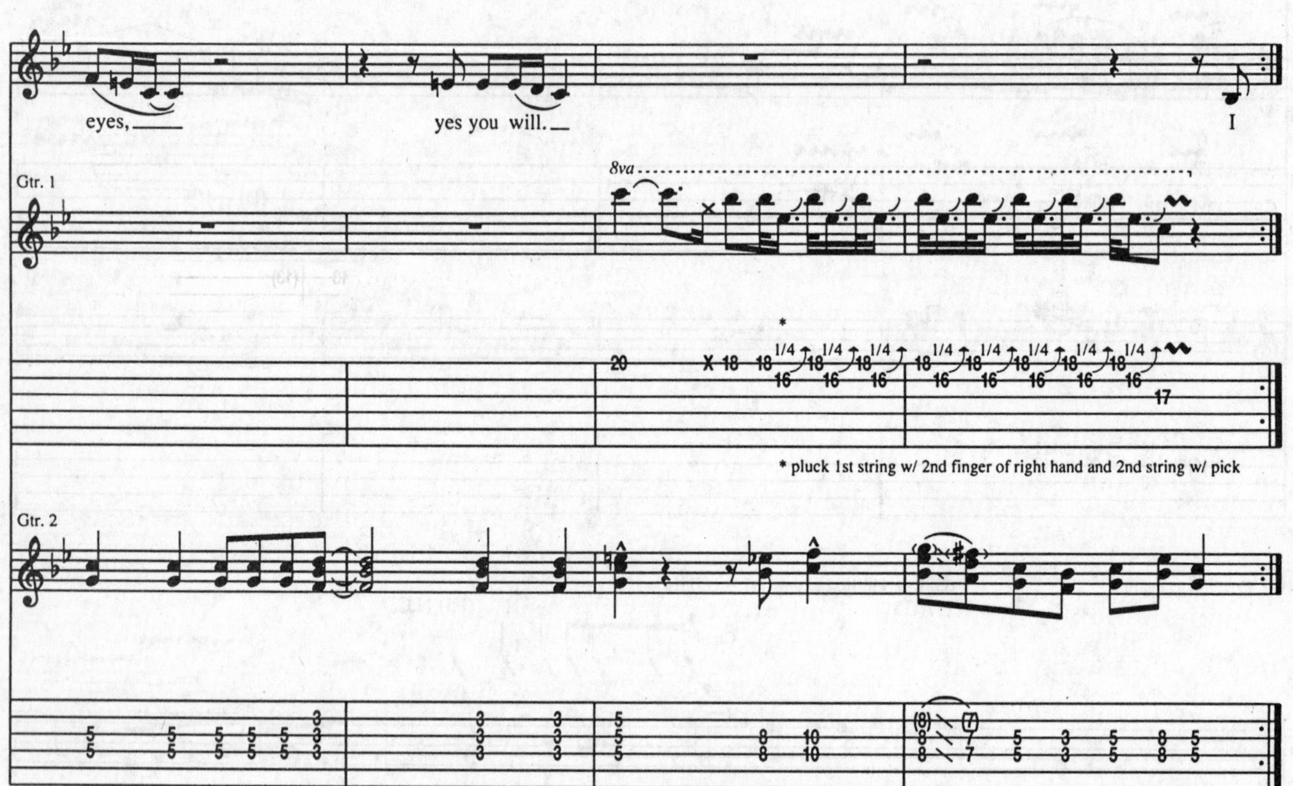
eyes,
yes you will.
I
Gtr. 1
8va
* pluck 1st string w/ 2nd finger of right hand and 2nd string w/ pick
Gtr. 2

Fill 8
Gtr. 2

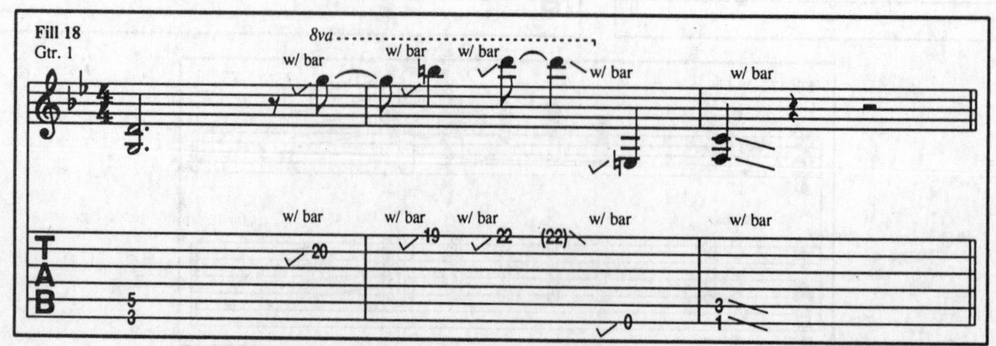
Fill 18
Gtr. 1
8va
w/ bar

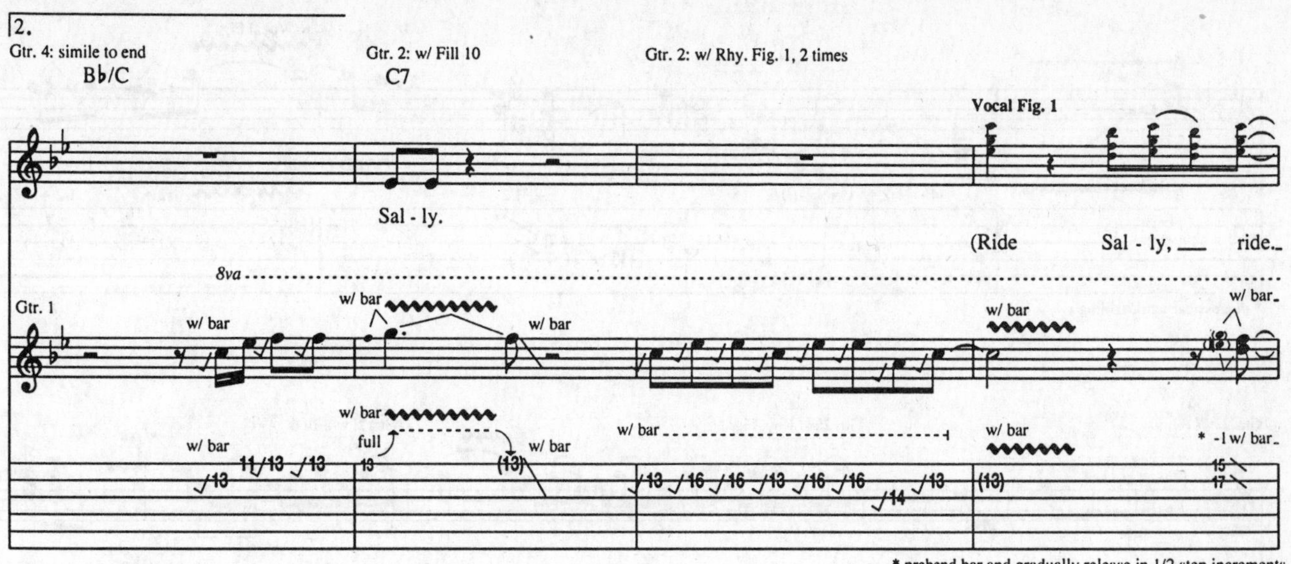
2.
Gtr. 4: simile to end
B♭/C
Gtr. 2: w/ Fill 10
C7
Gtr. 2: w/ Rhy. Fig. 1, 2 times
Vocal Fig. 1
Sal - ly.
(Ride
Sal - ly,
ride.
8va
Gtr. 1
w/ bar
full
* -1 w/ bar
* prebend bar and gradually release in 1/2 step increments

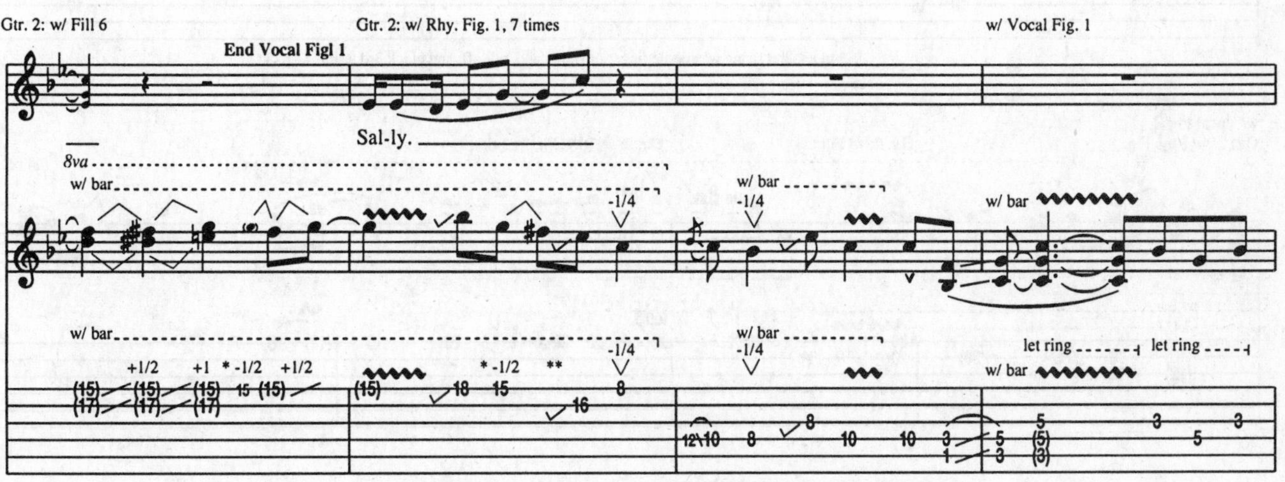
Gtr. 2: w/ Fill 6
End Vocal Figl 1
Gtr. 2: w/ Rhy. Fig. 1, 7 times
w/ Vocal Fig. 1
Sal-ly.
8va
w/ bar
let ring
* G is bent down 1/2 step w/ bar ** bar is held down while picking the E, then released

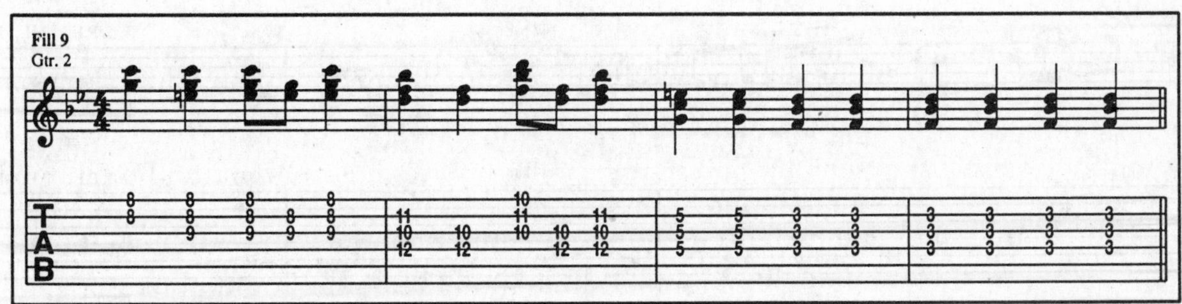
Fill 9
Gtr. 2

Fill 10
Gtr. 2

* w/bar
w/ Vocal Fig. 1
* w/bar
w/ bar
let ring
* depress bar while trilling

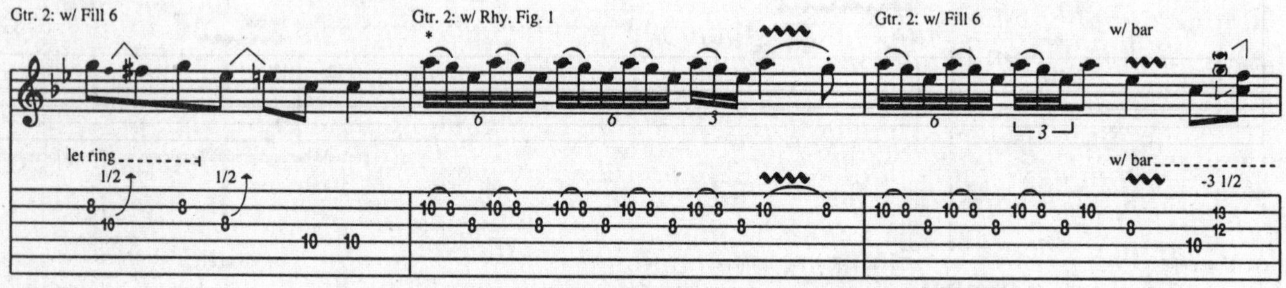

Gtr. 2: w/ Fill 6
Gtr. 2: w/ Rhy. Fig. 1
Gtr. 2: w/ Fill 6
w/ bar
let ring
w/ bar
* pluck 2nd string w/ middle finger of right hand, pulloff, and pluck 3rd string w/ pick

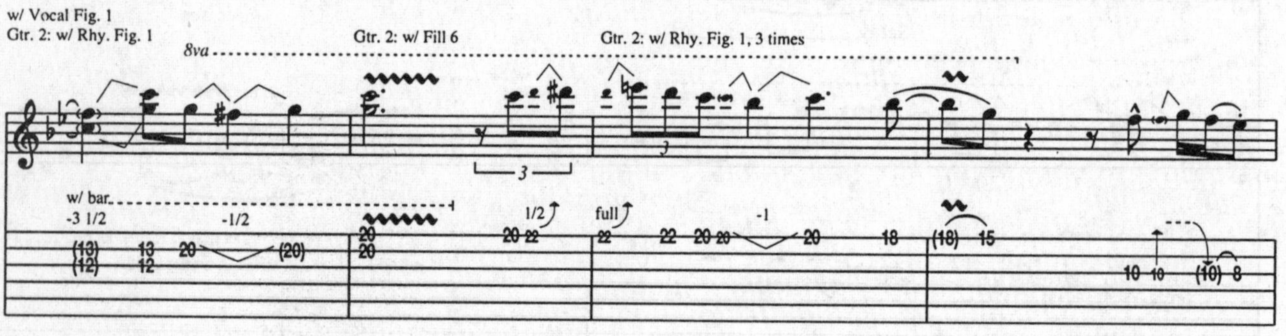

w/ Vocal Fig. 1
Gtr. 2: w/ Rhy. Fig. 1
Gtr. 2: w/ Fill 6
Gtr. 2: w/ Rhy. Fig. 1, 3 times
8va
w/ bar
full

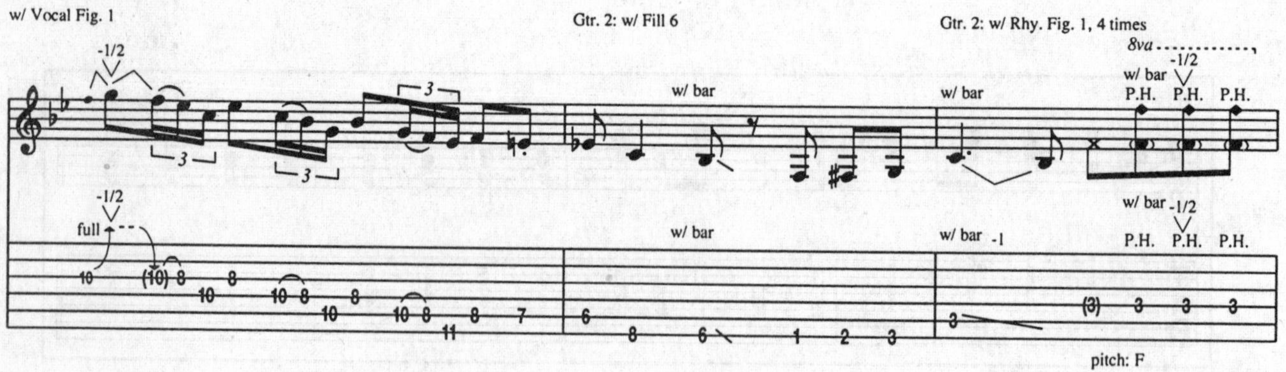

w/ Vocal Fig. 1
Gtr. 2: w/ Fill 6
Gtr. 2: w/ Rhy. Fig. 1, 4 times
8va
w/ bar
w/ bar
P.H.
full
pitch: F

Fade
full

No Excuses

Written by Jerry Cantrell

Aadd9
5fr
1342
Badd4
7fr
1342
G6
3fr
1342
E
342

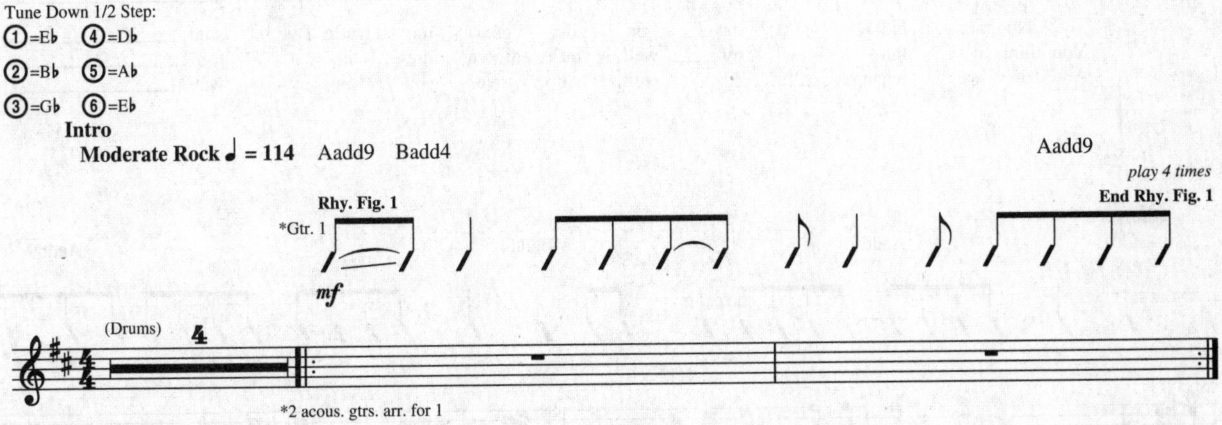

Tune Down 1/2 Step:
1=E♭ 4=D♭
2=B♭ 5=A♭
3=G♭ 6=E♭
Intro
Moderate Rock ♩ = 114
Aadd9 Badd4
Aadd9
play 4 times
Rhy. Fig. 1
End Rhy. Fig. 1
*Gtr. 1
mf
(Drums)
4
*2 acous. gtrs. arr. for 1

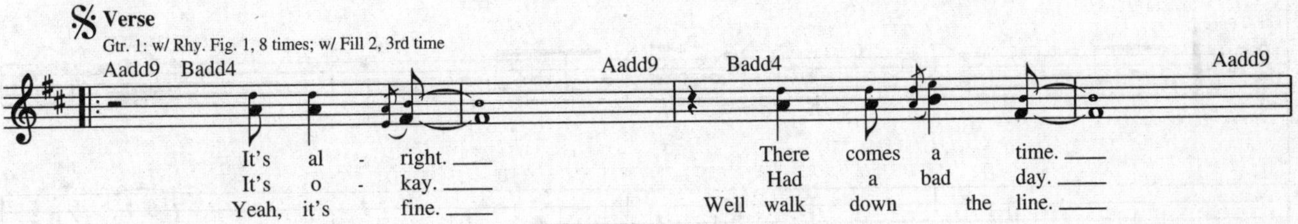

Verse
Gtr. 1: w/ Rhy. Fig. 1, 8 times; w/ Fill 2, 3rd time
Aadd9 Badd4
Aadd9 Badd4
Aadd9
It's al - right. There comes a time.
It's o - kay. Had a bad day.
Yeah, it's fine. Well walk down the line.

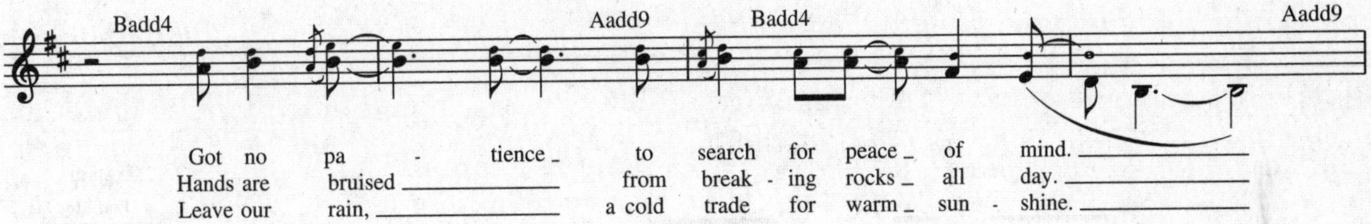

Badd4
Aadd9 Badd4
Aadd9
Got no pa - tience to search for peace of mind.
Hands are bruised from break - ing rocks all day.
Leave our rain, a cold trade for warm sun - shine.

Fill 2
Gtr. 1
7
7
7
TAB

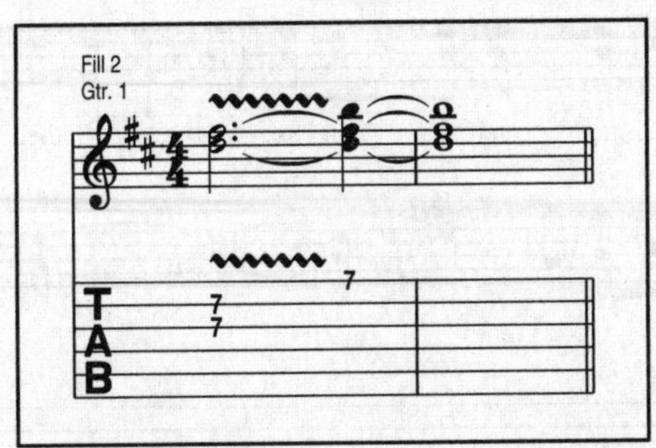

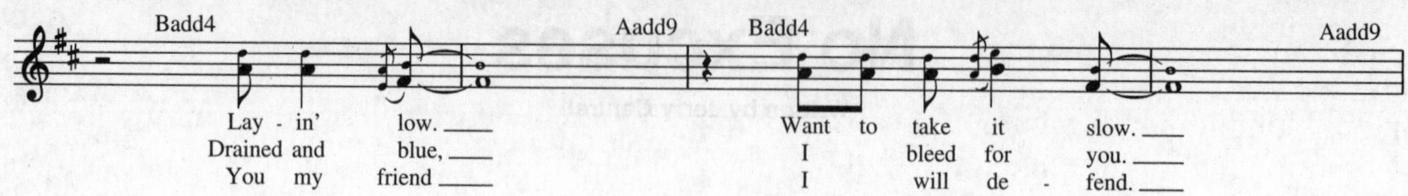
Badd4
Aadd9
Badd4
Aadd9
Lay - in' low.
Want to take it slow.
Drained and blue,
I bleed for you.
You my friend
I will de - fend.

To Coda
Badd4
Aadd9
Badd2
Aadd9
No more hid - ing or dis - guis - ing truths I've sold.
You think it's fun - ny well, you're drown - ing in it too.
And if we change, well, I love you an - y - way.

Chorus
G6
Aadd9
Badd4
Aadd9
Rhy. Fig. 2
Gtr. 1
Ev - 'ry day it's some - thing, hits me all so cold. You
Gtr. 2 (elec.)
full
full

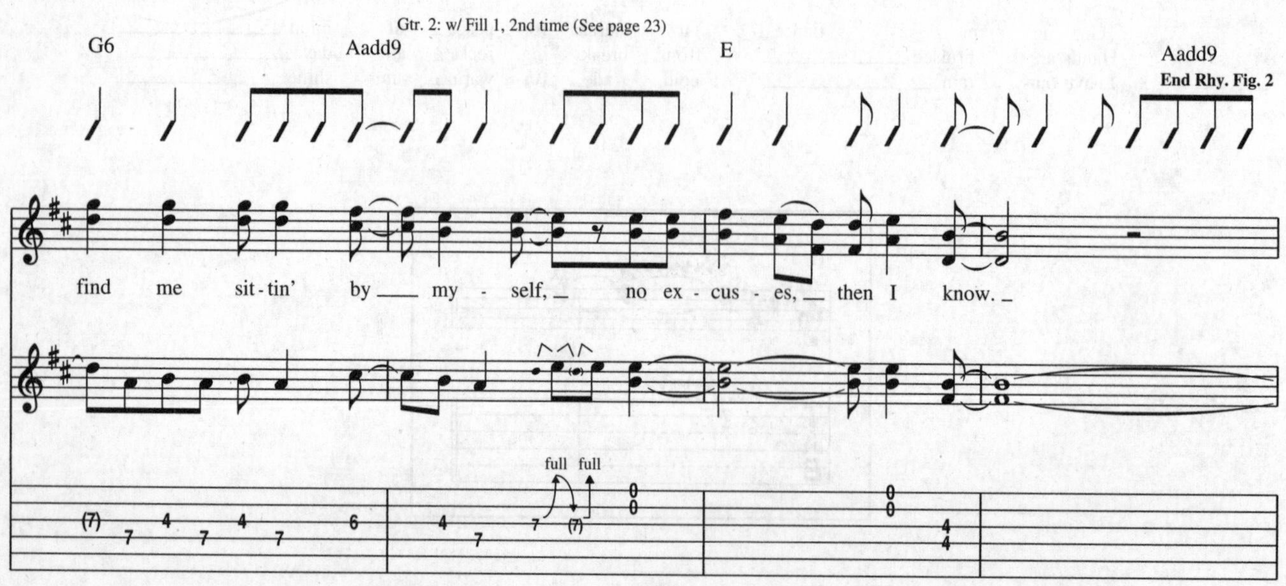
Gtr. 2: w/ Fill 1, 2nd time (See page 23)
G6
Aadd9
E
Aadd9
End Rhy. Fig. 2
find me sit - tin' by my - self, no ex - cus - es, then I know.
full full

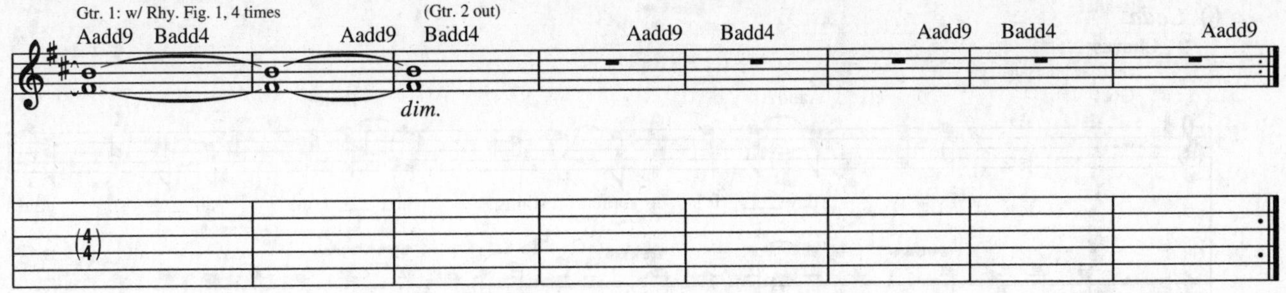
Gtr. 1: w/ Rhy. Fig. 1, 4 times
(Gtr. 2 out)
Aadd9 Badd4 Aadd9 Badd4 Aadd9 Badd4 Aadd9 Badd4 Aadd9
dim.

Guitar Solo

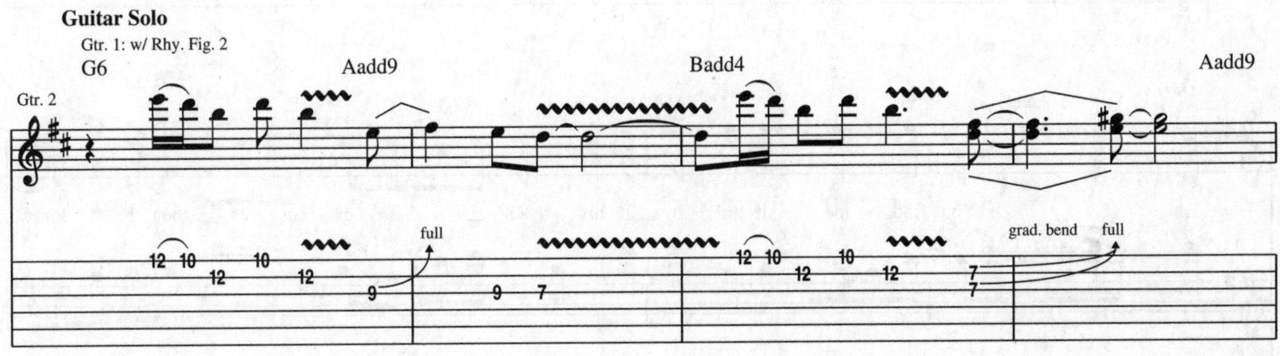
Gtr. 1: w/ Rhy. Fig. 2
G6 Aadd9 Badd4 Aadd9
Gtr. 2
full
grad. bend
full

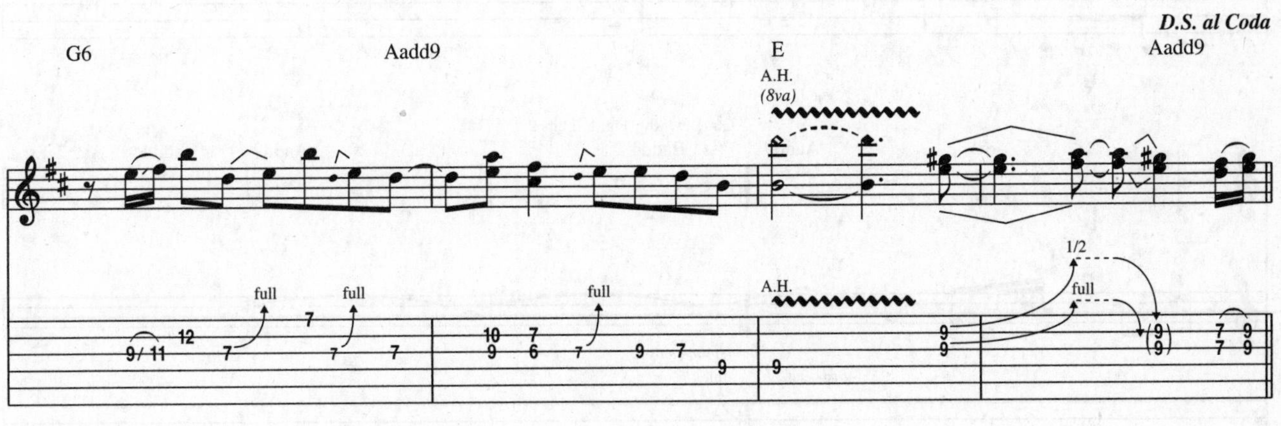
D.S. al Coda
G6 Aadd9 E Aadd9
A.H.
(8va)
full
full
full
A.H.
1/2
full

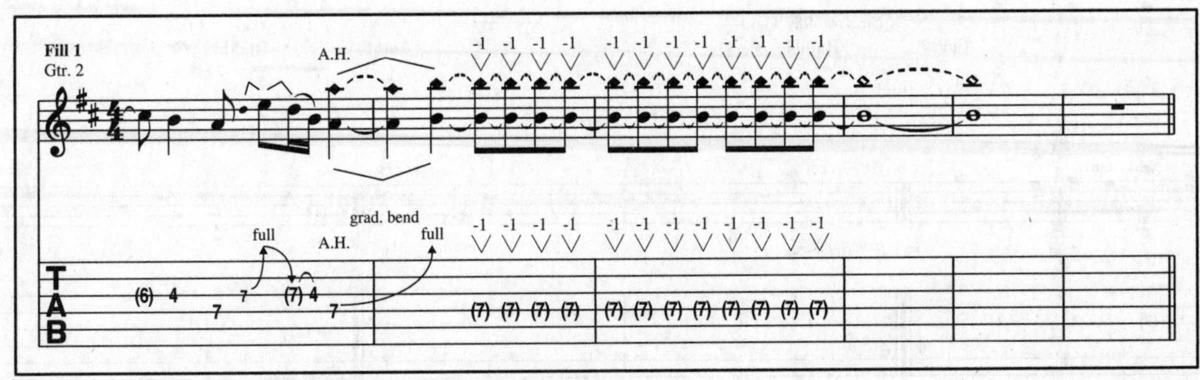
Fill 1
Gtr. 2
A.H.
full
grad. bend
full
A.H.

Coda

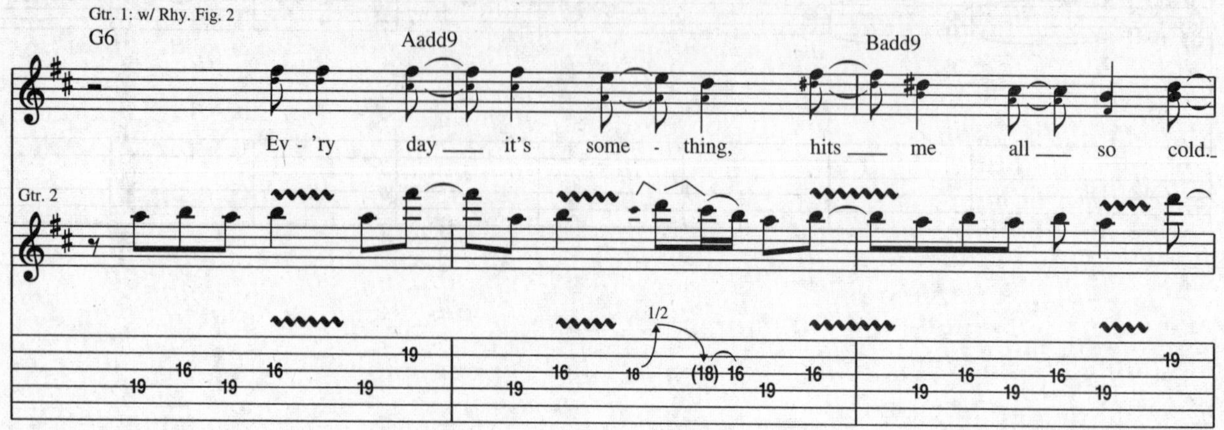
Chorus
Gtr. 1: w/ Rhy. Fig. 2
G6
Aadd9
Badd9
Ev - 'ry day it's some - thing, hits me all so cold.
Gtr. 2
1/2

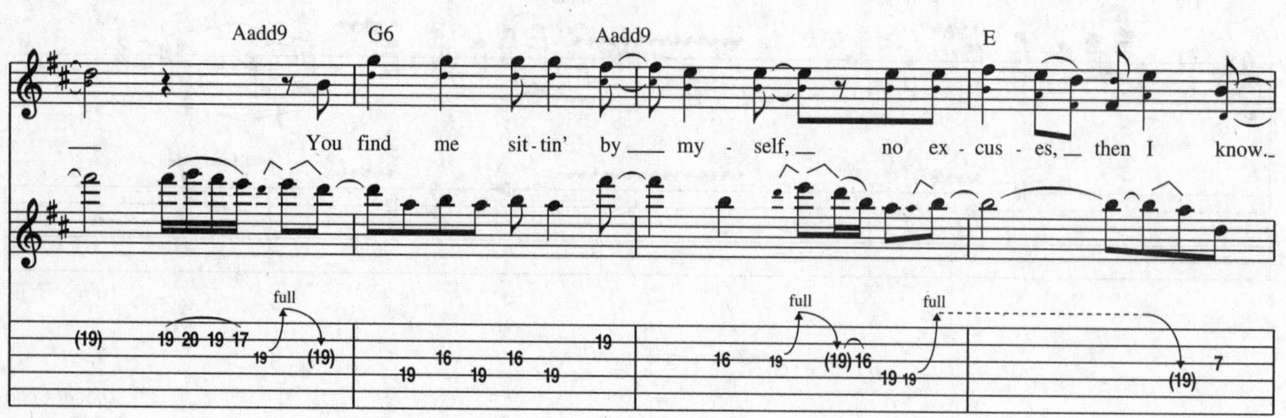
Aadd9
G6
Aadd9
E
You find me sit - tin' by my - self, no ex - cus - es, then I know.
full
full
full

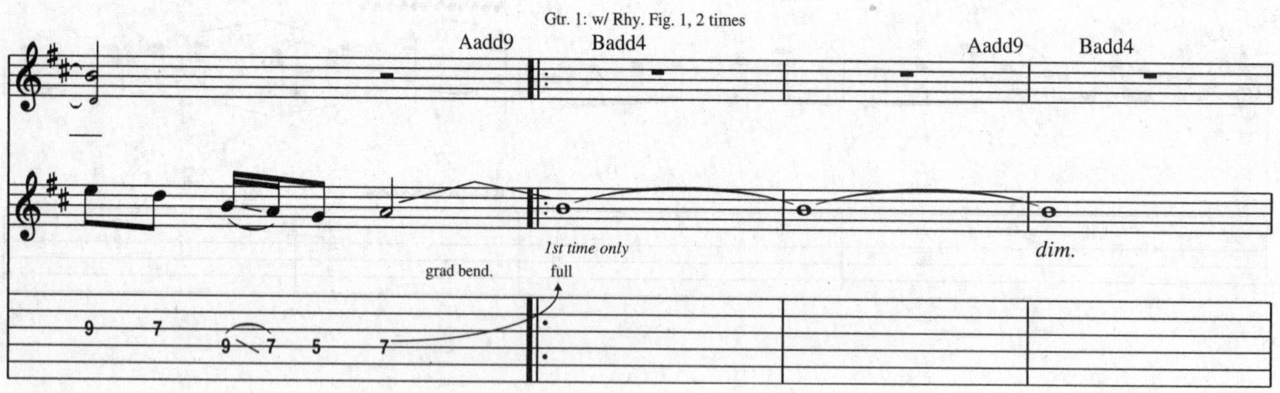
Gtr. 1: w/ Rhy. Fig. 1, 2 times
Aadd9
Badd4
Aadd9
Badd4
1st time only
dim.
grad bend.
full

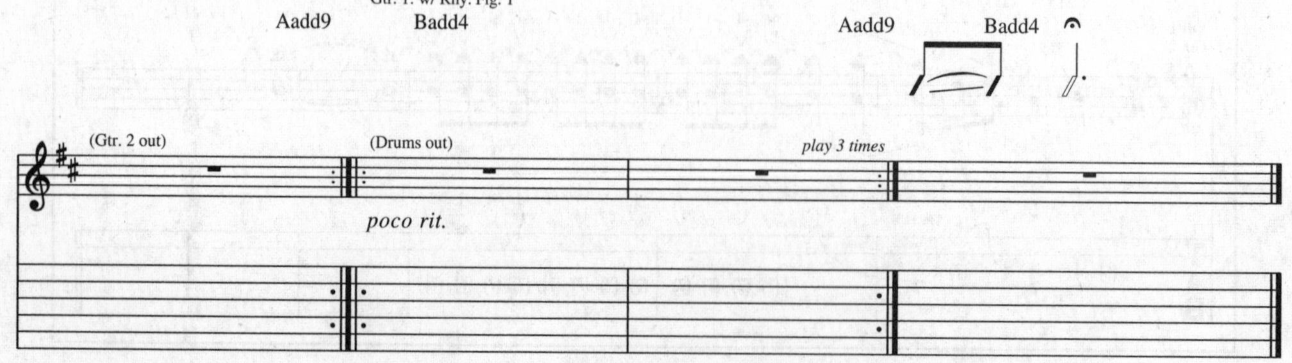
Gtr. 1: w/ Rhy. Fig. 1
Aadd9
Badd4
Aadd9
Badd4
(Gtr. 2 out)
(Drums out)
play 3 times
poco rit.

No More Tears

Words and Music by Ozzy Osbourne, Zakk Wylde, Randy Castillo, Michael Inez and John Purdell

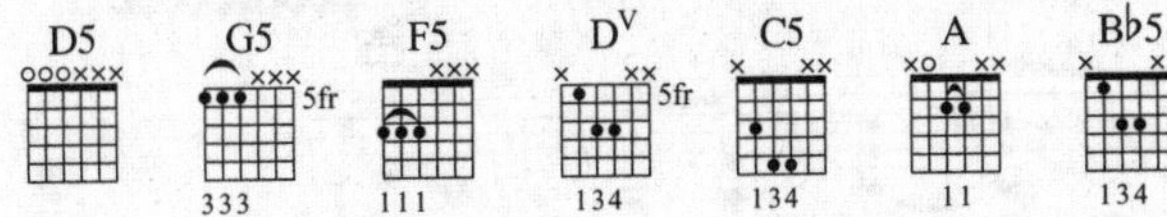

Drop D tuning, down 1/2 step:
(low to high) D♭-A♭-D♭-G♭-B♭-E♭

Intro

Moderate Rock ♩ = 104

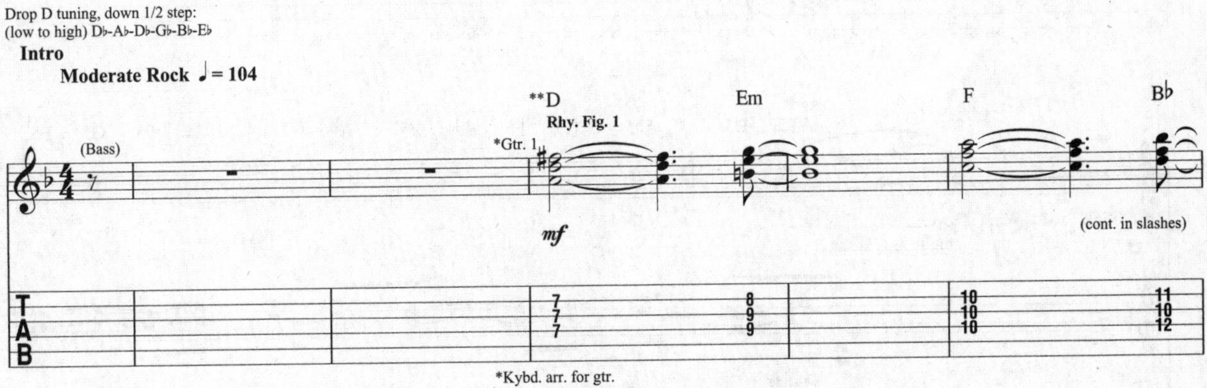

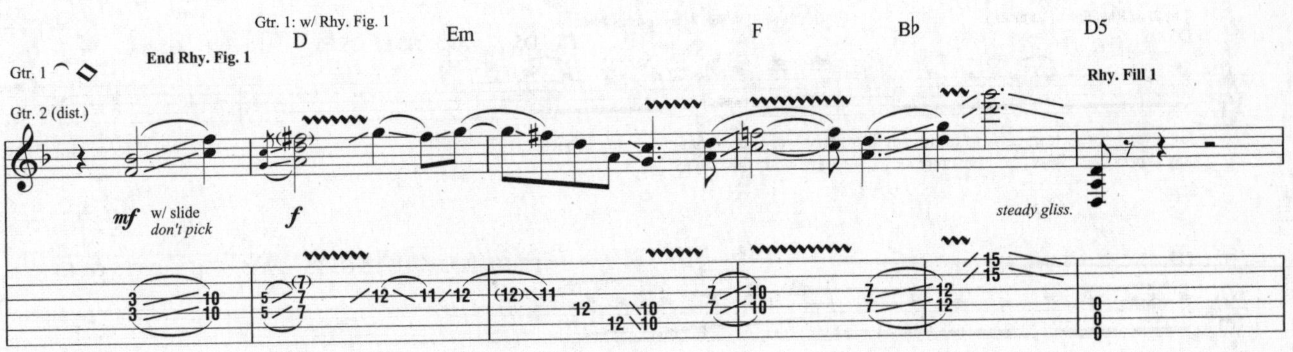

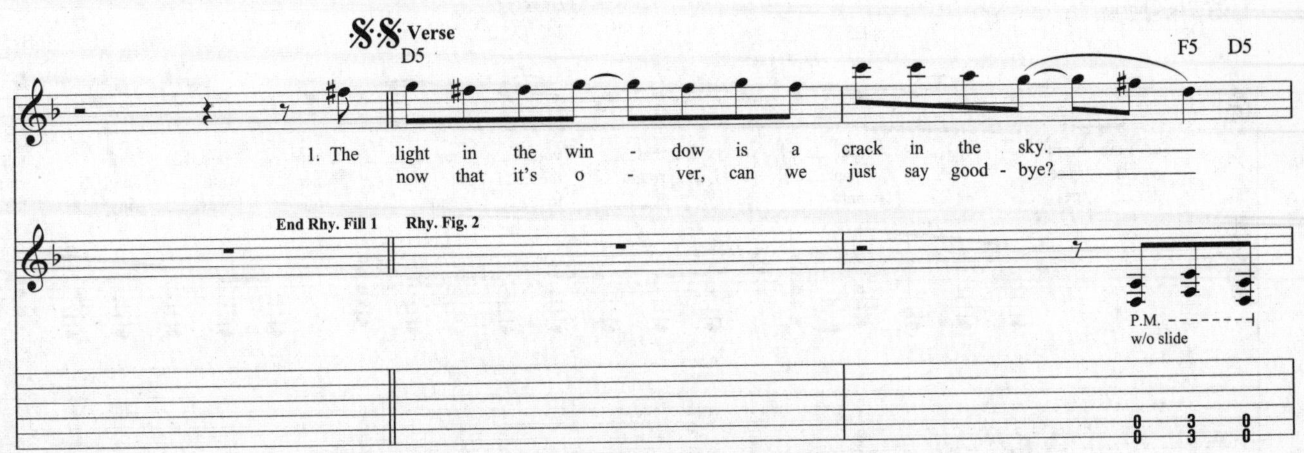

Ab5
G5
F5
D5
G5 N.C.
Bye, bye, bye, bye.
A stair - way to dark - ness in the
I'd like to move on and make the
P.M.
P.H.
Pitch: C D
blink of an eye.
most of the night.
A
End Rhy. Fig. 2
w/ slide
steady gliss.
Gtr. 2: w/ Rhy. Fill 1 (1st meas.)
Gtr. 2: w/ Rhy. Fig. 2 (last 7 meas.)
lev - ee of tears to learn she'll nev - er be com - ing back.
May - be a kiss be - fore I leave you this way.
The
Your
man in the dark will bring an - oth - er at - tack.
lips are so cold I don't know what else to say.
Pre-Chorus
E5
Bb5
Your mom - ma told you that you're not sup - posed to talk
I see the man a - round the cor - ner wait - ing, can
I nev - er want - ed it to end this way, my love,
Gtr. 2
w/o slide

2nd & 3rd times, Gtr. 2: w/ Fill 1
D5
E5
to strang - ers. Look in the mir - ror, tell me do
he see me? I close my eyes and wait to hear
my dar - ling. Be - lieve me when I say to you
P.M.
F5
B♭5
E
you think your life's in dan - ger? Yeah.
the sound of some - one scream - ing here.
in love I think I'm fall - ing here.
w/ slide
steady gliss.
To Coda 1
To Coda 2
Chorus
2nd & 3rd times, Bkgd. Voc.: w/ Voc. Fig. 1 (1 1/2 times)
F
N.C.
G5 A♭5 G5 F5
No more tears. No more
Rhy. Fig. 3
End Rhy. Fig. 3
steady gliss.
w/o slide
Voc. Fig. 1
No more tears.
Fill 1
Gtr. 2
tr

Gtr. 2: w/ Rhy. Fig. 3
N.C.
tears.
G5 A♭5 G5 F5 D5
Gtr. 2: w/ Rhy. Fill 1
2. An -
Verse
Gtr. 2: w/ Rhy. Fig. 2
D5
D5 F5 D5 A♭5 G5 F5 G5 F5 D5 A♭5
oth - er day pass - es as the night clos - es in.
G5 N.C.
D5
F5 D5 A♭5 G5 F5 G5 F5 A♭5
The red light goes on to say it's time to be - gin.
D.S. al Coda 1
G5 F5 G5 F5
Coda 1
Gtr. 2: w/ Rhy. Fig. 3 (3 times)*
N.C.
1., 2.
3.
G5 A♭5 G5 F5
G5 A♭5 G5 F5
tears.
No more
*3rd time, omit P.M.
Interlude
D5
Gtr. 2
Gtr. 2 tacet
N.C.
**Gtr. 3
mf
**Strings arr. for gtr.
***Gtr. 4
mf
***Strings and low brass arr. for gtr.
Interlude
Slower ♩ = 76
Gtrs. 3 & 4 tacet
Bm
G7
8va
†Gtr. 5
mf w/ fingers
†Kybds. arr. for gtr.

Spoken: He who laughs last, is just a hand in the bush.
Bm
G7
E
Esus4
E5
Gtr. 6 (clean)
w/ slide & delay**
*Vol. swell
**Set for eighth-note regeneration w/ four repeats.
Gtr. 5
8va
loco
D6
D
Dsus♯4
D/C♯
E
Esus4
E5
Fsus♯4
F/G
G
Gsus4
mf
D
Dsus4
D
C6
C
Cadd♯4
C
B♭
8va
f
w/ dist. delay off w/o slide
rake

G5
Gtr. 2
P.M.
8va
loco
acc.
acc.
Guitar Solo
Tempo I ♩ = 104
Gtr. 5 tacet
F5
G5
F5
D5
D
open
C5
Gtr. 6
P.M.

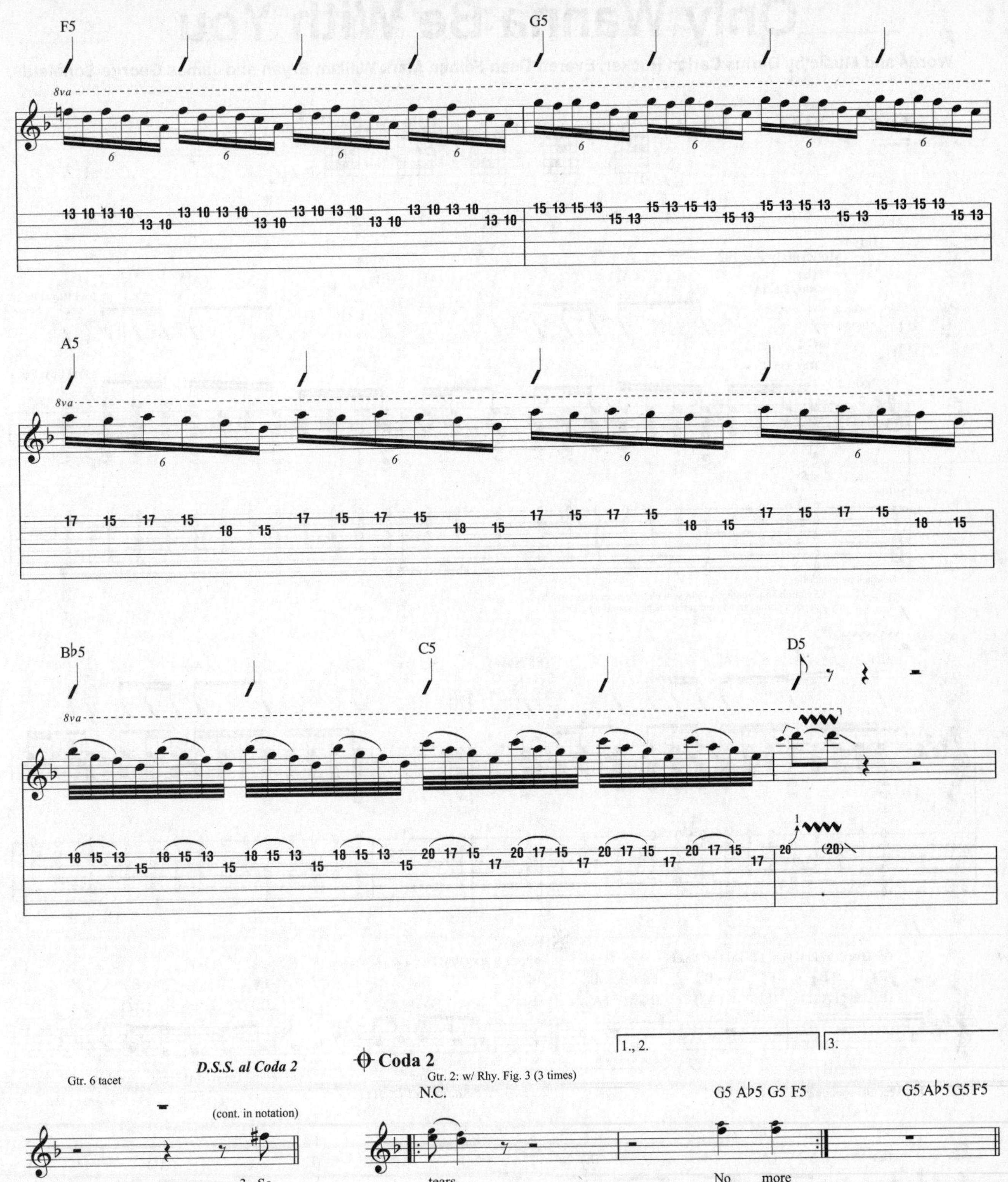
F5
G5
8va
A5
B♭5
C5
D5
Gtr. 6 tacet
D.S.S. al Coda 2
(cont. in notation)
3. So
Coda 2
Gtr. 2: w/ Rhy. Fig. 3 (3 times)
N.C.
tears.
1., 2.
3.
G5 A♭5 G5 F5
No more
Spoken: *...is just a hand in the bush.
Gtr. 2
P.M.
*w/ delay repeats

Only Wanna Be With You

Words and Music by Darius Carlos Rucker, Everett Dean Felber, Mark William Bryan and James George Sonefeld

Chorus
(F#7sus4)
Rhy. Fig. 2A
Gtr. 2
(Asus2)
End Rhy. Fig. 2A
To Coda
1.
Gtrs. 1 & 2: w/ Rhy. Figs. 1 & 1A
F#
(E)
B6/9
(A6/9)
no-thin' I can do,
help it if I'm luck-y,"
1. I've been look-in' for a girl like you.
2., 3., 4. I on-ly want to be with you.
Rhy. Fig. 2
Gtr. 1
End Rhy. Fig. 2
*Gtr. 3
Riff A
mf
* Piano arr. for gtr.
** Play when recalled only.
2.
Gtrs. 1 & 2: w/ Rhy. Figs. 1 & 1A
Gtr. 3: w/ Riff A
You can
End Riff A
Riff A1
Gtr. 4 (elec.)
mf w/ slight dist.
(Asus2)
Rhy. Fig. 3A
Gtr. 4 tacet
(Bsus4)
End Rhy. Fig. 3A
call me your fool,
I on-ly want to be with you.
Rhy. Fig. 3
End Rhy. Fig. 3
Gtr. 4
End Riff A1
3.
Gtrs. 1 & 2: w/ Rhy. Figs. 1 & 1A
Gtrs. 3 & 4: w/ Riffs A & A1

(Asus2)
(Bsus4)
Gtr. 2
Ain't Bob - by so ___ cool?
I on - ly want to be with you.
Gtr. 1
Guitar Solo
Gtrs. 1 & 2: w/ Rhy. Figs. 1 & 1A, 4 times
Gtr. 3: w/ Fill 1, 8 times
F♯
(E)
B6/9
(A6/9)
Gtr. 4
mf
let ring
full
1 1/2
Fill 1
Gtr. 3
TAB

Additional Lyrics

2. You look at me, you got nothing left to say.
I moan and pout at you until I get my way.
I won't dance, you won't sing.
I just want to love you, but you want to wear my ring.

3. Put on a little Dylan, sittin' on a fence.
I say, "That line is great." You ask me what I meant by
"Said I shot a man named Gray, took his wife to Italy.
She inherits a million bucks, and when she died it came to me.

4. Sometimes I wonder if we'll ever end.
You get so mad at me when I go out with my friends.
Sometimes you're crazy, and you wonder why
I'm such a baby, yeah, the Dolphins make me cry.

One Thing Leads to Another

Words and Music by Cy Curnin, Jamie West-Oram, Adam Woods, Rupert Greenall and Alfred Agius

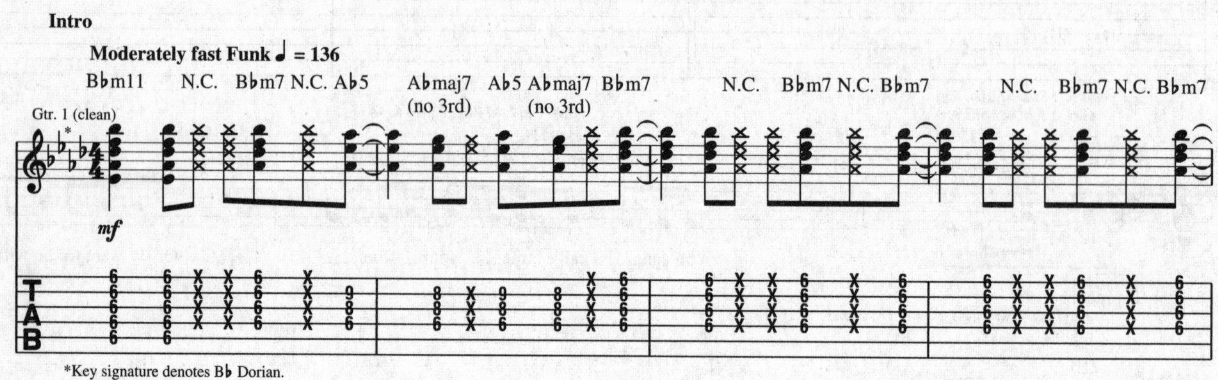

*Key signature denotes Bb Dorian.

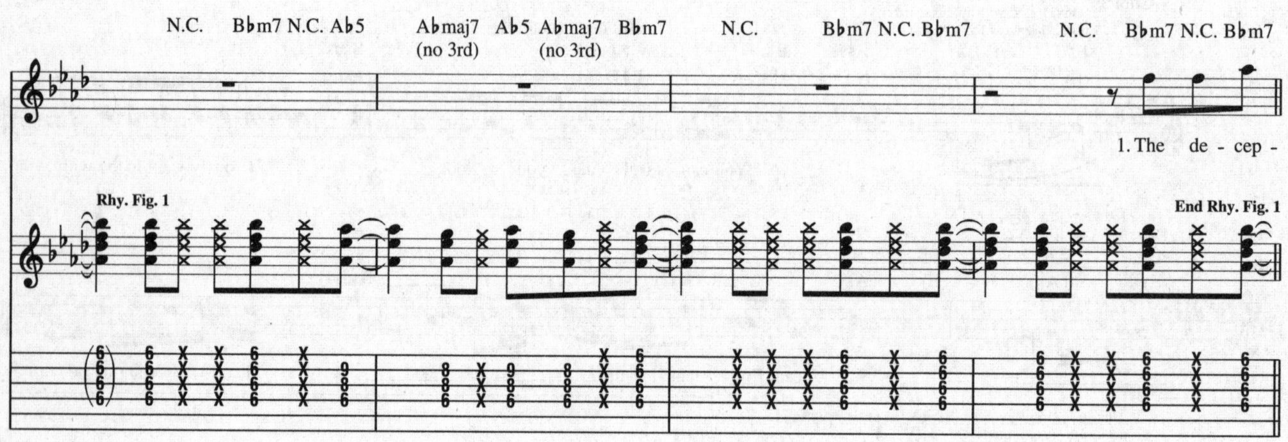

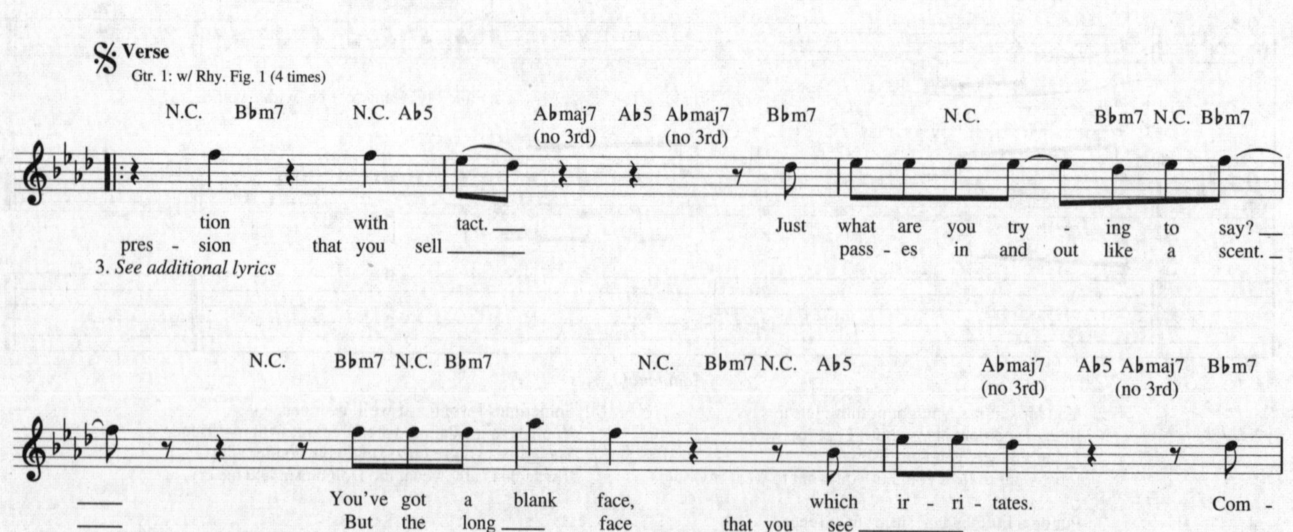

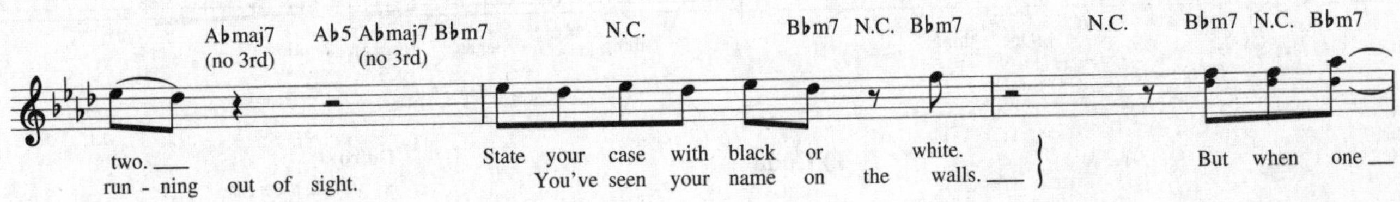

2nd & 3rd time, Bkgd. Voc.: w/ Voc. Fig. 1

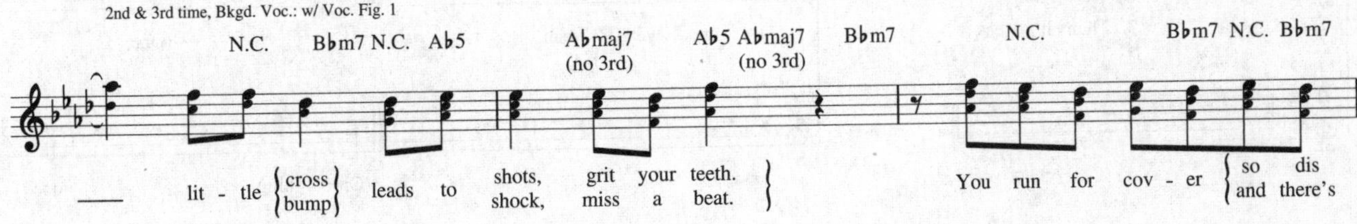

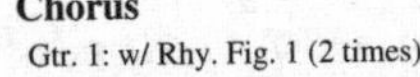

Gtr. 1: w/ Rhy. Fig. 1 (2 times)

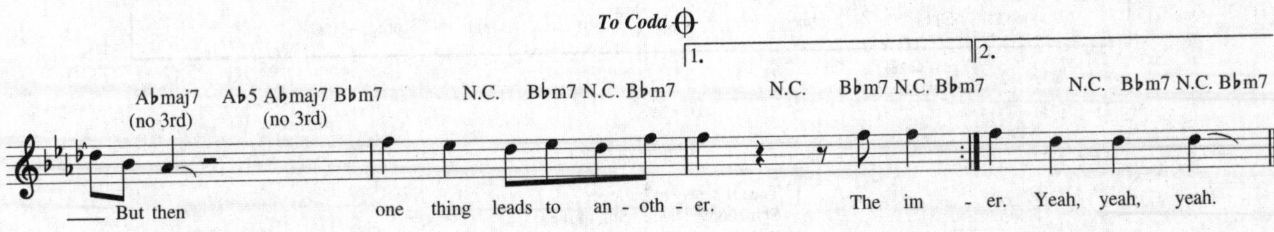

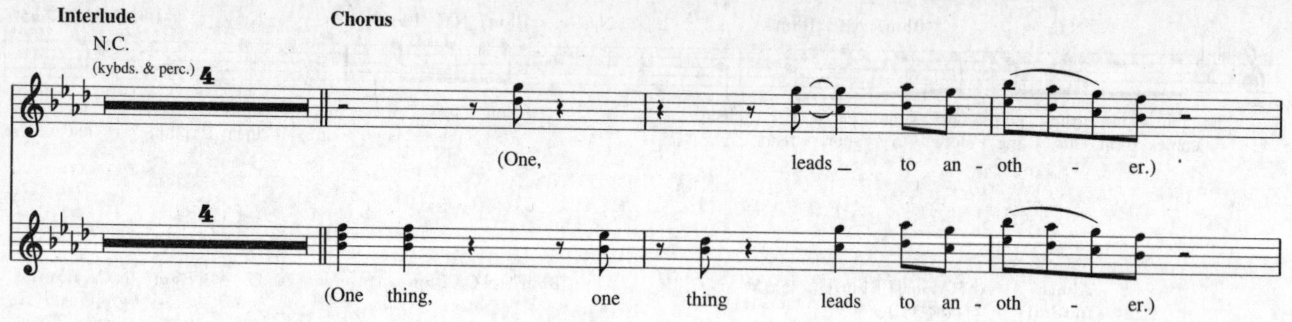

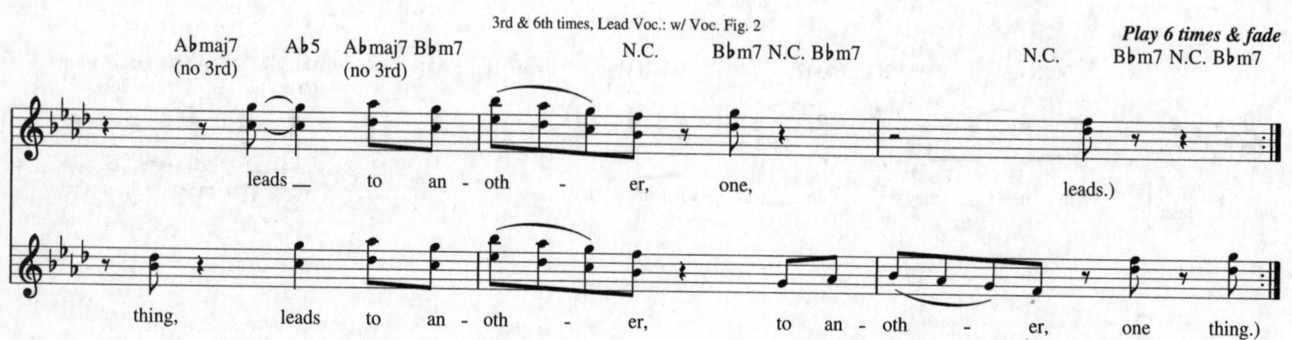

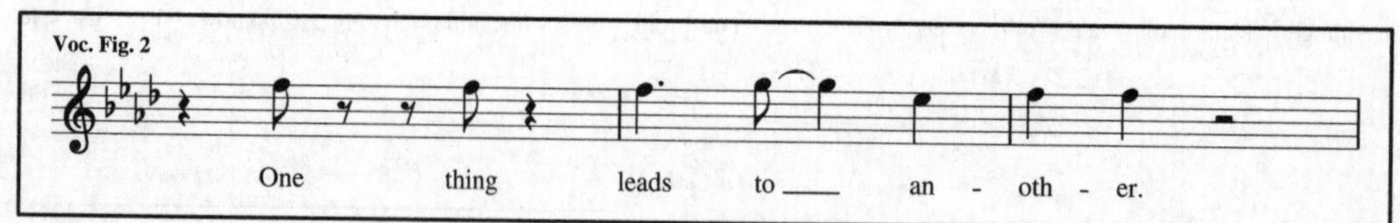

Additional lyrics

3. Then it's easy to believe,
Somebody's been lying to me.
But when the wrong word,
Goes in the right ear
I know why you've been lying to me.
It's gettin' rough, off the cuff,
I've got to say enough's enough.
Bigger, the harder he falls.
But when the wrong antidote,
Is like a baldge on the throat.
You run for cover in the heat,
Why don't they.....

Our House

Words and Music by Graham Nash

A/F♯ A/E D A/C♯ Bm7 D/F♯ D/E
your head for just five min-utes. Ev - 'ry - thing is done.
Gtr. 1: w/ Rhy. Fig. 1
A A/G♯ A/F♯ A/E D A/C♯
Such a co - zy room. The win - dows are il - lu - mi-nat - ed by the eve - ning
(Such a co - zy room.)
D/B D/C♯ D/E D/C♯ D/B D/C♯ D/E D/C♯ A A/G♯ A/F♯ A/E D F/C
sun - shine through them fier - y gems for you, on - ly for you.
Chorus
A A/G♯ A/F♯ A/E D A/C♯
Our house is a ver-y, ver-y, ver-y fine house, with two cats in the yard. Life
(Our house is a...)
Rhy. Fig. 2
Gtr. 1
D A/C♯ D A/C♯ D
used to be so hard. Now ev - 'ry-thing is eas - y 'cause of you

Interlude
Double-time feel
Bm7 D A A/G# A/F# A/E
and our La, la, la, la, la, la, la, la, la, la, la, la, la, la, la,
End Rhy. Fig. 2
1.
2.
End double-time feel
D A/C# Bm7 D/F# D/E D F/C
la, la, la, la, la, la, la, la, la, la, la, la, la, la, la. la, la, la, la, la, la, la, la.
Chorus
Gtr. 1: w/ Rhy. Fig. 2
A A/G# A/F# A/E D A/C#
Our house is a ver-y, ver-y, ver-y fine house, with two cats in the yard. Life
(Our house is a ver-y, ver-y, ver-y, ver-y, ver-y fine house, with. . .)
D A/C# D A/C# D Bm7 D
used to be so hard. Now ev-'ry-thing is eas-y 'cause of you and our. . .
rit.
Outro-Verse
Tempo I (♩ = 64)
A A/G# A/F# A/E D F/C
Slowly
A
3. I'll light the fi-re while you place the flow-ers in the vase that you bought to-day.
(Day.)
rit.
let ring

The Passenger

Words and Music by Iggy Pop and Ricky Gardner

1.
2.
To Coda 1
Gtr. 3: w/ Rhy. Fig. 1A
Am F/C C G/D Am F/C C E C E
2. And ev - 'ry-thing looks good to - night.
*Sing - ing,
*Sing 1st time only.
Chorus
Gtr. 1: w/ Rhy. Fig. 1, 2 1/2 times, simile
Gtr. 3: w/ Rhy. Fig. 1A, 2 1/2 times
Gtr. 2 tacet
la, la, la, la, la, la, la, la. La, la, la, la, la, la, la, la. La, la, la, la,
To Coda 2
D.S. al Coda 1
(take 2nd ending)
la, la, la, la, la, la, la.
Coda
Gtr. 1: w/ Rhy. Fig. 1, simile
Gtr. 2: w/ Riff A, simile
Gtr. 3: w/ Rhy. Fig. 1A
Verse
Gtr. 1: w/ Rhy. Fig. 1, 4 times, simile
Gtr. 2: w/ Riff A, 2 times, 1st time, simile
Gtr. 3: w/ Rhy. Fig. 1A, 4 times
4. O, the pas - sen - ger, how, how he rides.
5. He sees the cit - y's ripped back - sides, he sees the wind - ing o - cean drive.
*Gtr. 2
*Play 2nd time only.
O, the pas - sen - ger, and he rides and he rides.
And ev - 'ry-thing was made for you and me, all of it was made for you and me,
Gtr. 2 tacet 1st time
Gtr. 2: w/ Riff A, 2 times, 2nd time, simile
He looks through his win - dow. What does he see?
'cause it just be - longs to you and me, so let's take a ride and see what's mine.

Additional Lyrics

3. Get into the car,
We'll be the passenger.
We'll ride through the city tonight,
We'll see the city's ripped backsides.
We'll see the bright and hollow sky,
We'll see the stars that shine so bright.
Stars made for us tonight.

Poor Little Fool

Words and Music by Sharon Sheeley

Additional Lyrics

4. The next day she was gone and I knew she lied to me.
   She left me with a broken heart and won her victory.

5. Well, I've played this game with other hearts, but I never thought I'd see
   The day when someone else would play love's foolish game with me.

Pride and Joy

Written by Stevie Ray Vaughan

to the blind.
My ba - by loves my 'cause the sun does shine. And she's my
1/2
A7
sweet lit - tle thang,
E
she's my pride and joy.
full
B7
A7
She's my sweet lit - tle ba - by, I'm her lit - tle lov - er boy.
Verse
E
B7
E
2. Yeah, I love my ba - by, my
tr
tr

heart and __ soul. __ Love like ours, __ ah, won't __ nev - er grow __ old. ___ She's my
A7
sweet lit - tle thang, __ she's my
E
pride and joy. ___
She's my sweet
B7
lit - tle ba - by, I'm ___
A7
her ___ lit - tle lov - er boy. __
E
B7
Verse
E N.C.
3. Yeah, I love my ___ la - dy, she's
love my ___ la - dy, the
1/2
full
tr

E N.C. E N.C.

long and lean. You mess with her, you'll see a man get mean.
fin - est wine. Stick with her un - til the end of time. } And she's my

full

Gtr. 1: w/ Fill 1, 2nd time

A7 E

sweet lit - tle thang, she's my pride and joy. She's my

full

To Coda

B7 A7 E B7

sweet lit - tle ba - by. I'm her lit - tle lov - er boy.

tr

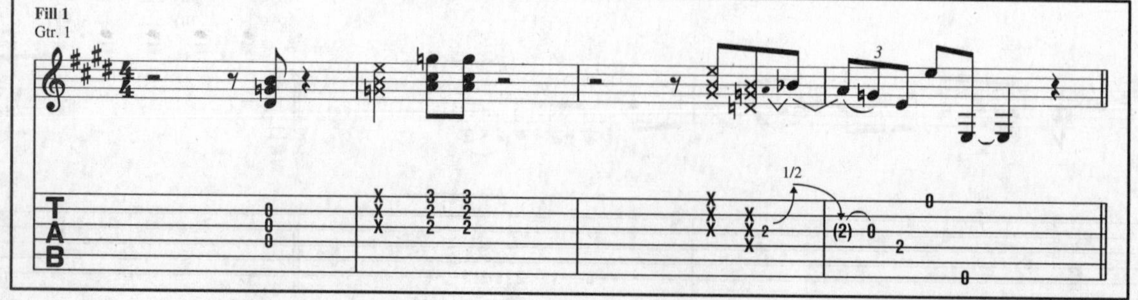

Guitar Solo
E
A7
8va
E
8va
B7
full
A7
loco
full
full
full
E
full
full
full
B7
E

A7
8va
loco
E
8va
loco
full
1/4
1/2
* Played behind the beat.
B7
A7
1/4
1/2
E
B7
E
1/2
full
1/2
A7

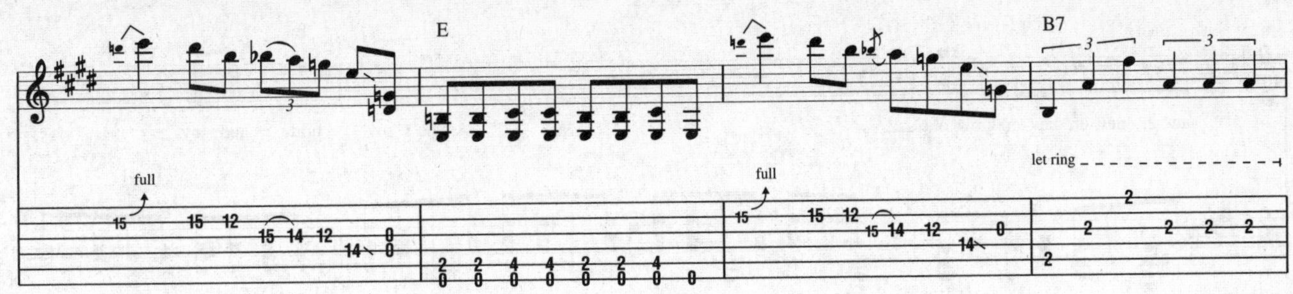
E
B7
full
full
let ring

D.S. al Coda
A7
E
B7
4. Yeah, I
let ring
tr

Coda
E
B7
5. Yeah, I
tr

Verse
E
love my ba - by, my heart and soul.
Love like ours ah, won't
1/2

A7
nev-er, nev-er, nev-er grow old.
E
She's my pride and joy.
1/2
B7
A7
She's my sweet lit-tle ba - by, I'm her lit-tle lov-er boy.
E
B7
Outro-Guitar Solo
E
full
A7

E
B7
full
A7
E
B7
E
full
A7
1/4
E
* even
B7
full
* Played as even eighth notes.
A7
N.C.(E)
full
1/4
fdbk.

The Promised Land

Words and Music by Chuck Berry

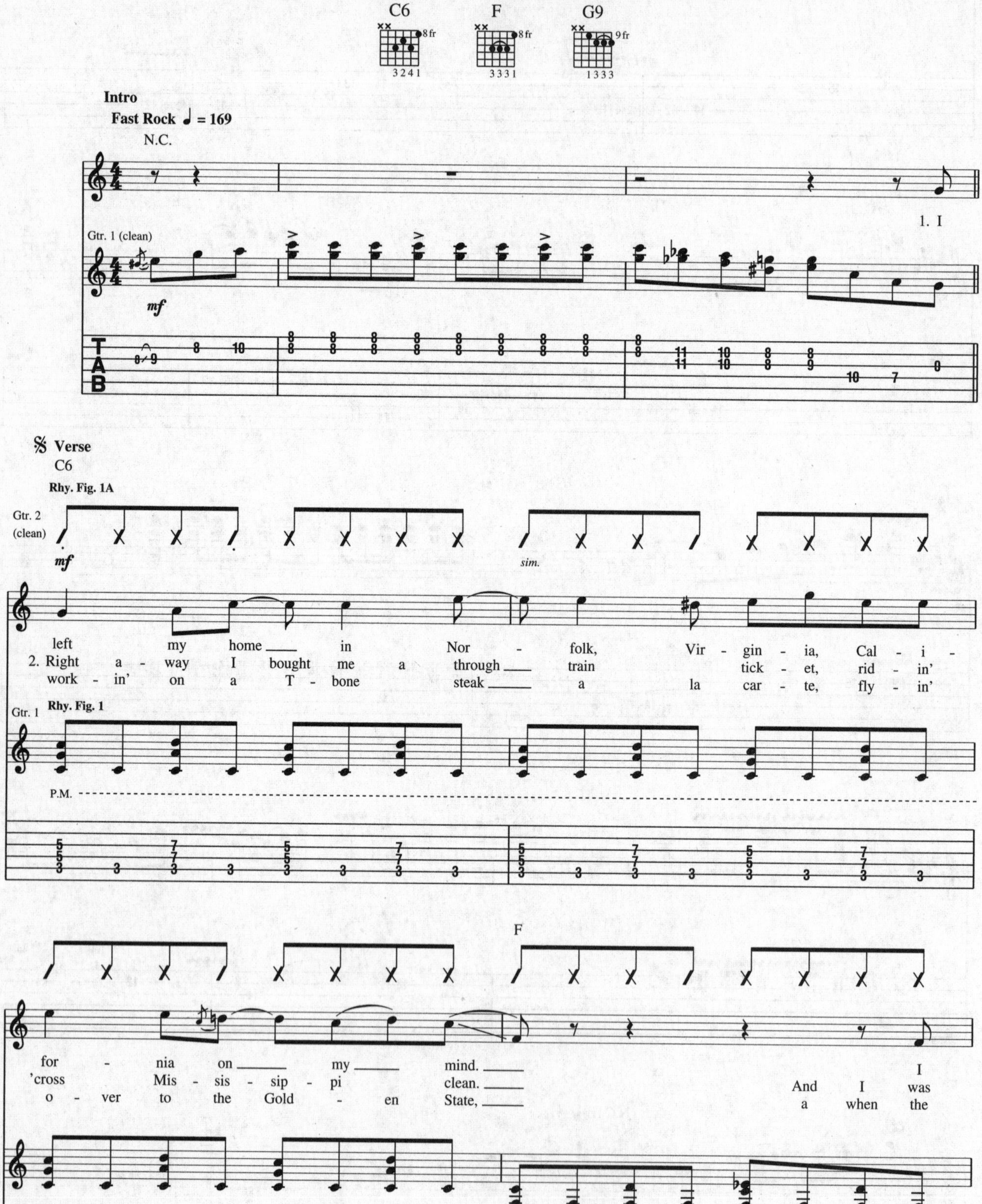

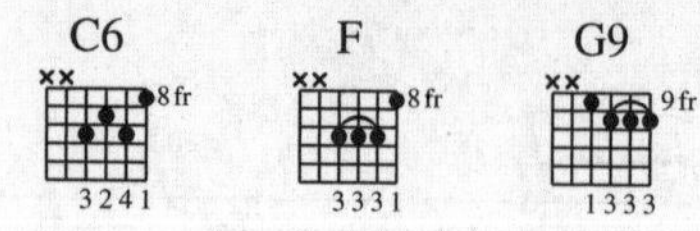

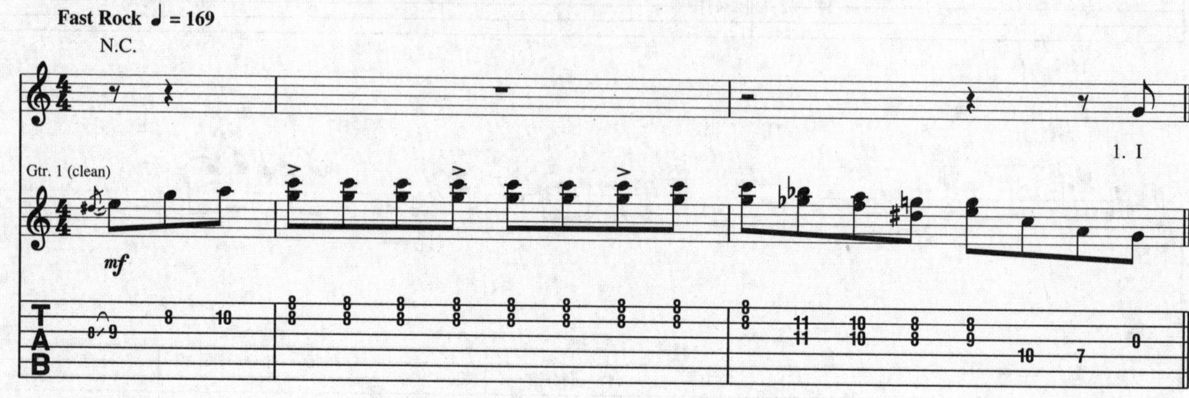

C6
8 fr
3241
F
8 fr
3331
G9
9 fr
1333
Intro
Fast Rock ♩ = 169
N.C.
Gtr. 1 (clean)
mf
1. I
𝄋 Verse
C6
Rhy. Fig. 1A
Gtr. 2 (clean)
mf
sim.
left my home in Nor - folk, Vir - gin - ia, Cal - i -
2. Right a - way I bought me a through train tick - et, rid - in'
work - in' on a T - bone steak a la car - te, fly - in'
Gtr. 1
Rhy. Fig. 1
P.M.
F
for - nia on my mind. I
'cross Mis - sis - sip - pi clean. And I was
o - ver to the Gold - en State, a when the
P.M.

G9
strad - dled that Grey - hound and rode him in - to Ral - eigh and on
on that Mid - night Fly - er out of Bir - ming - ham,
pi - lot told us in thir - teen min - utes he would
P.M.
C6
End Rhy. Fig. 1A
a - cross Car - o - line. We
smok - in' in - to New Or - leans.
set us at the ter - mi - nal gate.
End Rhy. Fig. 1
P.M.
Gtr. 1: w/ Rhy. Fig. 1 (1 3/4 times)
Gtr. 2: w/ Rhy. Fig. 1A (2 times)
stopped in Char - lotte, we by - passed Rock - hill, we nev - er was a min - ute late.
Some - bod - y help me get out of Lou - 'si - an - a, just help me get to Hous - ton town.
Swing low char - i - ot, come down eas - y, tax - i to the ter - mi - nal zone.
F
G9
A we was nine - ty miles out of At - lan - ta by sun - down, roll -
There are a peo - ple there who care a lit - tle 'bout me and they
Cut your en - gines and cool your wings and let me

C6
- in' out of Geor - gia State.
won't let the poor boy down.
make it to the tel - e - phone.
We had more trou - ble that turned
Sure as you're born they bought
Los An - gel - es, give me Nor -
F
in - to a strug - gle half - way a - cross Al - a - bam',
me a silk suit, put lug - gage in my hand,
- folk, Vir - gin - ia Tide - wa - ter four - ten - o - nine.
and that 'Hound
and I
Tell the
G9
To Coda 1
To Coda 2
broke down and left us all strand - ed in
woke up high o - ver Al - bu - quer - que on a
folks back home this is the Prom - ised Land call - in' and the
C6
down - town Bir - ming - ham.
Gtr. 1
P.M.
Guitar Solo
Gtr. 2: w/ Rhy. Fig. 1A
C6
F

G9
D.S. al Coda 1
C6
Coda 1
C6
jet to the Prom - ised Land.
Gtr. 1
P.M.
Guitar Solo
Gtr. 2: w/ Rhy. Fig. 1A
C6
F
G9

D.S. al Coda 2
C6
3. A
Coda 2
C6
poor boy's on the line.
Gtr. 1
P.M.
Outro-Guitar Solo
Gtr. 2: w/ Rhy. Fig. 1A
C6
F
G9
Begin fade
C6
Fade out

Push

Written by Rob Thomas with Matt Serletic

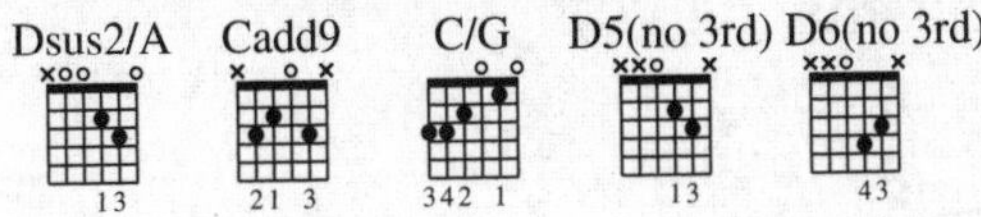

Tune Down 1/2 Step:
① = E♭ ④ = D♭
② = B♭ ⑤ = A♭
③ = G♭ ⑥ = E♭

Gtr. 2: Nashville Tuning: Bottom 4 strings tuned up 1 octave

Intro

Moderately Slow ♩ = 84

G Dsus4/F♯ Em C G Dsus4/F♯

Rhy. Fig. 1

*Gtrs. 1 & 2

mf

let ring throughout

**T

T

*composite arrangement

**T = Thumb on ⑥

Em C

Verse

G5 D/F♯

1. She said I don't know if I've ev - er been good e - nough.

End Rhy. Fig. 1 Rhy. Fig. 2

T

Em C G5 D/F♯ Em C

I'm a lit - tle bit rust - y, and I think my head is cav - ing in. And

End Rhy. Fig. 2

Gtrs. 1 & 2: w/ Rhy. Fig. 1

G5 D/F♯ Em C

I don't know if I've ev - er been real - ly loved by a hand that's touched me.

G5
D/F#
Em
C
Well, I feel like some-thing's gon - na give,
and I'm a lit - tle bit an - gry.
Pre-Chorus
Dsus2/A
Gtr. 3 (dist.)
mf
Cadd9
Well, this ain't o - ver, no, not here,
Oh, well, don't just stand there, say nice things to me
Gtr. 4 (dist.)
mf
let ring
Gtrs. 1 & 2
Dsus2/A
not while I still need you a - round.
'Cause I've been cheat - ed, I've been wronged. And you,
You don't owe
you don't know
let ring

D6(no 3rd)
D5(no 3rd)
C/G
(cont. in notation)
me, we might change, yeah.
me, yeah. Well, I can't change.
Yeah, we just might feel good.
Well, I won't do an-y-thing at all.
let ring
Chorus
Gtr. 4 tacet
G Dsus2/4 D Dsus2/4 C/G Dsus2/4 D Dsus2/4 5 G Dsus2/4 D Dsus2G
I wan-na push you a-round. Well, I will. Well, I will. I wan-na push you down.
Gtrs. 1, 2 & 3
To Coda 2
C/G Dsus2/4 D Dsus2 G Em Dsus2 C/G Dsus2 D Dsus2
Well, I will. Well, I will. I wan-na take you for grant-ed.
Gtr. 4
Harm.
Gtrs. 1, 2, & 3

To Coda 1
Em
Dsus2
C/G
D
Well, I wan - na take you for grant - ed. I, I will, I will.
Gtr. 4
Rhy. Fill 1
End Rhy. Fill 1
Harm.
Harm.
Harm.
Gtr. 5 (dist.)
mf
let ring
let ring
Gtrs. 1, 2 & 3
Guitar Solo
Gtrs. 1,2 & 3: w/ Rhy. Fig 1
Gtr. 4 tacet
G
Dsus4/F#
Em
C
G
Dsus4/F#
Em
C
I will.
2. She said
Gtr. 5
let ring

Verse
Gtrs. 1 & 2: w/ Rhy. Fig. 2, 2 times
G5
D/F#
Em
C
I don't know why you ev - er would lie to me.
Like I'm a lit - tle un - trust - ing when
Gtr. 5
Gtr. 4
Riff A
w/ clean tone
Gtr. 5 tacet
I think that the truth is gon - na hurt ya.
And
End Riff A
Gtr. 4: w/ Riff A
I don't know why you could - n't just stay with me.
You could - n't stand to be near me
D.S. al Coda 1
when my face don't seem to want to shine
cuz it's a lit - tle bit dirt - y.
Coda 1
Gtr. 4: w/ Rhy. Fill 1
C/G
D
Dsus2
Bridge
Dsus2/F#
ed. I, I will, I will.
Oh, but don't bowl me o - ver,
Gtrs. 1, 2 & 3

C/G
D
Dsus2
Em
Dsus2/F♯
just wait a min - ute. Well, it kind - a fell a - part. Things get so cra -
(Ah.
N.C.
- zy, cra - zy. Don't rush this, ba - by.
Ah.
Gtr. 5
fdbk.
Gtr. 4
Gtr. 5
divisi
Gtrs. 1, 2 & 3
D.S.S. al Coda 2
Don't rush this, ba - by, ba - by.
8va

Coda 2

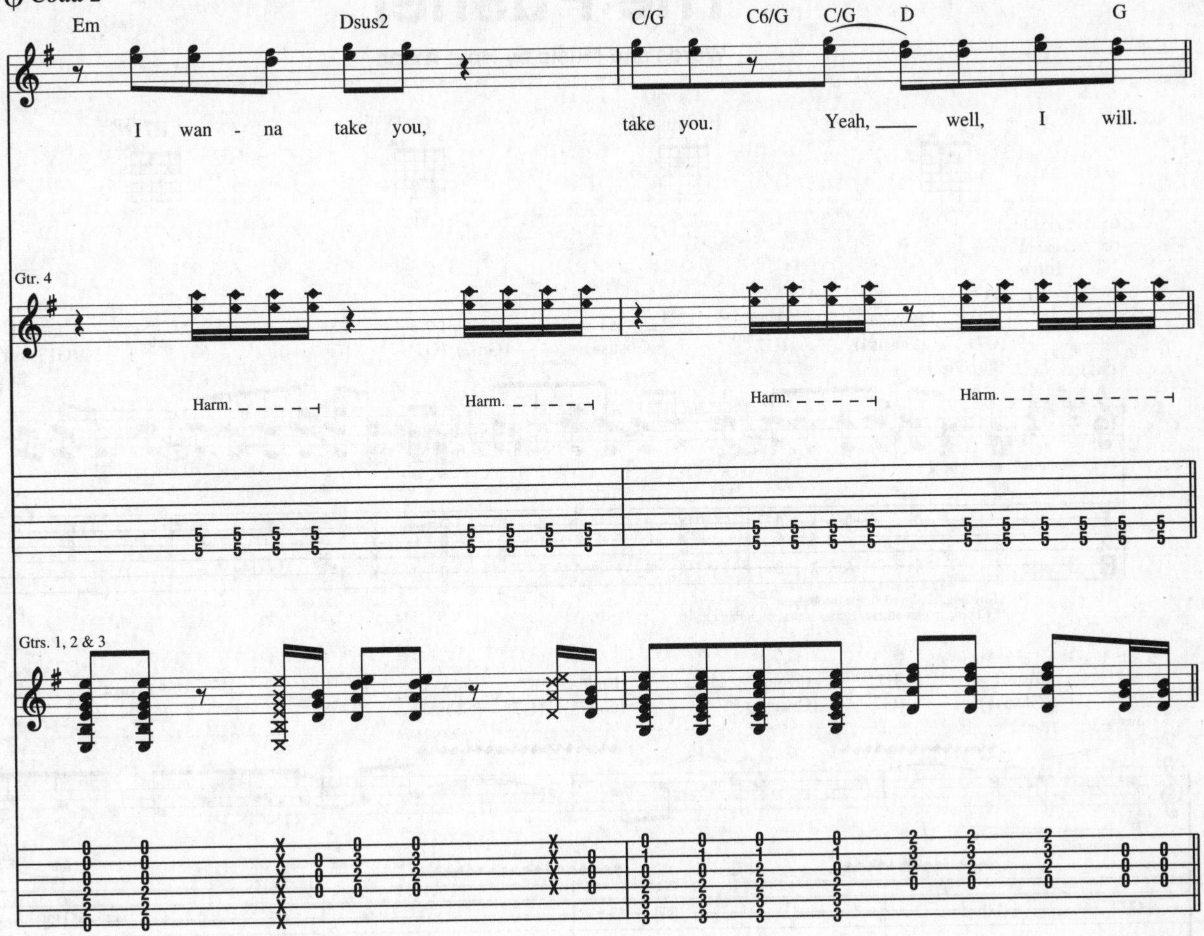

Em Dsus2 C/G C6/G C/G D G

I wan - na take you, take you. Yeah, ___ well, I will.

Gtr. 4

Harm. Harm. Harm. Harm.

Gtrs. 1, 2 & 3

Outro

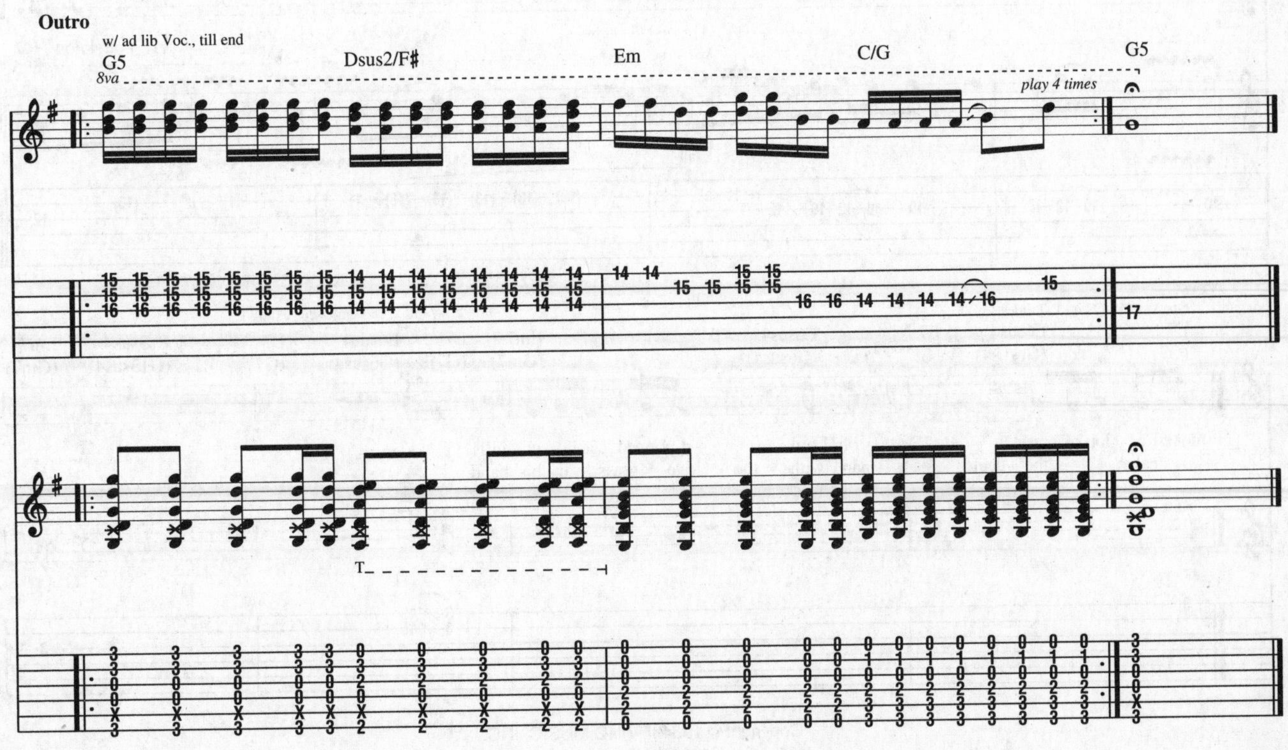

The Pusher

Words and Music by Hoyt Axton

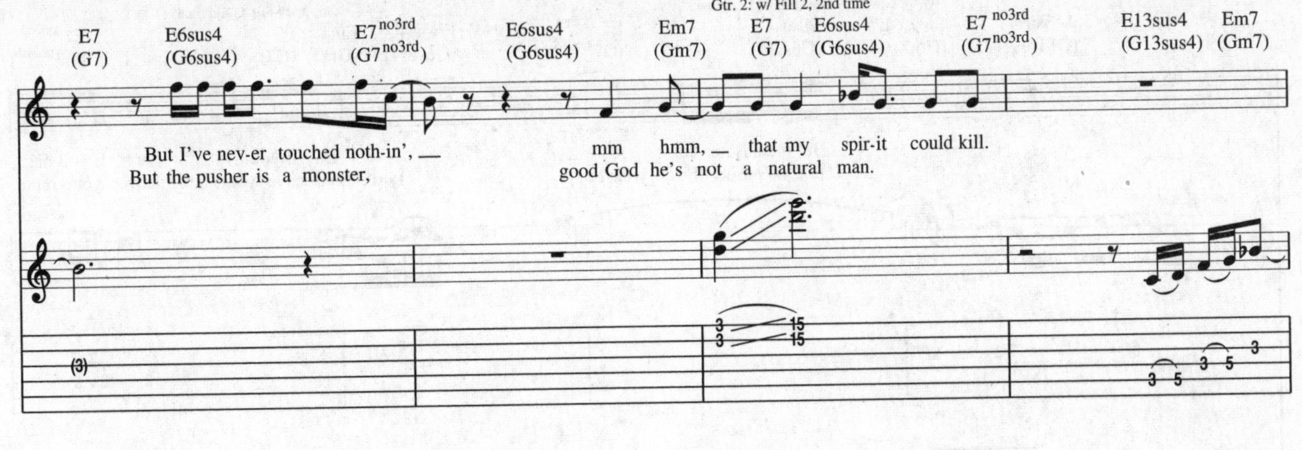

Gtr. 2: w/ Fill 2, 2nd time
E7
(G7)
E6sus4
(G6sus4)
E7no3rd
(G7no3rd)
E6sus4
(G6sus4)
Em7
(Gm7)
E7
(G7)
E6sus4
(G6sus4)
E7no3rd
(G7no3rd)
E13sus4
(G13sus4)
Em7
(Gm7)
But I've nev-er touched noth-in', mm hmm, that my spir-it could kill.
But the pusher is a monster, good God he's not a natural man.

Gtr. 2: w/ Fill 3, 2nd time
A7
(C7)
A13sus4
(C13sus4)
A7no3rd
(C7no3rd)
A13sus4
(C13sus4)
A7
(C7)
A13sus4
(C13sus4)
A7no3rd
(C7no3rd)
You know I've seen a lot of peo-ple walk-in' round with tomb-stones in their eyes.
The deal - er for a nick-el, Lord - he'll sell you lots of sweet dreams.
Gtr. 2

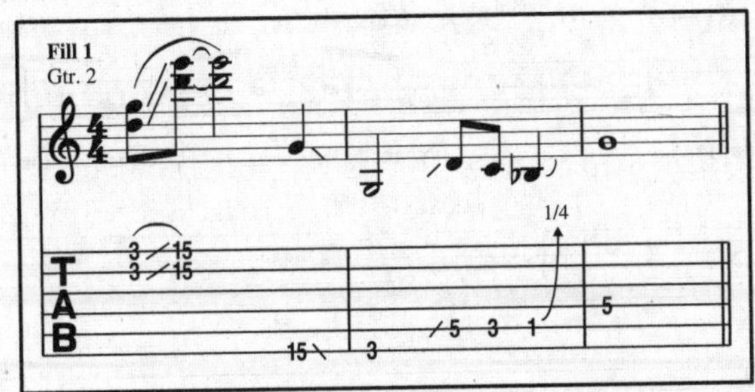

Fill 1
Gtr. 2
1/4

Fill 2
Gtr. 2
3/4

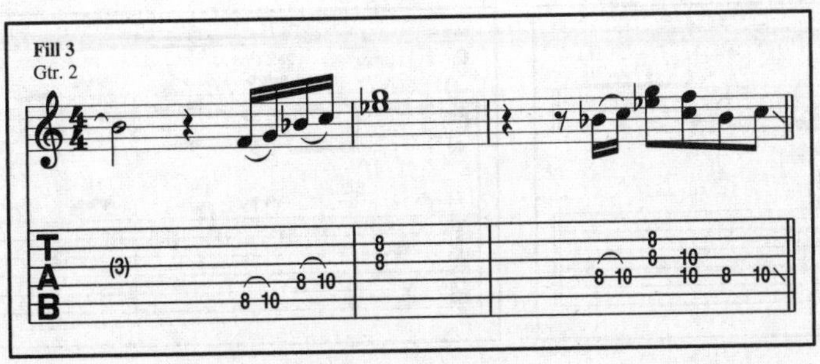

Fill 3
Gtr. 2

Gtr. 1: w/ Rhy. Fig. 1, 3 1/2 times
Gtr. 2: w/ Fill 4, 2nd time
A13sus4
(C13sus4)
Em7 E7
(Gm7) (G7)
E6sus4
(G6sus4)
E7 no3rd
(G7no3rd)
But the push-er don't care
But the pusher'll ruin your body.
aw, if you live or if you die.
Lord, he'll leave your, he'll leave your mind
Chorus
E13sus4
(G13sus4)
Gtr. 2: w/ Fill 5, 2nd time; w/ Riff A, 3rd time
to scream.
God damn
mm-hmm the push-er.
Gtr. 2
God damn,
yeah hey, I say the push -
Fill 4
Gtr. 2
Fill 5
Gtr. 2
8va
full
1/4

Gtr. 2: w/ Fill 6, 2nd time; w/ Fill 7, 3rd time
E7
(G7)
E6sus4
(G6sus4)
E7 no3rd
(G7 no3rd)
E13sus4
(G13sus4)
Em7 E7
(Gm7)(G7)
E6sus4
(G6sus4)
E7 no3rd
(G7 no3rd)
E6sus4
(G6sus4)
Em7
(Gm7)
- er.
I said God damn,
God damn
the push-er man.
Riff A
End Riff A
8va
full
full
Gtr. 1: w/ Rhy. Fig. 1
Gtr. 1
Gtr. 2
1/2
* Volume swell
2.
To Coda
Guitar Solo
N.C.
N.C.
2. You know the
mf
f
tr
1 1/2
slow release
* Attack note w/ volume control off, then quickly turn up to 10 on the first beat of the measure.
Fill 6
Gtr. 2
1 1/2
full
1/2
Fill 7
Gtr. 2
full
full
* volume swell

E6sus4 (G6sus4)
Em7 (Gm7)
E7 (G7)
E6sus4 (G6sus4)
E7 no3rd (G7no3rd)
E13sus4 (G13sus4)
Em7 (Gm7)
8va
hold bend
full
1/4
E7 (G7)
E13sus4 (G13sus4)
E7 no3rd (G7no3rd)
Rhy. Fig. 2
Gtr. 1
End Rhy. Fig. 2
loco
1/2
Gtr. 1: w/ Rhy. Fill 1
Gtr. 1: w/ Rhy. Fig. 2
3. Well now, if
Rhy. Fill 1
Gtr. 1
1.
2.

E7 (G7)
E6sus4 (G6sus4)
E7 no3rd (G7 no3rd)
E6sus4 (G6sus4)
Em7 (Gm7)
E7 (G7)
E13sus4 (G13sus4)
E7 no3rd (G7 no3rd)
E13sus4 (G13sus4)
I were the pres-i-dent - of this land - you know I'd de-clare to-tal war on the push er-man.
8va
full
* Volume swell
D.S. al Coda
(take 2nd ending)
Gtr. 1: w/ Rhy. Fig. 1, 1st 2 meas.
Gtr. 1: w/ Rhy. Fig. 2, last 2 meas only.
I'd cut him if he stands and I'd shoot him if he'd run, and I'd kill him with my Bi-ble. and my ra-zor and my gun. God
8va
3/4
full
Coda
Guitar Solo
Gtr. 1: w/ Rhy. Fig. 1, 1st meas.
E7 (G7)
E6sus4 (G6sus4)
E7 no3rd (G7 no3rd)
E13sus4 (G13sus4)
Gtr. 1: w/ Rhy. Fig. 1, 1st meas.
E7 (G7)
E6sus4 (G6sus4)
E7 no3rd (G7 no3rd)
E13sus4 (G13sus4)
Gtr. 1
Gtr. 2
8va
full
full
Gtr. 1: w/ Rhy. Fig. 1, 1st meas.
E7 (G7)
E6sus4 (G6sus4)
E7 no3rd (G7 no3rd)
E13sus4 (G13sus4)
E7 type2 (G7 type2)
8va
full
1/2
1/4

Rebel 'Rouser

By Duane Eddy and Lee Hazlewood

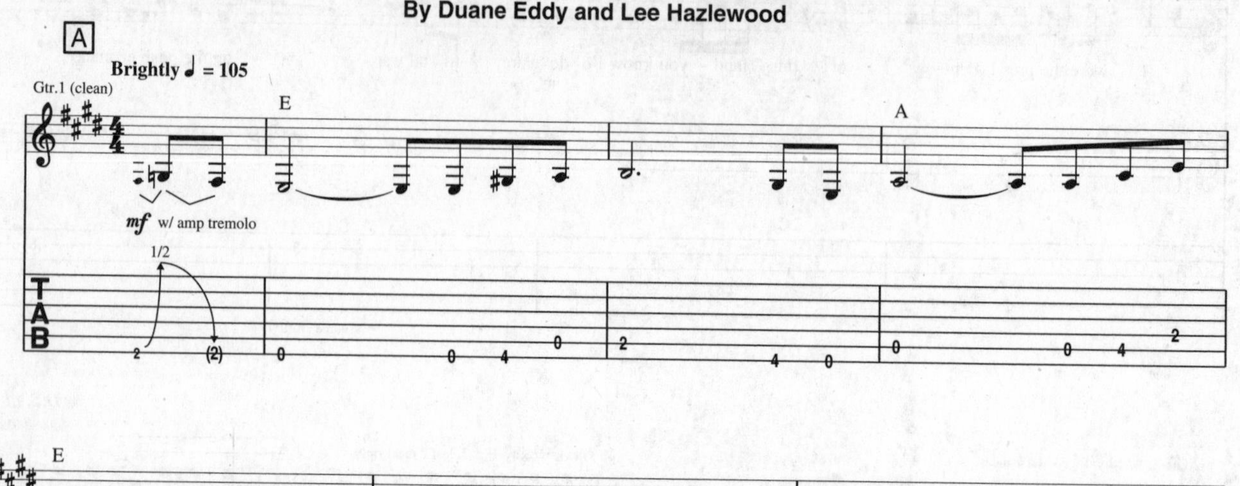

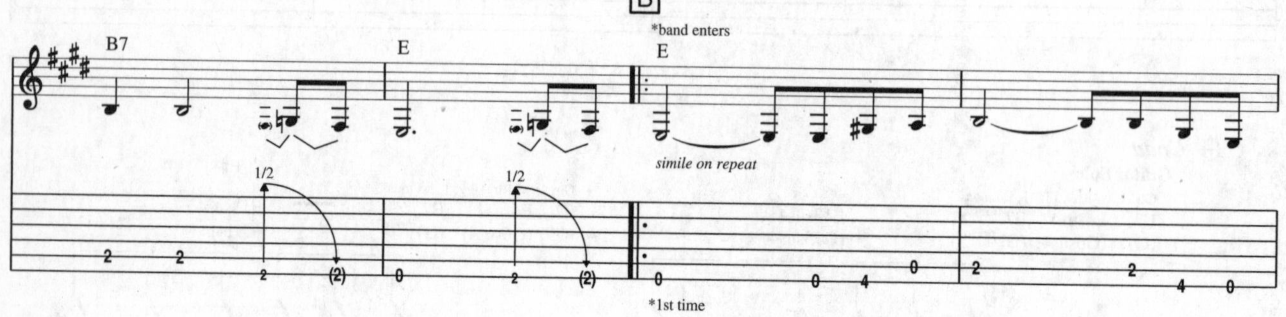

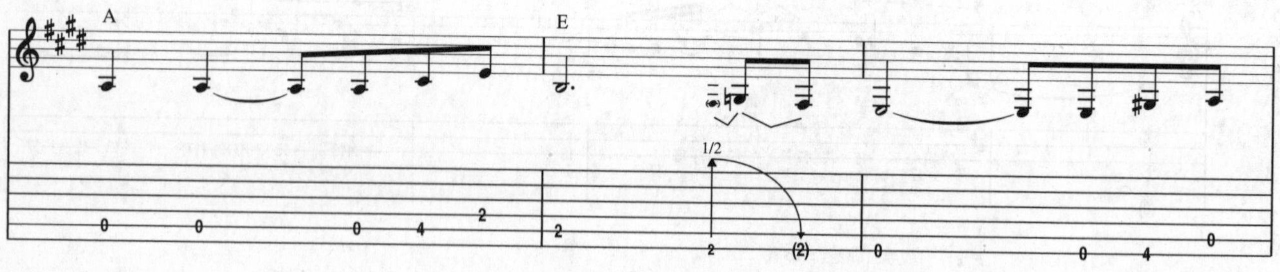

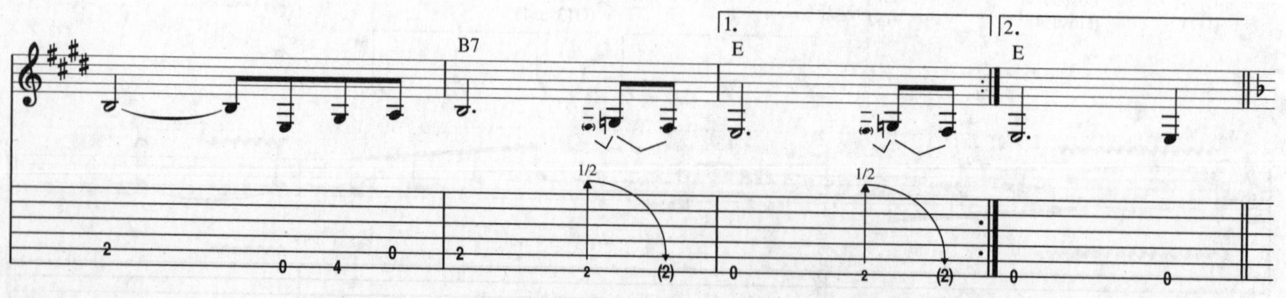

C
F
B♭
F
1/2
C7
F
D
F#
B
F#
1/2
C#7
F#
1/2
E
G
C
G
simile on repeats
1/2
Play 3 Times and Fade
D7
G
1/2
1/2

Refugee

Words and Music by Tom Petty and Mike Campbell

3rd time, Gtr. 3: w/ Fill 2
E
F#m
Gtr. 3 tacet
A
E
Ain't no real _ big se - cret, all ___ the same, _ some - how, we get a -
Tell me why ___ you wan - na lay ___ there, rev - el in your a - ban -
Who knows? _ May - be you were kid - napped, tied up tak - en a - way _ and held for ran -
Gtr. 3
mf
3rd time, Gtr. 3: w/ Fill 3
F#m
A
E
Pre-Chorus
D
round it.
don.
som.
Lis - ten,
Hon - ey,
Hon - ey,
it don't real - ly
it don't make no
it don't real - ly
* Gtrs. 1 & 2
f
* Composite arrangement.
B
mat - ter to me. _ Ba - by,
dif - f'rence to me. _ Ba - by,
mat - ter to me. _ Ba - by,
you be - lieve what you wan - na be - lieve. _
ev - 'ry - bod - y's had to fight to be free. _
ev - 'ry - bod - y's had to fight to be free. _
You see you
Chorus
Gtrs. 1 & 2: w/ Rhy. Figs. 1 & 1A
To Coda
1.
F#m
A5
E
F#m
A5
E
don't _ have _ to live like a ref - u - gee.
(Don't have to live like a ref - u - gee.) ____
Gtr. 3
f
Fill 2
Gtr. 3
mf
Fill 3
Gtr. 3

2.
F#m
A5
E
Gtrs. 1 & 2: w/ Rhy. Figs. 1 & 1A
(Don't have to live like a ref - u - gee.)
Now ba-by, you don't have to live like a ref - u - gee.
f
Bridge
Gtrs. 1 & 2
(Don't have to live like a ref - u - gee.)
Oh!
Ba - by, we ain't the first.
D
I'm sure a lot of oth - er lov - ers been burned.
Right now this seems real
to you, but it's one of those things you got to feel to be true.

Organ/Guitar Solo
Gtrs. 1 & 2: w/ Rhy. Figs. 1 & 1A (2 times)
F#m
A5
E
D.S. al Coda
Coda
Gtrs. 1 & 2: w/ Rhy. Figs. 1 & 1A, till fade
(Don't have to live like a ref - u - gee.)
No, you don't have to
Gtr. 3
let ring
live like a ref - u - gee.
(Don't have to live like a ref - u - gee.)
Ba-by, you

F#m
A5
E
don't have to live like a ref - u - gee.
(Don't have to live like a
ref - u - gee.)
Oh, oh, oh.
let ring
Begin fade
hold bend
A
Fade out

Renegade

Words and Music by Tommy Shaw

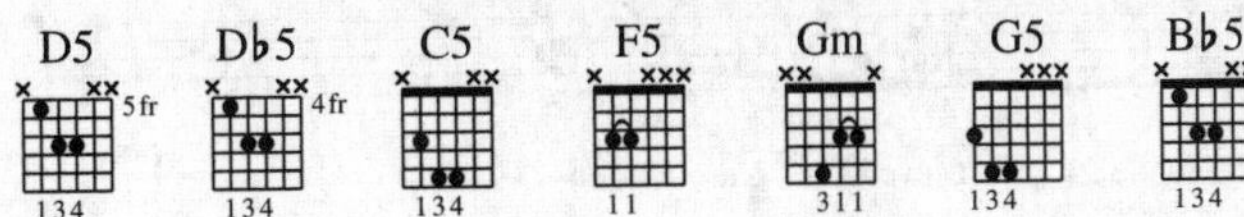

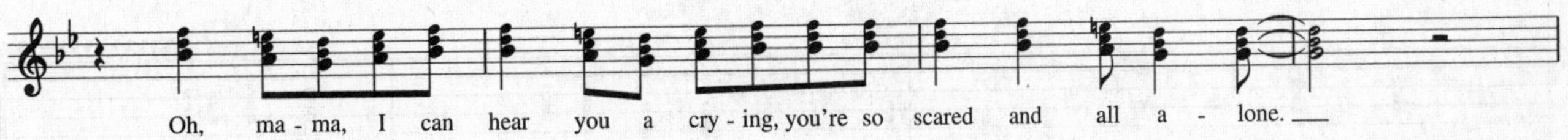

*Chord symbols reflect basic harmony.

*Omit this note when Riff C is recalled.

Gtr. 1: w/ Riff C (2 3/4 times)
Gm7
B♭/C
Gm
Law - man said, "Get him dead or a - live," now it's for sure he'll see me dead.
Gtr. 2
End Riff C1
let ring
6

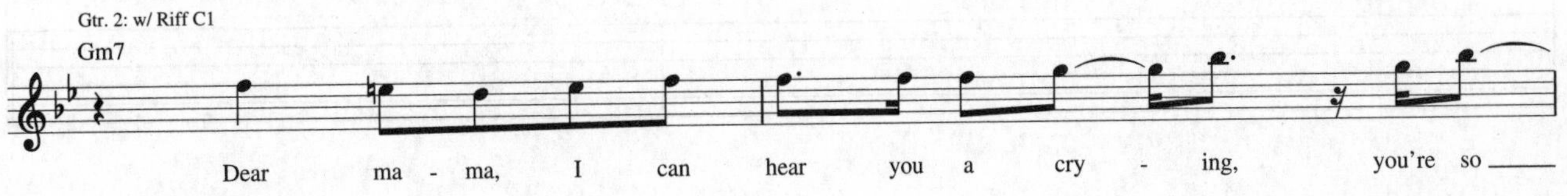
Gtr. 2: w/ Riff C1
Gm7
Dear ma - ma, I can hear you a cry - ing, you're so

B♭/C
Gm
Gm7
scared and all a - lone.
Hang - man is com-ing down

B♭/C
Gm
from the gal - lows and I don't have ver - y long.

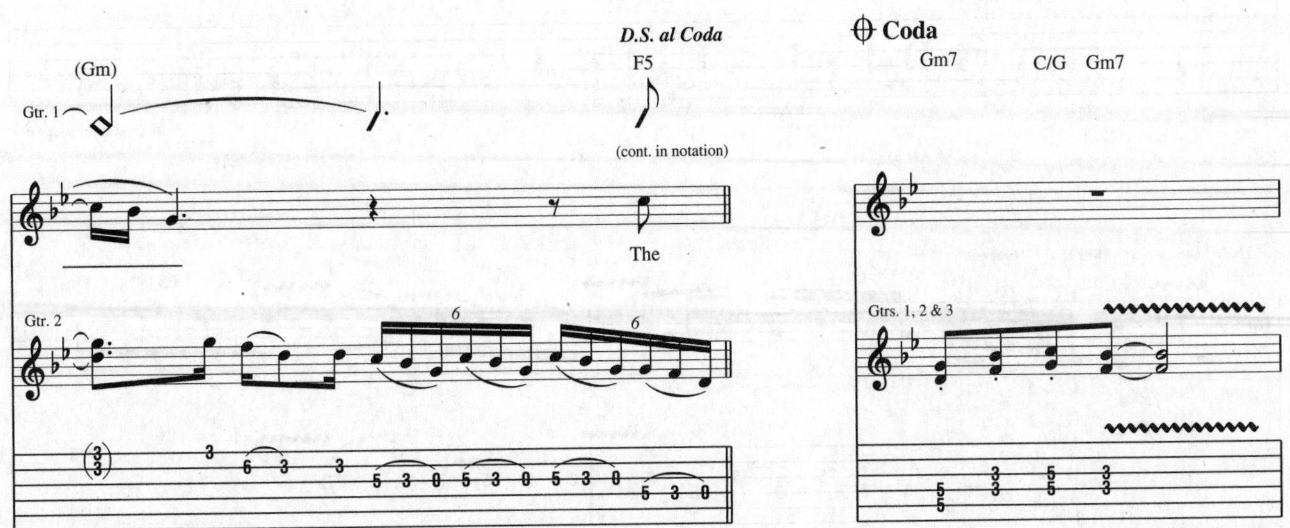
D.S. al Coda
Coda
(Gm)
F5
Gm7
C/G Gm7
Gtr. 1
(cont. in notation)
The
Gtr. 2
6
Gtrs. 1, 2 & 3

Guitar Solo

*Gtr. 2 tacet for beat 4 3/4.

F5
Gm7
w/ bar
slack

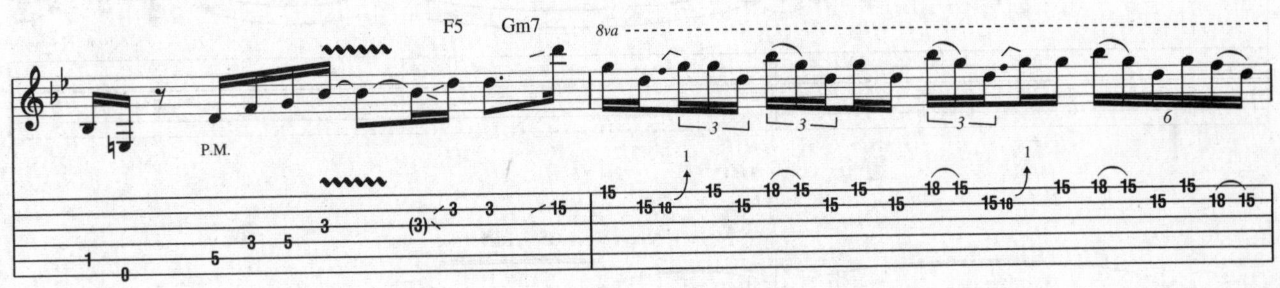
F5
Gm7
8va
P.M.

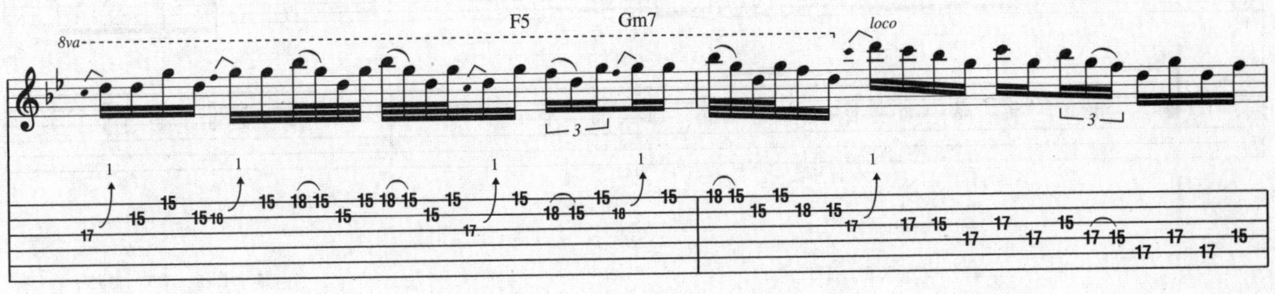
8va
F5
Gm7
loco

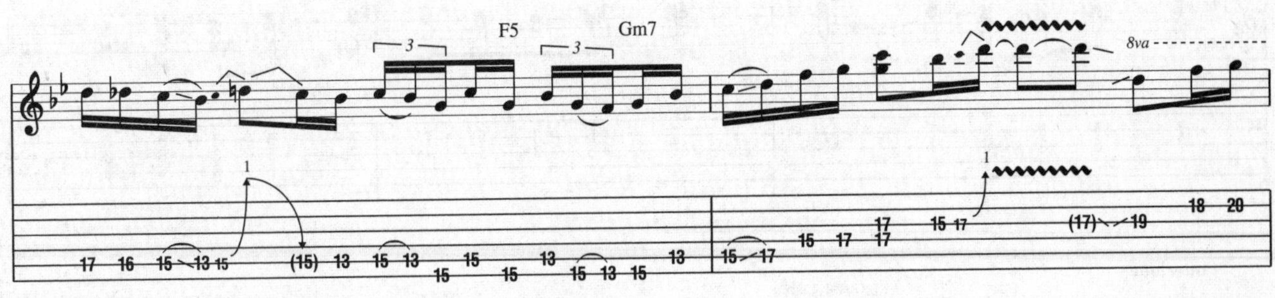
F5
Gm7
8va

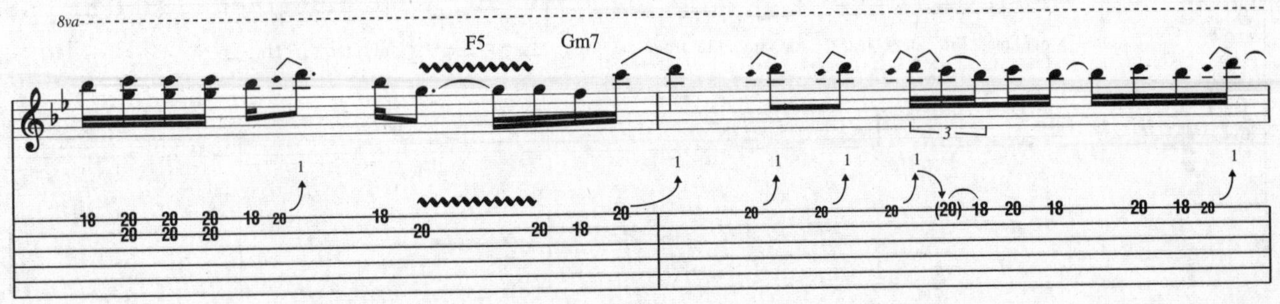
8va
F5
Gm7

8va
Gtr. 4
G5 B♭5 C5
Interlude
loco
Gtrs. 3 & 4
G5 B♭5 C5
Gtrs. 1 & 2
(cont. in slashes)
(C5)
Gtrs. 1 & 2
G5 B♭5 D5
Gtrs. 3 & 4
B♭5 C5 D5
C5 B♭5 C5 B♭5
(cont. in notation)
Interlude
G5
N.C.
Gtrs. 1-4 tacet
Oh ma - ma, I'm in fear for my life from the long ___ arm ___ of the law. ___
Gtrs. 1-4

Gtrs. 1 & 2: w/ Riff A
Hang - man is com - ing down from the gal - lows and I don't have ver - y long. The

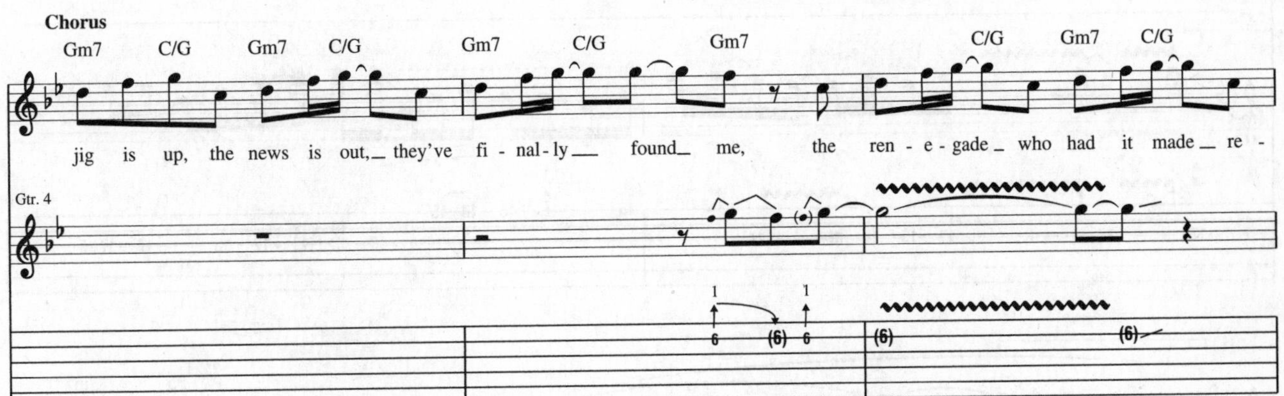
Chorus
Gm7 C/G Gm7 C/G Gm7 C/G Gm7 C/G Gm7 C/G
jig is up, the news is out, they've fi - nal - ly found me, the ren - e - gade who had it made re -
Gtr. 4

Gtr. 1: w/ Riff B
Gtrs. 2 & 3: w/ Rhy. Fig. 1
Gm7 C/G Gm7 D5 D♭5
trieved for a boun - ty. Nev - er more to go a - stray,

C5 Gm7 C/G Gm7 C/G Gm7 C/G Gm7
this will be the end to - day of the want - ed man, the want - ed man.
Gtr. 4
Gtrs. 1, 2 & 3

Outro-Guitar Solo

Gtrs. 1 & 2: w/ Riff D (till fade)
Gtr. 3 tacet

F5
Gm7
8va
w/ Voc. ad lib (next 5 meas.)
loco
Begin fade
w/ bar
Fade out
Yeah, yeah, yeah, I can't go.

Rock Me

Words and Music by Alan Niven, Mark Kendall, Jack Russell and Michael Lardie

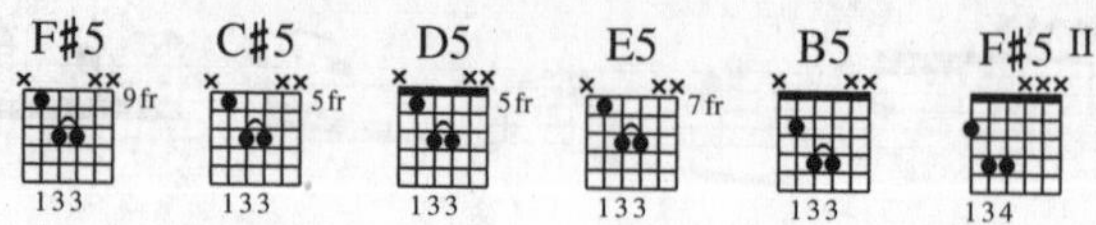

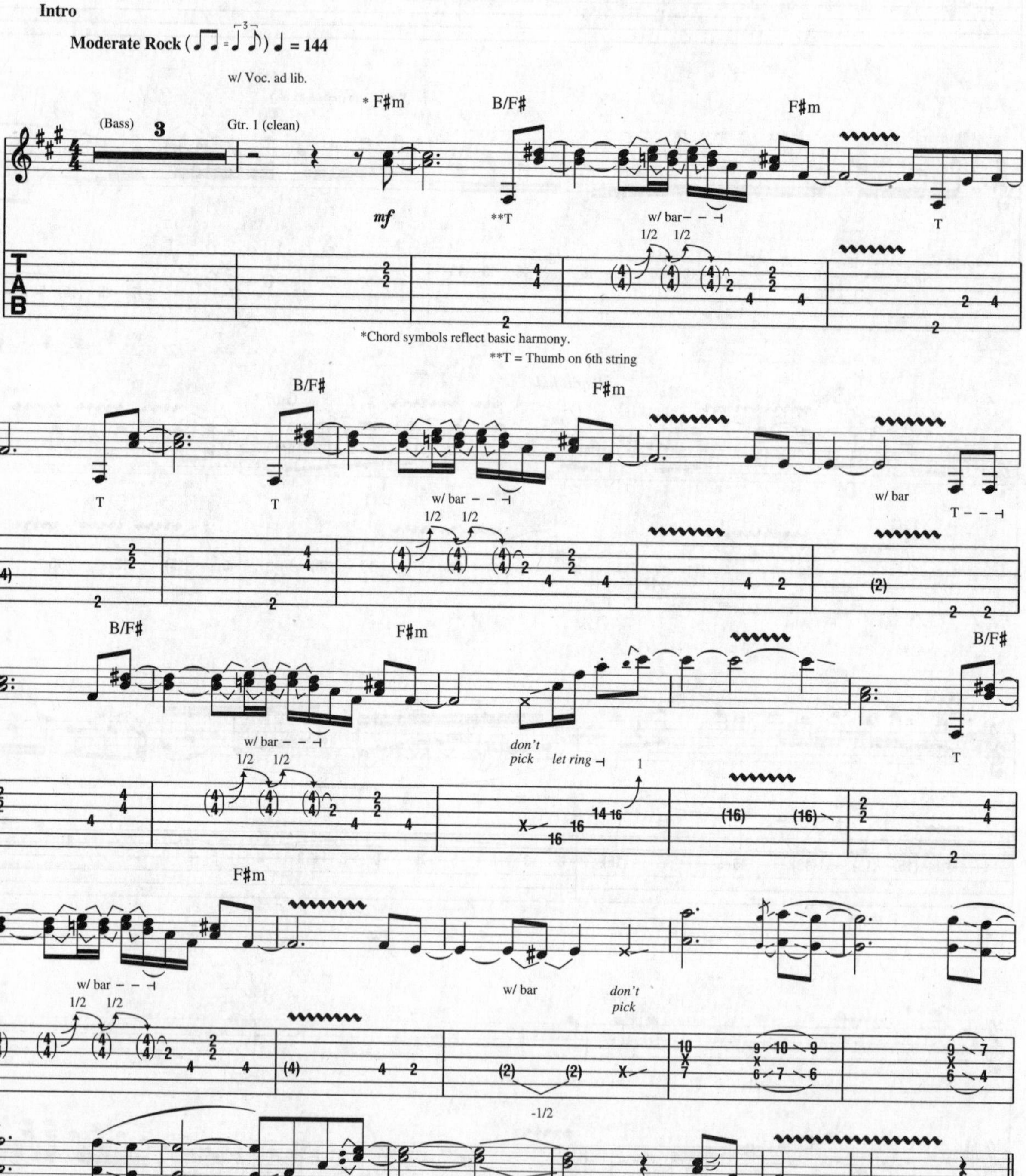

Intro

Moderate Rock (♫ = ♪♪) ♩ = 144

w/ Voc. ad lib.

(Bass) Gtr. 1 (clean)

*F#m B/F# F#m

mf

**T

w/ bar

*Chord symbols reflect basic harmony.

**T = Thumb on 6th string

B/F# F#m

w/ bar

B/F# F#m B/F#

don't pick let ring

F#m

w/ bar

don't pick

grad. release

Verse
F♯m
1. Sweet lit - tle ba - by, you don't have to go.
T w/ bar
1/2
1/2
Lit - tle ba - by, tell me you won't go.
Oh,
1/2 1
we'd be so good to - geth - er if we had the time.
Oh,
don't pick
let ring
1
1
1
be - in' a - lone's a no - where s - state of mind.

F#m
A
B7
D5
E
F#m
Oo, lov - in' ain't no crime, oh, no.
Rhy. Fig. 1
End Rhy. Fig. 1
A
B7
D5
E
F#m
I see your man ain't here, he don't care.
Rhy. Fig. 2
End Rhy. Fig. 2
A
B7
D5
E
F#m
uh, when the night is gone, uh, we'll move on.
A
B7
D5
E5
We'll have to find a way to face an - oth - er day.

Interlude

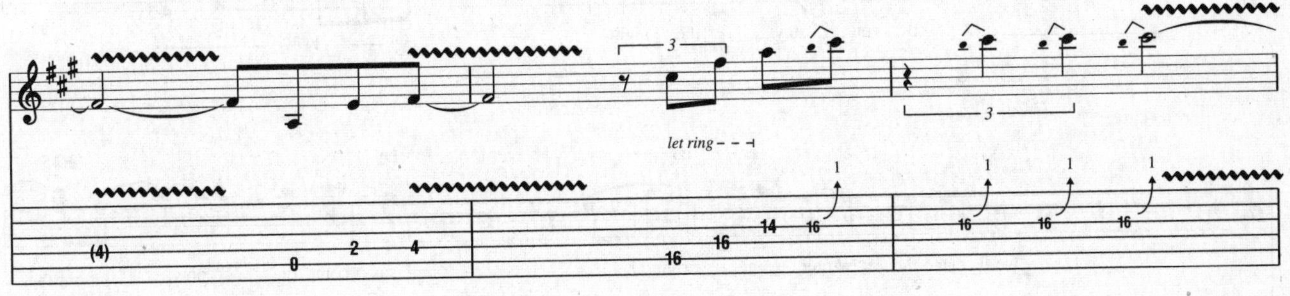

Verse

Chorus

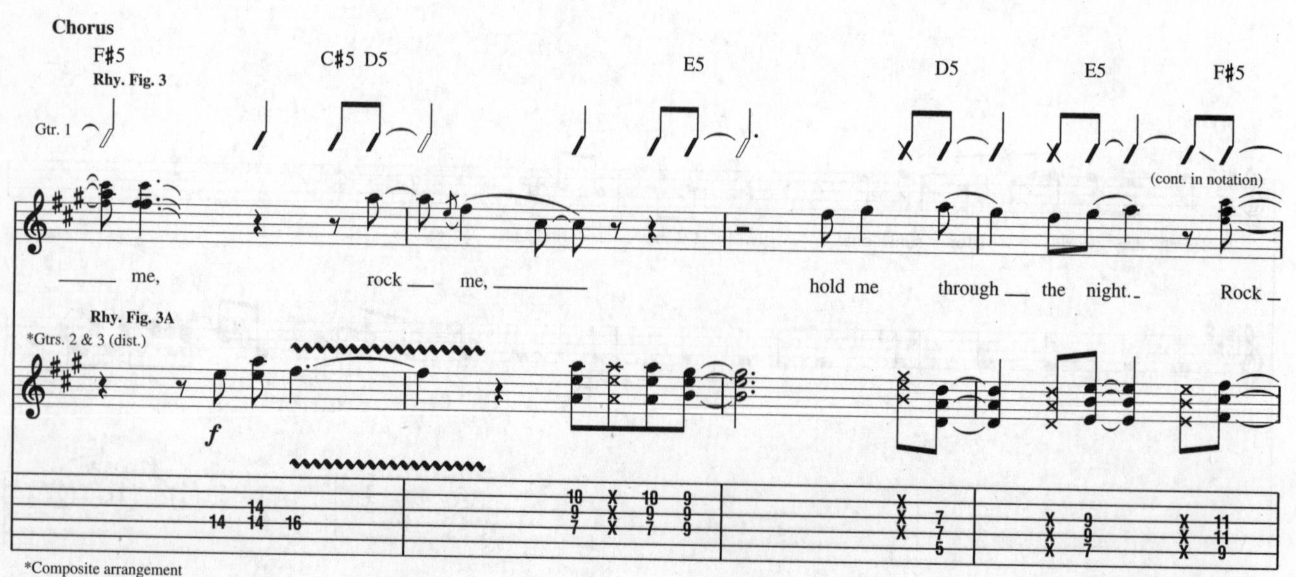

*Composite arrangement

C♯5 D5
E5
Esus4
E
F♯5
me,
rock me,
roll me
through the night.
Rock
Gtrs. 2 & 3
Gtr. 1
(cont. in slashes)
C♯5 D5
E5
D5
E5
B5
End Rhy. Fig. 3
me,
rock me,
roll me
through the night
End Rhy. Fig. 3A
Gtr. 1 tacet
F♯m
with burn - ing love to - night.
fdbk.
dim.
pitch: C♯

Interlude
F#m
Riff A
End Riff A
Gtr. 1
Gtrs. 2 & 3 w/ Riff A (5 times)
mp

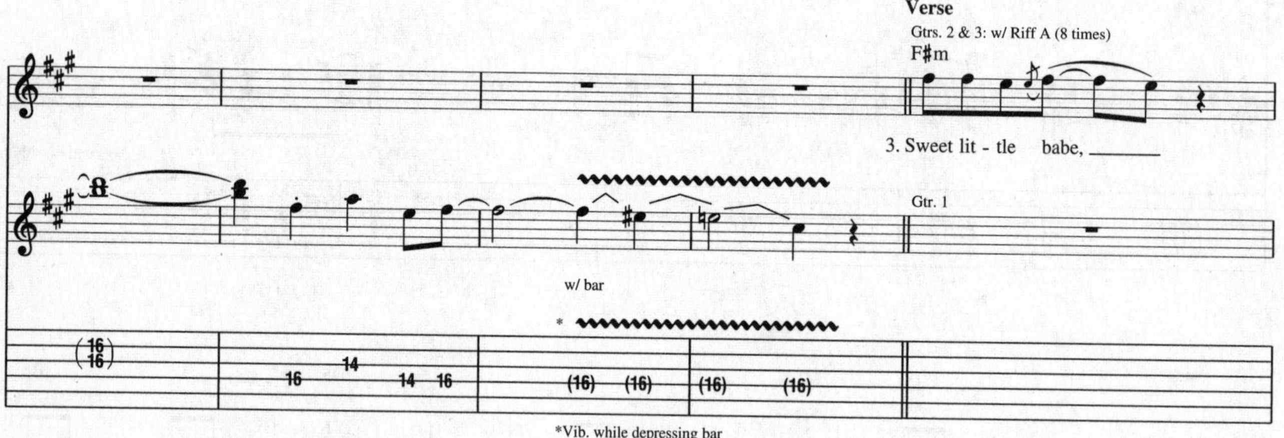
Verse
Gtrs. 2 & 3: w/ Riff A (8 times)
F#m
3. Sweet lit - tle babe,
Gtr. 1
w/ bar
*Vib. while depressing bar

oh, don't you go.
You ain't so, oo,
w/ bar
1/2
1/2

in - no - cent I know.
Gtr. 1: w/ Rhy. Fig. 1
F#m
A
Oo, I
Riff B
Gtr. 2
let ring

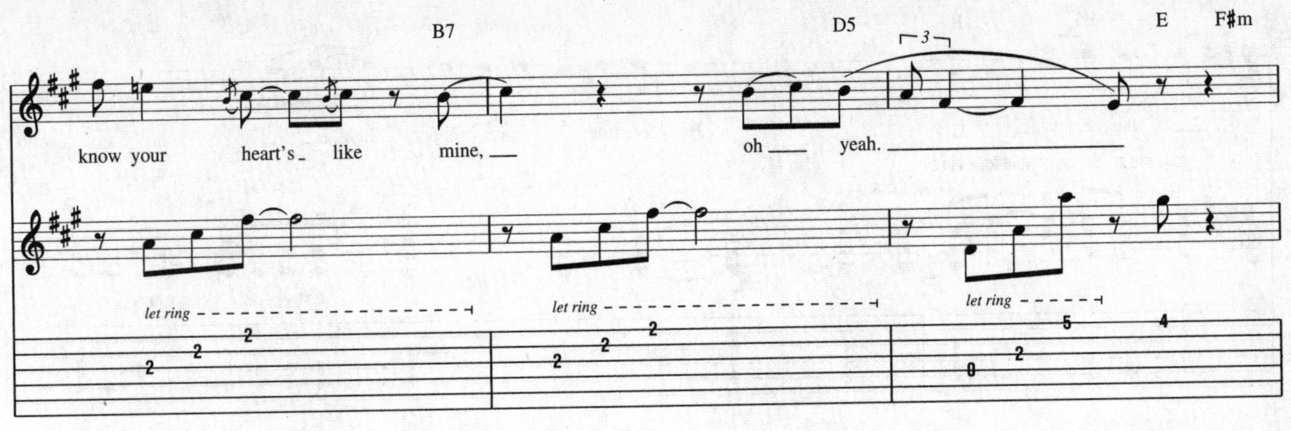
B7
D5
E
F#m
know your heart's like mine, oh yeah.
let ring
let ring
let ring

Gtr. 1: w/ Rhy. Fig. 2 (2 1/2 times)
Gtr. 2: w/ Riff B (2 3/4 times)
B7
D5
E
F#m
And I will find the time to make you mine. Oo,

A
B7
D5
E
F#m
and if your love goes bad, if it makes you sad,

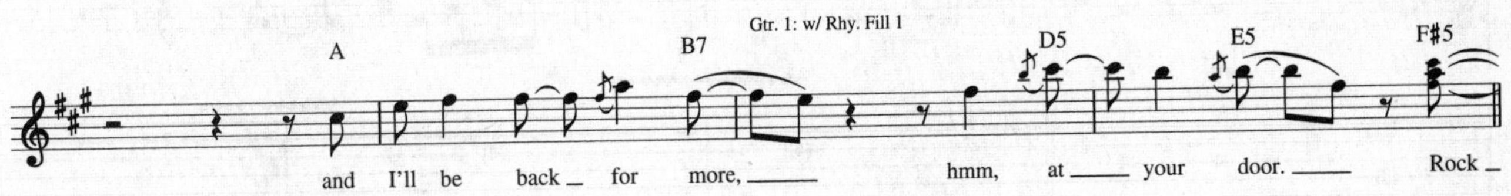
Gtr. 1: w/ Rhy. Fill 1
A
B7
D5
E5
F#5
and I'll be back for more, hmm, at your door. Rock

Chorus

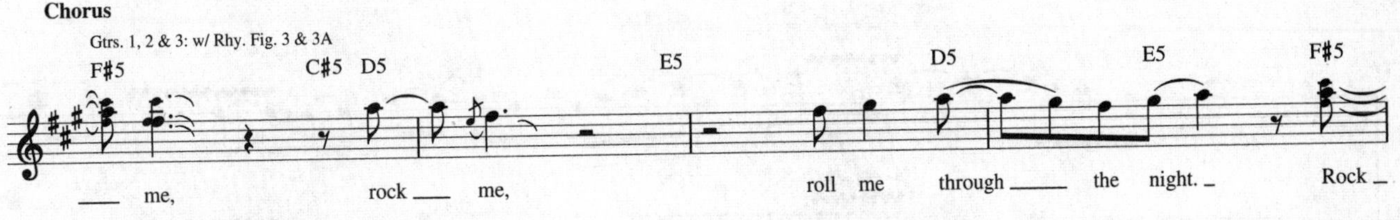
Gtrs. 1, 2 & 3: w/ Rhy. Fig. 3 & 3A
F#5
C#5
D5
E5
D5
E5
F#5
me, rock me, roll me through the night. Rock

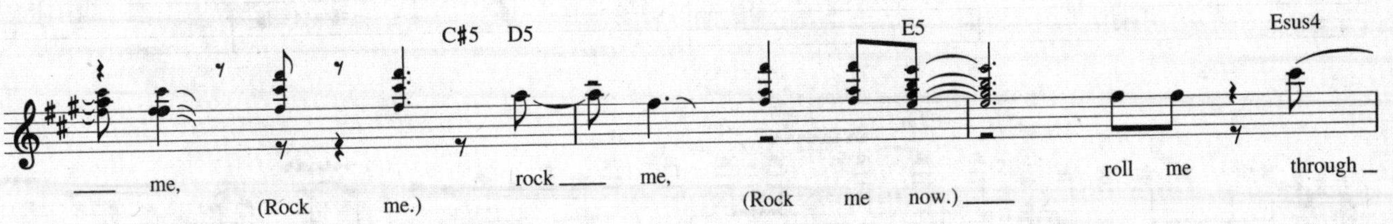
C#5
D5
E5
Esus4
me, rock me, roll me through
(Rock me.) (Rock me now.)

E
F#5
C#5
D5
E5
D5
the night. Rock me, rock me, roll me through

E5
B5
C#5
the night.
Be - fore the morn - ing light,
we'll
Rhy. Fill 2
End Rhy. Fill 2
Gtrs. 2 & 3
Gtrs. 1, 2 & 3
P.M.
D5
E5
Gtrs. 1, 2 & 3 tacet
F#m
burn with love to - night.
Burn with love to - night.
Gtr. 4 (dist.)
mf
dim.
Guitar Solo
F#m
f
let ring
Gtr. 1: w/ Rhy. Fig. 1
F#m
A
B7
D5

Gtr. 1: w/ Rhy. Fig. 2
E
F#m
A
B7
8va
Gtr. 4

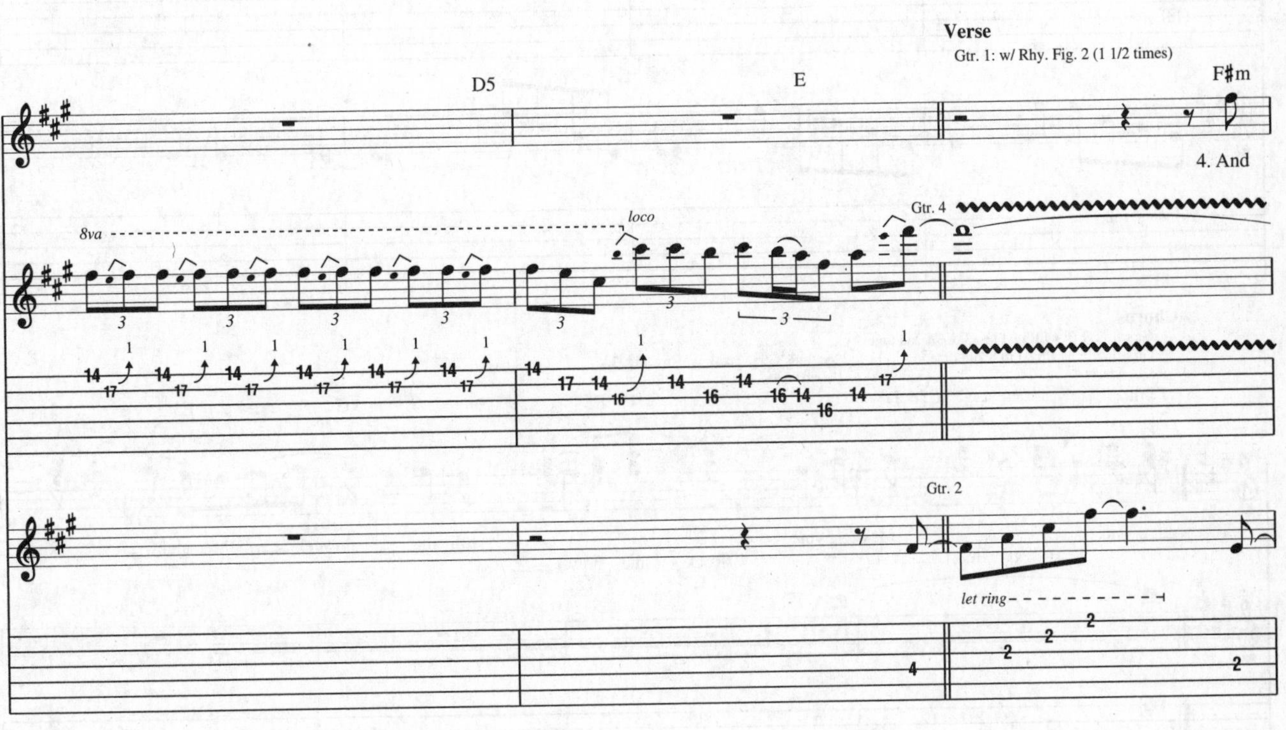

Verse
Gtr. 1: w/ Rhy. Fig. 2 (1 1/2 times)
D5
E
F#m
4. And
8va
loco
Gtr. 4
Gtr. 2
let ring

B7
D5
E
F#m
when your man don't care, I will be there.
dim.
let ring sim.

Gtr. 1: w/ Rhy. Fill 1
A
B7
D5
E5
F#m
You still be - long in real good love, so ba - by, now, rock
8va
Chorus
Gtrs. 1, 2 & 3: w/ Rhy. Figs. 3 & 3A 2nd time
Gtrs. 2 & 3: w/ Rhy. Fill 3 2nd time
Gtr. 4 tacet
2nd time, Gtrs. 2 & 3: w/ Rhy. Fig. 3A
(last 10 meas.)
Gtr. 4 tacet
F#m
C#5 D5
E5
D5
E5
F#5
me, rock me, roll me through the night. Rock
(Rock me.)
(Rock me now.)
2nd time, Gtr. 4: w/ Fill 1
C#5
D5
E5
Esus4
E
F#5
me, rock me, roll me through the night. Rock
(Come on.)
Gtrs. 2 & 3: w/ Rhy. Fill 2
C#5
D5
E5
D5
E5
B5
me, rock me, roll me through the night.
(Rock me.)
(Rock me now.)
Rhy. Fill 3
Gtrs. 2 & 3
Fill 1
Gtr. 4

1.
D5
E5
C#5
There's no wrong or right,
There's noth-ing left to do,
we'll burn with love.
but
Rock
Gtrs. 1, 2 & 3
P.M.
2.
Interlude
Gtrs. 2 & 3 tacet
D5
E5
F#m
B/F#
F#m
make sweet love to you.
Gtr. 1
mf
w/ bar
Gtrs. 2 & 3
w/ Voc. ad lib.
B/F#
F#m
let ring
F#m

B/F#
F#m
F#
14fr
F#5
Gtrs. 2 & 3
P.S.
Come on and rock me,
T
w/ bar
1/2
1/2
P.S.
*Roll up vol. knob
Outro-Guitar Solo
C#5
D5
E5
D5
yeah!
8va
E5
E
12fr
F#5
C#5
D5
E5
8va
loco

F#5
C#5 D5
E5
1/4
1
D5
E5
F#5
C#5 D5
8va
F#5
8va
8va

F#5
8va
Begin fade
C#5 D5
E5
D5
E5
F#5
Rhy. Fig. 4
End Rhy. Fig. 4
C#5 D5
E5
P.H.
pitch: E
w/ bar
-1 1/2
Gtrs. 2 & 3: w/ Rhy. Fig. 4 (till end)
F#5
C#5 D5
E5
w/ bar
-1 1/2
P.H.
pitch: E
Fade out
D5
E5
F#5
C#5
D5
P.H.
P.H.
pitch: E
pitch: E

Rock You Like a Hurricane

Words and Music by Herman Rarebell, Klaus Meine and Rudolf Schenker

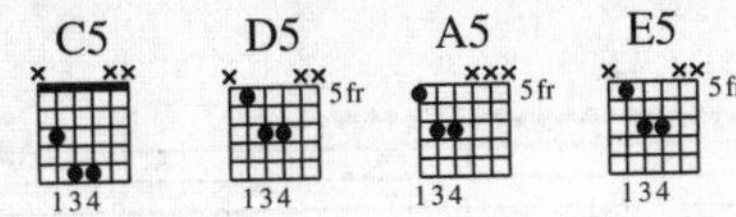

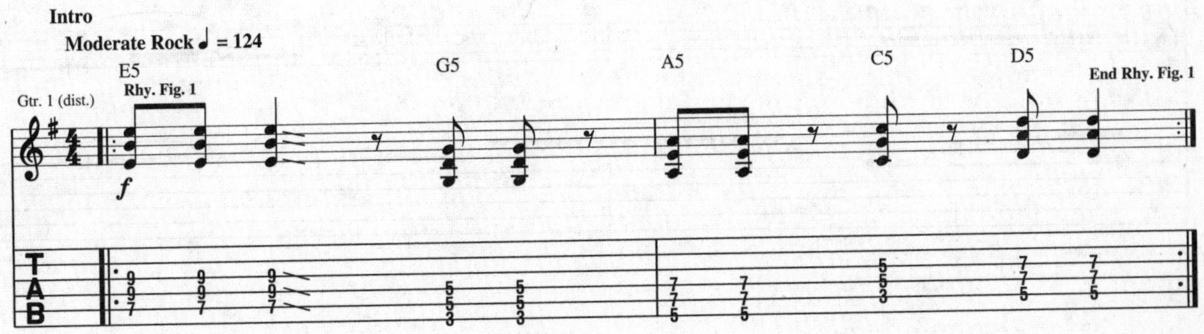

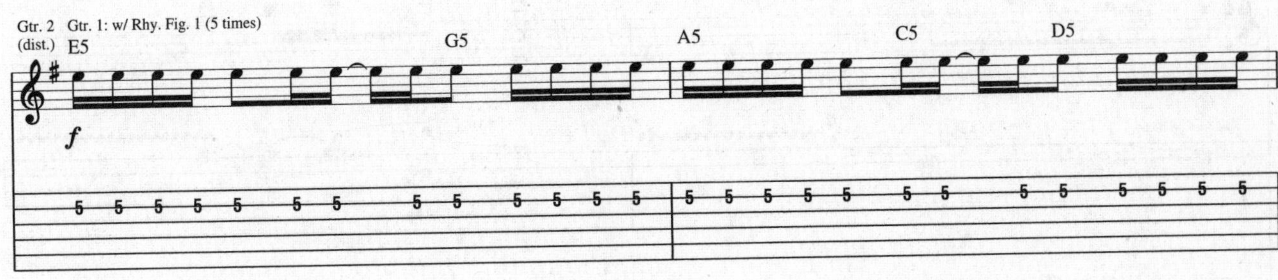

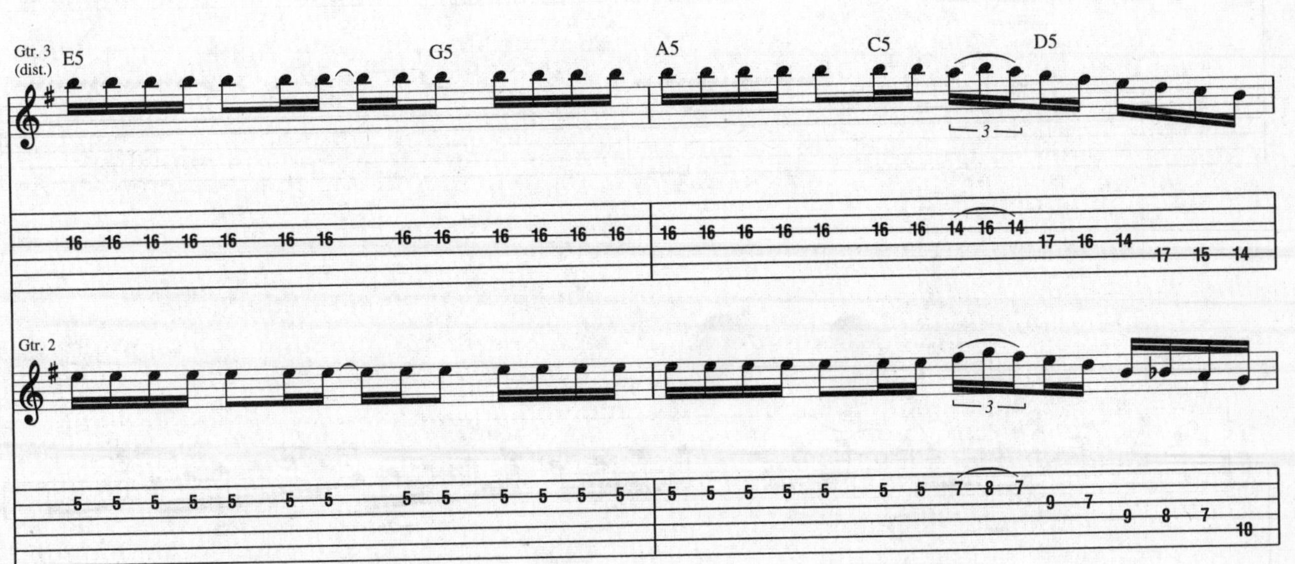

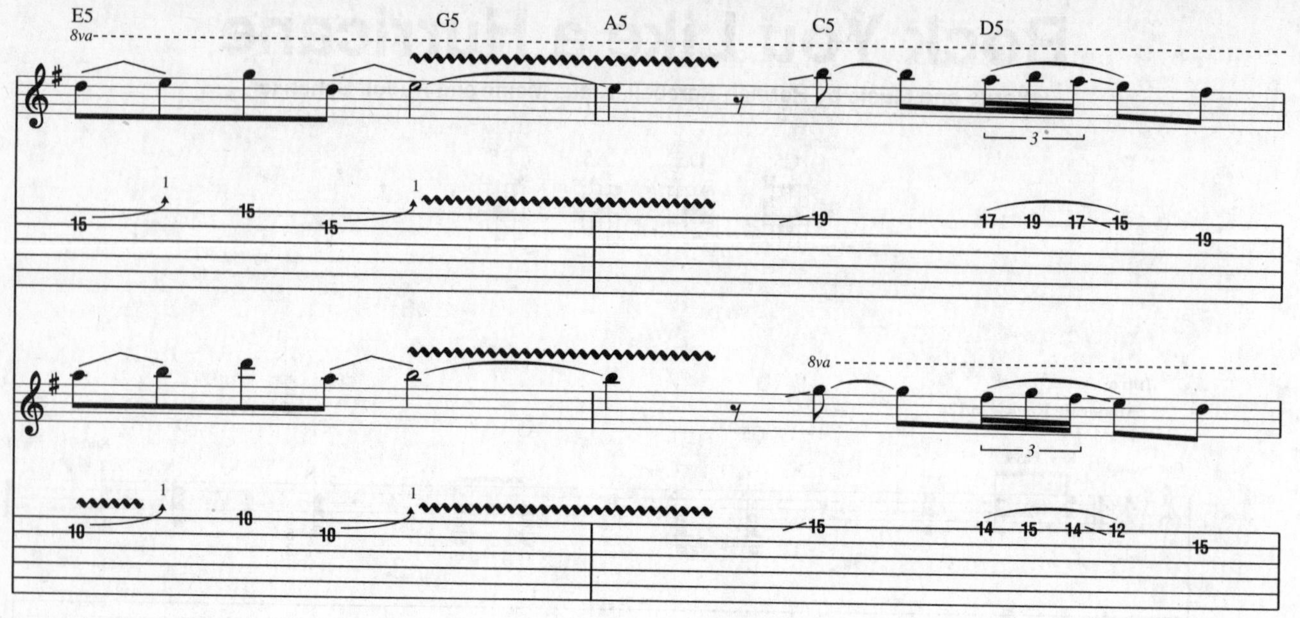
E5
8va
G5
A5
C5
D5
8va

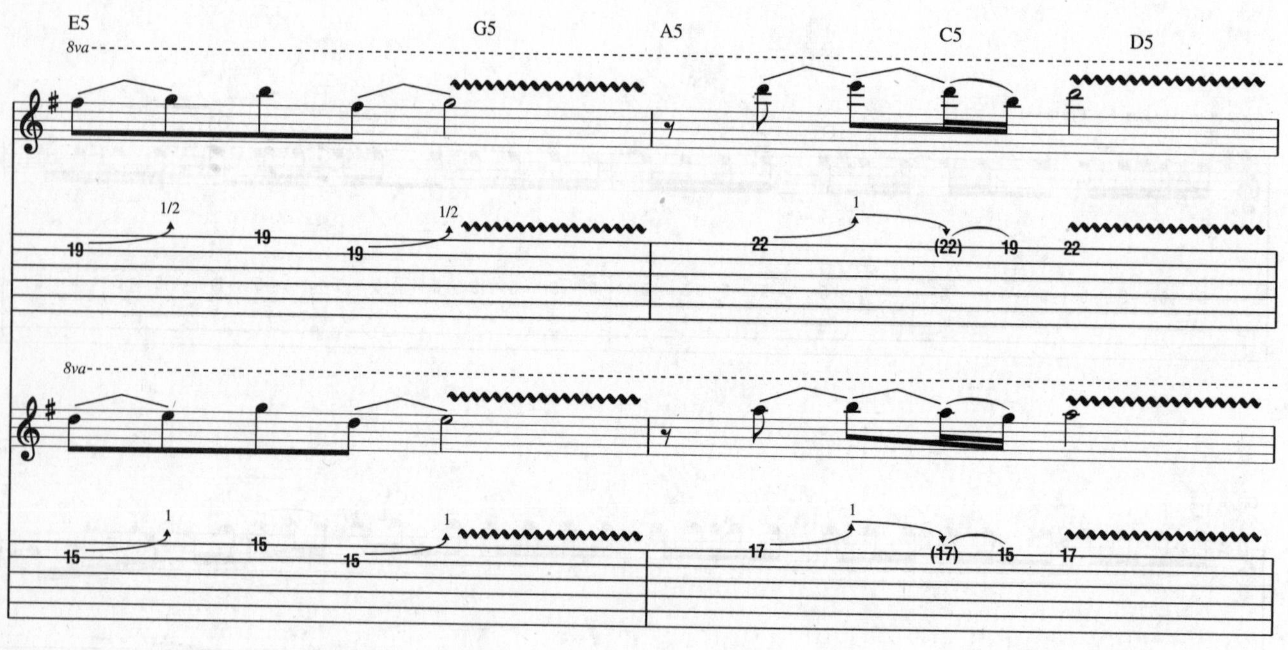
E5
8va
G5
A5
C5
D5
8va

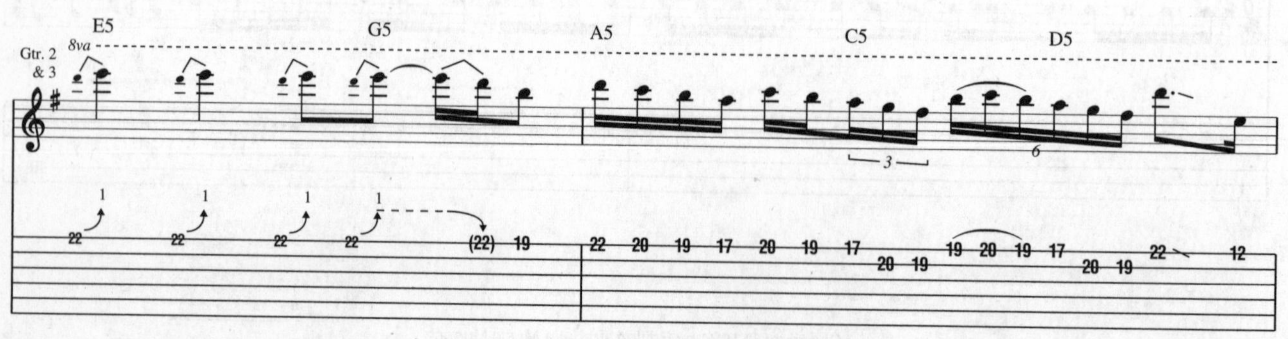
Gtr. 2
& 3
E5
8va
G5
A5
C5
D5

Gtrs. 2 & 3
E5
G5
A5
C5
D5
8va
loco
Gtr. 1
Rhy. Fill 1
Verse
Gtrs. 2 & 3 tacet
C5
E5
C5
E5
D5
1. It's ear - ly morn - ing, the sun comes out.
Last
End Rhy. Fill 2
Rhy. Fig. 2
P.M. throughout
C5
E5
C5
D5
night was shak - ing and pret - ty loud.
My
Gtr. 2
8va
Harm.
let ring
Pitch: A D B
End Rhy. Fig. 2

Gtr. 1: w/ Rhy. Fig. 2 (2 3/4 times)
C5
E5
C5
E5
D5
cat is pur - ring, it scratch - es my skin. So,
loco
Gtr. 2
w/ bar
0
Gtr. 2 tacet
C5
E5
C5
D5
* Gtr. 4 (dist.): w/ Rhy. Fig. 2 (1 3/4 times)
C5
E5
what is wrong with an - oth - er sin? The bitch is hun - gry, she
* mf
C5
E5
D5
C5
E5
C5
D5
needs to tell, so give her inch - es and feed her well. More
C5
E5
C5
E5
D5
C5
E5
days to come, new plac - es to go. I've got to leave, it's
C5
D5
Rhy. Fill 2
Gtr. 1
End Rhy. Fill 2
P.M.
time for a show.
Gtr. 4
Rhy. Fill 2A
End Rhy. Fill 2A
P.M.
P.S.
Chorus
Gtrs. 1 & 4: w/ Rhy. Fig. 1 (3 times)
E5
G5
A5
C5
D5
E5
G5
Chorus
Here I am, rock you like a hur - ri - cane.

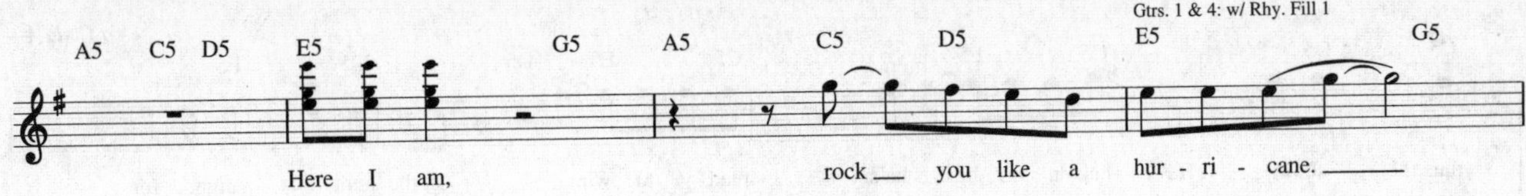

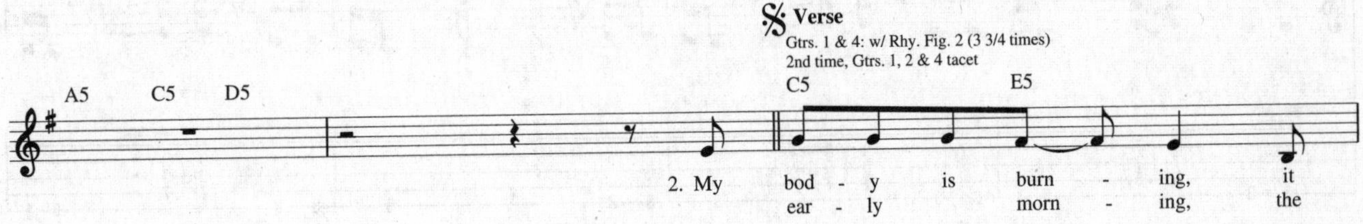

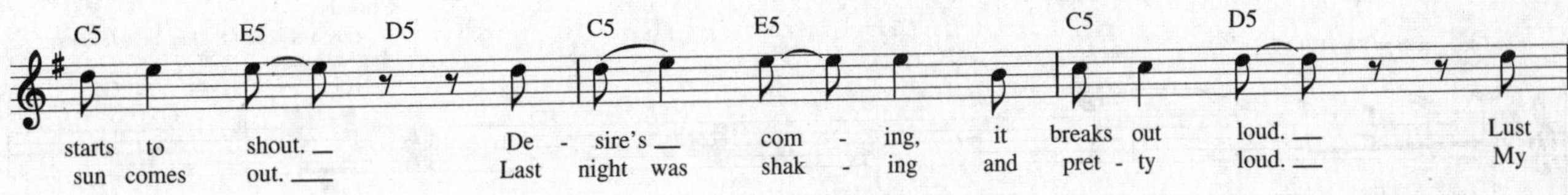

* Composite arrangement

To Coda

C5 D5 C5 E5 C5 E5 D5 C5 E5
runs the show. He's lick-in' his lips, he's read-y to win. On the hunt to - night for
* Gtr. 2 & 3
Gtrs. 1 & 4: w/ Rhy. Fill 2
C5 D5
love at first sting.
Chorus
Gtrs. 1 & 4: w/ Rhy. Fig. 1 (7 1/2 times)
Gtr. 3 tacet
E5 G5
Here I am,
Gtr. 2
Gtr. 3
Rhy. Fill 3
End Rhy. Fill 3
Gtr. 2 tacet
A5 C5 D5 E5 G5 A5 C5 D5
rock you like a hur - ri - cane. Are you read - y ba - by?
E5 G5 A5 C5 D5 E5 A5 C5 D5
Here I am, rock you like a hur - ri - cane.

Gtr. 2: w/ Fill 1
E5 G5 A5 C5 D5
Gtr. 2: w/ Fill 1
E5 G5 A5 C5 D5
Here I am, rock _ you like a hur - ri - cane. Come on, come on, come on, come on. ___
Gtr. 2: w/ Fill 1
E5 G5 A5 C5 D5
Gtr. 2: w/ Fill 1
E5 G5 A5 C5 D5 E5
Gtrs. 1 & 4
Here I am, rock _ you like a hur - ri - cane. ___

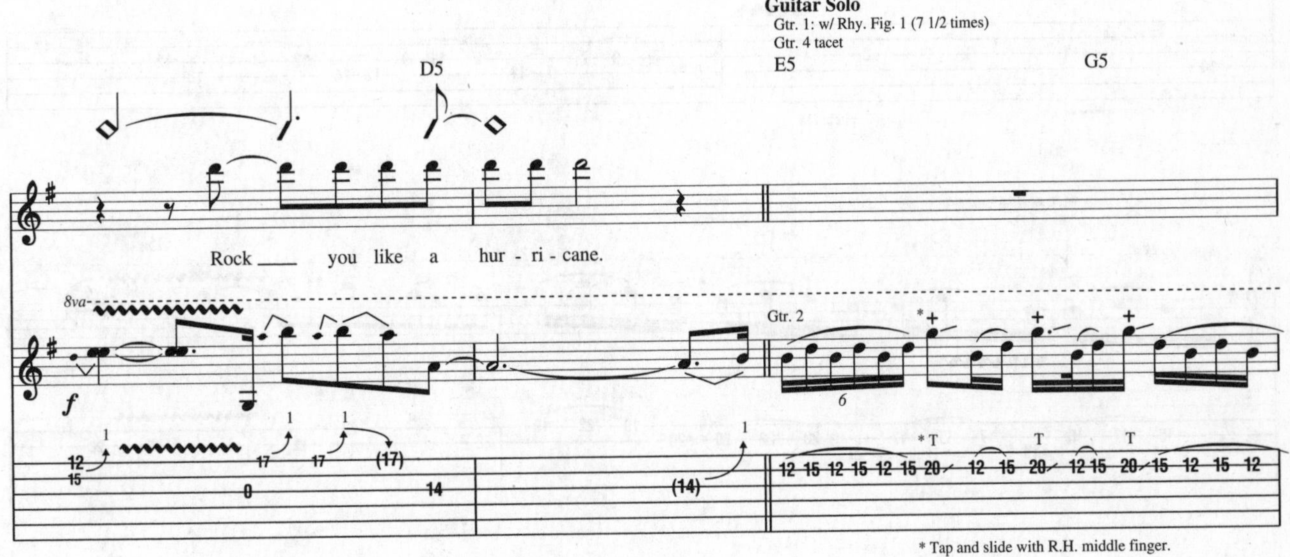

Guitar Solo
Gtr. 1: w/ Rhy. Fig. 1 (7 1/2 times)
Gtr. 4 tacet
D5
E5 G5
Rock ___ you like a hur - ri - cane.
8va
Gtr. 2
f
6
* Tap and slide with R.H. middle finger.

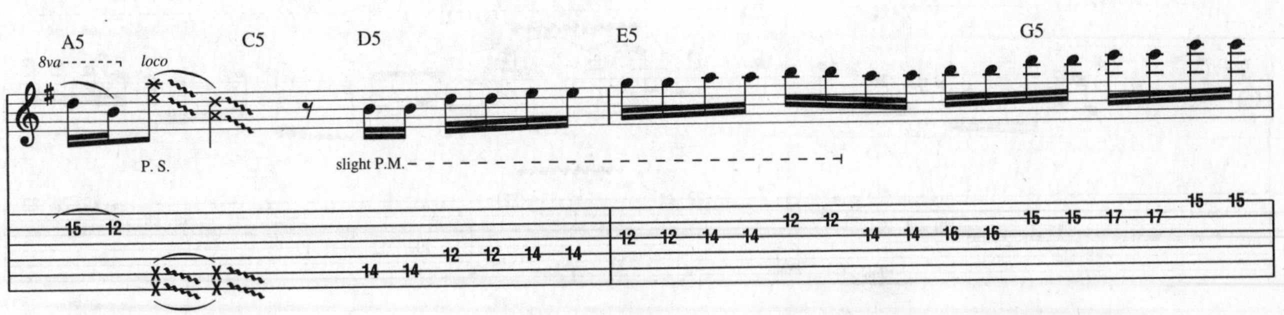

A5 C5 D5 E5 G5
8va
loco
P. S.
slight P.M.

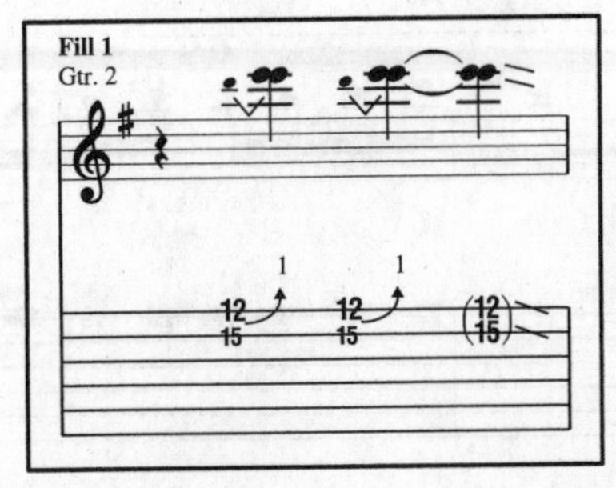

Fill 1
Gtr. 2

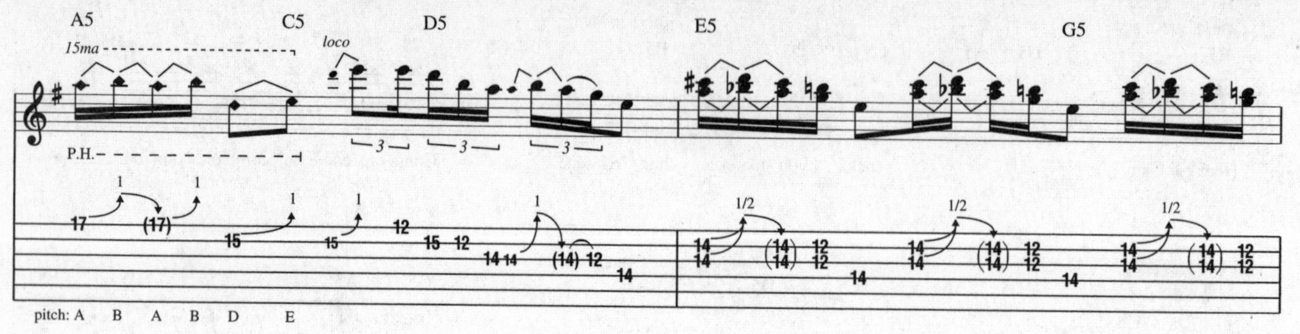
A5
C5
D5
E5
G5
15ma
loco
P.H.
pitch: A B A B D E
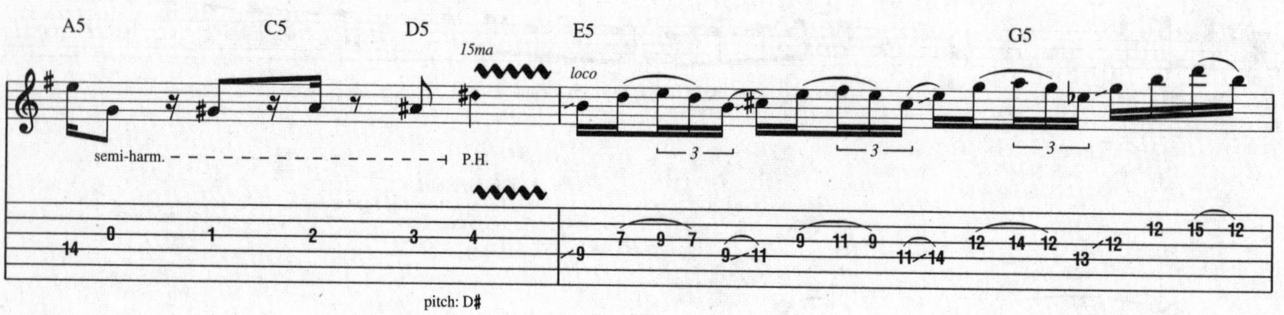
A5
C5
D5
15ma
E5
loco
G5
semi-harm.
P.H.
pitch: D♯
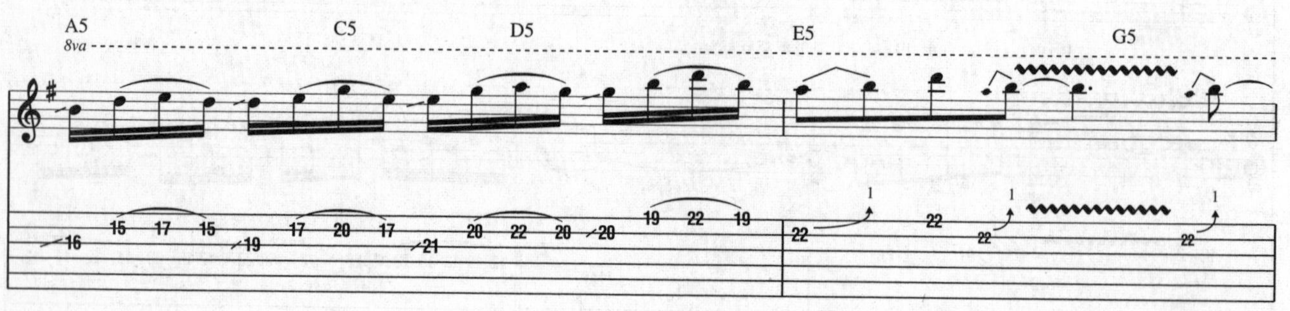
A5
8va
C5
D5
E5
G5
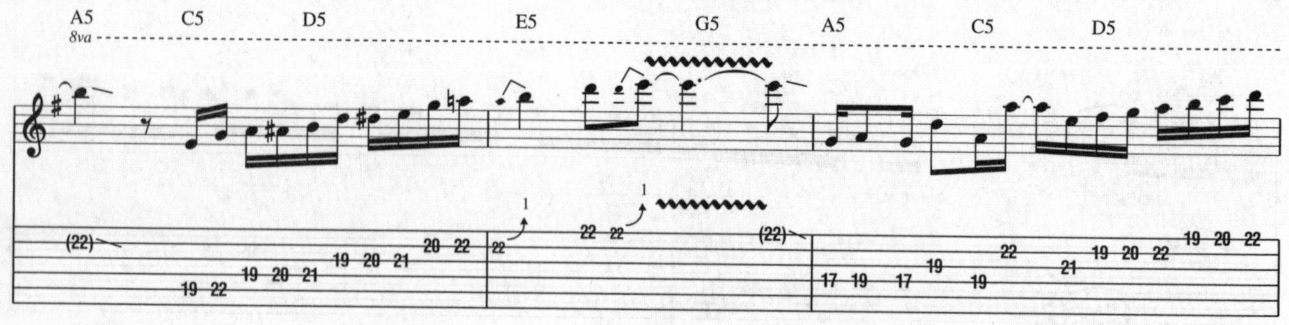
A5
C5
D5
8va
E5
G5
A5
C5
D5

E5
8va
G5
A5
C5
D5
loco

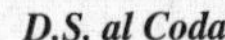
D.S. al Coda

E5
G5
A5
C5
D5
E5
Gtr. 1
3. It's
semi-harm.
grad. bend
1/2

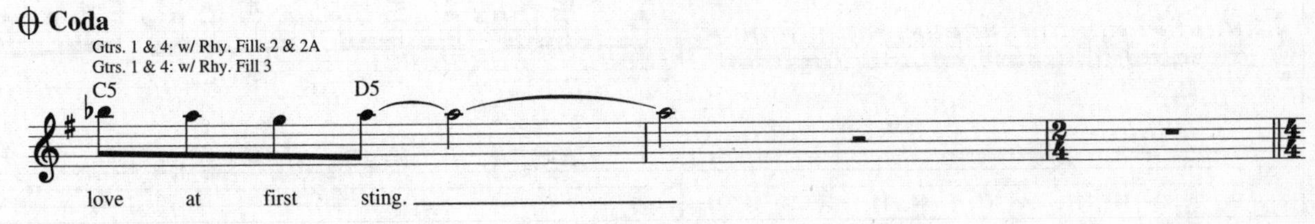
Coda
Gtrs. 1 & 4: w/ Rhy. Fills 2 & 2A
Gtrs. 1 & 4: w/ Rhy. Fill 3
C5
D5
love at first sting.

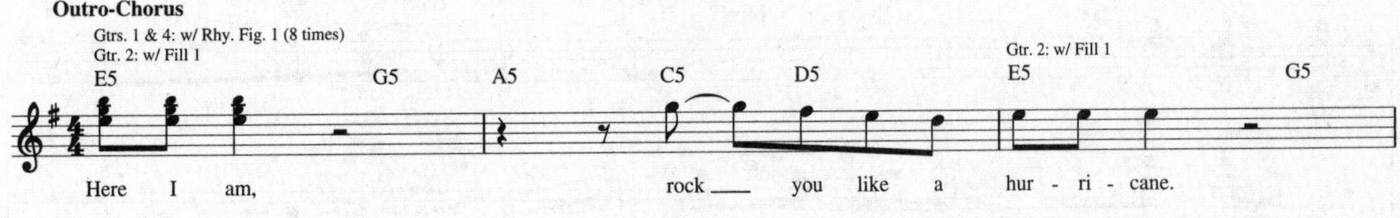
Outro-Chorus
Gtrs. 1 & 4: w/ Rhy. Fig. 1 (8 times)
Gtr. 2: w/ Fill 1
E5
G5
A5
C5
D5
Gtr. 2: w/ Fill 1
E5
G5
Here I am, rock you like a hur - ri - cane.

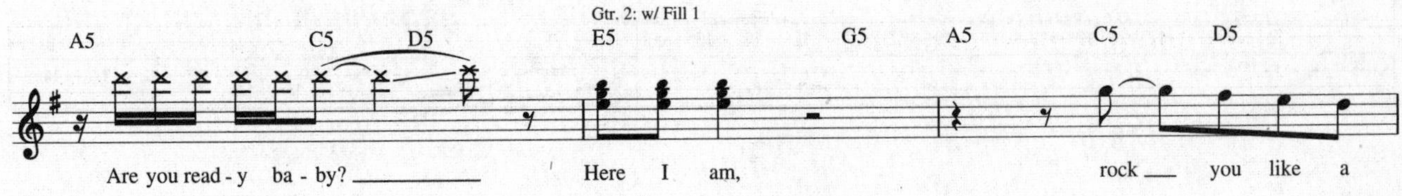
A5
C5
D5
Gtr. 2: w/ Fill 1
E5
G5
A5
C5
D5
Are you read - y ba - by? Here I am, rock you like a

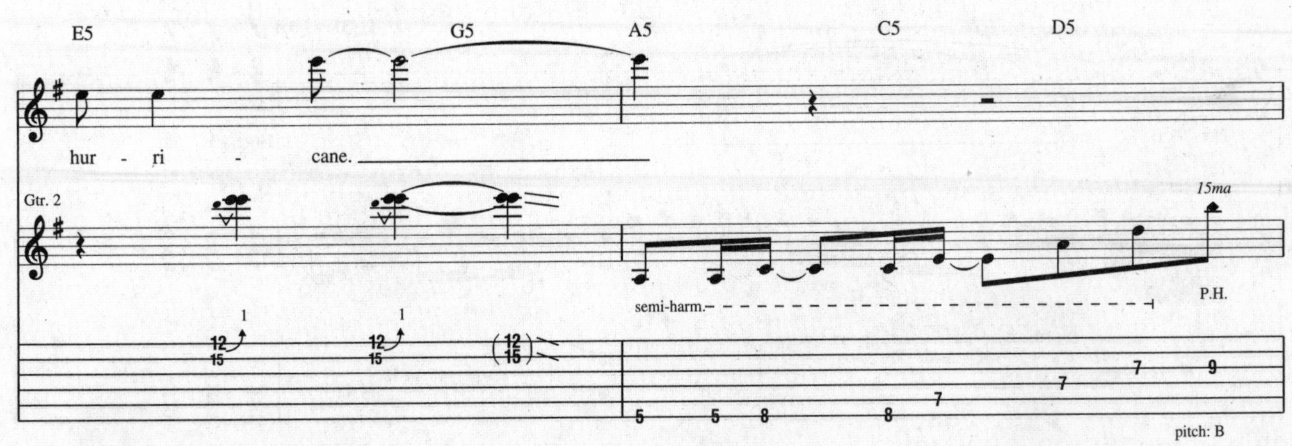
E5
G5
A5
C5
D5
hur - ri - cane.
Gtr. 2
15ma
semi-harm.
P.H.
pitch: B

E5
G5
A5
C5
D5
Here I am,
rock you like a
loco
hur - ri - cane.
Well, come on, come on, come on, come on, come on.
Here I am,
rock you like a
T
P.S.
slight P.M.
hur - ri - cane.
Gtrs. 1 & 4
Here I am.
8va
loco

Rollin' Stone (Catfish Blues)

Written by McKinley Morganfield (Muddy Waters)

A7/E
a whole deep blue sea. I will have all
E7
you good - look - in' wom - en fish - in', fish - in' af - ter me.
1/4
Sure 'nuff af - ter me, sure 'nuff af - ter me.
1/4
Oh, Lord. Oh, Lord.
1/2

Sure 'nuff.
Verse
E7
2. I went to my ba - by's house
4. See additional lyrics
told my fa - ther
1/2
A7/E
and I sit down, ho, on her step.
just be - fore, hmm, I was born,
E7
She said, "Come on in now, Mud - dy, you know my
"I got a boy - child com - in', gon - na be,
1/4

hus - band— just now left.—
he's gon - na be a roll - in' stone.
Sure 'nuff, he just now left.—
Sure 'nuff, he's a roll - in' stone.
To Coda
Sure 'nuff, he just now left."—
Sure 'nuff, he's a roll - in' stone.
Oh, Lord.—
Whoa, well, he's a,
Oh, well.—
Oh, well, he's a,
Oh, well.—
Oh, well, he's a
1.
tr

2.
3. Well, my moth - er
Oh, well, he's a."
Guitar Solo
A7/E
E7

Additional Lyrics

4. Well, I feel, yes I feel, baby,
   Like the low-down, ho, time ain't long.
   I'm gonna catch the first thing smokin'
   Back, back down the road I'm goin',
   Back down the road I'm goin',
   Back down the road I'm goin'.

Runnin' Down a Dream

Words and Music by Jeff Lynne, Tom Petty and Mike Campbell

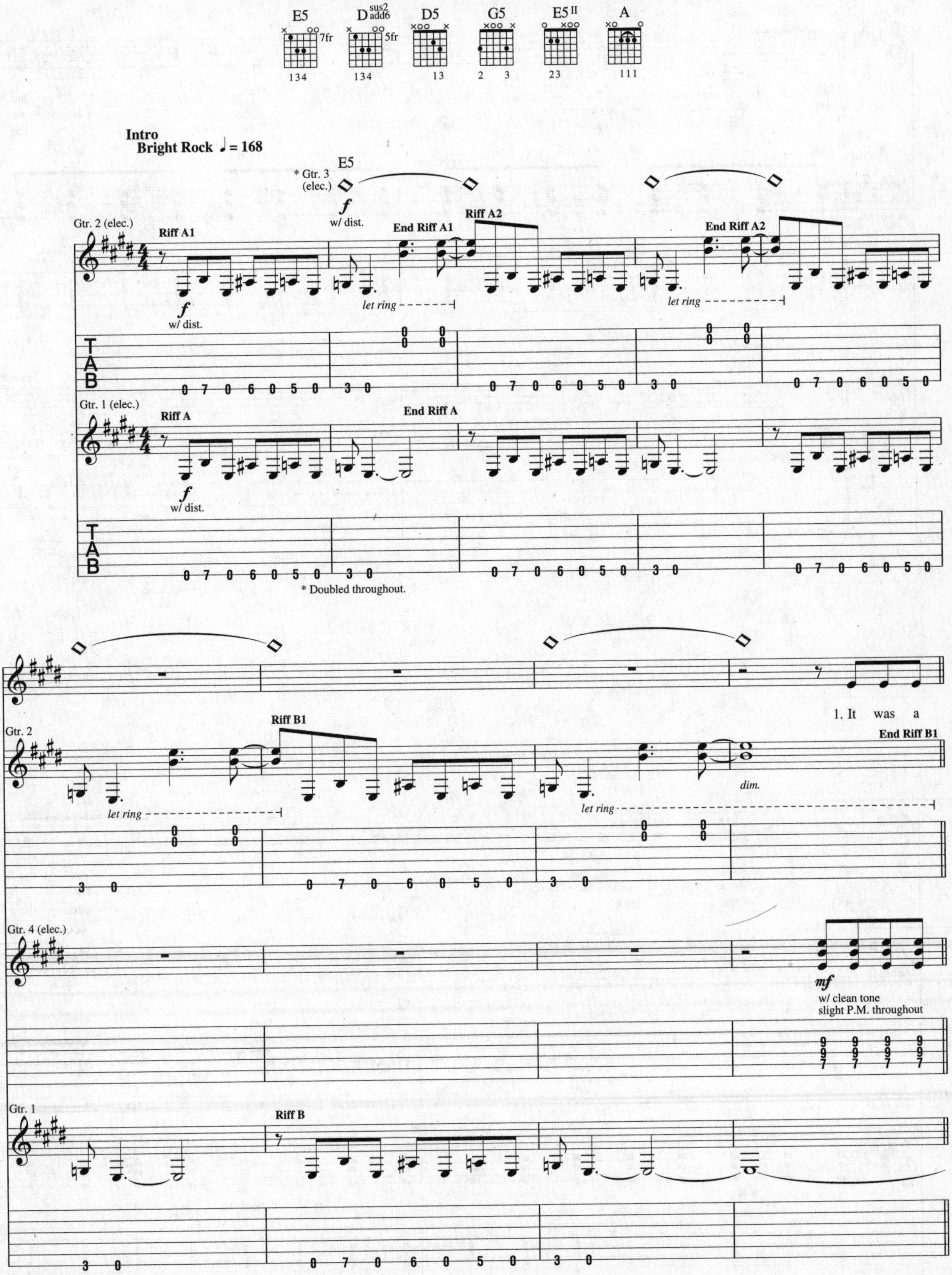

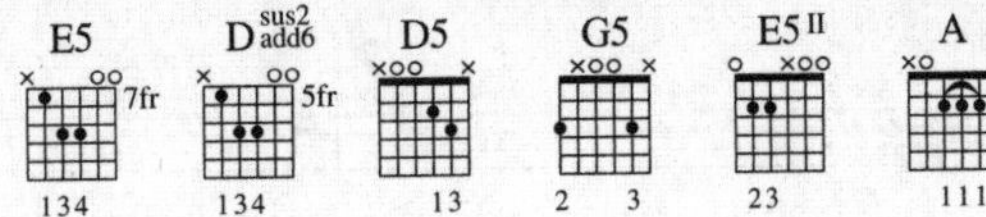

Intro
Bright Rock ♩ = 168

E5
* Gtr. 3 (elec.)
f w/ dist.
Gtr. 2 (elec.)
Riff A1
End Riff A1
Riff A2
End Riff A2
let ring
f w/ dist.

Gtr. 1 (elec.)
Riff A
End Riff A
f w/ dist.

* Doubled throughout.

1. It was a

Gtr. 2
Riff B1
End Riff B1
let ring
dim.

Gtr. 4 (elec.)
mf
w/ clean tone
slight P.M. throughout

Gtr. 1
Riff B

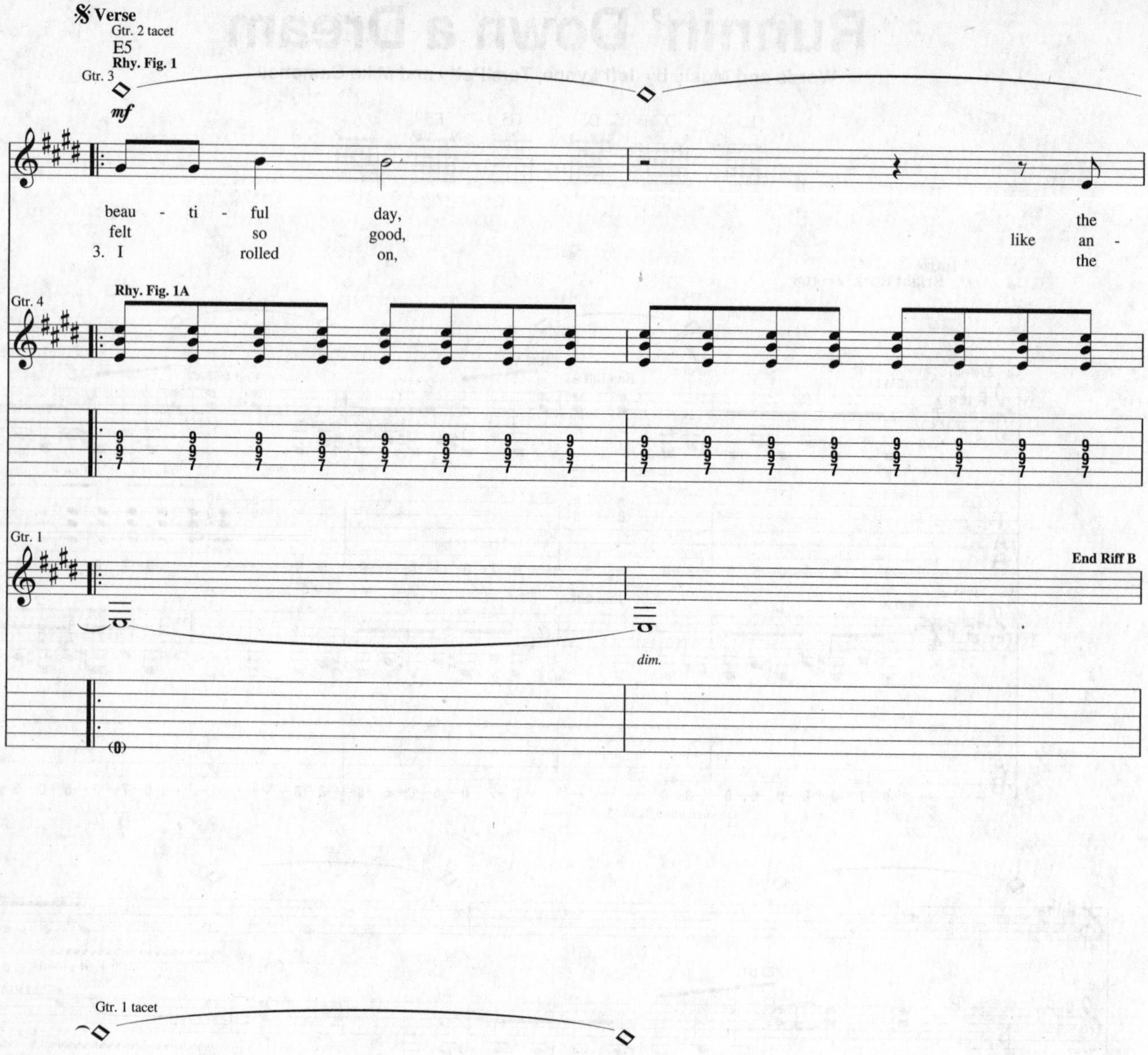

𝄋 Verse

Gtr. 2 tacet

E5

Rhy. Fig. 1

Gtr. 3

mf

beau - ti - ful day, the

felt so good, like an -

3. I rolled on, the

Gtr. 4

Rhy. Fig. 1A

Gtr. 1

End Riff B

dim.

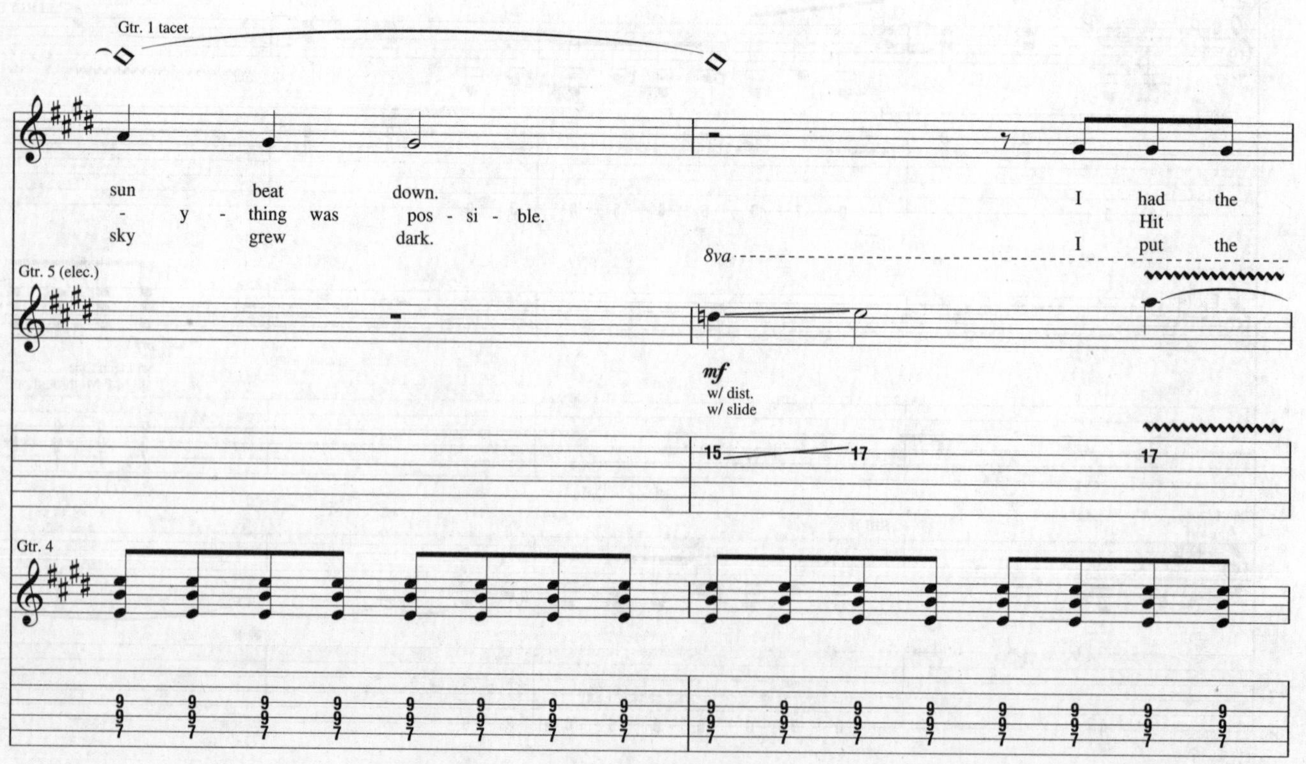

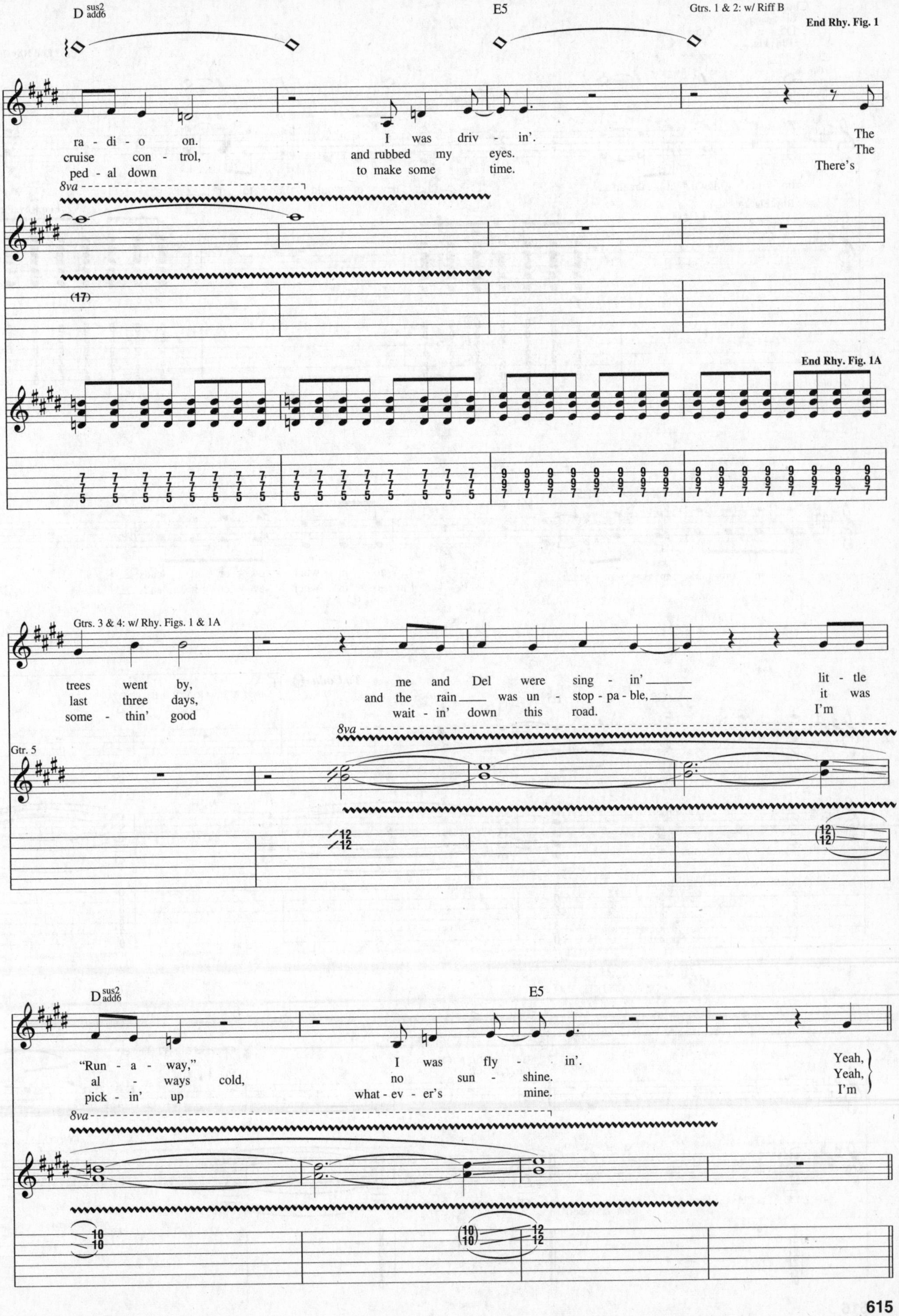

Dsus2 add6 E5 Gtrs. 1 & 2: w/ Riff B

End Rhy. Fig. 1

ra - di - o on. I was driv - in'. The
cruise con - trol, and rubbed my eyes. The
ped - al down to make some time. There's

8va

(17)

End Rhy. Fig. 1A

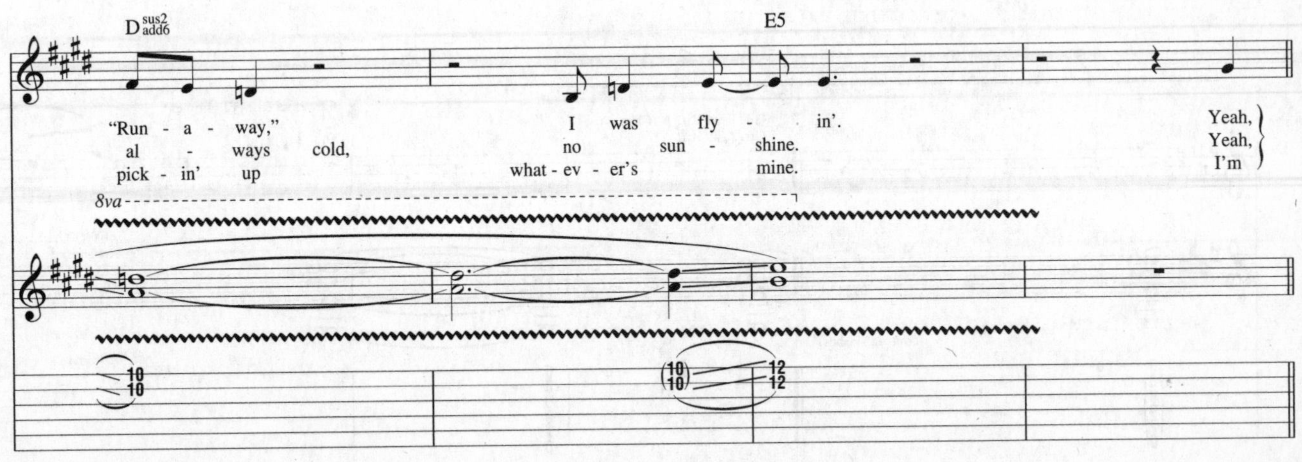

Chorus
Gtr. 5 tacet
D5
G5
E5II
A
Rhy. Fig. 2
Gtr. 3
End Rhy. Fig. 2
run - nin' down a dream
that nev - er would come to me.
Work -
Rhy. Fig. 2A
* Gtr. 6 (acous.)
End Rhy. Fig. 2A
* Doubled throughout

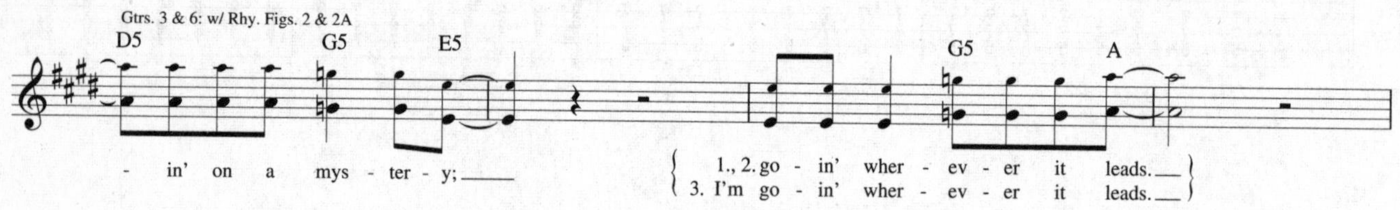
Gtrs. 3 & 6: w/ Rhy. Figs. 2 & 2A
D5
G5
E5
A
- in' on a mys - ter - y;
1., 2. go - in' wher - ev - er it leads.
3. I'm go - in' wher - ev - er it leads.

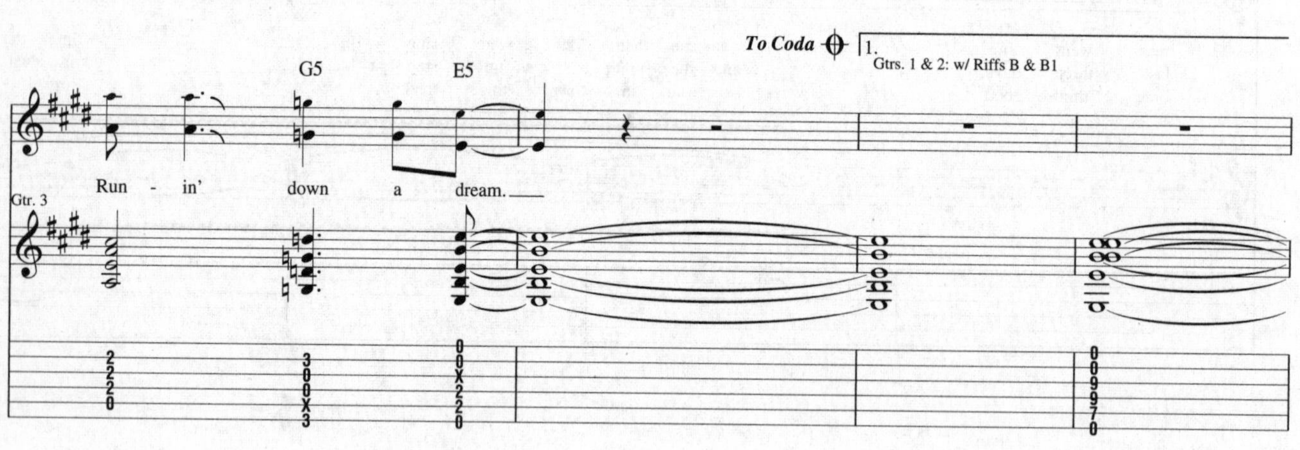
To Coda
1.
Gtrs. 1 & 2: w/ Riffs B & B1
G5
E5
Run - in' down a dream.
Gtr. 3

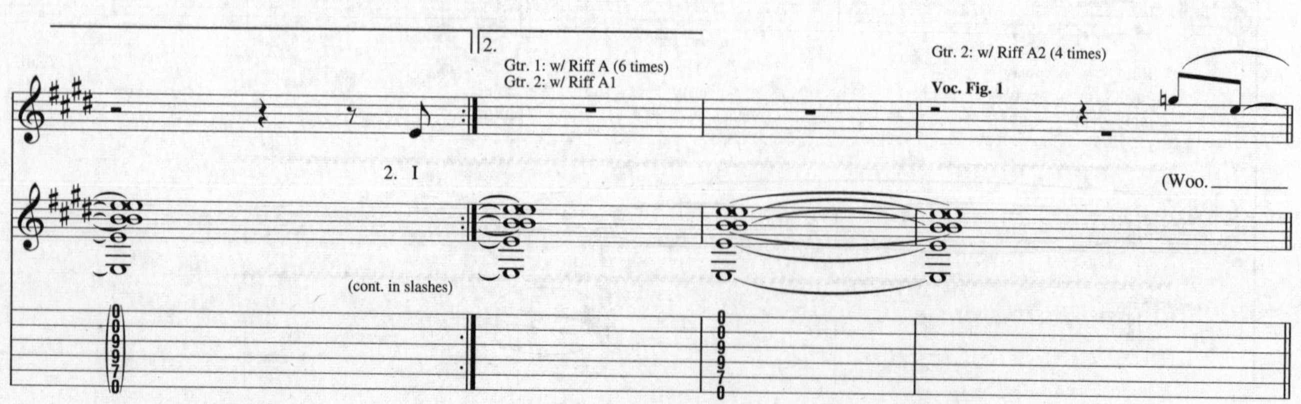
2.
Gtr. 1: w/ Riff A (6 times)
Gtr. 2: w/ Riff A1
Gtr. 2: w/ Riff A2 (4 times)
Voc. Fig. 1
2. I
(Woo.
(cont. in slashes)

Interlude

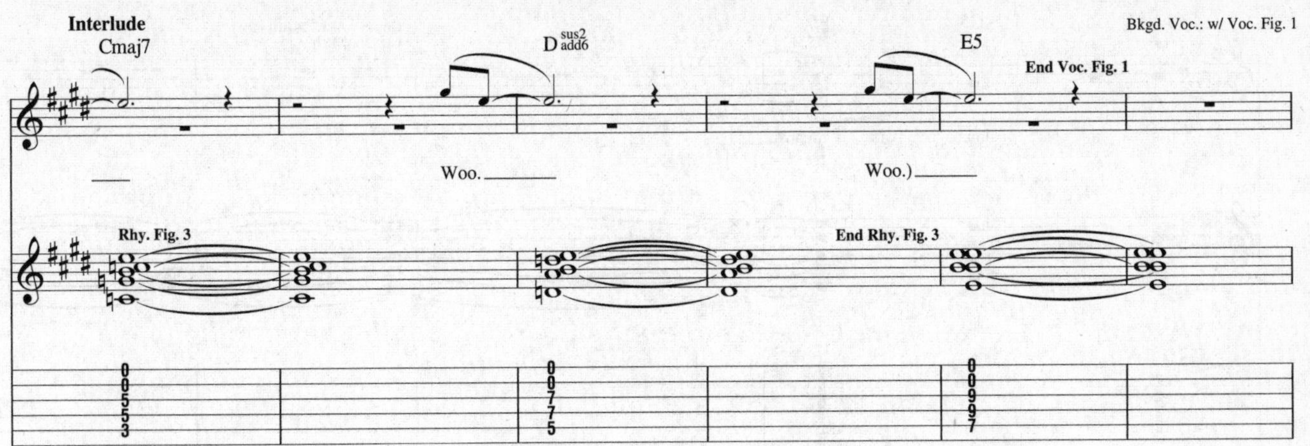

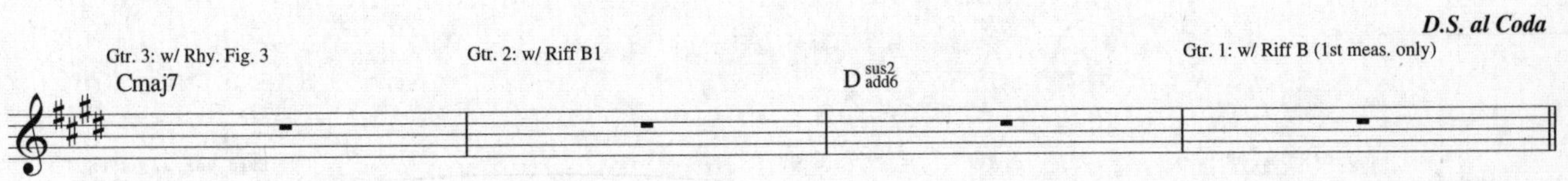

Coda

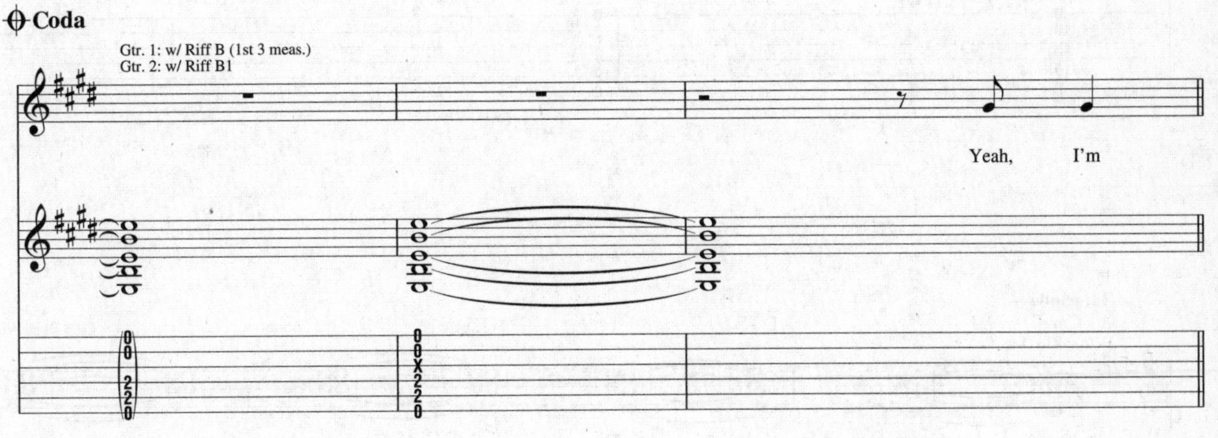

Chorus

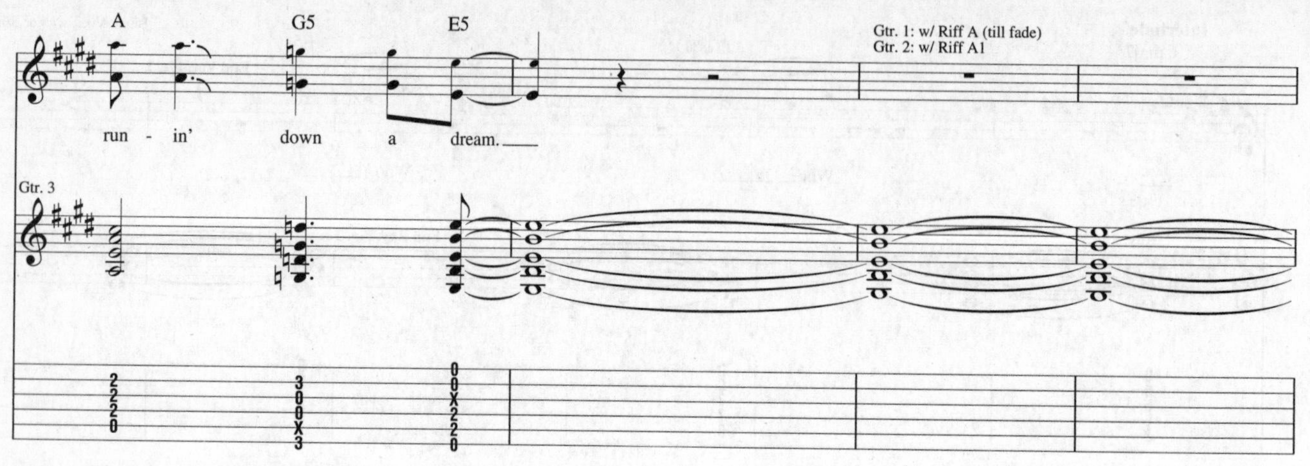

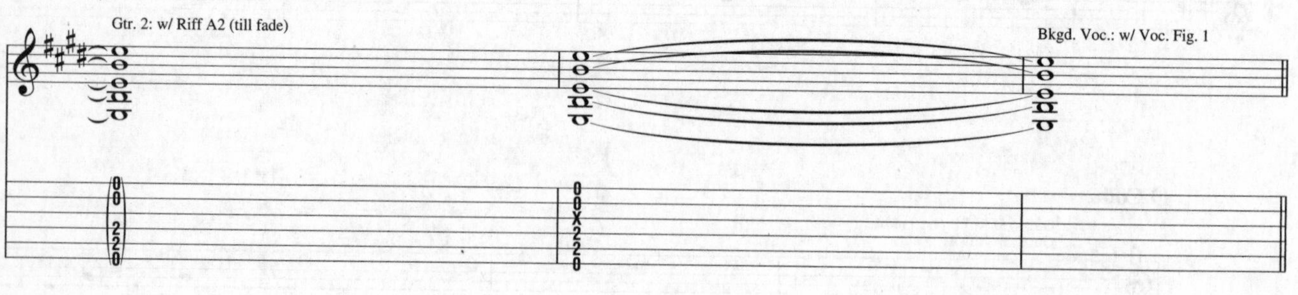

Interlude

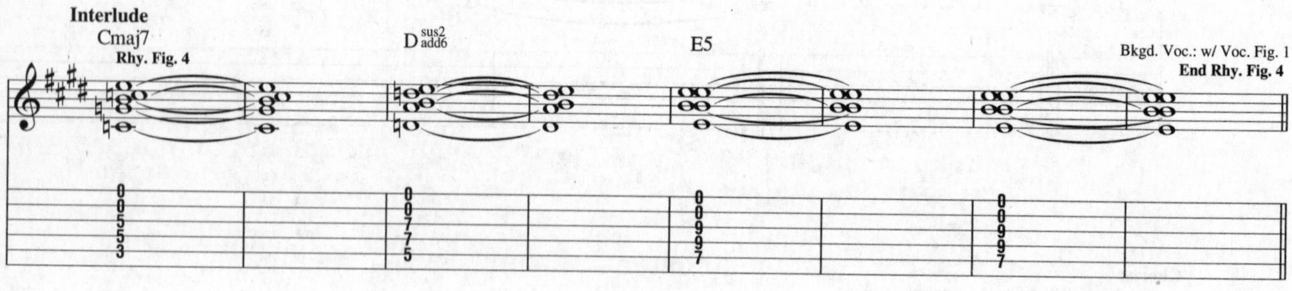

Outro - Guitar Solo

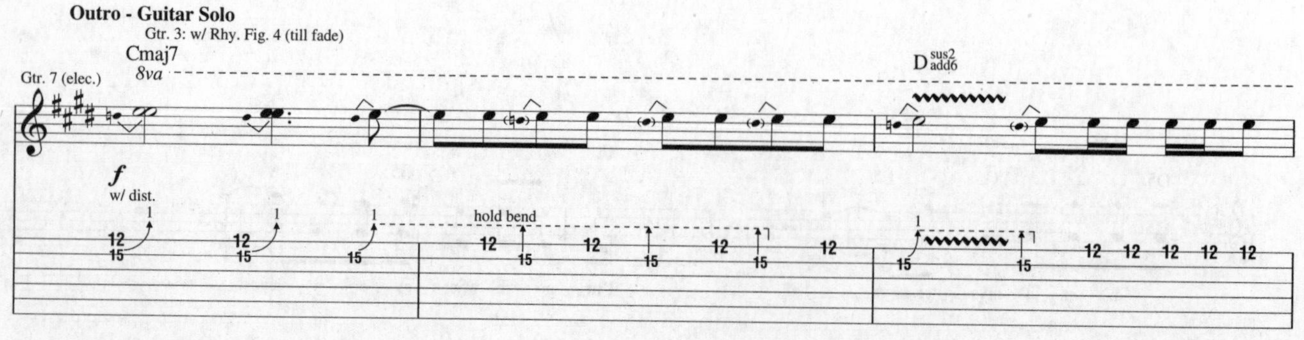

E5
8va
1
12
15
15
12 12 12 12 12
12
15
1
12
15
1
12
15
1
12
15
1
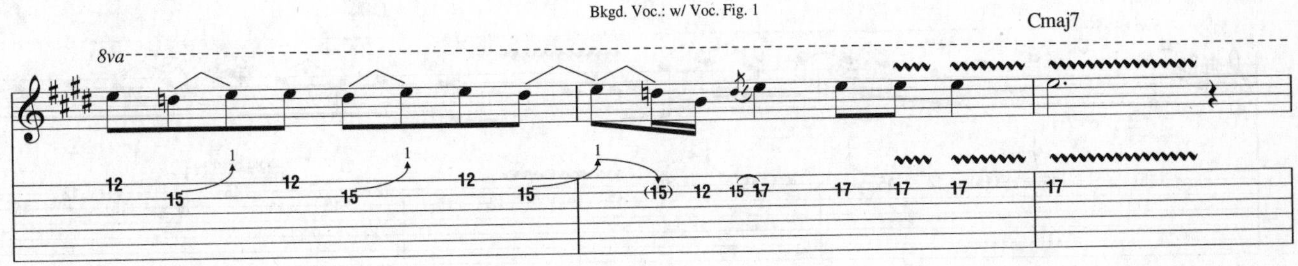
Bkgd. Voc.: w/ Voc. Fig. 1
Cmaj7
8va
12
15
1
12
15
1
12
15
1
(15) 12 15 17
17
17 17
17

D sus2 add6
8va
1
17
17
1
17
1
17
(17) 15 17
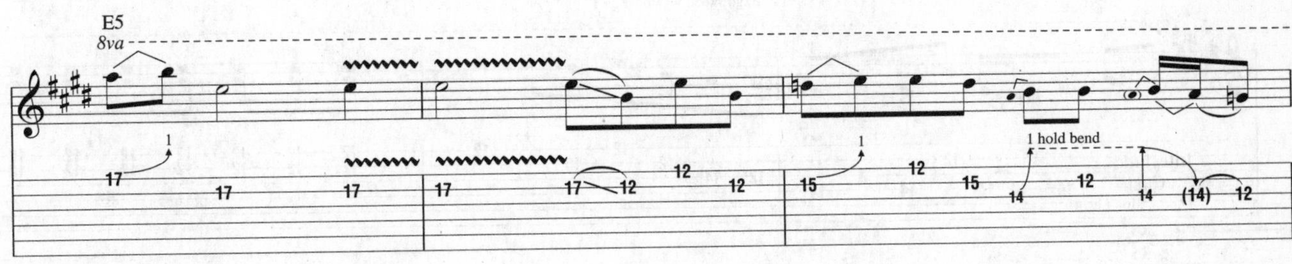
E5
8va
1
17
17
17
17
17 12
12
12
1
15
12
15
1 hold bend
14
12
14 (14) 12

Bkgd. Voc.: w/ Voc. Fig. 1
Cmaj7
8va
14 12 14
X
3
3
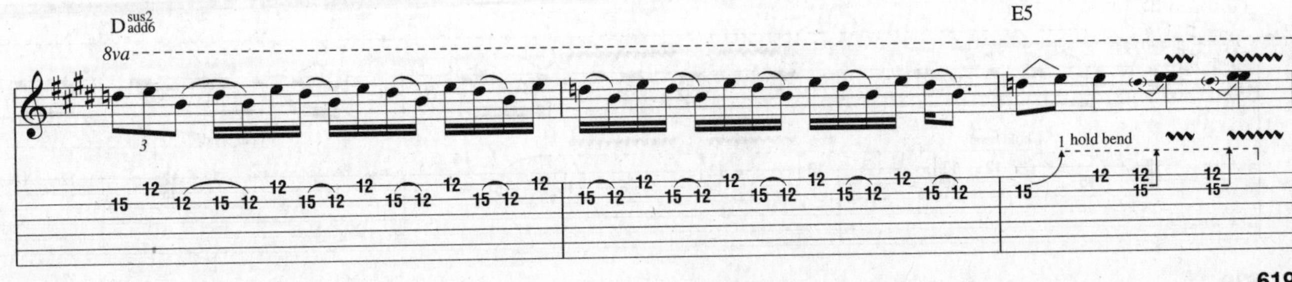
D sus2 add6
E5
8va
3
1 hold bend

8va
Bkgd. Voc.: w/ Voc. Fig. 1
Cmaj7
D sus2 add6
hold bend
E5
Bkgd. Voc.: w/ Voc. Fig. 1
Cmaj7
D sus2 add6
E5
hold bend
hold bend

Bkgd. Voc.: w/ Voc. Fig. 1
Cmaj7
8va
* grad. release
1/2
1/4
* over next 2 meas.
D sus2 add6
E5
Bkgd. Voc.: w/ Voc. Fig. 1
Cmaj7
Begin fade
D sus2 add6
E5
Fade out

Same Old Song & Dance

Words and Music by Steven Tyler and Joe Perry

Verse
loco
N.C.(E5)
1. Get your-self cool-er,
full
w/ wah wah
steady gliss.
mf
Rhy. Fig. 1A
End Riff A
Rhy. Fig. 1
End Rhy. Fig. 1
P.M.
Gtr. 1: w/ Rhy. Fig. 1, 6 times
Gtr. 3 tacet
lay your-self low. Co-in-ci-den-tal mur-der with noth-in' to show. When the judge-
Gtr. 2
-'s con-sti-pa-tion goes to his head, and his wife's ag-gra-va-tion, you

Chorus

G A C5 D5

soon end up dead. It's the same old sto - ry, same old song and dance,

Gtr. 2

End Rhy. Fig. 1A Rhy. Fig. 3A

Gtr. 1

Rhy. Fig. 2 End Rhy. Fig. 2 Rhy. Fig. 3

P.M.

N.C.(E5) G A C5

my friend. It's the same old sto - ry, same

End Rhy. Fig. 3A

1/4 1/4

End Rhy. Fig. 3

1/4 1/4

Gtr. 3: w/ Fill 1
D5
N.C.(E5)
old song and dance, my friend. 2. Sha -
1/4
Verse
Gtr. 1: w/ Rhy. Fig. 1, 3 times
Gtr. 2: w/ Rhy. Fig. 1A
N.C.(E5)
- dy look - in' los - er you played with my gun. No smooth face law - yer can
down and dir - ty from walk - in' the street with your old hur - dy gur - dy,
Gtr. 1: w/ Rhy. Fig. 1, 2 times
get you un - done.
no one to meet.
Say love ain't the same on the south side o' town. You could look
Gtr. 1
P.M.
Fill 1
Gtr. 3
w/ wah wah
steady gliss.

Gtr. 1: w/ Rhy. Fig. 2

but you ain't gon - na find it a - round. It's the same

Chorus

Gtrs. 1 & 2: w/ Rhy. Figs. 3 & 3A

G A C5

old sto - ry, same

Gtr. 3: w/ Fill 2, 1st time
Gtr. 3: w/ Fill 4, 2nd time

D5 N.C.(E5) G

old song and dance, my friend. It's the same

A C5 D5 F5 G5 A5

old sto - ry, same old sto - ry, same old song and dance.

Gtr. 2

Gtr. 1

(cont. in slash)

Fill 2
Gtr. 3

full full full full

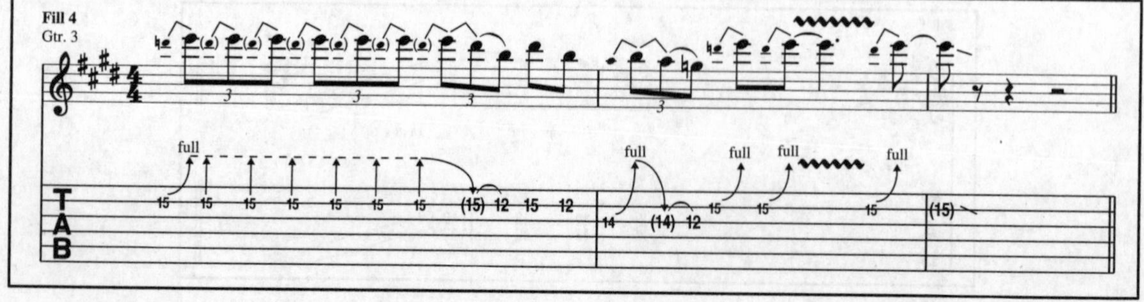

To Coda
Guitar Solo
Gtr. 3: w/ Fill 3, 1st time
Gtr. 3: w/ Fill 5, 2nd time
Gtrs. 1 & 2: w/ Riff A, 1 3/4 times, simile
C5
D5
N.C.(E5)
Gtr. 1
Gtr. 2
Gtr. 3
w/ slide
w/ delay
w/o slide
8va
full
Bridge
B5
A5
G5
A5
B5
A5
G5
A5
B5
1. Fate comes a - knock-in', doors start lock - in'. Your old
2. Saxophone solo
1/2
Gtrs. 1 & 2
Gtr. 1
Gtr. 2
divisi
Rhy. Fig. 4
End Rhy. Fig. 4
Rhy. Fig. 4A
End Rhy. Fig. 4A
1/4
*1st time only
**don't pick
†Gtr. 2 tabbed to right of slash.
Fill 3
Gtr. 3
Fill 5
Gtr. 3
1 1/2

Gtr. 3 tacet
Gtrs. 1 & 2: w/ Rhy. Figs. 4 & 4A, 2 times
A5 G5 A5 B5 A5 G5 A5 B5 A5 G5 A5 B5
time con - nec - tion, change your di - rec - tion. You ain't gon - na change it, can't
A5 G5 A5 B5 A5 G5 A5 B5 C#5 D5 D#5
re - ar - range it. Can't stand the pain when it's all the same to you
Gtr. 1
Gtrs. 1 & 2
Gtr. 2
divisi
1.
2.
D.S. al Coda
Gtrs. 1 & 2: w/ Riff A, simile
N.C.(E5)
N.C.(E5)
my friend.
3. When you're low
Gtr. 1
Gtr. 2
divisi
Coda
Gtr. 1: w/ Riff A, 2 times, simile
Gtr. 2: w/ Rhy. Fig. 1A, 1st 4 bars, 2 times
N.C.(E5)
Gtr. 3
full
1/4
hold bend
fdbk.

Santa Monica

Words by Art Alexakis
Music by Art Alexakis and Everclear

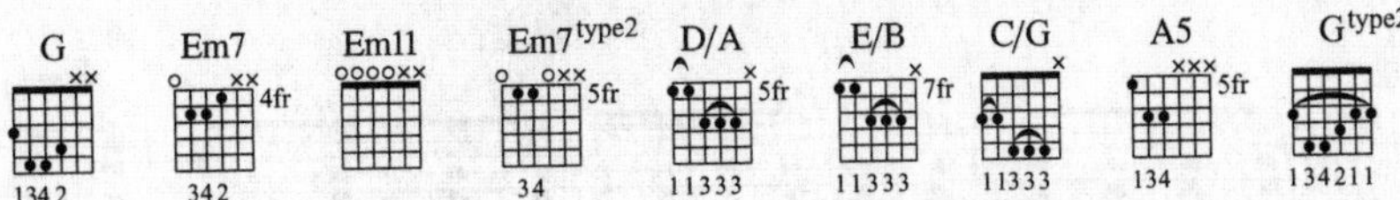

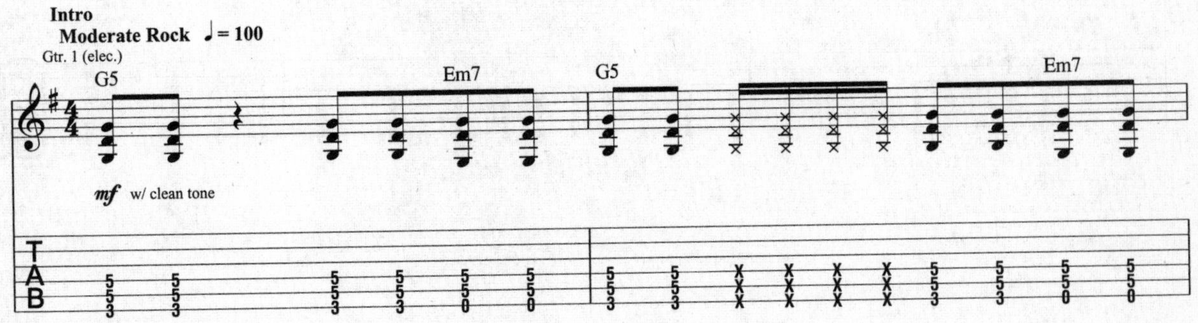

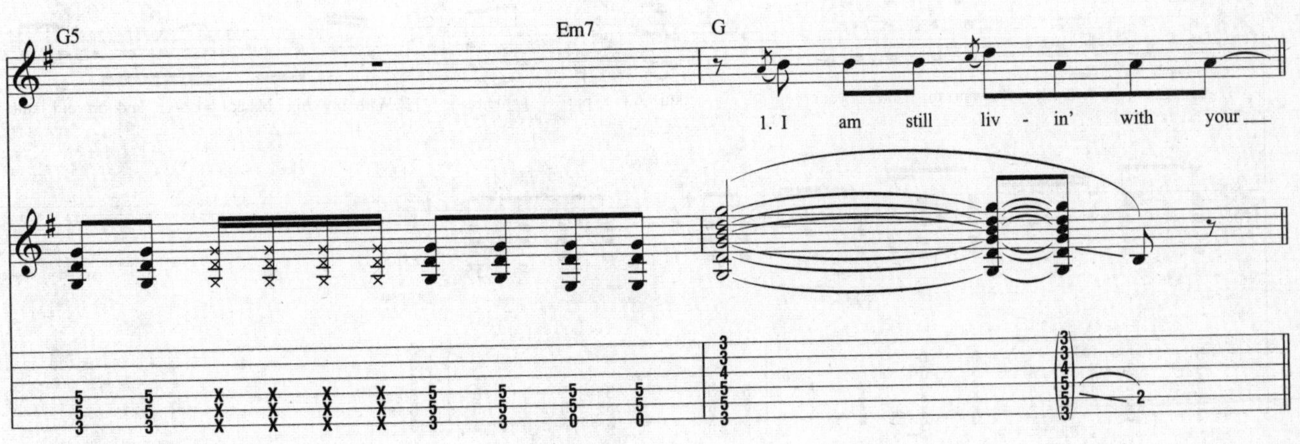

G5
Em7
G5
Em7
D/A
E/B
Coast.
I don't want to be your down - time,

Gtr. 2: w/ Rhy. Fill 1
C/G
A5
G5
Em7
G
I don't want to be your stu - pid game.
2. With my big black boots and an old suit -
(cont. in slashes)

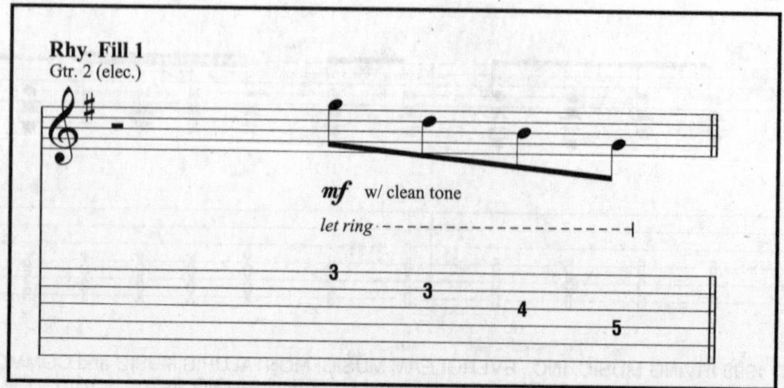
Rhy. Fill 1
Gtr. 2 (elec.)
mf w/ clean tone
let ring

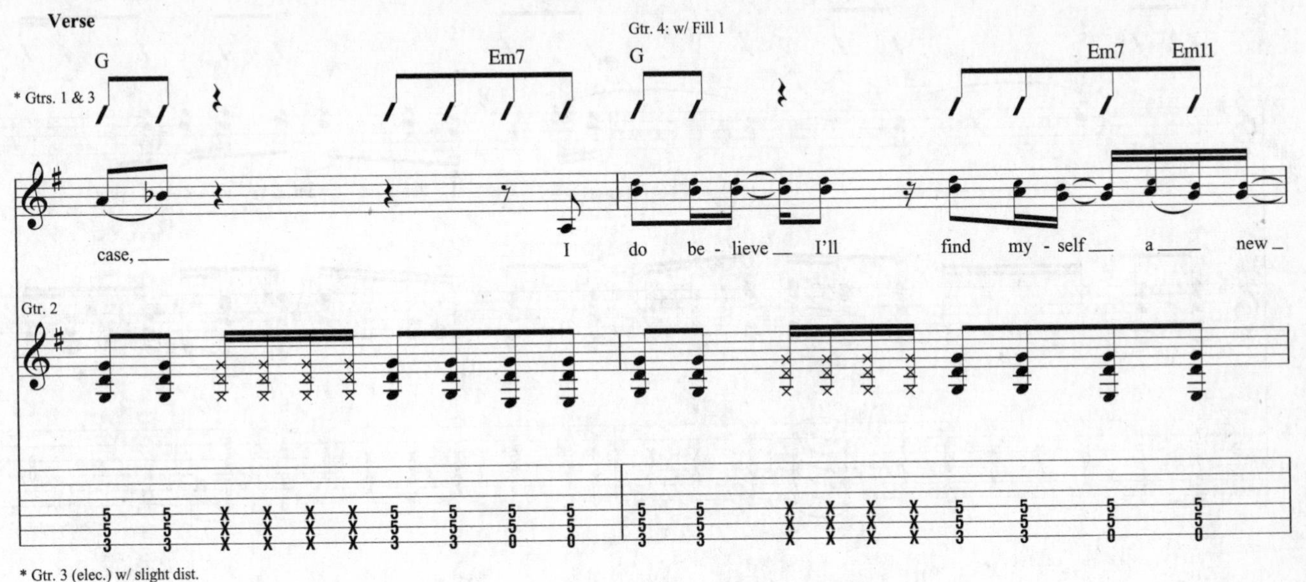
Verse
Gtr. 4: w/ Fill 1
G
Em7
G
Em7
Em11
* Gtrs. 1 & 3
case,
I
do
be - lieve
I'll
find
my - self
a
new
Gtr. 2
* Gtr. 3 (elec.) w/ slight dist.

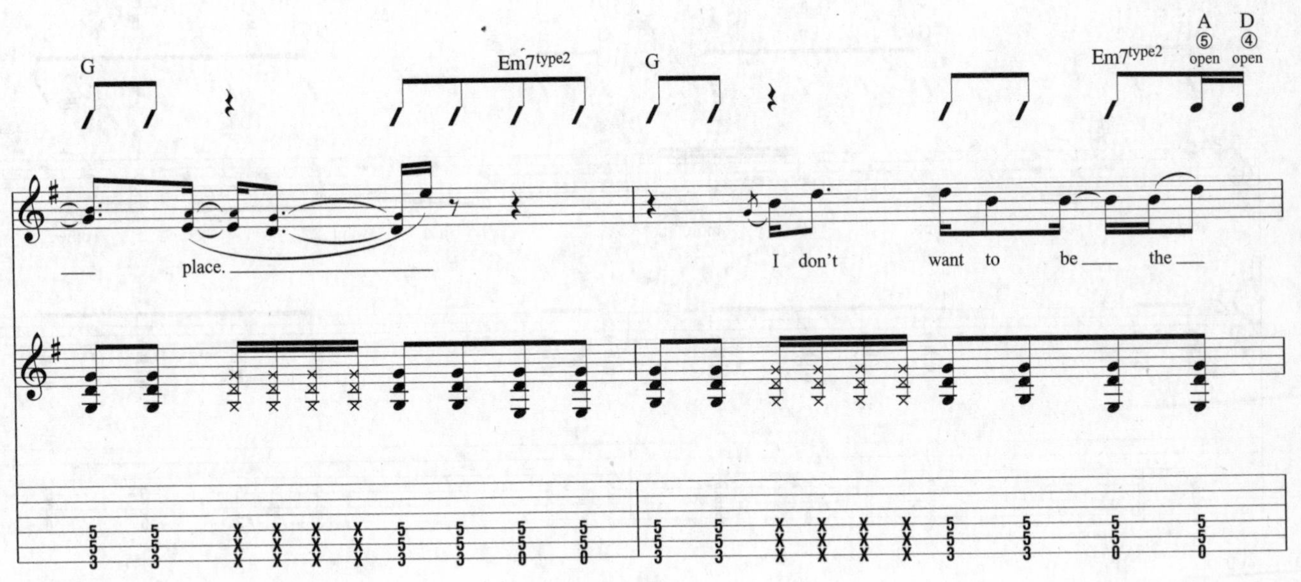
G
Em7type2
G
Em7type2
A
⑤
open
D
④
open
place.
I
don't
want
to
be
the

Fill 1
Gtr. 4 (elec.)
mf
w/ dist.

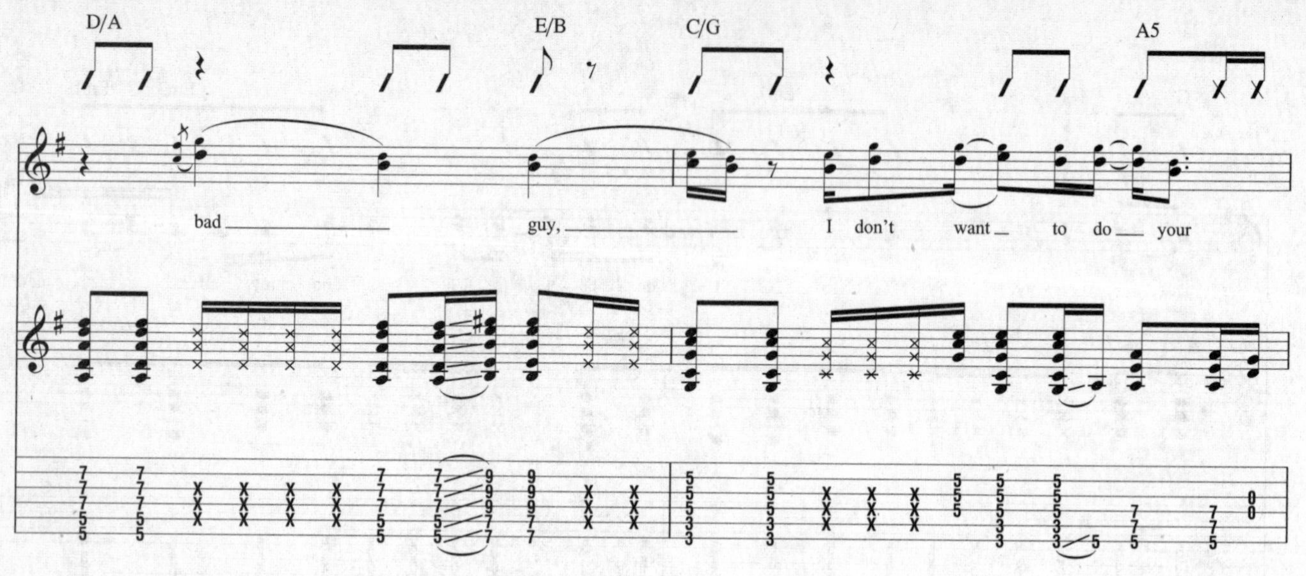
D/A
E/B
C/G
A5
bad guy, I don't want to do your

Gtr. 4: w/ Fill 2
G5
G
Em7
G
E
⑥
open
sleep - walk dance an - y - more. I just want to see some

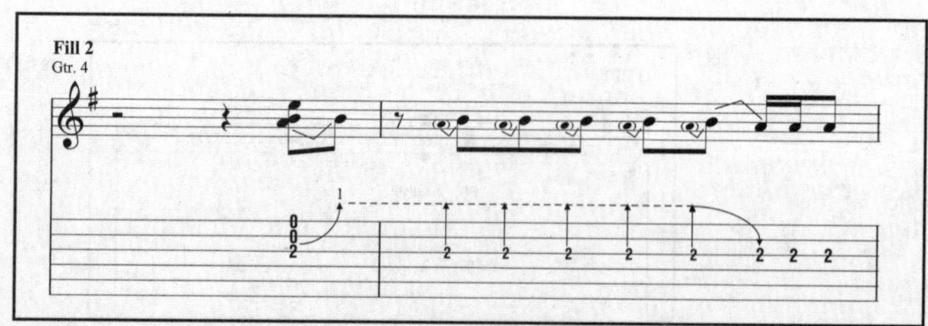
Fill 2
Gtr. 4

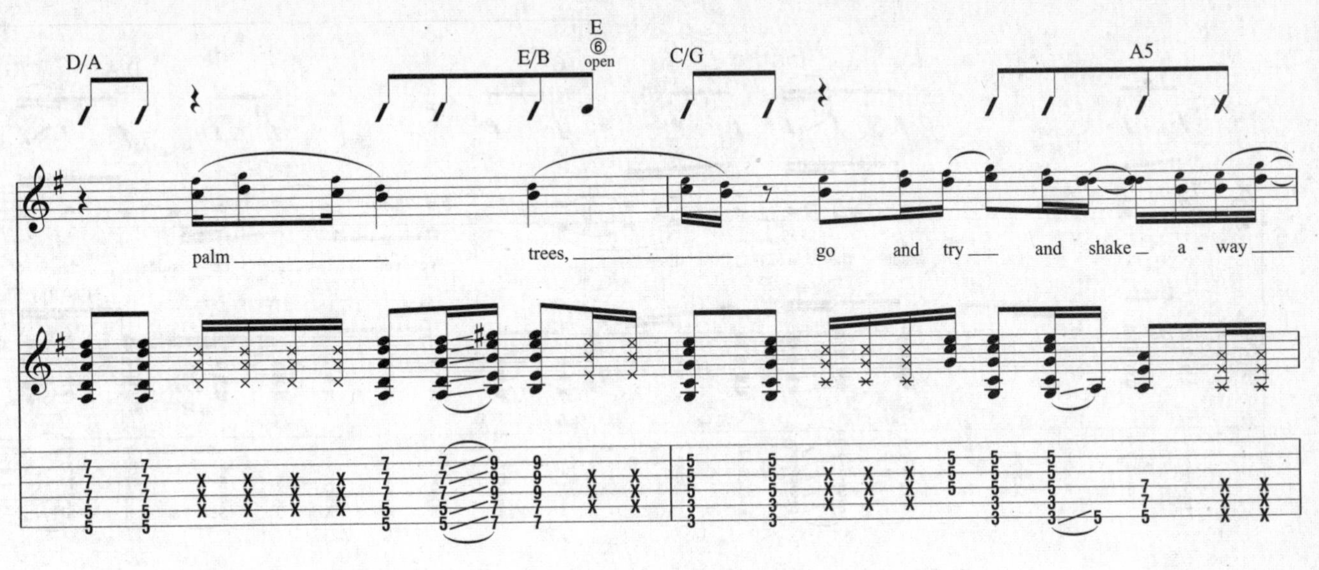
D/A
E/B
E
⑥ open
C/G
A5
palm
trees,
go and try and shake a - way

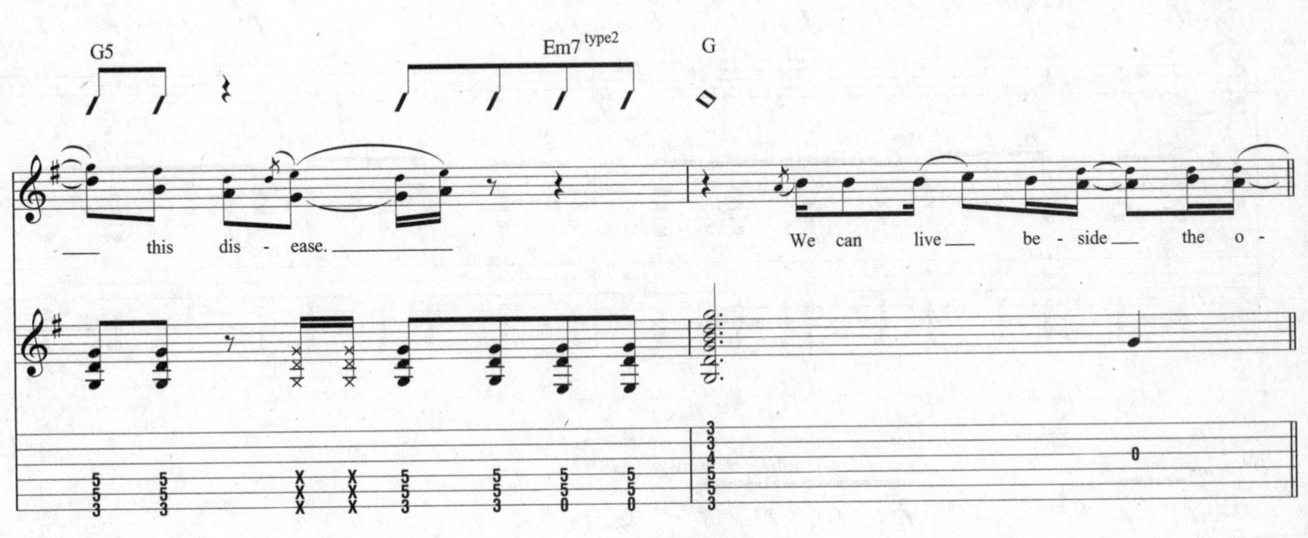
G5
Em7 type2
G
this dis - ease.
We can live be - side the o -

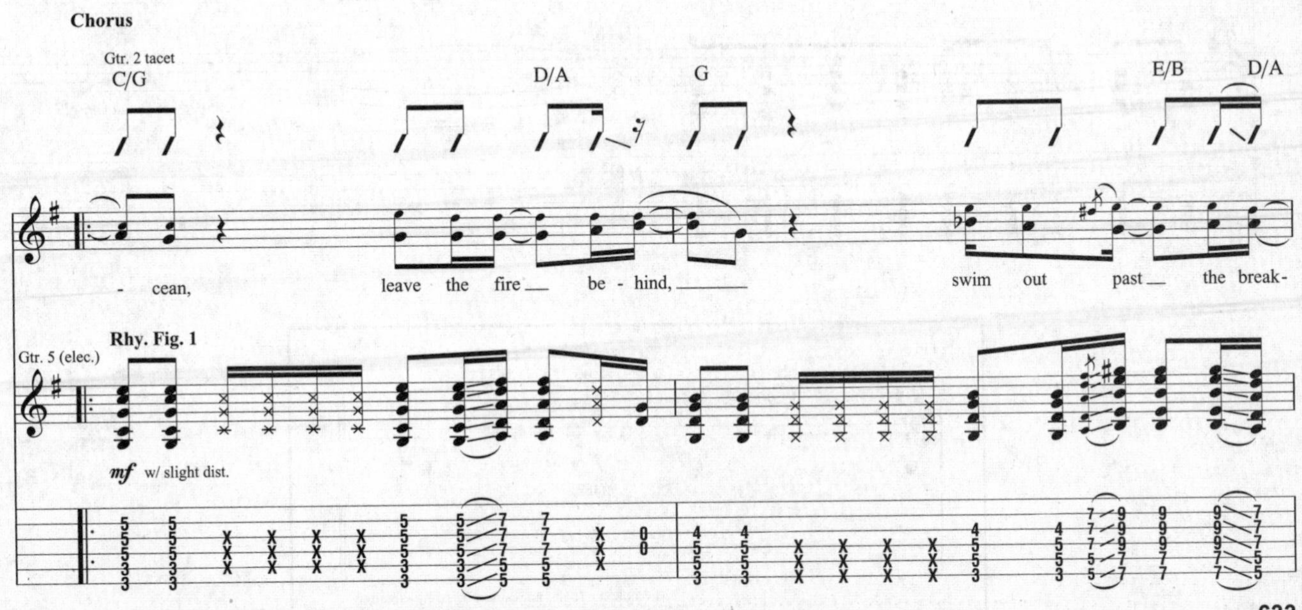
Chorus
Gr. 2 tacet
C/G
D/A
G
E/B
D/A
- cean, leave the fire be - hind, swim out past the break-
Rhy. Fig. 1
Gtr. 5 (elec.)
mf w/ slight dist.

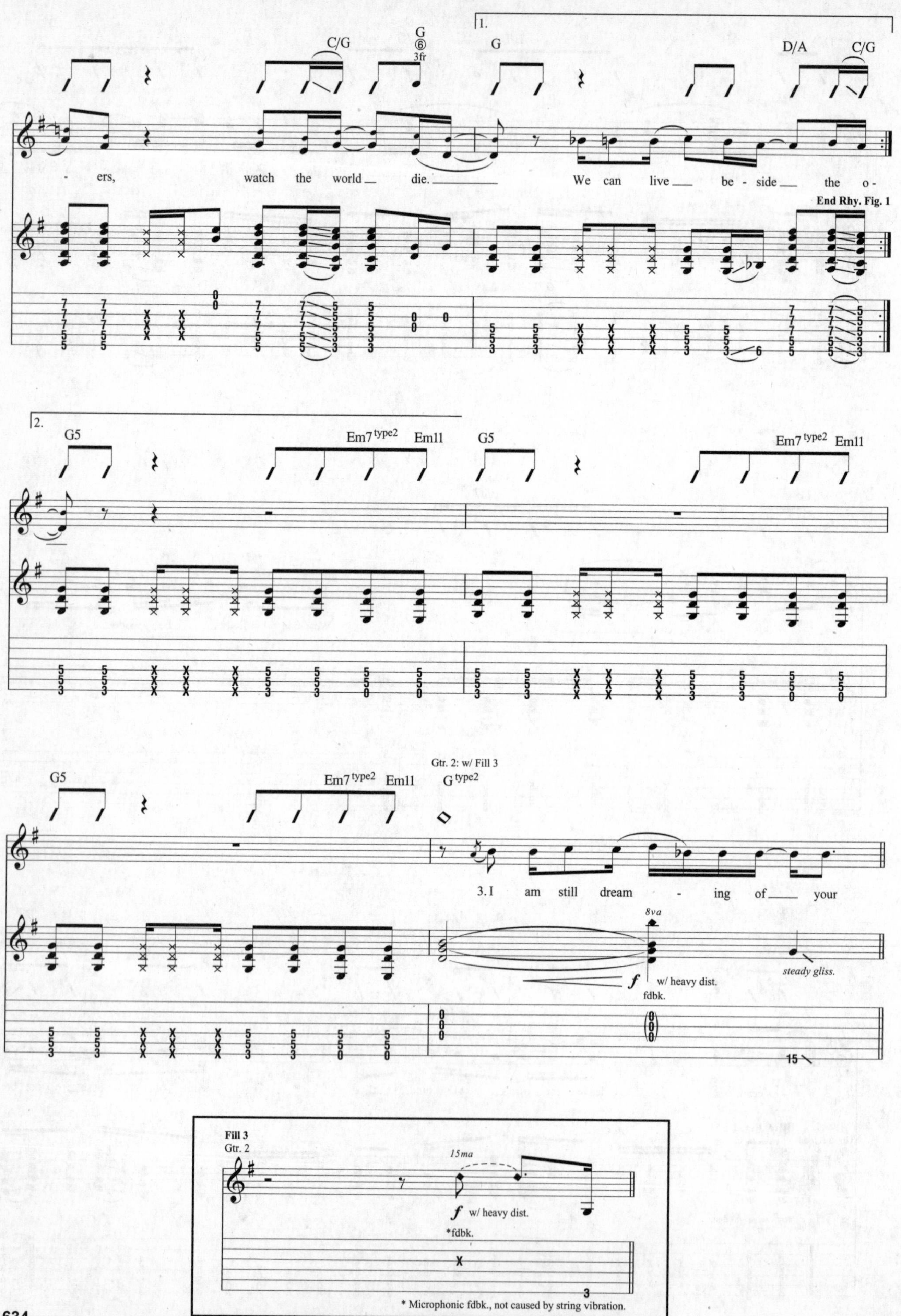
1.
C/G
G
⑥
3fr
G
D/A
C/G
- ers, watch the world die. We can live be - side the o -
End Rhy. Fig. 1
2.
G5
Em7 type2
Em11
G5
Em7 type2
Em11
G5
Em7 type2
Em11
Gtr. 2: w/ Fill 3
G type2
3. I am still dream - ing of your
8va
f w/ heavy dist.
fdbk.
steady gliss.
Fill 3
Gtr. 2
15ma
f w/ heavy dist.
*fdbk.
* Microphonic fdbk., not caused by string vibration.

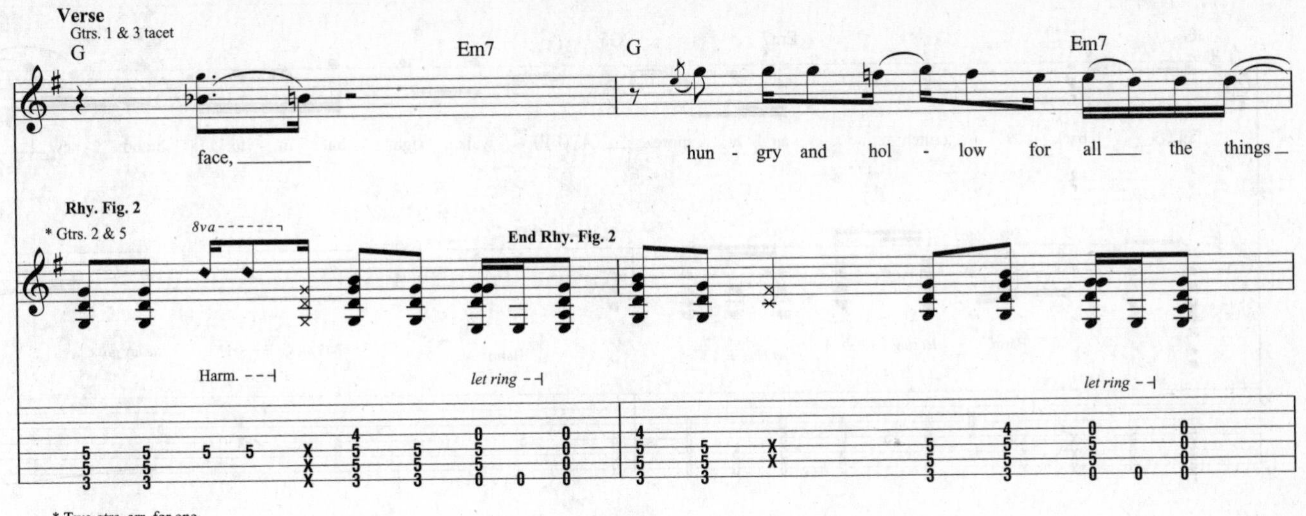

* Two gtrs. arr. for one.

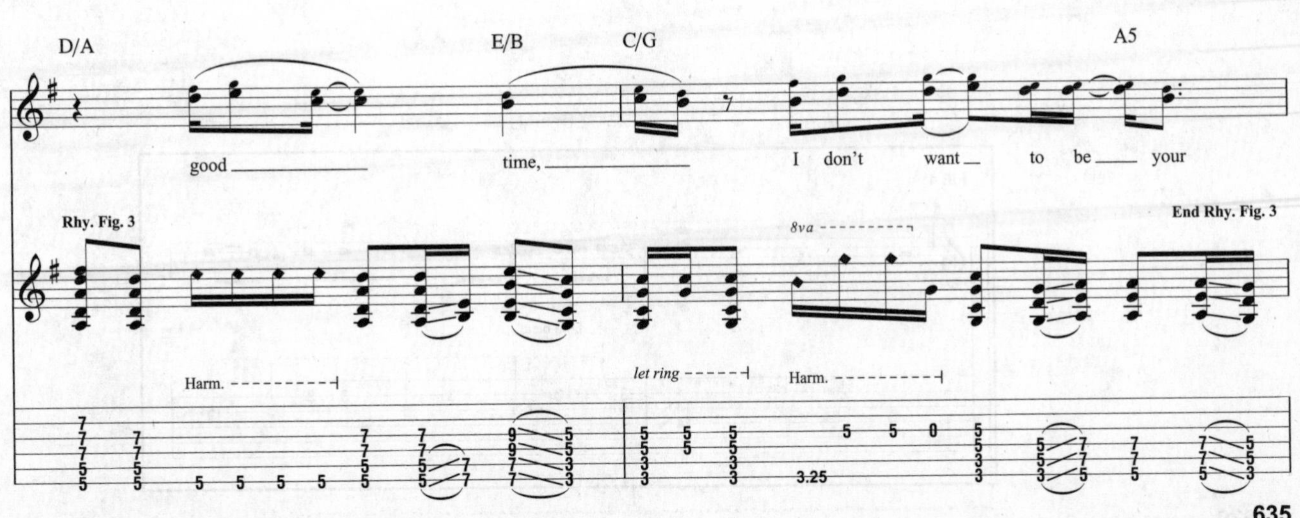

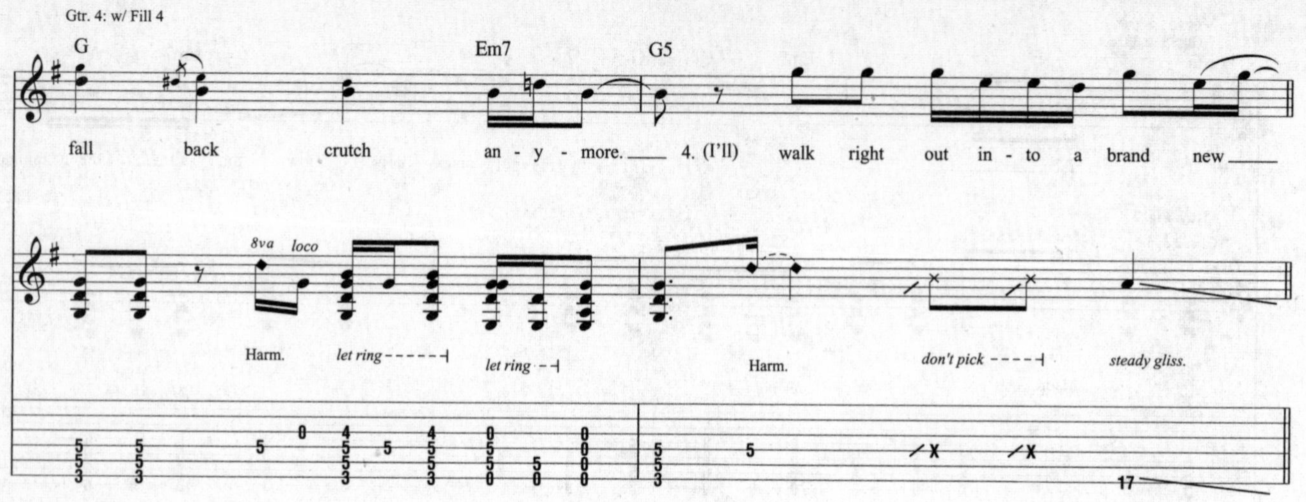

Gtr. 4: w/ Fill 4
G
Em7
G5
fall back crutch an - y - more. 4. (I'll) walk right out in - to a brand new
8va loco
Harm.
let ring
let ring
Harm.
don't pick
steady gliss.

Verse

Gtrs. 2 & 5: w/ Rhy. Fig. 2 (4 times)
G
Em7
G
Em7
Gtr. 4: w/ Fill 4
G
Em7
day, in - sane and ris - ing in my own weird way.
Gtr. 4
let ring

Fill 4
Gtr. 4
hold bend

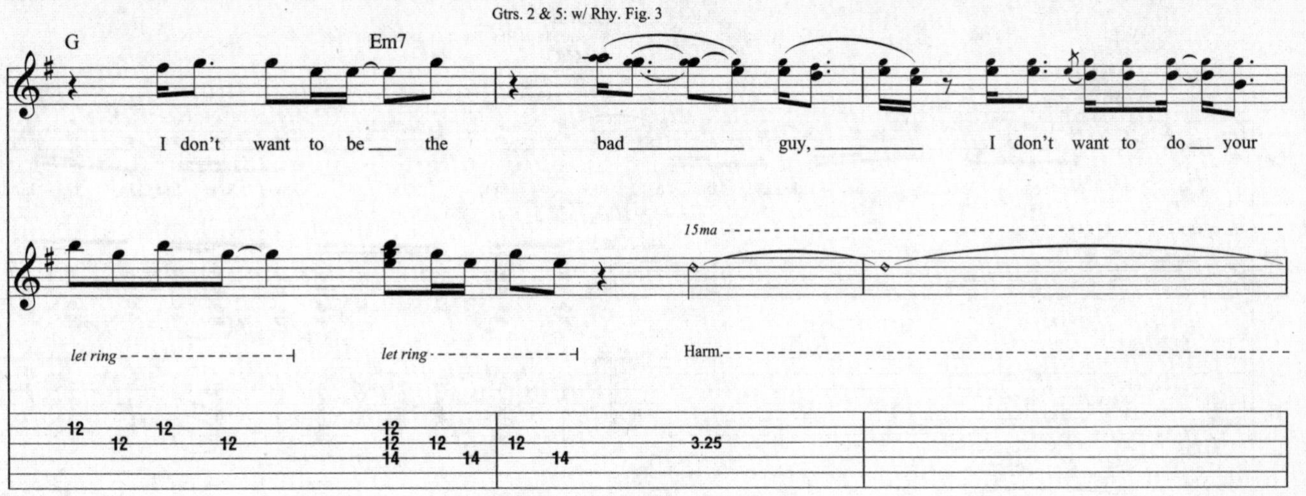
Gtrs. 2 & 5: w/ Rhy. Fig. 3
G
Em7
I don't want to be the bad guy, I don't want to do your
15ma
let ring
let ring
Harm.
12 12 12 12
12 12 14 12 14 12 14
3.25

Gtrs. 2 & 5: w/ Rhy. Fig. 2 (2 times)
Gtrs. 2 & 5: w/ Rhy. Fig. 3
sleep - walk dance an - y - more. I just want to feel some sun - shine,
Harm.
(3.25)

Gtrs. 2 & 5: w/ Rhy. Fig. 2
I just want to find some place to be a - lone.
8va
15 17 15 17 15 17 17

Chorus
Gtrs. 2 & 5: w/ Rhy. Fig. 2
Gtr. 3: w/ Fill 5
Gtr. 3: w/ Rhy. Fig. 1 (1 3/4 times)
C/G
D/A
Voc. Fig. 1
We can live beside the ocean,
leave the fire behind,
Rhy. Fig. 4
Gtrs. 2 & 5
Gtr. 4
8va
loco
fdbk.

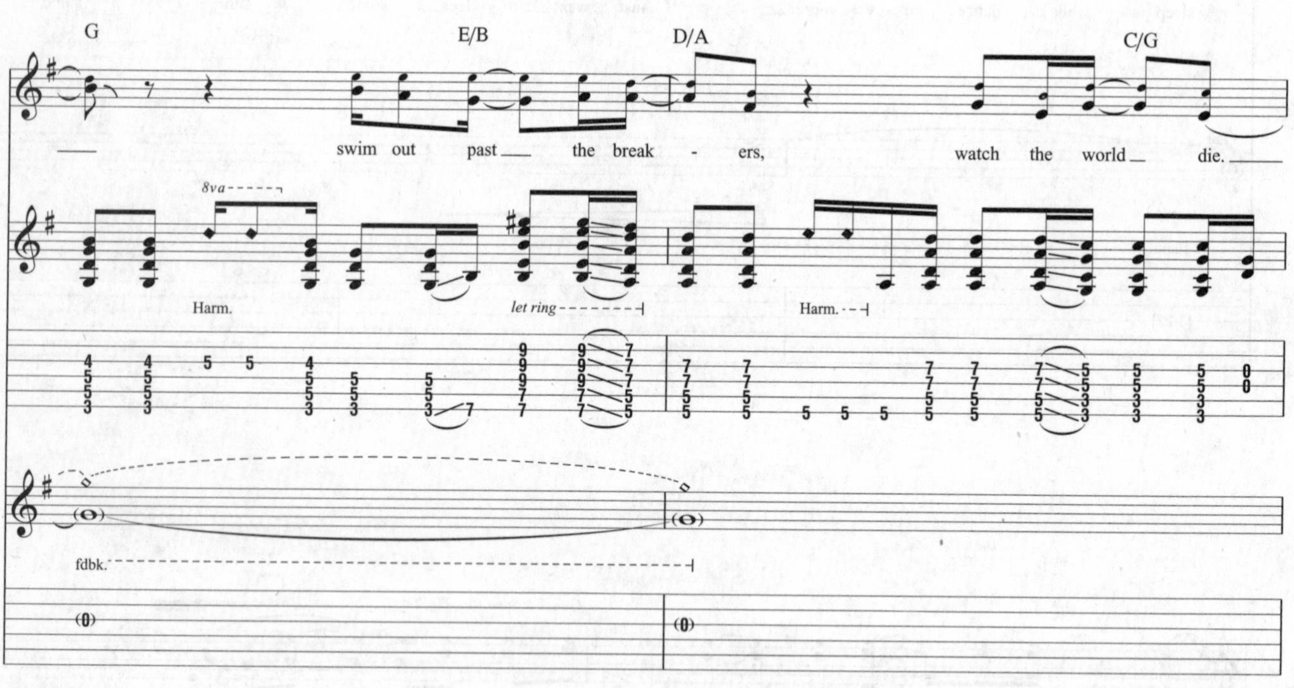
G
E/B
D/A
C/G
swim out past the breakers,
watch the world die.
8va
Harm.
let ring
Harm.
fdbk.

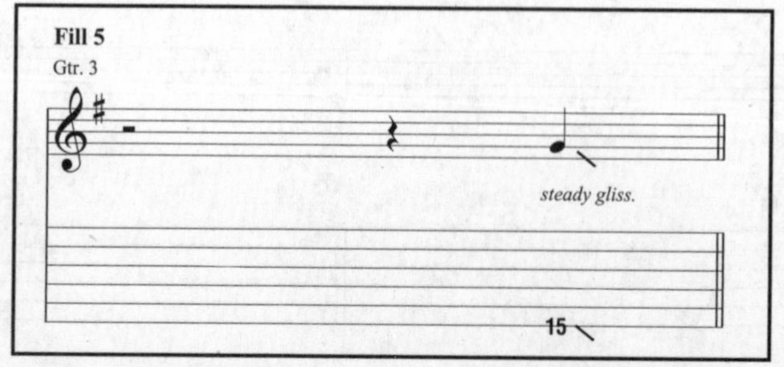
Fill 5
Gtr. 3
steady gliss.

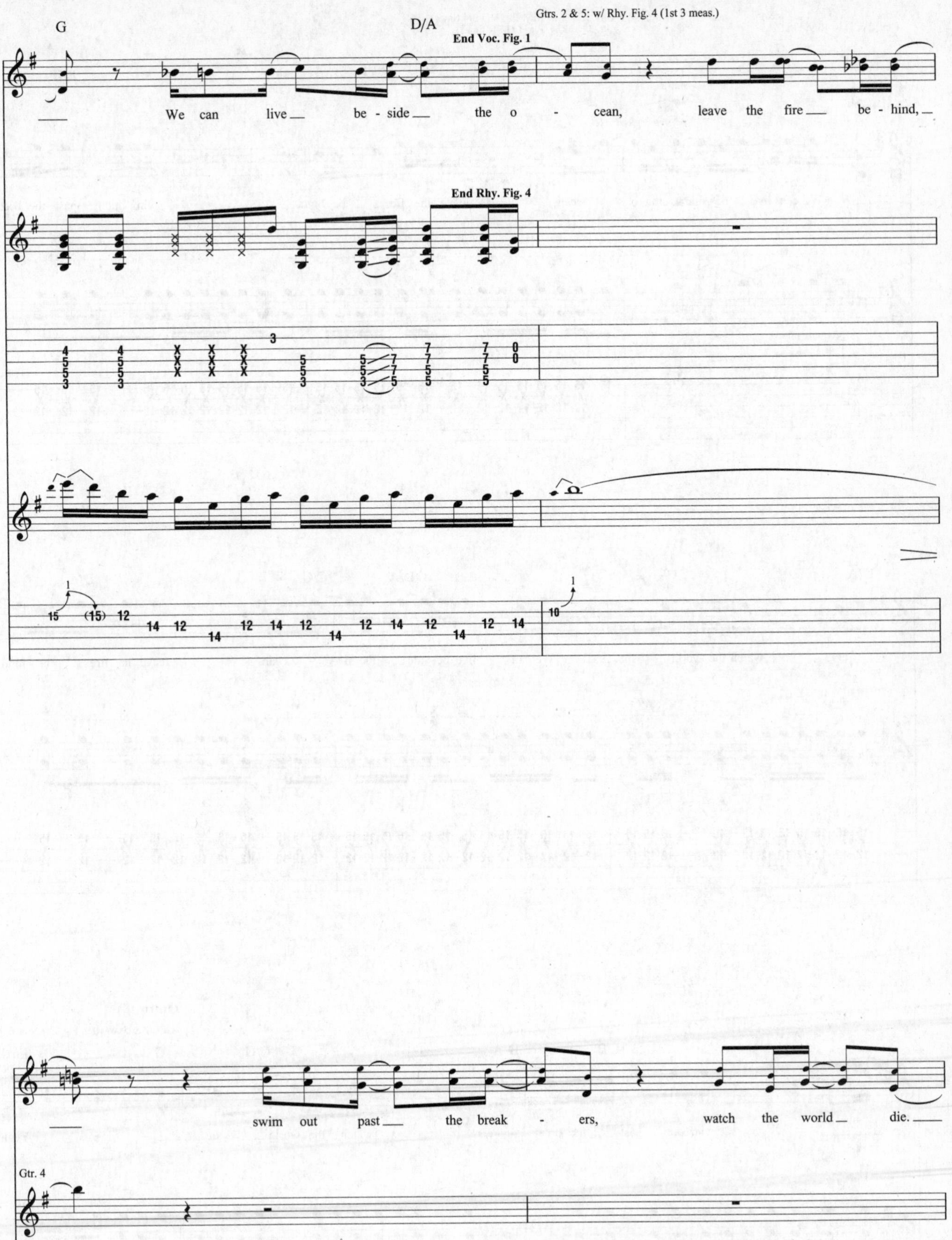

G D/A

Gtrs. 2 & 5: w/ Rhy. Fig. 4 (1st 3 meas.)

End Voc. Fig. 1

We can live__ be - side__ the o - cean, leave the fire__ be - hind,__

End Rhy. Fig. 4

Voc.: w/ Voc. Fig. 1 (2 times)
Gtrs. 2 & 5: w/ Rhy. Fig. 2
Gtrs. 2 & 5: w/ Rhy. Fig. 4 (1 3/4 times)
Gtr. 3: w/ Rhy. Fig. 1 (1 3/4 times)
G
C/G
D/G
G
E/B
15fr
steady gliss.
Gtr. 3
We can live be-side the o - cean, leave the fire be-hind, swim out past the break -
8va
grad. release

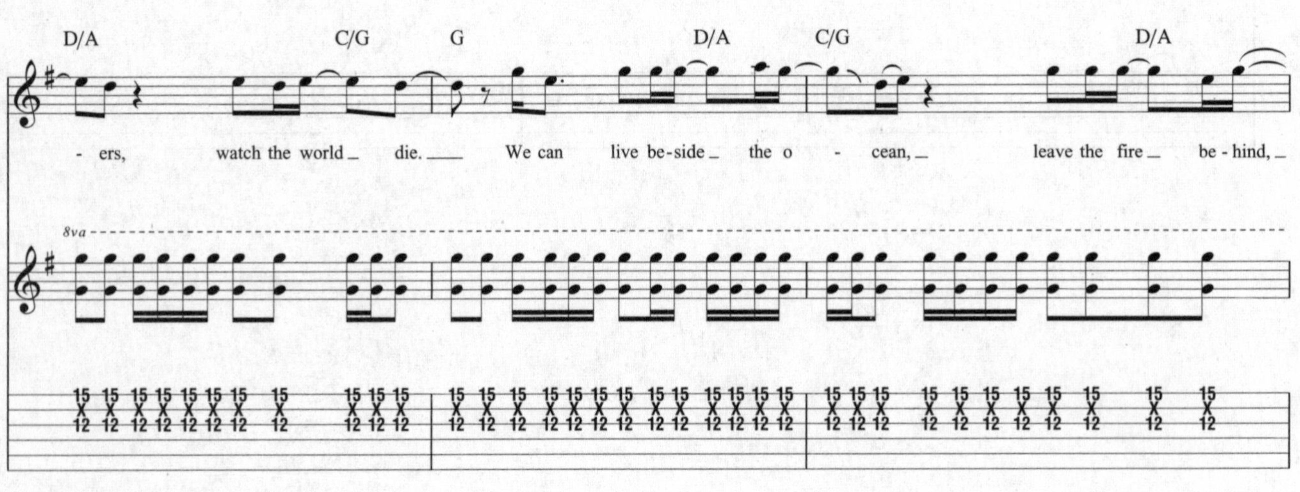
D/A
C/G
G
D/A
C/G
D/A
- ers, watch the world die. We can live be-side the o - cean, leave the fire be-hind,
8va

Outro
Gtrs. 2 & 5: w/ Rhy. Fig. 2 (8 times)
G
E/B
D/A
C/G
G
Em7
swim out past the break - ers, watch the world die. Yeah!
8va
loco
steady gliss.

G
Em7
G
Em7
G
Em7
Yeah, watch the world die.
Yeah.
Yeah, watch the world die.
steady gliss.
12 (12) 3

G
Em7
G
Em7
Whoa.
Yeah, watch the world die.
don't pick
12 12 12 12 12 12 12 (12) (12) 2 2 X

G
Em7
G
rit.
Em7
Gtr. 4 tacet
G5
Yeah, watch the world die.
Gtrs. 2 & 5
don't pick
steady gliss.
rit.
15 12 12 12 (12) (12) (12) X X 5 5 3 (5) (5) (3)

Scar Tissue

Words and Music by Anthony Kiedis, Flea, John Frusciante and Chad Smith

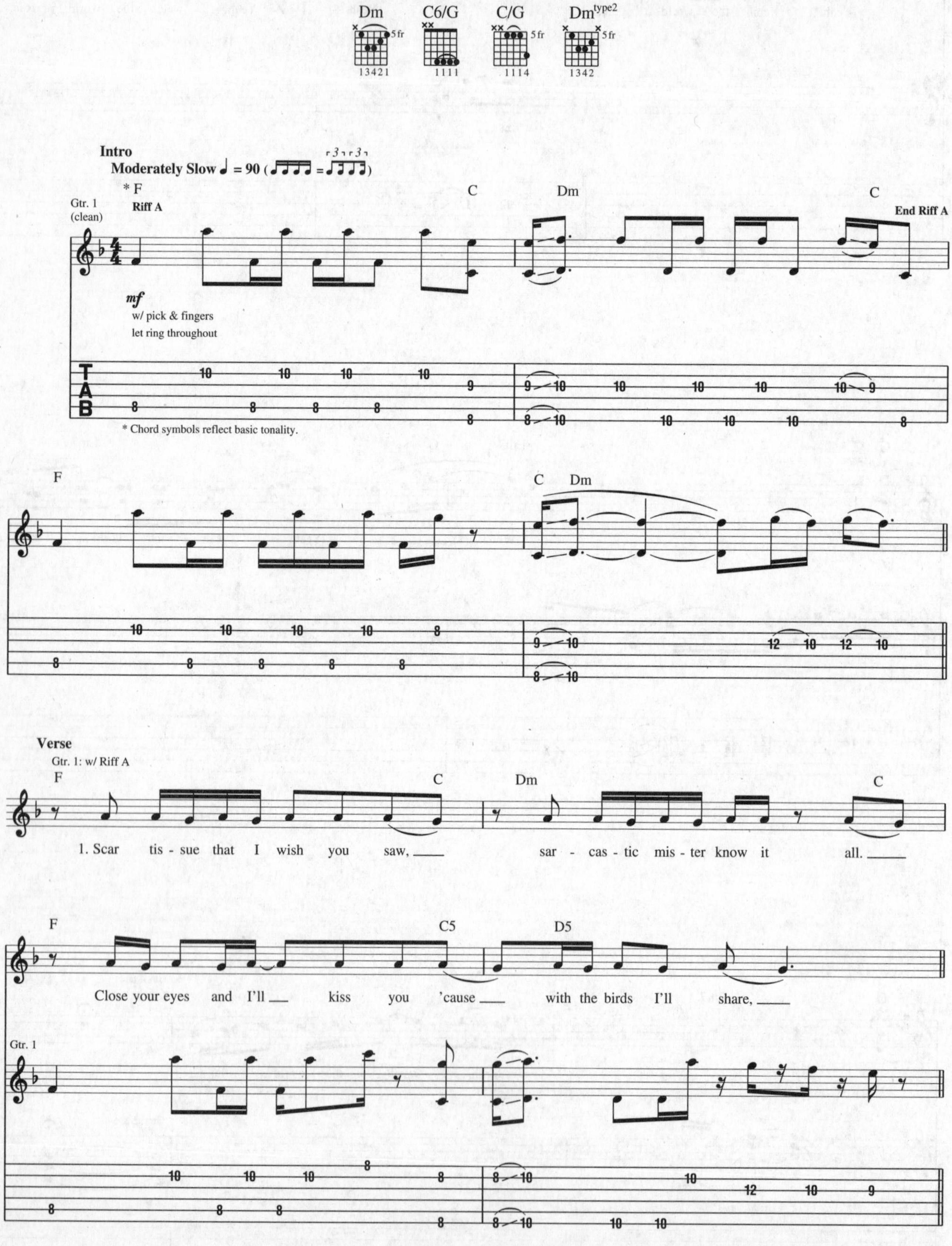

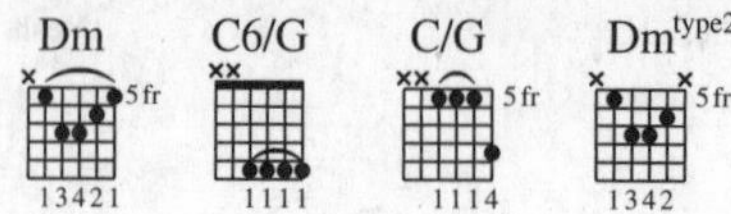

Intro

Moderately Slow ♩ = 90

*F C Dm C

Gtr. 1 (clean)

Riff A

End Riff A

mf

w/ pick & fingers

let ring throughout

* Chord symbols reflect basic tonality.

F C Dm

Verse

Gtr. 1: w/ Riff A

F C Dm C

1. Scar tis - sue that I wish you saw, sar - cas - tic mis - ter know it all.

F C5 D5

Close your eyes and I'll kiss you 'cause with the birds I'll share,

Gtr. 1

Chorus
F C Dm
with the birds I'll share this lone - ly view,
Rhy. Fig. 1
End Rhy. Fig. 1
F C Dm C
with the birds I'll share this lone - ly view.
Rhy. Fig. 2
End Rhy. Fig. 2
Verse
Gtr. 1: w/ Riff A
F C Dm C
2. Push me up a - gainst the wall, young Ken - tuck - y girl in a push up bra.
F C5 D5 C5
Fall - in' all o - ver my - self to lick your heart and taste your health 'cause
Gtr. 1
Chorus
Gtr. 1: w/ Rhy. Fig. 1, 2 times, simile
F C Dm C
with the birds I'll share this lone - ly view,
(Share this lone - ly...
F C Dm C
with the birds I'll share this lone - ly view,
Share this lone - ly...

F
Csus4
C
Dm
Interlude
Dm
with the birds I'll share this lone - ly view.
Share this lone - ly...)
Gtr. 2 (clean)
mf
w/ slide
Rhy. Fig. 3
End Rhy. Fig. 3
Gtr. 1
C
Dm
Em
Verse
F
C
Gtr. 2 tacet
Dm
C
3. Blood loss in a bath - room stall,
south-ern girl with a scar - let drawl.

F C5 D5
Wave good - bye to ma and pa 'cause with the birds I'll share,
Gr. 1
Chorus
Gtr. 1: w/ Rhy. Fig. 1
F C Dm C
with the birds I'll share this lone - ly view,
(Share this lone - ly...
Gtr. 1: w/ Rhy. Fig. 2, simile
F C
with the birds I'll share this lone -
Share this lone -
Dm C
- ly view.
- ly...)
Verse
Gtr. 1: w/ Riff A
F C Dm C
4. Soft spo-ken with a bro - ken jaw, step out - side, but not to brawl.
F C5 D5
Au-tumn's sweet, we call it fall, I'll make it to the moon if I have to crawl.
Gtr. 1
Chorus
Gtr. 1: w/ Rhy. Fig. 1, 2 times, simile
F C Dm C
With the birds I'll share this lone - ly view,
(I will share this lone - ly...
F C
with the birds I'll share this lone -
I will share this lone -
Dm C
- ly view,
- ly...
Gtr. 1: w/ Rhy. Fig. 3
F Csus4 C Dm
with the birds I'll share this lone - ly view.
I will share this lone - ly...)

Guitar Solo

Verse

Chorus

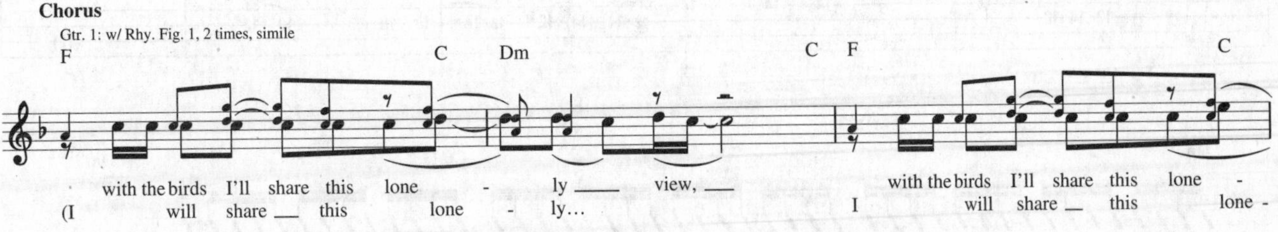

Outro-Guitar Solo

Self Esteem

Words and Music by Dexter Holland

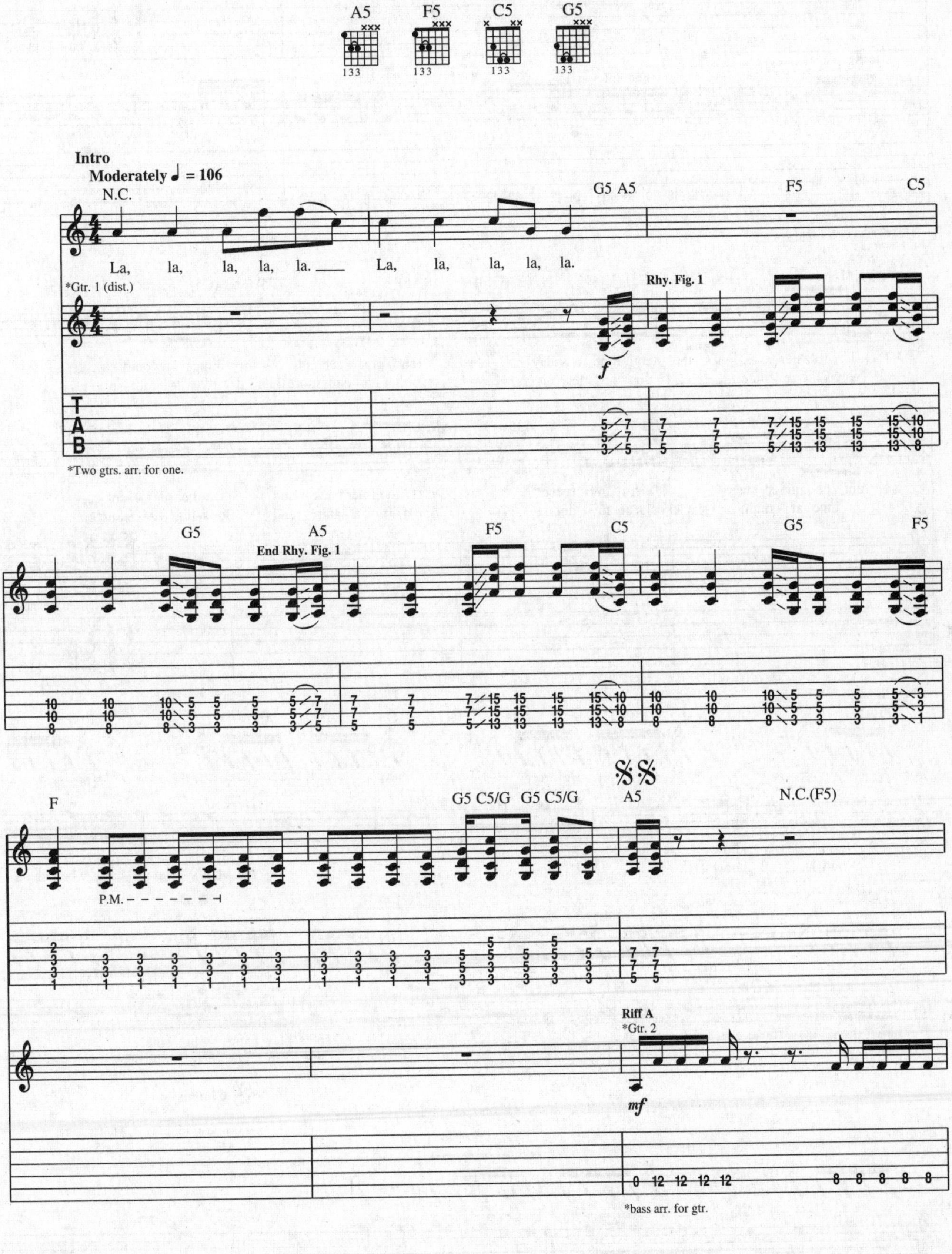

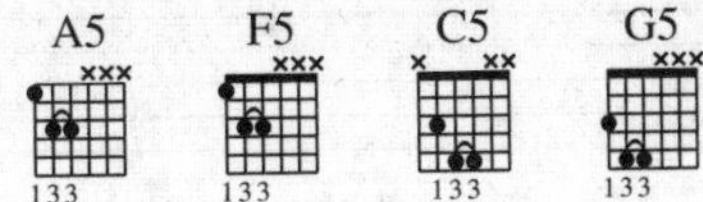

Intro

Moderately ♩ = 106

N.C. G5 A5 F5 C5

La, la, la, la, la. La, la, la, la, la.

*Gtr. 1 (dist.)

Rhy. Fig. 1

f

*Two gtrs. arr. for one.

G5 A5 F5 C5 G5 F5

End Rhy. Fig. 1

F G5 C5/G G5 C5/G

P.M.

𝄋𝄋 A5 N.C.(F5)

Riff A

*Gtr. 2

mf

*bass arr. for gtr.

(C5) (G5) (A5) (F5) (C5) G5
End Riff A
Verse
Gtr. 1 tacet
Gtr. 2: w/ Riff A, 8 times
N.C.(A5) (F5) (C5) (G5) (A5) (F5) (C5) (G5)
1. I wrote her off for the tenth time to - day (and) prac-ticed all the things I would say.
3. Now I'll re - late this lit - tle bit that hap-pens more than I'd like to ad - mit.
(A5) (F5) (C5) (G5) (A5) (F5) (C5) G5
But she came o - ver, I lost my nerve. I took her back and made her des - sert.
Late at night she knocks on my door. She's drunk a - gain and look-ing to score.
Gtr. 1
(cont. in slash)
Pre-Chorus
G5 A5 F5 C5 G5 A5 F5
Gtr. 1
P.M.
(Now) I know I'm be in' used. That's o - kay man 'cause I
(Now) I know I should say no, but that's kind of hard when she's
C5 G5 A5 F5 C5 G5
Rhy. Fig. 2
like the a - buse. I know she's play - ing with me.
read - y to go. I may be dumb but I'm not a dweeb.
Chorus
Gtr. 2 tacet
Gtr. 1: w/ Rhy. Fig. 1, 4 times
A5 F5 C5 G5 A5 F5 C5
End Rhy. Fig. 2
* P.M.
That's o - kay 'cause I've got no self es - teem.
I'm just a suck - er with no self es - teem.
Oh, hey, yeah, ay, yeah.
* gradually less P.M.

G5 A5 F5 C5 G5 A5 F5 C5 G5 A5
Yeah. Oh, yeah, yeah. Oh, yeah. Yeah.
To Coda
Verse
Gtr. 1 tacet
Gtr. 2: w/ Riff A, 4 times
F5 C5 G5 A5 N.C.(A5) (F5) (C5) (G5) (A5) (F5)
Oh, yeah, yeah. 2. We make plans to go out at night. I wait till two then I
Gtr. 1: w/ Rhy. Fig. 2
D.S. al Coda
G5 A5 F5 C5 G5 A5 F5 C5 G5
Gtr. 1
P.M.
turn out the light. This re-jec-tion's got me so low. (If) she keeps it up, I just might tell her so. Oh,
Coda
Bridge
D5 B♭5 F5 C5 D5 B♭5
When she's say - ing ah, that she wants on - ly me. Then I won - der why she
When she's say - ing oh, that I'm like a dis - ease. Then I won - der how much
Well I guess I should stick up for my - self, but I real - ly think it's
Gtr. 1
F5 C5 D5 B♭5 C5 G5 F5
play 3 times
sleeps with my friends. The more you suf - fer, the more it shows you real - ly
more I can spend.
bet - ter this way.
1. D.S.S. al Coda 2.
G5 C5/G G5 C5/G F5 G5 C5/G G5 C5/G A5
care. Right? Yeah. Right? Yeah.
P.M.

Semi-Charmed Life

Words and Music by Stephan Jenkins

Verse
Gtrs. 1 & 2 tacet
* Gtr. 4: w/ Rhy. Fig. 1, 4 times
G D G5/D Cadd9
hold-ing. I'm smil-ing, she's liv-ing, she's gold-en, she lives for me. Says she lives for me. O-
* Elec. w/ clean tone playing mf.
G D G5/D Cadd9
va-tion, her own mo-ti-va-tion. She comes 'round and she goes down on me.
G D G5/D Cadd9
And I make her smile like a drug for you. Do ev-er what you want to do. Com-ing o-ver
G D G5/D Cadd9
you. Keep on smil-ing, what we go through. One stop to the rhy-thm that di-vides you.
Gtrs. 1 & 2: w/ Rhy. Fill 2
Gtr. 4 tacet
* Gtr. 5: w/ Rhy. Fig. 1, 2 times
G D G5/D Cadd9
And I speak to you like the cho-rus to the verse. Chop an-oth-er line like a co-da with a
* Elec. w/ clean tone playing mf.
G D G5/D Cadd9
curse. Come on like a freak show takes the stage. We give them the games we play. She said,
Chorus
Gtrs. 1 & 2: w/ Rhy. Figs. 1 & 1A, 3 times
G D G5/D Cadd9 G D G5/D
"I want some-thing else to get me through this sem-i-charmed kind of life.".
Gtr. 3: w/ Riff A
Cadd9 G D G5/D Cadd9
Ba-by, a, ba-by, I want some-thing else. I'm not list'n-ing when you
Rhy. Fill 2
Gtrs. 1 & 2
T
A
B

G
D
G5/D
Cadd9
Gtr. 1
Rhy. Fill 3
End Rhy. Fill 3
say good - bye.
Gtr. 2
Rhy. Fill 3A
End Rhy. Fill 3A
Gtrs. 1 & 2: w/ Rhy. Figs. 1 & 1A, 1 1/2 times
Gtrs. 1 & 2: w/ Rhy. Fills 1 & 1A
(Do, do, do. Do, do, do, do. Do, do, do. Do, do, do, do. Do, do, do. Do, do, do, do. Do, do, do.)
2. The sky, it was gold,
Verse
Gtr. 4: w/ Rhy. Fig. 1, 4 times
it was rose. I was tak - ing sips of it through my nose. And I wish I could get back there, some place
Gtr. 3
mf w/ wah-wah as filter
let ring throughout
back there. Smil-ing in the pic-tures you would take. Do - ing crys - tal myth will lift you up un - til you break. It won't

Gtrs. 1 & 2: w/ Rhy. Fill 2
G
D
G5/D
Cadd9
stop. I won't come down. I keep stock with a tick - tock rhy - thm. A bump for the drop and then I
bumped up. I took the hit that I was giv - en then I bumped a - gain, then I bumped a - gain. You said,
wah off
Pre-Chorus
Gtr. 3 tacet
Rhy. Fig. 2
Gtr. 1
"How do I get back there to the place where I fell a - sleep in - side you?"
Rhy. Fig. 2A
Gtr. 2
End Rhy. Fig. 2
How do I get my - self back to the place where you said,
End Rhy. Fig. 2A

Chorus
Gtrs. 1 & 2: w/ Rhy. Figs. 1 & 1A, 3 1/2times
G D G5/D Cadd9 G D G5/D
"I want some - thing else to get me through this sem - i-charmed kind of life?"
Gtr. 3: w/ Riff A
Cadd9 G D G5/D
Ba - by, a, ba - by, I want some - thing else.
Cadd9 G D G5/D Cadd9
Gtrs. 1 & 2: w/ Rhy. Fills 3 & 3A
I'm not list'n - ing when you say good - bye.
Verse
*G5 Dadd4 C
3. I be - lieve in the sand be - neath my toes. The beach gives a feel - ing, an earth - y feel -
Gtr. 6 (acous.)
mf
let ring throughout
* Chord symbols reflect implied tonality.
G5 Dadd4 Cadd9
- ing. I be - lieve in the faith that grows. And the four right chords can make
Gtr. 6
Gtr. 7 (12-str. elec.)
mf
let ring throughout
Gtrs. 1 & 2: w/ Rhy. Figs. 1 & 1A
Gtrs. 6 & 7 tacet
G D G5/D
Gtr. 3: w/ Riff A
Cadd9
me cry. When I'm with you I feel like I could die

G D G5/D Cadd9
Gtr. 1
and that would be all right, all right. And when the
Gtr. 2
Bridge
Gtrs. 1 & 2: w/ Rhy. Figs. 2 & 2A, 1st & 2nd meas.
D G5/D Cadd9 D G5/D Cadd9
plane came in she said she was crash - ing. The vel - vet, it rips. In the cit - y we tripped.
D G5/D Cadd9 G
on the urge to feel a - live but now I'm strug - gling to sur - vive. Those
P.S.
Gtrs. 1 & 2: w/ Rhy. Figs. 2 & 2A, 1st & 2nd meas.
D G5/D Cadd9 D G5/D Cadd9
days you were wear - ing that vel - vet dress. You're the priest - ess, I must con - fess. Those
D G5/D Cadd9 G
lit - tle red pan - ties, they pass the test. Slide up a - round the bel - ly, face down on the mat - tress.

Gtrs. 1 & 2 tacet
G/D Gsus4/D G/C
G/D Gsus4/D G/C
G/D Gsus4/D G/C
Gtr. 5 tacet
G
One. And you hold me, and we are bro - ken. Still, it's all that I want to do, just a lit-tle now.
Gtr. 5
Gtrs. 1 & 2
w/ flanger & fingers
(flanger off)
Verse
Gtrs. 1 & 2: w/ Rhy. Figs. 1 & 1A, 3 1/2 times
G D G5/D Cadd9
4. Feel my - self, head made of the ground. I'm scared, I'm not com - ing down,
G D G5/D Cadd9 G D G5/D
no, no. And I won't run for my life.
Cadd9 G D G5/D
Gtrs. 1 & 2: w/ Rhy. Fills 1 & 1A
Cadd9
She's got her jaws just locked now in her smile but noth - ing is all right, all right. And
Chorus
Gtrs. 1 & 2 tacet
G N.C.(D) C G5 D C
I want some-thing else to get me through this life. Ba - by,
Gtr. 5
mp w/ amp tremolo
let ring throughout
Gtr. 7
mp
let ring throughout

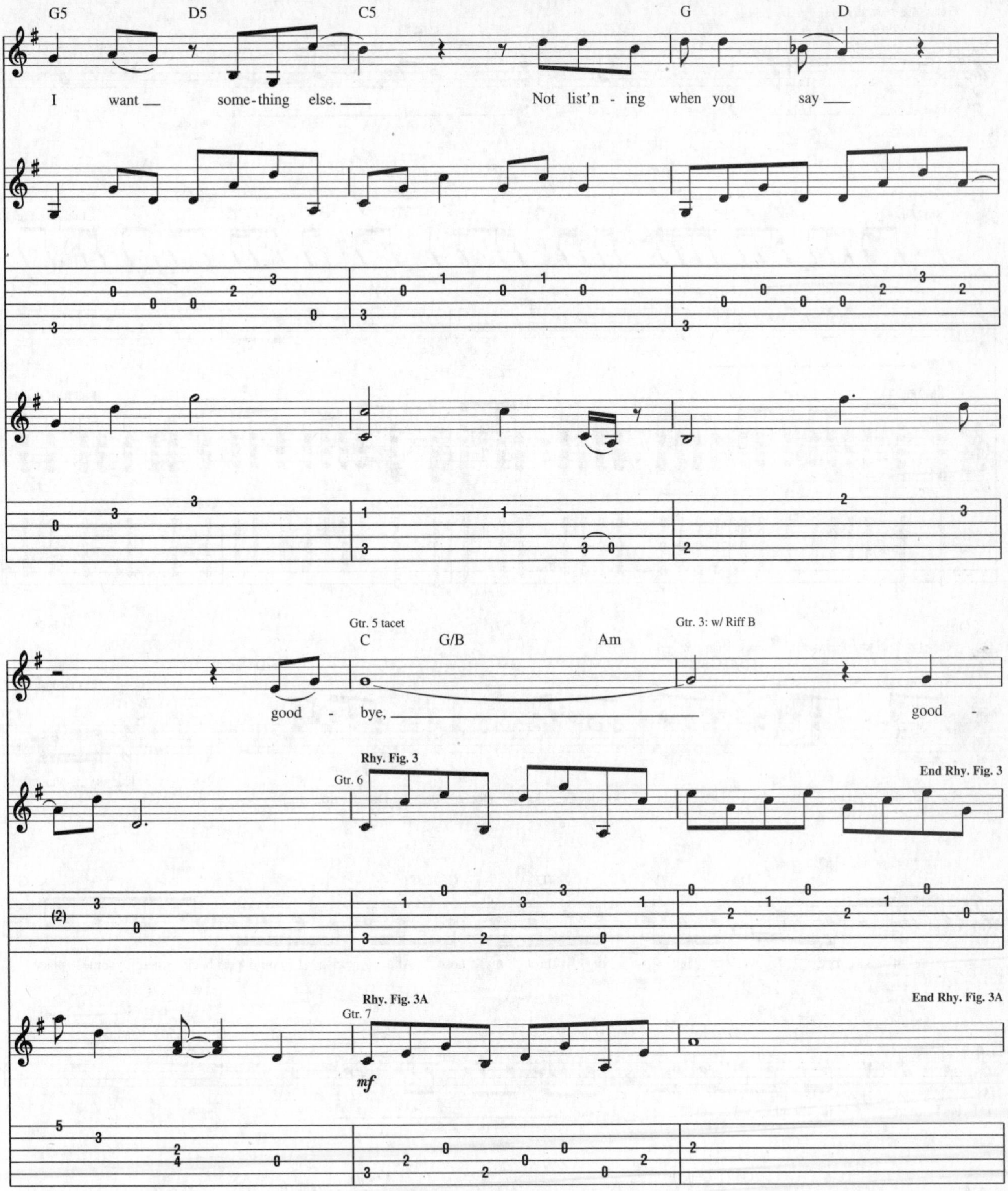

G5 D5 C5 G D

I want __ some-thing else. __ Not list'n - ing when you say __

Gtr. 5 tacet

C G/B Am

Gtr. 3: w/ Riff B

good - bye, __ good -

Rhy. Fig. 3

Gtr. 6

End Rhy. Fig. 3

Rhy. Fig. 3A

Gtr. 7

mf

End Rhy. Fig. 3A

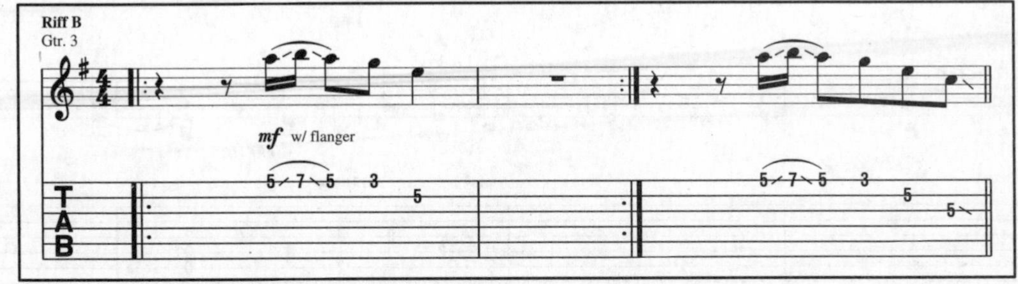

Gtrs. 6 & 7: w/ Rhy. Figs. 3 & 3A, 2 times
C G/B Am C G/B Am
bye, good - bye, good -
G D G5/D Cadd9 G D G/D Cadd9
Rhy. Fig. 4
Gtr. 1
End Rhy. Fig. 4
bye.
Rhy. Fig. 4A
Gtr. 2
End Rhy. Fig. 4A
Outro
Gtrs. 1 & 2: w/ Rhy. Figs. 4 & 4A, 3 times, simile
G D G5/D Cadd9 G D G5/D Cadd9
Voc. Fig. 1
End Voc. Fig. 1
(Do, do, do. Do, do, do,_ do. Do, do, do. Do, do, do,_ do. Do, do, do. Do, do, do,_ do.)
The sky, it was gold,
Bkgd. Voc.: w/ Voc. Fig. 1, 2 times
G D G5/D Cadd9 G
it was rose. I was tak - ing sips of it through my nose. And I wish I could get back there, some place
D G5/D Cadd9 G D G5/D Cadd9 G
back there in the place we used to stay.
D G5/D Cadd9 C G/B slight rit. A5
I want some - thing else.
Gtrs. 1 & 2
slight rit.
let ring
let ring

Seventeen

Words and Music by Kip Winger, Reb Beach and Beau Hill

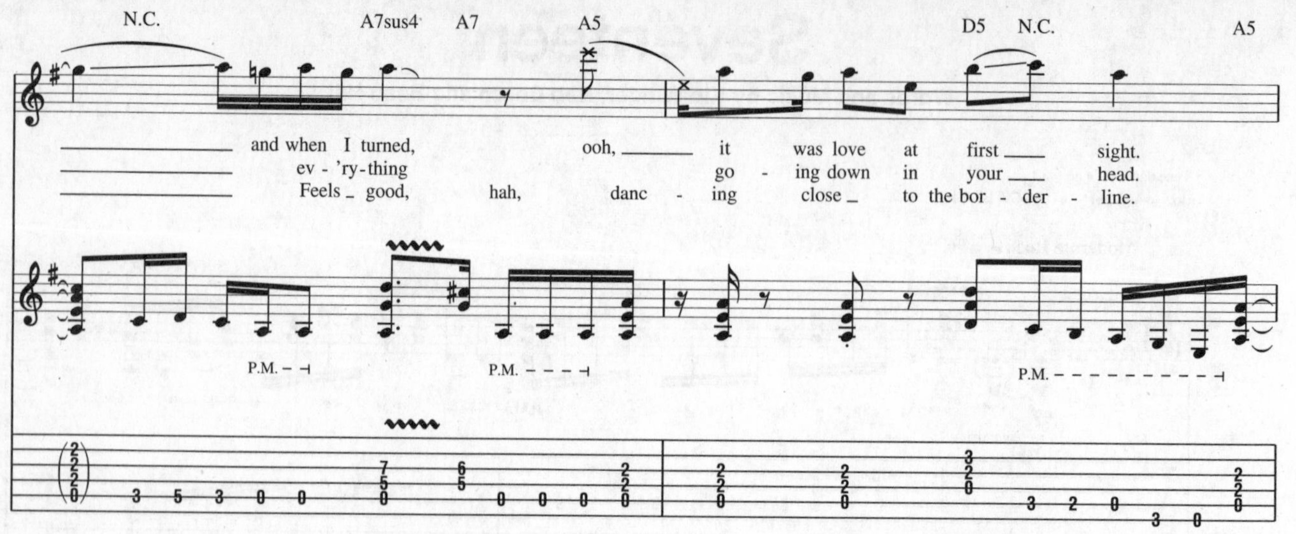
N.C.
A7sus4
A7
A5
D5
N.C.
A5
and when I turned, ooh, it was love at first sight.
ev - 'ry - thing go - ing down in your head.
Feels _ good, hah, danc - ing close _ to the bor - der - line.
P.M.
P.M.
P.M.

N.C.
A7sus4
A7
A
D/F#
G5
A
I said, "Please ex - cuse me, I did - n't catch your name. Whoa,
She says, "Take it eas - y, I need some time. Time
She's a mag - ic moun tain, she's a leath - er glove. Oh,
P.M.
P.M.
P.M.

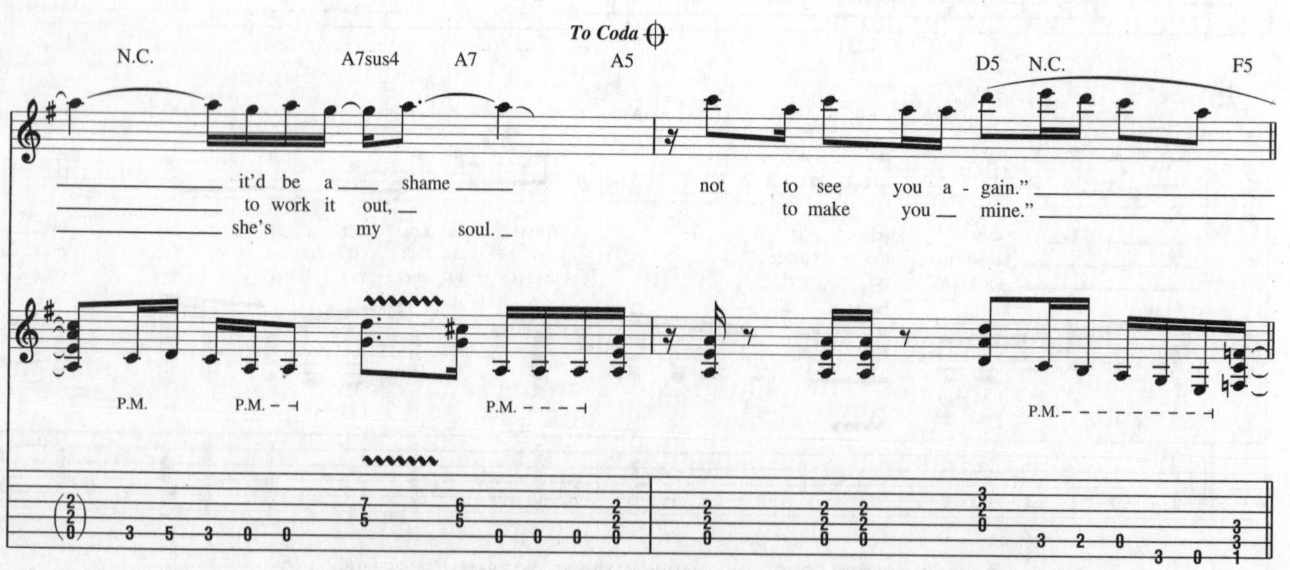
To Coda
N.C.
A7sus4
A7
A5
D5
N.C.
F5
it'd be a shame not to see you a - gain."
to work it out, to make you mine."
she's my soul.
P.M.
P.M.
P.M.
P.M.

Pre-Chorus
G
Gsus4
A5
Asus4
A
Asus2
A5
And just when I thought she was com - in' to my door,
Gtr. 1
P.M.
Gtr. 2
F5
G5
A5
B5
C5
N.C.
E
she whis - pered sweet and brought me to the floor. She said,
Chorus
D
D5
"I'm on - ly sev - en - teen."
(Sev - en - teen.)
Rhy. Fig. 1
Gtrs. 1 & 2

D
C5
G5
A5
N.C.
E
"I'll show you love like you've nev - er seen, ow."
You ain't seen love, ain't seen noth-in' like me.
End Rhy. Fig. 1
P.M.
She's on - ly sev - en - teen.
* (Sev - en - teen.)
D5
* Sung 1st time only.
1.
Dad - dy says she's too young, but she's old e - nough for me.
2. Mm,
2.
Sev - en - teen, ay, yeah.
Gtr. 3 (dist.)
8va
mf
w/ slight delay
w/ bar
Harm.
Gtrs. 1 & 2
P.S.

Guitar Solo
B5
loco
A5
G5
P.M.
A5
D5
A5
B5
A5

G5
F♯m7
(add4)
1/4
1
P.M.
N.C.
8va
w/ bar
let ring
loco
Gtr. 1
Gtr. 2
divisi

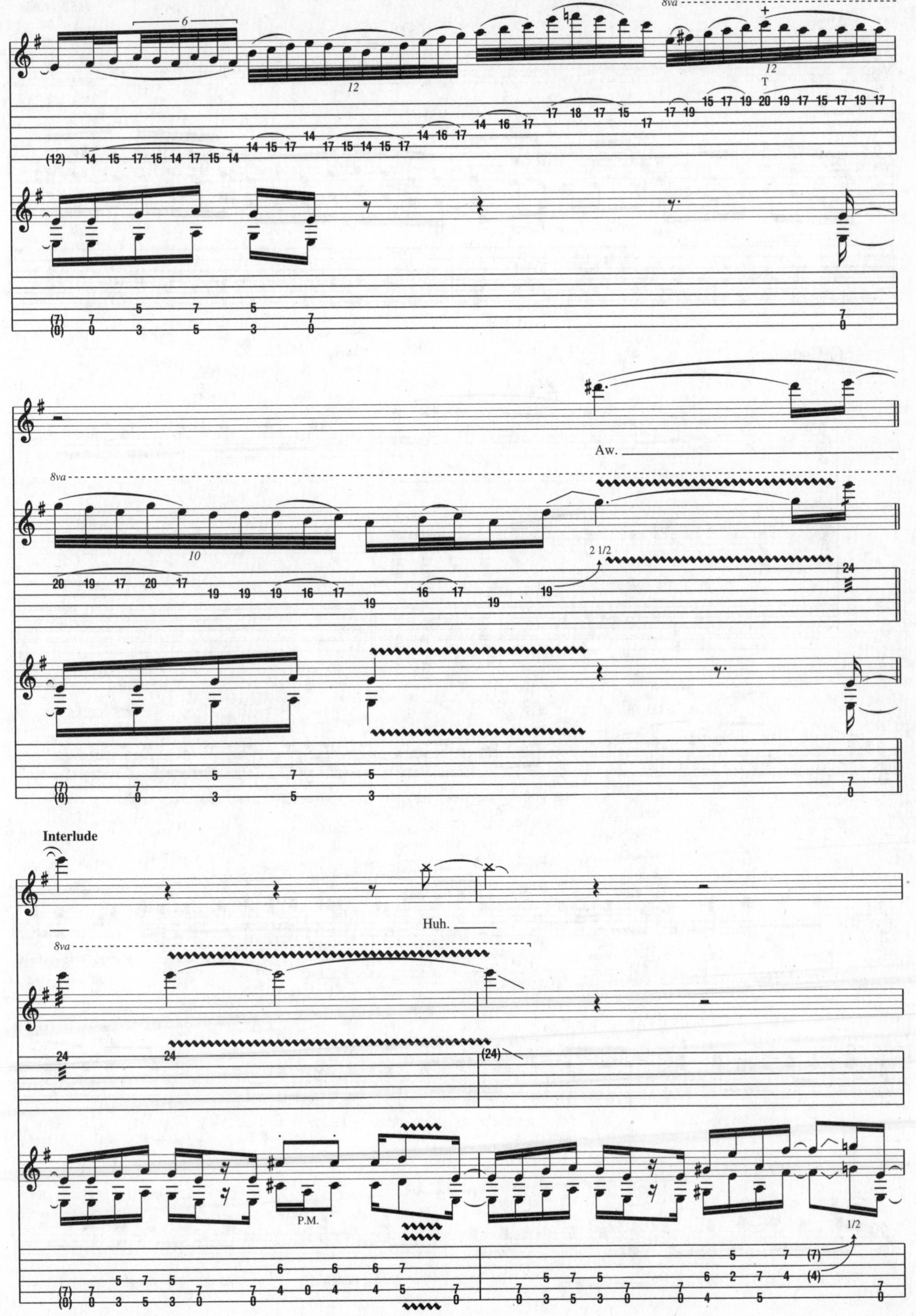
8va
Aw.
8va
Interlude
Huh.
8va
P.M.

D.S. al Coda
Gtr. 3 tacet
A5
3. Yeah,
Gtr. 1
Gtr. 2 divisi
P.M.
P.M.
1/2
Coda
Chorus
Gtrs. 1 & 2: w/ Rhy. Fig. 1 (till fade)
D5 N.C.
E
D
It must be love.
She's on - ly sev - en - teen.
Gtrs. 1 & 2
P.M.
C5
D5 E
D
C5 G5 A5
E
(Sev - en - teen.
That girl, she gives me love like I've nev - er seen.
D
C5
D5 E
D
She's on - ly sev - en - teen.
Sev - en - teen.
Dad - dy says she's too young, but she's
C5 G5 A5
E
D
C5
D5 E
old e - nough for me.
Sev-en - teen.
She's ev - 'ry - thing I need.
Sev - en - teen.).
D
C5
G5
A5
E
Dad - dy says she's too young, but she's old e - nough,
old e - nough for me.

* In one motion, tap the note indicated with the index finger of the pick hand, then pluck the adjacent strings with the same finger while pulling off.

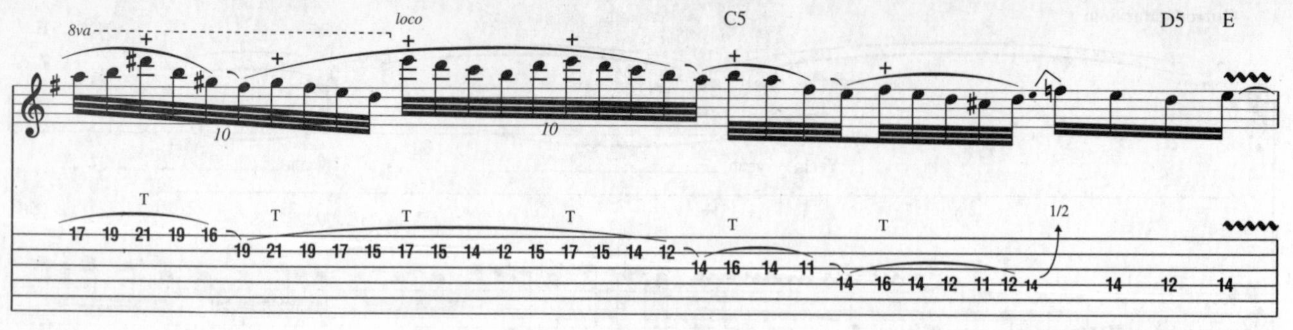
8va
loco
C5
D5
E
T
1/2

Begin Fade
D
C5
G5
A5
E
1/4

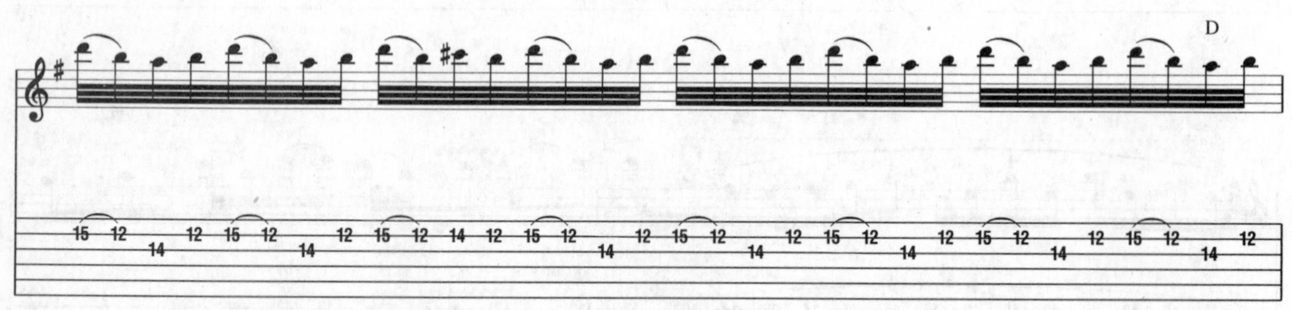
D

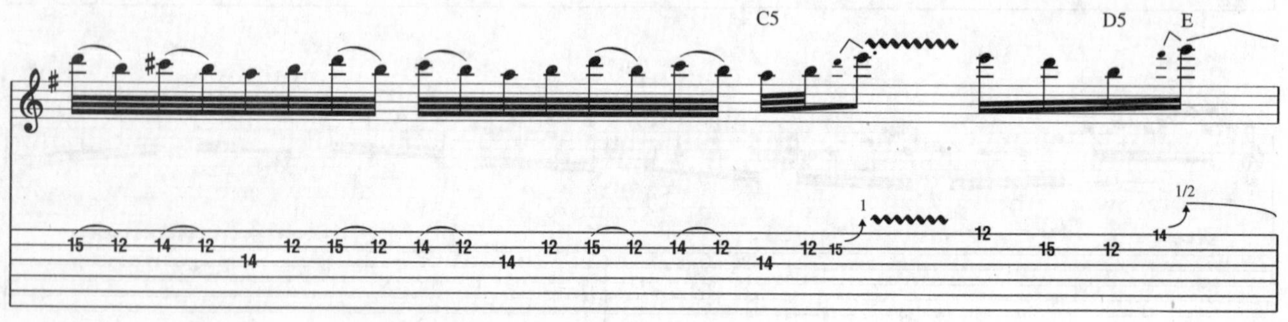
C5
D5
E
1
1/2

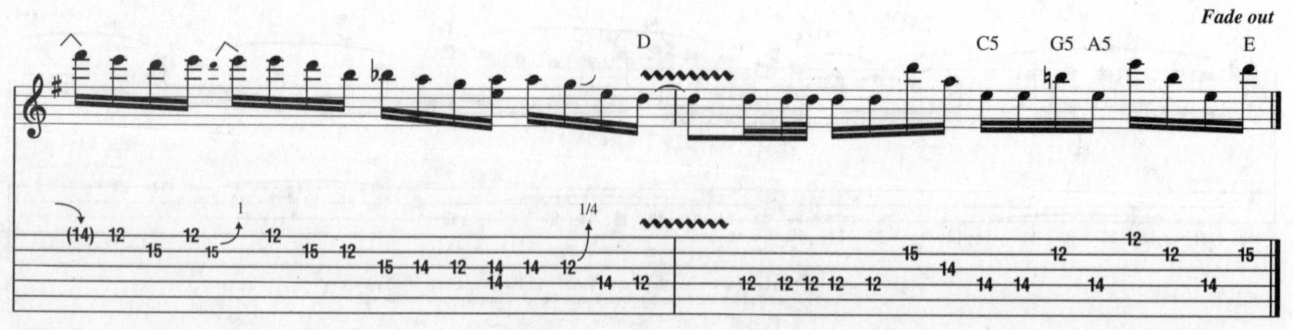
Fade out
D
C5
G5
A5
E
1
1/4

Shattered

Words and Music by Mick Jagger and Keith Richards

A5
E5
B5
E5
I'm in tat - ters.
(Tat - ters.)
I been shat - tered.
(Shat - tered.)
P.M.
let ring
P.M.
B5
Verse
E5
B5
Spoken: 1. Friends are so a-larm - ing and my lov - er's nev - er charm - ing.
(Shat - tered.)
Rhy. Fig. 1
P.M.
let ring
E5
B5
E5
Life's just a cock - tail part - y on the street.
Big Ap - ple peo - ple dressed in plas - tic bags
(Sha - doo - be.)
P.M.
let ring
P.M.
B5
E5
B5
dir - ec - ting traf - fic.
(Shat - tered.)
Some kind - a fash - ion.
(Sha - doo - be.)
(Shat - tered.)
End Rhy. Fig. 1
let ring
P.M.
let ring

Chorus
A5
B5
E5
Spoken: Laugh-ter, joy and lone - li - ness and sex, and sex, and sex, and sex and look at me!
Rhy. Fig. 2
let ring
A5
E5
B5
E5
I'm in tat - ters.
(Tat - ters.)
I'm a shat - tered.
(Shat - tered.)
P.M.
let ring
P.M.
B5
Verse
E5
B5
(Shat - tered.)
Spoken: 2. All this chit - ter chat - ter, chit - ter chat - ter, chit - ter chat - ter, 'bout
End Rhy. Fig. 2
let ring
E5
B5
E5
Shmat-ter, shmat-ter, shmat-ter. I can't give it a-way on Sev-enth Av - e - nue. This town's been wear - in'
(Sha-doo-bee.)
P.M.
let ring
P.M.

Chorus
B5
E5
B5
A5
tat-ters.
Uh, huh.
(Shat - tered.)
(Sha-doo-bee.)
(Shat - tered.)
Work and work for love and sex.
let ring
P.M.
let ring
Ain't you hun-gry for suc-cess? Suc - cess, suc-cess, suc - cess!
Does it mat - ter?
(Mat - ter?)
P.M.
Gtr. 2: w/ Rhy. Fill 1
I'm shat - tered.
(Shat - tered.)
Does it mat - ter?
(Shat-tered.)
P.M.
let ring
(cont. in slash)
Rhy. Fill 1
Gtr. 2 (clean)
mf

Guitar Solo

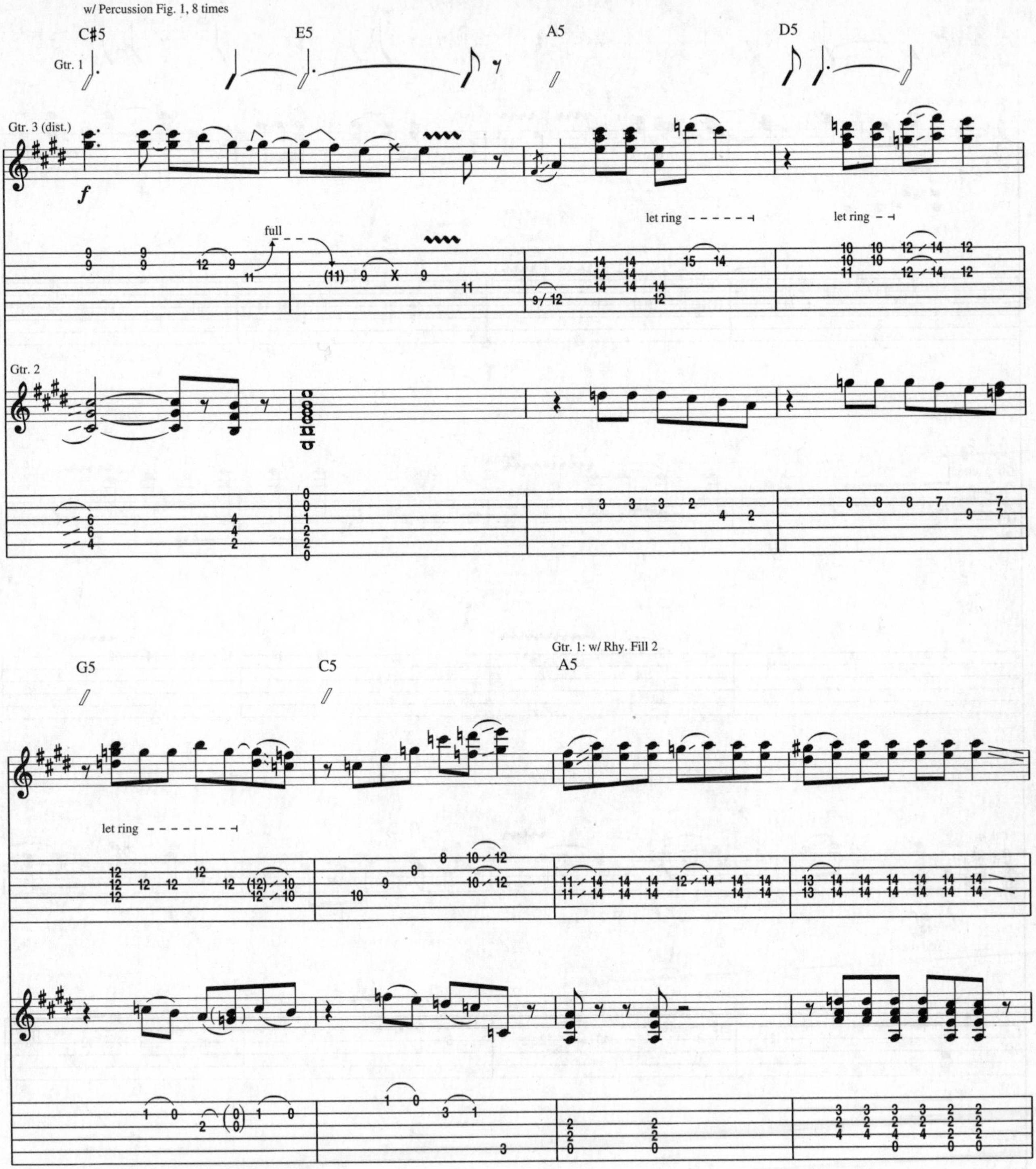

w/ Percussion Fig. 1, 8 times
C#5
E5
A5
D5
Gtr. 1
Gtr. 3 (dist.)
f
full
let ring
let ring
Gtr. 2
G5
C5
Gtr. 1: w/ Rhy. Fill 2
A5
let ring

Percussion Fig. 1
Handclaps

Rhy. Fill 2
Gtr. 1
(cont. in slash)

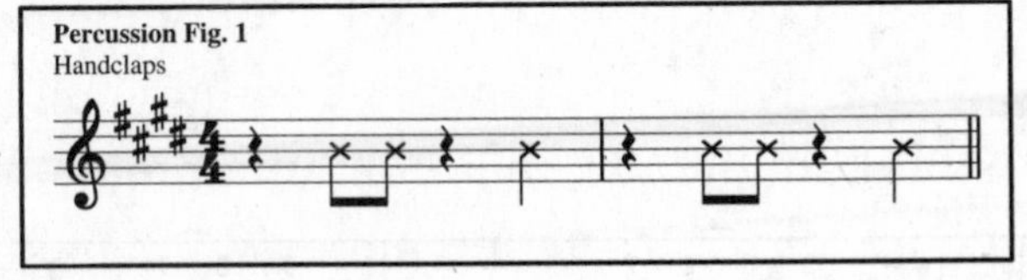

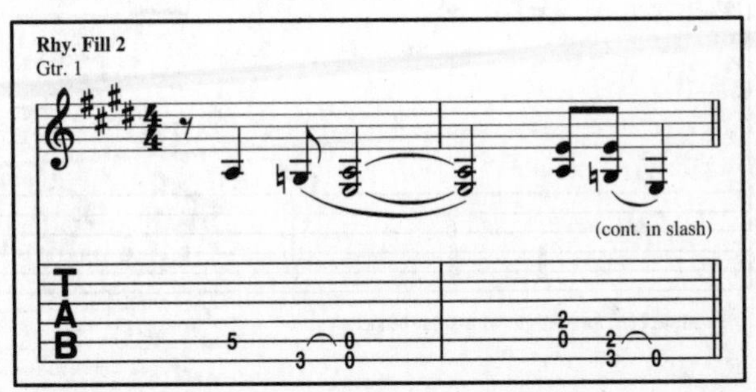

* Pedal steel arr. for elec. gtr. w/ B-string bender.

* Pull down on the neck w/ frethand (behind slide) to activate B-Bender.

E
B
E
B
Look at me!
I been shat - tered.
(Shat - tered)
Yeah!
(Shat - tered)
Gtr. 7 (clean)
mf
w/ slide
Gtr. 6 (clean)
mf

Gtr. 1: w/ Rhy. Fig. 2, simile
Gtr. 7 tacet
A
B
E
Spoken: Pride and joy and greed and sex, that's what makes our town the best.
Pride and joy and dir - ty dreams are
Gtr. 6
let ring

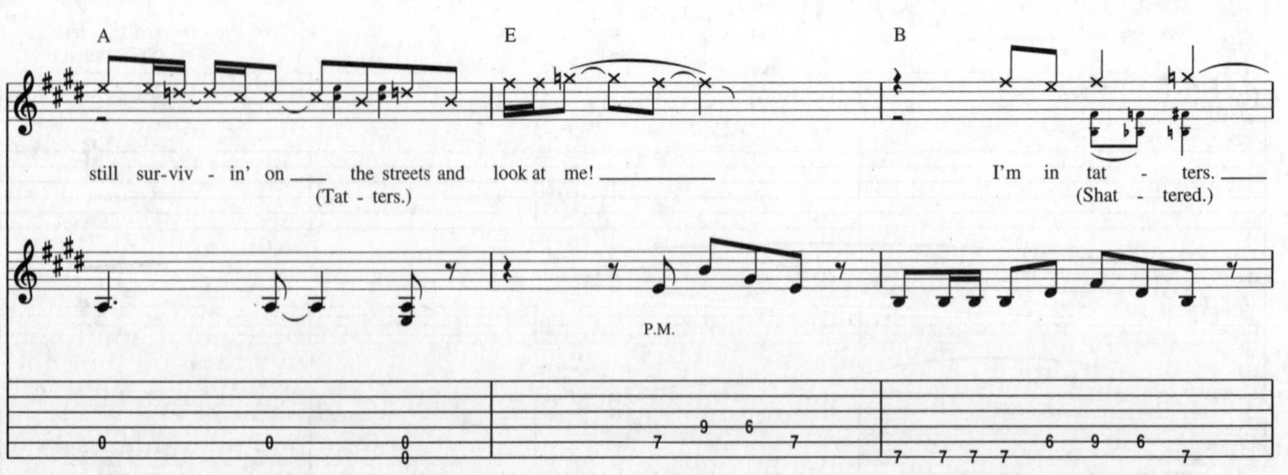
A
E
B
still sur-viv - in' on the streets and look at me!
(Tat - ters.)
I'm in tat - ters.
(Shat - tered.)
P.M.

Gtr. 1: w/ Rhy. Fig. 1, 6 times, simile
E
B
E
B
Yeah!
I been bat - tered.
(Shat - tered.)
What does it mat - ter?
(Shat - tered.)
Does it mat - ter?
(Shat - tered.)
Uh huh.
Does mat - ter?
P.M.
Uh huh.
I'm, uh, shat - tered.
Mm.
I'm, shat - tered.
Huh!
Sha - doo - bee.
(Sha - doo - bee.)
Shat-tered. Huh!
(Shat - tered.)
Sha - doo - bee.
Shat - tered.
(Shat - tered.)

E
B
E
Sha - doo - bee.
(Sha - doo - bee.)
(Shat - tered.)
(Shat - tered.)
Spoken: Don't you know the crime rate's go in' -
(Sha - doo - bee.)
B
E
B
up, up, up, up, up?
(Shat - tered.)
(Sha - doo - bee.)
To live in this town you must be
(Shat - tered.)
E
B
E
tough, tough, tough, tough, tough, tough, tough!
(Sha - doo - bee.)
(Shat - tered.)
(Shat - tered.)
We got rats on the West Side,
(Sha - doo - bee.)
B
E
B
bed - bugs up - town.
(Shat - tered.)
What a mess! This town's in tat - ters.
(Sha - doo - bee.)
I been shat - tered.
(Shat - tered.)

E
B
E
My brain's been bat - tered,
splat-tered all o - ver
Man - hat - tan.
Uh
(Sha - doo - bee.)
(Shat - tered.)
(Sha - doo - bee.)
B
E
B
E
huh.
What say?
Sha - doo - bee.
Shat - tered.
(Shat - tered.) (Shat - tered.)
(Sha - doo - bee.)
(Shat - tered.)
(Oh!)
(Sha - doo - bee.) (Oh!)
B
E
B
E
Shat - tered.
Sha - doo - bee.
Spoken: Uh, huh.
This town's full of
(Shat - tered.) (Oo!)
(Sha - doo - bee.)
(Shat - tered.)
(Sha - doo - bee.)
B
E
B
E
mon - ey grab - bers.
Go a - head!
Bite
the Big Ap - ple.
Don't mind the mag - gots!
Uh huh.
(Shat - tered.) (Shat - tered.)
(Sha - doo - bee.)
(Shat - tered.)
(Sha-doo-bee.)

B E B

(Shat - tered.) Sha - doo - bee. (Sha - doo - bee.) My brain's been bat - tered! (Shat - tered.) (Shat - tered.)

full

E B E

My fam - 'ly come a-round 'n' flat - ter, flat - ter, flat - ter, flat - ter, flat - ter, flat - ter, flat - ter.
(Sha - doo - bee.) (Shat - tered.) (Sha - doo - bee.)

Gtr. 1: w/ Rhy. Fig. 2, 1st meas., simile

B E B E

Pile it up! Pile it up! Pile it high ___ on the plat - ter!
(Shat - tered.) (Sha-doo-bee.) (Shat - tered.) (Shat - tered.)

Gtr. 6

Show Me the Way

Words and Music by Peter Frampton

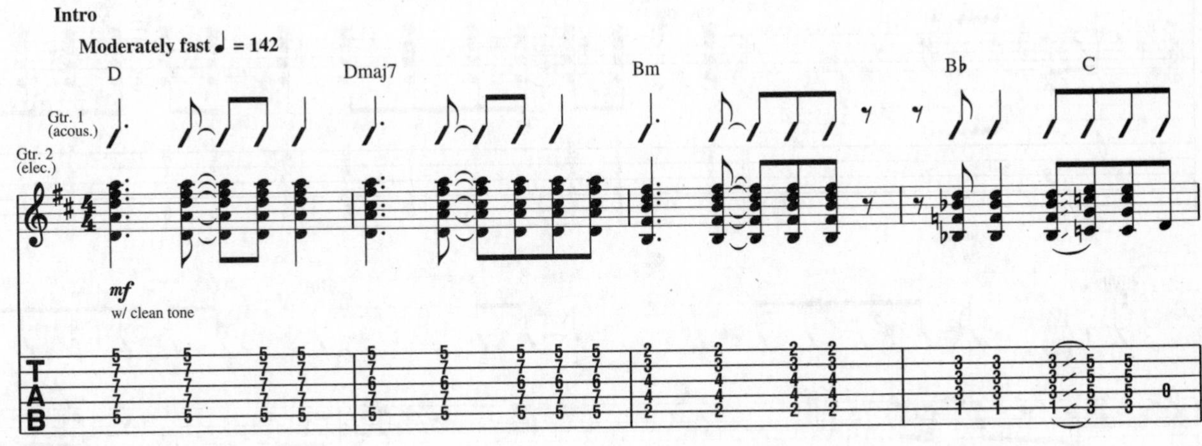

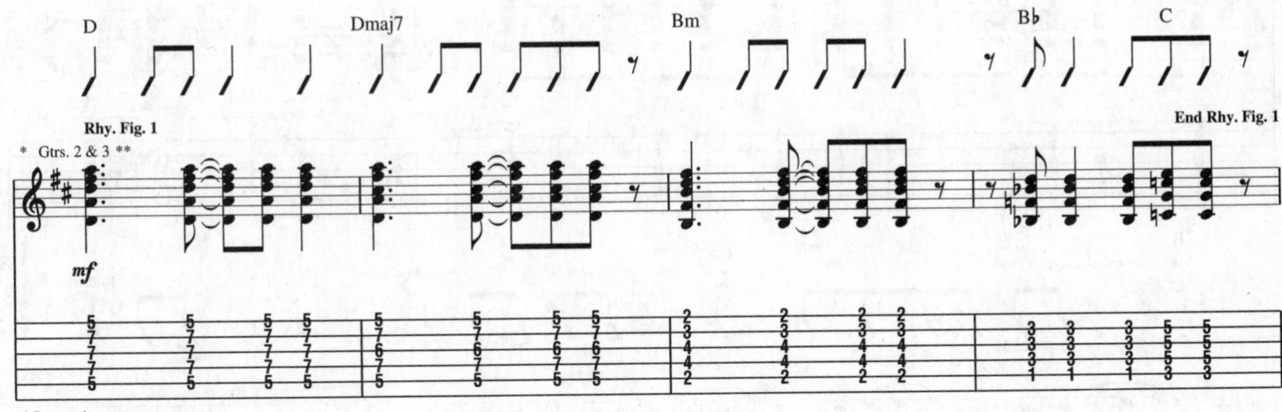

*Composite arrangement

**Gtr. 3 (elec.) w/ clean tone

2.
Verse
B♭
C
D
Rhy. Fig. 3
Gtr. 1
1. I wonder how you're feeling, there's
I can see no reason, you
Gtrs. 2 & 3
Rhy. Fig. 3A
1/2
Dmaj7
Bm
ringing in my ears. And no one to relate
living on your nerves. when someone drops a cup
let ring
B♭
C
End Rhy. Fig. 3
to 'cept the sea.
and I submerge. I'm
End Rhy. Fig. 3A
let ring
Verse
Gtrs. 1, 2 & 3: w/ Rhy. Figs. 3 & 3A (1st 7 meas.)
D
Dmaj7
2. Who can I believe in? I'm kneeling on the floor. There
swimming in a circle, I feel I'm going down. There
wonder if I'm dreaming, I feel so unashamed. I

Bm
has to be a force,
has to be a fool
can't be - lieve this is hap - pen - ing
who do I phone?
to play my part.
to me.
Bb
Bridge
Bb
A7sus4
Asus4
A7sus4 Asus4
A7sus4
Gtr. 1
The stars are out and shin - ing,
Some - one thought of heal - ing
I watch you when you're sleep - ing,
but all I
but all I
oh then I
Gtrs. 2 & 3
let ring
G
G
B
G
open
3fr
Chorus
Bm
Rhy. Fig. 4
Gtr. 1
let ring
real - ly wan - na know...
real - ly wan - na know...
wan - na take your love...
Oh, won't
you
Rhy. Fig. 4A
Gtr. 3
let ring
Rhy. Fig. 4A
Gtr. 2

G
End Rhy. Fig. 4
Gtr. 1
show me the way, ev - 'ry day. I want
Gtrs. 2 & 3
End Rhy. Fig. 4A
To Coda 1
To Coda 2
Bm
G
you to show me the way, yeah.
Interlude
Gtr. 2: w/ Rhy. Fig. 2
Gtr. 2: w/ Rhy. Fig. 1
G/A D Dmaj7 Bm B♭ C
D.S. al Coda 1
3. Well
Gtr. 3
w/ talk box
1/2
Gtr. 2

Coda 1
G
Bm
Rhy. Fig. 5
Gtr. 1
way, oh. I want you
Rhy. Fig. 5A
Gtrs. 2 & 3
G
G/A
End Rhy. Fig. 5
Gtr. 1
day af - ter day, hey.
Gtr. 3
let ring
End Rhy. Fig. 5A
Gtr. 2

Guitar Solo
Gtrs. 1 & 2: w/ Rhy. Figs. 3 & 3A
D
Gtr. 3
Dmaj7
w/ talk box
1/2
Bm
B♭
C
P.M.
3/4
Gtrs. 1 & 2: w/ Rhy. Figs. 3 & 3A (1st 6 meas.)
D
Dmaj7
Bm
G
D.S.S. al Coda 2
Gtr. 1
5. An', ___ I
Gtr. 3
Gtr. 2

Coda 2

G
way,
one more time.
I want

Gtrs. 1, 2 & 3: w/ Rhy. Figs. 4 & 4A
Bm
G
you
day af - ter day,
hey. I want

Gtr. 1: w/ Rhy. Fig. 5 (1st 3 meas.)
Gtr. 2: w/ Rhy. Fig. 5A
Gtr. 3: w/ Rhy. Fig. 5A (1st 3 meas.)
Bm
G
G/A
you
day af - ter day,
hey.
Gtr. 1
Gtr. 3

Interlude
D
Dmaj7
Bm
G
Gtr. 1
I want
Gtrs. 2 & 3
Outro-Chorus
Gtrs. 1, 2 & 3: w/ Rhy. Figs. 4 & 4A (2 times)
Bm
G
you
to show me the way ev - 'ry day.
I want
Bm
G
you
to show me the way, night and day.
I want
Gtrs. 1, 2 & 3: w/ Rhy. Figs. 5 & 5A
Bm
G
G/A
you
day af - ter day,
hey, hey,
D
Dmaj7
Bm
B♭
C
D
Gtr. 1
rit.
oh.
Gtrs. 2 & 3
rit.

Silent Lucidity

Words and Music by Chris DeGarmo

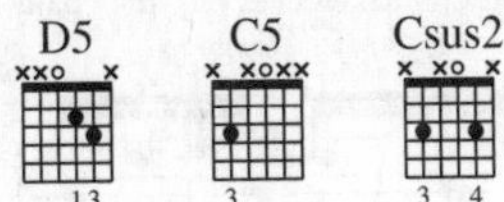

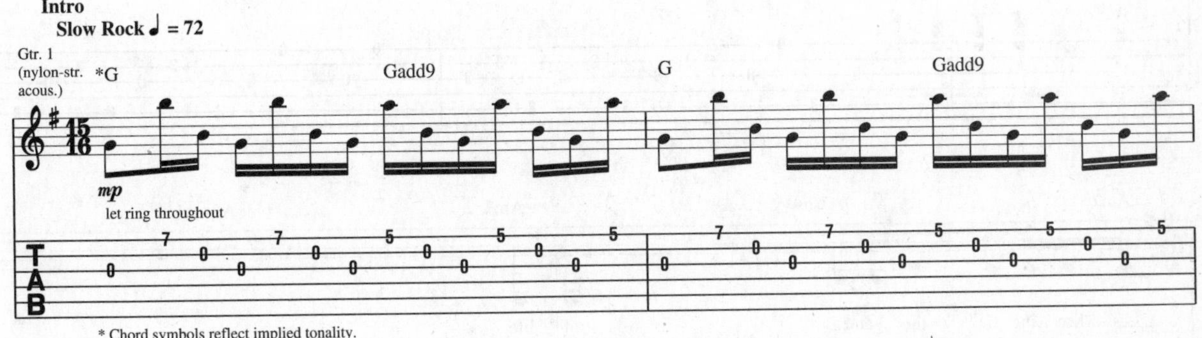

* Chord symbols reflect implied tonality.

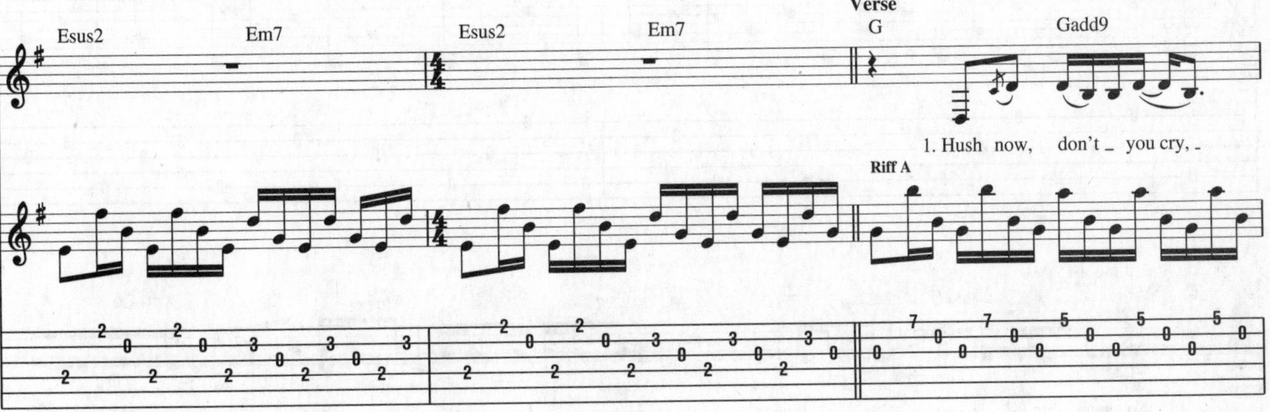

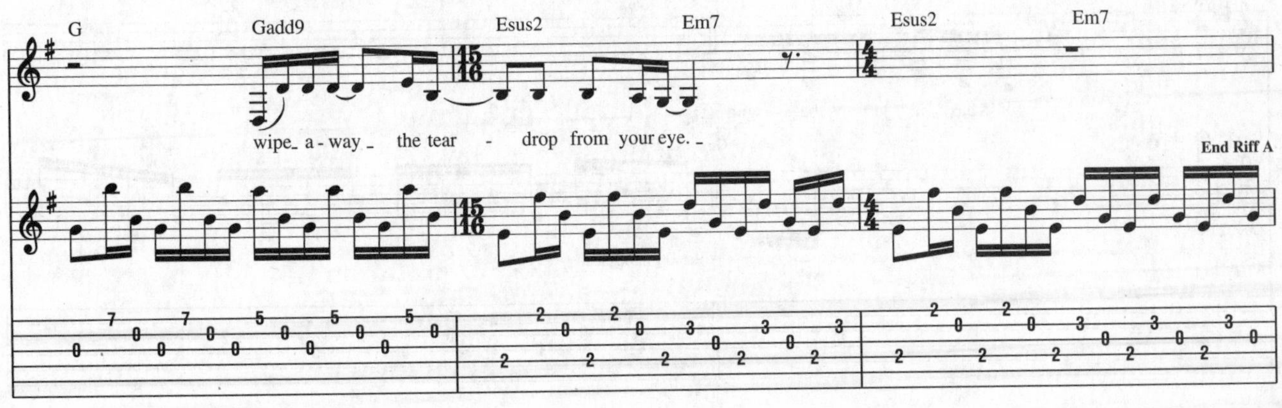

Esus2 Em7 C Csus2 C Csus2
Your mind tricked you to feel the pain of some - one close to you
Riff B
Gtr. 1
Am7 A7sus4 Am7 A7sus4
leav - ing the game of life.
End Riff B
Gtr. 1: w/ Riff B, 1st 3 meas.
C Csus2 C Csus2 Am7 A7sus4
So here it is, an - oth - er chance, wide a - wake you face the day, your dream is o - ver...
Interlude
G Gsus2
or has it just be - gun?
Gtr. 1
Gtrs. 1 & 2
Gtr. 2
(12-str. acous.)
divisi
mf
let ring throughout
G Gsus2 Esus2 Em7 Esus2 Em7

Verse
Gtr. 4: w/ Fill 1, 2nd time
Gtr. 5 tacet, 2nd time
G
Gsus2
G
Gsus2
2. There's a place I like to hide, a door-way that I
3. If you o-pen your mind for me, you won't re-ly on
Riff C
Esus2
Em7
Esus2
Em7
run through in the night.
o-pen eyes to see.
End Riff C
Gtrs. 1 & 2: w/ Riff C
G
Gsus2
G
Gsus2
Esus2
Em7
Re-lax, child, you were there, but on-ly did-n't re-al-ize (it), and you were scared.
The walls you built with-in, come tumb-ling down and a new world will be-gin.
Esus2
Em7
Gtrs. 1 & 2: w/ Riff B, 1 3/4 times
C
Csus2
C
Csus2
It's a place where you will learn to face your fears, re-
Liv-ing twice at once, you learn you're safe from pain in the
Am7
A7sus4
Am7
A7sus4
C
Csus2
trace the years and ride the whims of your mind. Com-mand-ing in an-oth-er world,
dream do-main. A soul set free to fly. A round-trip jour-ney in your head,
C
Csus2
Am7
A7sus4
sud-den-ly, you hear and see this mag-ic new di-men-
mas-ter of il-lus-sion, can you re-al-ize your
Fill 1
Gtr. 4
TAB
(4)

Chorus
Gtrs. 1 & 2 tacet
Am7
A7
D5
Gtr. 4 (elec.)
mf w/ dist.
sion.
dream's a - live, you can be the guide but... (I
Gtrs. 1 & 2
Gtr. 3 (elec.)
f
w/ clean tone
let ring throughout
C5
D5
...will be watch - ing o - ver you.
I...
C5
D5
...am gon-na help to see it through.
I...
C5
D5
...will pro-tect you in the night.
I...
End Riff D

To Coda
Csus2
am smil - ing next to you,
in si - lent lu - cid - i - ty.
Gtr. 1
Gtr. 3
divisi
Guitar Solo
Gtr. 1: w/ Riff A, 1st 2 meas.
Gtrs. 3 & 4 tacet
G
Gadd9
G
Gadd9
Gtr. 1 tacet
E♭
E♭sus2
Gtr. 4
full
1 1/2
Gtr. 2
E♭
E♭sus2
Csus2
C
full
P.M.

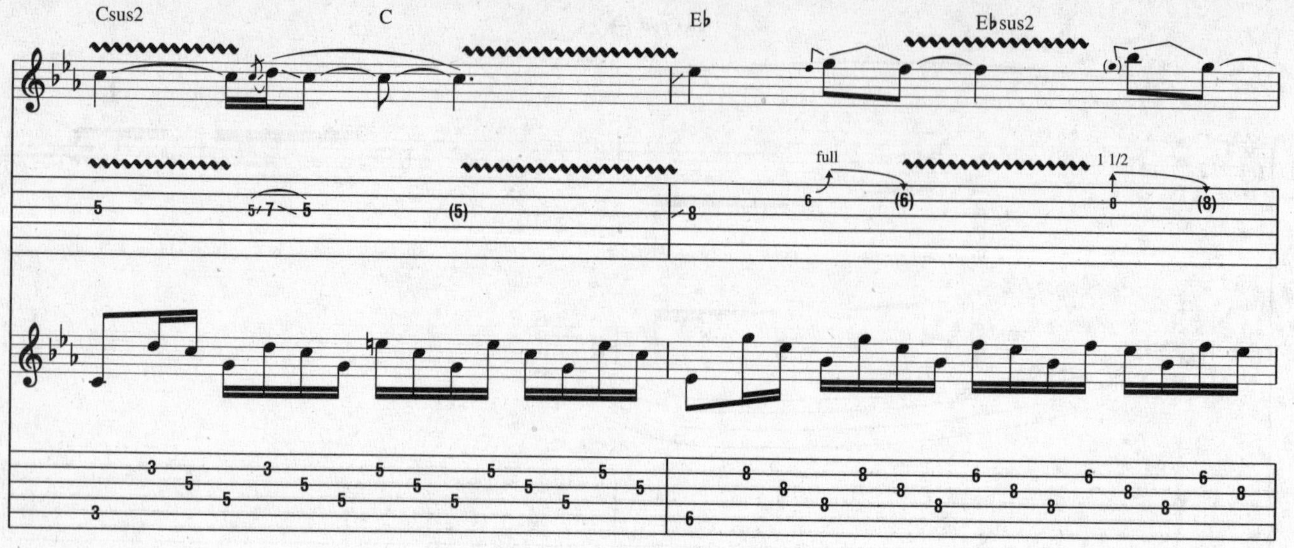

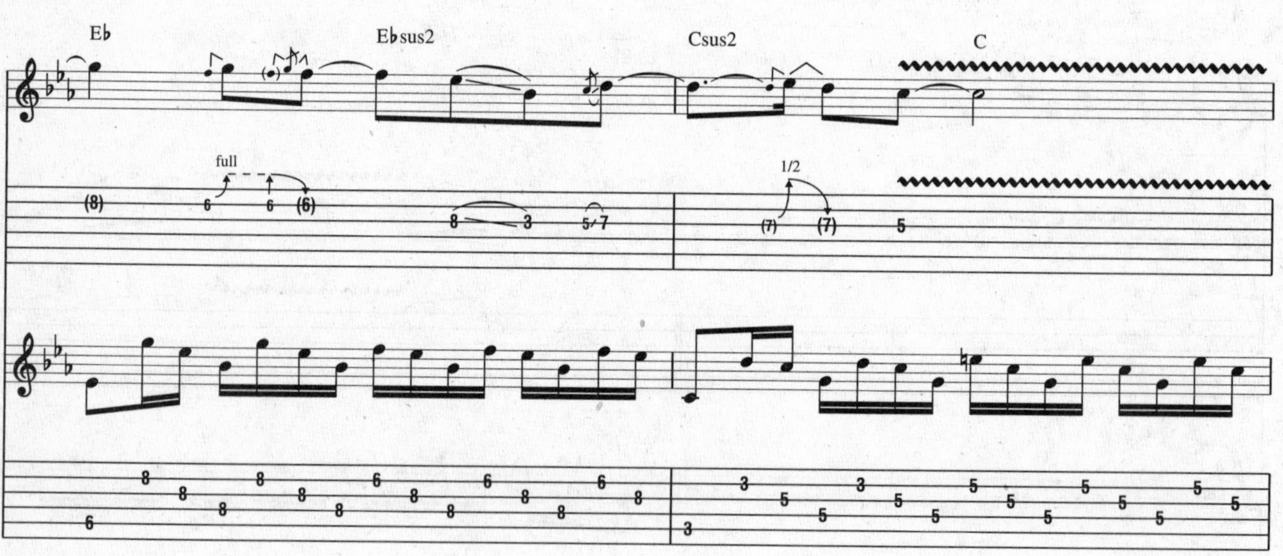

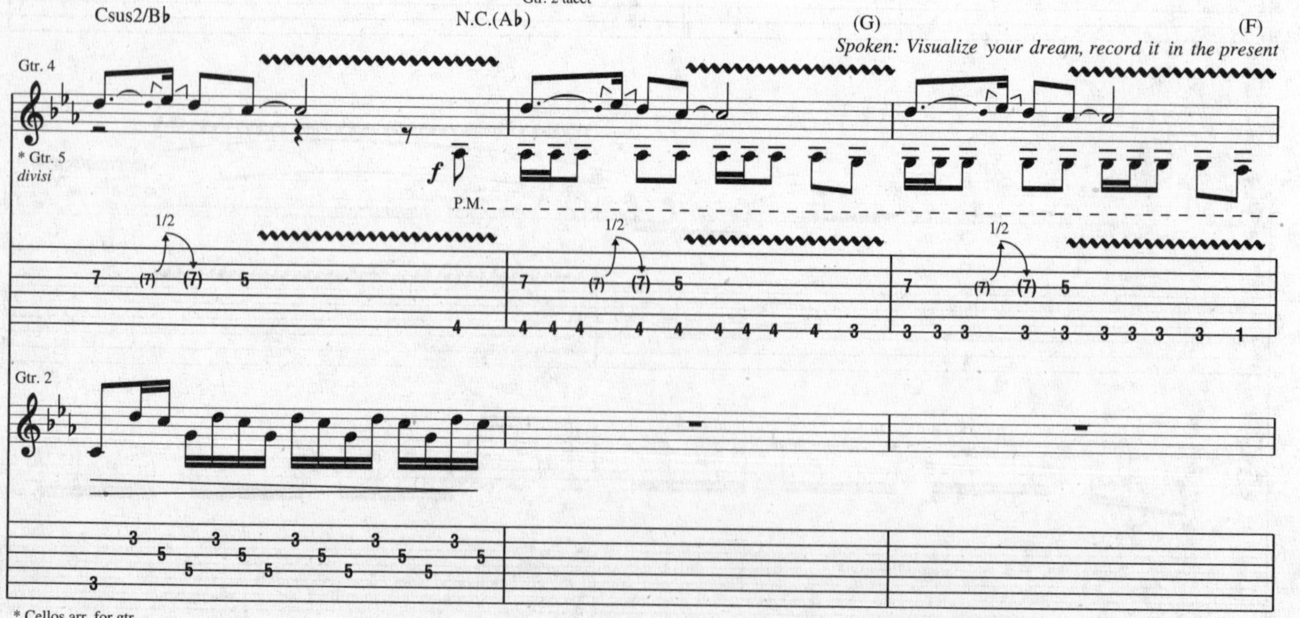

* Cellos arr. for gtr.

(E♭)
(D)
(C)
tense, put it into a permanent form. If you persist in your efforts, you can achieve dream control... control...
P.M.
1/2
D.S. al Coda
(B♭)
(A♭)
(G)
dream control . . .
dream control... dream control . . .
dream control.
Coda
Outro
Gtrs. 3 & 4 tacet
G
Gadd9
Gtr. 1
Gtr. 5 (nylon-str. acous.)
p

(Sittin' On) The Dock of the Bay

Words and Music by Steve Cropper and Otis Redding

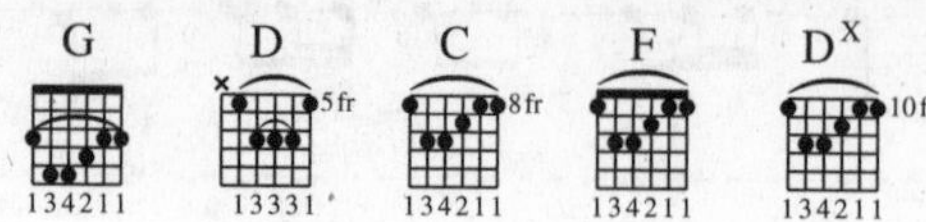

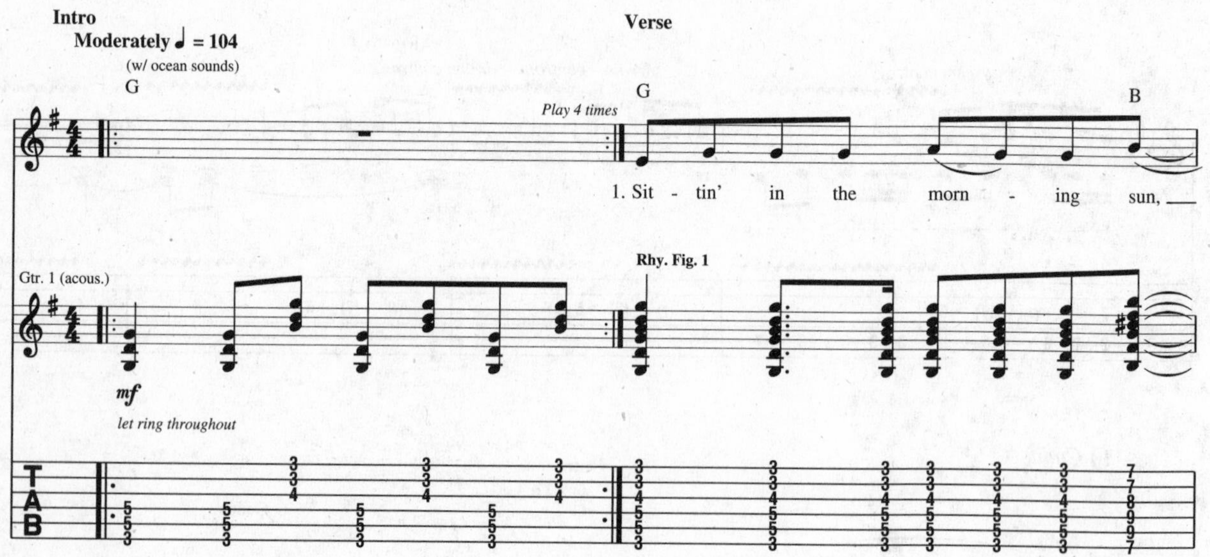

Chorus
G
E
G
E
sit - tin' on the dock of the bay,
sit on the dock of the bay,
sit at the dock of the bay,
watch-ing the tide roll a - way.
Gtr. 2 (elec.)
mf w/ clean tone
Gtr. 1
G
A
G
Oo, I'm just sit-tin' on the dock of the bay, wast - ing time.
let ring
let ring

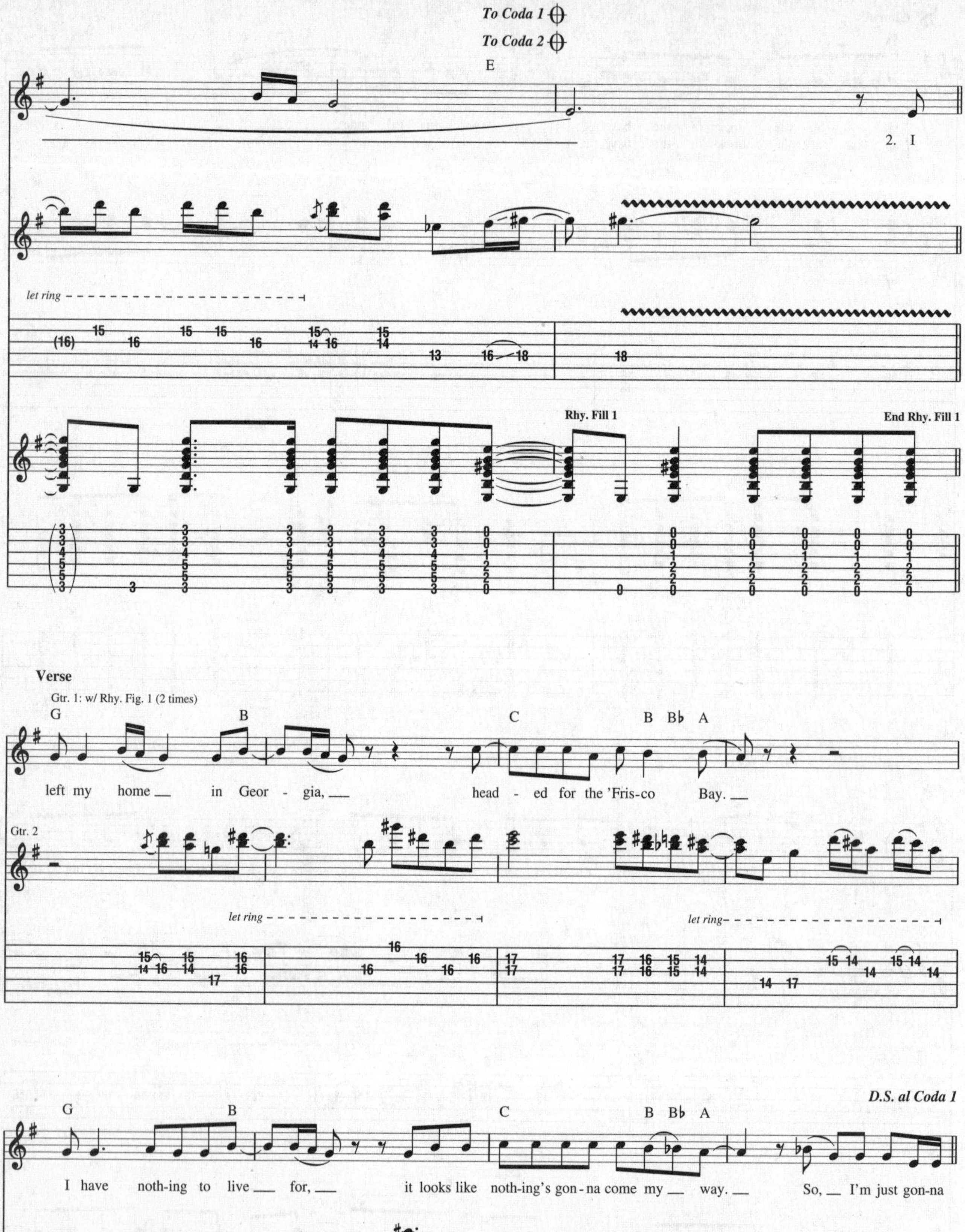

To Coda 1

To Coda 2

E

2. I

let ring

Rhy. Fill 1

End Rhy. Fill 1

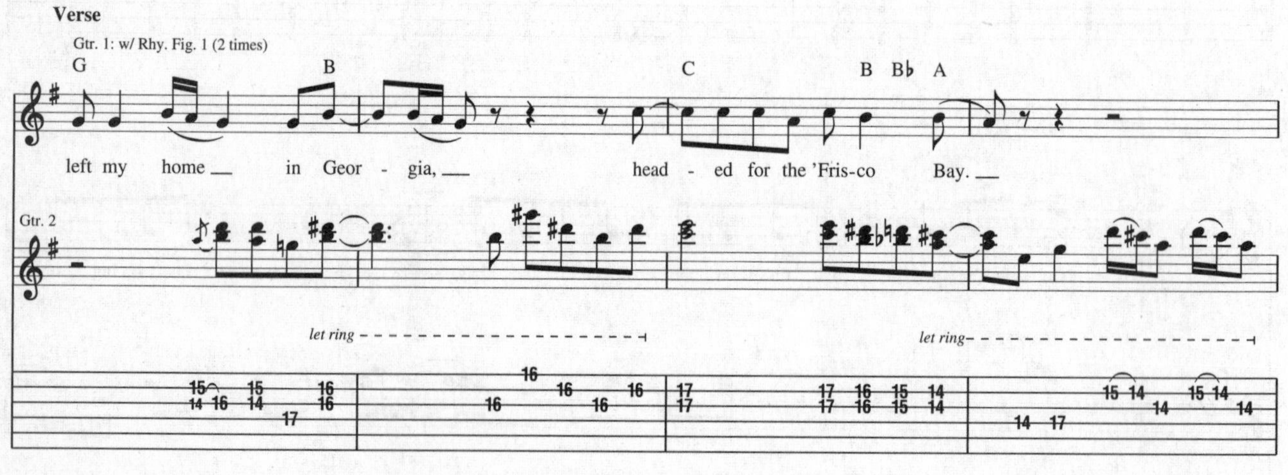

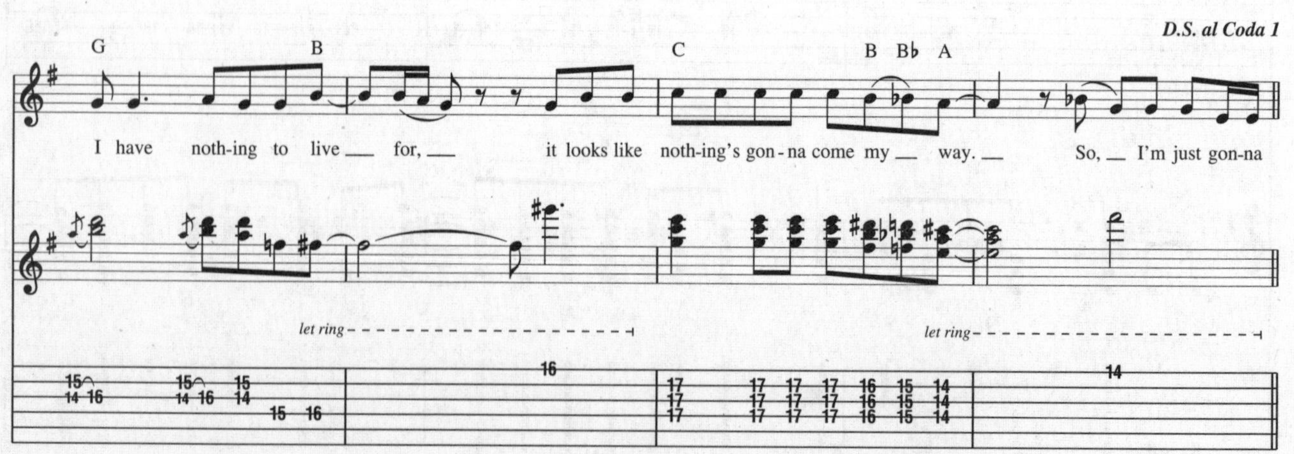

Coda 1
Bridge
Gtr. 1: w/ Rhy. Fill 1
G
D
C
Gtr. 1
Looks like nothing's gonna change.
Gtr. 2
* w/ pick & fingers
* next 8 meas.
Ev - 'ry thing still remains the same.
I can't do what
let ring
ten peo-ple tell me to do,
so I guess I'll re-main the same, yes. 3. I'm
F
let ring
Verse
Gtr. 1: w/ Rhy. Fig. 1 (2 times)
B
B B♭ A
sit-tin' here rest-ing my bones,
and this lone - li-ness won't leave me a-lone,
yes.

D.S. al Coda 2
G
B
C
B B♭ A
Two thou - sand miles I roamed
just to make this a dock my home.
Now, I'm just gon-na
let ring

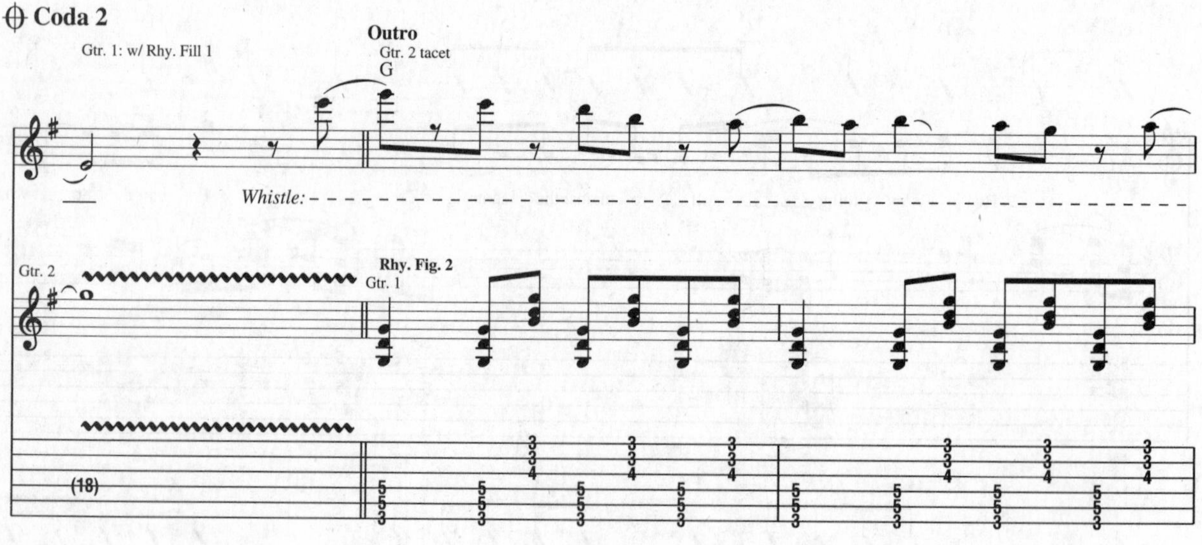
Coda 2
Gtr. 1: w/ Rhy. Fill 1
Outro
Gtr. 2 tacet
G
Whistle:
Gtr. 2
Rhy. Fig. 2
Gtr. 1

E
Begin fade
Gtr. 1: w/ Rhy. Fig. 2 (till fade)
G
Whistle:
End Rhy. Fig. 2

E
G
Fade out
Whistle:

Smells Like Teen Spirit

Words and Music by Kurt Cobain, Chris Novoselic and David Grohl

Pre-Chorus
3rd time, Gtr. 3 tacet
(F5) (B♭5) (A♭5) (D♭5) (F5) (B♭5) (A♭5) (D♭5)
Hel - lo, hel - lo, hel - lo, how low? Hel - lo, hel - lo, hel - lo, how low?
Gtrs. 1 & 2
let ring
(F5) (B♭5) (A♭5) (D♭5) (F5) (B♭5) (A♭5) (D♭5)
Hel - lo, hel - lo, hel - lo, how low? Hel - lo, hel - lo, hel - lo. With the lights
let ring
w/ dist.
Chorus
Gtrs. 1 & 2: w/ Rhy. Fig. 1 (6 times)
Fsus4 B♭ G/A A♭sus4 D♭ G/A Fsus4 B♭ G/A A♭sus4 D♭ G/A
out it's less dan - g'rous. Here we are now, en - ter - tain us. I feel stu -
Fsus4 B♭ G/A A♭sus4 D♭ G/A Fsus4 B♭ G/A A♭sus4 D♭ G/A
- pid and con - ta - gious. Here we are now, en - ter - tain us. A mul - la -
To Coda
Fsus4 B♭ G/A A♭sus4 D♭ G/A Fsus4 B♭ G/A A♭sus4 D♭ G/A
- to, an al - bi - no, a mos - qui - to, my li - bi - do. Yeah,
Bridge
F5 E5 F5 G♭5 N.C. F5/C E5/B F5/C B♭5 A♭5 C/E F5 E5 F5 G♭5 N.C
yay, yay.
Gtrs. 1 & 2

1.
2.
F5/C E5/B F5/C B♭5 A5 A♭5
Gtr. 3 (dist.)
w/ chorus & compression
fdbk.
don't pick
*Vol. swell
Gtrs. 1 & 2
Guitar Solo
Gtrs. 1 & 2: w/ Rhy. Fig. 1 (8 times)
Fsus4 B♭ G/A A♭sus4 D♭ G/A

Interlude
N.C.(F5) (B♭5) (A♭5) (D♭5) (F5) (B♭5) (A♭5) (D♭5)
compressor off
*fdbk.
pitch: C
*cresc. poco a poco
Verse
N.C.(F5) (B♭5) (A♭5) (D♭5) (F5) (B♭5) (A♭5) (D♭5)
3. And I for - get just why I taste. Oo, yeah, I guess it makes you smile,
fdbk.
pitches: D♭ C
(F5) (B♭5) (A♭5) (D♭5) (F5) (B♭5) (A♭5) (D♭5)
D.S. al Coda
I found it hard it's hard to find. Oh well, what ev - er, nev - er mind.
pitches: E D♭ C
Coda
Outro
Gtrs.1 & 2: w/ Rhy. Fig. 1 (4 times)
A♭sus4 D♭ G/A Fsus4 B♭ G/A A♭sus4 D♭ G/A Fsus4 B♭ G/A A♭sus4 D♭ G/A
- do, a de-ni - al, a de-ni - al, a de-ni - al, a de-ni - al, a de-ni -
F5
- al!
Gtrs. 1 & 2
fdbk.
pitch: C
C A

Smokin' in the Boys Room

Words and Music by Michael Koda and Michael Lutz

C5
B5
C5
D♯5
Lis - ten - in' to the teach - er rap just ain't my bag. But when
Look - in' in the stalls, nah, there ain't no - bod - y here.
E5
B5
two bells ring, you know it's my cue. I'm
My bud - dies Sixx. Mick, and Tom, to
Chorus
C5
B5
C5
A5
A6
A5
A6
gon - na meet the boys on floor num - ber two.
get caught would sure - ly or the death of us all.
Smok - in' in the boy's room.
Rhy. Fig. 1
P.M.

1st time, Gtr. 2 (dist.): w/ Fill 1
2nd time, Gtr. 2: w/ Fill 2

A5 A6 A5 A6 E5 E6 E5 E6 E5 E6 E5 E6

Smok - in' in the boy's room. Now, teach -

P.M.

Gtr. 2 tacet

To Coda

B5 B6 B5 B6 B5 A5 A6 A5 A6 B5 B6 B5 B6

- er, don't fill me up with your rules, 'cause ev - 'ry - bod - y knows that

End Rhy. Fig. 1

P.M.

Fill 1
Gtr. 2

15 ma *loco*

f 1/2 1/2 1 1/4 1/4

P.H.

Pitch: F♯ E

Fill 2
Gtr. 2

15ma *loco*

1/2 1/4 1/4 1/4

P.H.

Pitch: E

1.
A5
D♯5
E5
D♯5
E5
D♯5
smok - in' ain't al - lowed in school.
2.
A5
D♯5
E5
smok - in' ain't al - lowed in school. Spoken: Hey, can I be excused?
Harmonica Solo
A5 A6 A5 A6 A5 A6 A5 A6 A5 E5 E6 E5 E6 E5 E6 E5 E6 E5
Rhy. Fig. 2
P.M. throughout
A5 A6 A5 A6 A5 A6 A5 A6 A5 B5 B6 B5 B6 B5 B6 B5 B6 B5
Gtr. 3 (dist.)
w/ slide
Gtr. 1
End Rhy. Fig. 2

Guitar Solo
Gtr. 1: w/ Rhy. Fig. 2
Gtr. 3 tacet
Gtr. 3
Gtr. 2
Gtr. 2 tacet
Gtr. 1: w/ Rhy. Fig. 2 (1st 6 meas.)
A5 A6 A5 A6 A5 A5 A6 A5 A6 A5 E5 E6 E5 E6 E5
E6 E5 E6 E5 A5 A6 A5 A6 A5 A6 A5 A6 A5
B5 B6 B5 B6 B5 B6 B5 B6 B5 A5 A6 A5 A6 A5
A6 A5 A6 A5 E5 E6 E5 E6 E5 E6 E5 E6 E5
15ma
loco
8va
P.H.
Pitch: E F♯
B
A5 A6 A5 A6 A5 A6 A5 A6 A5
loco

Gtr. 3 tacet
F#5
F#6
F#5
B5
D#5
Verse
Gtr. 2 tacet
E5
D#5
2. Well,
put me to work in the
Gtr. 2
Gtr. 1
E5
B5
C5
B5
C5
D#5
school book store
check - out count - er, and I got bored.
Gtr. 1
E5
D#5
E5
B5
C5
B5
C5
D.S. al Coda
Teach - er was look - in' for me all a - round.
Two hours lat - er, you know where I was found.

Coda
A5
D#5
E5
F#5
G5
G#5
smok - in' ain't al - lowed in school.
Outro-Chorus
Gtr. 1 tacet
N.C.
Smok - in' in the boy's room.
Smok - in' in the boy's room.
1.
2.
I tell you, I was
Hey, teach -
B5
B6
A6
- er, don't ya fill me up with your rules, 'cause ev - 'ry - bod - y knows that
Gtr. 1
P.M.
Gtr. 1: w/ Rhy. Fig. 1
Smok - in' in the boy's room.
Gtr. 2
15ma
P.H.
Pitch: F#

A5 A6 A5 A6 E5 E6 E5 E6 E5 E6 E5 E6
Smok - in' in the boy's room. Now, teach -
loco
P.H.
1 1/4 1/4
(7) 5 5 5 7
14 13 12 14 13 12 12 14 (14)
Pitch: G♯
Gtr. 2 tacet
B5 B6 B5 B6 B5 A5 A6 A5 A6 A5
er, I ain't fool - in' a - round with your rules, 'cause
Gtr. 1: w/ Rhy. Fill 1
B5 B6 B5 B6 A5
ev - 'ry - bod - y knows that smok - in' ain't al - lowed in school.
Slower
E9
Free time
Gtr. 2
w/ bar & misc. fdbk.
7 6 9 7 7 (7) 7 7 7 7 6 7
Gtr. 1
2 4 2 2 (2) 0 0
Rhy. Fill 1
Gtr. 1
7
5

Smooth

Words by Rob Thomas
Music by Rob Thomas and Itaal Shur

Am
F
E7
my Span - ish Har - lem Mo - na Li - sa.
Well, you're my rea - son for
full
full
full
Dm7
Dm7/C Bm7♭5
E/G♯
Am
F
E7
rea - son,
the step in my groove,
yeah.
And if you said
Chorus
Gtr. 1 tacet
this life ain't good e - nough,
I would give
my world
to lift you up.
I could change
G7
my life to bet - ter suit your mood
be-cause you're so
Gtr. 1
let ring
F♯7sus4
smooth.
Well, and it's just like the o - cean

Gtr. 1 tacet
Am F E7
un - der the moon. Well, it's the same as the e - mo - tion that I get from you. You
Am F E7 Dm7 E7
got the kind of lov - in' that can be so smooth, yeah. Gim - me your heart, make it real.
Gtr. 1
N.C.
Interlude
Am F E7 Am F E7
Or else for - get a - bout it.
fdbk.
1/2
fdbk.
full
Verse
Am F E7
3. Well, I'll tell you one thing, if you would leave it'd be a
Am F E7 Dm7 Dm7/C Bm7♭5 E/G♯
cry - in' shame. In ev - 'ry breath and ev - 'ry word I hear your name call - in' me
full

Am
F
E7
out,
yeah.
Verse
Am
F
E7
4. Well, out from the bar - ri - o
1/2
Am
F
E7
you hear my rhy - thm on your ra - di - o.
And you feel the turn - ing of the
Dm7
Dm7/C
Bm7♭5
E/G♯
Am
F
E7
world, so soft and slow, turn - in' you round and
mp
mf
full
* roll tone control off.
Chorus
Gtr. 1 tacet
Am
F
E7
round. And if you said this life ain't good e - nough, I would give
full
Am
F
E7
Am
F
E7
my world to lift you up. I could change my life to bet - ter suit your mood.

Dm7
Dm7/C Bm7♭5
G7
F♯7sus4
E7
be - cause you're so ___ smooth. ___
full
full
full
Am
F
E7
Well, and it's just like the o - cean un - der the moon. _ Well, it's the
same as the e - mo - tion that I get from you. ___ You got the kind of lov - in' that can
be so smooth _ yeah.
Dm7
E+7
N.C.
Gim - me your heart, _ make it real. Or else for - get a - bout it.

Guitar Solo

Am F E7
Am F E7
Am F E7
Am F E7
Am F E7
Am F E7
Am F E7
8va
Dm7 Dm7/C Bm7♭5
G7 F#7sus4 E7
And it's
loco
full
1/2
hold bend

Chorus
Am F E7 Am F E7
just like the o - cean un - der the moon. Well, it's the same as the e - mo - tion that I
Am F E7
get from you. You got the kind of lov - in' that can be so smooth, yeah.
Outro-Guitar Solo
Dm7 E7 N.C. Am F E7
Gim - me your heart, make it real. Or else for - get a - bout it. Or else for - get a - bout it.
fdbk.
1/2
Am F E7 Am F E7
Ah, let's all for - get a - bout it. Ah, let's all for - get a - bout it.
fdbk.
full
fdbk.
full

Am F E7 Am F E7
Ah, let's all for - get a - bout it, yeah.
(Gim - me your heart, make it real. Or else for - get a - bout it.
Ah,
Let's all for - get a - bout it.
let's all for - get a - bout it.
Am F E7
Yeah, ah no. Oh, let's all for - get a - bout it.
Am F E7
Oh, no, no. Oh, let's all for - get a - bout it.
8va
Am F E7
Hey, ah. Oh, let's all for - get a - bout it.
8va

Am
F
E7
8va
full
Am
F
E7
full
8va
loco
Am
F
E7
Am
F
E7
Begin Fade
Am
F
E7
8va
Am
8va
F
E7
full
Am
8va
F
E7
1/2
Am
F
E7
Fade Out
8va
Am
F
E7

Somebody to Love

Words and Music by Darby Slick

A
E
F#m
B VII
E
Bsus2/E
End Rhy. Fig. 1
F#m
Bsus2/E
love some-bod-y to love?
You bet-ter find some - bod-y to love.
hold bend
1/2
1
f
Interlude
F#m
B6/E
F#m
Love.
Verse
F#m
Rhy. Fig. 2
B
E
F#m
2. When the gar - den flow-ers, ba - by, are
mf

B
E
A
F#m
5
open
B
E
F#m
End Rhy. Fig. 2
dead. Yes, and your mind, your mind is so full of red.
Chorus
Gtr. 1: w/ Rhy. Fig. 1
B
E
A
E
F#m
B
Don't you want some - bod - y to love? Don't you
let ring
A
E
F#m
B
A
E
need some - bod - y to love? Would - n't you love some - bod - y to love?
F#m
B
E
Bsus2/E
F#m
Gtr. 1
You bet - ter find some - bod - y to love.
3. Your eyes,

Verse
A
B VII
I say, your eyes may look like his. Yeah, but
p
F♯m
B
E
A
5
open
F♯m
in your head, baby, I'm a-fraid you don't know where it is.
Chorus
Gtr. 1: w/ Rhy. Fig. 1
A
B VII
A
E
F♯m
B
Don't you want some-bod-y to love? Don't you
(Don't you
let ring
1/2

A
E
F♯m
B
A
E
need some-bod-y to love?
need some - bod-y to love?)
Would - n't you love some - bod - y to love?
F♯m
B
E
Bsus2/E
F♯m
E
Interlude
Gtr. 1
You bet-ter find some - bod - y to love.
B VII
A
E
F♯m
E5
open
let ring
Verse
Gtr. 1: w/ Rhy. Fig. 2
F♯m
B
E
F♯m
4. Tears are run - ning, they're all run - ning down your breast.

B E F#m B E
And your friends, baby, they treat you
F#m B E
Chorus
A E
Rhy. Fig. 3
Gtr. 1
like a guest. Don't you want some-bod-y to love?
B5 E A E B5
6 open
mp f
Don't you need some-bod-y to love? Would-n't you
(Don't you?)

* Microphonic fdbk., not caused by string vibration.

Outro-Guitar Solo
Gr. 1: w/ Rhy. Fig. 4 (2 times)
F♯m
E
B
E
open
Rhy. Fig. 4
End Rhy. Fig. 4
fdbk.
1/2
1
mf
f
Gtr. 1
Gtr. 1: w/ Rhy. Fig. 3
A
B5
A5
let ring

Soul Man

Words and Music by Isaac Hayes and David Porter

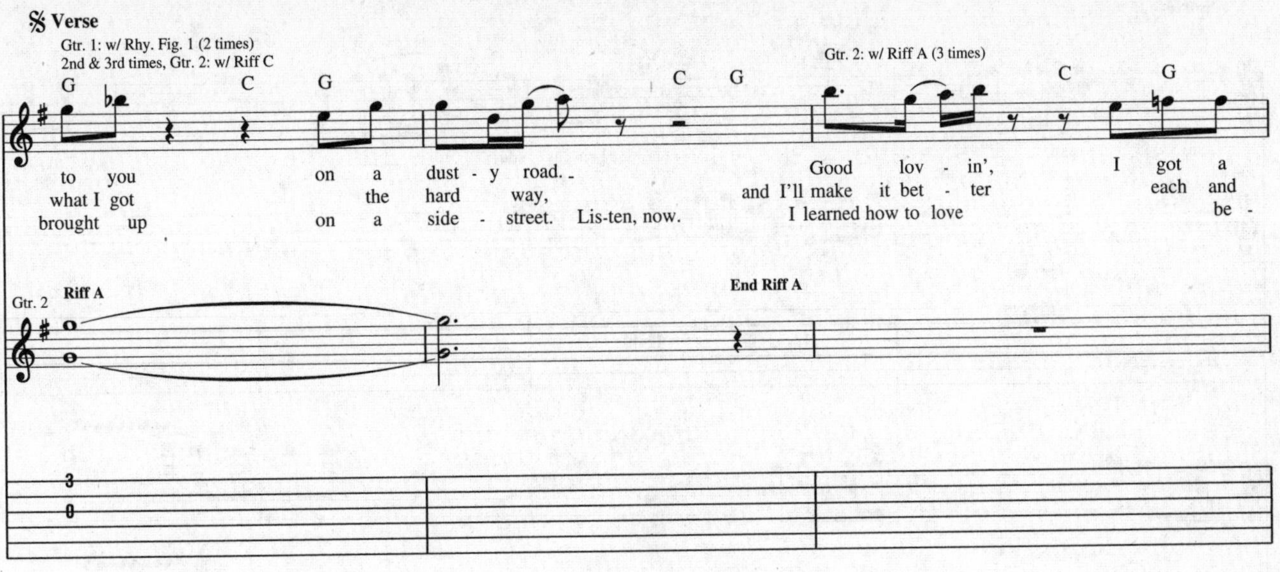
Verse
Gtr. 1: w/ Rhy. Fig. 1 (2 times)
2nd & 3rd times, Gtr. 2: w/ Riff C
Gtr. 2: w/ Riff A (3 times)
G C G C G C G
to you on a dust - y road. Good lov - in', I got a
what I got the hard way, and I'll make it bet - ter each and
brought up on a side - street. Lis-ten, now. I learned how to love be -
Gtr. 2
Riff A
End Riff A
3
0

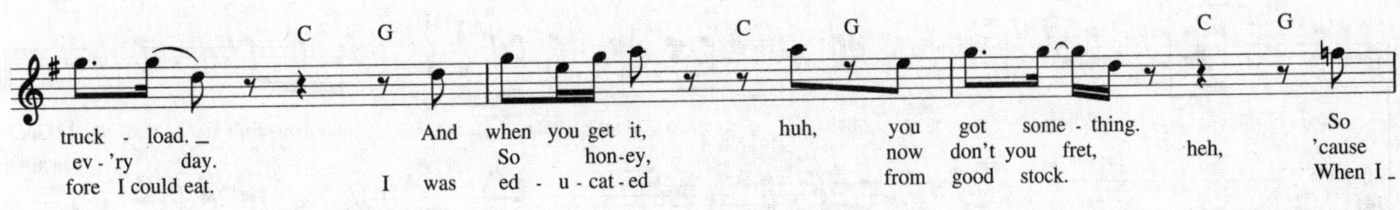
C G C G C G
truck - load. And when you get it, huh, you got some - thing. So
ev - 'ry day. So hon-ey, now don't you fret, heh, 'cause
fore I could eat. I was ed - u - cat - ed from good stock. When I

2nd time, To Coda 1
3rd time, To Coda 2
C G C G
don't wor - ry, 'cause I'm com - in'.
you ain't seen noth - ing yet. I'm a
start lov - in', oh, I can't stop.

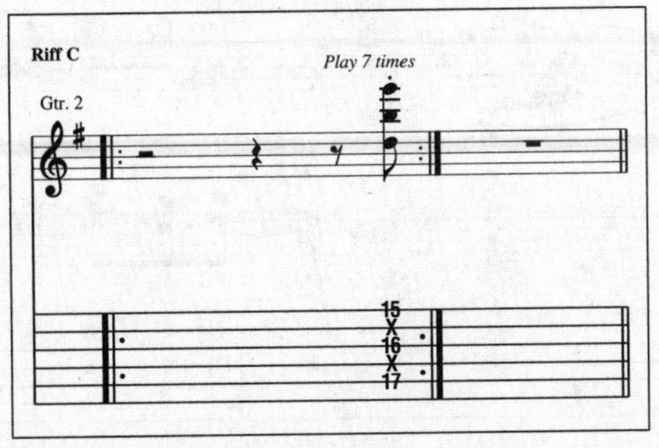
Riff C
Play 7 times
Gtr. 2
15
X
16
X
17

Chorus
G
F
G
soul
man.
Ow.
I'm a
soul
man.
I'm a
Gtr. 2
Riff B
Gtr. 1
w/ slide
D.S. al Coda 1
F
G
C
D
soul
man.
Whoa,
heh.
I'm a
soul
man,
and that ain't all,
huh.
2. Got
End Riff B
Coda 1
Chorus
Gtr. 2: w/ Riff B
G
F
soul
man.
Oh,
Lord.
I'm a
Gtr. 1

G
soul
man.
Spoken: Play it, Steve.
I'm a
soul
man.
w/ slide
D.S. al Coda 2
F
Huh.
I'm a
G
soul
man.
C
Oh.
(Oh.)
D
3. I was
Coda 2
Chorus
Gtr. 2: w/ Riff B
G
soul
man.
F
I'm a
Gtr. 1
G
soul
man.
I'm a
soul
man.
w/ slide

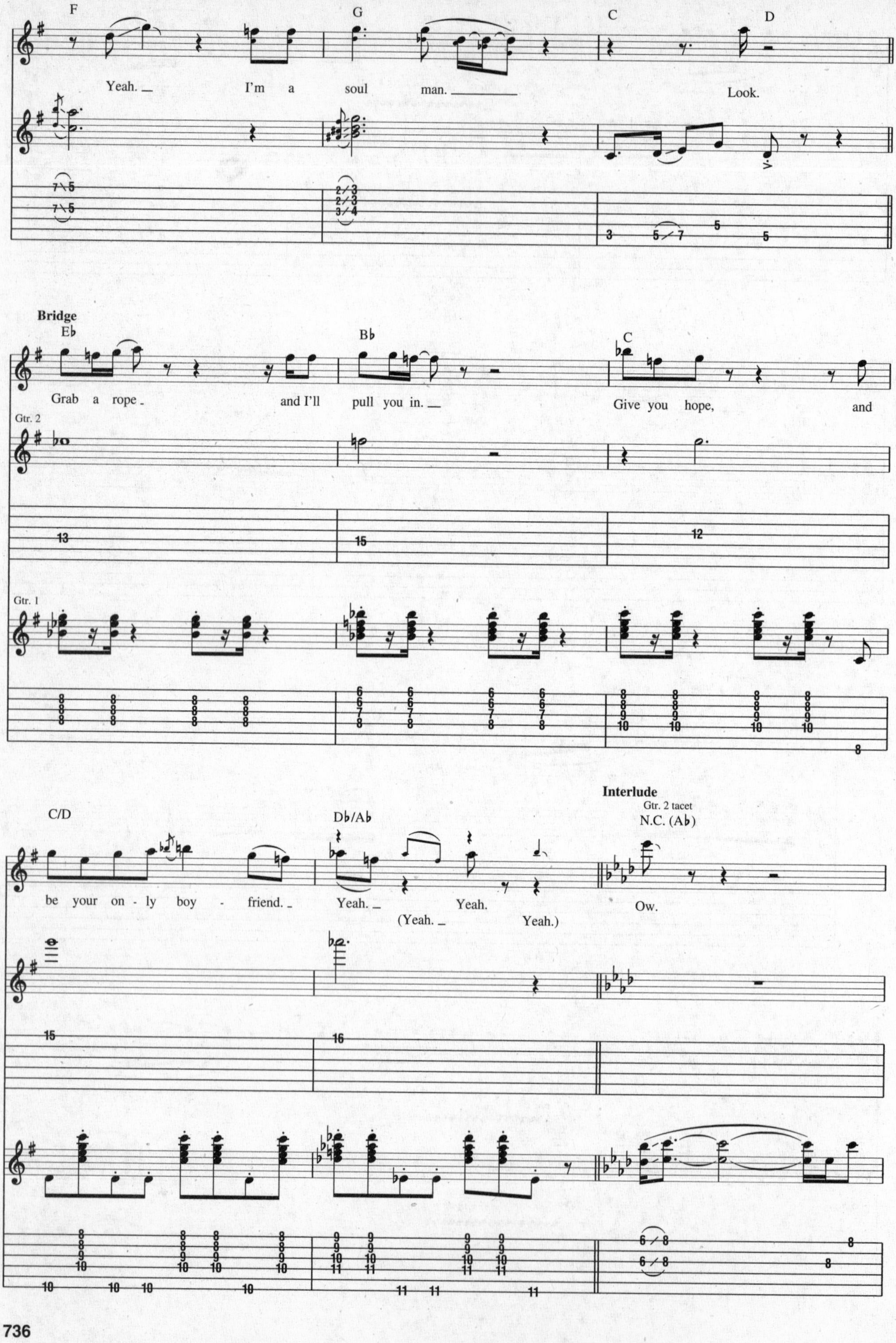

F G C D

Yeah. I'm a soul man. Look.

Bridge

Eb Bb C

Grab a rope and I'll pull you in. Give you hope, and

Gtr. 2

Gtr. 1

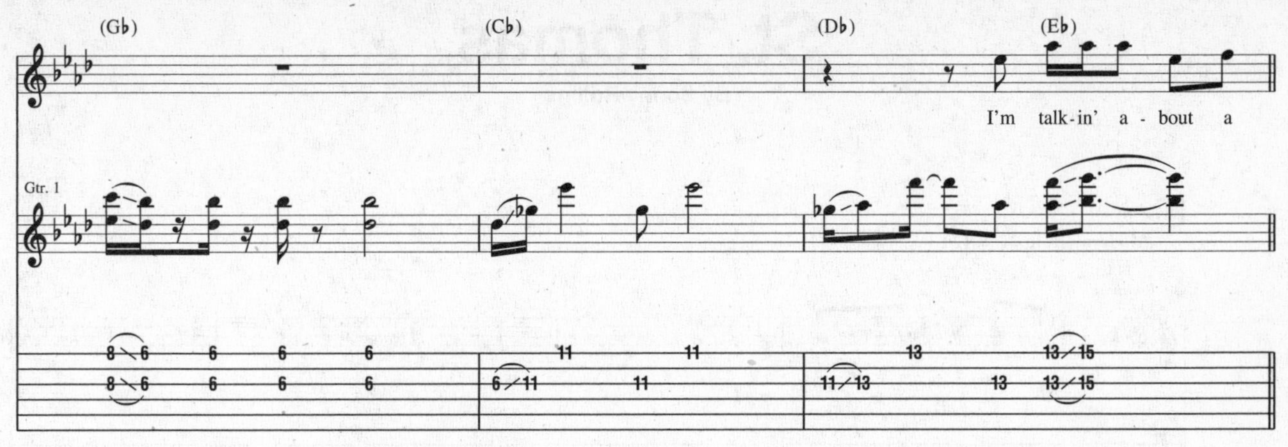

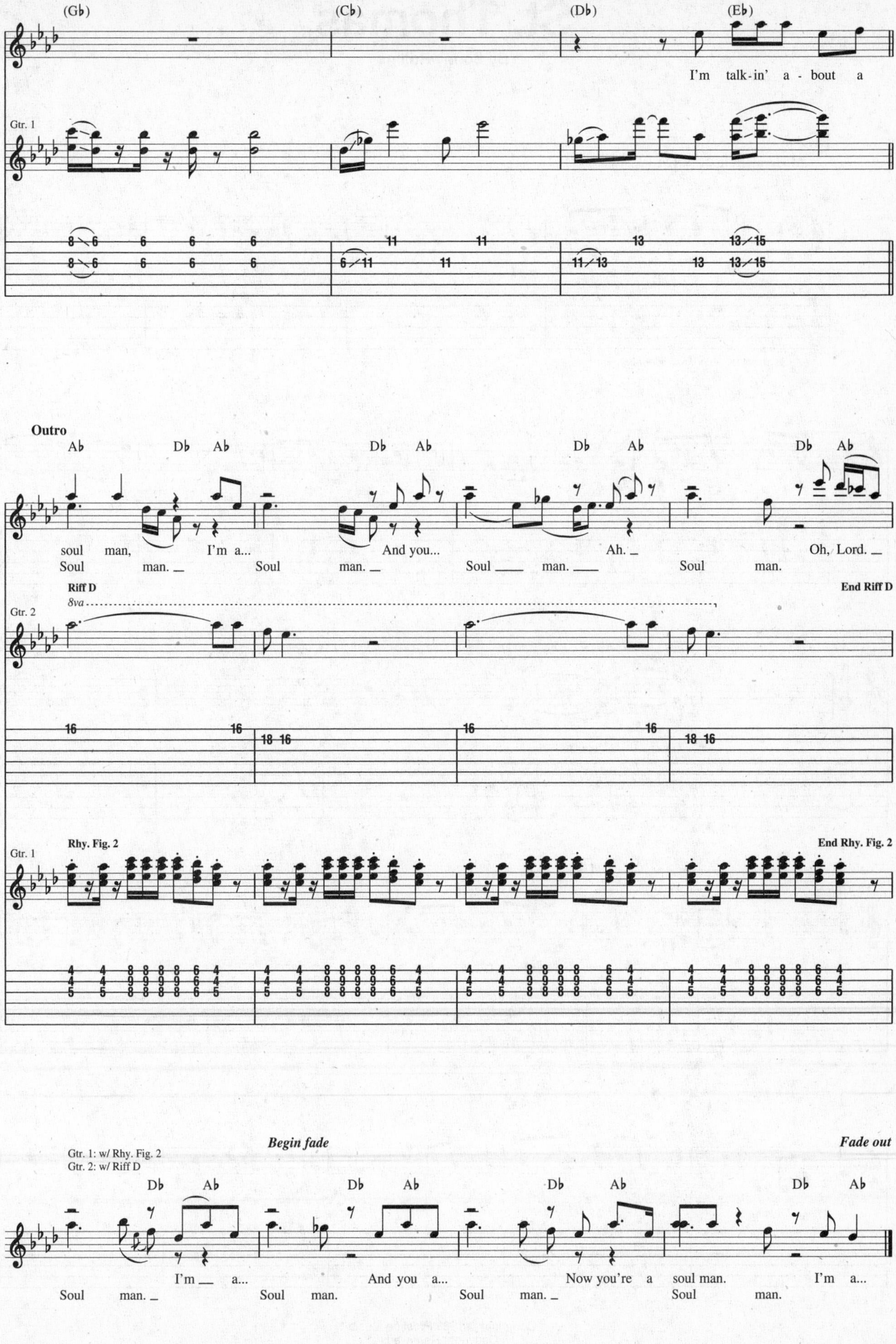

Outro

A♭ D♭ A♭ D♭ A♭ D♭ A♭ D♭ A♭

soul man, I'm a... And you... Ah. Oh, Lord.

Soul man. Soul man. Soul man. Soul man.

Riff D

Gtr. 2

8va

End Riff D

Rhy. Fig. 2

Gtr. 1

End Rhy. Fig. 2

St. Thomas

By Sonny Rollins

Em7
A7
Dm7
G7
C
C/E
F
F#°
G
N.C.
C
C
P.M.
let ring
Dm7
G7
C
let ring
let ring simile
Dm7
G7
C
Em7
A7
Dm7
G7
C
C/E
F
F#°
G
D
C
Dm7
G7
C

Dm7
G7
C
Em7
A7
Dm7
G7
C
C/E
F
F#°
G
C/G
E
C
G
C
G
C
Em7
A7
Dm7
G7
C
C/E
F
F#°
G
F/G
F
C
Dm7
G7
Dm7
G7

C
Em7
A7
Dm7
G7
C
Em7
let ring
A7
Dm7
G7
C
C/E
F
F#°
let ring
G
G
C/G
G
C
G
C
G
Em7
A7
Dm7
G7
C
C/E
F
F#°
G
H
C

C#°
C
C#°
Em7
A7#9#5
Dm7
A♭7
G7#9
C
C/E
F
F#°
C/G
Am7
Dm7
G7
I
C6/9
Dm11/G
mp
* w/ vol. knob
C6/9
Dm11/G
Em7#5
A7
Dm7♭5
G7
C
C/E
F
F#°

J
G
C6/9
F6/9/D
F6/9/G
C6/9
F6/9/D
F6/9/G
Em7♭5
A7
Dm7
G13
C
C/E
K
F
F#°
G
C
D♭
C
B♭add9
Em7
B♭7
A7
Dm7
G7

C
C/E
F
F♯°
G
L
C6/9
Dm11/G
C6/9
Dm11/G
Em7♭5
A7
Dm7
G13
C
C/E
F
F♯°
G
M
C
Dm7
G7
C

G
Em7
A7
Dm7
G7
C
C/E
F
F#°
G
G#°
Am7
D7
G7
N
N.C.
E7#9
A7
Dm7
G13
C7#9
C7#9/E
F
F#°
G

O
C
Dm7 G7 C
mf
Dm7 G7 C
Em7
A7
Dm7
G7
C C/E
F F#°
C/G
G7 C
P
C
P.M.
Dm7
D♭
C
P.M.
Am7
D
Em7
A7
Dm7
let ring
G7
C C/E
F F#°
A♭
A♭+ Csus2
let ring
let ring

Stayin' Alive

from the Motion Picture SATURDAY NIGHT FEVER

Words and Music by Barry Gibb, Maurice Gibb and Robin Gibb

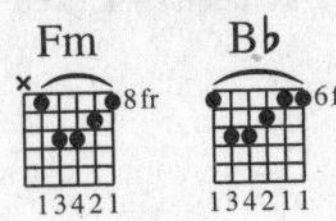

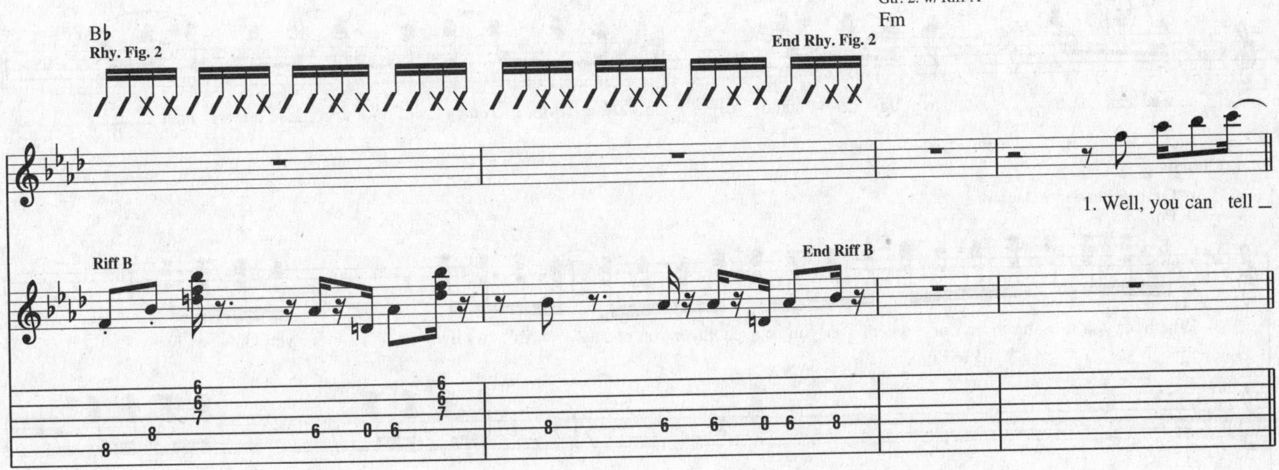

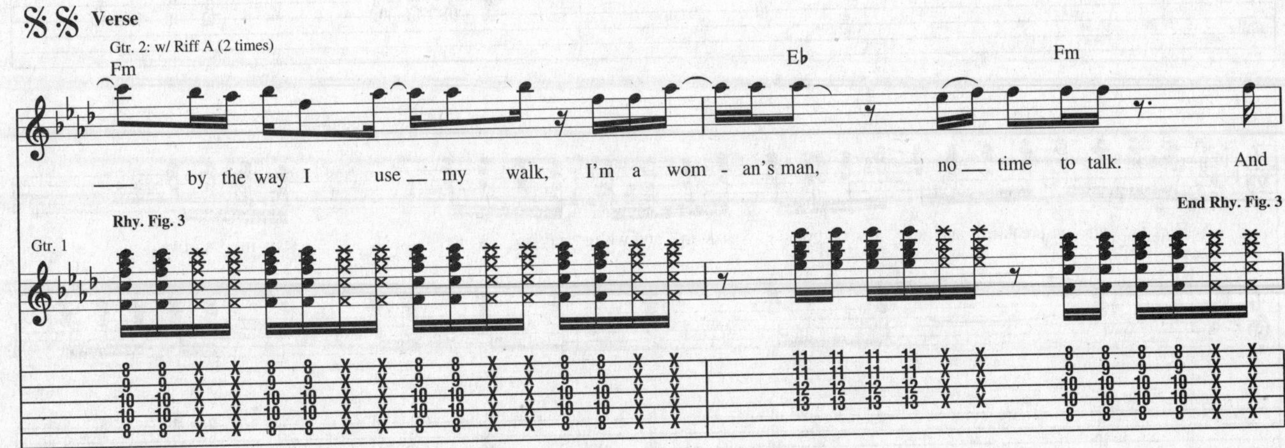

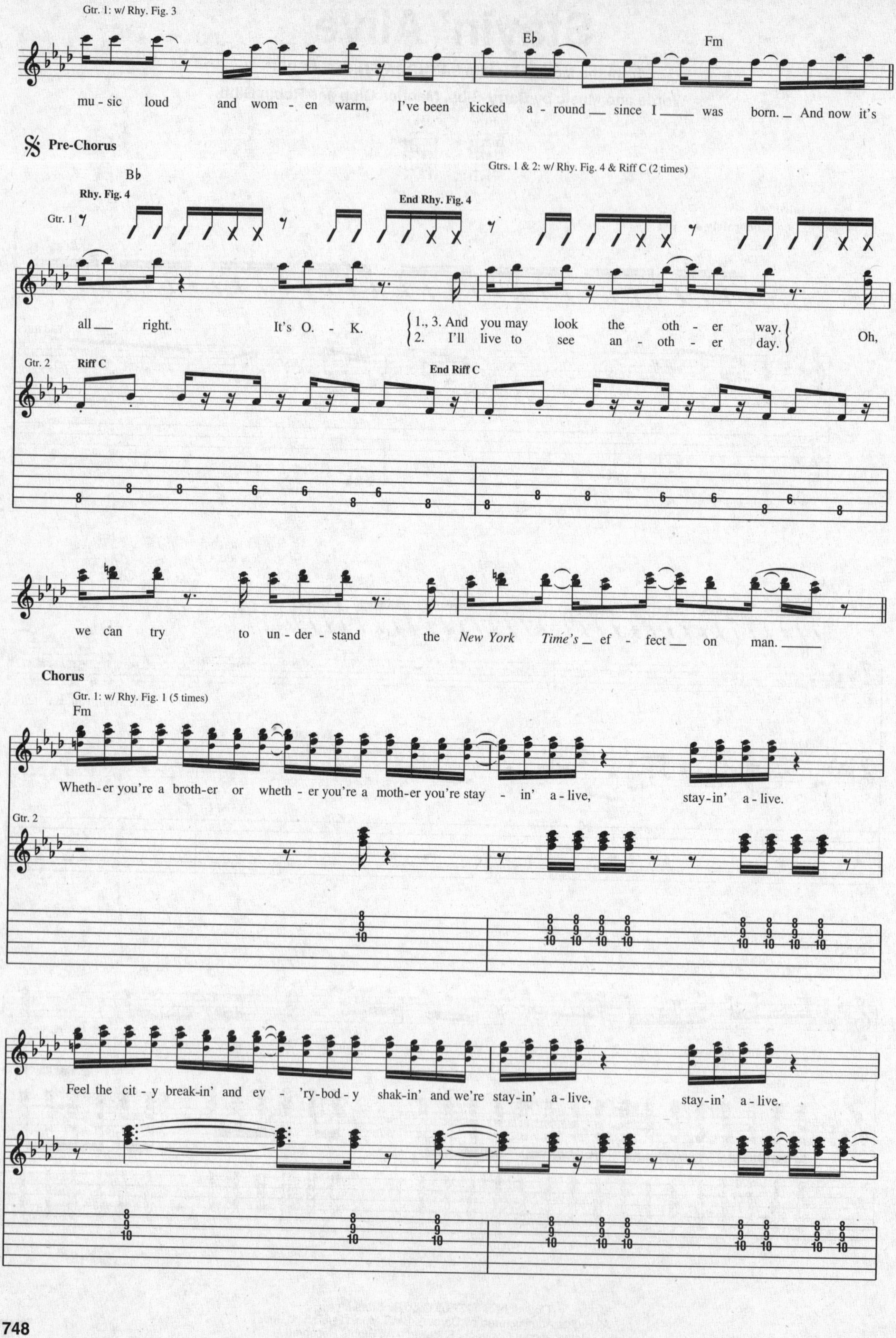

Gtr. 1: w/ Rhy. Fig. 3

E♭ Fm

mu-sic loud and wom-en warm, I've been kicked a-round since I was born. And now it's

𝄋 Pre-Chorus

B♭

Gtrs. 1 & 2: w/ Rhy. Fig. 4 & Riff C (2 times)

Rhy. Fig. 4 End Rhy. Fig. 4

Gtr. 1

all right. It's O. - K. {1., 3. And you may look the oth-er way. / 2. I'll live to see an-oth-er day.} Oh,

Gtr. 2 Riff C End Riff C

we can try to un-der-stand the *New York Time's* ef-fect on man.

Chorus

Gtr. 1: w/ Rhy. Fig. 1 (5 times)

Fm

Wheth-er you're a broth-er or wheth-er you're a moth-er you're stay-in' a-live, stay-in' a-live.

Gtr. 2

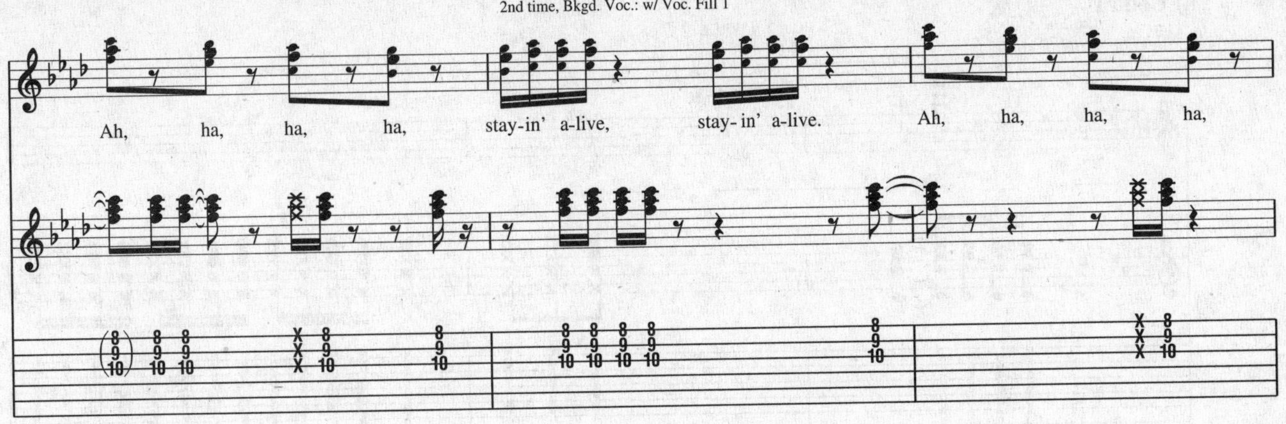
2nd time, Bkgd. Voc.: w/ Voc. Fill 1
Ah, ha, ha, ha, stay-in' a-live, stay-in' a-live. Ah, ha, ha, ha,

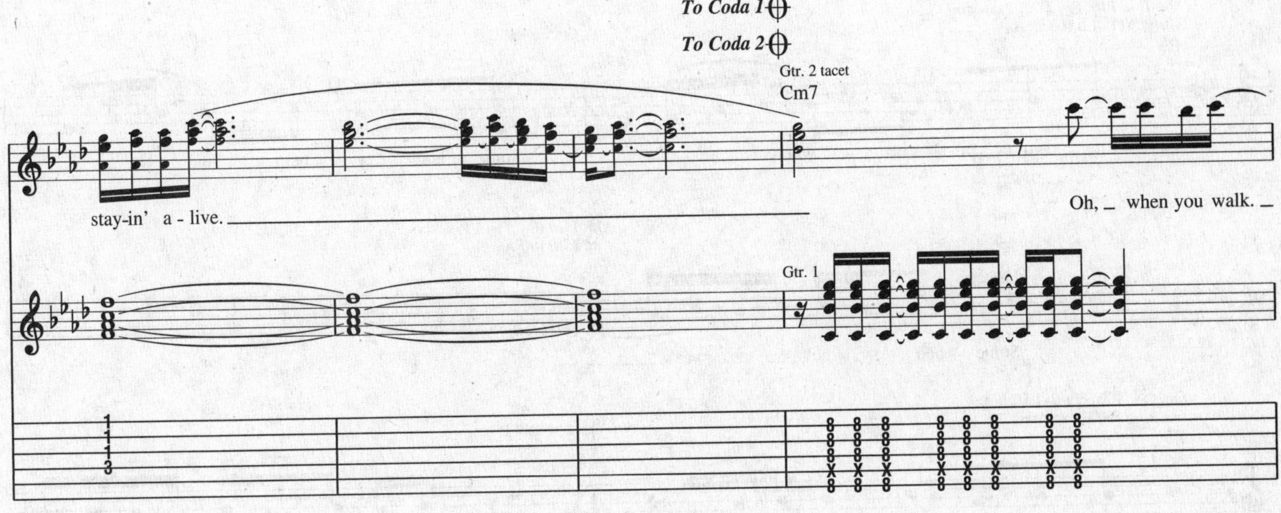
To Coda 1
To Coda 2
Gtr. 2 tacet
Cm7
stay-in' a - live.
Oh, when you walk.
Gtr. 1

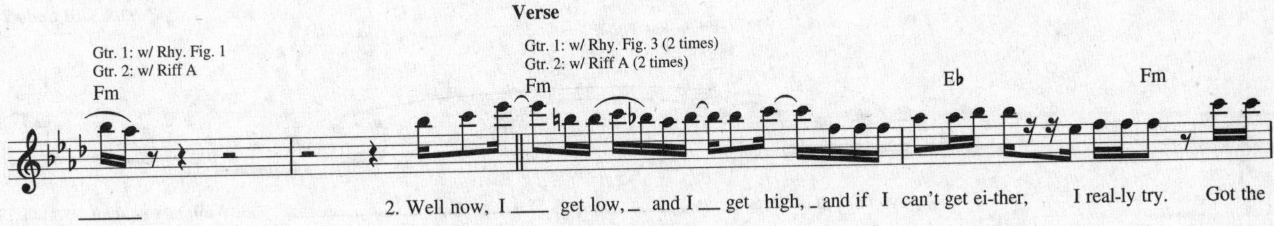
Verse
Gtr. 1: w/ Rhy. Fig. 1
Gtr. 2: w/ Riff A
Fm
Gtr. 1: w/ Rhy. Fig. 3 (2 times)
Gtr. 2: w/ Riff A (2 times)
Fm
Eb
Fm
2. Well now, I get low, and I get high, and if I can't get ei-ther, I real-ly try. Got the

D.S. al Coda 1
Eb
Fm
wings of heav - en on my shoes. I'm a danc - in' man, and I just can't lose. You know it's

Voc. Fill 1
(Oh.)

Coda 1
Gtr. 2 tacet
Cm7
Gtr. 2: w/ Riff A
N.C.
Fm
Ah.
Gtr. 1
Bridge
Gtr. 1: w/ Rhy. Fig. 2 (1 1/2 times)
Gtr. 2: w/ Riff B (1st meas.)
B♭
Gtr. 2: w/ Riff B
Life go - in' no - where.
Some - bod - y help me
Some - bod - y help me, yeah.
Gtr. 1: w/ Rhy. Fig. 1
Gtr. 2: w/ Riff A
Fm
Gtr. 1: w/ Rhy. Fig. 2 (1 1/2 times)
Gtr. 2: w/ Riff B (1st meas.)
B♭
Gtr. 2: w/ Riff B
Life go - in' no - where.
Some - bod - y help me, yeah.
D.S.S. al Coda 2
Gtr. 1: w/ Rhy. Fig. 1
Gtr. 2: w/ Riff A
Fm
I'm stay - in' a - live.
3. Well, you can tell
Coda 2
Gtr. 2 tacet
Cm7
Gtr. 2: w/ Riff A
Fm
Oh, yeah.
Gtr. 1

Outro

Gtr. 1: w/ Rhy. Fig. 2 (1 1/2 times)
Gtr. 2: w/ Riff B (1st meas.)
Gtr. 2: w/ Riff B
B♭
Life go - in' no - where.
Some - bod - y help me

Gtrs. 1 & 2: w/ Rhy. Fig. 1 & Riff A
2nd time, Bkgd. Voc.: w/ Voc. Fill 2
3rd time, Bkgd. Voc.: w/ Voc. Fill 3
4th time, Bkgd. Voc.: w/ Voc. Fill 4
Fm
Some - bod - y help me, yeah.
Yeah.

Gtrs. 1 & 2: w/ Rhy. Fig. 2 & Riff B
B♭
Life go - in' no - where.
Some - bod - y help me, yeah.

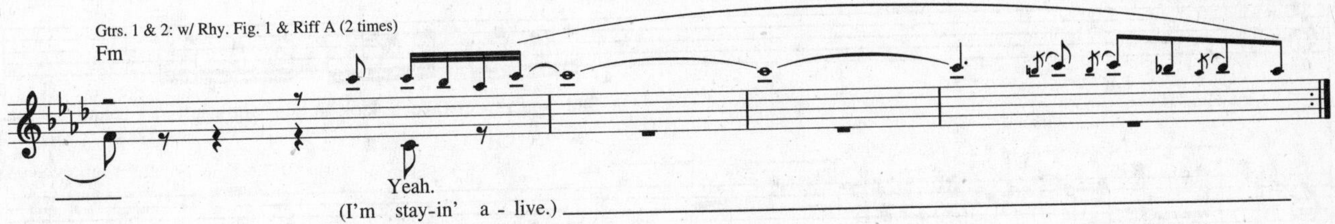
Play 4 times and fade
Gtrs. 1 & 2: w/ Rhy. Fig. 1 & Riff A (2 times)
Fm
Yeah.
(I'm stay-in' a - live.)

Voc. Fill 2
(Ah, ah, ah.)

Voc. Fill 3
(Ah, ah, ah, ah.)

Voc. Fill 4
8va
loco
(Oh, ha, ha.)

Still Alive and Well

Words and Music by Rick Derringer

(C5)
(G5)
E
They tried to get me lots of times and now they're
1/4
sl.
F♯m
N.C.(G)
com-in' af-ter you.
I got out and I'm here to say,
*T T T T T T
H
H P
*T=thumb.
D5
E5
Chorus
A
Ba-by, you can get out too.
I'm still a-live and well,
I'm
sl.
*2nd and 3rd times, play w/slight variations ad lib (next 7 bars).
D
E
A
E
still a-live and well.
Ev-'ry now and then I know it's kind of hard to tell, but I'm
P

2nd time substitute Rhy. Fill 1
3rd time substitute Rhy. Fill 2
D5 C5 A5
A7 D A7
still a - live_ and well.___
Still a - live_ and well,___
D7 G D7
E7 A E7
2nd time to Coda I;
3rd time to Coda II
still a - live_ and well.___
Ev - 'ry now and then I know it's kind of hard to tell,
(2nd, 3rd times:) but I'm
D5 C5 A5
N.C(*E)
still a - live_ and well.___
Woo!
*Chord symbol implied by Bass.
Rhy. Fill 1
Rhy. Fill 2

2nd Verse
N.C.(A5)
(C5)
(G5)
When I think a-bout the past it on-ly brings me down.
Let's
(A5)
make love in the grass while the sun is shin-ing down.
It

E5
N.C.(F♯m)
feels so good, your long, blonde hair, ba - by, when you're way down low.
Full
let ring
G7
D5
E5
D.S. al Coda I
Make me shake, make the whole earth quake so ev - 'ry - one will know I'm
H
P
T
sl.
*T=thumb.
Coda I
D5
C5
A5
N.C.(*E)
still a - live and well. Ow!
*Chord symbol implied by Bass.
hold bend

Guitar solo
N.C.(*A5)
Spoken: Yeah!
*Some chord symbols implied by Bass, next 16 bars.
(C5)
(G5)
(A5)
(A)
(D)
(E)
(C)
Full
1/2
sl.
H
P
steady gliss.

(D) *Full
1/2
sl.
H
*Slightly bend 4th stg. along w/1st; bend 4th stg. 1/2 step only.
(E)
Full
hold bend
(D) (C) (A)
D.S. al Coda II
Coda II
D5 C5 A5
still a - live__ and well,__
still a - live__ and well,____
still a - live__ and well.____
Outro
I'm a - live__ and well.__

D5
N.C.(*A5)
D
Am7
I want to tell you, ba - by, I'm a-live and well.
Full
Full
sl.
*Some chord symbols implied by Bass, next 5 bars.
D5
N.C.(A5)
D5
N.C.(A5)
D5
N.C.(A5)
You know I don't mean may-be.
I'm a-live and well.
Ooh.
H
D5
A5
D5
Oh, I'm a-live and well.
I'm still a-live and well.
sl.
Free time
N.C.(A7)
sl.
sl.

Suffragette City

Words and Music by David Bowie

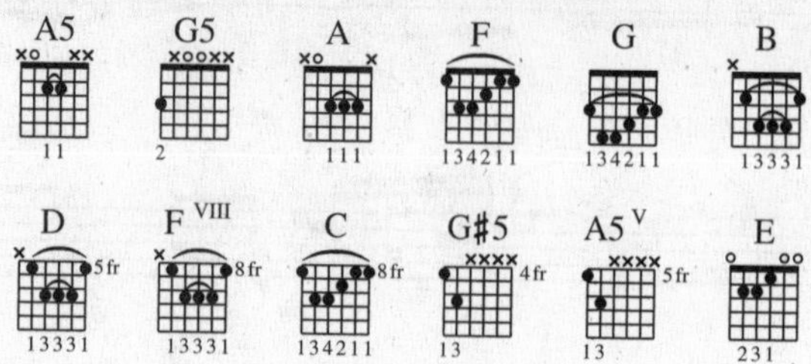

Intro

Moderate Rock ♩ = 138

A5 G5 A

Gtr. 2 (acous.)

Gtr. 1 (elec.)

mf w/ slight dist.

Gtr. 3 (elec.)

mf w/ dist.

1 1/2

Verse

Gtr. 3 tacet

A F G

Rhy. Fig. 1A

* **Voc. Fig. 1**

(Hey, man!

1. Ah, leave me a - lone, you know.

Rhy. Fig. 1

*Pertains to bkgd. vocs. only.

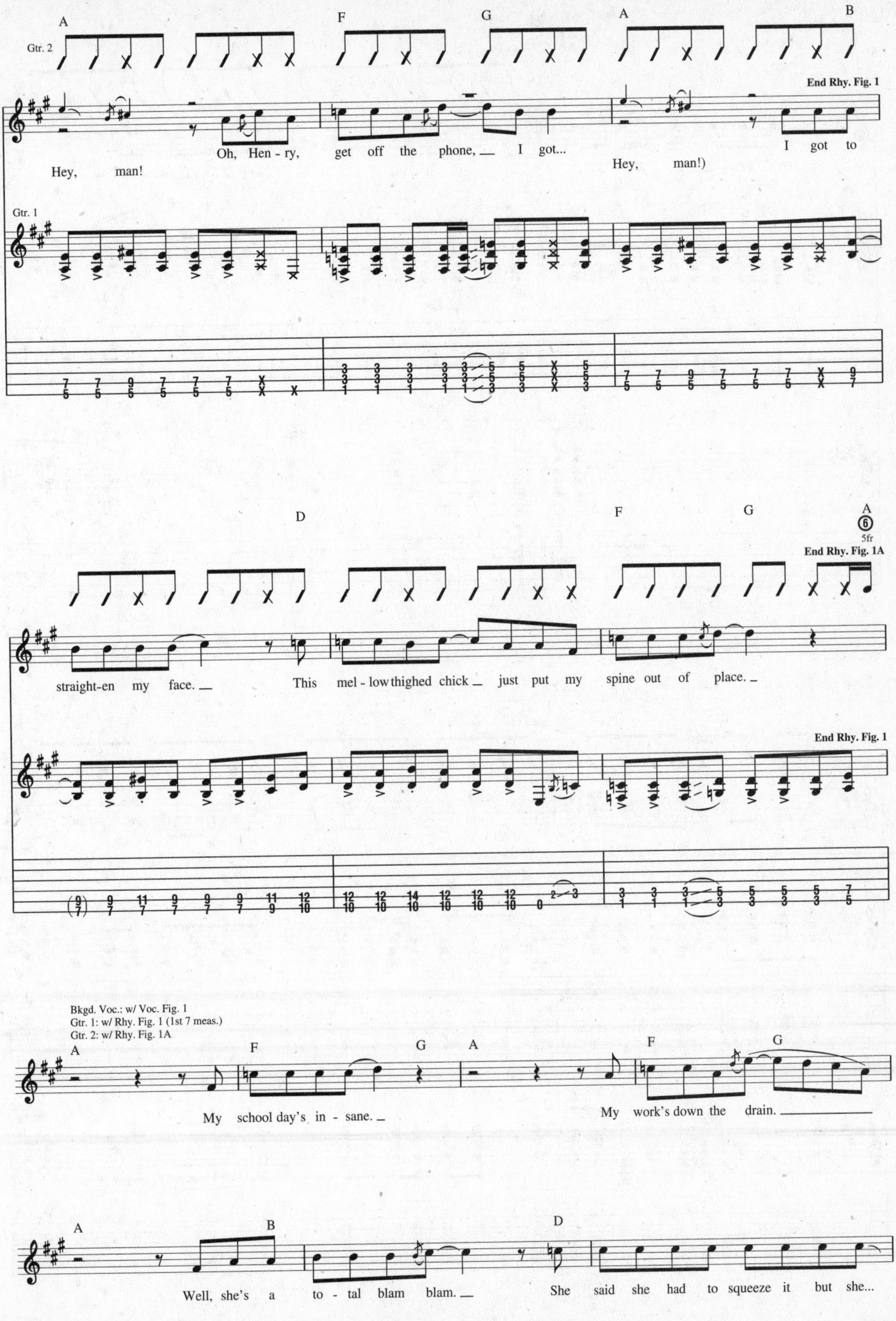

A F G A B

Gtr. 2

End Rhy. Fig. 1

Oh, Hen - ry, get off the phone, __ I got... I got to

Hey, man! Hey, man!)

Gtr. 1

D F G A

⑥ 5fr

End Rhy. Fig. 1A

straight-en my face. __ This mel - low thighed chick __ just put my spine out of place. _

End Rhy. Fig. 1

Bkgd. Voc.: w/ Voc. Fig. 1
Gtr. 1: w/ Rhy. Fig. 1 (1st 7 meas.)
Gtr. 2: w/ Rhy. Fig. 1A

A F G A F G

My school day's in - sane. _ My work's down the drain. ______

Chorus

F G A A D

Rhy. Fig. 2A

Gtr. 2

an' then she... Ah, _ don't _ lean on me, man, 'cause you can't af - ford the tick - et

Gtr. 1 (dist.)

Gtr. 1 Rhy. Fig. 2

Gtr. 3

Gtr. 3 Rhy. Fig. 2B

VIII F C G A

back from Suf - fra - gette Cit - y! Uh, don't _ lean on me, man, 'cause you

3rd time, To Coda 2
D
F VIII
C
G
G#5
A5 V
ain't got time to check it. You know my Suf - fra - gette Cit - y is out - ta
1/2
2nd time, To Coda 1
A5
G
3fr
A
End Rhy. Fig. 2A
sight! She's al - right!
End Rhy. Fig. 2
End Rhy. Fig. 2B
1/2

Hmm.

Verse
Bkgd. Voc.: w/ Voc. Fig. 1
Gtrs. 1 & 2: w/ Rhy. Figs. 1 & 1A
Gtr. 3: tacet
A F G A
2. Ah, Hen - ry, don't be un - kind, go 'way! I can't take

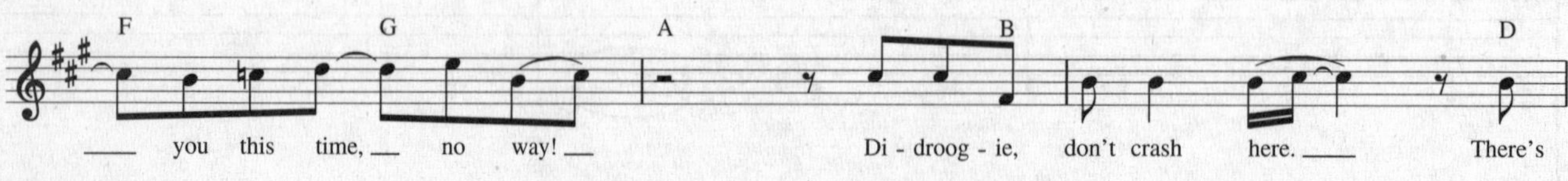
F G A B D
you this time, no way! Di - droog - ie, don't crash here. There's

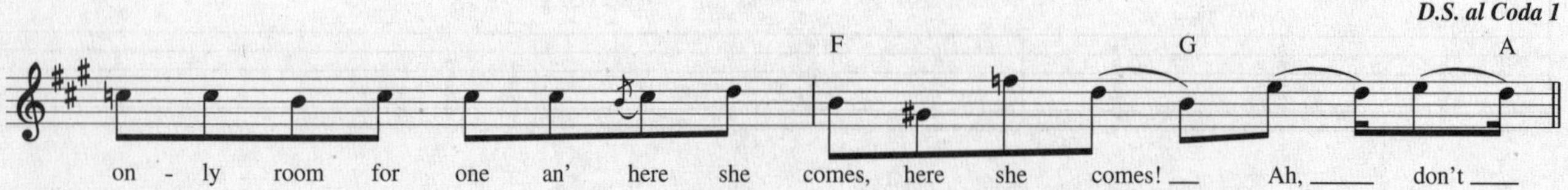
D.S. al Coda 1
F G A
on - ly room for one an' here she comes, here she comes! Ah, don't

Coda 1
A
F
G
Gtr. 2
right!
Oh,
hit
Gtr. 3
w/ pick & finger
hold bend
Gtr. 4 (elec.)
w/ dist.
hold bend
Gtr. 1
A
F
G
A
B
me.
w/ pick & finger
hold bend
hold bend
let ring
w/ pick & fingers
hold bend

D.S. al Coda 2
D
F
G
A
Uh, don't
steady gliss.
steady gliss.
Coda 2
Gtrs. 1 & 3: w/ Rhy. Fills 1 & 1A
G
G#5
A5
Gtrs. 1, 2 & 3: w/ Rhy. Figs. 2, 2A & 2B
A
y! Don't lean on me, man, 'cause you can't af - ford the tick - et
Rhy. Fill 1
Gtr. 1
Rhy. Fill 1A
Gtr. 3

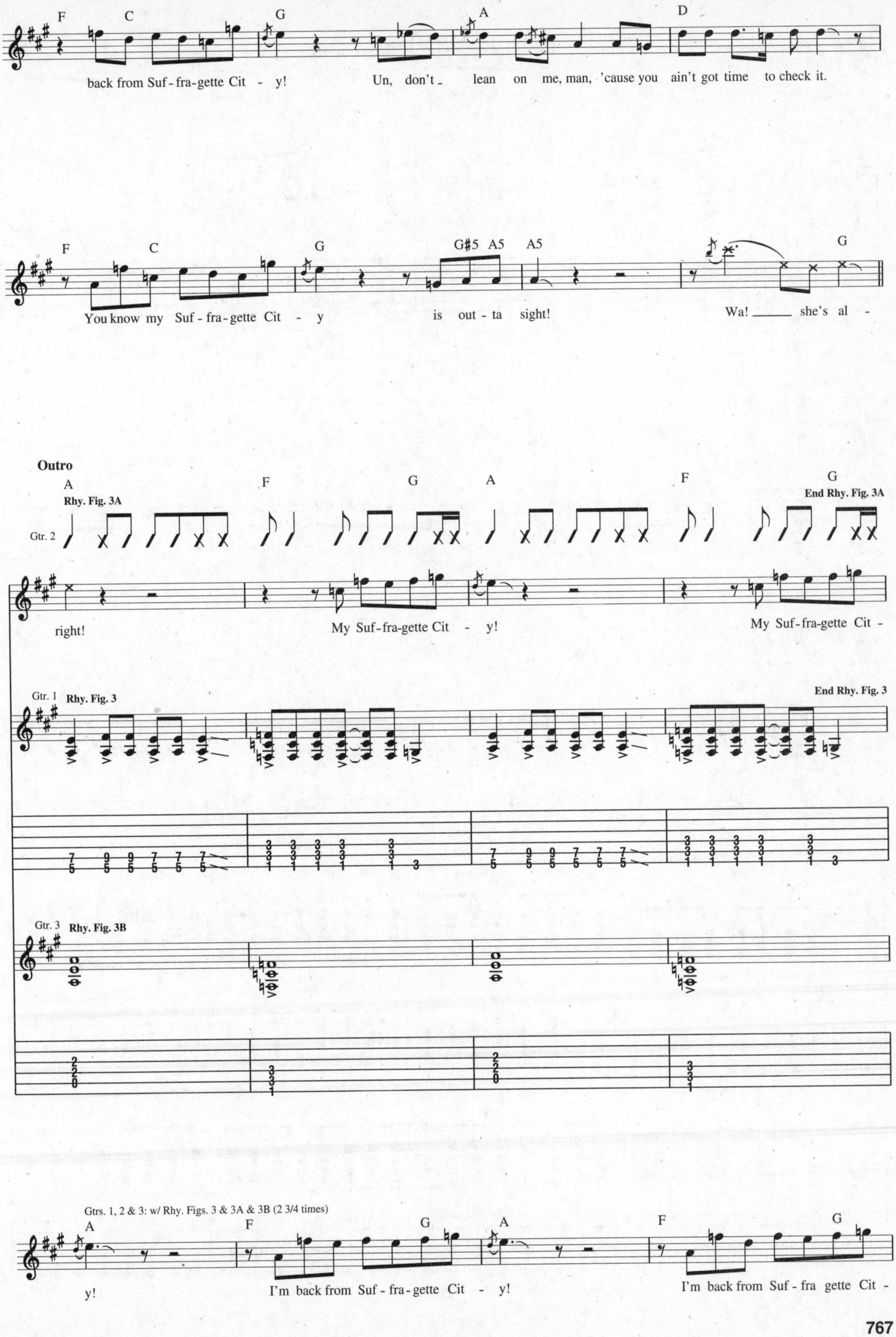

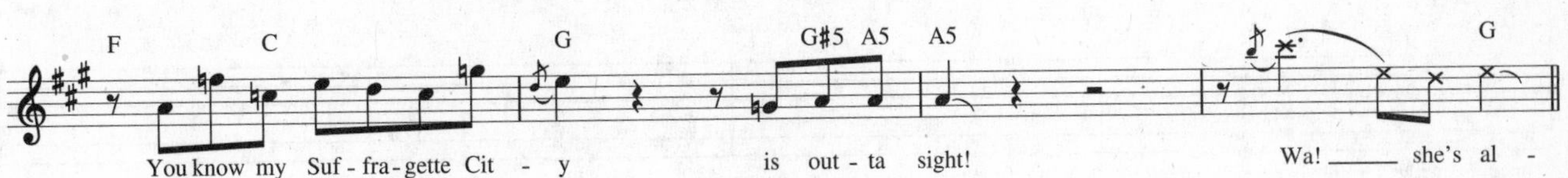

Outro

A F G A F G

Rhy. Fig. 3A

End Rhy. Fig. 3A

Gtr. 2

right! My Suf - fra - gette Cit - y! My Suf - fra - gette Cit -

Gtr. 1 Rhy. Fig. 3

End Rhy. Fig. 3

Gtr. 3 Rhy. Fig. 3B

Gtrs. 1, 2 & 3: w/ Rhy. Figs. 3 & 3A & 3B (2 3/4 times)

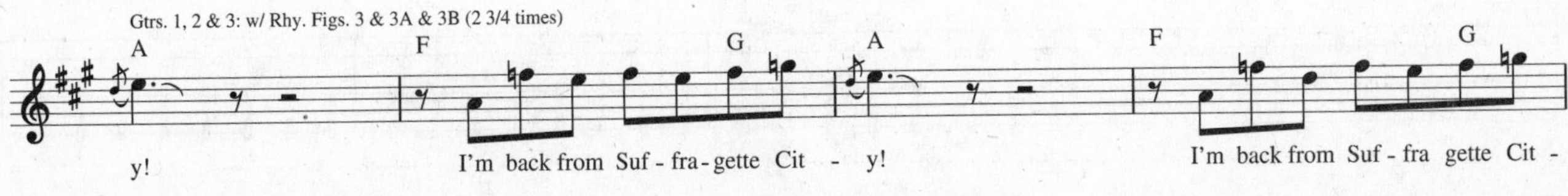

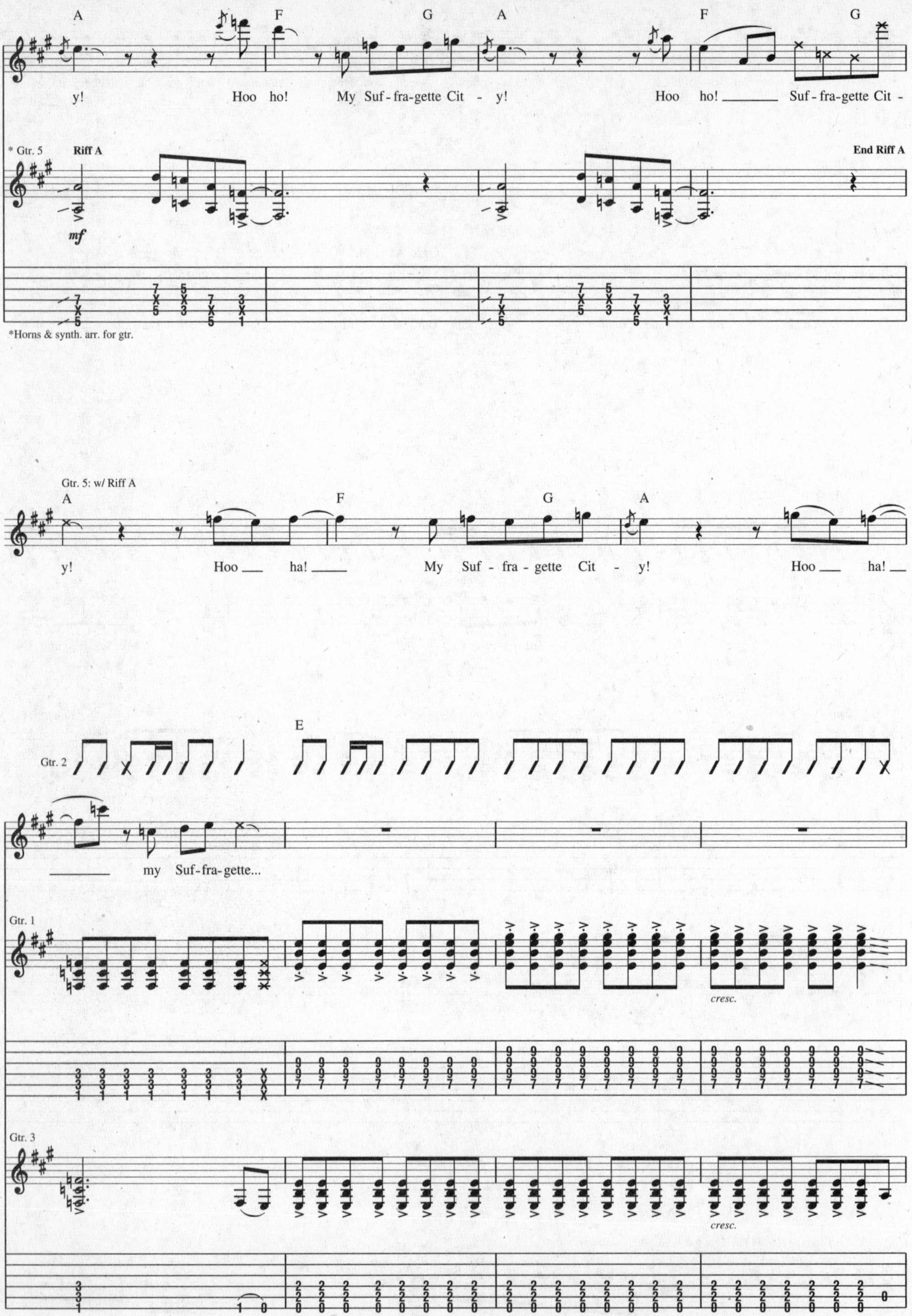

*Horns & synth. arr. for gtr.

E

Gtr. 2

my Suf-fra-gette...

Gtr. 1

cresc.

Gtr. 3

cresc.

A N.C.
A
F
Rhy. Fig. 4A
End Rhy. Fig. 4A
Ah, wham bam, thankyou, ma'am!
My Suf-fra-gette Cit -
Rhy. Fig. 4
End Rhy. Fig. 4
Gtrs. 3 & 4
Rhy. Fig. 4B
Gtr. 4
End Rhy. Fig. 4B
P.S.
Gtr. 3
divisi
1/2
*Pertains to both gtrs.
Gtrs. 1, 2, 3 & 4: w/ Rhy. Figs. 4, 4A & 4B (6 times)
y! my Suf - fra - gette Cit - y! Quite al - right!
(Oo, yeah, oo! Oo!
My Suf - fra - gette Cit - y! Too fine! Uh, Suf - fra - gette Cit -
Too fine!
Gtr. 5: w/ Riff A (4 times)
y! Oh, my Suf - fra - gette Cit - y! Yeah!
Oo, oo! Oo, hoo, hoo!
Ho! My Suf - fra - gette Cit - y! Ah! Woo! My Suf - fra - gette Cit -
Oo, oo!

A F E

Gtr. 2

ty!
Oo, oo!) ___ Ah, ___ Suf - fra-gette...

Gtr. 1

Gtrs. 3 & 4

Gtr. 4

Gtr. 3
divisi

Gtrs. 3 & 4

A

cresc.

Suf - fra - gette!

cresc.

cresc.

Sweet Talkin' Woman

Words and Music by Jeff Lynne

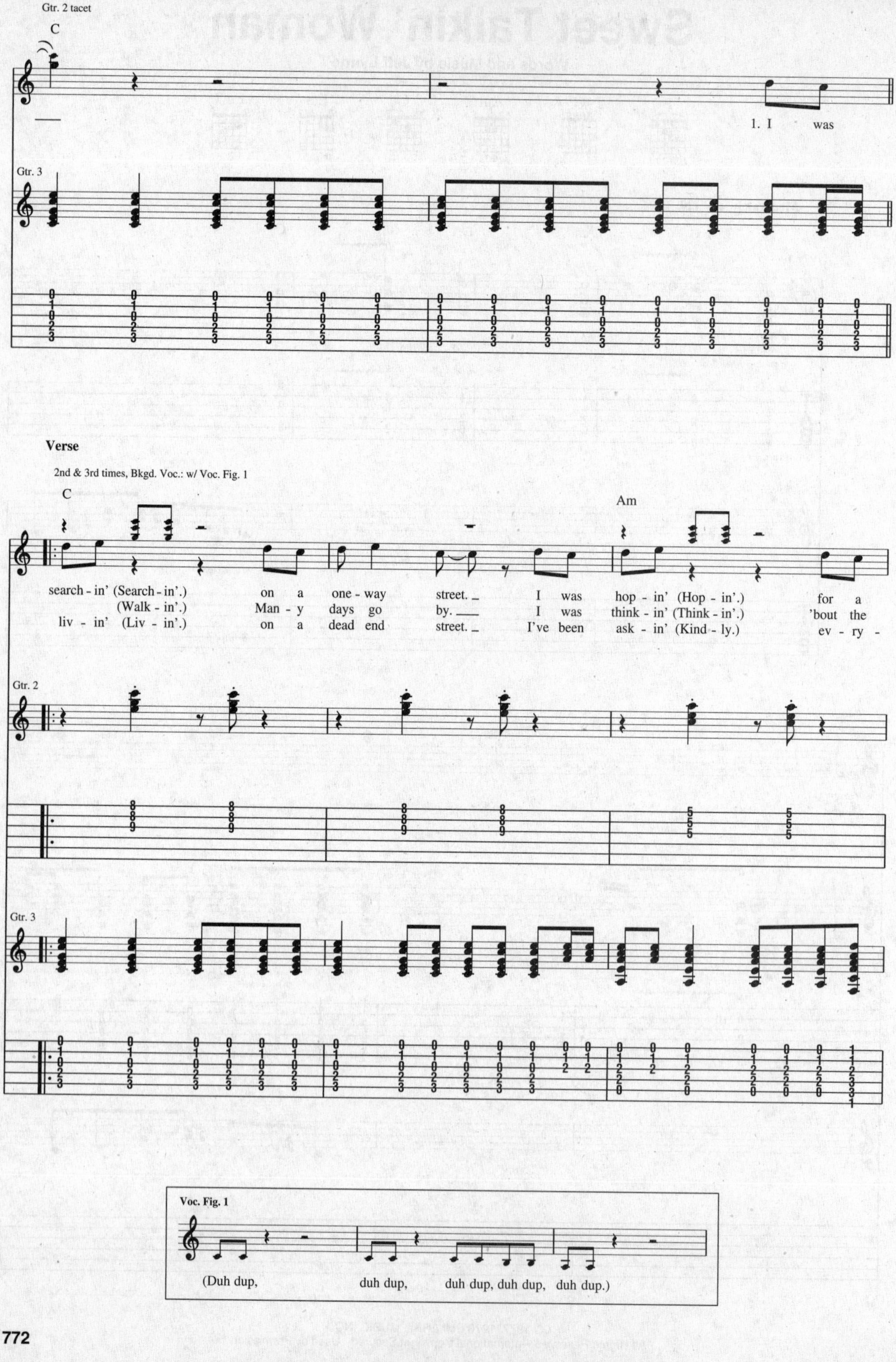

Verse

2nd & 3rd times, Bkgd. Voc.: w/ Voc. Fig. 1

C | | | Am

search - in' (Search - in'.) on a one - way street. I was hop - in' (Hop - in'.) for a
(Walk - in'.) Man - y days go by. I was think - in' (Think - in'.) 'bout the
liv - in' (Liv - in'.) on a dead end street. I've been ask - in' (Kind - ly.) ev - ry -

Gtr. 2

Gtr. 3

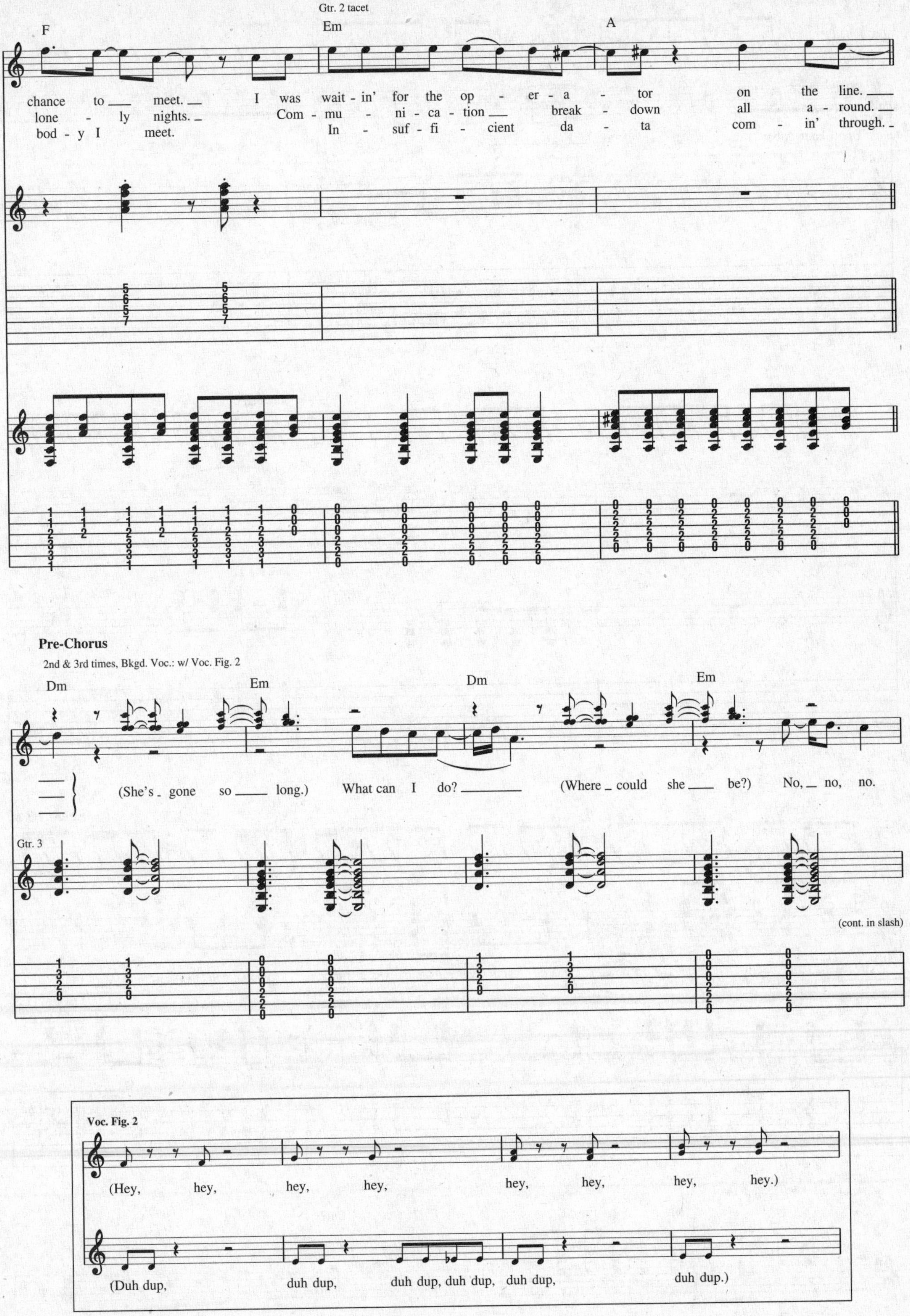

Gtr. 2 tacet

F Em A

chance to ___ meet. ___ I was wait - in' for the op - er - a - tor on the line. ___
lone - ly nights. _ Com - mu - ni - ca - tion ___ break - down all a - round. ___
bod - y I meet. In - suf - fi - cient da - ta com - in' through. _

F
G
Am
F
G
Gtr. 3
Don't know what I'm gon - na do, I got - ta get back to you.
Gtr. 2
Chorus
C
G
C
Rhy. Fig. 1A
You got - ta slow down, (Slow down.)
Rhy. Fig. 1
Am
Em
F
Em7
F
G
End Rhy. Fig. 1A
sweet talk - in' wom - an. (Slow down.) You got me run - nin', (Run, run.) you got me search - in'.
End Rhy. Fig. 1
Gtrs. 2 & 3: w/ Rhy. Figs. 1 & 1A
C
Am
Em
F
Em7
F
G
Hold on, (Hold on.) sweet talk - in' lov - er. (Hold on.) It's so sad if that's the way it's o - ver.

1.
F G Am F G
Rhy. Fig. 2
End Rhy. Fig. 2
Gtr. 3
Vocoder:
Sweet talk - in' wom - an.
2. I was...
Gtr. 2 Riff A
End Riff A
2.
Gtrs. 2 & 3: w/ Riff A & Rhy. Fig. 2
F G Am
Vocorder:
Sweet talk - in' wom - an.
3. I've been
3.
F G Am
Gtr. 1 tacet
G
Gtr. 3
Sweet talk - in' wom - an.
Gtr. 1
Gtr. 2
Chorus
Gtrs. 2 & 3: w/ Rhy. Figs. 1 & 1A (3 times)
C Am Em F Em7 F G
Slow down, (Slow down.) sweet talk - in' wom - an. (Slow down.) You got me run - nin', you got me search - in'.
(Do, do.)
C Am Em F Em7 F G
Hold on, (Hold on.) sweet talk - in' lov - er. (Hold on.) It's so sad if that's the way it's o - ver.
(Do, do.)

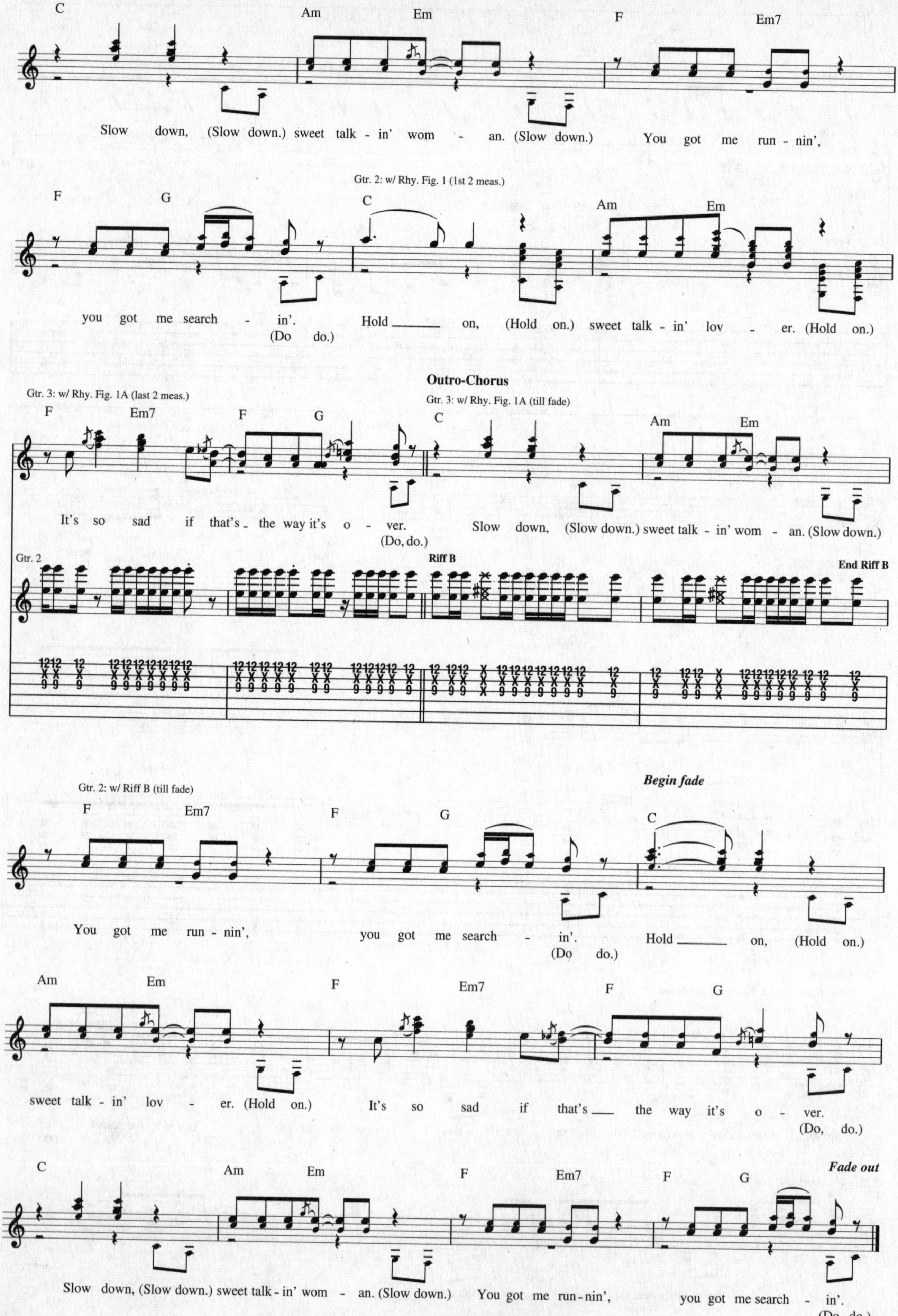

C Am Em F Em7

Slow down, (Slow down.) sweet talk - in' wom - an. (Slow down.) You got me run - nin',

Gtr. 2: w/ Rhy. Fig. 1 (1st 2 meas.)

F G C Am Em

you got me search - in'. Hold ___ on, (Hold on.) sweet talk - in' lov - er. (Hold on.)
(Do do.)

Outro-Chorus

Gtr. 3: w/ Rhy. Fig. 1A (last 2 meas.)

Gtr. 3: w/ Rhy. Fig. 1A (till fade)

F Em7 F G C Am Em

It's so sad if that's_ the way it's o - ver. Slow down, (Slow down.) sweet talk - in' wom - an. (Slow down.)
(Do, do.)

Gtr. 2

Riff B

End Riff B

Gtr. 2: w/ Riff B (till fade)

Begin fade

F Em7 F G C

You got me run - nin', you got me search - in'. Hold ___ on, (Hold on.)
(Do do.)

Am Em F Em7 F G

sweet talk - in' lov - er. (Hold on.) It's so sad if that's ___ the way it's o - ver.
(Do, do.)

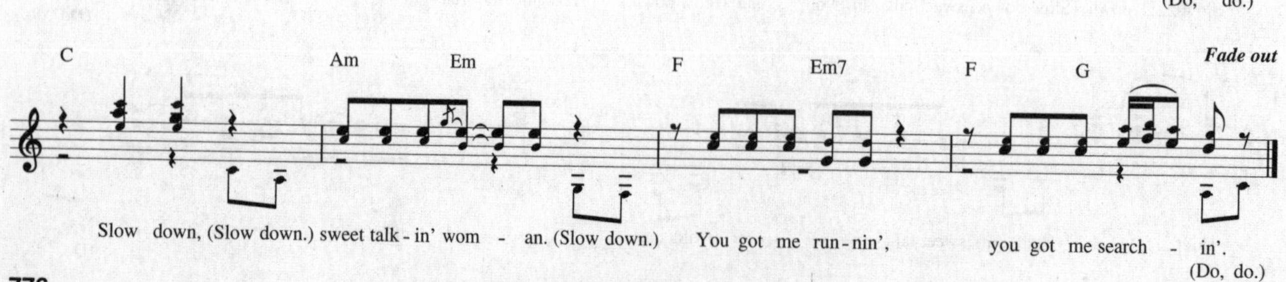

Take Five

By Paul Desmond

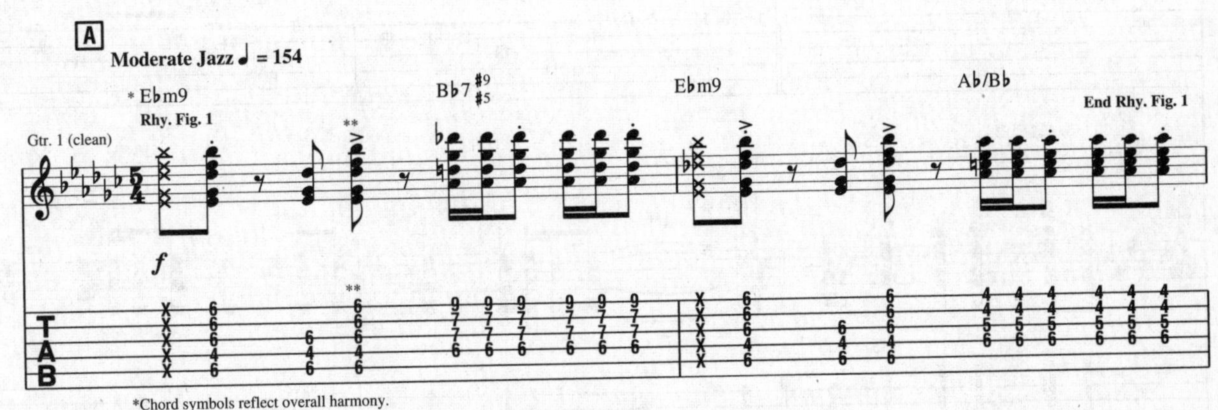

*Chord symbols reflect overall harmony.

**This chord is played staccato, 1st time only.

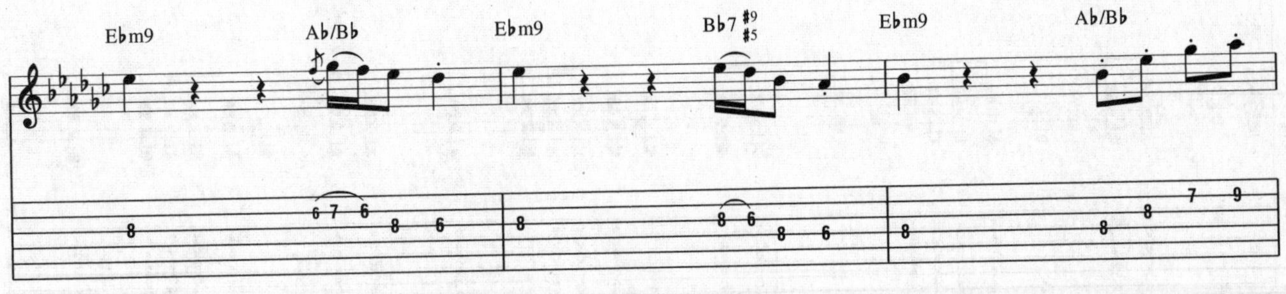

2nd time, Gtr. 1: w/ Rhy. Fill 1
C
Ebm9
Am7
Abm7
Abm6
Bbm7
Eb9
Gtr. 2
Gtr. 1
Rhy. Fig. 2

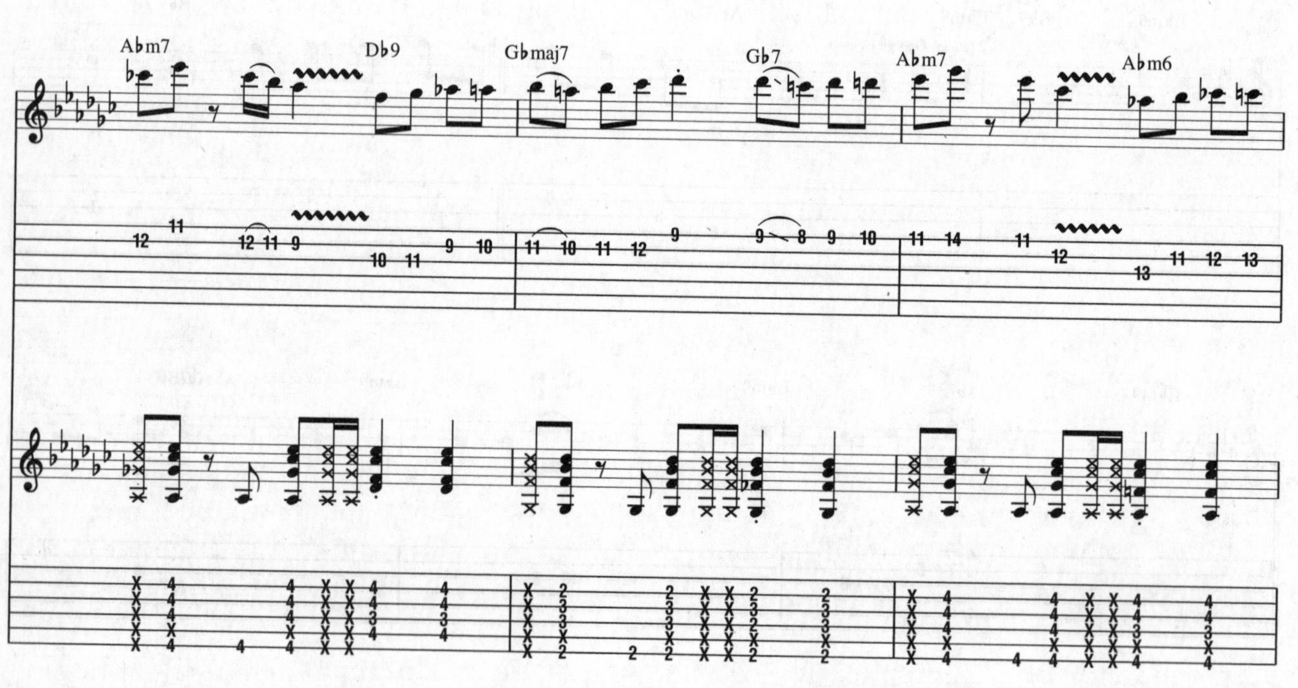
Abm7
Db9
Gbmaj7
Gb7
Abm7
Abm6

Rhy. Fill 1
Gtr. 1

To Coda
Bbm7
Eb9
Abm7
Db9
Fm7
End Rhy. Fig. 2
D
Gtr. 1: w/ Rhy. Fig. 1 (4 times)
Gtr. 2
Ebm9
Ab/Bb
E
Gtr. 1: w/ Rhy. Fig. 1 (34 times)
let ring
let ring simile

Ebm9
Ab/Bb
Ebm9
Bb7#9#5
Ebm9
Ab/Bb

Ebm9
Ab/Bb
Ebm9
Bb7 #9 #5
8va

Ebm9
8va
Bb7#9#5
Ebm9
Ab/Bb
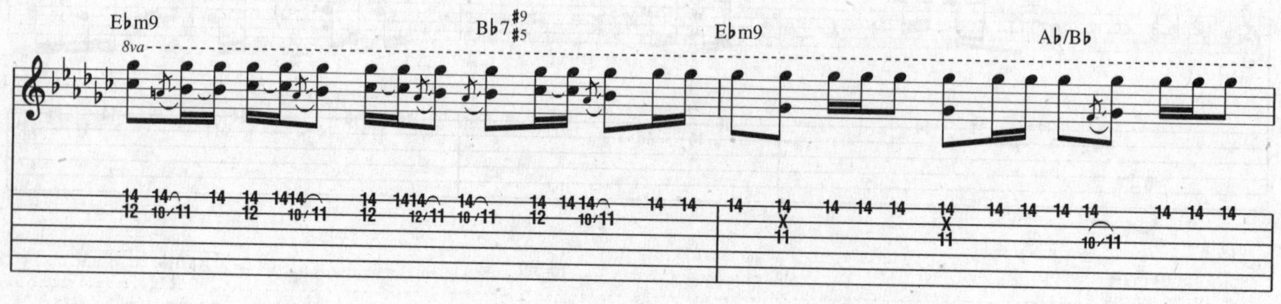
Ebm9
8va
Bb7#9#5
Ebm9
Ab/Bb
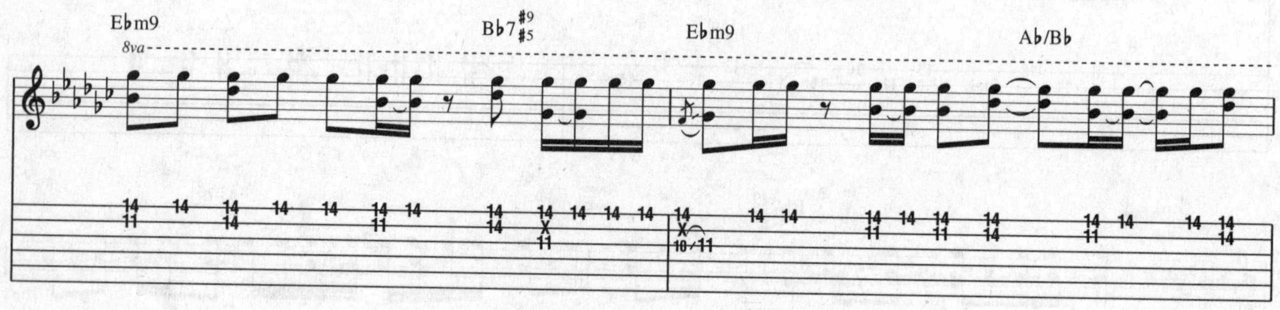
Ebm9
8va
Bb7#9#5
Ebm9
Ab/Bb
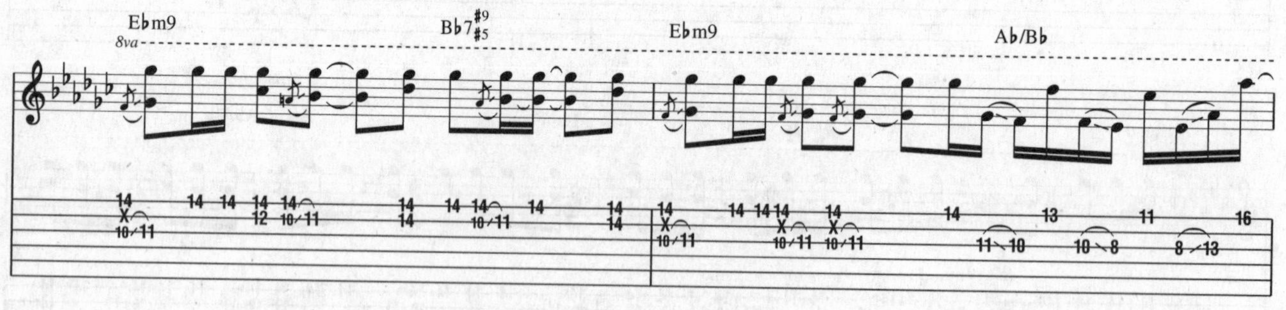
Ebm9
8va
Bb7#9#5
Ebm9
Ab/Bb
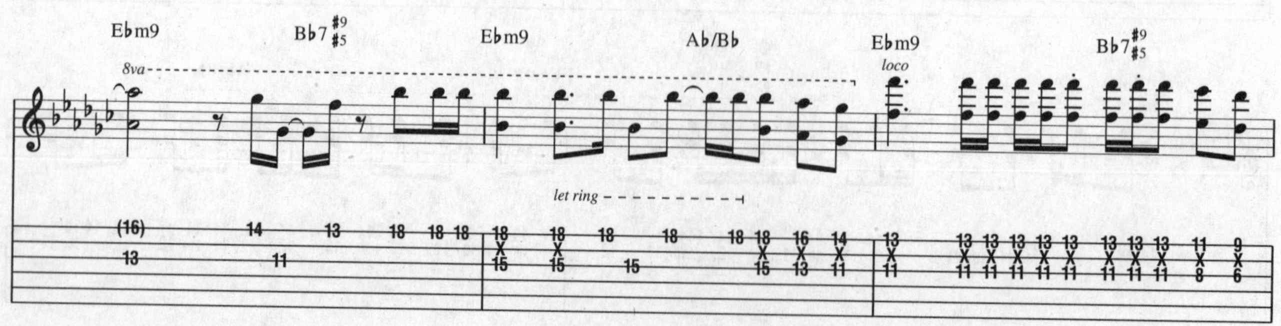
Ebm9
8va
Bb7#9#5
Ebm9
Ab/Bb
let ring
Ebm9
loco
Bb7#9#5

Ebm9
Ab/Bb
Ebm9
Bb7#9#5
Ebm9
Ab/Bb
Ebm9
Bb7#9#5
Ebm9
Ab/Bb
Ebm9
Bb7#9#5
Ebm9
Ab/Bb
Ebm9
Bb7#9#5
Ebm9
Ab/Bb
Ebm9
Bb7#9#5
Ebm9
Ab/Bb
Ebm9
Bb7#9#5

Ebm9
Ab/Bb
Bb7 #9 #5
8va
loco
*Note is pulled off fretboard.
F
Gtr. 1: w/ Rhy. Fig. 2
Abm7
Abm6
Bbm7
Eb9

Abm7
Db9
Gbmaj7
Gb7
Abm7
Abm6
G
Gtr. 1: w/ Rhy. Fig. 1 (2 times)
Bbm7
Eb9
Abm7
Db9
Fm7
Bb7#9#5
Ebm9
Bb7#9#5
Ebm9
Ab/Bb
Ebm9
Bb7#9#5
Ebm9
Ab/Bb
mp
H
Gtrs. 1 & 2: w/ Rhy. Fig. 1 (4 times) Gtrs. 1 & 2: w/ Rhy. Fig. 2
D.S. al Coda
Gtrs. 1 & 2: w/ Rhy. Fig. 1 (16 times)
Gtrs. 1 & 2: w/ Rhy. Fig. 2
Gtr. 1: w/ Rhy. Fig. 1 (2 times)
Gtr. 2: w/ Rhy. Fig. 1 (1 1/2 times)
Ebm9
Gtr. 2
Ab/Bb
f
Coda
I
Gtr. 1: w/ Rhy. Fig. 1 (2 times)
Fm7
Bb7#9#5
Ebm9
Bb7#9#5
Ebm9
Ab/Bb
Ebm9
Bb7#9#5
J
Gtr. 1: w/ Rhy. Fig. 1 (14 times)
Ebm9
Ab/Bb
Ebm9
Bb7#9#5
Ebm9
Ab/Bb
Ebm9
Bb7#9#5

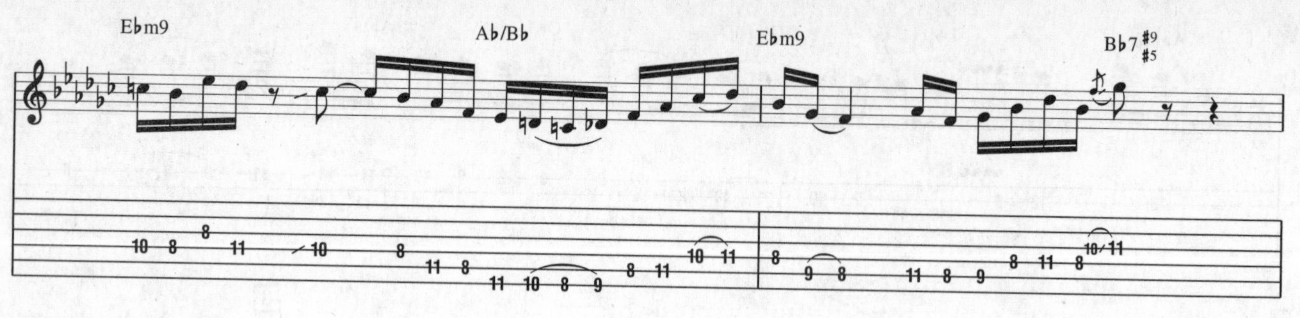
E♭m9
A♭/B♭
E♭m9
B♭7#9#5

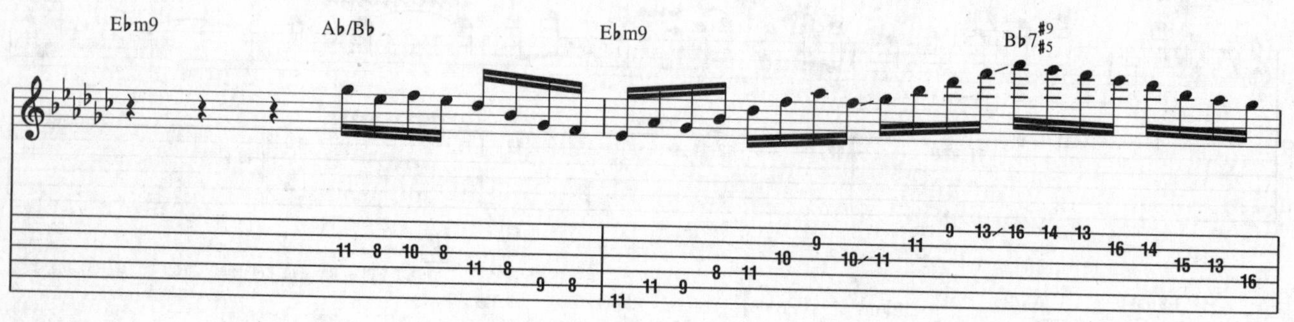
E♭m9
A♭/B♭
E♭m9
B♭7#9#5

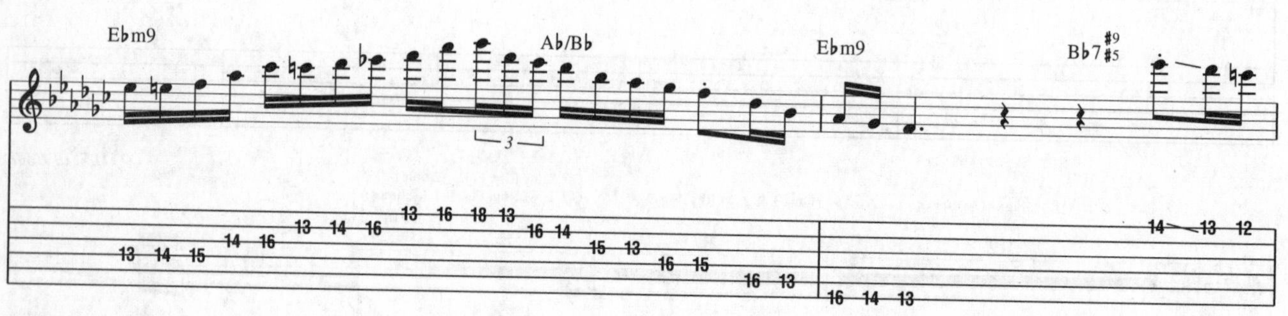
E♭m9
A♭/B♭
E♭m9
B♭7#9#5

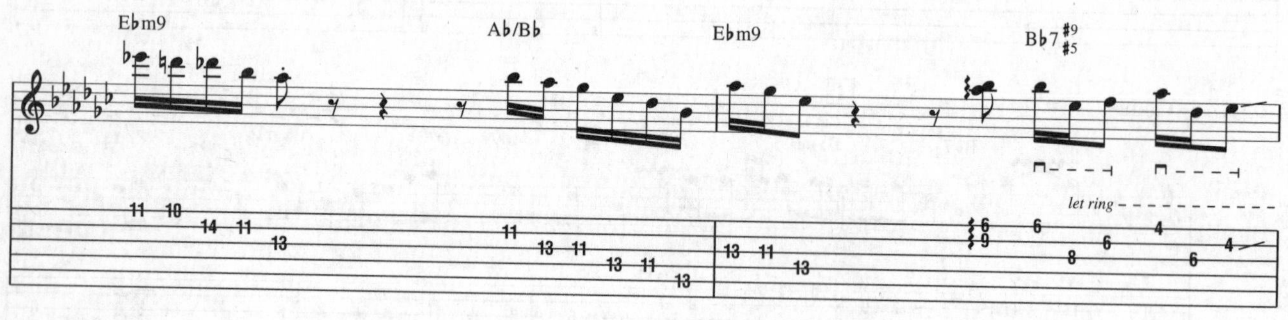
E♭m9
A♭/B♭
E♭m9
B♭7#9#5
let ring

E♭m9
A♭/B♭
E♭m9
8va
loco
B♭7#9#5
let ring

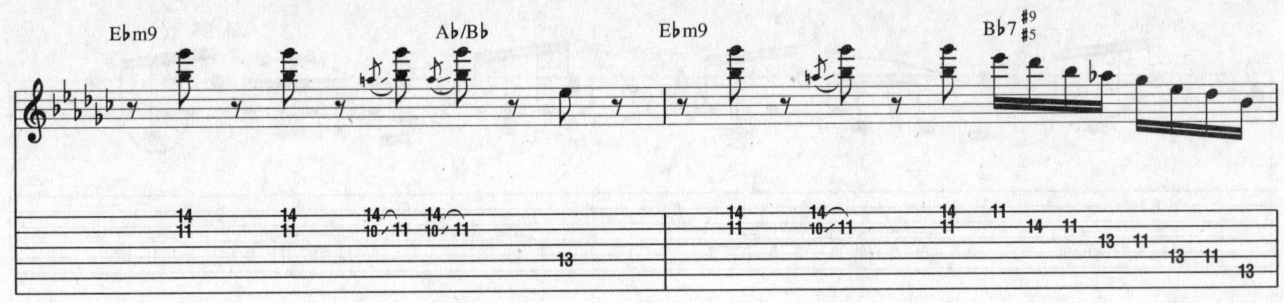
Ebm9
Ab/Bb
Ebm9
Bb7#9#5

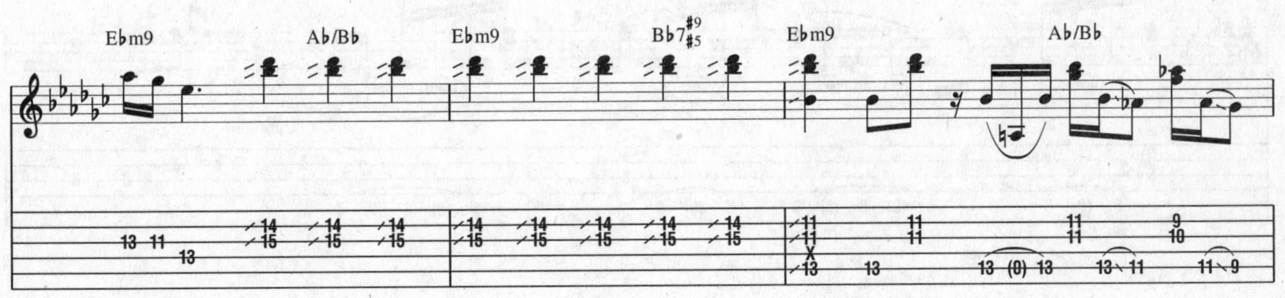
Ebm9
Ab/Bb
Ebm9
Bb7#9#5
Ebm9
Ab/Bb

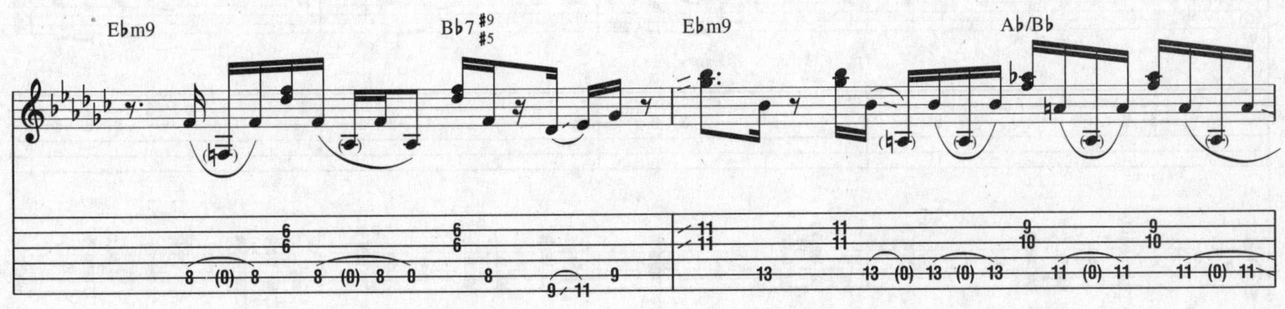
Ebm9
Bb7#9#5
Ebm9
Ab/Bb

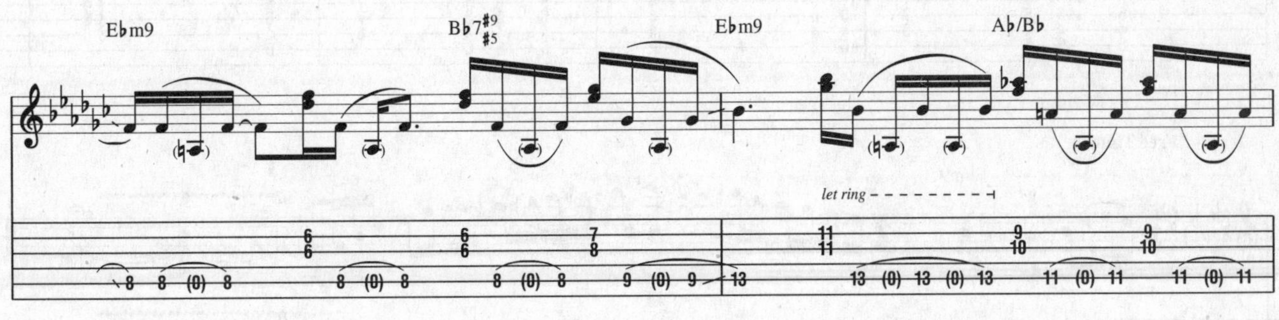
Ebm9
Bb7#9#5
Ebm9
Ab/Bb
let ring

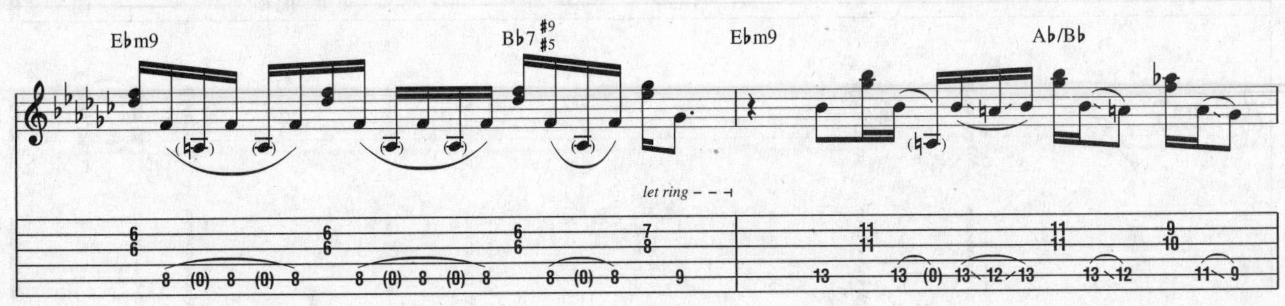
Ebm9
Bb7#9#5
Ebm9
Ab/Bb
let ring

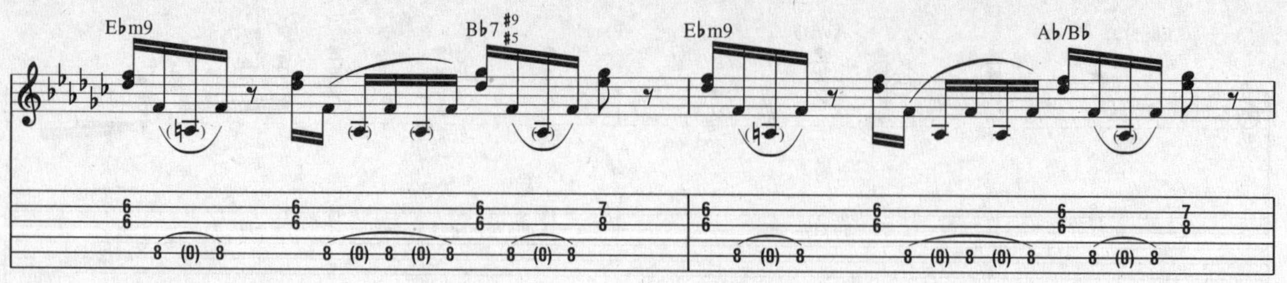
Ebm9
Bb7 #9 #5
Ebm9
Ab/Bb
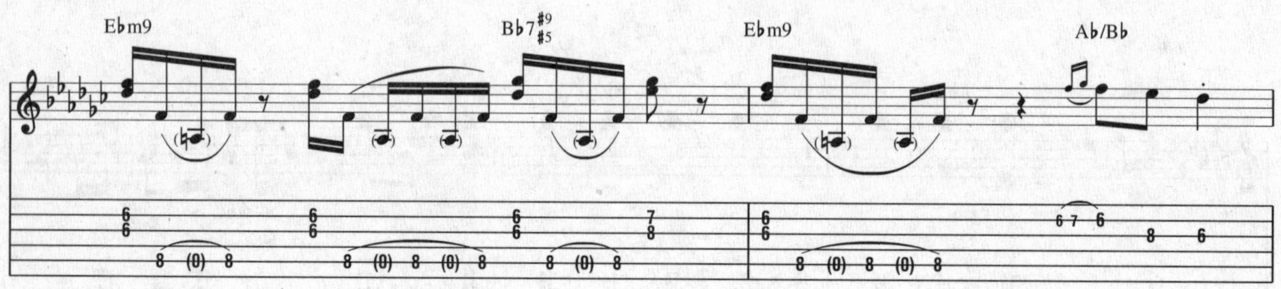
Ebm9
Bb7 #9 #5
Ebm9
Ab/Bb

Gtr. 2
Ebm9
Bb7 #9 #5
Ebm9
Abadd9/Bb
Ebm9
Bb7 #9 #5
Ebm9
Abadd9/Bb
rit.
Gtr. 1
let ring
rit.
let ring
p

Free Time
Ebm9
tr

Talk to Your Daughter

Written by John Lee Hooker

G5 G6 G5 G6 G5 G6 G5 G6 G5 G6 G5 G6
Verse
Gtr. 1: w/Rhy. Fig. 1, 2¾ times
G5 G6 G5 G6 G5 G6 G5 G6 G5 G6 G5 G6
1. Ma - ma, pa - pa, please talk to your daugh - ter for me.
1/4
G5 G6 G5 G6 G5 G6 G5 G6 G5 G6 G5 G6
Ma - ma, pa - pa, please talk to your daugh - ter for me.
G5 G6 G5 G6 G5 G6 G5 G6 G5 G6 G5 G6
She done made me love her and I

G5
G6
G5
G6
G5
G6
G5
G6
Gtr. 1 tacet
*G13
ain't
gon - na
leave
her
be.
f
w/dist.
*Chord symbols reflect overall tonality.
Interlude
G13
1/2
1/2
1/2
Verse
G13
2. Yeah,
ba - by,
please
don't dog me a - round.
C13
Yeah,
ba - by,
please
grad. bend
full

G13
don't dog me a - round.
If you don't
let ring
full
1/2
D13
C13
G13
pitch up wom - an, put you six feet in the ground.
P.M.
full
1½
Chorus
G13
You should talk to your daugh - ter.
You should talk
full
C13
to your daugh - ter.
You should talk to your daugh - ter.

G13
You should talk to your daugh - ter.
She done made
Harm.
D13
C13
G13
me love her and I ain't gon - na leave her be.
Talk to your daugh -
full
Guitar Solo
G13
ter.
rake
full
1/2
C13
tr

G13
1/2

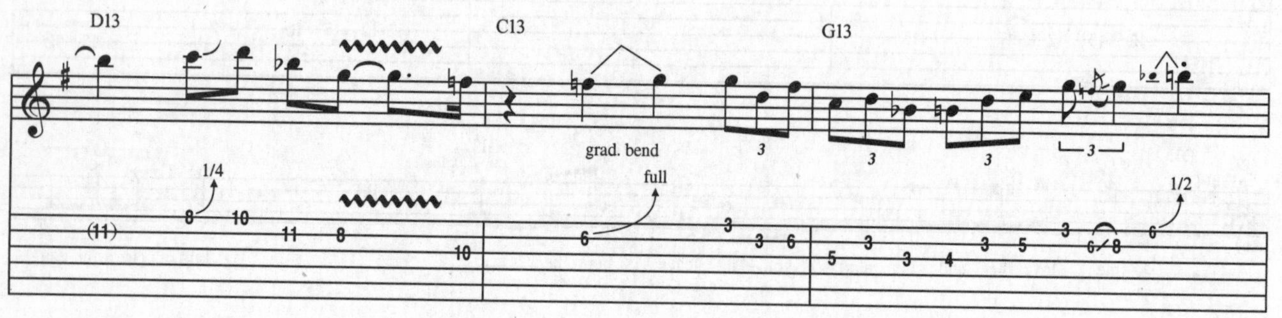
D13
C13
G13
grad. bend
full
1/4
1/2

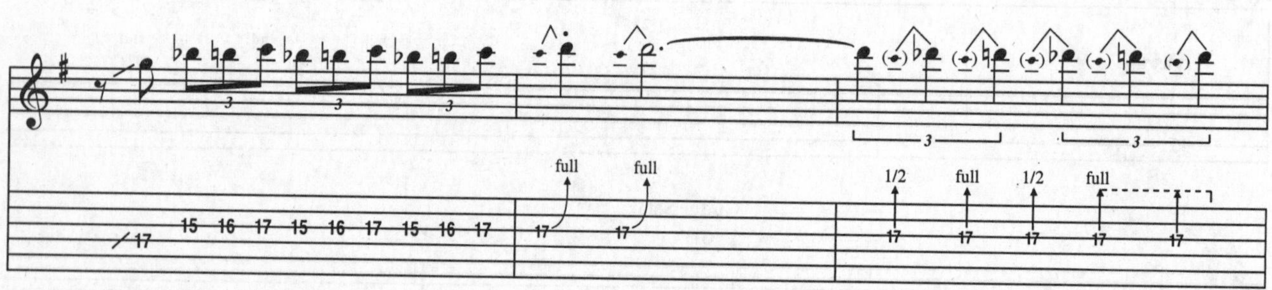
full
1/2

C13
full
1/2
grad. bend

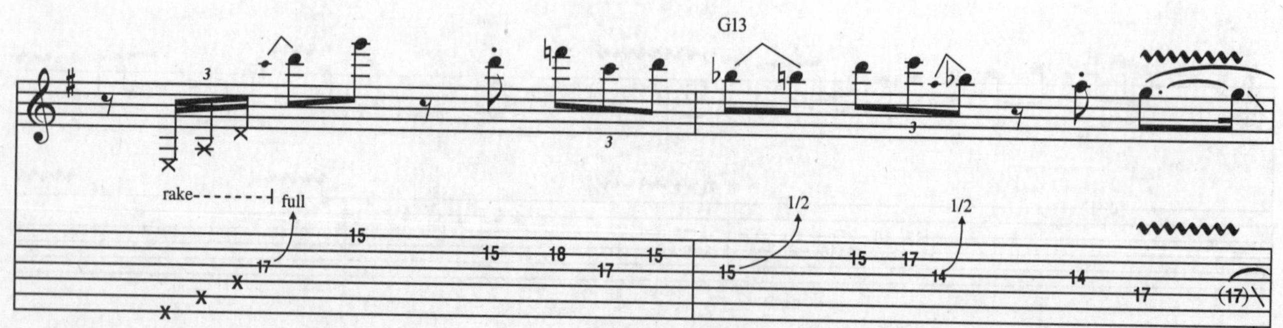
G13
rake-
full
1/2

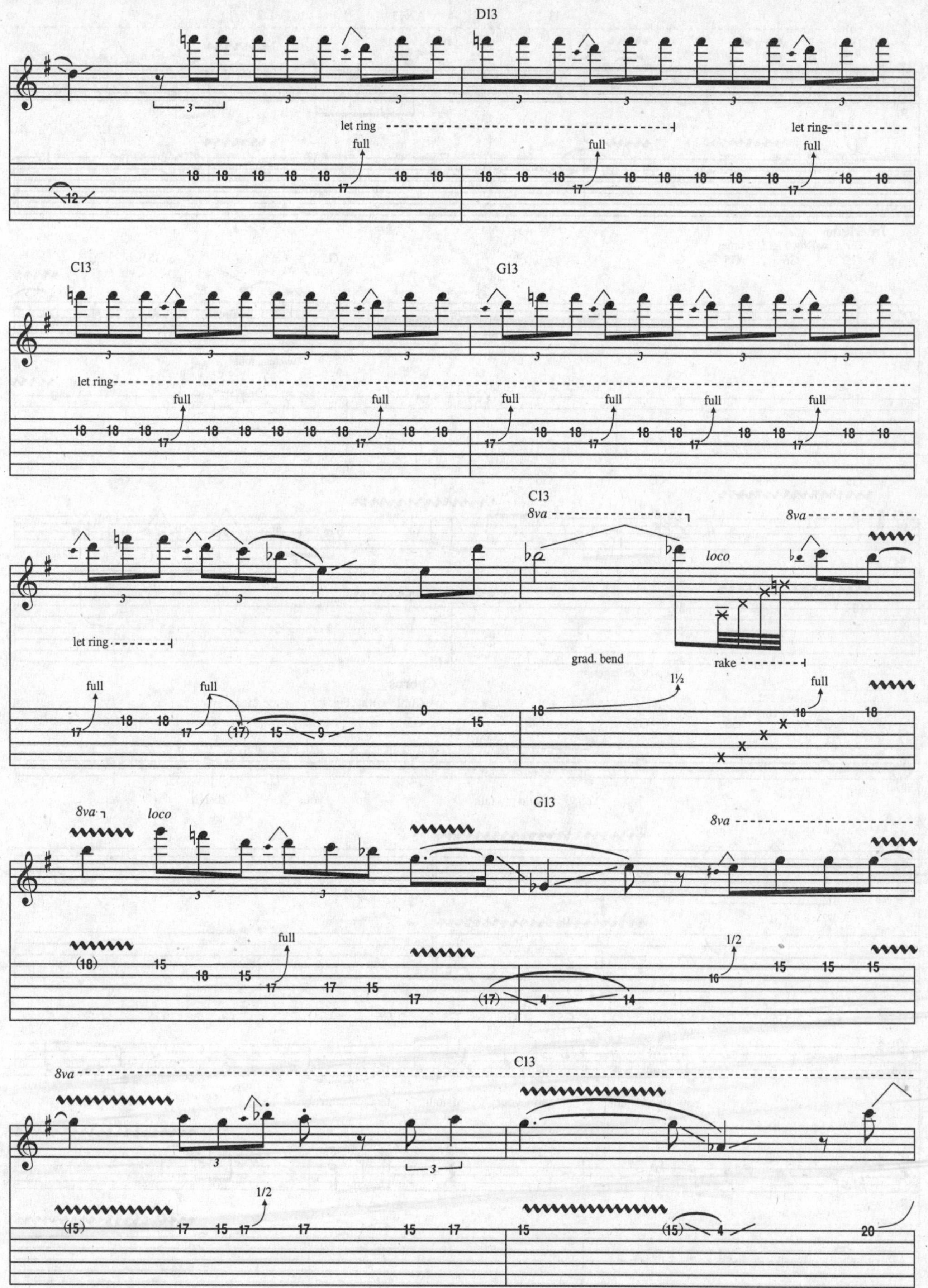
D13
let ring
full
C13
G13
let ring
full
C13
8va
loco
grad. bend
rake
1½
full
8va
loco
G13
8va
full
1/2
8va
C13
1/2

A13
A7♭13
D7
8va
full
1/2
Interlude
Gtr. 1: w/Rhy. Fig. 1, 2 times
G5 G6 G5 G6
loco
mf
w/clean tone
*w/pick & finger
Chorus
Gtr. 1: w/Rhy. Fig. 1
You should talk to your daugh - ter.
You should talk to your daugh - ter.
You should talk

C5
C6
G5
G6
D5
D6
to your daugh - ter.
You should talk to your daugh - ter.
She done made me love her and I
Gtr. 2
Gtr. 1
P.M.
*w/octaver
full
*Set to produce pitches one octave below.

Gtr. 1 tacet
C5
C6
C5
C6
G5
G6
G5
G6
G5
G13
ain't gon - na leave her be.
You should talk
full
full
full
full
full
w/dist.
P.M.
to your daugh - ter.
You should talk
to your daugh - ter.
full
C13
G13
You should talk
to your daugh - ter.
You should talk
1/2
full

D13
to your daugh - ter.
She done made — me love her and I
1/2
C13
G13
ain't gon - na leave her be.
You should talk
1/2
to your daugh - ter.
You should talk
to your daugh - ter.
8va
1/2
1/2
full
full
C13
G13
You should talk
to your daugh - ter.
You should talk
8va
loco
full

D13
to your daugh - ter.
She done made me love her and I
8va
loco
C13
G13
ain't gon-na leave her be.
Free Time

Tequila

By Chuck Rio

F
Eb/C
F
Eb/C
F
Eb/C
F
Eb/C
End Riff A
F
Eb/C
F
Eb/C
F
Eb/C
F
Eb/C
F
Eb/C
F
Eb/C
F
Eb/C
F
Eb/Bb
Rhy. Fill 1
End Rhy. Fill 1
Gtr. 1
mf
steady gliss.

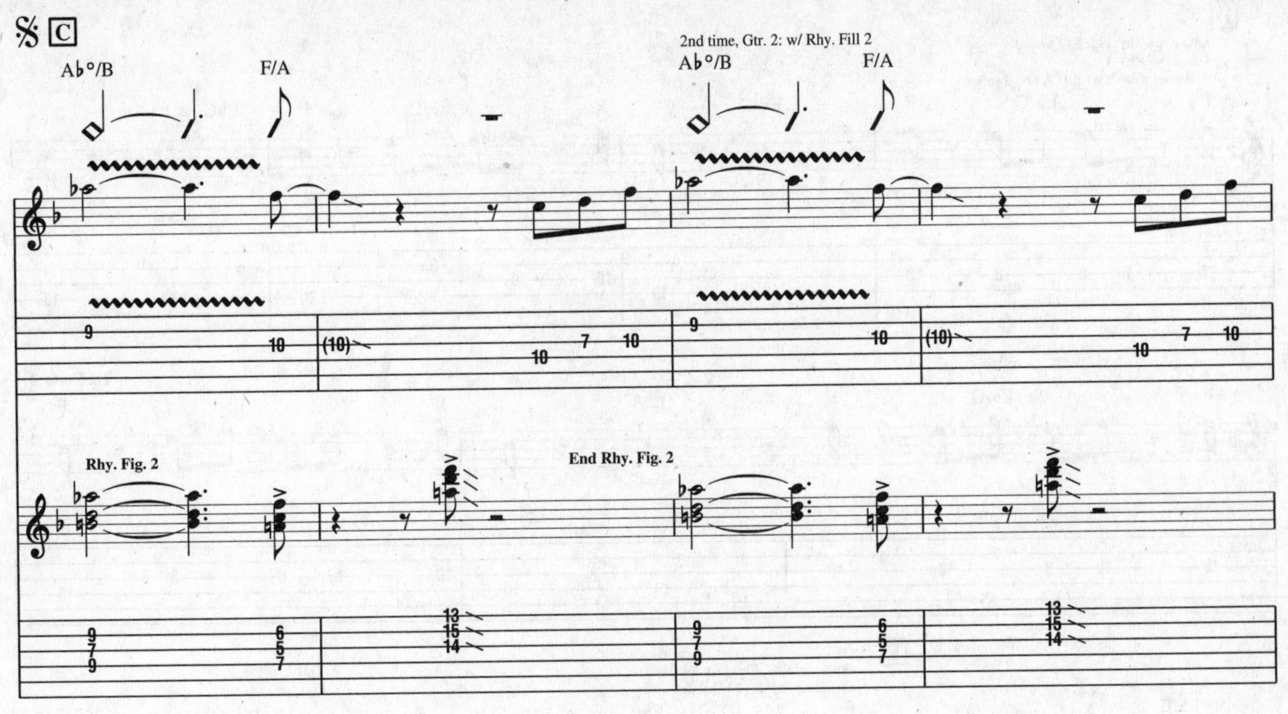
C
Ab°/B
F/A
2nd time, Gtr. 2: w/ Rhy. Fill 2
Rhy. Fig. 2
End Rhy. Fig. 2

2nd time, Gtr. 2: w/ Rhy. Fig. 2
Ab°/B
F/A
G
Spoken: Tequila.
C

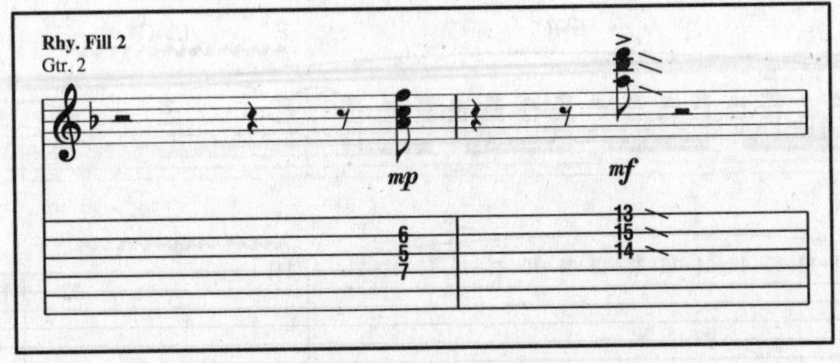
Rhy. Fill 2
Gtr. 2
mp
mf

D
Gtr. 1: w/ Rhy. Fig. 1 (2 times)
Gtr. 2: w/ Riff A
2nd time, Gtr. 2: w/ Riff A (1st 7 meas.)
Gtr. 3
F
Eb/C
To Coda
E
Gtr. 1: w/ Rhy. Fig. 1 (3 3/4 times)
Gtr. 2: w/ Riff A (1 1/2 times)

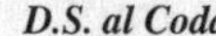

Gtr. 1: w/ Rhy. Fill 1

F Eb/C F Eb/C F Eb/C F Eb/Bb

Gtr. 3

(8) 6 5 8 5 6 5 8 8 6 8 6 8 5 8 6 8 6 8 5 5 10 7 10

Gtr. 2

mf

steady gliss.

3 1 3 1 1 1 1 1 1 3 2 3 1 3 1 3 1 3

Coda

F

Gtr. 3 tacet

Gtr. 1: w/ Rhy. Fig. 1 (1 1/4 times)

Gtr. 2 Eb/C F Eb/C F Eb/C F Eb/C F

* T

T

P.M.

1 1 1 0 3 0 2 1 1 1 3 0 3 1 3 1 2 1 1 3

* T = Thumb on 6th string

Gtr. 2 tacet

Eb/C F Eb/C F Eb/C F Eb/C F

Gtr. 1

T

P.M.

3 3 3 3 3 1

Eb/C F Eb/C F Eb/C F Eb/C F

Tequila!

Eb/C F Eb F Eb F Eb F N.C.

That'll Be the Day

Words and Music by Jerry Allison, Norman Petty and Buddy Holly

Verse
E7 (B7) A (E) D (A) A (E)
when I die. 1. Well, you give me all your lov-in' and your tur - tle dov-in' a
when I die.) 2. Well, a, when Cu-pid shot his dart, he shot it at your heart,
(Oo.
P.M.
D (A) A (E) D (A)
all your hugs and kiss-es and your mon-ey too. Well, a, you know you love me, ba-by.
so if we ev-er part then I'll leave you. You sit and hold me and you
Oo. Oo.
To Coda
A (E) Bm (F♯m) B (F♯) E7 (B7)
Still you tell me may-be that some-day, well, I'll be blue. Well,
tell me bold-ly
Oo. Oo, oo.)
Chorus
Gtr. 1: w/ Rhy. Fig. 1
D (A) A (E)
that-'ll be the day when you say good-bye. Yes, that-'ll be the day when
(That-'ll be the day. Ah. That-'ll be the day.
Gtr. 1: w/ Rhy. Fig. 2
D (A) A (E)
you make me cry. You say you're gon-na leave. You know it's a lie 'cause that-'ll be the day
Ah. That-'ll be the day. Ah. Oo,

Guitar Solo
E7
(B7)
A
(E)
when I die.
when I die.)
Gr. 1
let ring
f
A7
(E7)
D
(A)
P.M.
let ring
D7
(A7)
D.S. al Coda
Well,
1/4
Coda
Chorus
Gtr. 1: w/ Rhy. Fig. 1, 1st 3 meas.
That - 'll be the day when you say good - bye. Yes, that - 'll be the day when
(That - 'll be the day. Ah. That - 'll be the day.

Gtr. 1: w/ Rhy. Fill 1
Gtr. 1: w/ Rhy. Fig. 2
you make me cry. You say you're gon - na leave. You know it's a lie 'cause that - 'll be the day
Ah. That - 'll be the day. Ah. Oo,
Outro
when I die. Well, that - 'll be the day. Oo, oo. Well,
when I die.) (Oo.
Gtr. 1
let ring
that - 'll be the day. Oo, oo. Well, that - 'll be the day.
Oo. Ah.
Oo, oo. Well, that - 'll be the day.
Ah.)
N.C.
Rhy. Fill 1
Gtr. 1
P.M.

(They Call It) Stormy Monday

(Stormy Monday Blues)

Words and Music by Aaron "T-Bone" Walker

Gtr. 1: w/ Rhy. Fill 2. 2nd time
G9
A♭9/B G9/B B♭
D7/A
D7
D+7/A
D7
Wednes - day's worse, _
Sun-day I go to church,
and _ Thurs-day's al - so sad. _
then I kneel down and
even
full
full
full

1.
G
D7
G
D7
2. Yes, _
full
1/2
let ring
6

2.
G
D7
G
D7
pray.
5:4
6
even
full
1/4
let ring
full

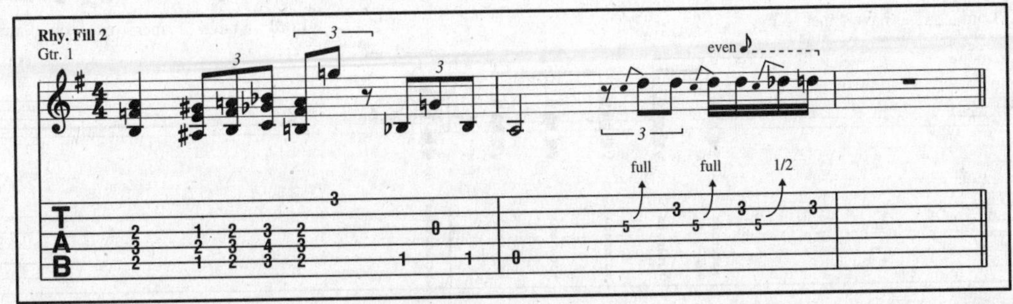
Rhy. Fill 2
Gtr. 1
even
full
full
1/2

Guitar Solo
G6
even
C7
full
let ring
1/4
G6
even
G7
C9
G7
D7
Bm7
B♭
D7/A
D7♯9
1/2
D7/A
D7
G7
G7/D
G7
G7/D
Verse
G9
C9
3. Lord ___ have mer - cy,
Lord have mer - cy on me. ___

G9
D+7
G9
G9/B
B9/F
C9
B9
Lord have mer - cy,
C9
G6
D7
my heart's in mis - er - y.
even
1/2
G7
Bm7
E♭9/B♭
D7/A
D7
Cra - zy 'bout my ba - by,
1/4
full
D7/A
D7
G7
D7
G7
A♭9
G13
yeah, send her back to me.
* Played behind the beat.

The Thrill Is Gone

Words and Music by Roy Hawkins and Rick Darnell

Verse
Bm
2. The thrill is gone,
it's gone a - way _ from me. ___
Gtr. 1
mp
Em
The thrill is gone, ___ ba - by,
the thrill has
Bm
gone a - way _ from me. ___
Gmaj7
Al - though I'll ___ still live on, ___
F#7
Bm
but so ___ lone - ly ___ I'll ___ be.
mf

Guitar Solo
Bm
1/2
1/2
1
1/4
1/4
1/4
Em
8va
Bm
loco
1
Gmaj7
F#7
Bm
1
1/2
Verse
Bm
Gtr. 1 tacet
3.The thrill is gone, it's gone a-way for good.
Oh,
Em
Bm
the thrill is gone, ba-by, it's gone a-way for good.
Gmaj7
F#7
Bm
Some-day I know I'll be hold-in' on, ba-by, just like I know a good man

Verse
Bm
should.
4. You know I'm free, free now, ba - by,
Gtr. 1
I'm free from your spell.
Em
Whoa, I'm free free, free now, I'm free
Bm
from your spell.
Gmaj7
And now that it's all o - ver
F#7
Bm
all I can do is wish you well.

Outro-Guitar Solo
Bm
Em
8va
Bm
loco
Gmaj7
F#7
Bm
8va
8va
loco

Begin fade
Fade out

Throwing It All Away

Words and Music by Tony Banks, Phil Collins and Mike Rutherford

*Chord symbols reflect overall harmony.

**Set for eighth-note regeneration w/ 1 repeat.

*Synth arr. for gtr. (Synth sound is flute-like.)

G♭9
A♭sus4
a - way,
throw - ing it all
a - way.
End Riff A
18
16
18
End Rhy. Fig. 3
Gtr. 1: w/ Rhy. Fig. 3
Gtr. 2: w/ Riff A
To Coda
D♭maj7
D♭sus4/B
G♭9
A♭sus4
Is there
And there's
noth-ing that I can say
to make you change your mind?
Bsus2
G♭
I watch the world go 'round and 'round
Gtr. 1
Bsus2
G♭
and see mine turn - ing up - side down.
Ooh,

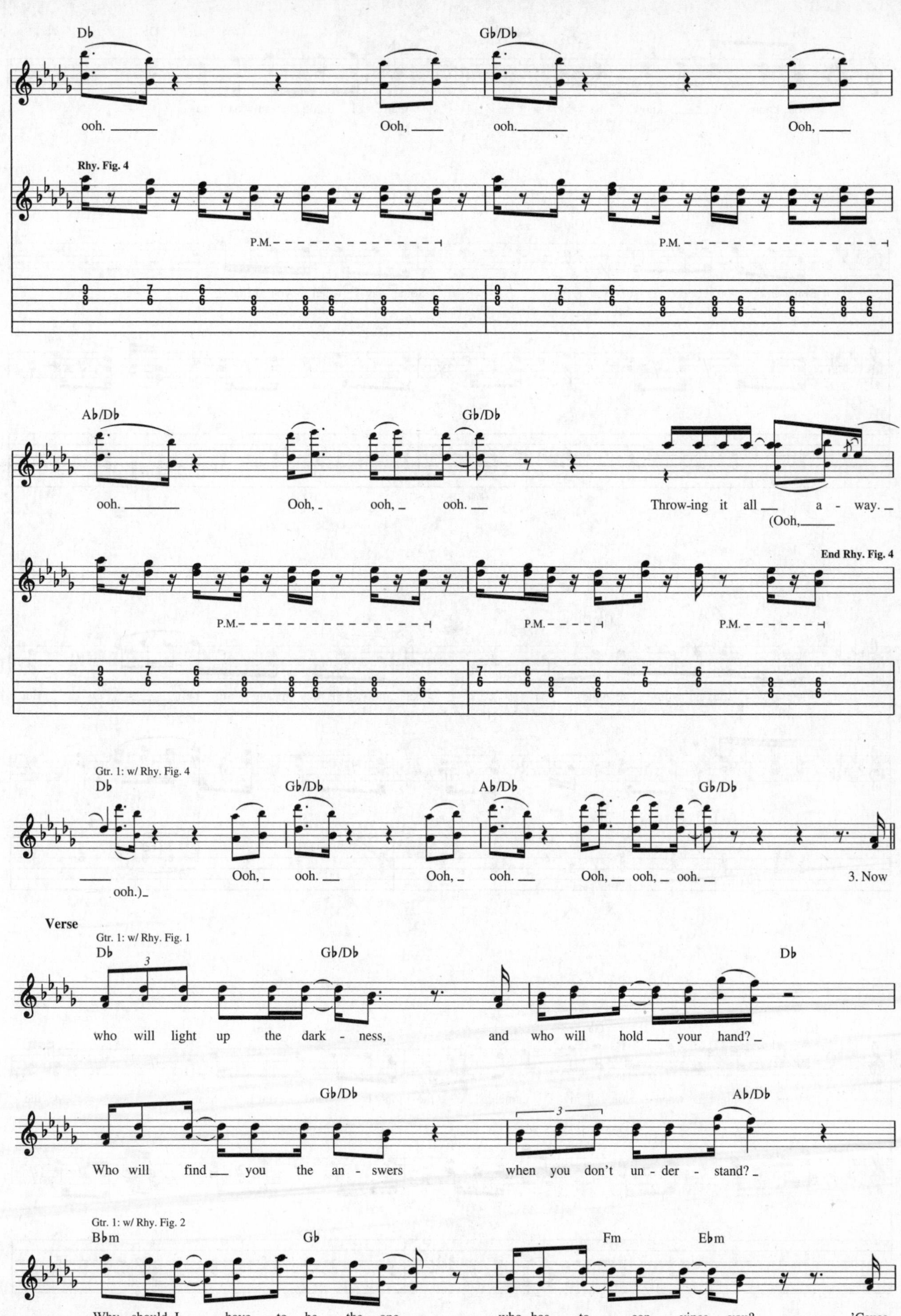

Db
Gb/Db
ooh.
Ooh,
ooh.
Ooh,
Rhy. Fig. 4
P.M.
Ab/Db
Gb/Db
ooh.
Ooh,
ooh,
ooh.
Throw-ing it all a - way.
(Ooh,
End Rhy. Fig. 4
Gtr. 1: w/ Rhy. Fig. 4
Db
Gb/Db
Ab/Db
Gb/Db
ooh.)
Ooh,
ooh.
Ooh,
ooh.
Ooh, ooh, ooh.
3. Now
Verse
Gtr. 1: w/ Rhy. Fig. 1
Db
Gb/Db
Db
who will light up the dark - ness,
and who will hold your hand?
Gb/Db
Ab/Db
Who will find you the an - swers
when you don't un - der - stand?
Gtr. 1: w/ Rhy. Fig. 2
Bbm
Gb
Fm
Ebm
Why should I have to be the one
who has to con - vince you?
'Cause

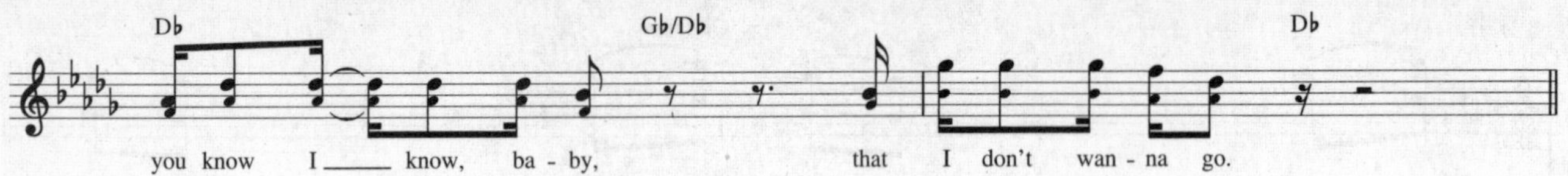
Db
Gb/Db
Db
you know I ___ know, ba - by, that I don't wan - na go.

Verse
Gb/Db
Db
4. Some - day you'll _ be sor - ry. Some - day when _ you're free. _
Gtr. 1

Gb/Db
Ab/Db
Mem - o - ries _ will re - mind you that our love was meant to be. ___ But

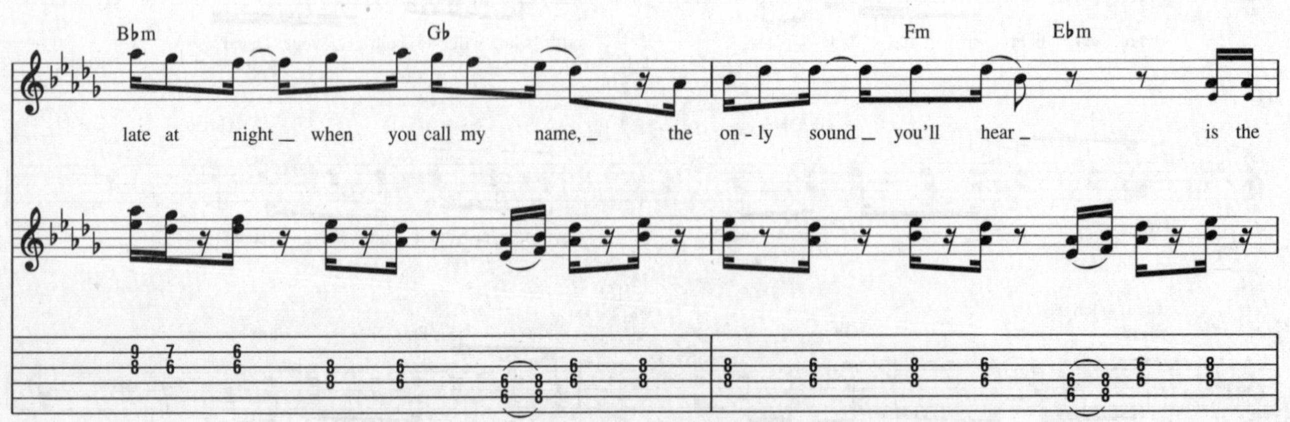
Bbm
Gb
Fm
Ebm
late at night _ when you call my name, _ the on - ly sound _ you'll hear _ is the

D.S. al Coda
D♭
E♭m/D♭
G♭/D♭
D♭
sound of your voice call - ing, call - ing af - ter me.
Coda
G♭
A♭
I can say.
Ay.
Ah.
(Ooh,
Gtr. 1
Outro
D♭
G♭/D♭
ooh.
Ooh,
ooh.
Ooh,
* Sing 2nd, 3rd & 4th times only.
Play 4 times and fade
A♭/D♭
G♭/D♭
ooh.
Ooh,
ooh,
ooh.
We're throw-ing it all a - way.
Ooh,)

Time Is on My Side

Words and Music by Jerry Ragovoy

F
B♭
6fr
C
8fr
Dm
5fr
C^III
G
C^III type2
134211
134211
134211
1342
1333
13421
13331

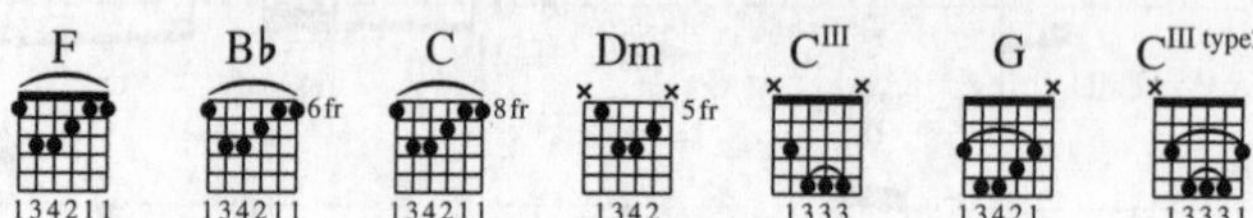

Intro
Moderately Slow ♩. = 70
** B♭
Dm
G
C
* Gtr. 1
mf

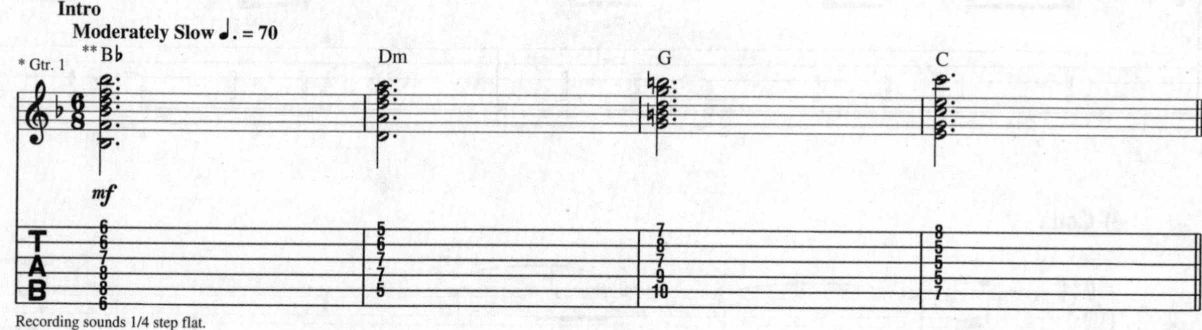

Recording sounds 1/4 step flat.
* Organ arr. for gtr.
** Chord symbols reflect basic harmony.

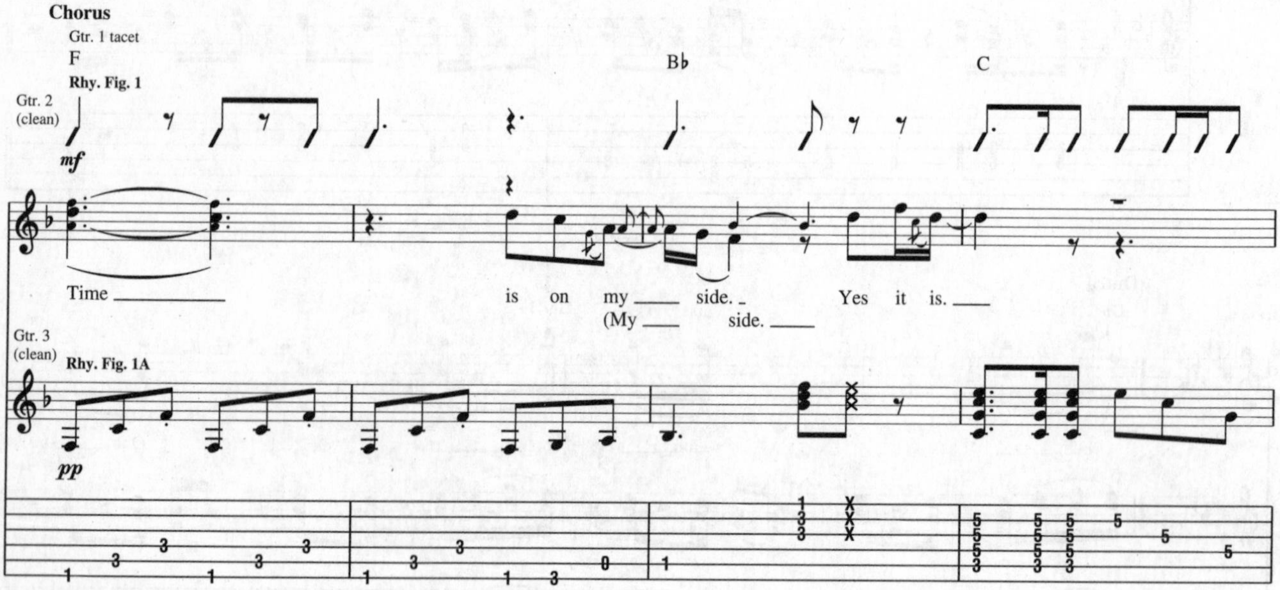

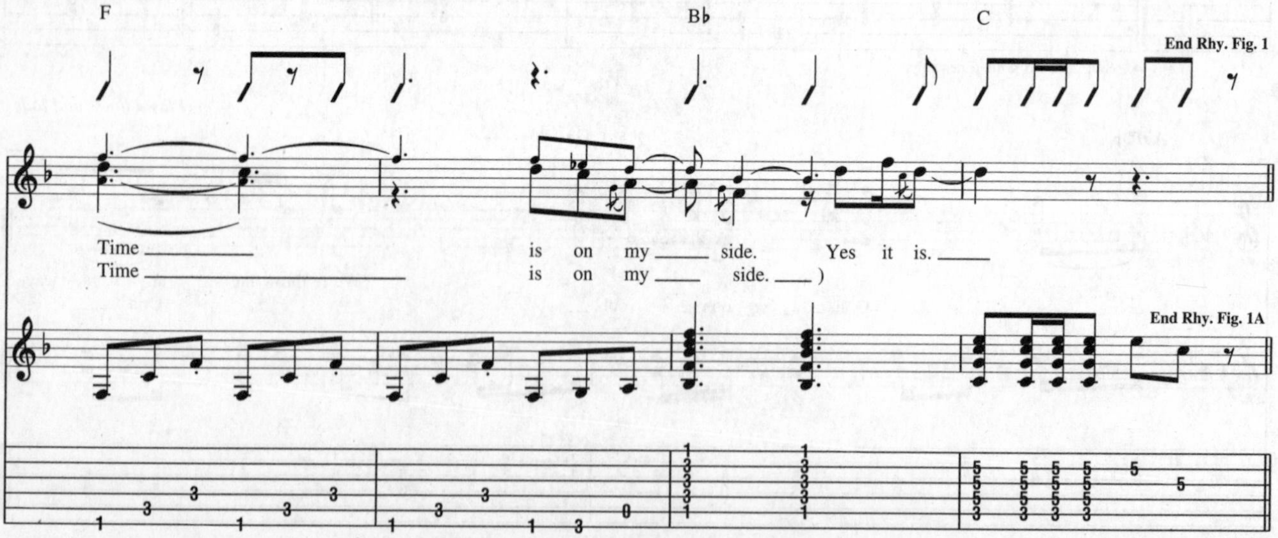

Chorus
Gtr. 1 tacet
F
B♭
C
Rhy. Fig. 1
Gtr. 2 (clean)
mf
Time
is on my side.
Yes it is.
(My side.
Gtr. 3 (clean)
Rhy. Fig. 1A
pp

F
B♭
C
End Rhy. Fig. 1
Time
is on my side.
Yes it is.
Time
is on my side.)
End Rhy. Fig. 1A

Verse
Dm
Rhy. Fig. 2
C^{III}
Dm
1. Now you al - ways say ___ that you want to be
(Oo. ___ Oo. ___
Rhy. Fig. 2A
G
C^{III}
B♭
free, but you'll come run-ning back. Said you will ba - by.
You'll come run-ning back.)
C^{III}
B♭
C^{III}
I said so man - y times be - fore. ___ Come
(You'll come run-ning back. You'll come

B♭
C III type2
End Rhy. Fig. 2
run-ning back to me. Oh.
run-ning back to me.)
End Rhy. Fig. 2A
Chorus
Gtrs. 2 & 3: w/ Rhy. Figs. 1 & 1A, simile
F
B♭
C
Time is on my side. Yes it is.
F
B♭
C
Time is on my side. Yes it is.
(Time is on my side.)
To Coda
Verse
Gtrs. 2 & 3: w/ Rhy. Figs. 2 & 2A, simile
Dm
C
Dm
G
2. You're search - ing for good times, but just wait and see.
3. 'Cause I got the real love, the kind that you need.
(Oo.)
C
B♭
C
You'll come run - ning back. I won't have to wor - ry no more.
(You'll come run - ning back. You'll come

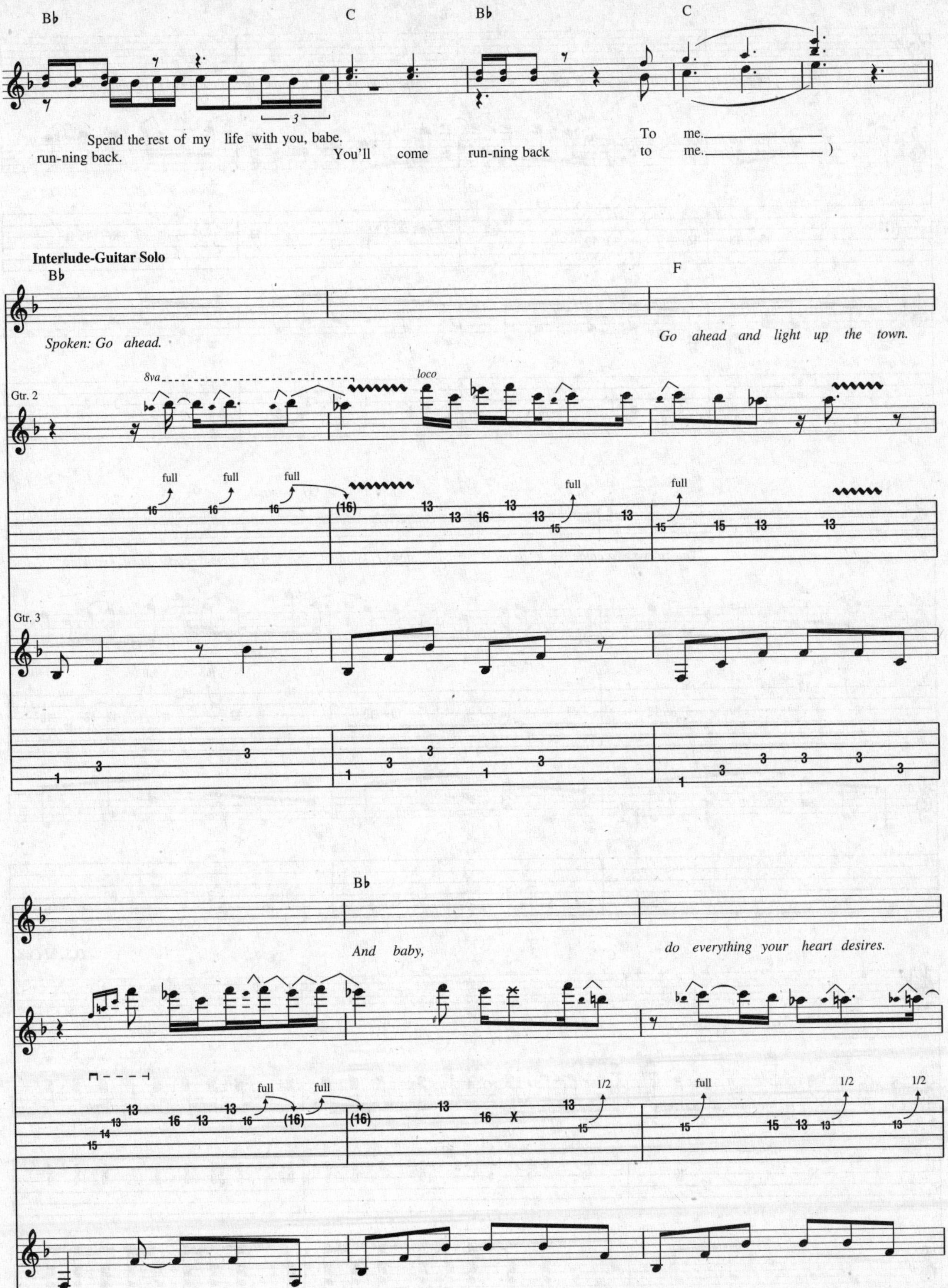

Interlude-Guitar Solo

B♭ F

Spoken: Go ahead.

Go ahead and light up the town.

Gtr. 2

8va loco

full full full full full

Gtr. 3

B♭

And baby,

do everything your heart desires.

full full 1/2 full 1/2 1/2

F
B♭
Remember I'll always be around.
And I know, I know like I told you so many times before
Dm
G7
You're gonna come back baby.
'Cause I know you're gonna come back knocking.
C
D.S. al Coda
Yeah, knocking right on my door.
Yes, yes.
Well,

Coda
C
Bb
You'll come run - ning back I said you would, ba - by.
(You'll come run - ning back.
You'll come
run - ning back.
I al - ways said you would.
You'll come run - ning back
I won't have to wor - ry no more.
to
Outro
Gtrs. 1 & 2: w/ Rhy. Figs. 1 & 1A, till fade, simile
F
Yes. Time, time, time is on my
)
side. Yes it is.
Time, time, time is on my
side. Yes it is. Oh, time, time. Oh, is on my
(Time.)
side. Yes it is. I said time, time, hey, is on my
(Time. My
Begin Fade
side. Yes it is. Oh, time, time, time is on my
side.)
Fade Out
side. Yeah, time, time, time is on my side.

Torn

Words and Music by Phil Thornalley, Scott Cutler and Anne Previn

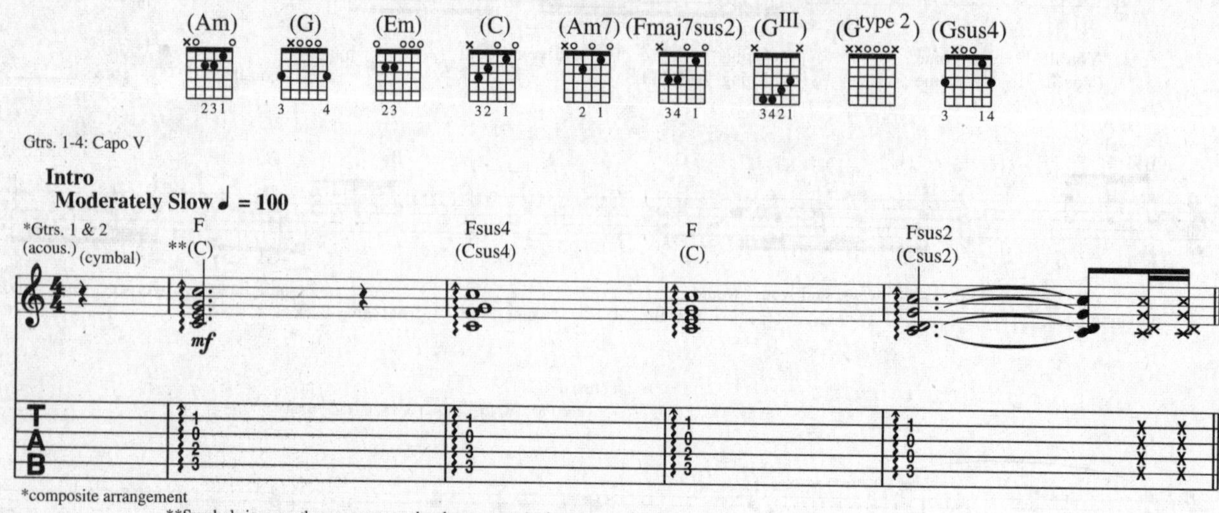

*composite arrangement

**Symbols in parentheses represent chord names respective to capoed guitar. Symbols above reflect actual sounding chord. Capoed fret is "0" in TAB.

B♭7
(F7)
- ni - fied.
He showed me what it was to cry.
End Rhy. Fig. 1
Gtrs. 1 & 2: w/ Rhy. Fig. 1, simile
F
(C)
Well, you could-n't be that man I a - dored.
Am
(Em)
You don't seem to know, seem to care what your heart is for.
B♭7
(F7)
I don't know him an - y - more. There's
Pre-Chorus
(Am)
Rhy. Fig. 2
Gtrs. 1 & 2
(G)
noth-in' where he used to lie.
My com - ver - sa - tion has run dry.
Gtr. 3 (elec.)
Rhy. Fig. 2A
mf
w/ clean tone & Leslie
let ring
(Em)
(G)
End Rhy. Fig. 2
That's what's go - in' on.
Noth - ing's fine, I'm torn.
End Rhy. Fig. 2A

𝄋 Chorus

(C)
Rhy. Fig. 3
(G)
Voc. Fig. 1
(Ah.
I'm all out of faith,
this is how I feel.
Rhy. Fig. 3A
let ring

(Am7)
(Fmaj7sus2)
End Rhy. Fig. 3
I'm cold and I am shamed,
ly - ing na - ked on the floor.
End Voc. Fig. 1
)
End Rhy. Fig. 3A
let ring

Gtrs. 1, 2 & 3: w/ Rhy. Figs. 3 & 3A, simile
Bkgd. voc.: w/ Voc. Fig. 1
F
(C)
C
(G)
Dm7
(Am7)
Il - lu - sion nev - er changed in - to some - thing real.
I'm wide a - wake and I

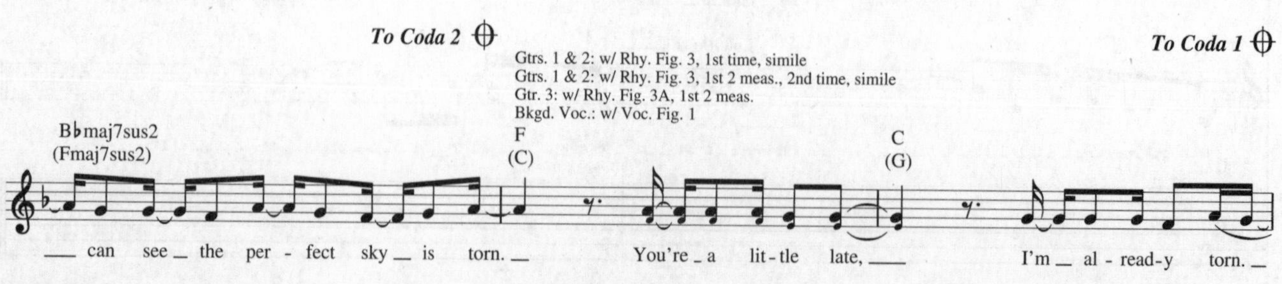

To Coda 2
To Coda 1
Gtrs. 1 & 2: w/ Rhy. Fig. 3, 1st time, simile
Gtrs. 1 & 2: w/ Rhy. Fig. 3, 1st 2 meas., 2nd time, simile
Gtr. 3: w/ Rhy. Fig. 3A, 1st 2 meas.
Bkgd. Voc.: w/ Voc. Fig. 1
B♭maj7sus2
(Fmaj7sus2)
F
(C)
C
(G)
can see the per - fect sky is torn.
You're a lit - tle late,
I'm al - read - y torn.

Verse
Gtrs. 1 & 2: w/ Rhy. Fig. 1, simile
Gtr. 3 tacet
Dm7
(Am7)
B♭maj7sus2
(Fmaj7sus2)
F
(C)
2. So I guess the for-tune-tell-er's right.
Gtr. 3
Gtr. 4 (elec.)
mf
w/ dist. & Leslie
let ring
Am
(Em)
B♭7
(F7)
I should have seen just what was there and not some ho-ly light, but you
let ring
Pre-Chorus
Gtrs. 1, 2, & 3: w/ Rhy. Figs. 2 & 2A
Dm
(Am)
C
(G)
crawled be-neath my veins and now, I don't care, I have no luck. I don't miss it all that much.
D.S. al Coda 1
Am
(Em)
Gtr. 3
(cont. in notation)
There's just so man-y things that I can't touch. I'm torn.
mp
mf

Coda 1
(Am7)
(G type 2)
(Fmaj7sus2)
Gtrs. 1 & 2
Gtr. 3
let ring
(Am7)
(G type 2)
(Fmaj7sus2)
(Gtr. 1, cont. in notation)
Torn.
let ring
Interlude
Gtr. 3 tacet
(Am)
Gtr. 2
(Oo,
oo.
Gtr. 1
(C)
p
(G)
)
There's

Pre-Chorus

Gtrs. 1 & 2: w/ Rhy. Fig. 2
Dm
(Am)
C
(G)
noth - ing where _ he used to lie. ___ My in - spi - ra - tion has run dry.
Gtr. 4

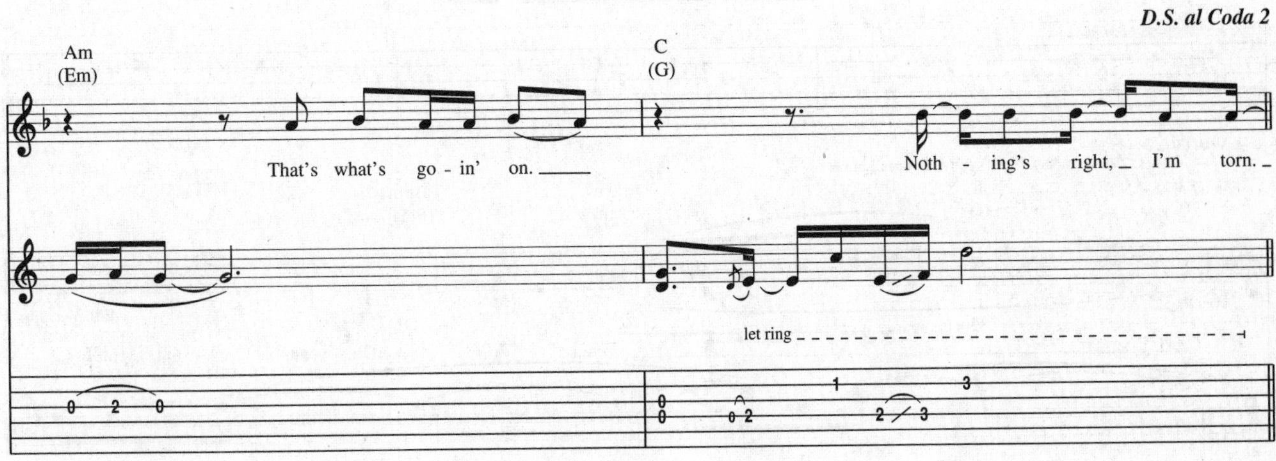
D.S. al Coda 2
Am
(Em)
C
(G)
That's what's go - in' on. ___ Noth - ing's right, _ I'm torn. _
let ring

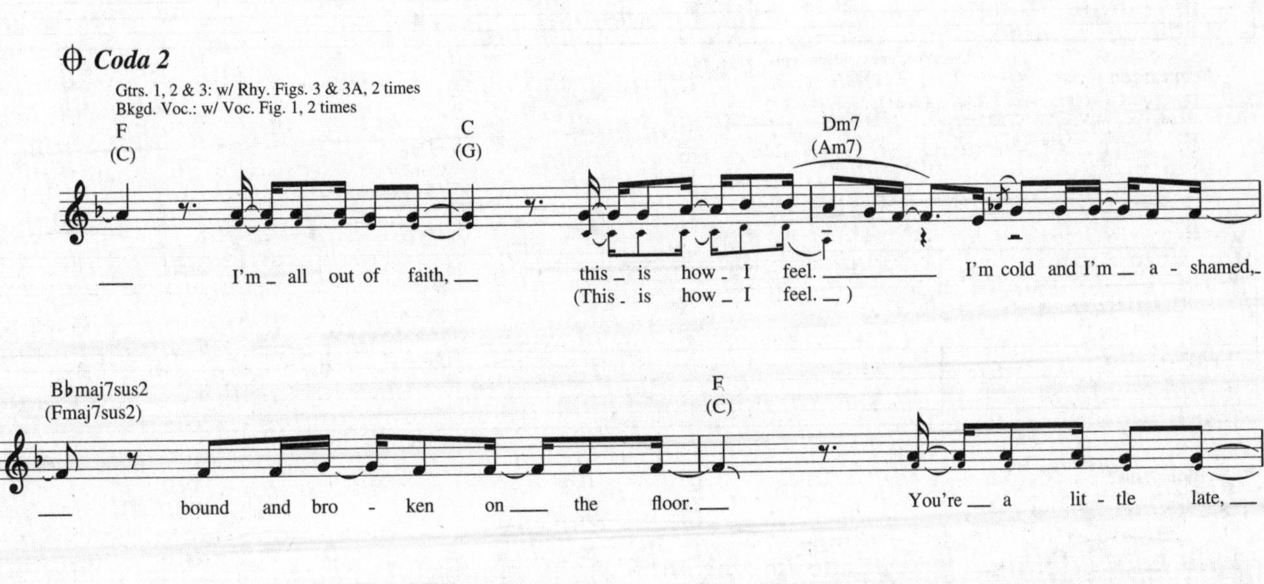
Coda 2
Gtrs. 1, 2 & 3: w/ Rhy. Figs. 3 & 3A, 2 times
Bkgd. Voc.: w/ Voc. Fig. 1, 2 times
F
(C)
C
(G)
Dm7
(Am7)
___ I'm _ all out of faith, ___ this _ is how _ I feel. ___ I'm cold and I'm _ a - shamed, _
(This _ is how _ I feel. _)
B♭maj7sus2
(Fmaj7sus2)
F
(C)
___ bound and bro - ken on ___ the floor. ___ You're _ a lit - tle late, _
C
(G)
Dm7
(Am7)
B♭maj7sus2
(Fmaj7sus2)
___ I'm ___ al - read - y torn. ___

(Am7)
(G type 2)
(G)
(Gsus4)
Gtrs. 1 & 2
Torn.
(Ah, ah. Ah, ah.)
Oh.
Gtr. 5 (elec.)
mf
w/ dist. & slide
Gtr. 3
let ring
Outro
Gtrs. 1, 2 & 3: w/ Rhy. Figs. 3 & 3A, 2 times, simile
F
(C)
C
(G)
Dm7
(Am7)
B♭maj7sus2
(Fmaj7sus2)
Voc. Fig. 2
End Voc. Fig. 2
Oo.
(Ah.
Oh, yeah. Oh, yeah.)
Gtr. 5
*Lead Voc. sings 2nd time only.
Begin Fade
Gtrs. 1, 2 & 3: w/ Rhy. Figs. 3 & 3A, till fade, simile
Bkgd. Voc.: w/ Voc. Fig. 2, till fade
Fade Out

T-R-O-U-B-L-E

Words and Music by Jerry Chesnut

Gtrs. 1 & 2: w/ Rhy. Figs. 1 & 1A, 3 times
G6 G5
Gtr. 3
1. Well, I play an
Verse
Gtr. 1 tacet
Gtr. 3 tacet
C5 C6 C5 G5 D5 D6
old gui - tar from nine 'til half past one.
Gtr. 1
let ring
Gtr. 2
Rhy. Fig. 2
I'm just try'n' to make a liv - ing watch - ing ev - 'ry - bod - y else hav -

Gtr. 2: w/ Rhy. Fig. 2
G5
G6 G5
G6 G5
G6 G5
G6 G5
C5
C6 C5
C6 C5
ing fun.
Well, I don't miss much if it
let ring
End Rhy. Fig. 2
C6 C5
C6 C5
G5
G6 G5
G6 G5
G6 G5
G6 G5
hap - pens on the dance hall floor.
Gtr. 1
let ring
let ring
D5
D6 D5
D6 D5
C5
C6 C5
C6 C5
G5
G6 G5
G6 G5
Mer - cy, look what just walked through that door.
Chorus
Gtr. 2: w/ Rhy. Fig. 2, 1 3/4 times, simile
G6 G5
G6 G5
C5
C6 C5
C6 C5
C6 C5
C6 C5
Well, hel - lo T - R - O - U - B - L - E,

G5
G6
G5
G6
G5
G6
G5
G6
G5
D5
D6
D5
D6
D5
tell me what in the world — you do - in'
Gtr. 1
Gtr. 3
C5
C6
C5
C6
C5
G5
G6
G5
G6
G5
G6
G5
G6
G5
A - L - O - N - E?
Yeah, say hey
C5
C6
C5
C6
C5
C6
C5
C6
C5
G5
G6
G5
G6
G5
good L - dou - ble O - K - I - N - G.

G6 G5 G6 G5 D5 D6 D5 D6 D5 C5 C6 C5 C6 C5
Well, I smell T - R - O - U - B - L -
Gtr. 2 tacet
C
E.
Yeah.
Gtr. 2: w/ Rhy. Fig. 1A
G5 G6 G5 G6 G5 G6 G5 G6 G5
2. I was a
Verse
Gtrs. 2 & 3 tacet
N.C. (G)
Gtr. 1: w/ Rhy. Fig. 3, 7 times, simile
lit - tle bit - ty ba - by when my pa - pa hit the skids. Ma - ma had a time try'n' to
sweet talk - in', sex - y walk - in', hon - ky tonk - in' ba - by. The men are gon - na love you and the
Gtr. 1
Rhy. Fig. 3
End Rhy. Fig. 3

raise nine kids. She told me not to stare 'cause it was im - po - lite. She
wom - en gon - na hate you. Re - mind - ing them of ev - 'ry - thing they're nev - er gon - na be
Gtr. 3
steady glisses
did the best she could to try to raise ___ me right, but then ma - ma nev - er told me 'bout
may be the be - gin - ning of a World ___ War Three 'cause the world ___ ain't read - y for
Gtr. 2: w/ Rhy. Fig. 2
C5 C6 C5 C6 C5
Gtr. 1
Gtr. 3
C6 C5 C6 C5 G5 G6 G5 G6 G5 G6 G5 G6 G5
noth - in' like ___ Y - O - U. Bet your ma -
noth - in' like ___ Y - O - U. I bet your

Gtr. 3: w/ Fill 1, 2nd time
D5 D6 D5 D6 D5 C5 C6 C5 C6 C5 G5 G6 G5 G6 G5
- ma may have been an - oth - er good look - in' hon - ey, too.
ma - ma must have been an - oth - er good look - in' ma - ma, too.
8va

Chorus

Gtr. 2: w/ Rhy. Fig. 2, 1st 6 meas. only
G6 G5 G6 G5 C5 C6 C5 C6 C5 C6 C5 C6 C5
Yeah, hey good L - dou - ble O - K - I - N - G.
8va

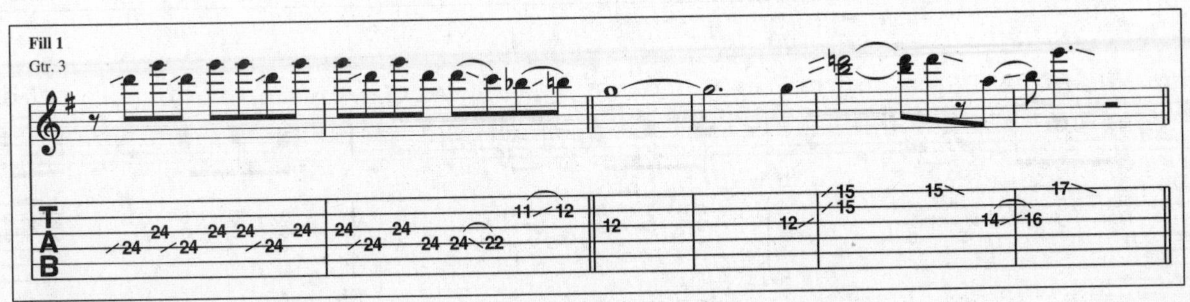
Fill 1
Gtr. 3

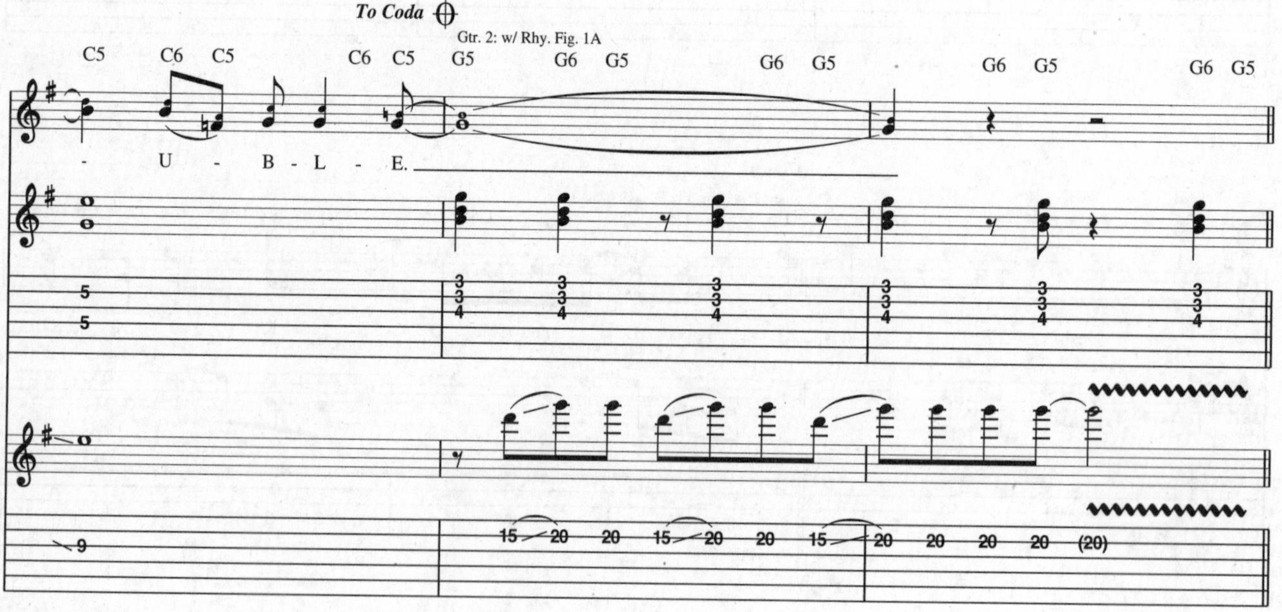

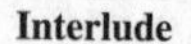
Interlude

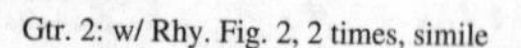
Gtr. 2: w/ Rhy. Fig. 2, 2 times, simile

Gtr. 3 tacet

Gtr. 1 C5 C6 C5 C6 C5 C6 C5 C6 C5 G5 G6 G5 G6 G5 G6 G5 G6 G5

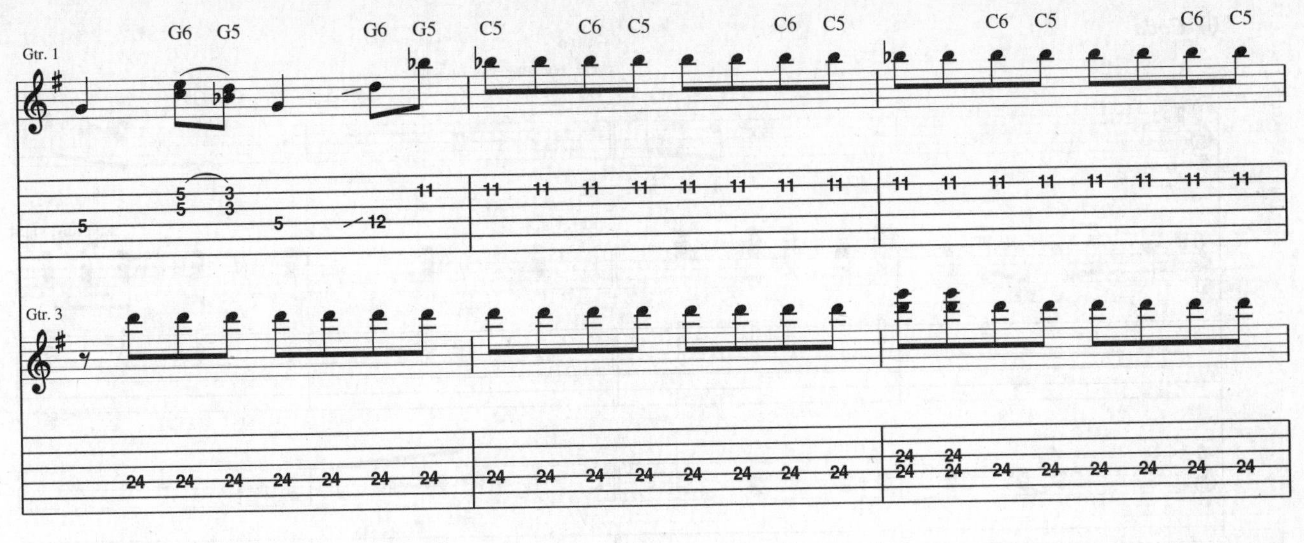
Gtr. 1
G6 G5
G6 G5
C5
C6 C5
C6 C5
C6 C5
C6 C5
Gtr. 3

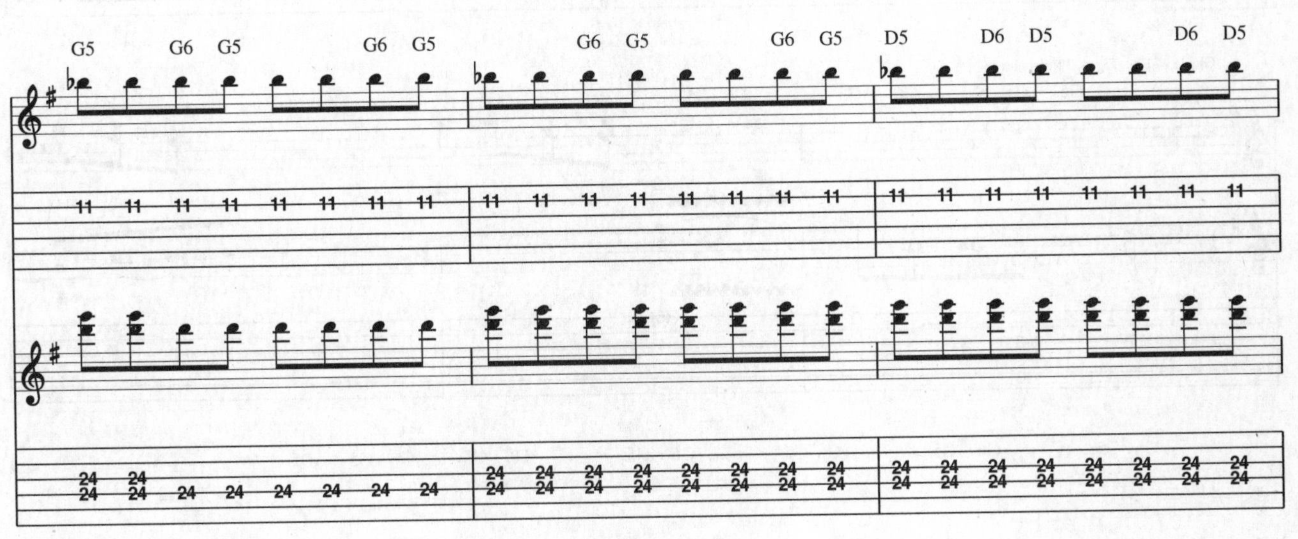
G5
G6 G5
G6 G5
G6 G5
G6 G5
D5
D6 D5
D6 D5

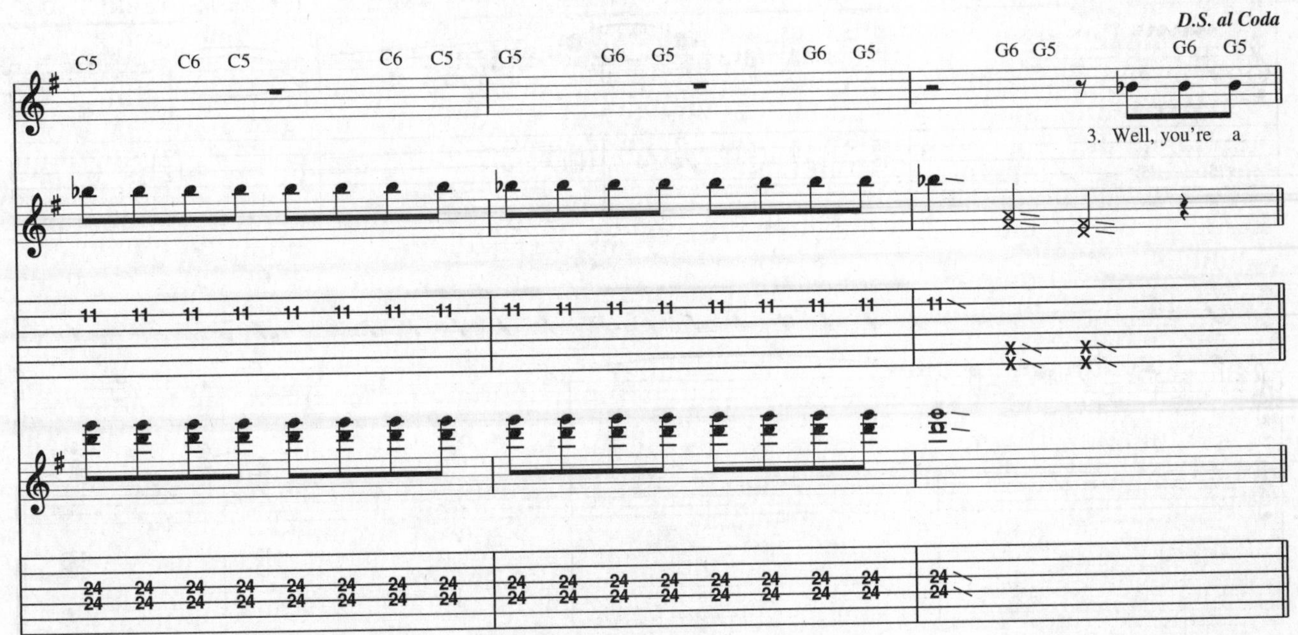
D.S. al Coda
C5
C6 C5
C6 C5
G5
G6 G5
G6 G5
G6 G5
G6 G5
3. Well, you're a

Coda
Outro
Gtr. 2 tacet
C
Gtr. 2: w/ Rhy. Fig. 1A, 4 times
G5 G6 G5 G6 G5 G6 G5 G6 G5
I say, hey.
I say, hey.
Rhy. Fig. 4
End Rhy. Fig. 4
Gtr. 1: w/ Rhy. Fig. 4, 3 times, simile
G6 G5 G6 G5 G6 G5 G6 G5 G6 G5 G6 G5
I say, hey.
I say, hey.
G6 G5 G6 G5 G6 G5 G6 G5 G6 G5 G6 G5 D5
Gtrs. 1 & 2
I say, hey.
Yeah.
Well,
I smell T - R - O -
G5
C5
G
G7
G
- U - B - L - E.

Tuff Enuff

Words and Music by Kim Wilson

Chorus
Gtr. 3: w/ Fill 1 (4 times)
B
D E
B
D E
tough e - nough? _
Ain't _ that
tough e - nough? _
Ain't _ that
Gtr. 2
Rhy. Fig. 2
End Rhy. Fig. 2
Riff B
Gtr. 1
End Riff B
*w/ octaver
*Set for one octave below
Gtrs. 1 & 2: w/ Riff B & Rhy. Fig. 2
2nd & 3rd times, Gtrs. 1 & 2: w/ Riff B & Rhy. Fig. 2 (1st 3 meas.)
1.
To Coda
B
D E
B
D E
tough e - nough? _
Ain't _ that
tough e - nough? _
2.
D
Gtrs. 1* & 2
E
Gtrs. 1 & 2
Fill 2
End Fill 2
8va
Gtr. 3
f
(cont. in slashes)
*Octave off
Fill 1
Gtr. 3
mf
** w/ delayed reverb
* vol. swell
** Set for quarter note regeneration w/ 4 repeats.

B
D
(Gtr. 1 cont. in notation)
(8va)
loco
8va
D.S. al Coda
E
B^II
Gtr. 2
3. I would
Gtr. 3
(8va)
Gtr. 1
slight P.M.
Coda
Verse
Gtrs. 1 & 2: w/ Riff A & Rhy. Fig. 1 (2 times)
B
4. I'd lay in a pile of burn - in' mon-ey that I've earned and
Gtr. 2
Gtr. 1
divisi
Octave off
not e - ven wor - ry a - bout get - ting burned. I'd climb the Em - pire State, fight Mu -
ham-med Al - i just to have you ba - by close to me.

Interlude
D
E
B
Ain't _ that
Gtr. 3
8va
loco
Gtrs. 1 & 2
Chorus
Gtr. 1 & 2: w/ Riff B & Rhy. Fig. 2 (1 3/4 times)
Gtr. 3: w/ Fill 1 (4 times)
tough e - nough? _
Ain't _ that tough e - nough? _
Ain't _ that
Gtrs. 1 & 2: w/ Fill 2
Outro-Chorus
tough e - nough? _
Ain't _ that
Gtr. 3
delay off
Gtr. 1
Riff C
End Riff C

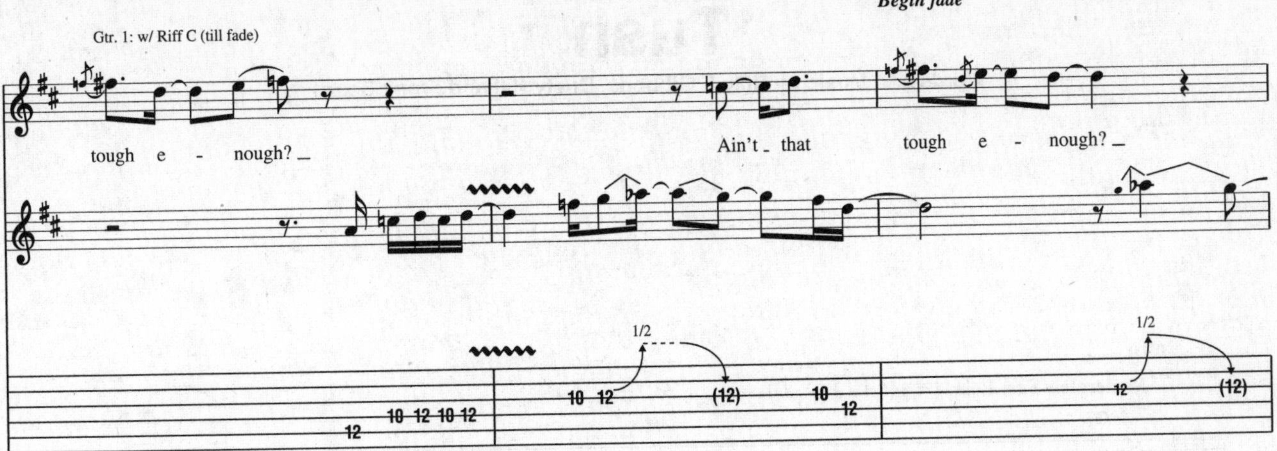

Begin fade
Gtr. 1: w/ Riff C (till fade)
tough e - nough?
Ain't that
tough e - nough?
1/2
10 12
(12)
10
12
10 12 10 12
12
1/2
12
(12)

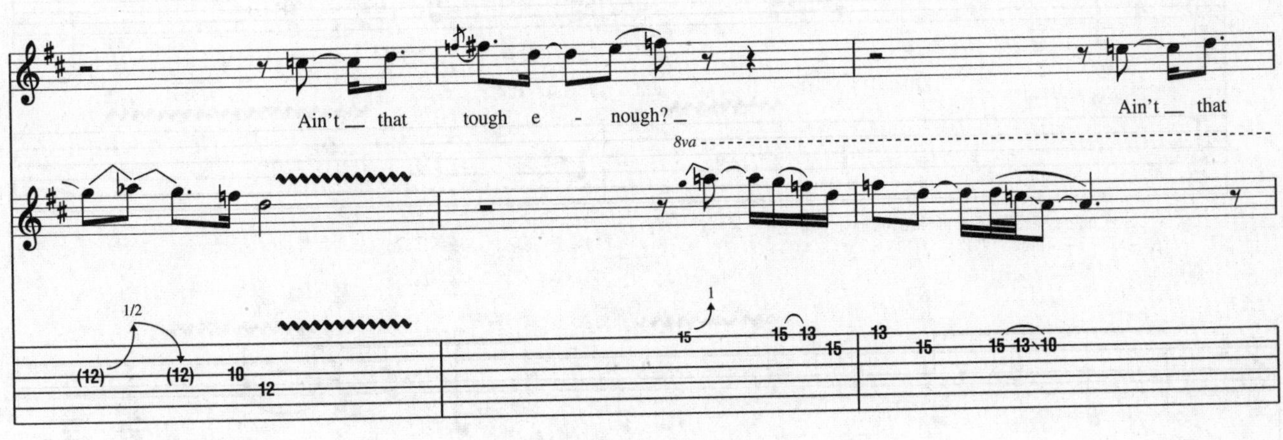

Ain't that
tough e - nough?
Ain't that
8va
1/2
(12)
(12)
10
12
1
15
15 13
15
13
15
15 13 10

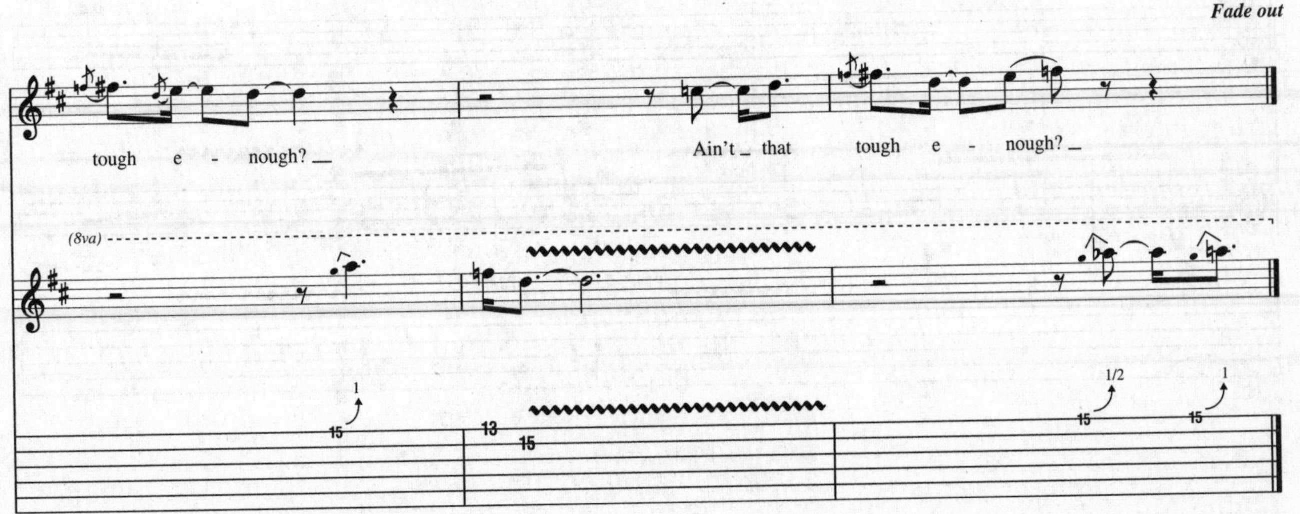

Fade out
tough e - nough?
Ain't that
tough e - nough?
(8va)
1
15
13
15
1/2
15
1
15

Tush

Words and Music by Billy F Gibbons, Dusty Hill and Frank Beard

Verse
G7
I've been down,
take my word,
my why 'round.
I've been good,
Dal - las, Tex - as,
Hol - ly - wood.
P.M.
C7
E7
F7
F♯7
I ain't ask - in' for much.
G7
D7
Mm.
I said, Lord, take me down - town,
C7
1.
G7
C7
C♯7
D7
I'm just look - in' for some tush
2. I've been bad,

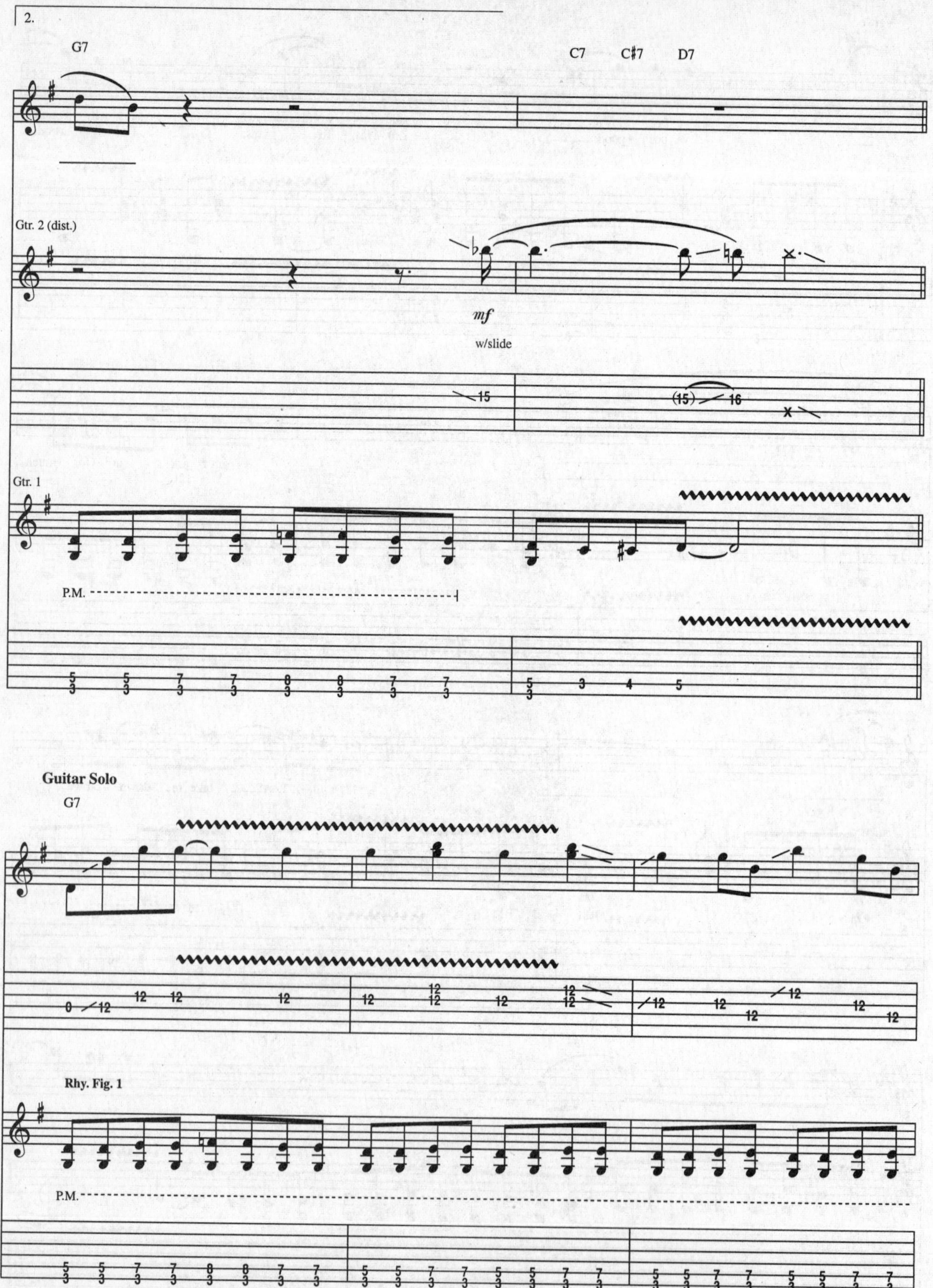

2.
G7
C7
C♯7
D7
Gtr. 2 (dist.)
mf
w/slide
Gtr. 1
P.M.
Guitar Solo
G7
Rhy. Fig. 1
P.M.

G♯7
A7
B♭7
C7
E7
F7
F♯7
P.M.
G7
D7
w/o slide
w/slide
C7
G7
C7 C♯7 D7
End Rhy. Fig. 1

Gtr. 1: w/Rhy. Fig. 1
G7
Gtr. 2
let ring
G♯7
A7
B♭7
C7
E7
F7
F♯7
G7
D7
C7
G7
C7
C♯7
D7
3. Take me back,

Verse
Gtr. 2 tacet
G7
way back home,
not by my - self,
not a - lone
Gtr. 1
P.M.
C7
E7
F7
F♯7
I
ain't
ask - in' for much.
Gtr. 2
Gtr. 2 tacet
G7
D7
Mm.
I said, Lord,
take me down - town,

C7
G7
N.C.
I'm just look - in' for some tush.
Gtr. 2
Gtr. 1
P.M.
P.M.
Outro-Guitar Solo
G7
P.M.

G♯7
A7
B♭7
C7
E7
F7
F♯7
P.M.
G7
D7
C7
G7 N.C.
A♭9 G9

Under the Bridge

Words and Music by Anthony Kiedis, Flea, John Frusciante and Chad Smith

* Symbols in parenthesis represent chord names respective to capoed guitar. Symbols above reflect actual sounding chord, and overall tonality.

C♯m A E B C♯m G♯m A
my on - ly friend is the cit - y I live in, the cit - y of an - gels.
Gtr. 2
band enters
E B C♯m A Emaj7
Lone - ly as I am, to - geth - er we cry. 2. I
Verse
E B C♯m G♯m A E B
drive on her streets 'cause she's my com - pan - ion. I walk through her hills 'cause she
hard to be - lieve that there's no - bod - y out there. It's hard to be - lieve that
Rhy. Fig. 1
simile 2nd time
let ring
C♯m A E B C♯m G♯m A
knows who I am. She sees my good deeds, and she kiss - es me wind - y.
I'm all a - lone. At least I have her love, the cit - y, she loves me.
End Rhy. Fig. 1
let ring

Pre-Chorus
E B C#m A Emaj7 F#m E
I nev - er wor - ry, now, that is a lie.
Lone-ly as I am, to-geth - er we cry.
I don't ev-er wan-na feel
let ring
B F#m E B F#m
like I did that day. Take me to the place I love, take me all the way.
Rhy. Fig. 2
End Rhy. Fig. 2
Gtr. 2: w/ Rhy. Fig. 2, 2 times
E B F#m E
I don't ev - er wan - na feel like I did that day. Take me to the place I love,
1.
Gtr. 2: w/ Rhy. Fig. 1, simile
B F#m E B C#m G#m A E B C#m A
take me all the way, yeah. Yeah, yeah.
3. It's
Bridge
2.
B F#m A Am G6 Fmaj7
take me all the way, yeah. Yeah, yeah.
Gtr. 2
Rhy. Fig. 3
End Rhy. Fig. 3
w/ chorus

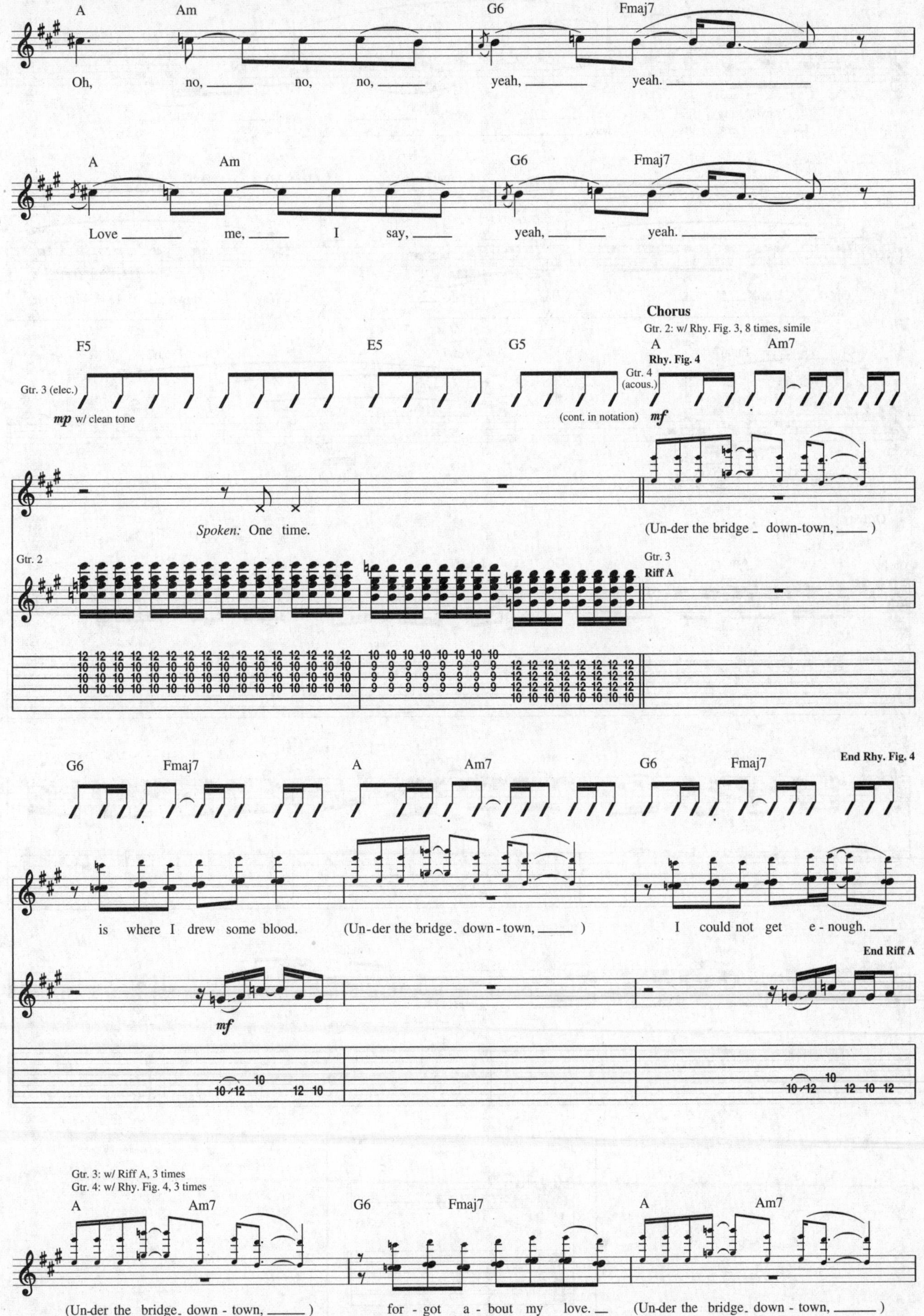

Gtr. 2: w/ Rhy. Fig. 3, 2 times, simile
A
Am
G6
Fmaj7
Oh, no, no, no, yeah, yeah.
A
Am
G6
Fmaj7
Love me, I say, yeah, yeah.
Chorus
Gtr. 2: w/ Rhy. Fig. 3, 8 times, simile
F5
E5
G5
A
Am7
Rhy. Fig. 4
Gtr. 3 (elec.)
mp w/ clean tone
Gtr. 4 (acous.)
(cont. in notation)
mf
Spoken: One time.
(Un-der the bridge down-town,)
Gtr. 2
Gtr. 3
Riff A
G6
Fmaj7
A
Am7
G6
Fmaj7
End Rhy. Fig. 4
is where I drew some blood.
(Un-der the bridge down-town,)
I could not get e-nough.
End Riff A
mf
Gtr. 3: w/ Riff A, 3 times
Gtr. 4: w/ Rhy. Fig. 4, 3 times
A
Am7
G6
Fmaj7
A
Am7
(Un-der the bridge down-town,)
for-got a-bout my love.
(Un-der the bridge down-town,)

G6
Fmaj7
A
Am7
I gave my life a - way,
yeah,
yeah,
yeah.
I gave my life a - way.
A -
Oh,
no,
no, no, no,
way.
Way down I said, oh,
A - way.
Spoken: Will I stay?
Outro
Gtr. 3: w/ Fill 1
Gtr. 4 tacet
Gtr. 2
Gtr. 3 tacet
Am
let ring
rit.
Fill 1
Gtr. 3

Wait

Words and Music by Mike Tramp and Vito Bratta

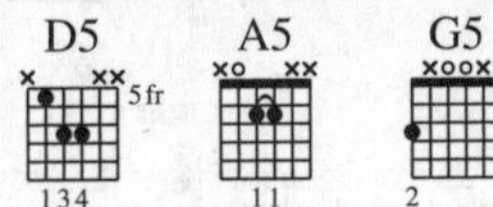

Intro

Moderate Rock ♩ = 144

*D A/D C/D

Wait, wait, I nev - er had a chance to love

Gtr. 1 (12 str. acous.)

mp

w/ pick & fingers

let ring throughout

*Chord symbols reflect implied tonality.

G/D B♭/D A5

you. Now I on - ly wan - na say I love you one more time.

Gtr. 1

Gtr. 2 (elec.)

mp P.M.

w/ dist.

f

Verse
A
1. Wait
Riff A
mf
w/ pick

Gtr. 2 tacet
A7
D/A
Dm(add9)/A
A
just a mo - ment be - fore our love will die, 'cause I must
Gtr. 1

A7
D
Dm(add9)/A
A
know the rea - son why we say good - bye. Wait

A7
D
Dm(add9)/A
A
just a mo - ment and tell me why, 'cause I can
A7
D
Dm/A
show you lov - in' that you won't de - ny.
End Riff A
Gtr. 1
(cont. in slashes)
Gtr. 2
Interlude
Gtr. 1 tacet
A
A7
D/F#
Dm/F
*w/ delay
delay off
P.M.
*Set for quarter-note regeneration w/ 3 repeats
Dm/F N.C.
A5
2. I said wait,

Verse

A
A/G
D/F#
Dm/F
and show your lov - in' like it was be - fore,
P.M.
A5
A
A/G
D/F#
'cause I won't let that feel - in' walk
Dm/F
A5
A
A7
out through the door. I said wait just
D/F#
Dm/F
A
a mo - ment and try once more, 'cause babe,
let ring

Pre-Chorus

2nd time, Gtr. 4 tacet

B5 B/A E5 F#5 G5

So if you go __ a-way, I know that I __ will fol-

Gtr. 1

P.M. - ⊣

let ring - - ⊣

p *mf* *p*

Gtr. 2

Gtr. 3 (elec.)

f

w/ dist.

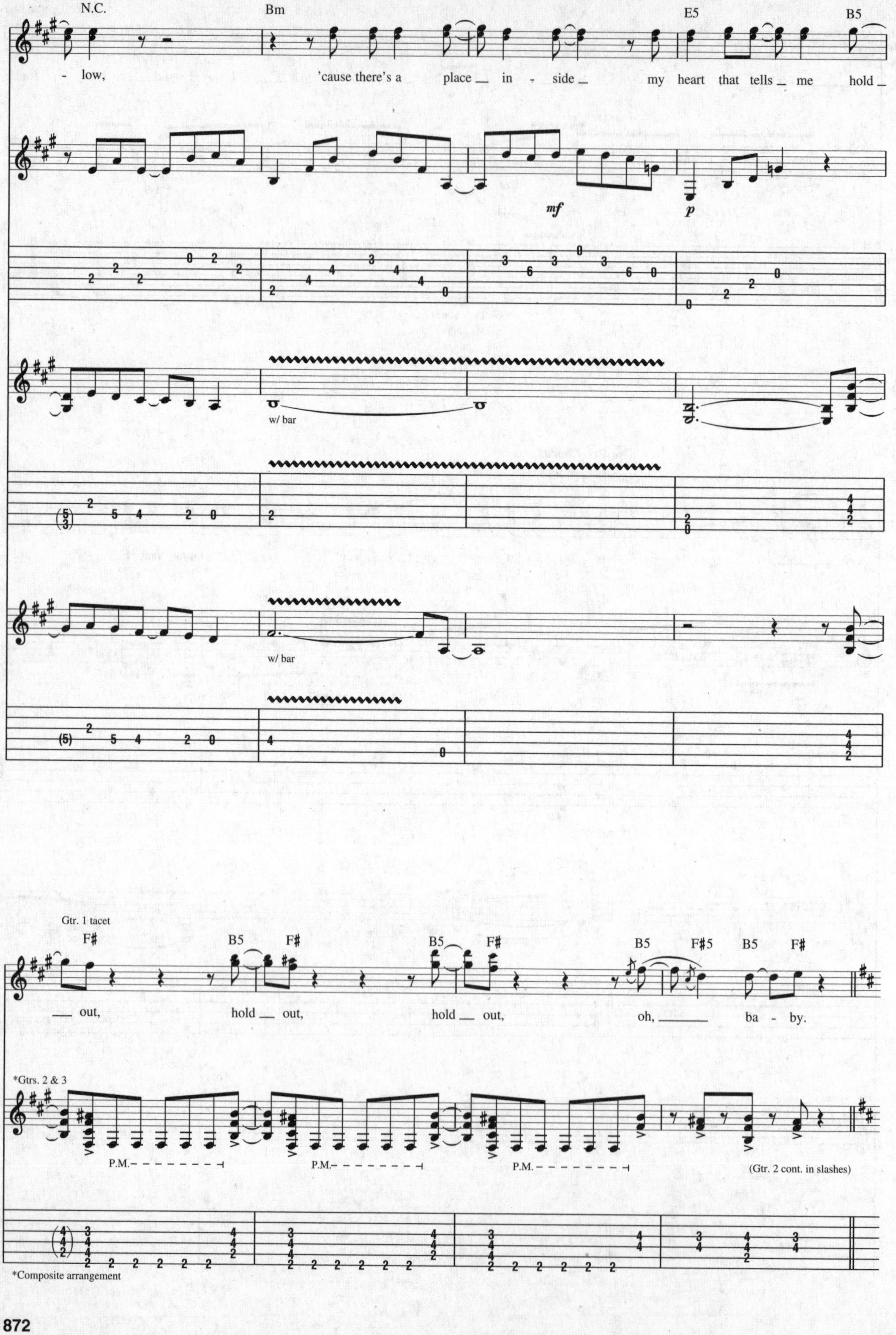

N.C. Bm E5 B5

-low, 'cause there's a place in - side my heart that tells me hold

mf *p*

w/ bar

w/ bar

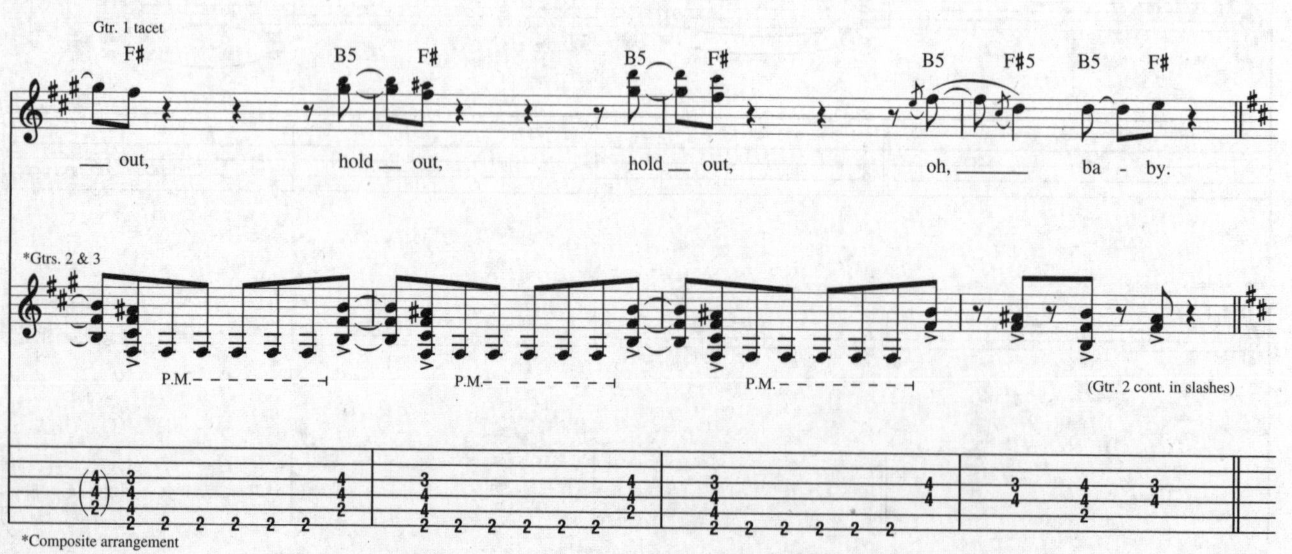

Chorus

D5 A5 G5 A5

Rhy. Fig. 1 End Rhy. Fig. 1

Gtr. 2

Wait, wait, ____ I nev - er had a chance to love ____ you.

Gtr. 3

P.M. P.M. P.M. P.M.

Gtrs. 2 & 3: w/ Rhy. Fill 1 (2nd time)

D5 A5 G F♯ E5 A

⑥ ⑥

3fr 2fr

(cont. in notation)

Wait, wait, ____ if on - ly our love could show ____ you.

Gtrs. 2 & 3

P.M. P.M.

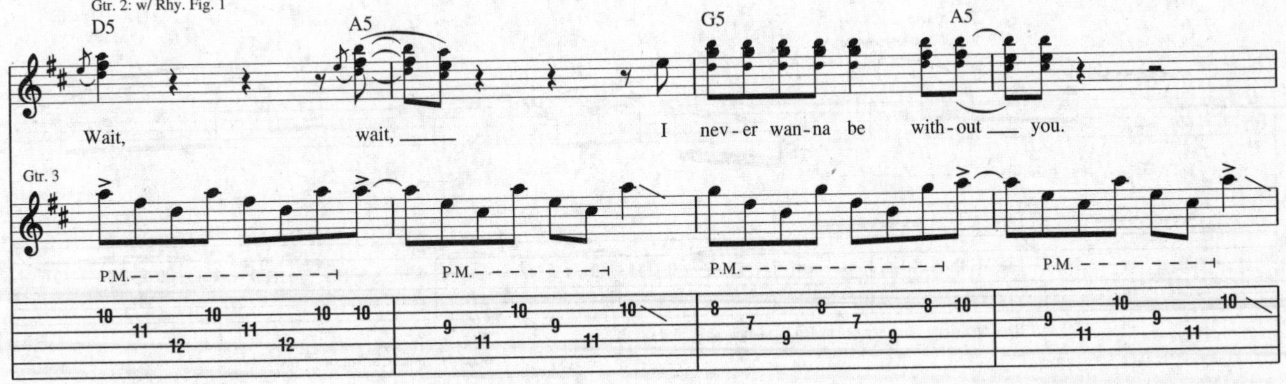

Guitar Solo

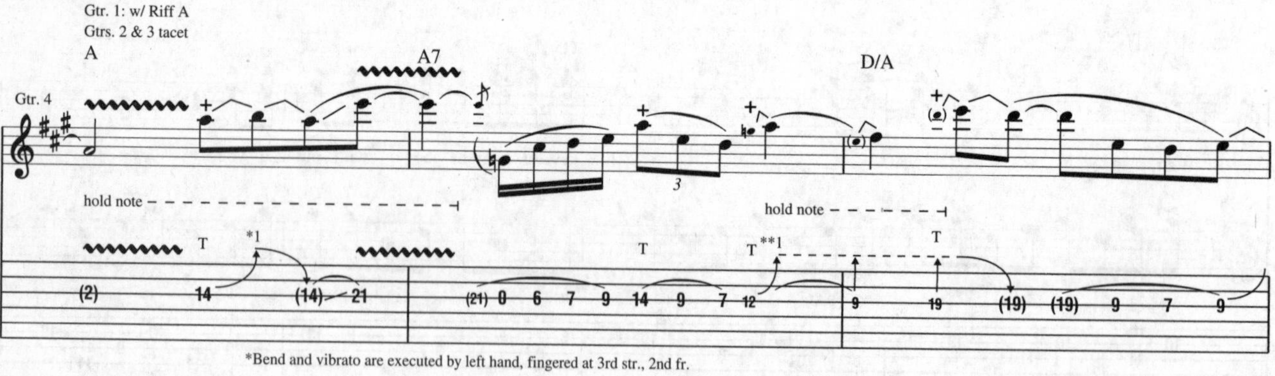

*Bend and vibrato are executed by left hand, fingered at 3rd str., 2nd fr.

**Bend w/ left hand at 3rd str., 9 fr.

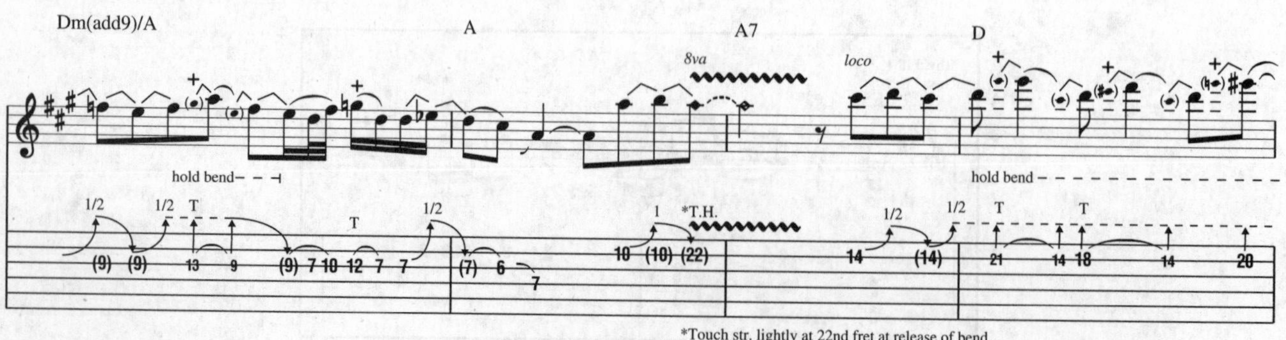

*Touch str. lightly at 22nd fret at release of bend.

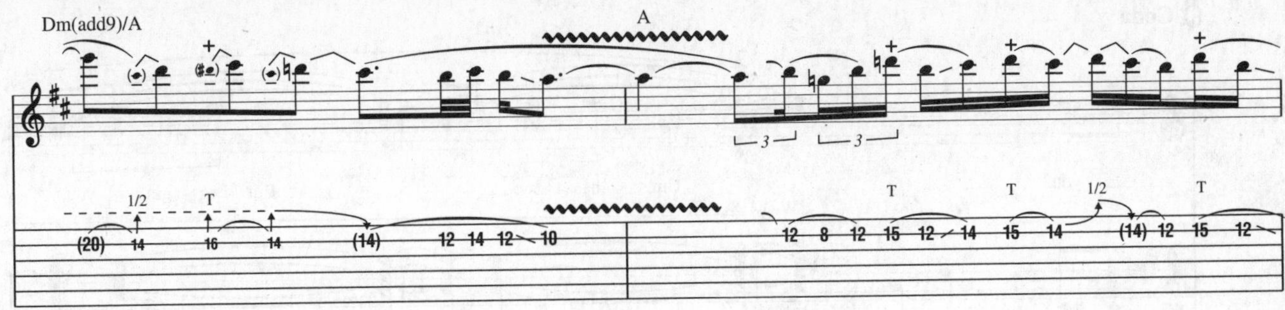
Dm(add9)/A
A
steady gliss.

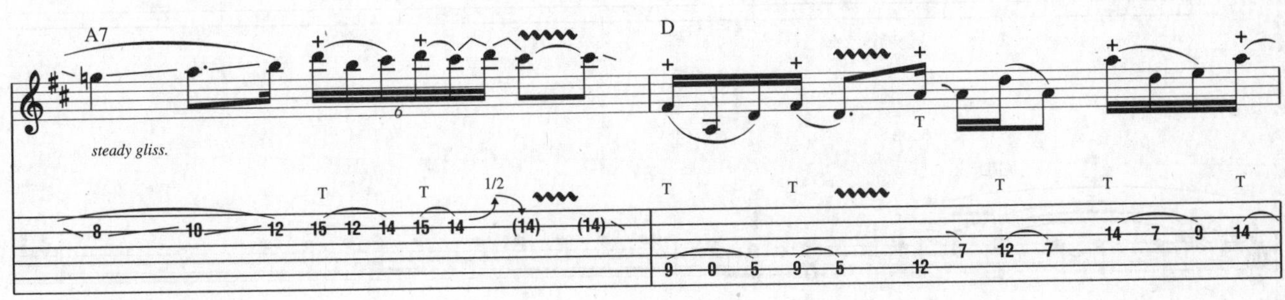
A7
D
steady gliss.

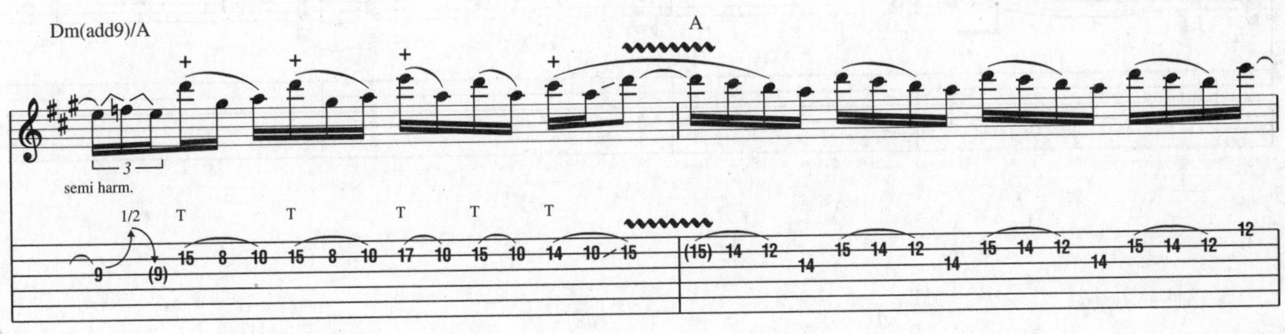
Dm(add9)/A
A
semi harm.

A7
D
8va
D.S. al Coda
Gtr. 4
w/ delay
Gtr. 1

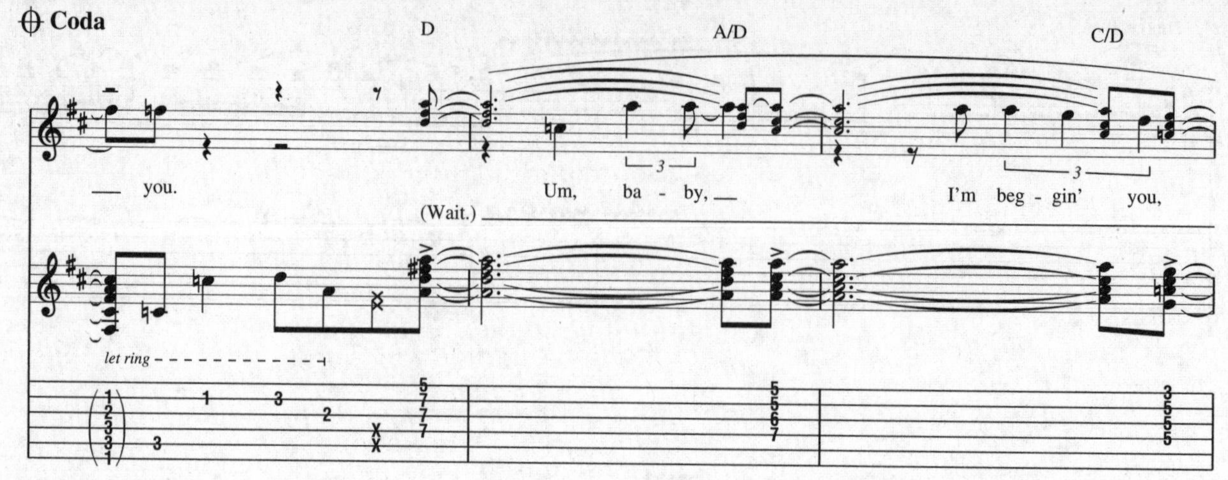
Coda
D
A/D
C/D
you.
(Wait.)
Um, ba - by,
I'm beg - gin' you,
let ring

G/D
B♭
F/A
wait - ing.
No, I nev - er had a chance to love you.

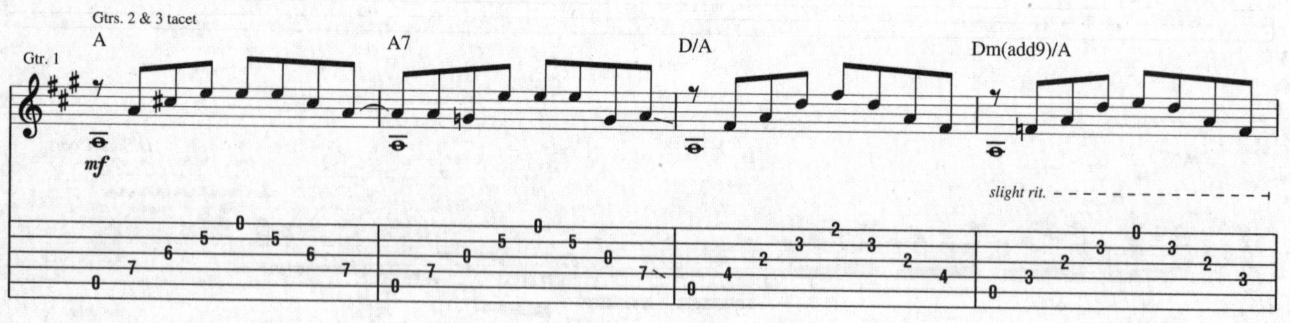
Gtrs. 2 & 3 tacet
A
A7
D/A
Dm(add9)/A
Gtr. 1
mf
slight rit.

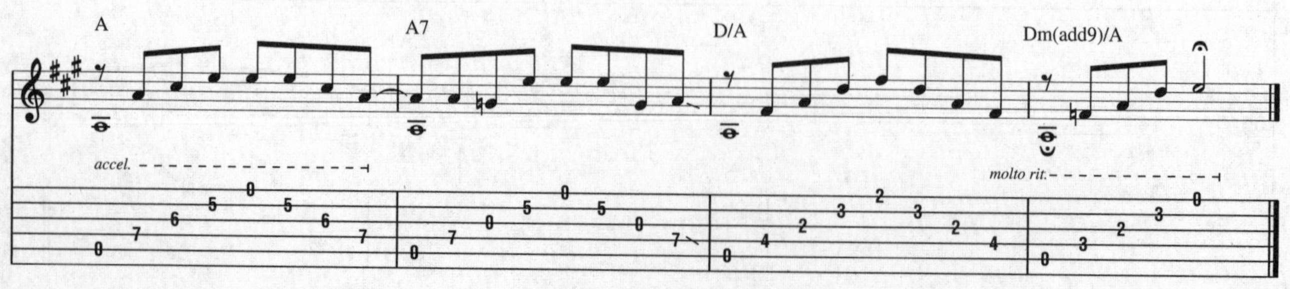
A
A7
D/A
Dm(add9)/A
accel.
molto rit.

Walk Don't Run

By Johnny Smith

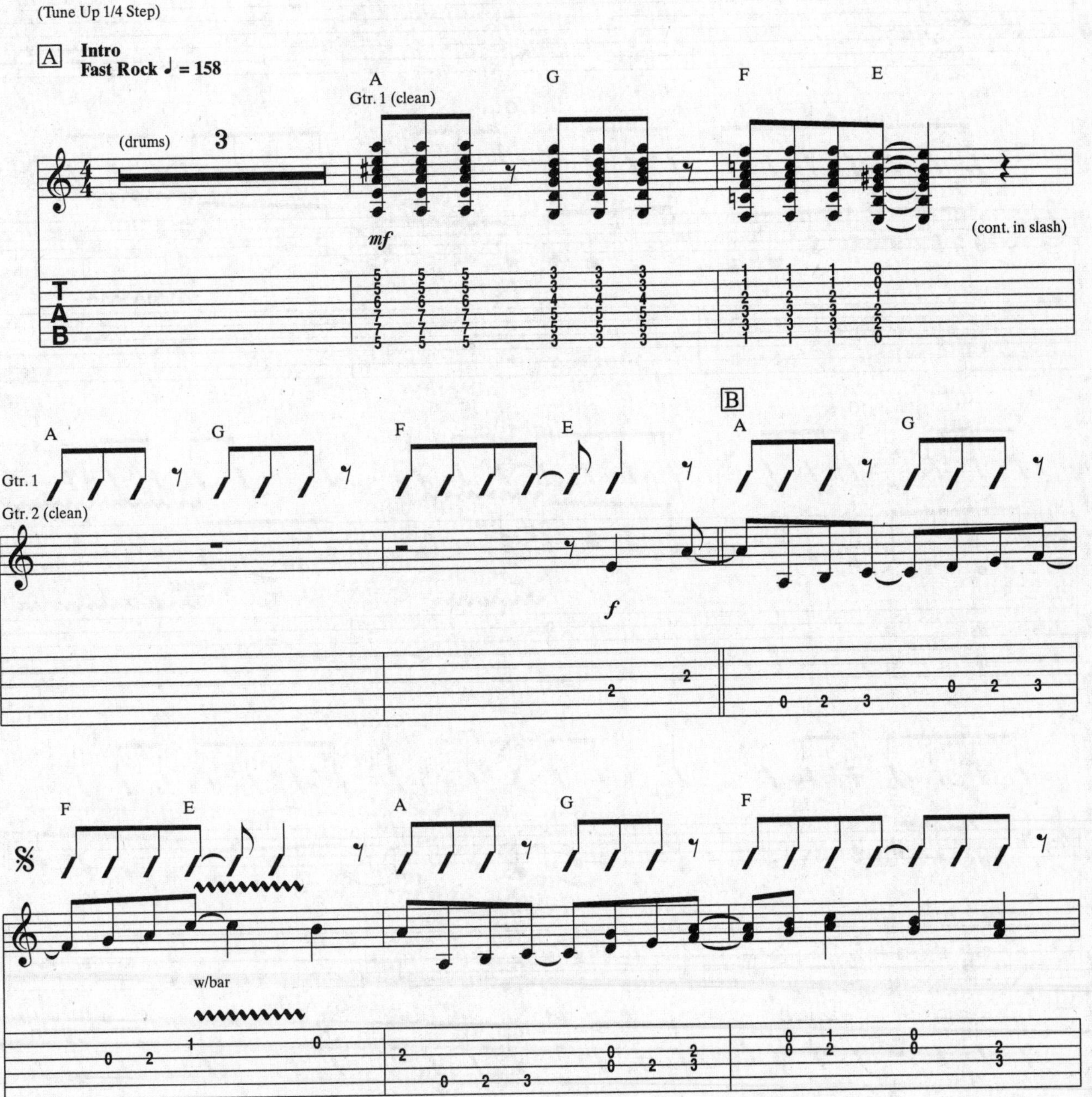

To Coda 1
C
G open
E
A
G
F
w/bar
Am
-1/2

F
E
-1/2
w/bar
let ring
B
D.S. al Coda 1
To Coda 2
Am
A
G
Coda 1
C
F
Gopen
D.C. al Coda 2
Coda 2

War Pigs

(Interpolating Luke's Wall)

Words and Music by Frank Iommi, John Osbourne, William Ward and Terence Butler

D5 E5
sor - cer - er of death's con - struc - tion.
Hand of God has struck the hour.
In the fields the bod - ies
Day of judge - ment, God is call -
burn - ing.
- ing,
as the war mach - ine keeps turn - ing.
on their knees, the war pigs crawl - ing.
Gtr. 2
Death and hat - red to man - kind,
Beg - ging mer - cies for their sins,
Em
pois - on - ing their brain - washed
Sat - an laugh - ing, spreads his
Interlude
4th time, To Coda
G5 F#5 F5 E5
minds.
wings.
Oh, Lord, yeah!
Gtrs. 1 & 2
1.
2.
N.C.
Rhy. Fig. 2
End Rhy. Fig. 2
P.M.

N.C.
Em
P.M.
Bridge
Gtr. 2: w/ Rhy. Fig. 2, 1st time
N.C.(E5)
1. Pol - i - ti - cian's hide them - selves a - way,
2. Time will tell on their pow - er minds,
Gtr. 1
Gtrs. 1 & 2
1/2
they on - ly start - ed the war.
mak - ing war Just for fun.
Riff A
End Riff A
Gtrs. 1 & 2: w/ Riff A, 2 times
Why should they go out to fight?
Treat - ing peo - ple just like pawns in chess,
They leave that all to the poor! Yeah!
Wait till their Judge-ment Day comes. Yeah!
Interlude
D5 E5
F5 F#5
F5
E5
G5 F#5

Guitar Solo
1.
F5
E5
2.
F5
E5
N.C.(E5)
Gtr. 1
Gtr. 2
Gtr. 3 (dist.)
mf

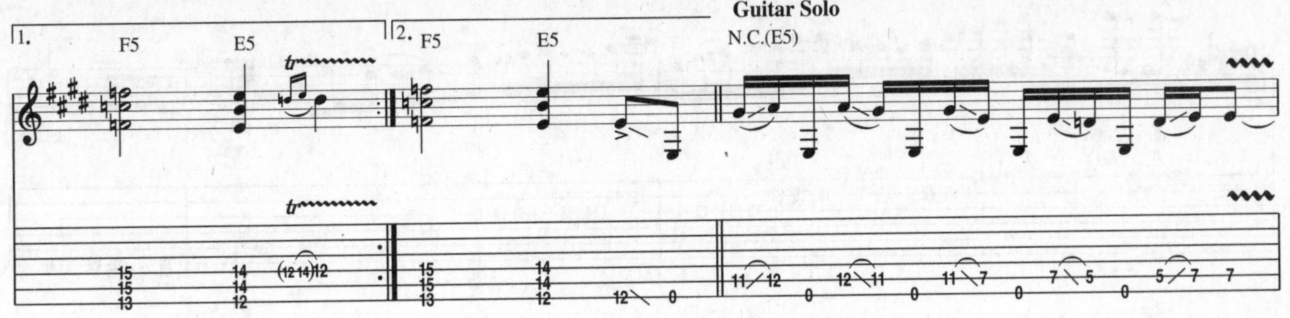

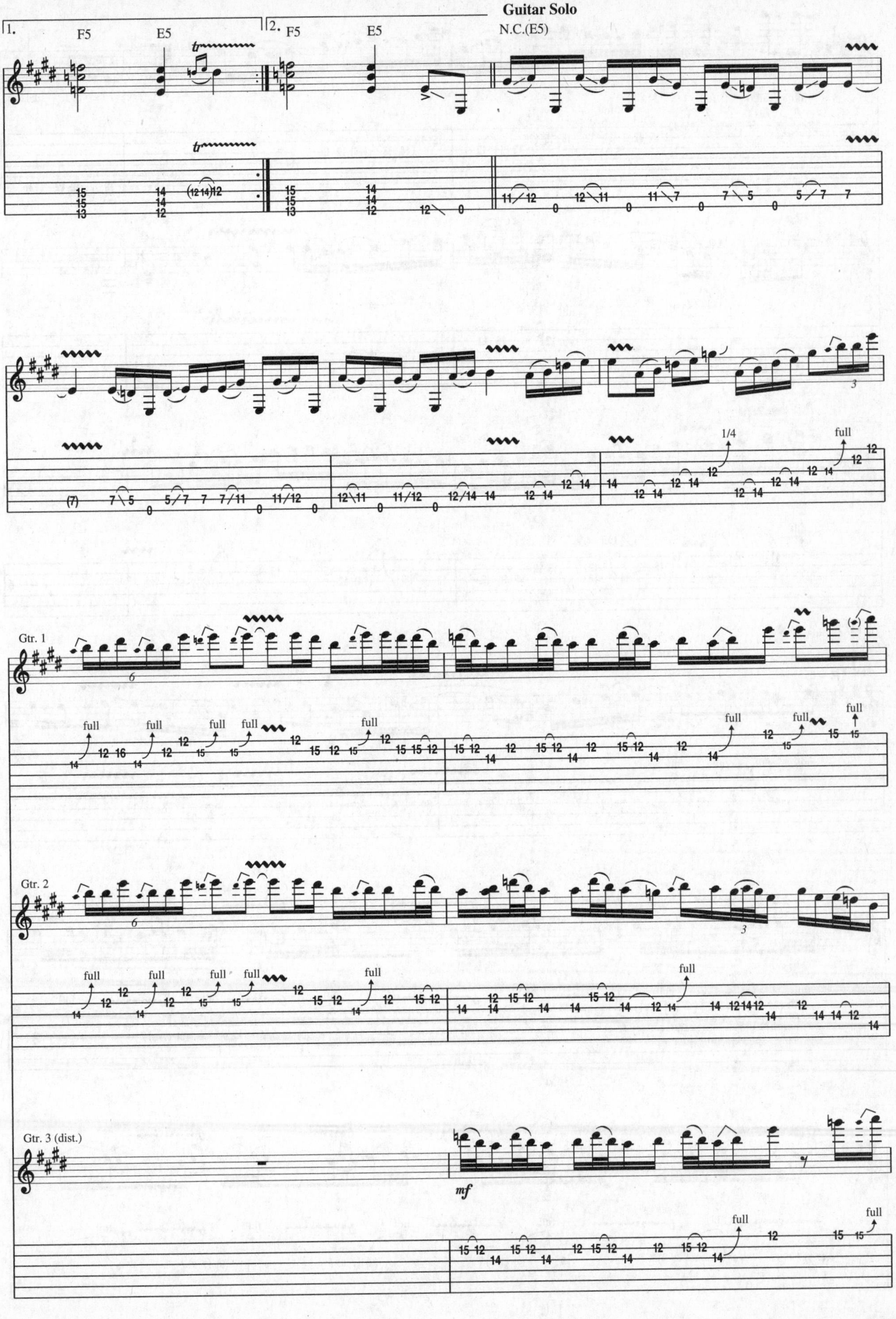

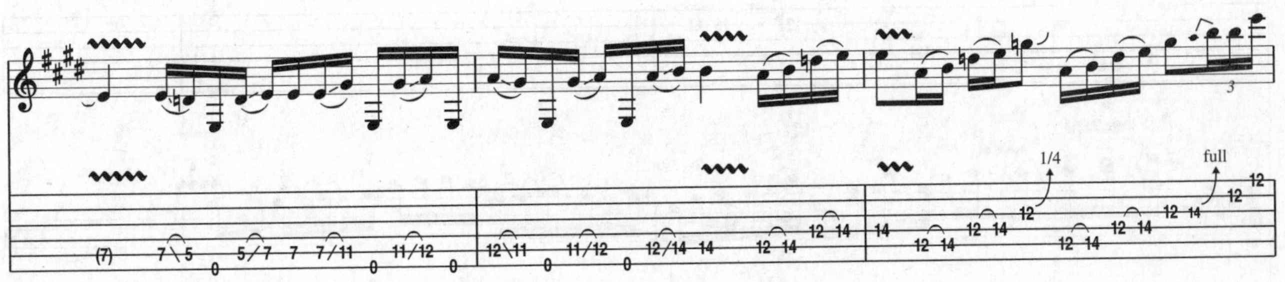

full
fdbk.
1/4
1/2
Gtrs. 1 & 2
Gtr. 3 tacet
tr

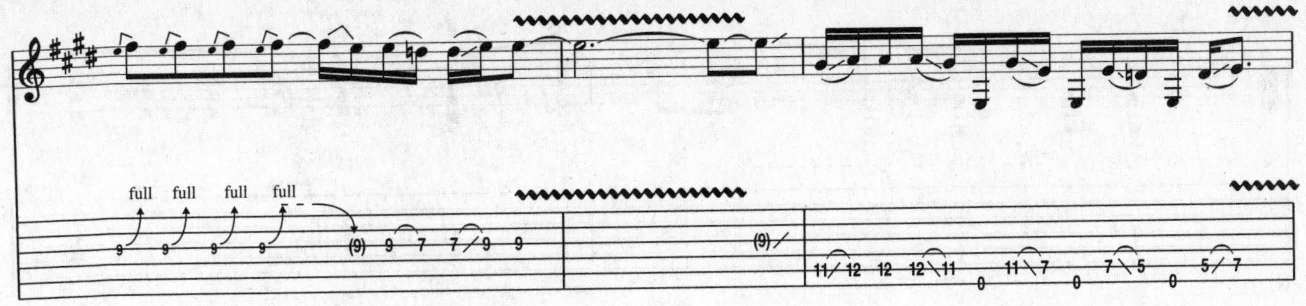
full
full
full
full

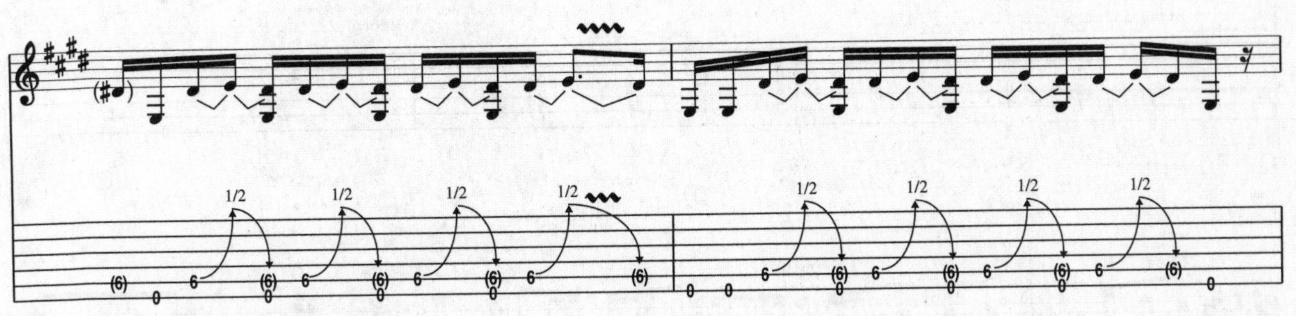
1/2
1/2
1/2
1/2
1/2
1/2
1/2
1/2

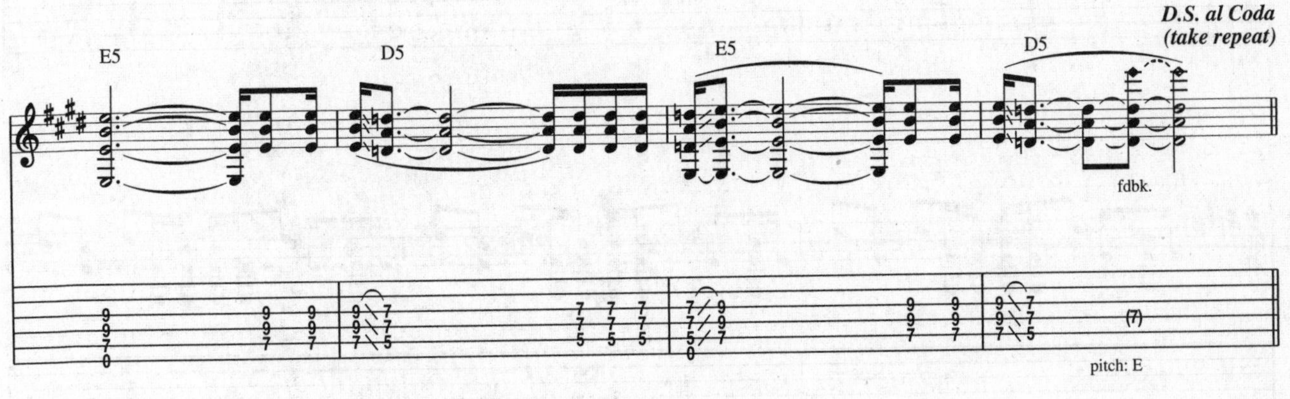
D.S. al Coda
(take repeat)
E5
D5
E5
D5
fdbk.
pitch: E

Coda
A "Luke's Wall"
Gtrs. 1 & 2
E7(no 3rd)
let ring

E5
B5
D5
let ring

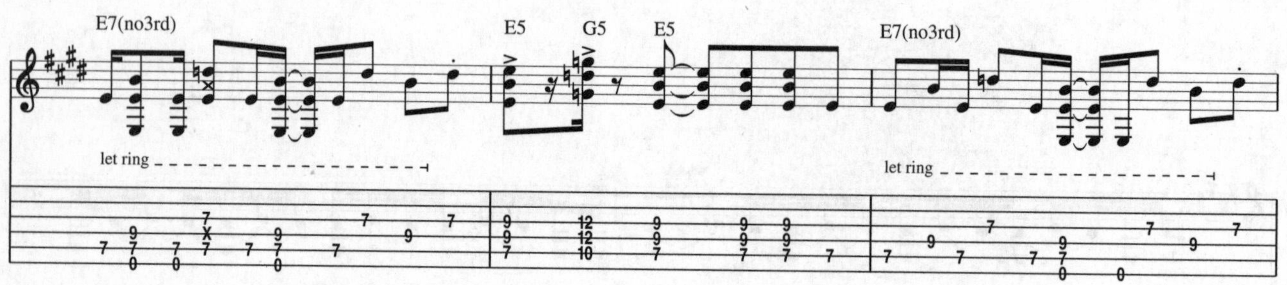
E7(no3rd)
E5
G5
E5
E7(no3rd)
let ring
let ring

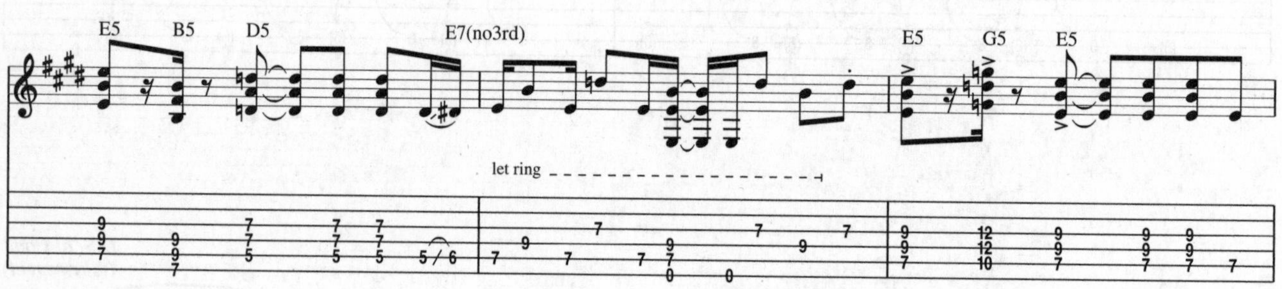
E5
B5
D5
E7(no3rd)
E5
G5
E5
let ring

E7(no3rd)
let ring

D7(no3rd)
C7(no3rd)
let ring
let ring
let ring

B
B5
C5
B5
E5
let ring
N.C.(D)
E5
N.C.(D)
E5
N.C.(D)
E5
C
(E5)
full
(D)
(E5)
Gtr. 1
(D)
(E5)
Gtr. 2

*Tape speeds up; last chord sounds 10 1/2 steps higher.

Wasting My Time

Words and Music by Danny Craig, Dallas Smith, Jeremy Hora and Dave Benedict

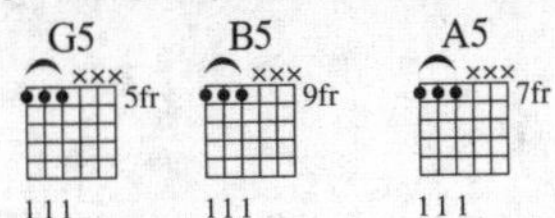

Gtrs. 1, 2 & 4: Drop D tuning:
(low to high) D-A-D-G-B-E

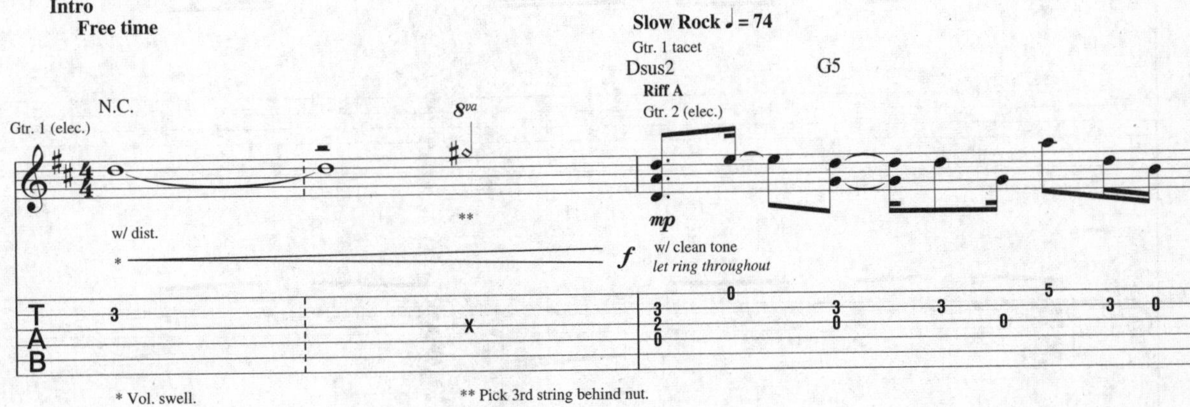

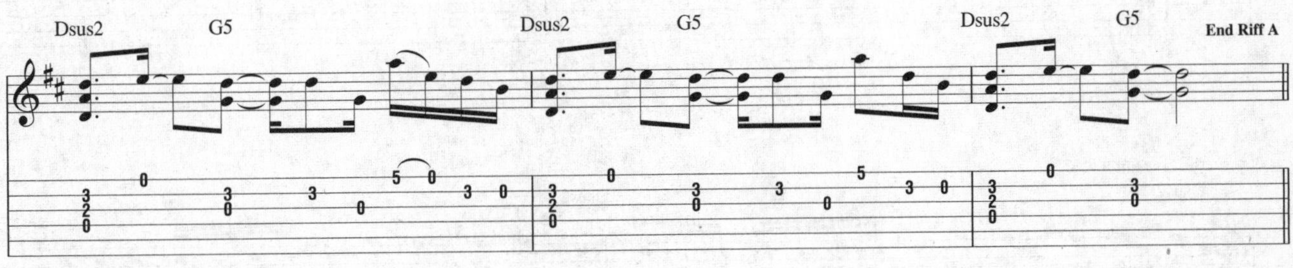

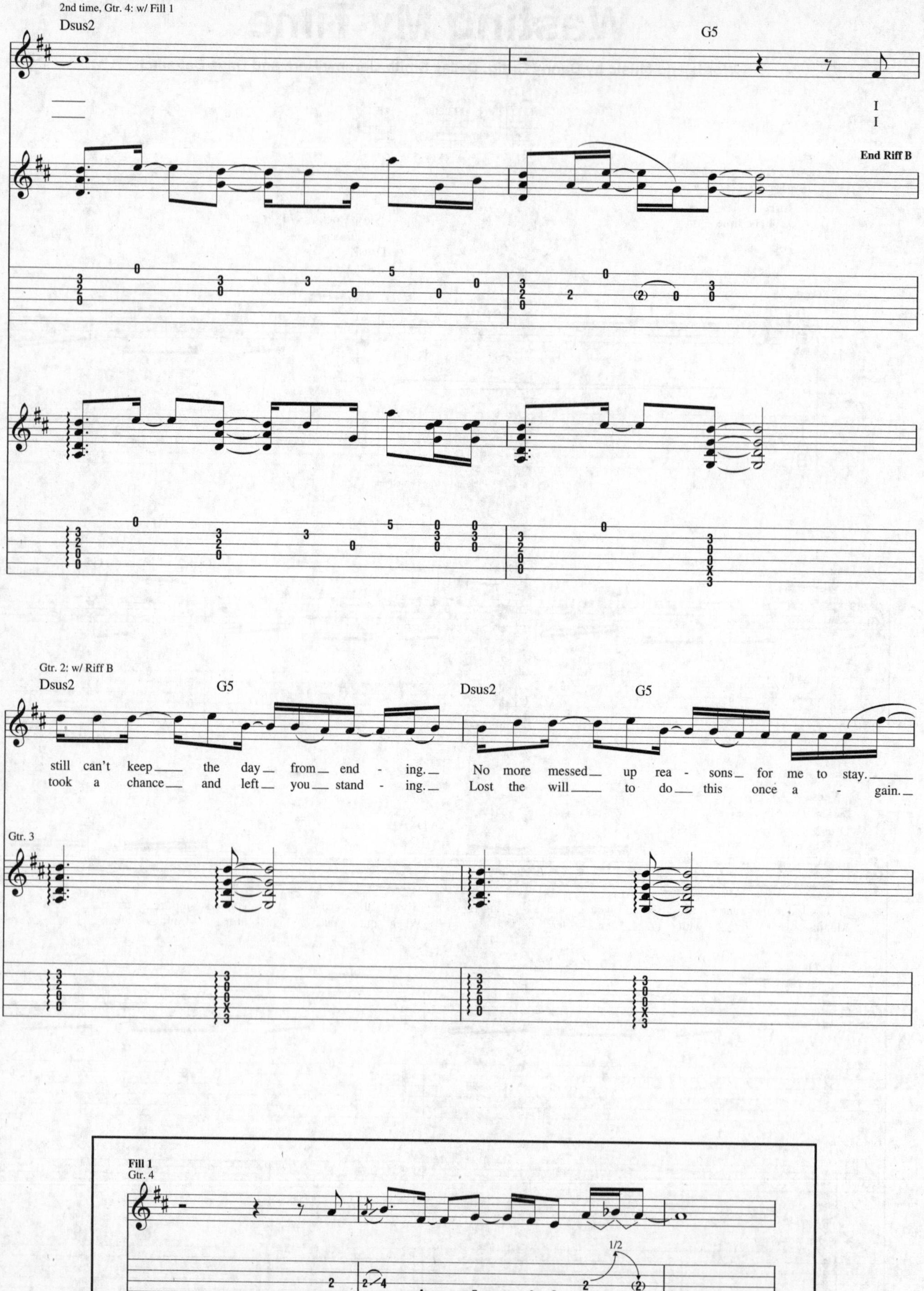

2nd time, Gtr. 4: w/ Fill 1

Dsus2

G5

End Riff B

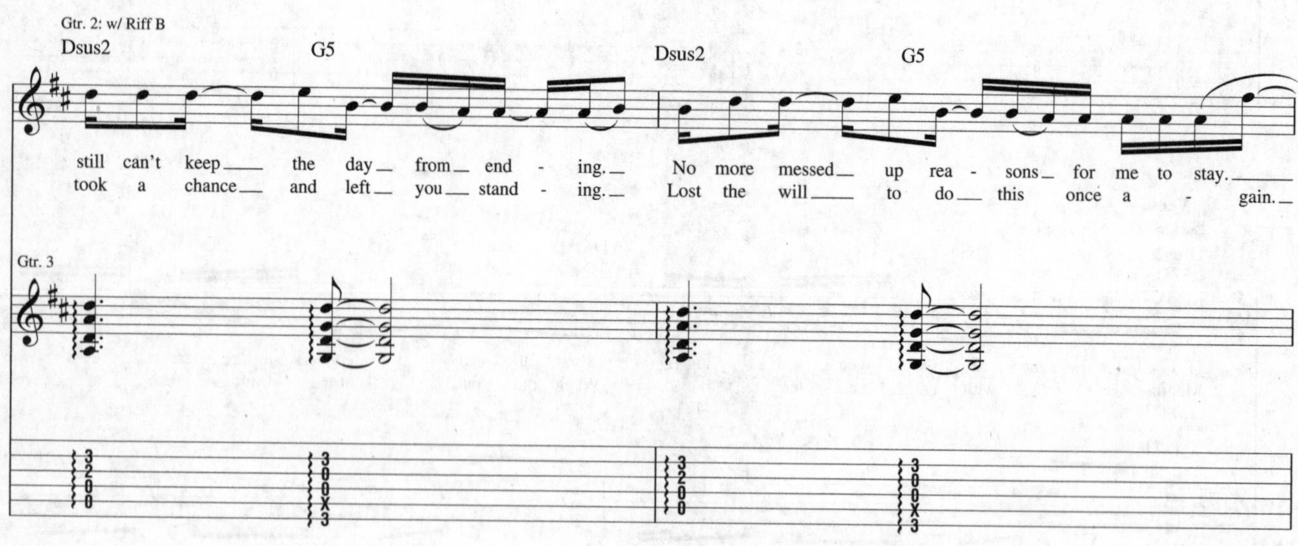

2nd time, Gtr. 4: w/ Fill 2

Dsus2 G5 Dsus2 G5

Well this is

Gtr. 3

Gtrs. 1 & 4 (elec.)

Rhy. Fill 1

End Rhy. Fill 1

mf *f*

w/ dist.

𝄋𝄋 Chorus

Gtrs. 2 & 3 tacet

G5

not for real, a - fraid to feel. I just hit the floor, don't ask for more. I'm

Gtrs. 1 & 4

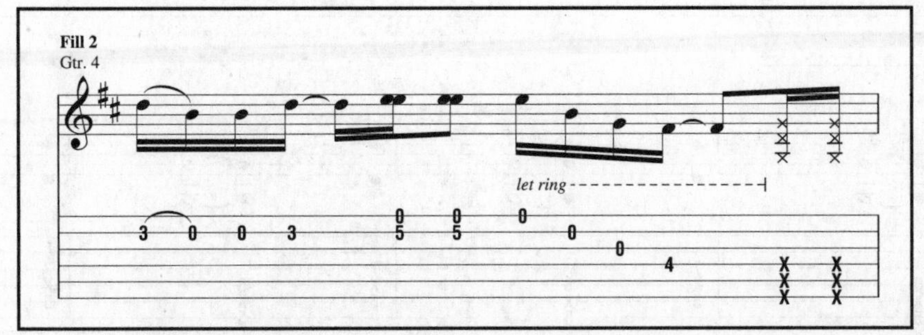

B5
wast - in' my time, I'm wast - in' my time. You can't
To Coda 1
To Coda 2
G5
stop
drop
the feel - in', there is no rea - son. Just make the call, and take it all a - gain.
A5
Whoa, ho, a - gain.
Interlude
Gtr. 2: w/ Riff A
Dsus2
G5
D.S. al Coda 1

Coda 1
B5
make the call, and take it all. I'm wast - in' my time, I'm

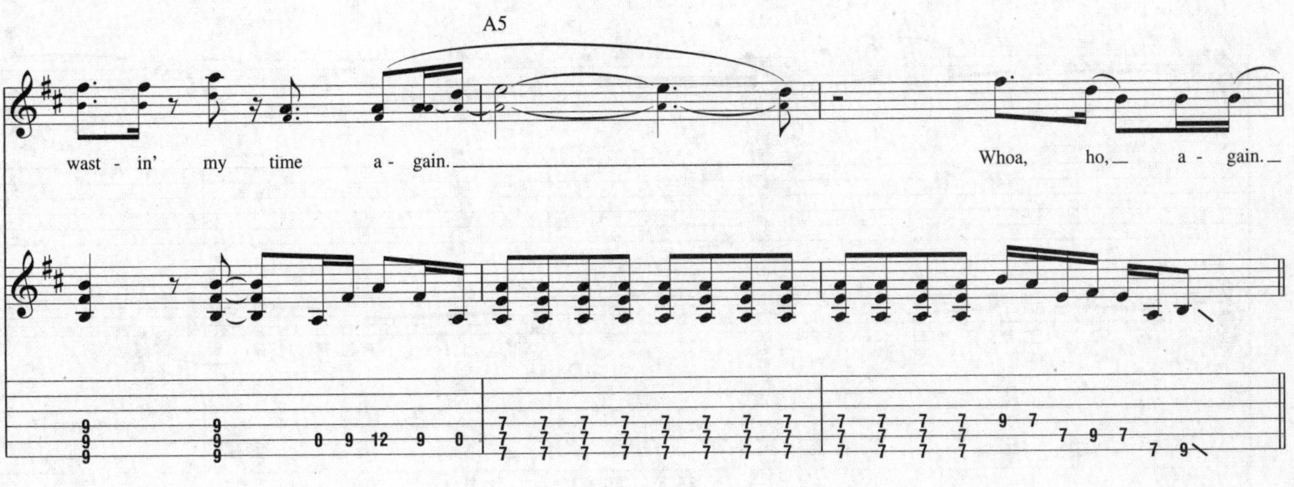
A5
wast - in' my time a - gain. Whoa, ho, a - gain.

Guitar Solo
N.C.
Gtr. 4
w/ wah-wah
1/2
Gtr. 1

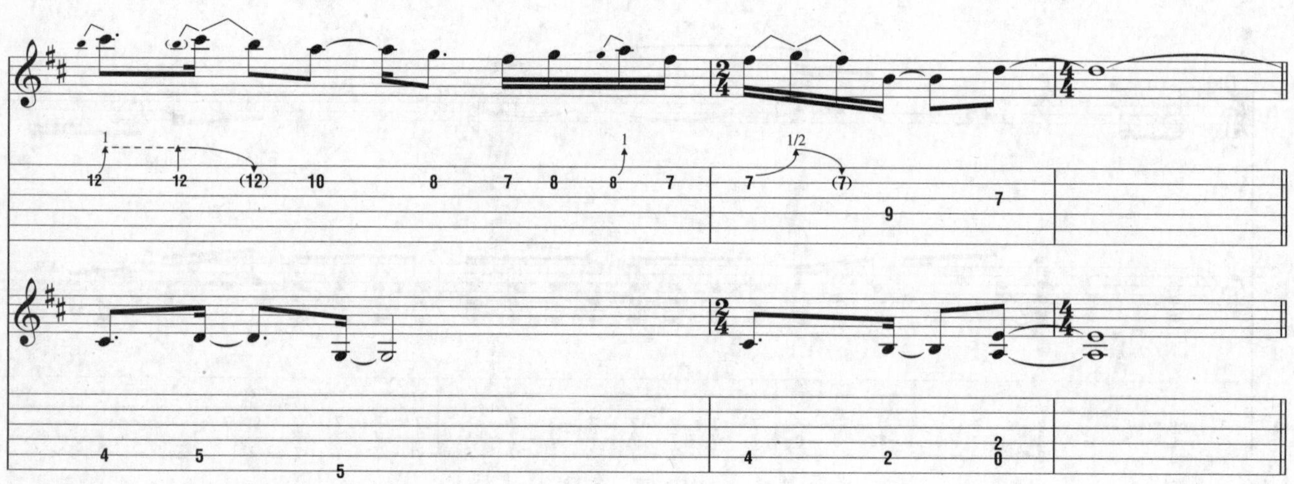

Verse
Gtr. 2: w/ Riff A (1st 2 meas.) (3 1/2 times)
Gtr. 1 tacet
Dsus2
G5
Dsus2
G5
Dsus2
G5
3. I see you wait - in'.
Gtr. 4

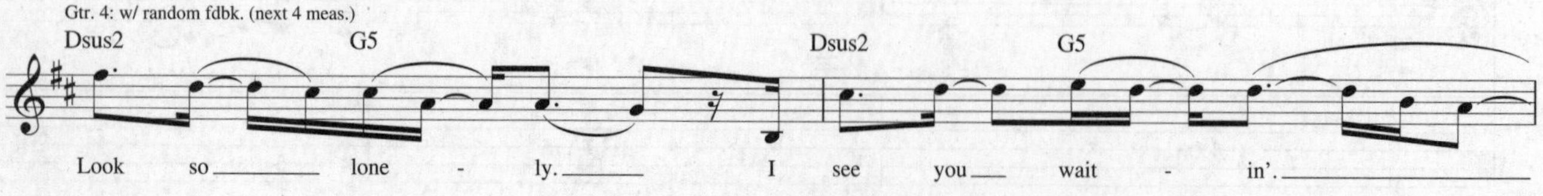
Gtr. 4: w/ random fdbk. (next 4 meas.)
Dsus2
G5
Dsus2
G5
Look so lone - ly. I see you wait - in'.

Gtrs. 1 & 4: w/ Rhy. Fill 1
Gtr. 2: w/ Riff A (last meas.)
Dsus2
G5
Dsus2
G5
I see you wait - in'. Well, this is

Coda 2
B5
make the call, and take it all. I'm wast - in' my time, I'm

G5
Gtr. 4
wast - in' my... Well, this is not for real, a - fraid to feel. I just
Gtr. 1
(Gtr. 4 cont. in slashes)

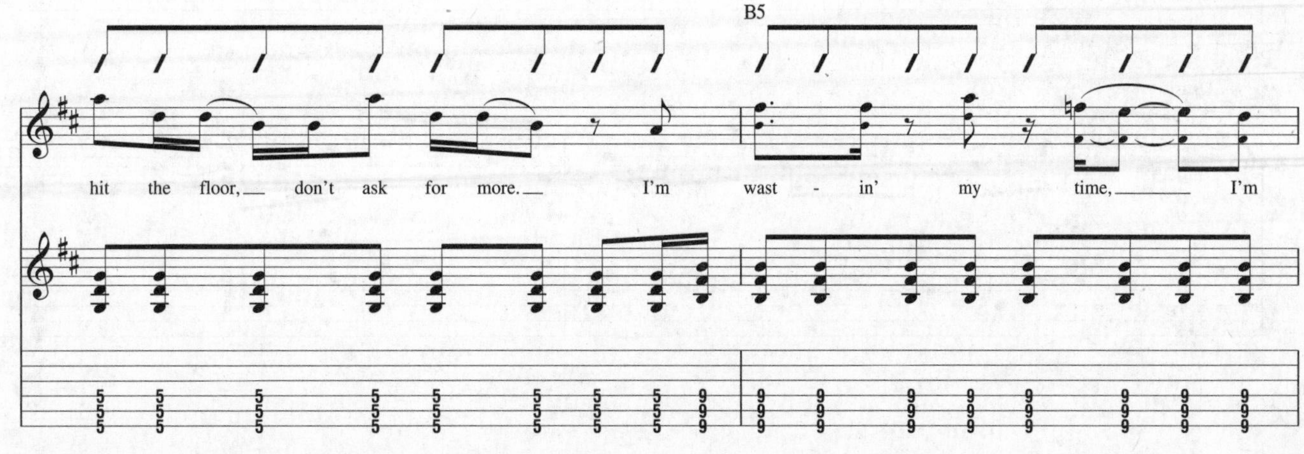
B5
hit the floor, don't ask for more. I'm wast - in' my time, I'm

G5
wast - in' my time. You can't stop the feel - in', there is no rea - son. Just
A5
make the call, and take it all a - gain.
Whoa, ho, a - gain.
(cont. in slashes)
Outro
Gtrs. 1 & 4
Gtrs. 1 & 4 tacet
Dsus2
G5
Gtr. 2
Dsus2
G5
rit.
Dsus2
G5

We Will Rock You

Words and Music by Brian May

Outro-Guitar Solo

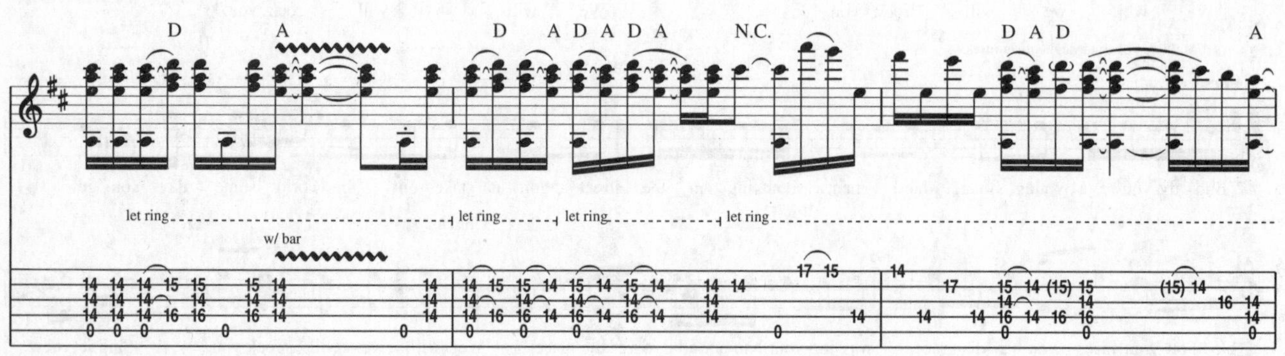

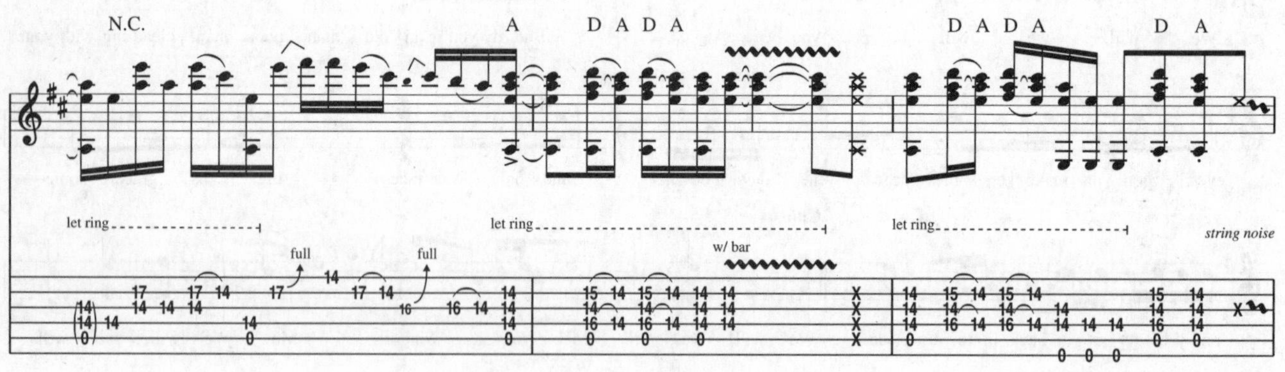

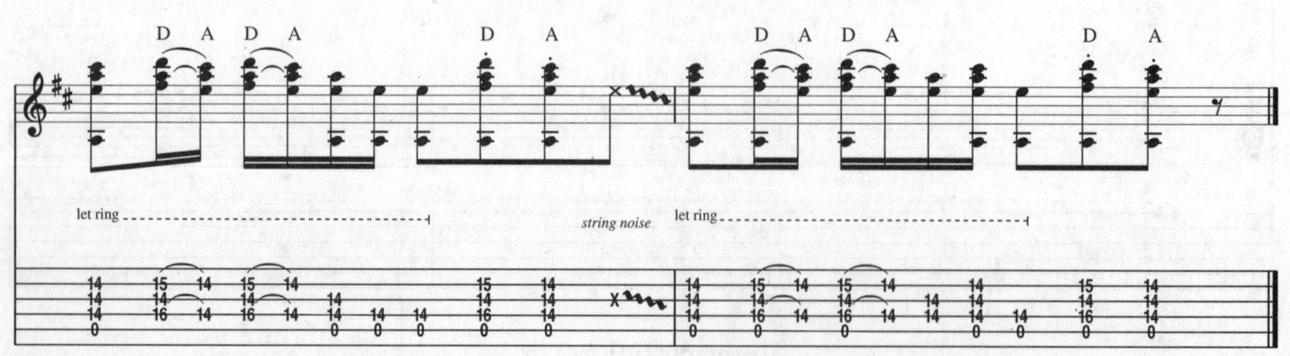

Welcome to the Jungle

Words and Music by W. Axl Rose, Slash, Izzy Stradlin', Duff McKagan and Steven Adler

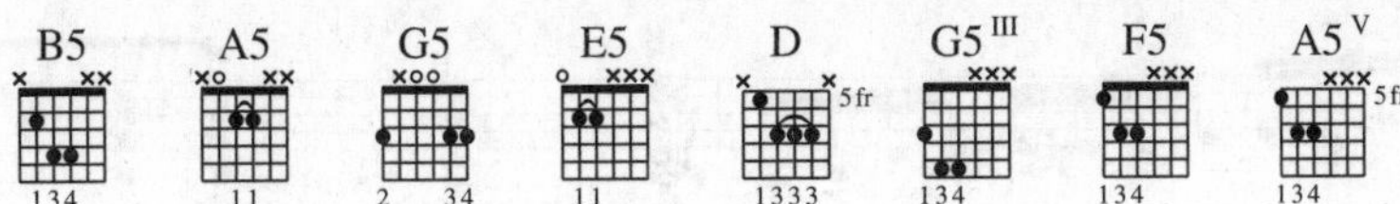

Tune down 1/2 step:
(low to high) E♭–A♭–D♭–G♭–B♭–E♭

* Set delay for sixteenth-note regeneration w/ multiple repeats.

* Roll back vol. knob

Faster ♩ = 124
E5
Gtr. 1 tacet
D5 A5 B
(cont. in notation)
Gtr. 2
P.M.
Cha!
A5 G5 A5 G5 F#5 E5 A5 G5 A5 G5 F#5 E5
cresc.
f
1/2
A5 G5 A5 G5 F#5 E5 A5 G5 A5 G5 F#5 E5
P.H.
pitch: A B A

Verse
A5
G5
F#5
E5
1. Wel-come to the jun - gle, we got fun 'n' games.
Rhy. Fig. 1
P.M.
1/2
Rhy. Fig. 1A
We got ev - 'ry - thing you want, hon - ey, we know the names. We are the
D5
C#5
B5
peo - ple that can find what - ev - er you may need.
Harm.

E5
D5
C♯5
B5
If you got the mon - ey, hon - ey, we got your dis - ease. In the jun -
End Rhy. Fig. 1
End Rhy. Fig. 1A
Chorus
C
C/B
C/A
C/G
D
D/C♯
D/B
D/A
Voc. Fig. 1
End Voc. Fig. 1
gle. Wel - come to the jun - gle. Watch it bring you to your...
(Ah, ah.
Gtr. 1
Fill 1
End Fill 1
** w/ delay
* Gtrs. 2 & 3
Rhy. Fig. 2
let ring
* Composite arrangement
** Set for quarter-note regeneration with 2 repeats.
Gtr. 1 tacet
B♭5
A5
G5
sha, na, na, na, na, na, na, na, na, na, na, na, knees, knees.
Gtrs. 2 & 3
P.M.

E5 D5 B♭5 A5 G5 E5 D5 B♭5 A5 G5 G♯5
Uh, ah. I wan - na watch you bleed.
End Rhy. Fig. 2
P.H.
pitch: F
Verse
Gtrs. 2 & 3: w/ Rhy. Figs. 1 & 1A
A5 G5 A5 G5 F♯5 E5 A5 G5 A5 G5 F♯5 E5 A5 G5 A5 G5 F♯5 E5
2. Wel - come to the jun - gle, we take it day by day. If you want it, you're gon - na bleed, but
A5 G5 A5 G5 F♯5 E5 D5 E5 D5 C♯5 B5 E5 D5 E5 D5 C♯5 B5
it's the price you pay. And you're a ver - y sex - y girl who's ver - y hard to please.
E5 D5 E5 D5 C♯5 B5 E5 D5 E5 D5 C♯5 B5
You can taste the bright lights, but you won't get them for free. In the jun -
Chorus
Bkgd. Voc: w/ Voc. Fig. 1
Gtrs. 2 & 3: w/ Rhy. Fig. 2
C C/B C/A C/G D D/C♯ D/B D/A E5 D5 B♭5 A5 G5 E5
- gle. Wel - come to the jun - gle. Feel my, my, my,
E5 D5 B♭5 A5 G5 E5 D5 B♭5 A5 G5 E5 B5 A5
Gtr. 2
(cont. in notation)
my ser - pen - tine. Uh, ah. I wan - na hear you scream!
Gtr. 3

* refers to harmonic note

Verse

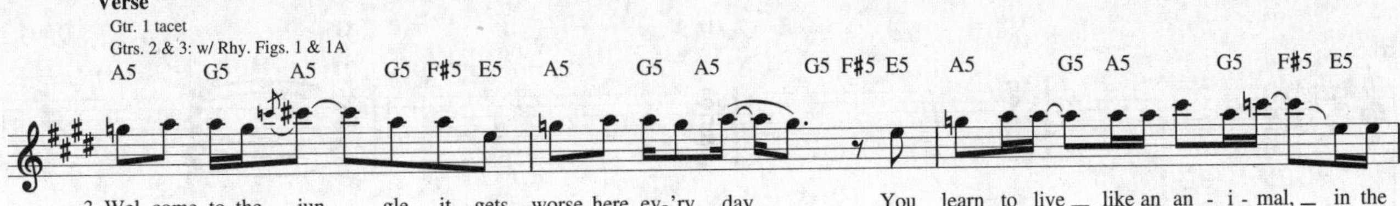
Gtr. 1 tacet
Gtrs. 2 & 3: w/ Rhy. Figs. 1 & 1A
A5 G5 A5 G5 F#5 E5 A5 G5 A5 G5 F#5 E5 A5 G5 A5 G5 F#5 E5
3. Wel-come to the jun - gle, it gets worse here ev-'ry day. You learn to live like an an - i - mal, in the

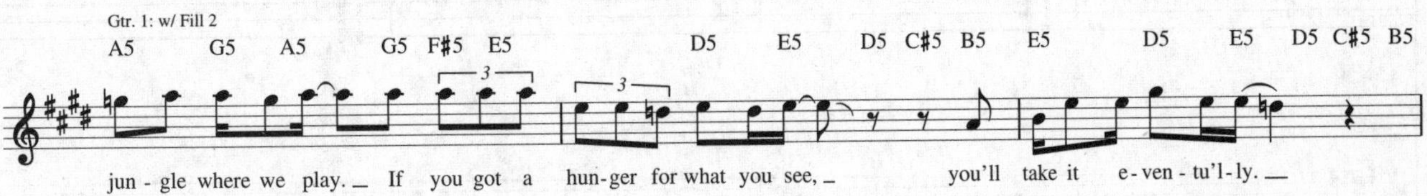
Gtr. 1: w/ Fill 2
A5 G5 A5 G5 F#5 E5 D5 E5 D5 C#5 B5 E5 D5 E5 D5 C#5 B5
jun - gle where we play. If you got a hun-ger for what you see, you'll take it e - ven - tu'l - ly.

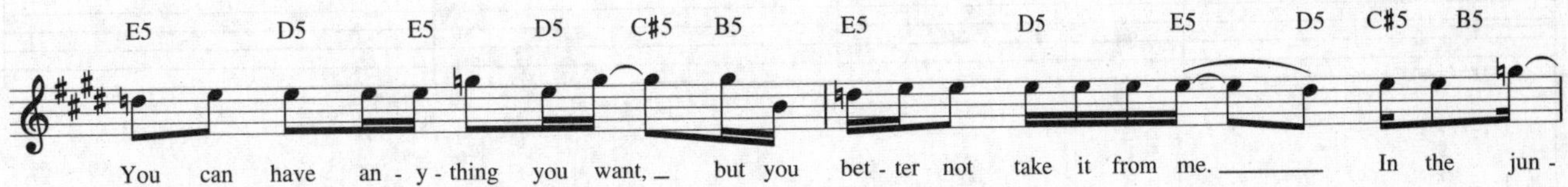
E5 D5 E5 D5 C#5 B5 E5 D5 E5 D5 C#5 B5
You can have an - y - thing you want, but you bet - ter not take it from me. In the jun -

Bkgd. Voc.: w/ Voc. Fig. 1
Gtrs. 2 & 3: w/ Rhy. Fig. 2
Gtr. 1: w/ Fill 1
C C/B C/A C/G D D/C# D/B D/A E5 D5 Bb5 A5 G5 E5
- gle, wel-come to the jun - gle. Watch it bring you to your... sha, na, na, na, na, na, na, na, na, na, na, na,

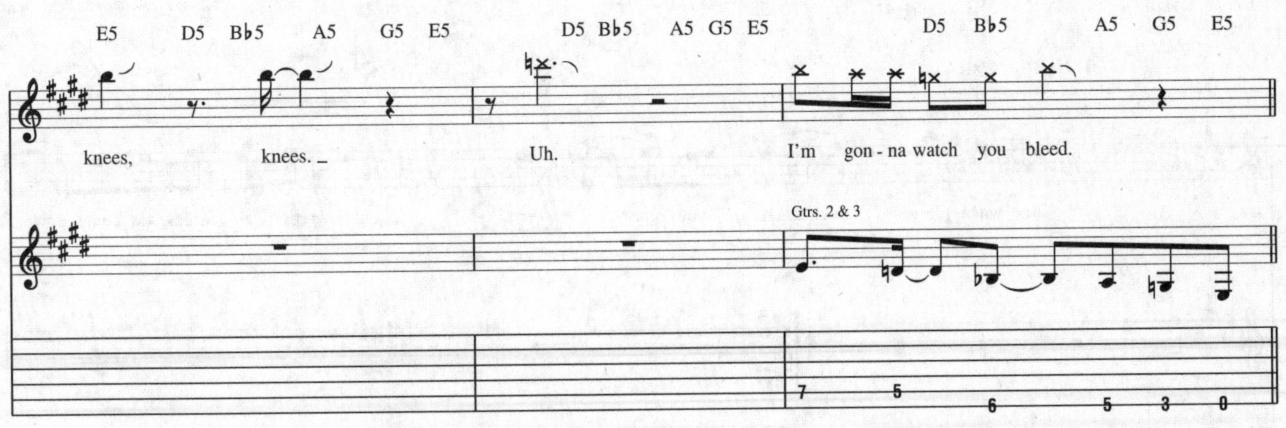
E5 D5 Bb5 A5 G5 E5 D5 Bb5 A5 G5 E5 D5 Bb5 A5 G5 E5
knees, knees. Uh. I'm gon-na watch you bleed.
Gtrs. 2 & 3
7 5 6 5 3 0

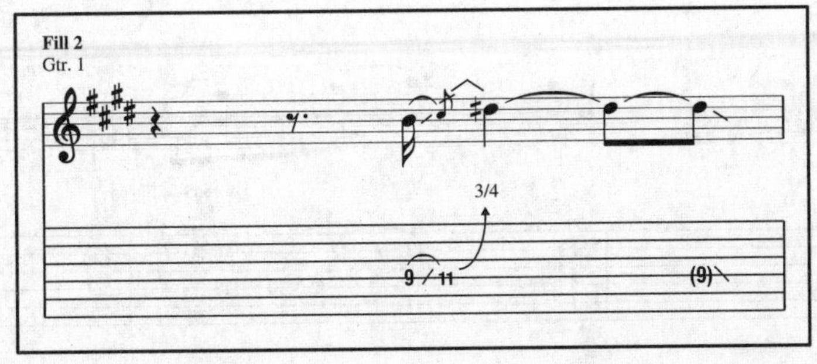
Fill 2
Gtr. 1
3/4
9 11 (9)

Bridge
D
G5
D
G5
Dsus4
Gtr. 1
mf
w/ clean tone
delay off
let ring
Gtr. 2
Gtr. 3
mf
let ring
Gtr. 2 tacet
D
G5
D
Gtr. 2
P.S.
And when you're high you nev - er ev - er want to come down,
Gtr. 1
let ring
Gtr. 3
let ring
w/ pick & finger

G5 III F5 G5 III F5 G5 III F5 A5 V G5 III

(cont. in notation)

so down, so down, so down.

f w/ dist. *grad. bend*

1 2 2 1/2

f

E

Yeah!

Gtr. 1

1 1 1 1 1/2

Gtrs. 2 & 3

P.M. P.M. P.M. P.M. P.M.

Guitar Solo

C♯5 B5 C5

Now!

8va

P.H.

pitch: E♯

P.M.

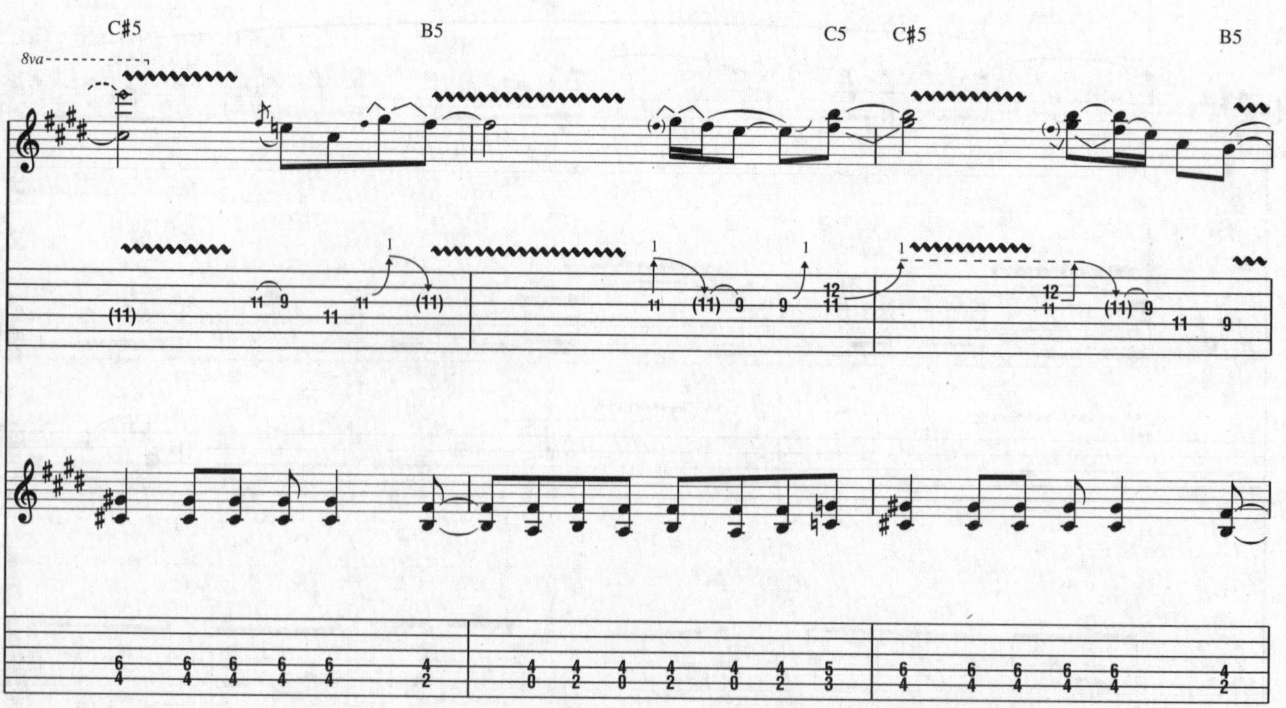

E5
B5
P.M.
P.M.
E5
B5
F#5

B

N.C.

Gtr. 1

15ma

w/ slide & delay
steady gliss.

T.H.

* Hypothetical fret location

Gtr. 2

steady gliss.

Gtr. 3

15ma

T.H.

let ring

15ma

steady gliss.

P.M.

You know where you are?
8va
steady gliss.
Harm.
P.M.
You're in the jun - gle, ba - by!
You're gon - na die!
loco

Outro-Chorus
Bkgd. Voc.: w/ Voc. Fig. 1
Gtrs. 2 & 3: w/ Rhy. Fig. 2, 1st 4 meas. (3 times)
Gtr. 1 tacet
F♯5 F5 F♯5 G5 A5 G♯5 A5 B♭5 C C/B C/A C/G
In the jungle. Welcome to the jun-
Gtrs. 2 & 3
D D/C♯ D/B D/A E5
-gle. Watch it bring you to your sha, na, na, na, na, na, na, na, na, na, na, na, knees, knees. In the jun-
Bkgd. Voc.: w/ Voc. Fig. 1
C C/B C/A C/G D D/C♯ D/B D/A E5
-gle. Welcome to the jungle. Feel my, oh, my, my,
C C/B C/A C/G D DF/C♯ D/B D/A
my serpentine. Jungle. Welcome to the jungle. Watch it bring you to your
Bkgd. Voc.: w/ Voc. Fig. 1
Gtrs. 2 & 3: w/ Rhy. Fig. 2 (1st 2 meas.)
E5 C C/B C/A C/G
sha, na, na, na, na, na, na, na, na, na, na, na, knees, knees. Down in the jungle. Welcome to the jun-
D D/C♯ D/B D/A E5 D5 B♭5 A5 G5 E5 A G E E7♯9
-gle. Watch it bring you to your... It's gonna bring you down! Huh!
Gtrs. 2 & 3
* Slowly detune ⑥ str.

Wheel in the Sky

Words and Music by Robert Fleischman, Neal Schon and Diane Valory

Dsus2
C
Cadd4/B♭
Gtrs. 1 & 2: w/ Riff A
D5
year or more. I hope she holds on a lit - tle long - er.
fore too long. Oo, I can't take this ver - y much long - er, no.
Gtrs. 1 & 2
Rhy. Fig. 2
End Rhy. Fig. 2
Gtr. 3
End Rhy. Fig. 1

Gtrs. 1 & 2: w/ Riff A (1 1/2 times)
Gtr. 3: w/ Rhy. Fig. 1
Sent a let - ter on a long sum-mer day made of sil - ver,
I'm strand - ed in the sleet and rain. Don't think I'm ev - er gon - na

Gtrs. 1 & 2: w/ Rhy. Fig. 2
Dsus2
C
2nd time, Gtr. 3: w/ Rhy. Fill 1
Cadd4/B♭
not of clay. Oo, I've been run - nin' down this dust -
make it home a - gain. The morn - in' sun is ris - in',

Rhy. Fill 1
Gtr. 3

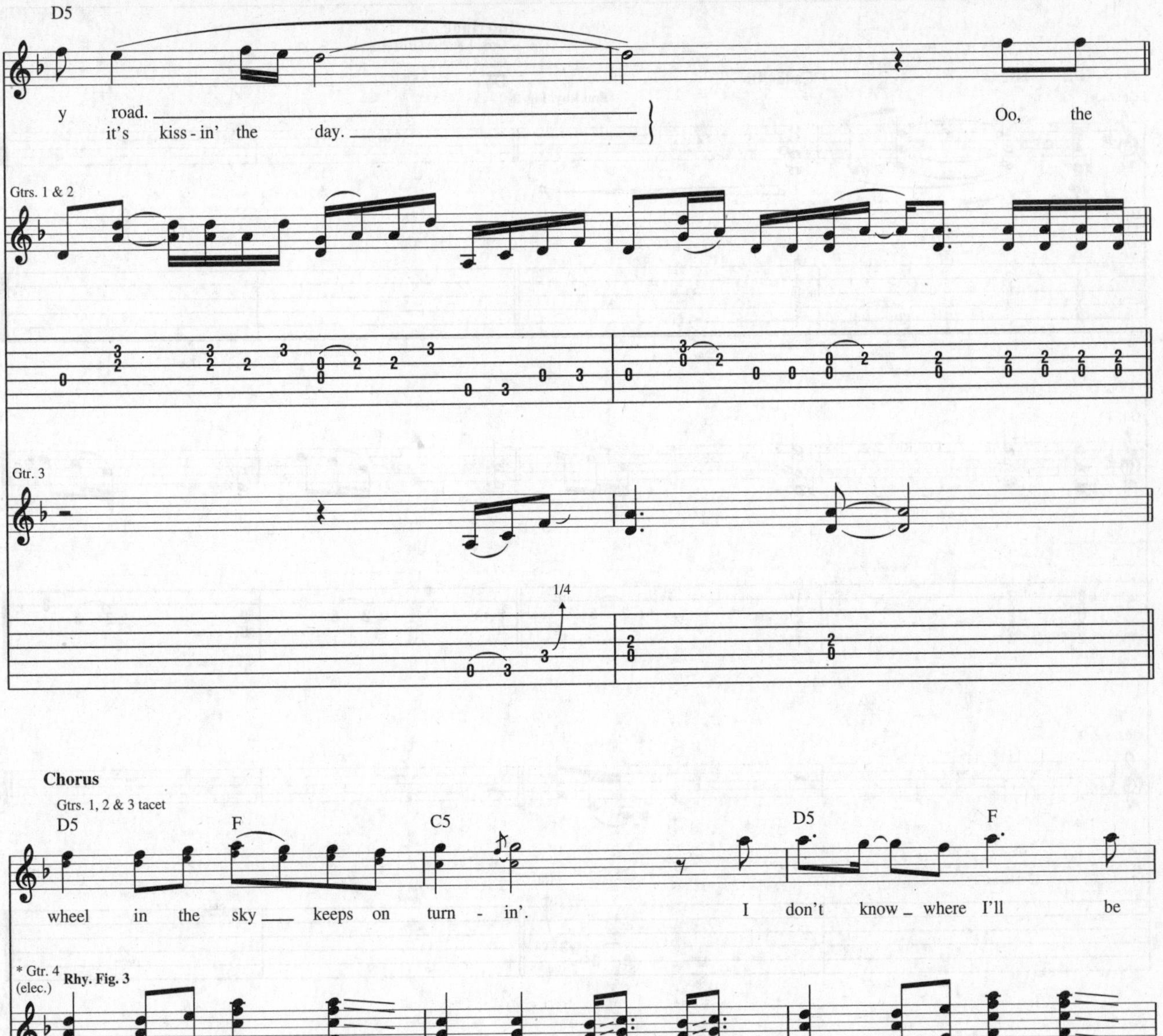

D5

y road.
it's kiss-in' the day.
Oo, the

Gtrs. 1 & 2

Gtr. 3

1/4

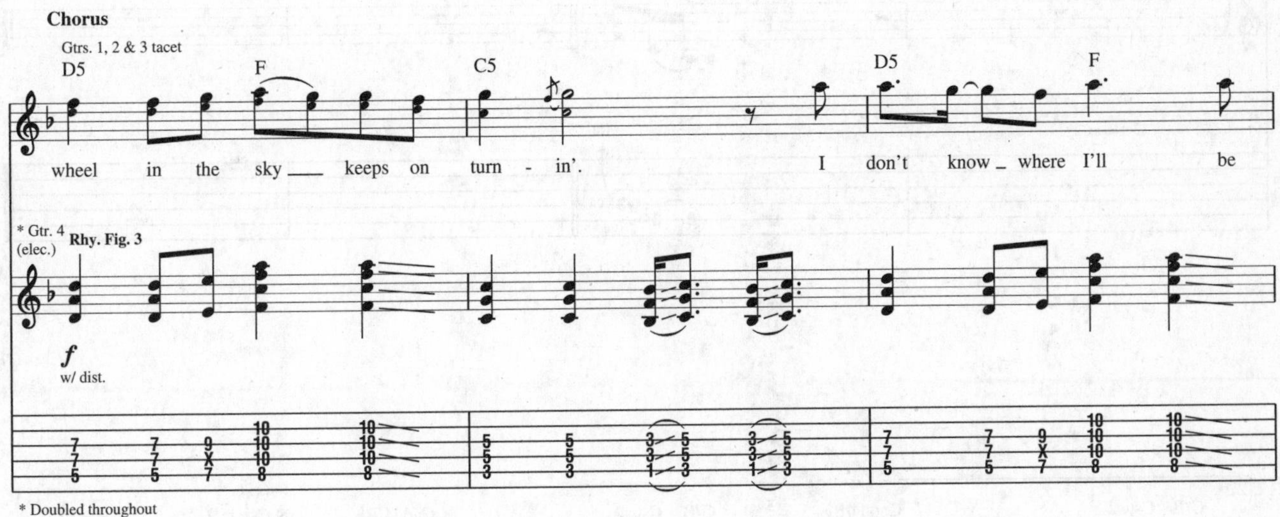

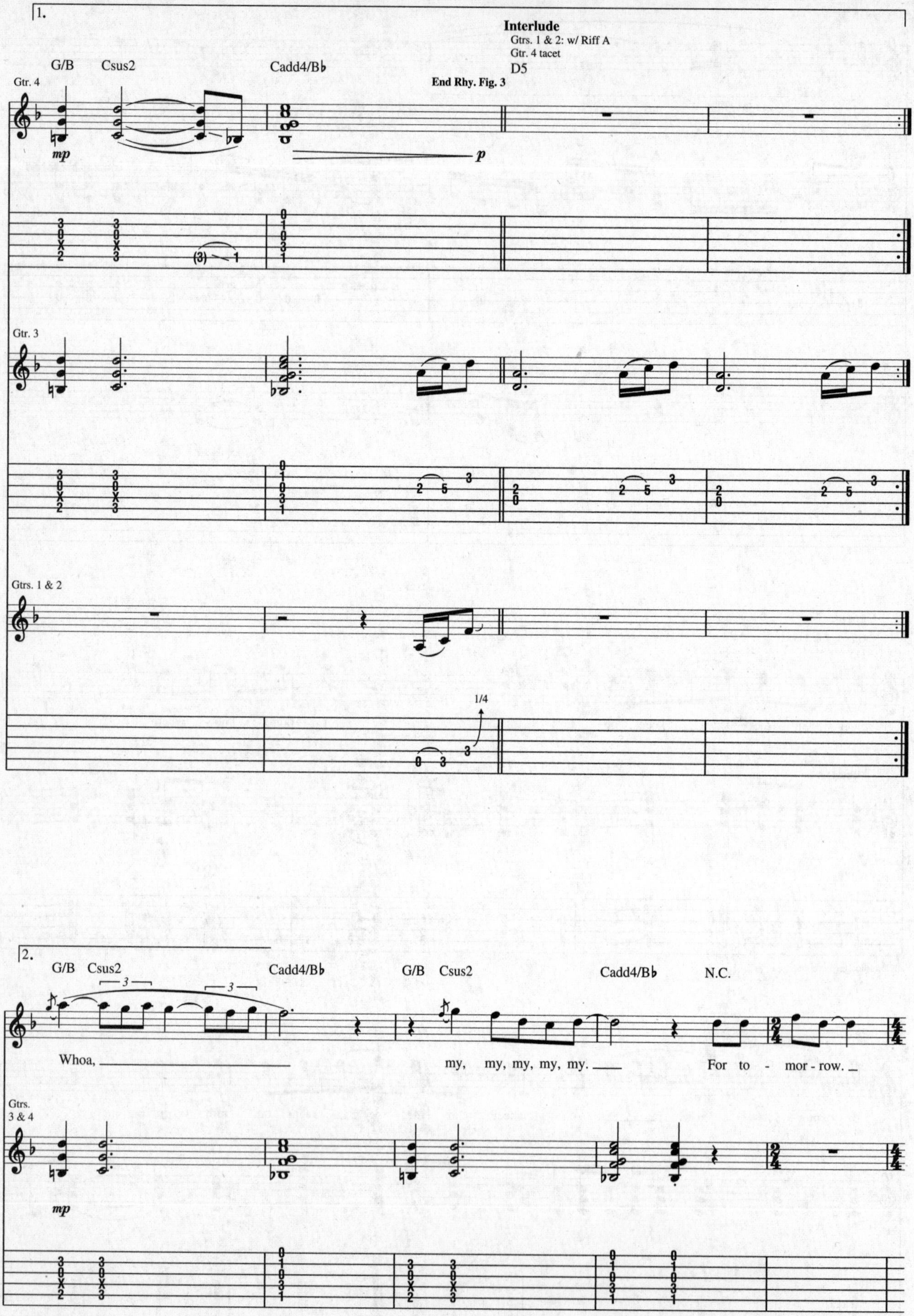

1.

Interlude

Gtrs. 1 & 2: w/ Riff A

Gtr. 4 tacet

G/B Csus2 Cadd4/B♭ D5

Gtr. 4

End Rhy. Fig. 3

mp

p

Gtr. 3

Gtrs. 1 & 2

1/4

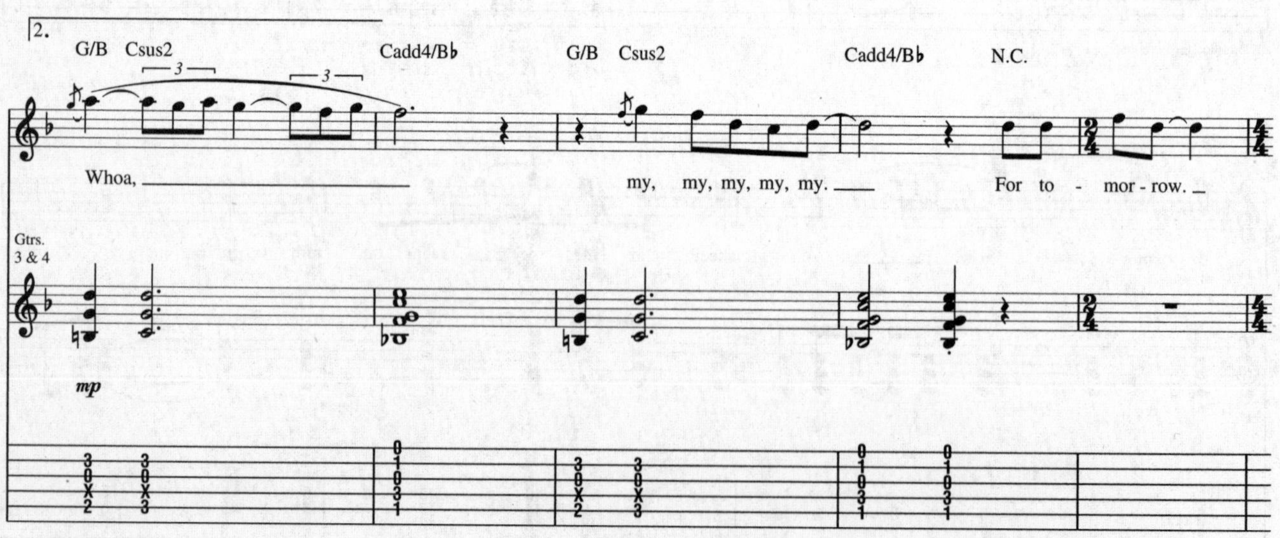

Guitar Solo
Gtr. 5 (elec.)
D5
w/ dist.
Gtr. 3
Gtr. 4 divisi
Gtrs. 1 & 2
Rhy. Fig. 4
Gtrs. 3 & 4 tacet
Csus2
Gtrs. 1 & 2: w/ Rhy. Fig. 4 (2 times)
End Rhy. Fig. 4

Gtr. 5
B♭6
Csus2
D5
Csus2
Gtrs. 1 & 2
B♭6
Csus2
D5
Csus2
B♭6
8va
Chorus
Gtrs. 1 & 2 tacet
Gtr. 4: w/ Rhy. Fig. 3
G/B
Csus2
D5
F
C5
D5
F
Oh, the wheel in the sky keeps on turn - in.' Oo, I don't know where I'll be to -
8va
loco
mf

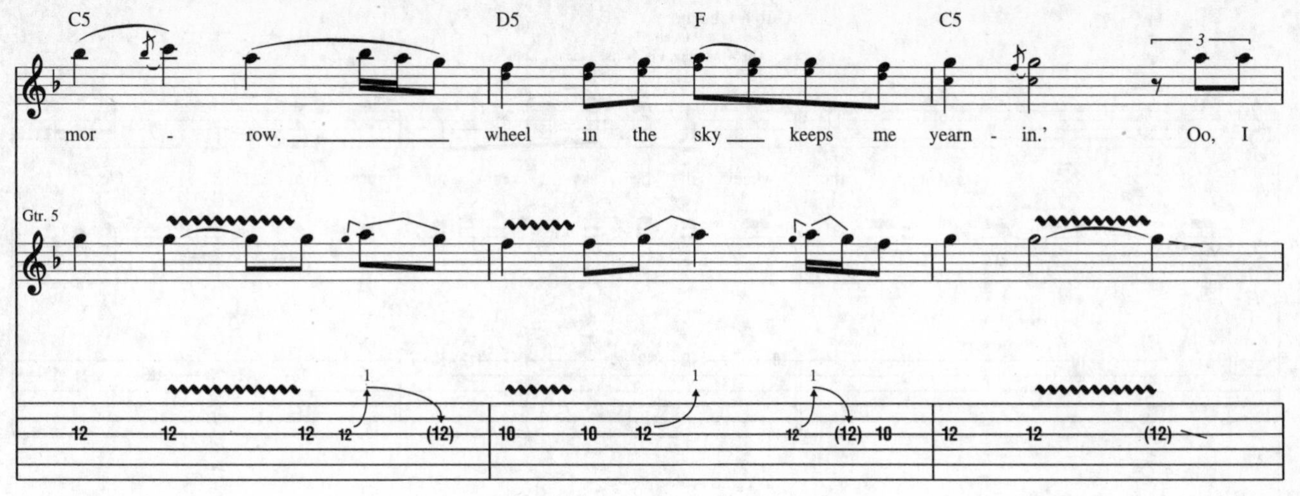

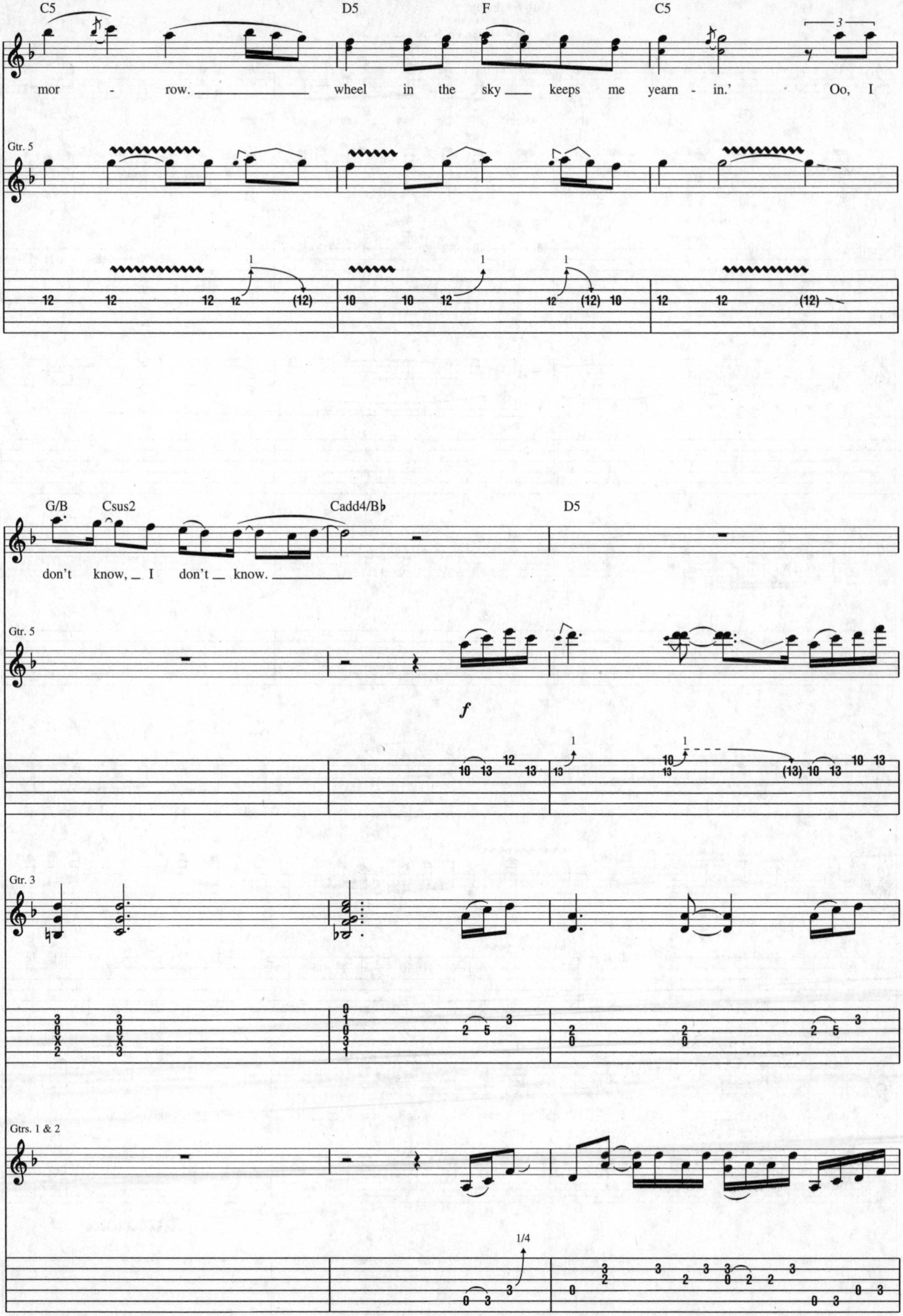

G/B Csus2 Cadd4/B♭ D5

don't know, I don't know.

Gtr. 5

f

Gtr. 3

Gtrs. 1 & 2

Outro-Chorus
Gtrs. 1 & 2 tacet
Gtr. 4: w/ Rhy. Fig. 3 (1st 4 meas., 4 times)
D5
F
C5
Oh, the wheel in the sky keeps on turn - in.' Oo, I
pp
Gtr. 3 tacet
don't know where I'll be to - mor - row.
Wheel in the sky keeps on
Gtr. 5
turn - in.' Oo, I don't know I don't know, I don't know.
8va

D5 F C5
Wheel in the sky keeps on turn - in'.
8va
D5 F C5
Don't know where I'll be to - mor - row. Oo, the
8va
D5 F C5 D5 F
wheel in the sky keeps turn - in'. Wheel in the sky keeps on
loco
8va
Begin fade
Repeat and fade
C5 B♭
turn - in'.
8va
Gtr. 5
loco
Gtr. 4

Where It's At

Words by Beck Hansen

Music by Beck Hansen, Mike Simpson and John King

Chorus
Gtr. 2 tacet, 2nd time
Bkgd. Voc.: w/ Voc. Fig. 1, 3 times, 1st time
Bkgd. Voc.: w/ Voc. Fig. 1, 2nd & 3rd times
Voc. Fig. 1
End Voc. Fig. 1
Em A Em A Em A
I got two turn-tab-les and a mic-ro-phone. I got
(Where it's at!)
Gtr. 1
To Coda 2
1.
Gtr. 1 tacet
N.C.(E5)
two turn-tab-les and a mic-ro-phone. Got two turn-tab-les and a mic-ro-phone.
Interlude
N.C.
Got two turn-tab-les and a mic-ro-phone. Take me home with my L O leave 'em come o's.
That was a good drum break.
2.
Interlude
G E G E
Gtr. 3: w/ Fill 1, 1st time
To Coda 1
Spoken: What about those who swing both ways? AC/DCs.
Fill 1
Gtr. 3 (dist.)
full
1 1/4

Gtr. 1: w/ Rhy. Fig. 1, 2 times
Am7
A
Am7
Let's make it out, ba - by.
Ah.
Guitar Solo
Gtr. 1: w/ Rhy. Fig. 1, 2 times
A
Gtr. 2
Am7
full
full
w/ Voc. Fig. 2, 6 times, simile
A
Am7
full
full
full
D.S. al Coda 1
(take 2nd ending)
A
Spoken: We're all part of the total scene.
1/2
1/2
Coda 1
Saxophone Solo
Gtr. 1 tacet
Gtr. 2: w/ Riff A, 2 times
Am7
D.S.S. al Coda 2
Spoken: That's beautiful, dad.
(Got my mic - ro-phone.)
3.There's a
Coda 2
Outro
Gtr. 1: w/ Rhy. Fig. 1, till fade
w/ ad Lib voc., kybd., organ, sound effects, & dist. harmonica, till fade
Am7
A
(Do, do, do, do, do, do, do, do, do do.
Am7
Play 7 Times and Fade
A
(Do, do, do, do, do, do, do, do, do do.)
Voc. Fig. 2
Two turn - tab - les and a mic - ro - phone.

Wherever You Will Go

Words and Music by Aaron Kamin and Alex Band

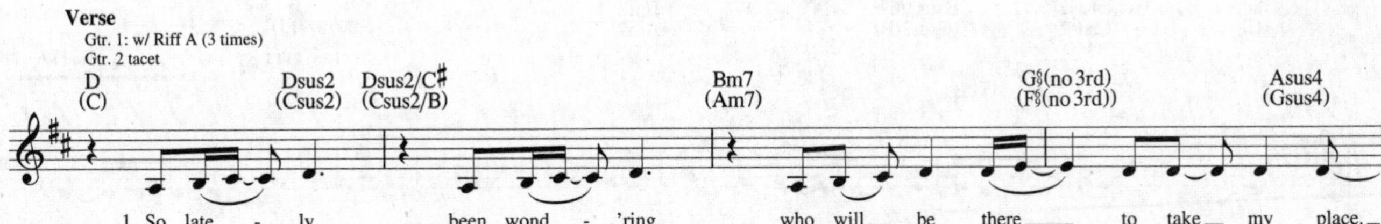

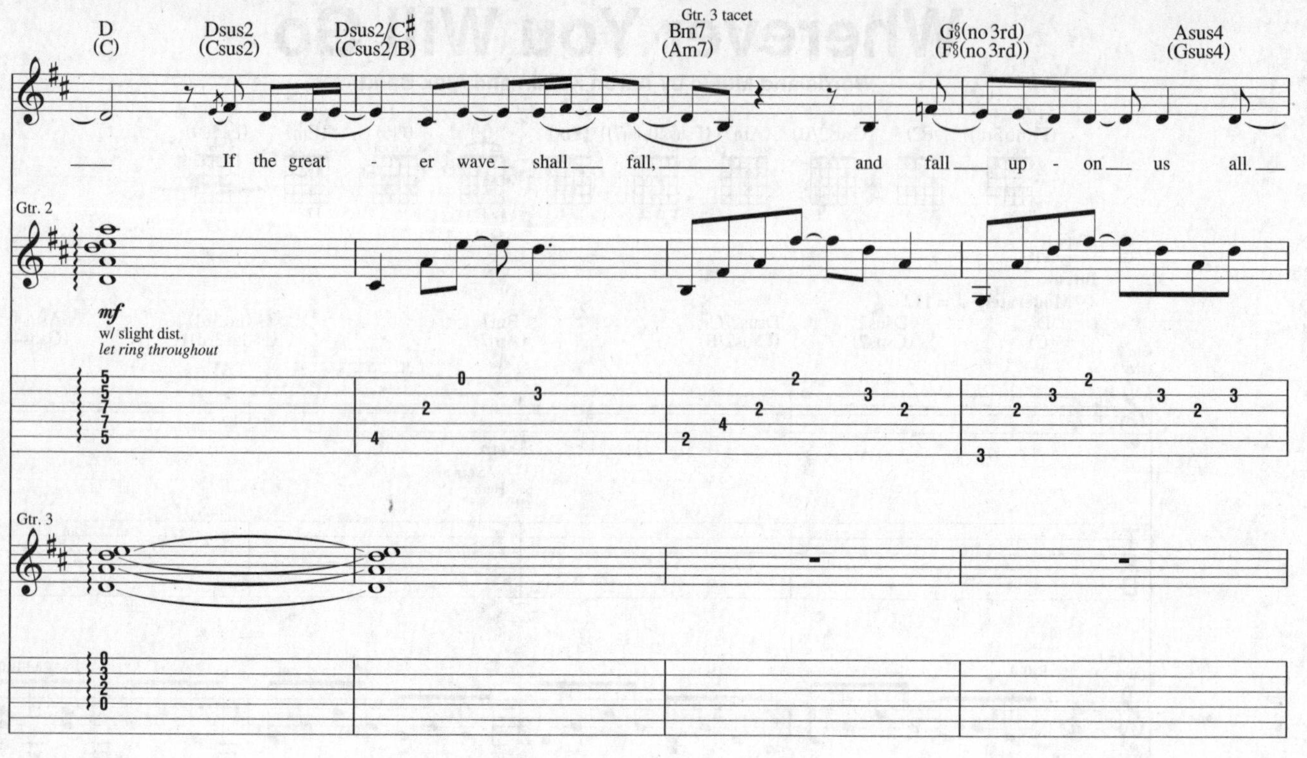

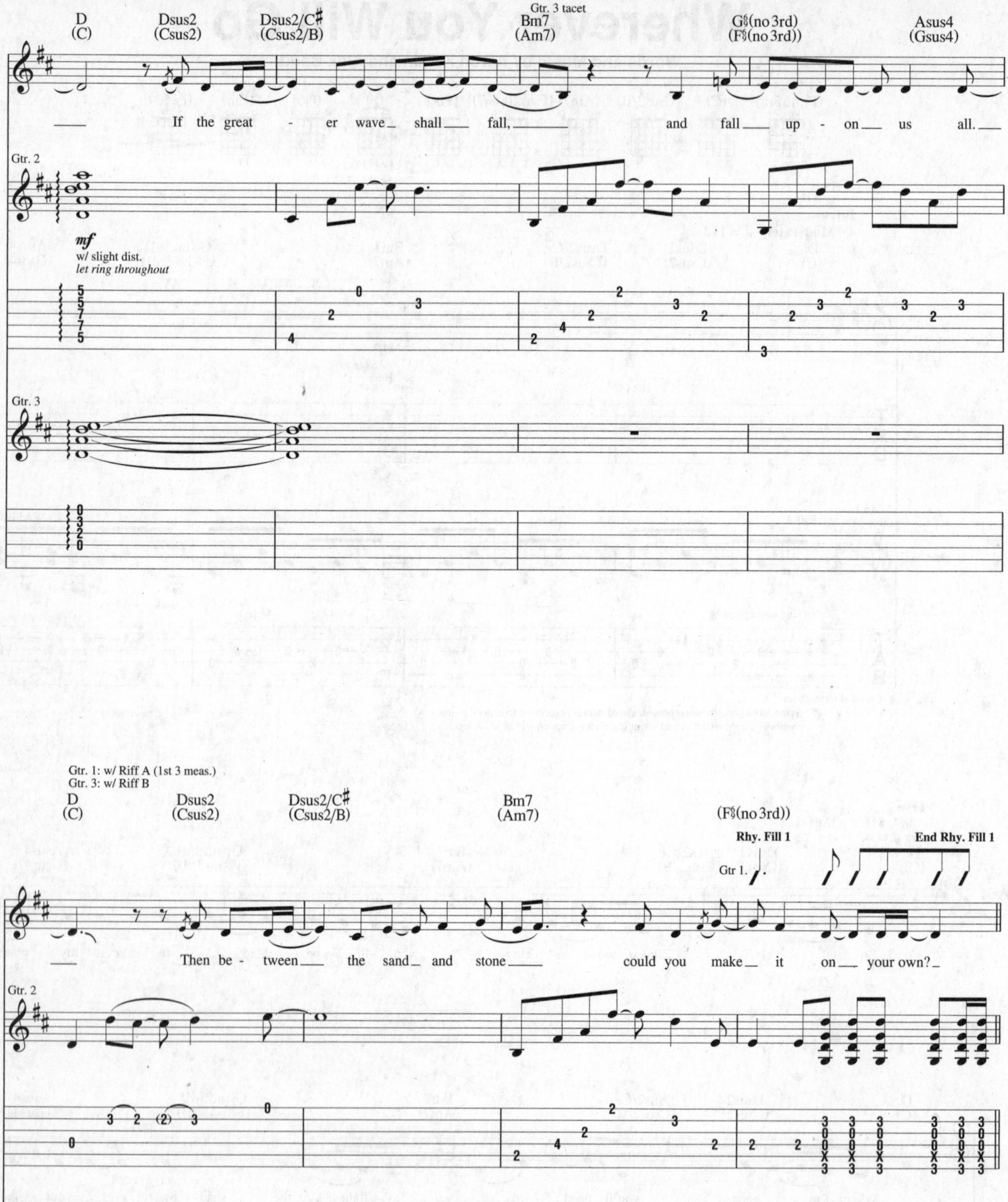

Gtr. 1: w/ Riff A (1st 3 meas.)
Gtr. 3: w/ Riff B

D (C) Dsus2 (Csus2) Dsus2/C♯ (Csus2/B) Bm7 (Am7) (F6/9(no 3rd))

Rhy. Fill 1 End Rhy. Fill 1

Gtr 1.

Then be - tween the sand and stone could you make it on your own?

Gtr. 2

Gtr. 4 (elec.)

mf
w/ dist.

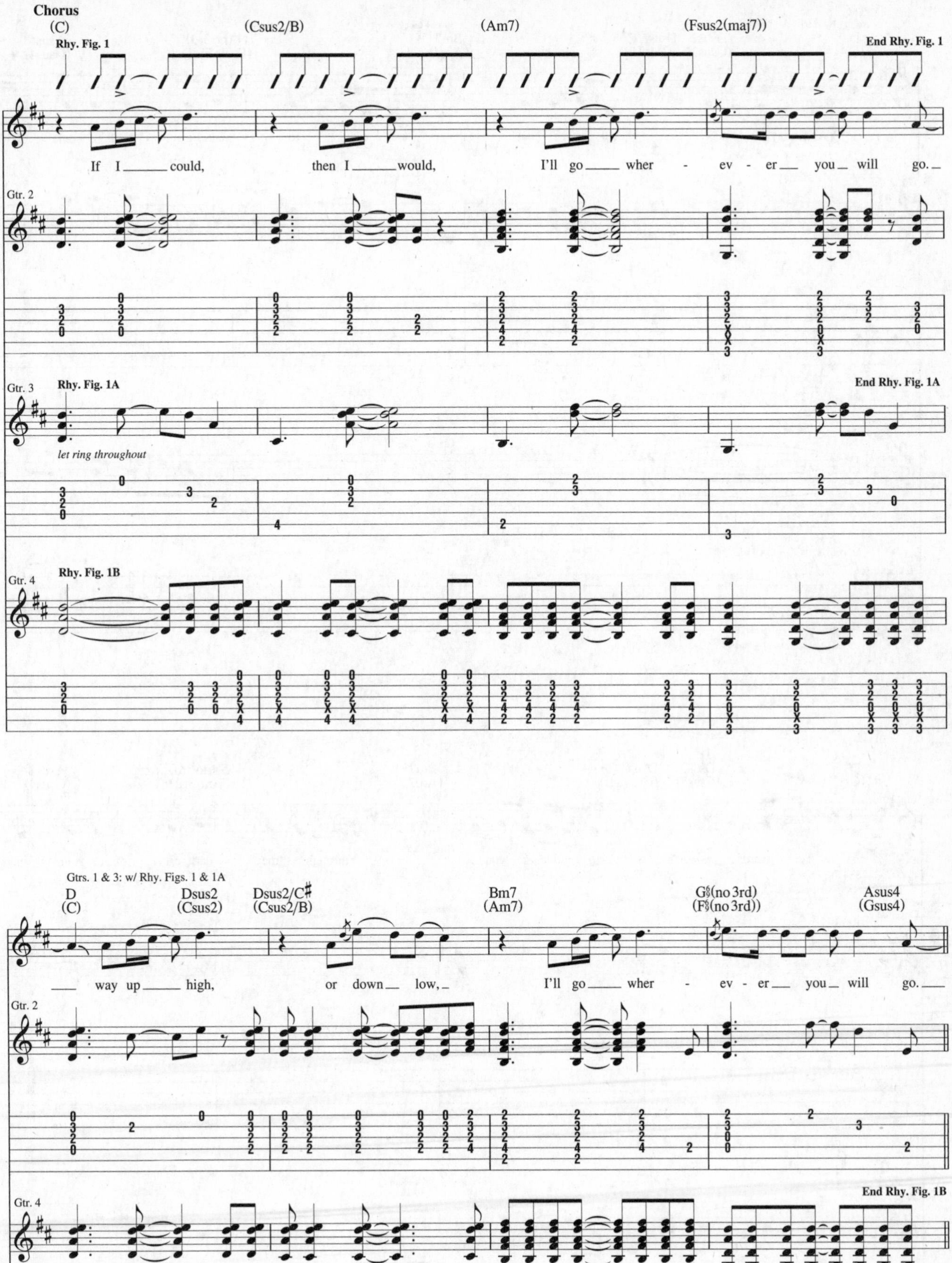

Chorus

(C) (Csus2/B) (Am7) (Fsus2(maj7))

Rhy. Fig. 1 End Rhy. Fig. 1

If I ___ could, then I ___ would, I'll go ___ wher - ev - er ___ you ___ will go. ___

Gtr. 2

Gtr. 3 Rhy. Fig. 1A End Rhy. Fig. 1A

let ring throughout

Gtr. 4 Rhy. Fig. 1B

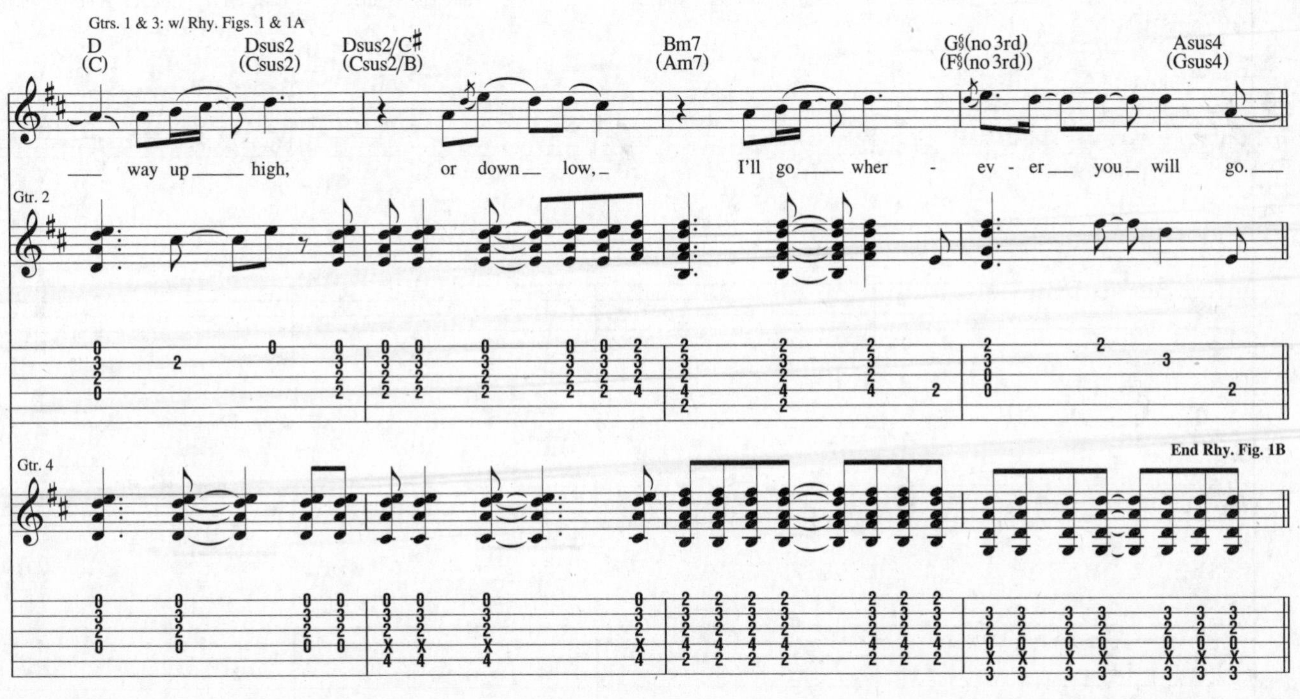

Verse

Gtr. 1: w/ Riff A (3 times)

Gtr. 4 tacet

D (C) Dsus2 (Csus2) Dsus2/C♯ (Csus2/B) Bm7 (Am7) G6/9(no 3rd) (F6/9(no 3rd)) Asus4 (Gsus4)

2. And may - be I'll find out a way to make it back some day.

Gtr. 2

Gtrs. 3 & 4

Gtr. 3

let ring throughout

D (C) Dsus2 (Csus2) Dsus2/C♯ (Csus2/B) Bm7 (Am7) G6/9(no 3rd) (F6/9(no 3rd)) Asus4 (Gsus4)

To - wards you, to guide you through the dark-est of your days.

Gtr. 3 (elec.)

Riff B

mf

Gtr. 2

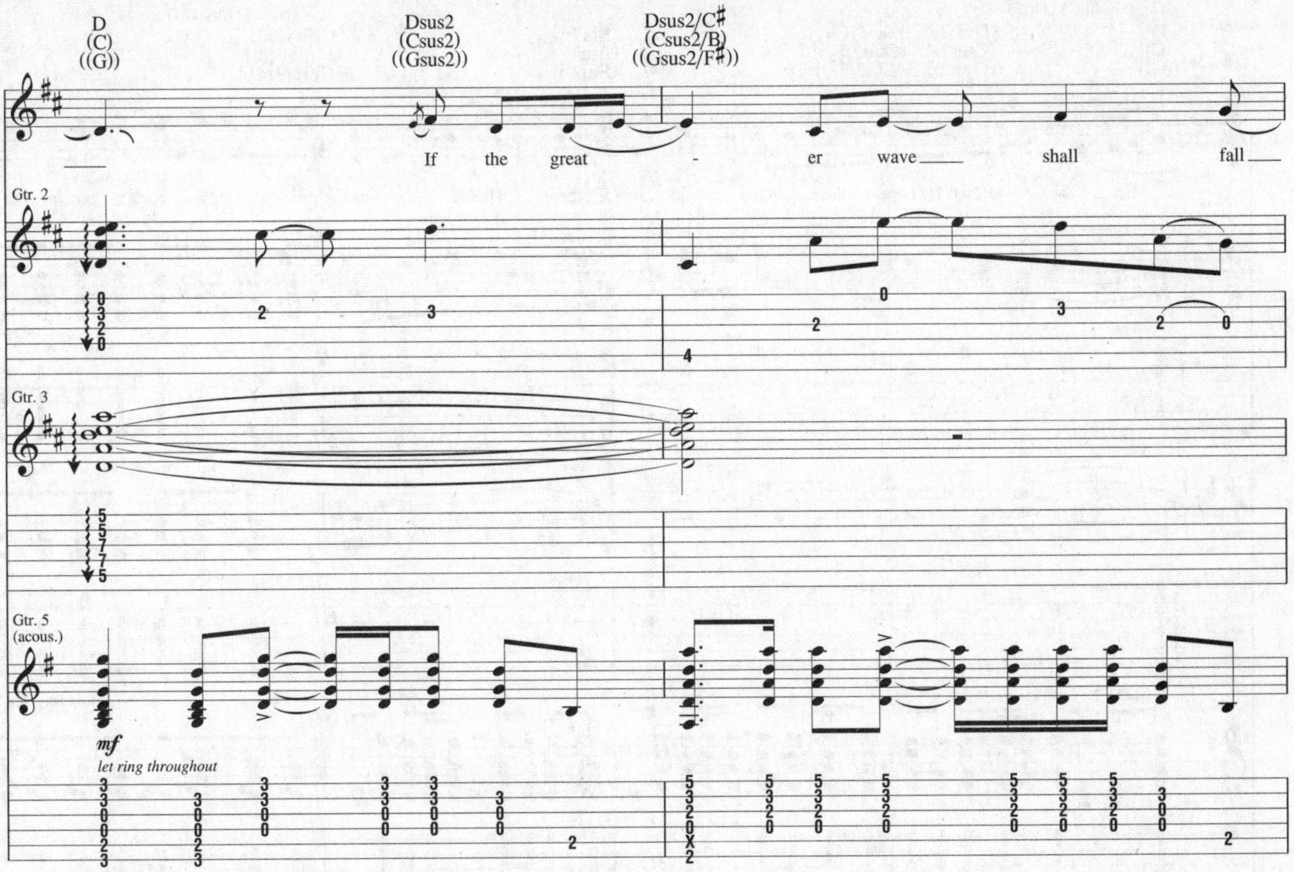

D
(C)
((G))

Dsus2
(Csus2)
((Gsus2))

Dsus2/C♯
(Csus2/B)
((Gsus2/F♯))

If the great - er wave shall fall

Gtr. 2

Gtr. 3

Gtr. 5
(acous.)

mf
let ring throughout

*Chord symbols in double parentheses represent chord names respective to Gtr. 5.

Bm7
(Am7)
((Em7))

G6/9(no 3rd)
(F6/9(no 3rd))
((C6/9(no 3rd)))

Asus4
(Gsus4)
((Dsus4)

and fall up - on us all.

Gtr. 1: w/ Riff A (1st 3 meas.)
Gtr. 1: w/ Rhy. Fill 1
D
(C)
((G))
Dsus2
(Csus2)
((Gsus2))
Dsus2/C#
(Csus2/B)
((Gsus2/F#))
Bm7
(Am7)
((Em7))
Well then I hope there's some - one out there, who can bring me back too.
Gtrs. 3 & 4
Rhy. Fig. 2
End Rhy. Fig. 2
Chorus
Gtrs. 1 & 3 w/ Rhy. Figs. 1 & 1A (2 times)
Gtr. 4: w/ Rhy. Fig. 1B
Gtr. 5 tacet
Gsus2(maj7)
(Fsus2(maj7))
If I could, then I would, I'll go wher - ev - er you will go.
Gtr. 2
Rhy. Fig. 3
Way up high or down low, I'll go wher - ev - er you will
End Rhy. Fig. 3

Bridge
(Bm)
(F)
(G6)
(Em)
Gtr. 1
go.
Run a - way with my heart,
run a - way with my heart.
Gtr. 2
Gtr. 3
Gtr. 4
let ring throughout
(Bm)
(F)
(G6)
(Bm)
Run a - way with my love.
P.M.

Verse

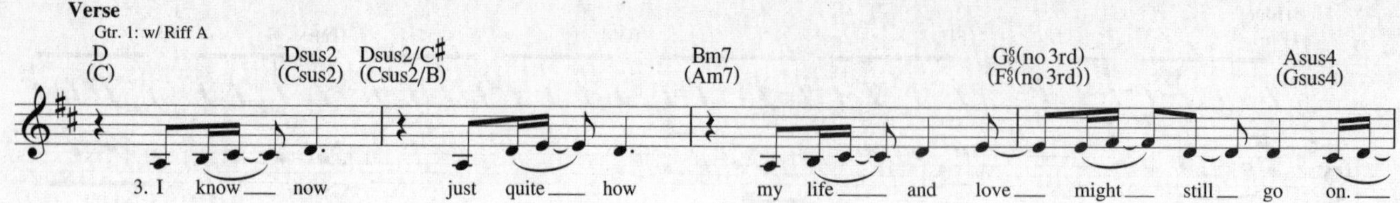

Chorus

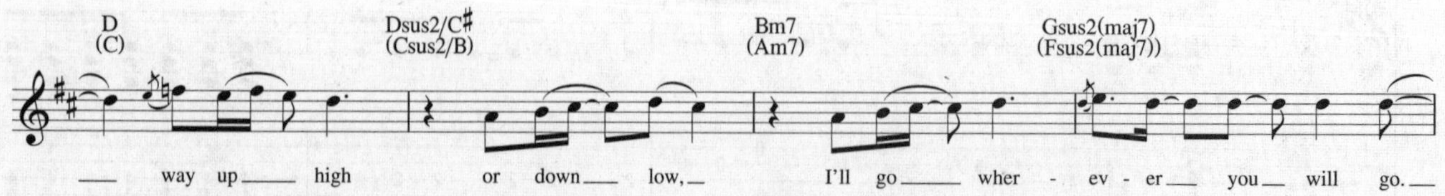

D
(C)
Dsus2/C♯
(Csus2/B)
Bm7
(Am7)
Gsus2(maj7)
(Fsus2(maj7))
If I could turn back time, I'll go wher - ev - er you will go.
If I could make you mine, I'll go wher - ev - er you will go.
(Go.
I'll go wher -
Gtr. 6
(elec.)
Riff C
End Riff C
mf
w/dist.
Gtr. 6: w/ Riff C (4 times)
(Fadd9)
ev - er you will go.
Go.)
Gtr. 6
Gtrs. 2 & 3
Gtr. 4

White Room

Words and Music by Jack Bruce and Pete Brown

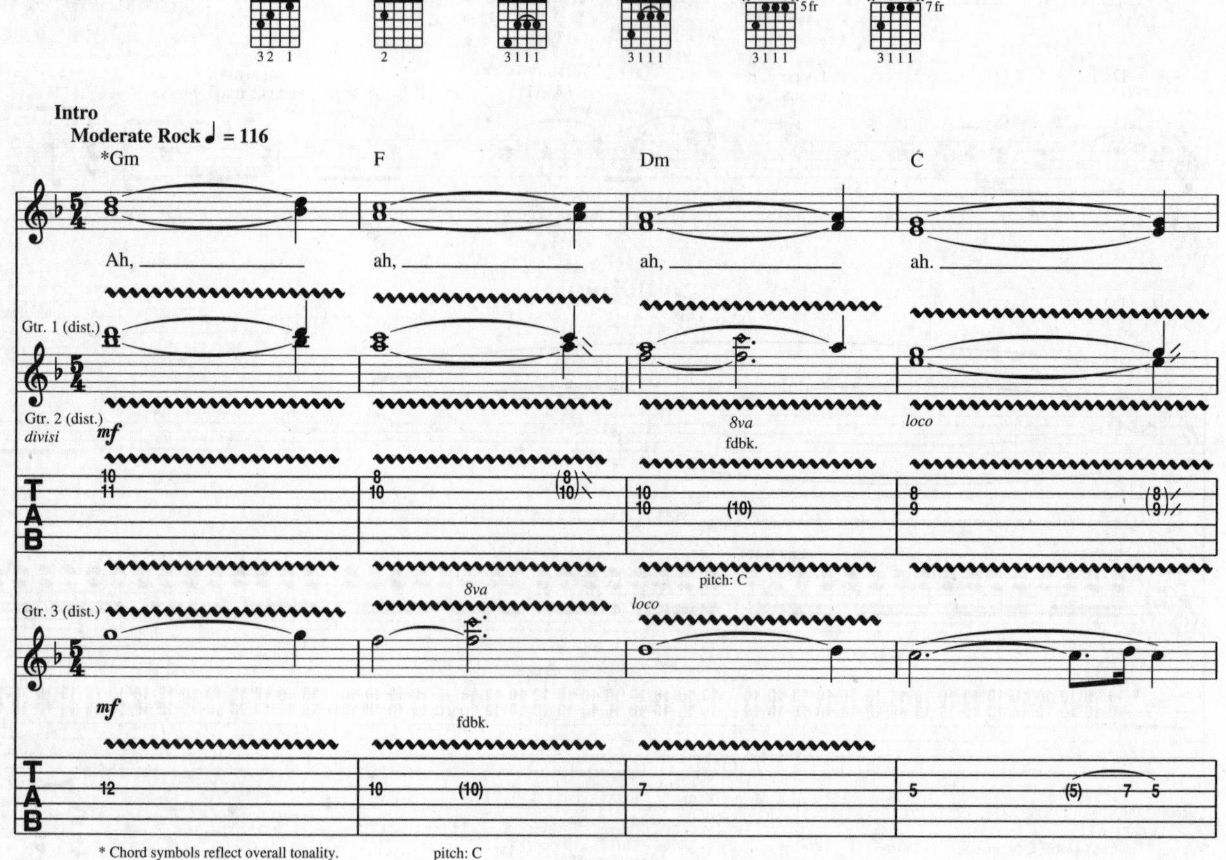

* Chord symbols reflect overall tonality.

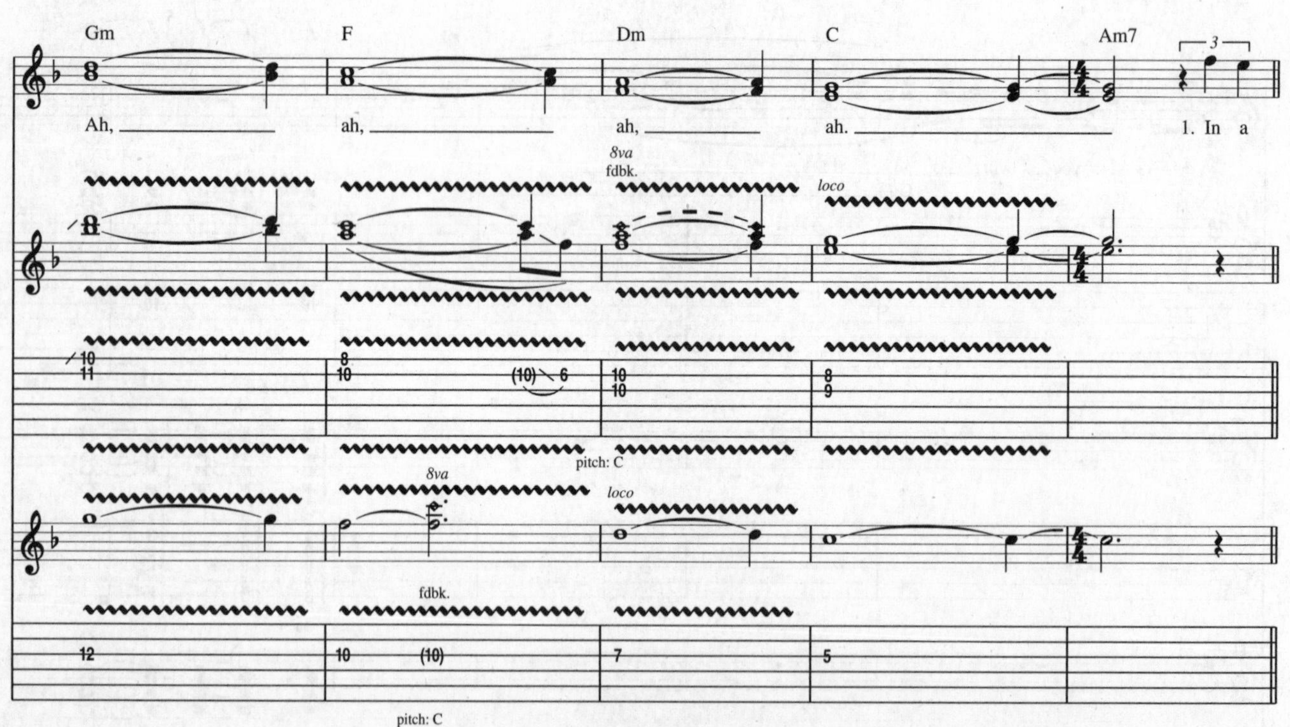

Verse

Gtrs. 2 & 3 tacet
D C5 G/B B♭5 C5 D5 Csus2 G/B B♭5 C5
white room with black cur - tains near the sta - tion. Black roof
Rhy. Fig. 1
Gtr. 1
let ring
let ring

D C5 G/B B♭5 C5 D Csus2 G/B B♭5 C5
coun - try, no gold pave - ments, tired star - lings. Sil - ver
let ring
let ring

D Csus2 G/B B♭5 C5 D5 Csus2 G/B B♭5 C5
hors - es ran down moon - beams in your dark eyes. Dawn - light
let ring
let ring

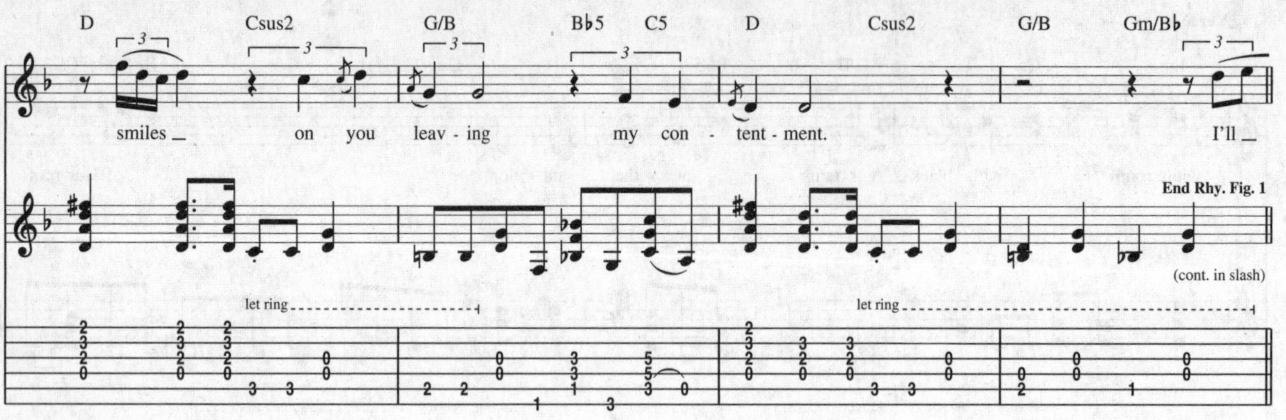
D
Csus2
G/B
B♭5
C5
D
Csus2
G/B
Gm/B♭
smiles on you leav - ing my con - tent - ment. I'll
End Rhy. Fig. 1
let ring
let ring
(cont. in slash)

Bridge

C
A G/B
open
C B♭/D
3fr
B A/C#
2fr
C
Rhy. Fig. 2A
Gtr. 1
wait in this place where the sun nev - er shines, wait in this
Gtr. 2
Rhy. Fig. 2
w/ wah-wah

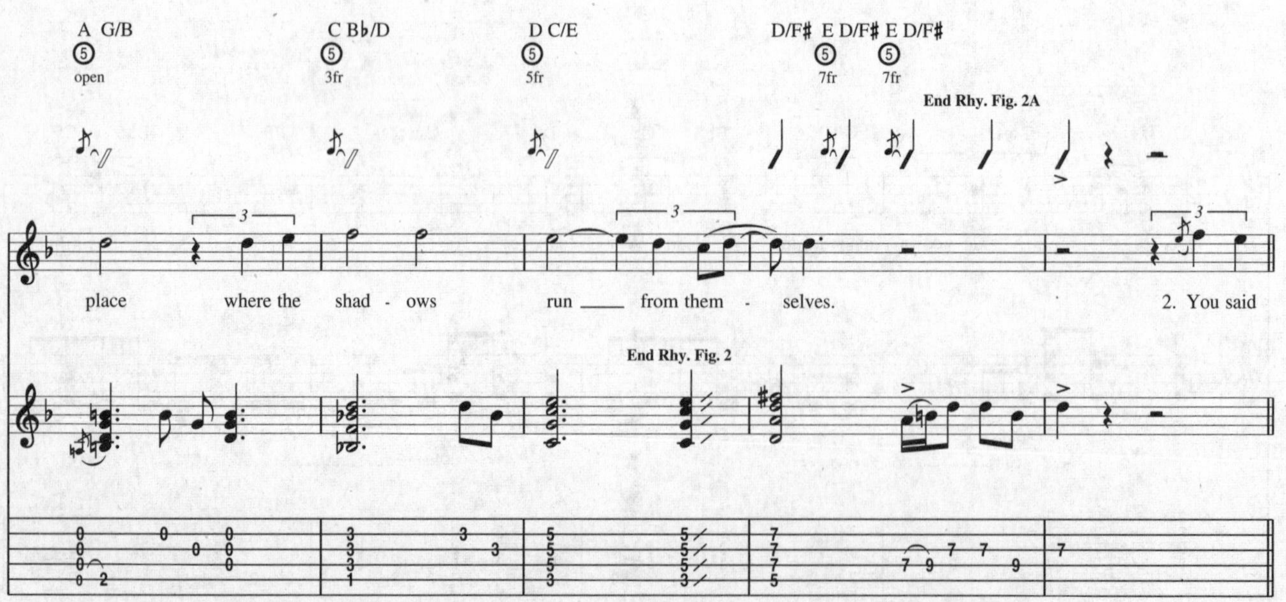
A G/B
open
C B♭/D
3fr
D C/E
5fr
D/F# E D/F# E D/F#
7fr
7fr
End Rhy. Fig. 2A
place where the shad - ows run from them - selves. 2. You said
End Rhy. Fig. 2

Verse

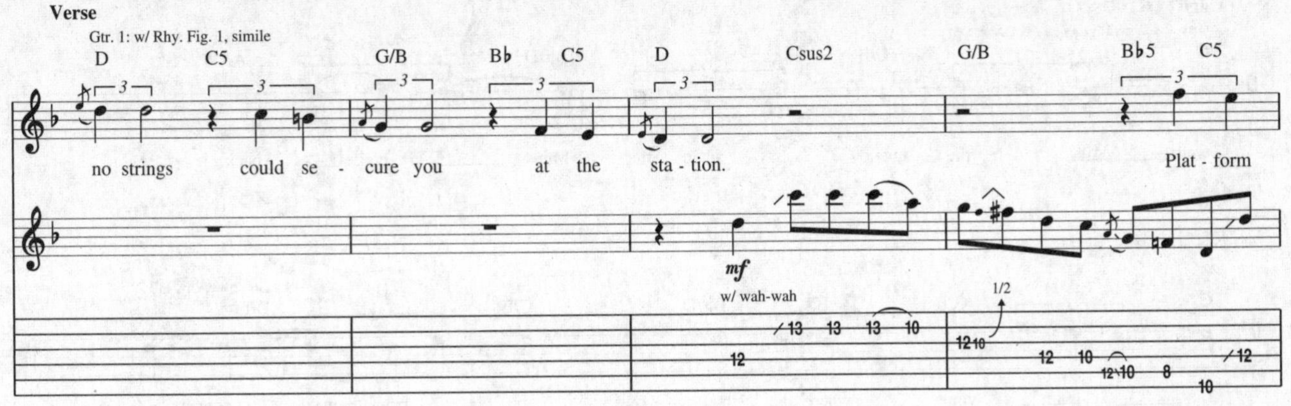
Gtr. 1: w/ Rhy. Fig. 1, simile
D C5 G/B B♭ C5 D Csus2 G/B B♭5 C5
no strings could se - cure you at the sta - tion. Plat - form
mf
w/ wah-wah
1/2

D C5 G/B B♭5 C5 D Csus2 G/B B♭5 C5
tick - et, rest - less die - sel, good - bye win - dows. I walked
full full full full full

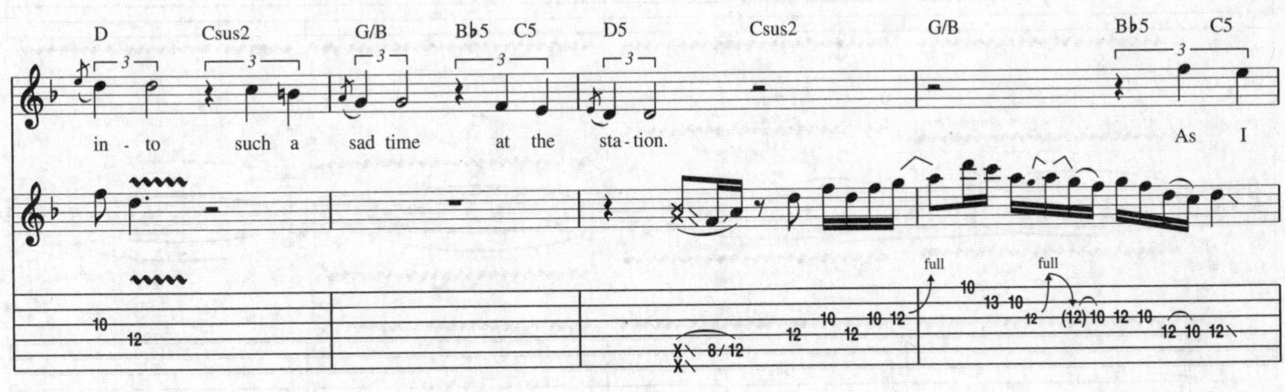
D Csus2 G/B B♭5 C5 D5 Csus2 G/B B♭5 C5
in - to such a sad time at the sta - tion. As I
full full

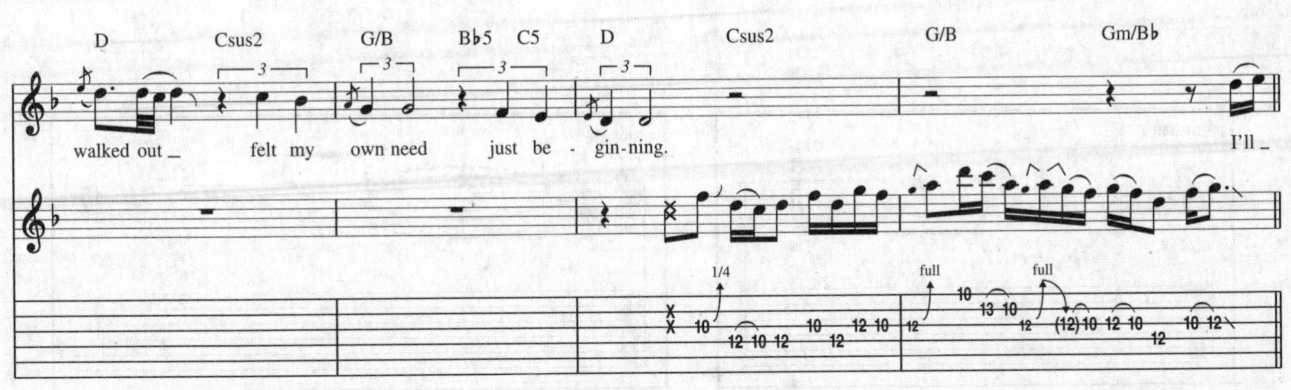
D Csus2 G/B B♭5 C5 D Csus2 G/B Gm/B♭
walked out felt my own need just be - gin - ning. I'll
1/4 full full

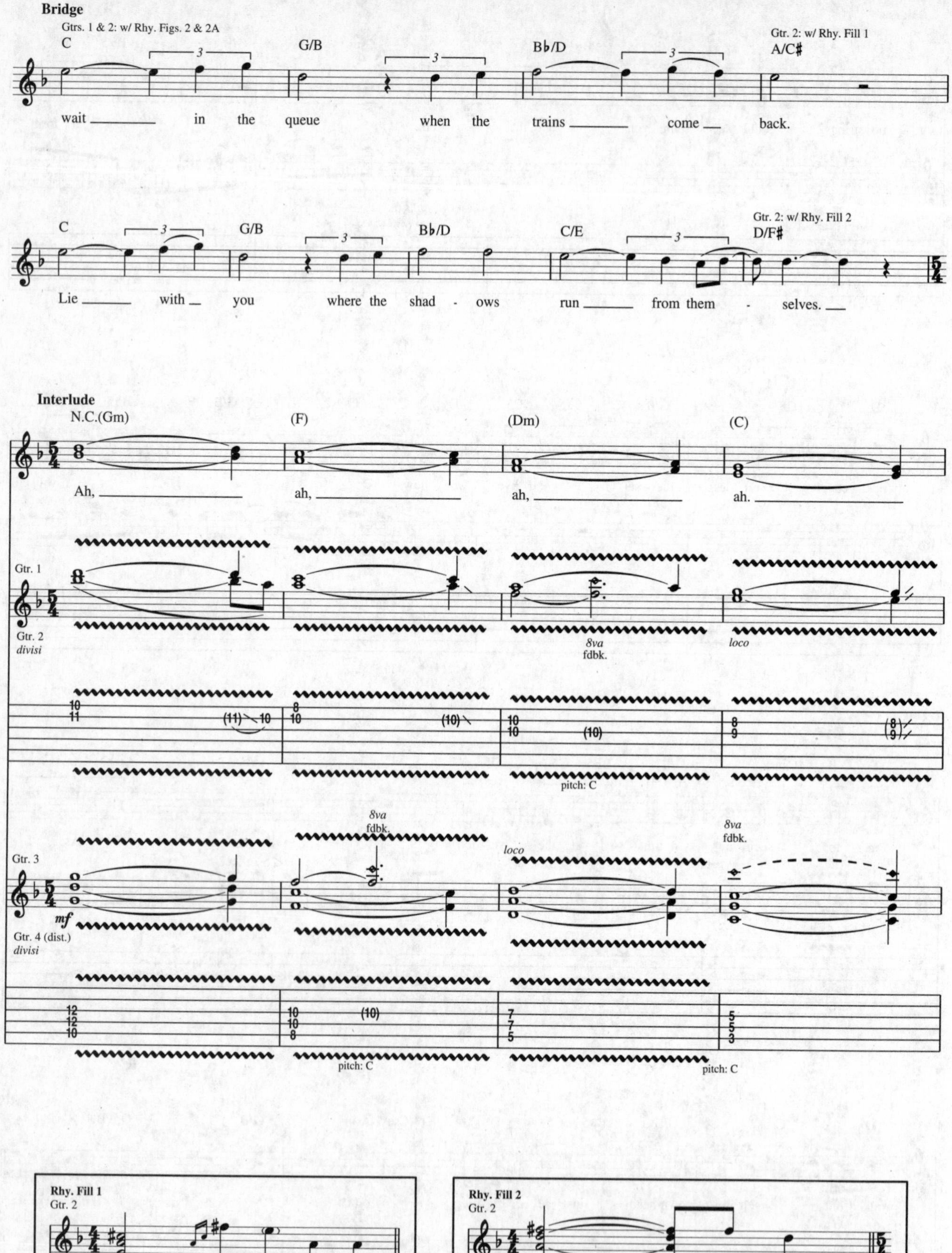

Bridge

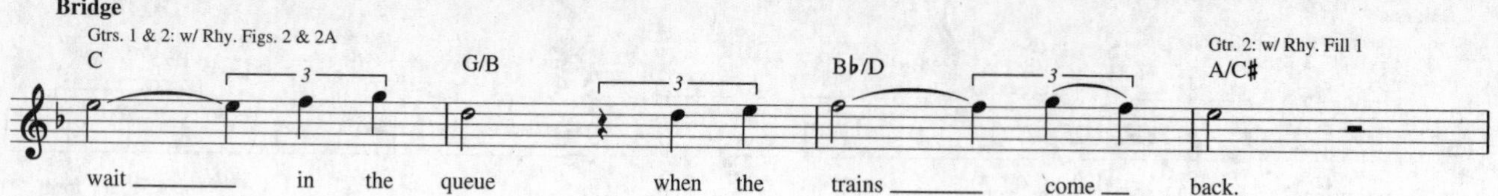

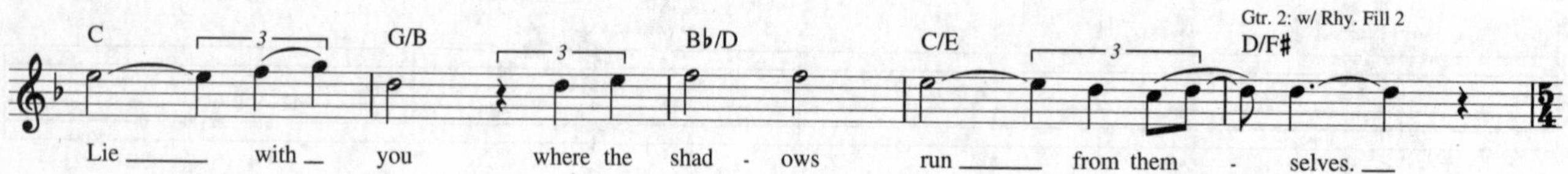

Interlude

N.C.(Gm) (F) (Dm) (C)

Ah, ___ ah, ___ ah, ___ ah. ___

Gtr. 1
Gtr. 2
divisi

8va fdbk. *loco*

10 11 (11) 10 | 8 10 (10) | 10 10 (10) | 8 9 (8 9)

pitch: C

Gtr. 3
mf
Gtr. 4 (dist.)
divisi

8va fdbk. *loco* *8va* fdbk.

12 12 10 | 10 10 8 (10) | 7 7 5 | 5 5 3

pitch: C pitch: C

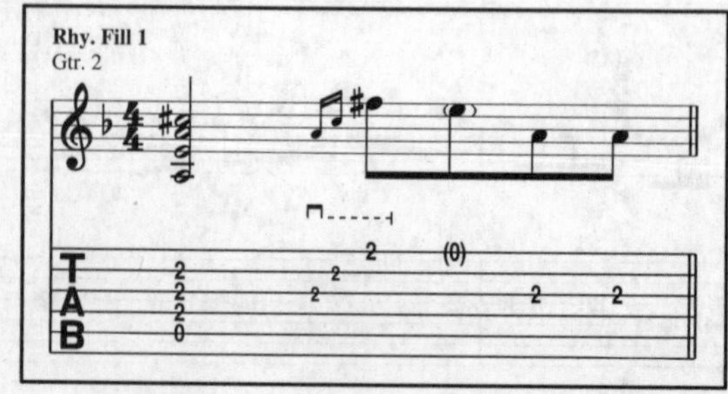

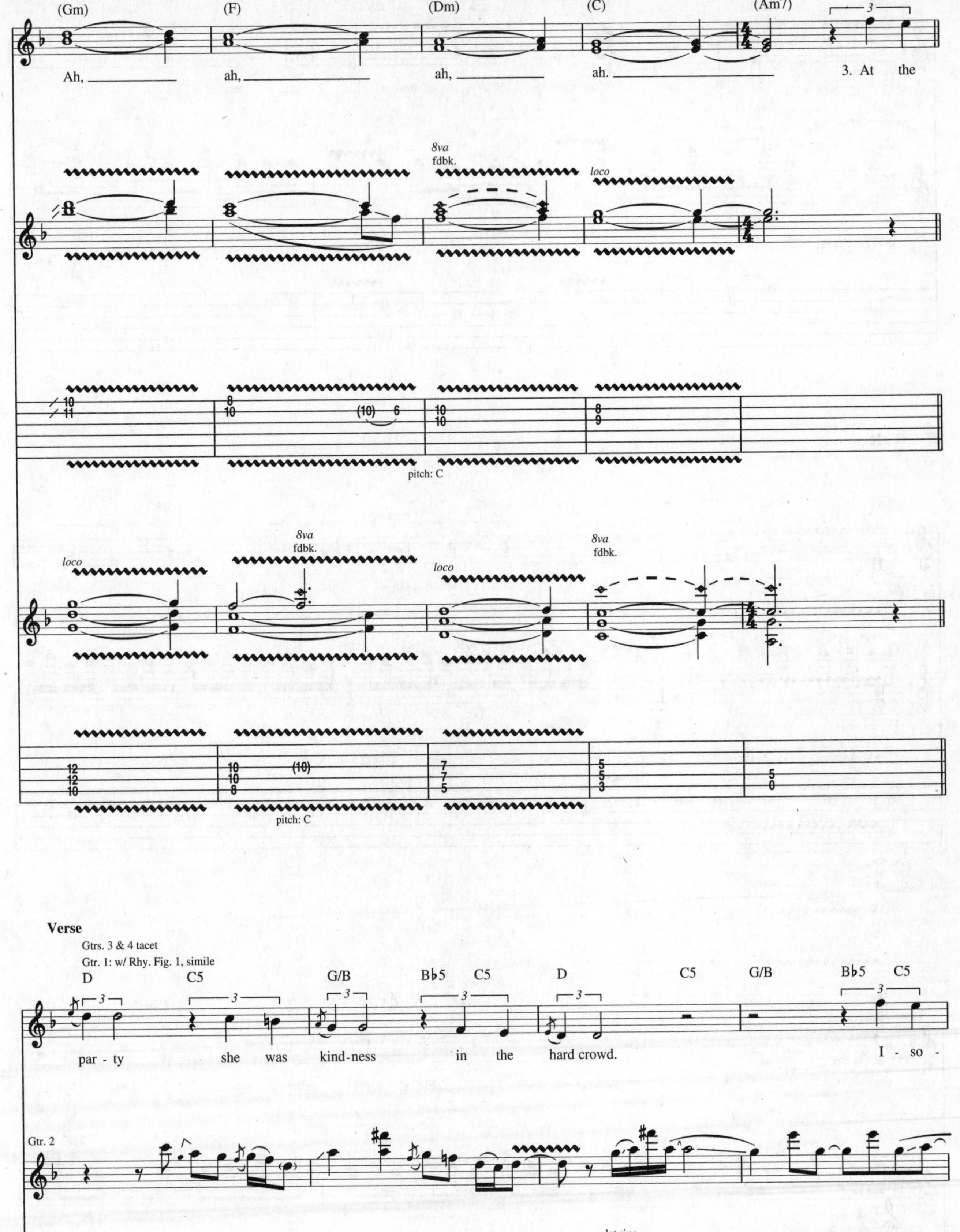
(Gm)
(F)
(Dm)
(C)
(Am7)
Ah,
ah,
ah,
ah.
3. At the
8va
fdbk.
loco
pitch: C
loco
8va
fdbk.
loco
8va
fdbk.
pitch: C
Verse
Gtrs. 3 & 4 tacet
Gtr. 1: w/ Rhy. Fig. 1, simile
D
C5
G/B
B♭5
C5
D
C5
G/B
B♭5
C5
par - ty
she
was
kind - ness
in
the
hard crowd.
I - so -
Gtr. 2
let ring
full

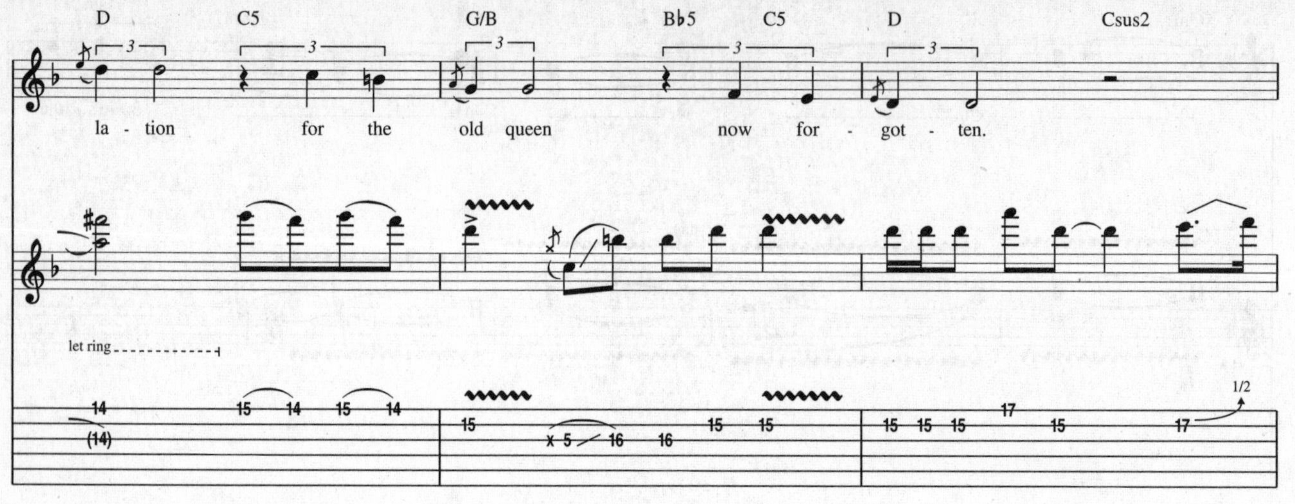
D
C5
G/B
B♭5
C5
D
Csus2
la - tion for the old queen now for - got - ten.
let ring
1/2

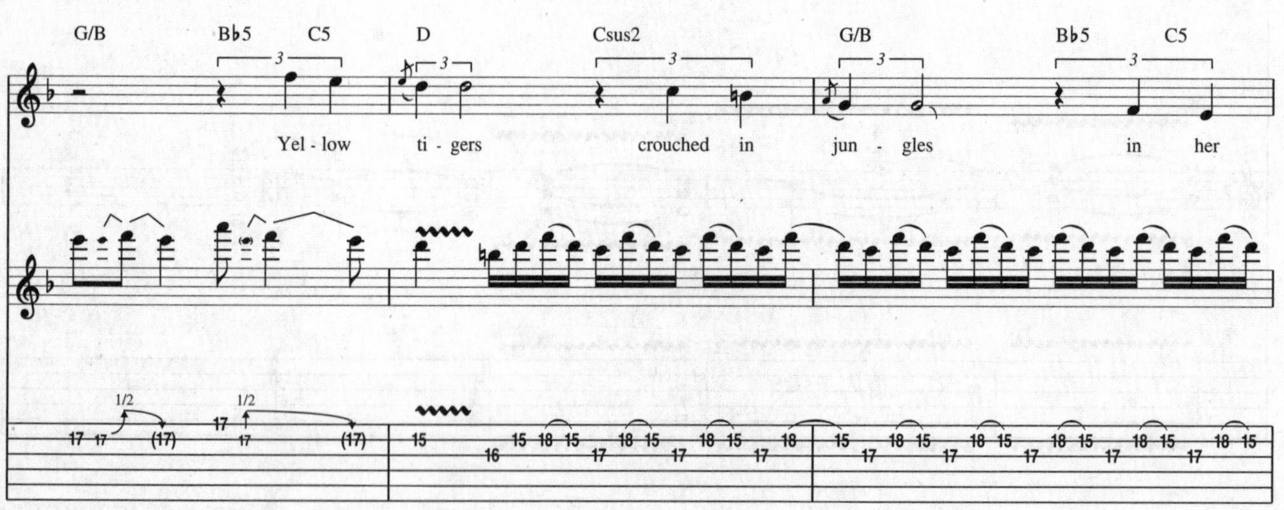
G/B
B♭5
C5
D
Csus2
G/B
B♭5
C5
Yel - low ti - gers crouched in jun - gles in her
1/2
1/2

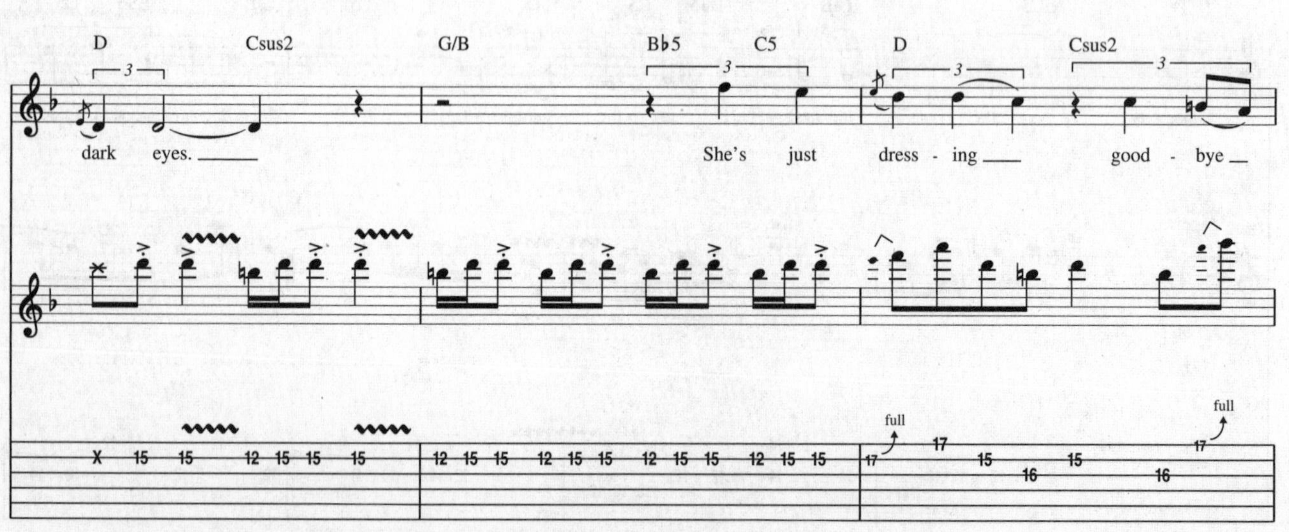
D
Csus2
G/B
B♭5
C5
D
Csus2
dark eyes.
She's just dress - ing good - bye
full
full

G/B
B♭5
C5
D
Csus2
G/B
Gm/B♭
win - dows,
tired
star - ling.
I'll
full
1/2
full
full
Bridge
Gtrs. 1 & 2: w/ Rhy. Figs. 2 & 2A
C
G/B
B♭/D
A/C♯
sleep in this place with the lone - ly crowd.
C
G/B
B♭/D
C/E
Lie in the dark, where the shad - ows run from them -
Interlude
Gtr. 1: w/ Rhy. Fill 3
D/F♯
N.C.(Gm)
(F)
(Dm)
- selves.
Ah,
ah,
ah,
Gtr. 1
Gtr. 2
divisi
8va
fdbk.
pitch: C
loco
Gtr. 3
Gtr. 4
divisi
mf
Rhy. Fill 3
Gtr. 1
let ring
T
A
B

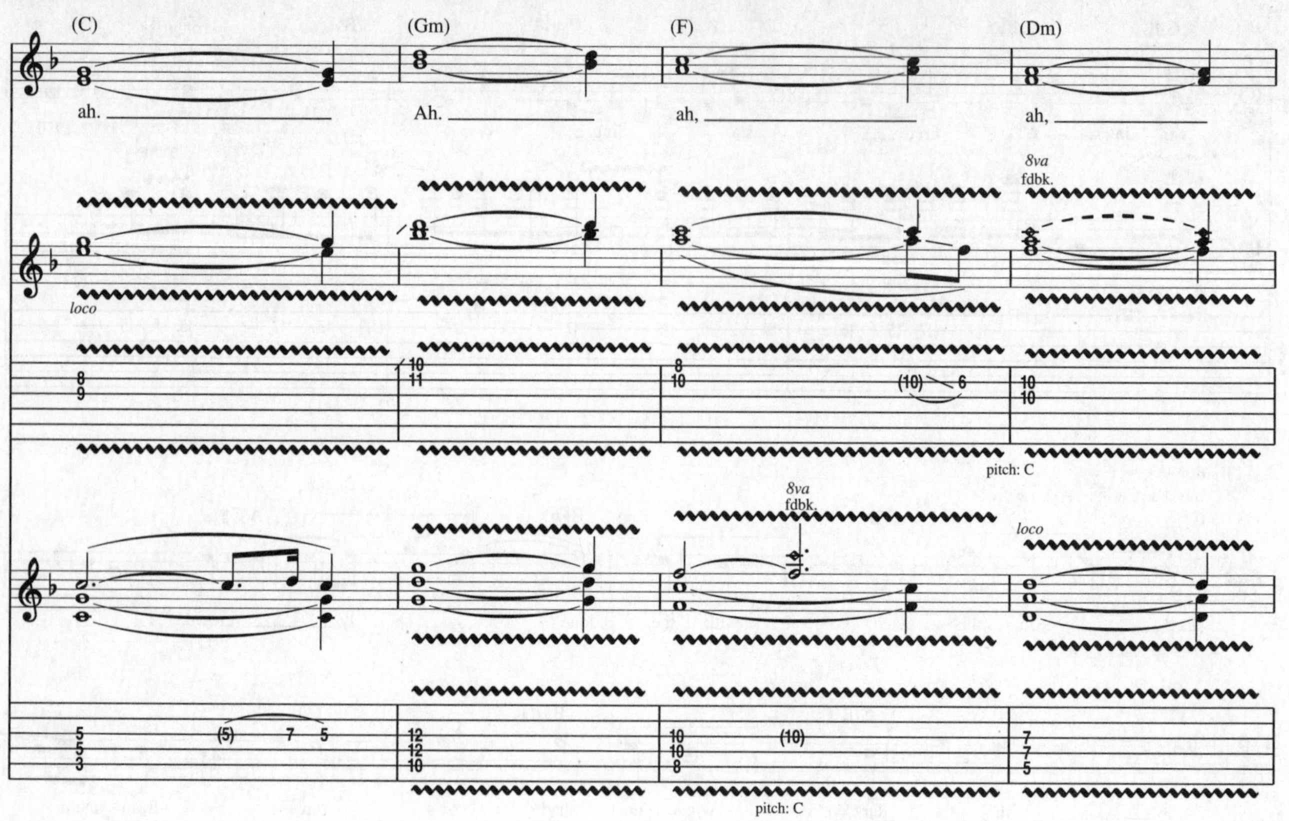

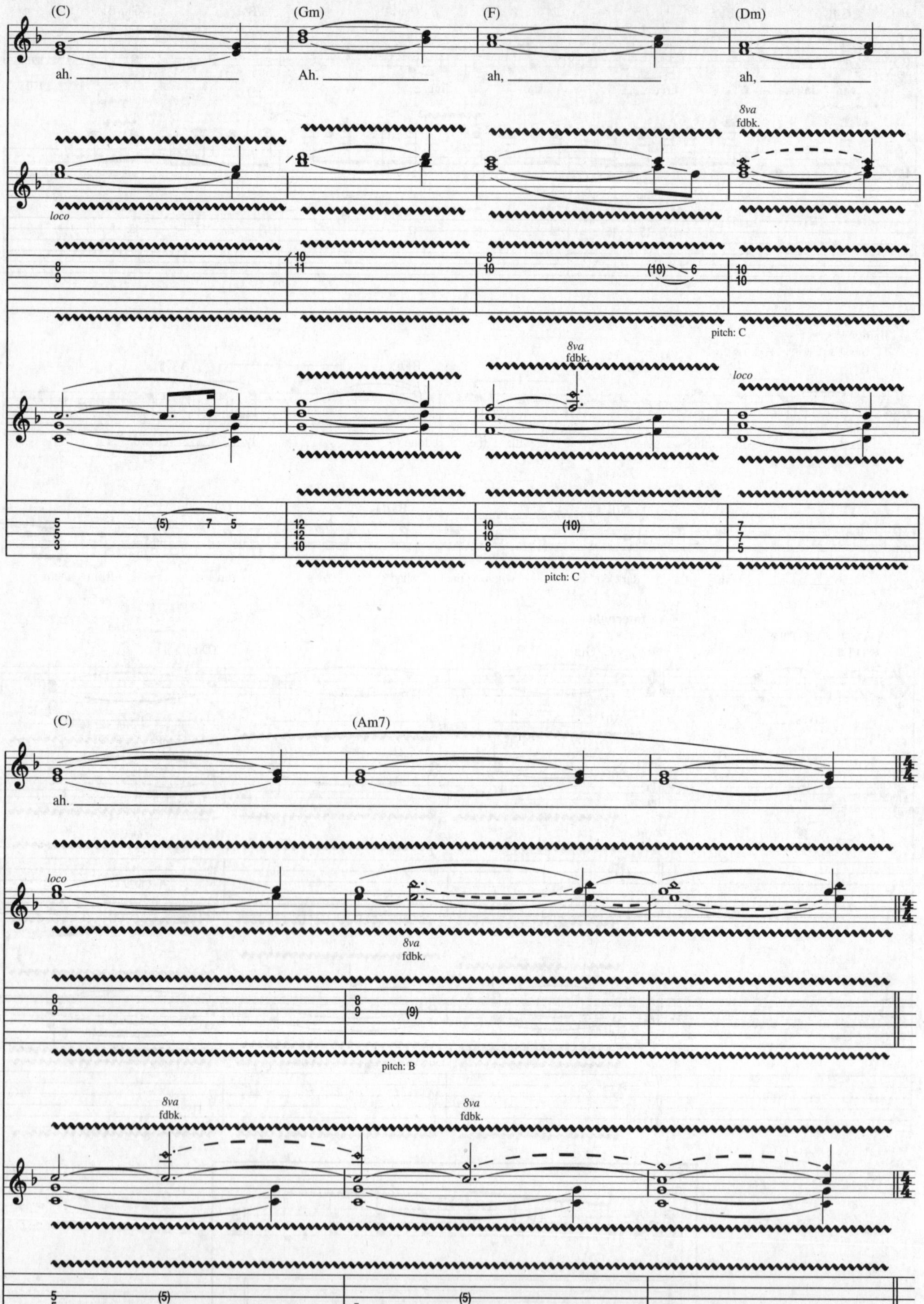

(C)
(Am7)
ah.
loco
8va
fdbk.
pitch: B
8va
fdbk.
8va
fdbk.
pitch: C
pitch: G

Outro-Guitar Solo

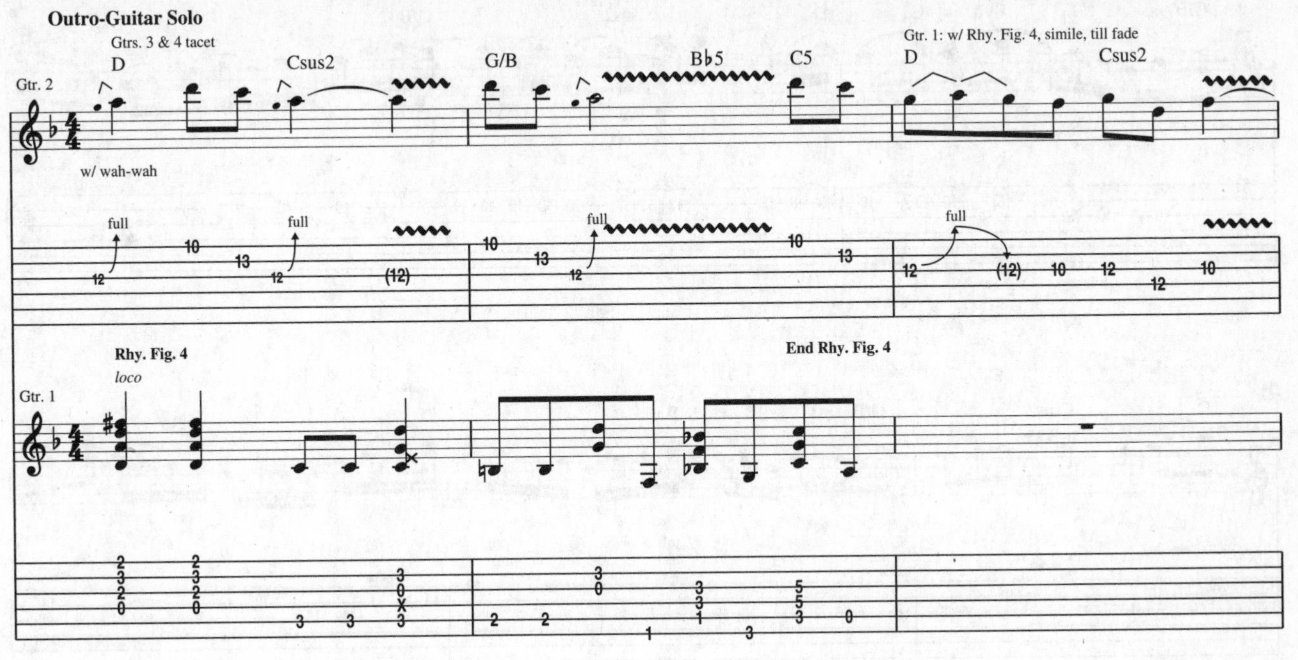

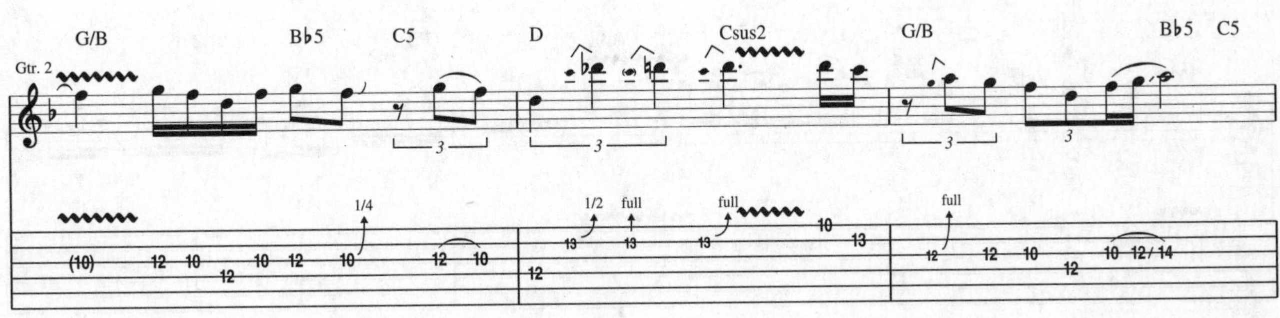

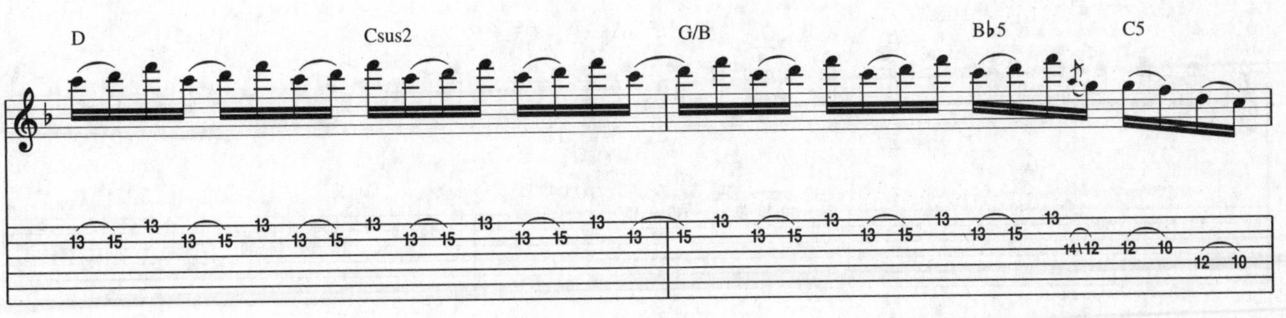

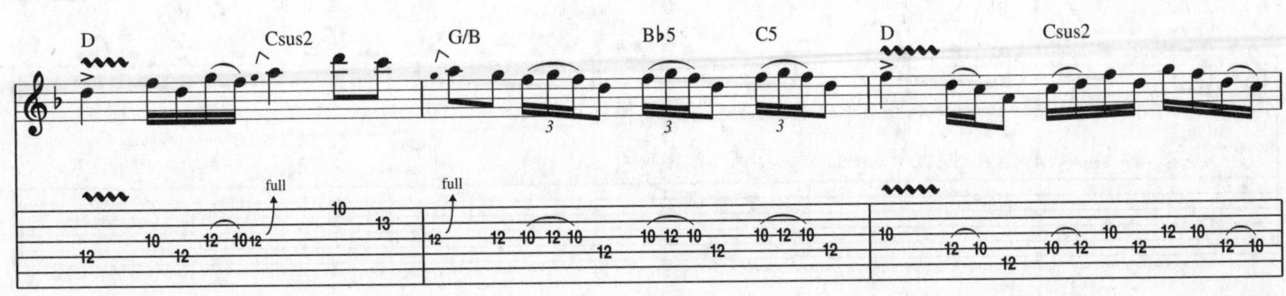

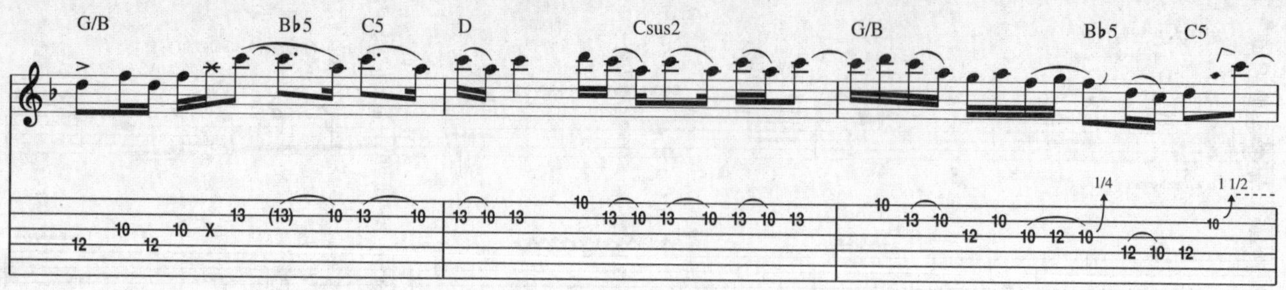
G/B
B♭5
C5
D
Csus2
G/B
B♭5
C5
1/4
1 1/2

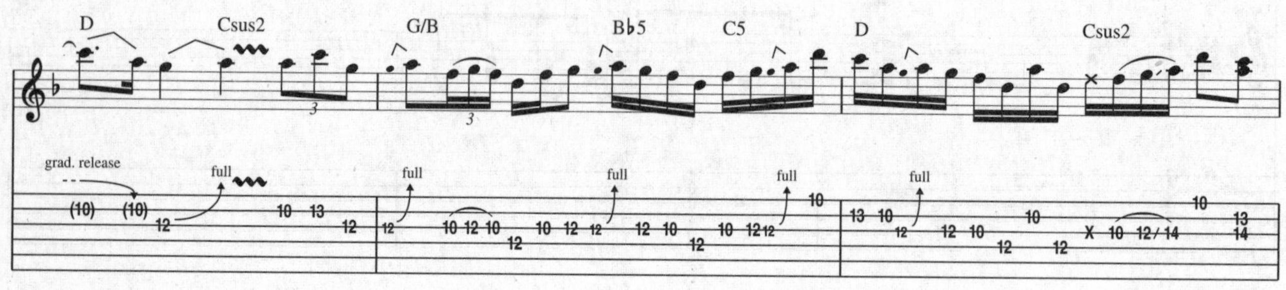
D
Csus2
G/B
B♭5
C5
D
Csus2
grad. release
full
full
full
full
full

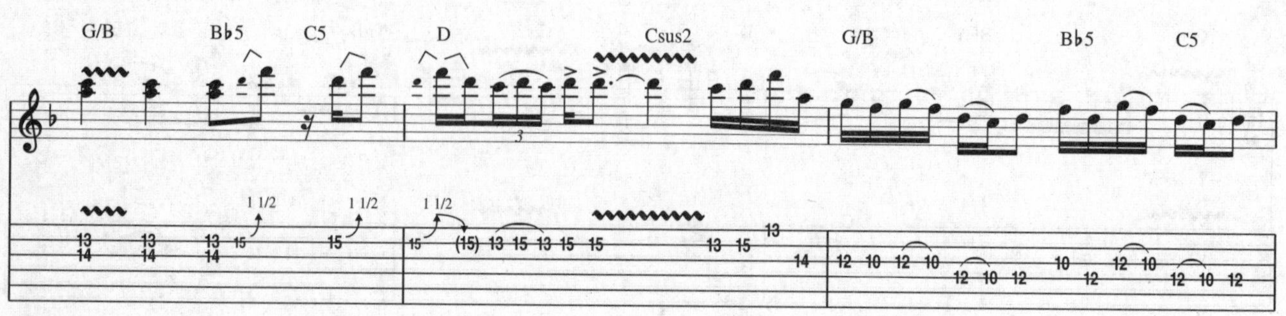
G/B
B♭5
C5
D
Csus2
G/B
B♭5
C5
1 1/2
1 1/2
1 1/2

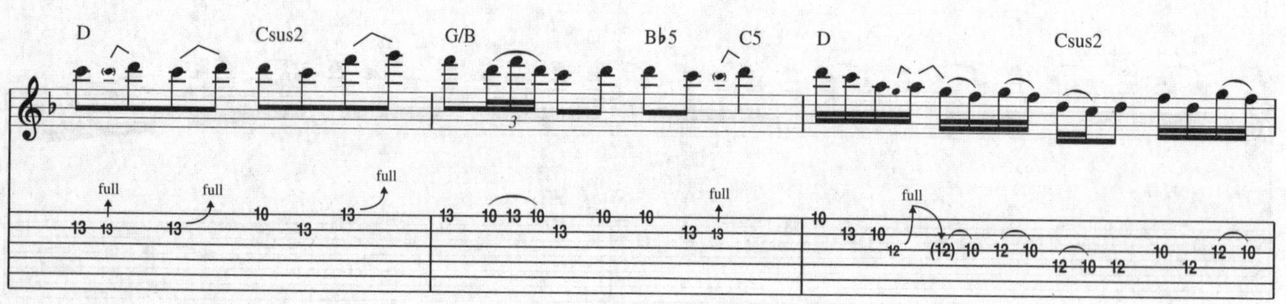
D
Csus2
G/B
B♭5
C5
D
Csus2
full
full
full
full
full

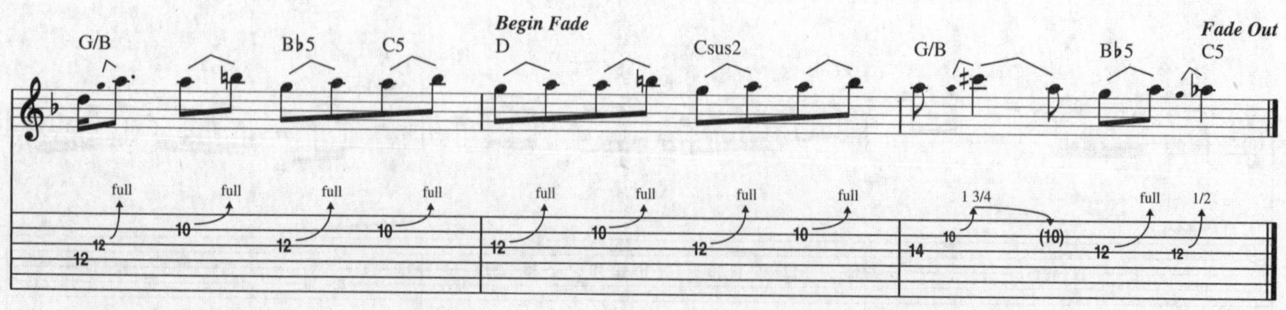
G/B
B♭5
C5
Begin Fade
D
Csus2
G/B
B♭5
Fade Out
C5
full
1 3/4
1/2

Wildwood Flower

Words and Music by A.P. Carter

Verse
C
E7
1. Oh, I'll twine with my ming - led and wav - ing black
2., 3., 4. See Additional Lyrics

C
hair with the ros - es so red and the

G7
C
lil - ies so fair. And the myr - tle so

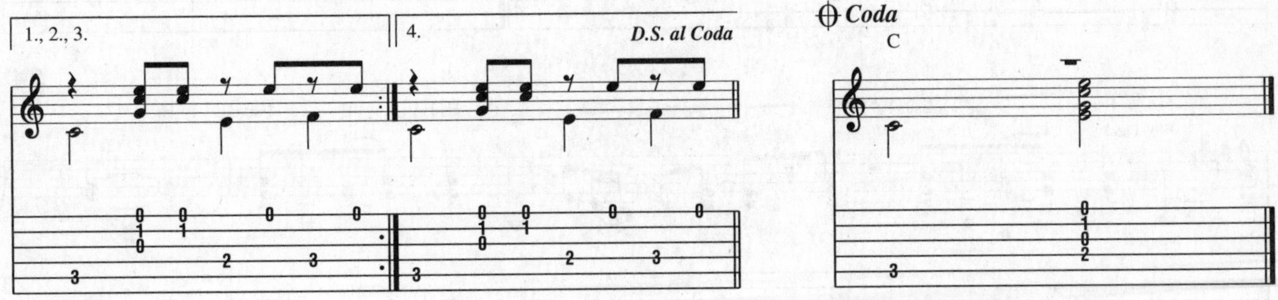

Additional Lyrics

2. I will dance, I will sing and my life shall be gay.
I will charm ev'ry heart, in his crown I will sway.
When I woke from dreaming, my idols was clay.
All portion of love had all flown away.

3. Oh, he taught me to love him and promised to love,
And to cherish me over all others above.
How my heart is now wond'ring, no misery can tell.
He's left me no warning, no words of farewell.

4. Oh, he taught me to love him and called me his flower,
That's blooming to cheer him through life's dreary hour.
Oh, I long to see him and regret the dark hour.
He's won and neglected this pale wildwood flower.

Woman from Tokyo

Words and Music by Ritchie Blackmore, Ian Gillan, Roger Glover, Jon Lord and Ian Paice

Verse

*G Fsus2/G G5 Fsus2/G

1. Fly ___ in - to the ris - in' sun. ___ Fac - es smil - in' ev - 'ry one. ___

let ring throughout

T T T

* Chord symbols reflect overall tonality.

G5 F6/G G N.C.

Yeah! She is a whole new tra - di - tion. Ow! ___ I feel it in my heart! ___

T T

Chorus

Gtr. 1: w/ Rhy. Fig. 1, 1st time
Gtr. 1: w/ Rhy. Fig. 1, 1st 7 meas., 2nd & 3rd times
Gtr. 2: w/ Fill 3, 3rd time

N.C. Esus4 E Esus4 E Esus4 E Esus4

My wom - an from To - ky - o. ___ She makes me see. ___

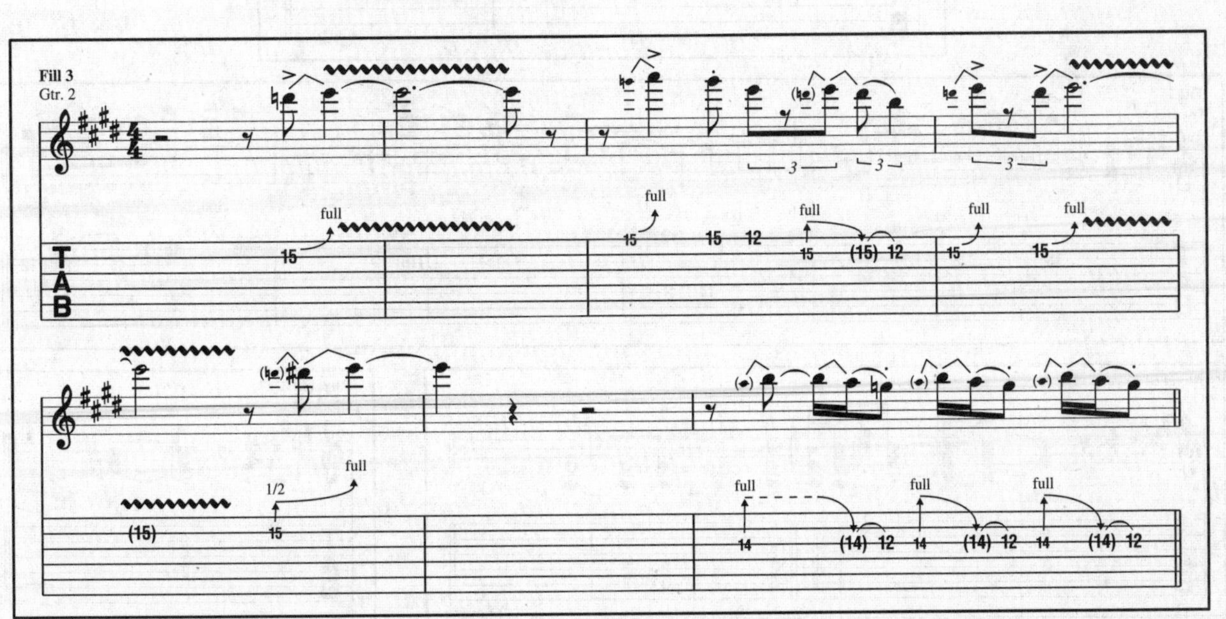

To Coda 1
To Coda 2
Gtr. 2: w/ Fill 1, 1st time
Gtr. 2: w/ Fill 2, 2nd time
Gtr. 1: w/ Rhy. Fill 1, 2nd time
Gtr. 1: w/ Rhy. Fill 2, 3rd time
E Esus4 E Esus4 E Esus4 E Esus4 E
My wom-an from To - ky - o. She's so good to me.
Verse
G G7sus4 G5 Gsus4 G G7
2. Talk a-bout her like a queen, danc - ing in a east - ern dream.
Gtr. 1
let ring throughout
8va
flutter bar
pitch: C
G5 Gsus4 G Gsus4 G N.C.
D.S. al Coda 1
Yeah, shemakesme feel like a riv - er, ow! That car-ries me a - way.
loco
Fill 1
Gtr. 2 (dist.)
mf
full
Fill 2
Gtr. 2
full
1/2
Rhy. Fill 1
Gtr. 1
let ring
Rhy. Fill 2
Gtr. 1

Coda 1
A5
Gtr. 2 tacet
Gm7
When I'm at home an' I, I just don't - be - long.
Gtr. 2
Gtr. 1
dim.
p
let ring throughout
w/ bar
full
Bridge
Gm6
G
So far a - way from the
F
G
gar - den we love.
She is what
F
moves in the soul of a dove.

G
F
Oo,
oo,
oo.
G
Soon I shall see just how black was my
F
G
night, when we're - a - lone in her
T
F
G
cit - y of light.
Oo,

C
C7
oo,
oo.
Interlude
G
Dsus4
G6
C
mp
G
C
Dsus4
G
Gtr. 1: w/ Rhy. Fig. 1, simile
8
Verse
G5
Fsus2/G
G5
Gsus4
3. Ris - in' from the ne - on gloom,
shin - in' like a
Gtr. 1
mf

G7
G5
G7sus4
cra - zy moon.
Yeah, she turns me on like a fire.
Ow!
8va
w/ bar fdbk.
loco
pitch: C
G
D.S. al Coda 2
I get high!
steady gliss.
Coda 2
Gtr. 2
B
A
E
Gtr. 2 tacet
full
1/2
Gtr. 1
* P.M.
* next 14 meas.

Guitar Solo
E
B
A
C
full
Chorus
Gtr. 1: w/ Rhy. Fig. 1, 1st 4 meas., 2 times, simile
Esus2 E Esus4 E
My wom-an from To - ky - o.
Esus4 E Esus4 E
She makes me see.
Esus4 E Esus4 E
My wom-an from To - ky - o.
Esus4 E Esus4 E
She's so good to me.
Outro-Chorus
Gtr. 1: w/ Rhy. Fig. 1, 1st 4 meas., 4 times, simile
Voc. Fig. 1
End Voc. Fig. 1
(My wom-an from To - ky - o.
Bkgd. Voc.: w/ Voc. Fig. 1, till fade
My wom-an from To - ky - o.)
Begin Fade
N.C.
Gtr. 1
P.M.
w/ bar
Fade Out

Wonderful Tonight

Words and Music by Eric Clapton

Intro
Moderately Slow ♩ = 95
Half-Time Feel

Verse
G
Gtr. 3 tacet
D/F#
C/E
D
1. It's late in the eve - ning. She's won-d'ring what clothes to wear.
2. We go to a par - ty and ev - 'ry - one turns to see.
3. It's time to go home now and I've got an ach-ing head.
mp
simile on repeats
She puts on her make - up and brush-es her long blond hair.
This beau - ti - ful la - dy is walk-in' a - round with me.
So I give her the car keys and she helps me to bed.
Gtr. 1
Gtr. 2

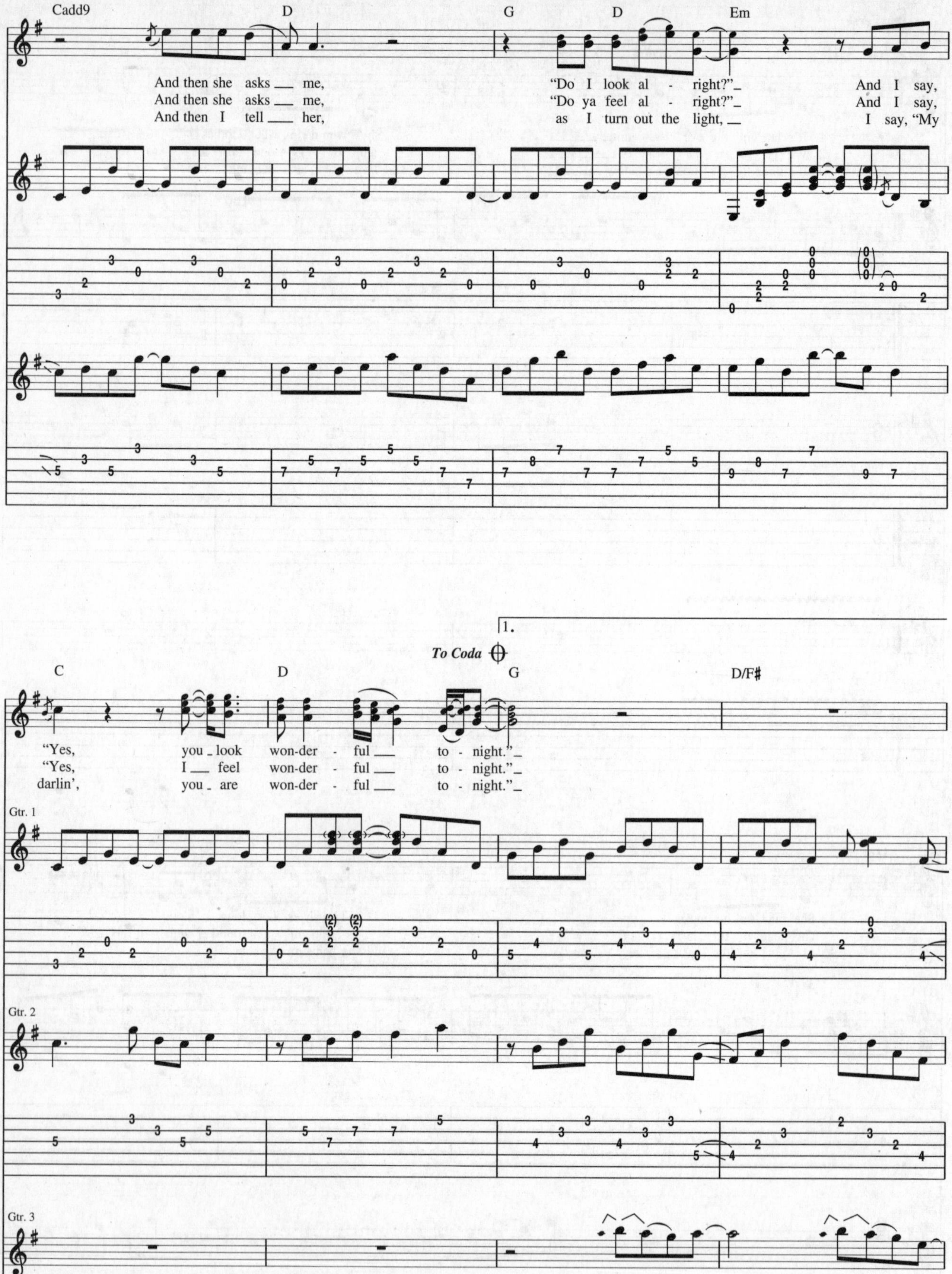

1.
To Coda

C D G D/F#

"Yes, you look won-der - ful ___ to - night."
"Yes, I ___ feel won-der - ful ___ to - night."
darlin', you are won-der - ful ___ to - night."

Gtr. 1

Gtr. 2

Gtr. 3

full
full

C/E D 2. G

full

Bridge

C

Gtr. 3 tacet

D Csus2

I feel won - der - ful __ be - cause I see __ the love _

(Oo, oo,

G D/F# Em C

___ light in ___ your ___ eyes. ___ And the won - der of it ___ all ___

oo, oo, oo, oo,

Gtr. 1

Gtr. 2

D C D

___ is that you just don't ___ re - al - ize ___ how ___ much ___ I love ___

oo, oo, oo.)

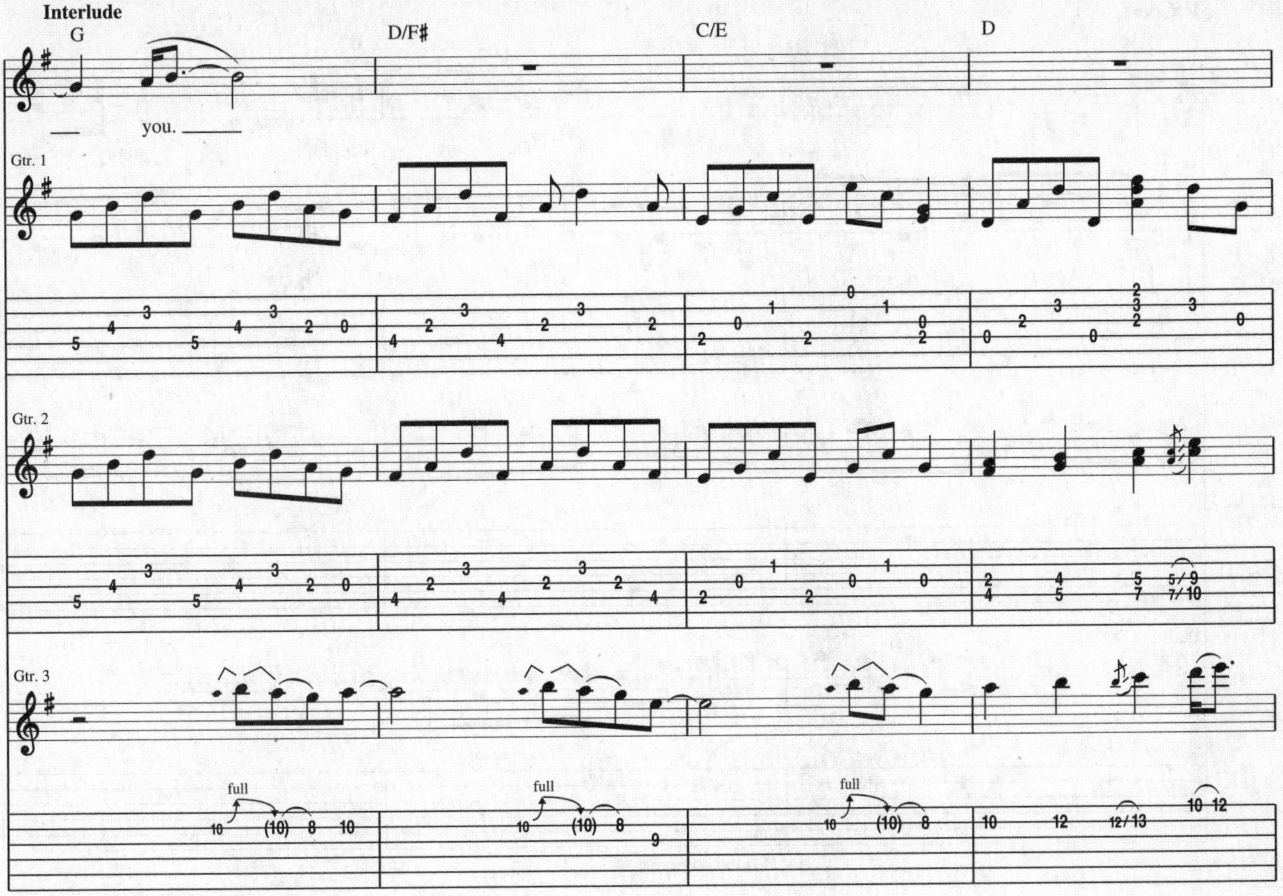

Interlude
G
D/F♯
C/E
D
you.
Gtr. 1
Gtr. 2
Gtr. 3
full
full
full

D.S. al Coda
G
D/F♯
C/E
D
full
full
full

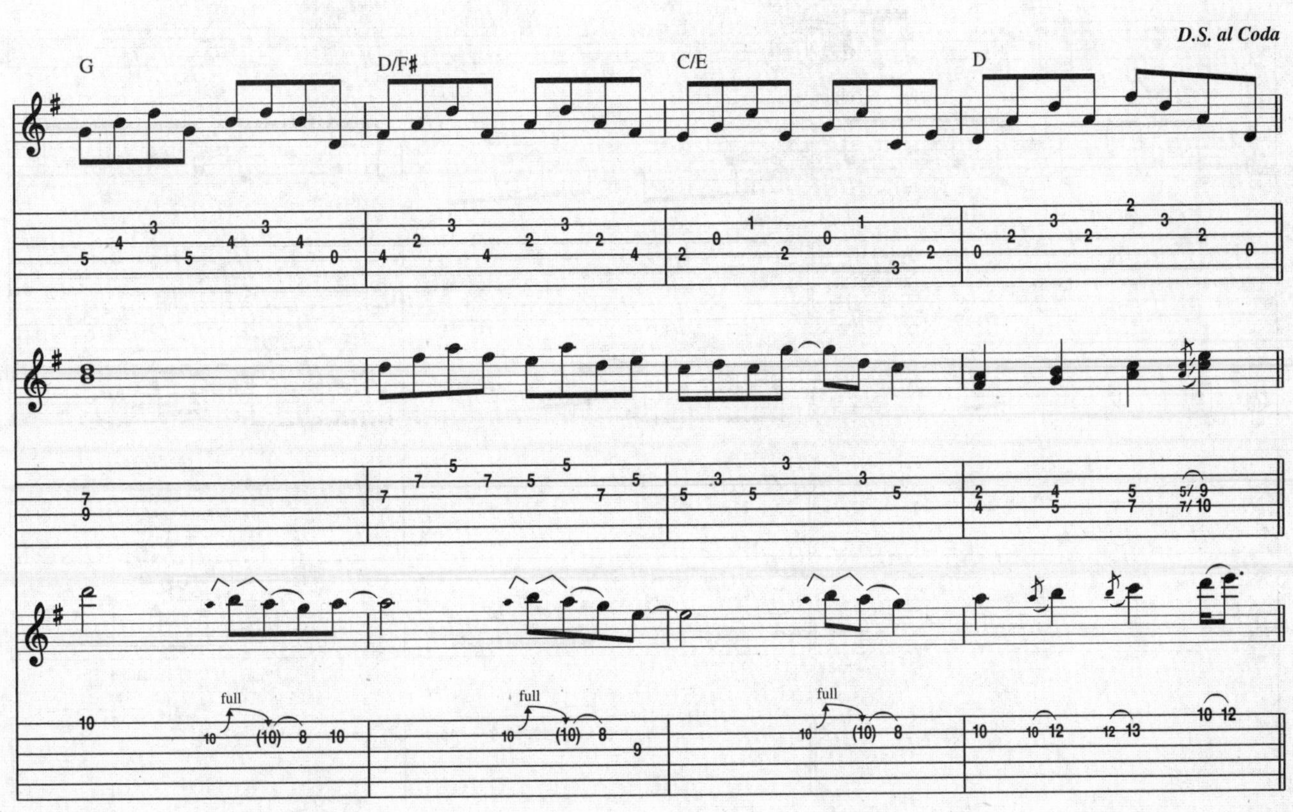

Coda

G D Em7 C

Oh my darlin', you are

Gtr. 1

Gtr. 2

Gtr. 3

3/4 full

* Played behind the beat.

Outro

D G D/F#

won - der - ful to - night.

full

hold bend full

C/E D G

rit.

D/F# C/E D G

rit.

rit.

Working for the Weekend

Words and Music by Paul Dean, Matthew Frenette and Michael Reno

Pre-Chorus
D5
N.C. G5
N.C.
Ev - 'ry - bod - y's work - ing for the week - end.
P.M.
N.C. G5
Ev - 'ry - bod - y wants a new ro - mance.
Ev - 'ry - bod - y's go - ing off the deep end.
D5
Ev - 'ry - bod - y needs a sec - ond chance, oh.
You want a piece of my heart?

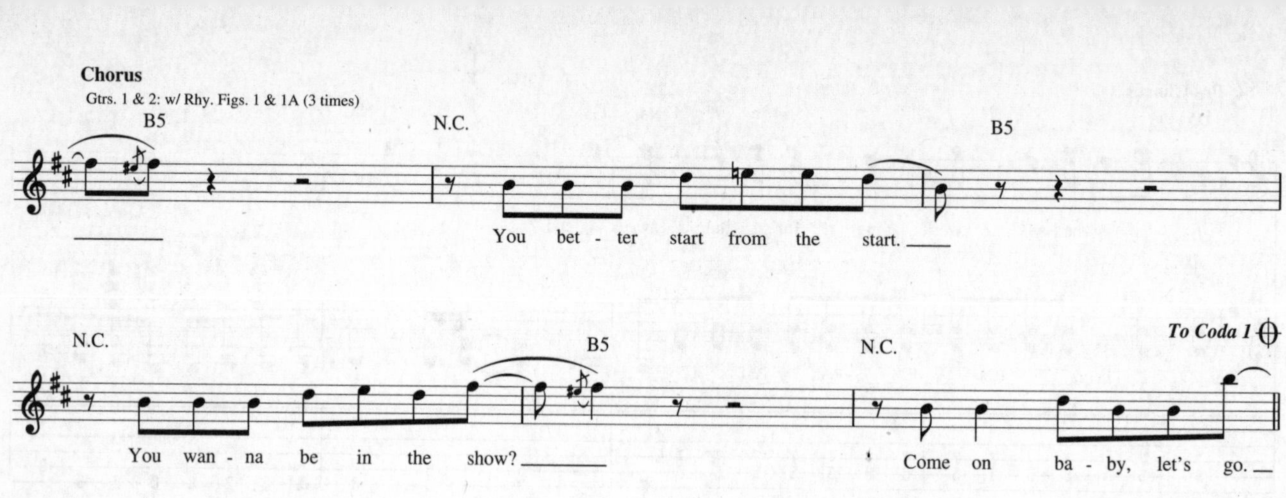
Chorus
Gtrs. 1 & 2: w/ Rhy. Figs. 1 & 1A (3 times)
B5
N.C.
B5
You bet - ter start from the start.
N.C.
B5
N.C.
To Coda 1
You wan - na be in the show?
Come on ba - by, let's go.

Interlude
N.C.
Gtr. 1
P.M.
P.M.

To Coda 2
B5
N.C.
P.M.
P.M.

Verse
2. Ev - 'ry-one's look - ing to see if it was you.
Rhy. Fig. 2
mf
P.M.
P.M.

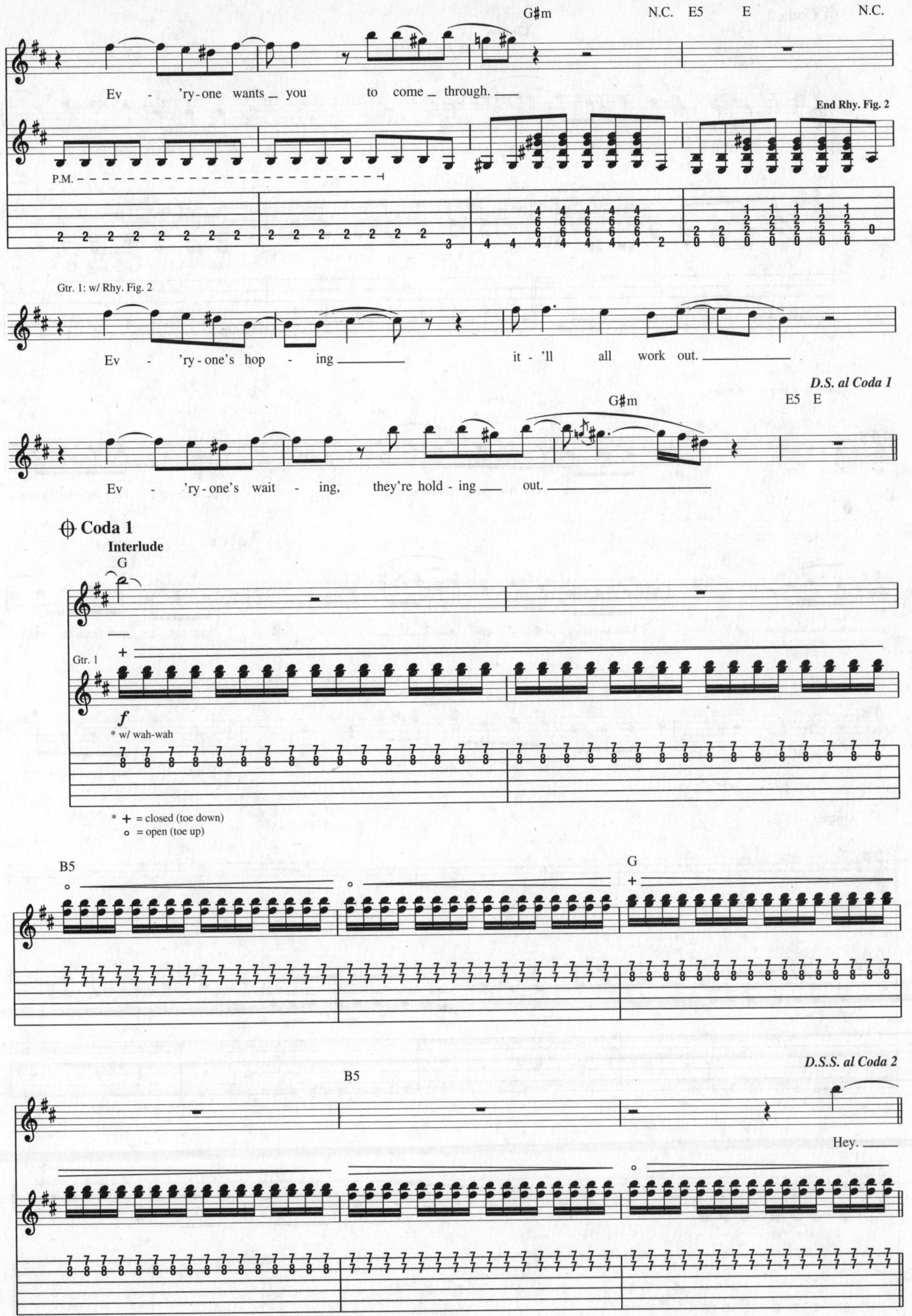
G♯m
N.C.
E5
E
N.C.
Ev - 'ry-one wants _ you to come _ through. ___
End Rhy. Fig. 2
P.M.
Gtr. 1: w/ Rhy. Fig. 2
Ev - 'ry-one's hop - ing ______ it-'ll all work out. ______
D.S. al Coda 1
G♯m
E5 E
Ev - 'ry-one's wait - ing, they're hold-ing _ out. ______
Coda 1
Interlude
G
Gtr. 1
f
* w/ wah-wah
* + = closed (toe down)
○ = open (toe up)
B5
G
D.S.S. al Coda 2
B5
Hey. ___

Coda 2
Chorus
Gtr. 2: w/ Rhy. Fig. 1A (7 times)
N.C.
B5
N.C.
You want a piece of my heart?
You bet - ter start from the start.
Gtr. 1
P.M.
Gtr. 1: w/ Rhy. Fig. 1 (6 times)
B5
N.C.
B5
N.C.
You wan - na be in the show?
Come on ba - by, let's go.
You want a piece of my heart?
You bet - ter start from the start.
You wan - na be in the show?
Come on ba - by, let's go.
Outro
Gtr. 1
f
P.M.
B5
rit.

Yellow

Words and Music by Guy Berryman, Jon Buckland, Will Champion and Chris Martin

F#6add11
3/4
Emaj7
3/4
B
Badd4
End Riff A
3/4
End Rhy. Fig. 2

Verse
Gtrs. 1 & 4: w/ Rhy. Fig. 2, 1st 6 meas. (3 times)
Gtr. 3 tacet
B
F♯6add11
1. Look at the stars. Look how they shine for you
Gtr. 3
Fill 1
End Fill 1
Emaj7
and ev - 'ry - thing you do. Yeah, they were all yel - low.
B
F♯6add11
I came a - long. I wrote a song for you
Gtr. 2
Rhy. Fig. 3
mf
w/ clean tone
Emaj7
and all the things you do, and it was called "Yel - low."
End Rhy. Fig. 3
Gtr. 2: w/ Rhy. Fig. 3
B
F♯6add11
So then I took my turn.
Emaj7
Oh, what a thing to have done, and it was all yel - low.

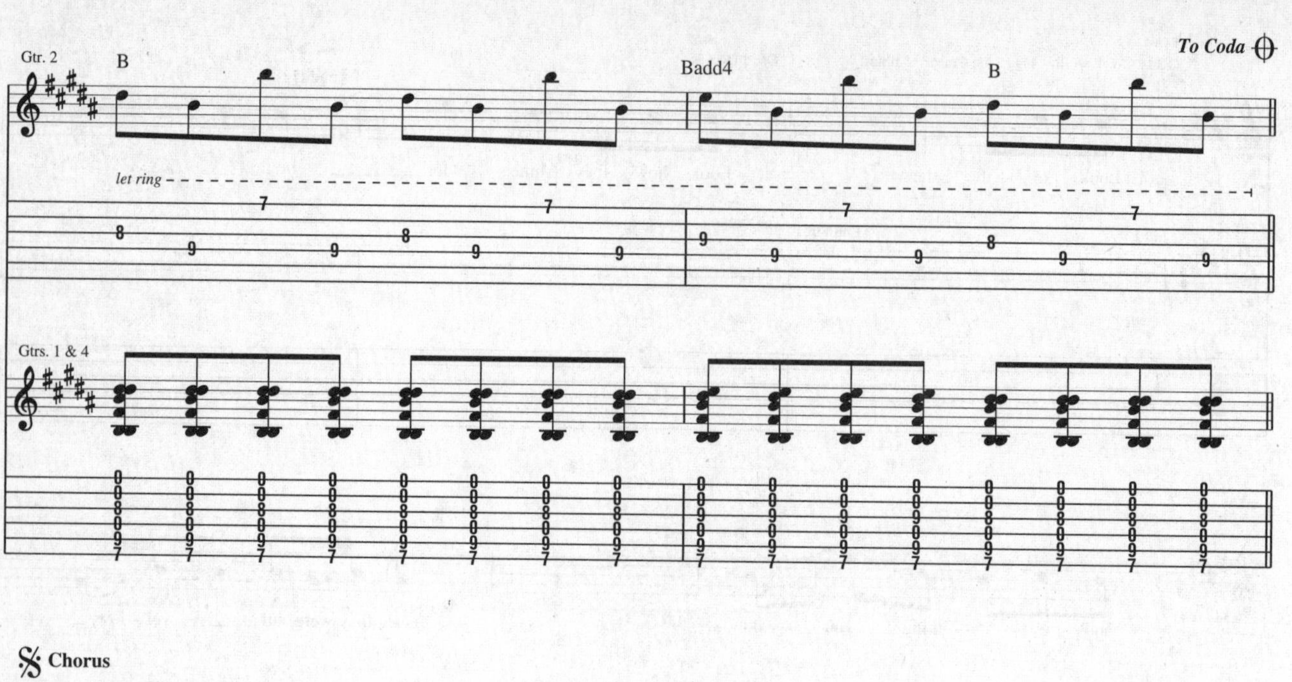
Gtr. 2
B
Badd4
B
To Coda
let ring
Gtrs. 1 & 4

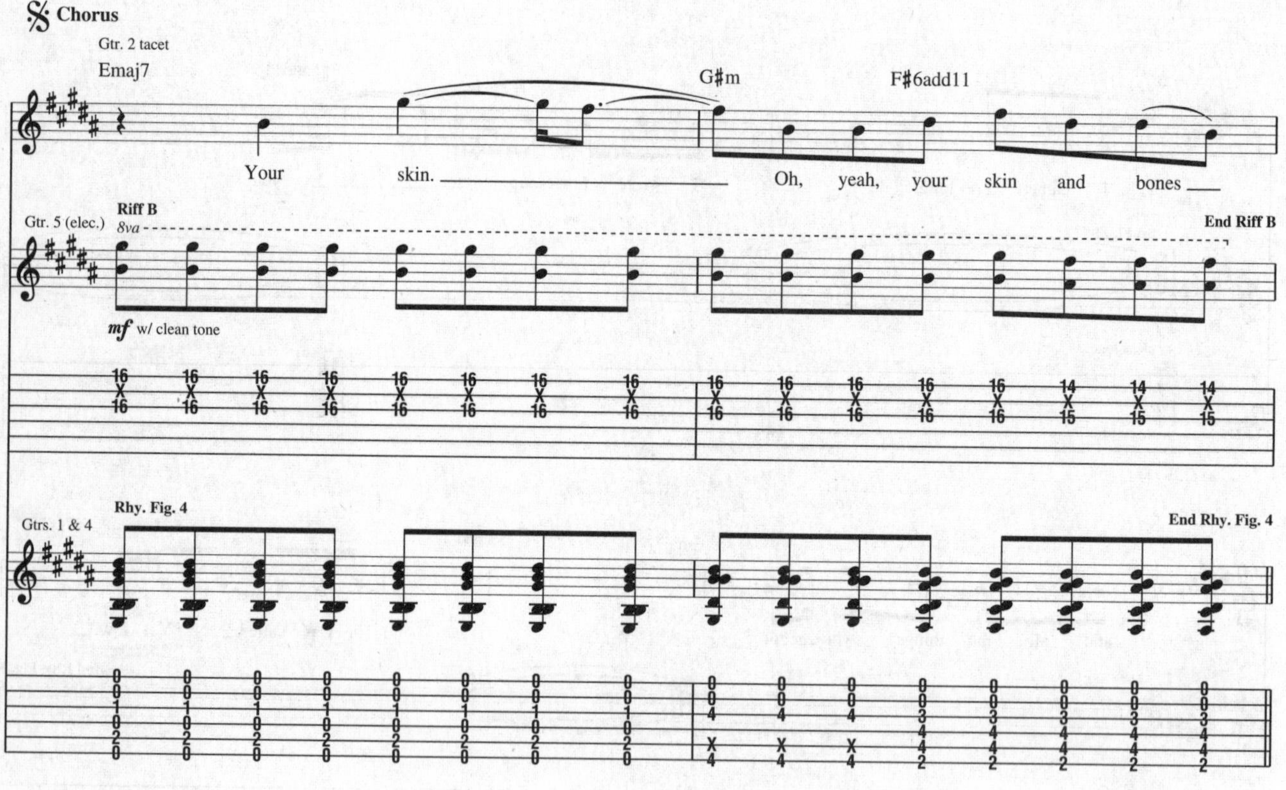
Chorus
Gtr. 2 tacet
Emaj7
G#m
F#6add11
Your skin. Oh, yeah, your skin and bones
Riff B
Gtr. 5 (elec.)
8va
End Riff B
mf w/ clean tone
Rhy. Fig. 4
Gtrs. 1 & 4
End Rhy. Fig. 4

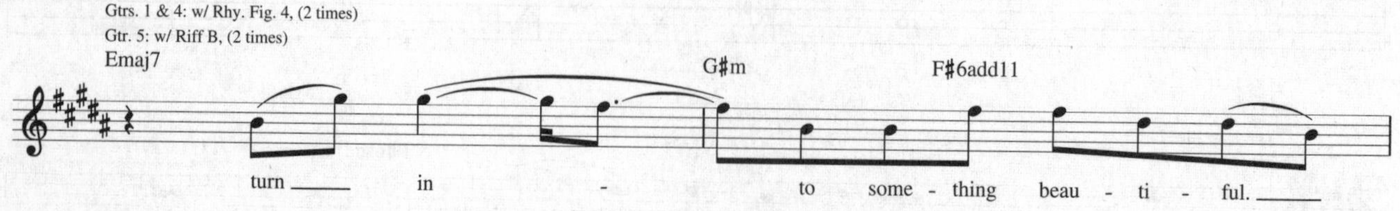
Gtrs. 1 & 4: w/ Rhy. Fig. 4, (2 times)
Gtr. 5: w/ Riff B, (2 times)
Emaj7
G#m
F#6add11
turn in - to some - thing beau - ti - ful.

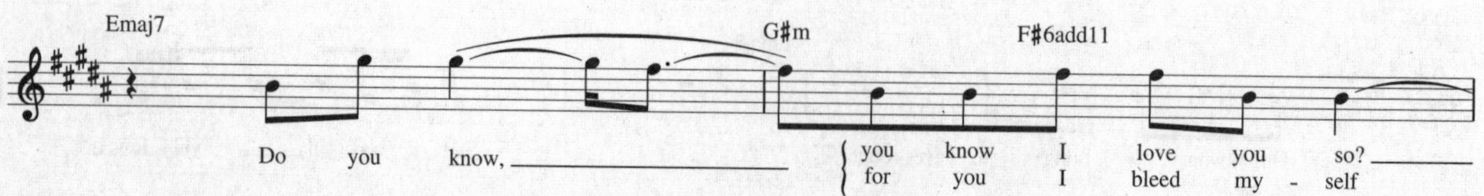
Emaj7
G#m
F#6add11
Do you know, you know I love you so?
for you I bleed my - self

To Coda

Gtr. 4 tacet
Emaj7
dry.
Gtr. 5 tacet
You know I love you so.
For you I bleed my - self
Gtr. 5
8va
Gtr. 1
Interlude
Gtrs. 1 & 4: w/ Rhy. Fig. 2
Gtr. 3: w/ Riff A
8
Verse
Gtrs. 1 & 4: w/ Rhy. Fig. 2, 1st 6 meas. (2 times)
Gtr. 3: w/ Fill 1
Gtr. 2: w/ Rhy. Fig. 3, (2 times)
B
F♯6add11
2. I swam a - cross, I jumped a - cross for you.
Emaj7
Oh, what a thing to do, 'cause you were all yel - low.
B
F♯6add11
I drew a line, I drew a line for you.
Emaj7
Oh, what a thing to do. And it was all yel - low.
D.S. al Coda
Gtr. 2
B
Badd4
let ring
Gtrs. 1 & 4

Coda
Interlude
Gtrs. 1 & 4: w/ Rhy. Fig. 2
Gtr. 3: w/ Riff A
B
6
B
dry.
It's
Outro
Gtrs. 1 & 4: w/ Rhy. Fig. 2, 1st 6 meas. (2 times)
Gtr. 3: w/ Riff A, 1st 6 meas. (2 times)
B
F#6add11
true.
Look how they shine for you.
Emaj7
Look how they shine for you.
Look how they shine for...
B
F#6add11
Look how they shine for you.
Emaj7
Look how they shine for you.
Look how they shine.
Gtr. 3: w/ Fill 1
B
Look at the stars.
Look how they shine for
Gtr. 1
F#m11
Emaj7
you
and all the things that you do.

Yesterday

Words and Music by John Lennon and Paul McCartney

Tune Down 1 Step:
①= D ④= C
②= A ⑤= G
③= F ⑥= D

Intro

Moderately ♩ = 98

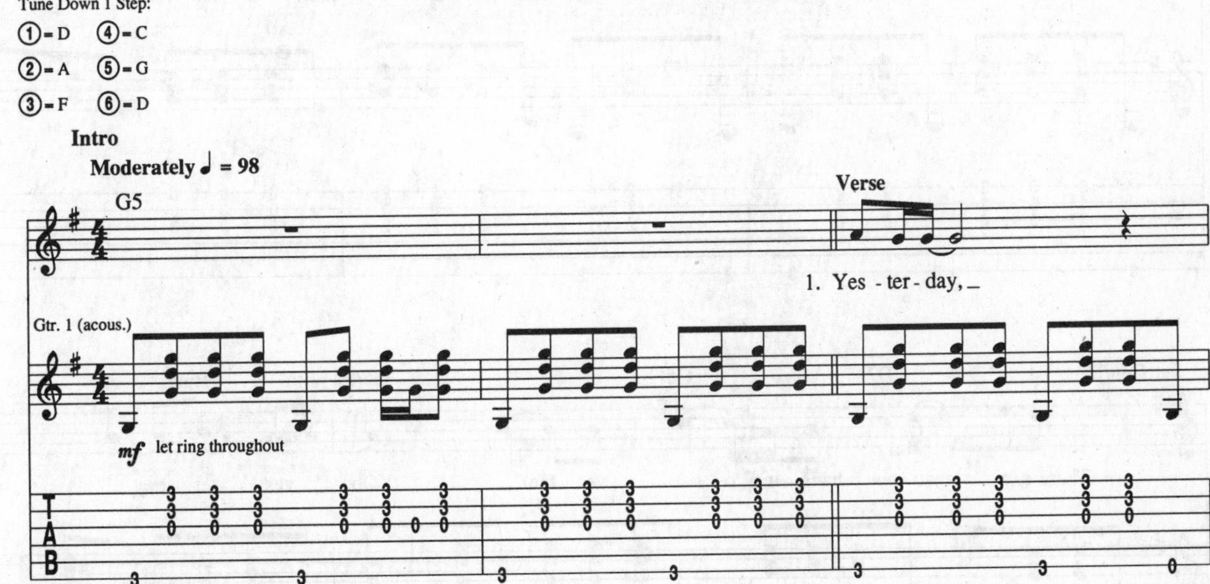

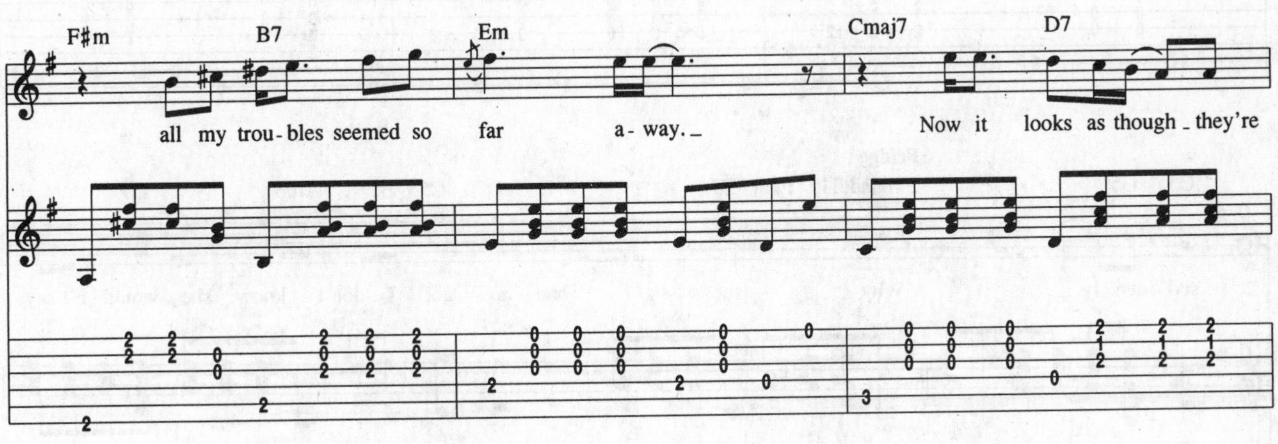

Verse
G5
F♯m
B7
Em
2. Sud - den - ly,
I'm not half the man I used to be.
Cmaj7
D7
G5
G5/F♯
Em
Em7
A
There's a shad - ow hang - ing o - ver me.
Oh, yes - ter - day came
C5
G5
Bridge
F♯m(add11)
F♯m
B7
E
D
C5
B5
Am6
D7
sud - den - ly.
Why she had to go, I don't know, she would - n't say.
G5
F♯m
B7
E
D
C5
B5
Am6
D7
I said some - thing wrong, now I long for yes - ter -

G5
Verse
F♯m
B7
- day. 3. Yes - ter - day, love was such an eas - y
Em
Em/D
Cmaj7
D7
G5
F♯m
game to play. Now I need a place to hide a - way. Oh,
Bridge
Em7
A
C5
G5
F♯m
B7
E
D
C5
B5
I be - lieve in yes - ter - day. Why she had to go, I don't
Am6
D7
G5
F♯m
B7
know, she would - n't say. I said

E D C5 B5 Am6 D7 G5
some - thing wrong, _ now I long _ for _ yes - ter - day. _
Verse
F#m7 B7 Em Em/D
4. Yes - ter - day, _ love was such an eas - y game to play. _
Cmaj7 D7 G5 F#m Em7 A
Now I need _ a place _ to hide a - way. _ Oh, I be - lieve _ in
C5 G5 A7/G C5 G5
yes - ter - day. _ Hmm. _

You Ain't Seen Nothin' Yet

Words and Music by Randy Bachman

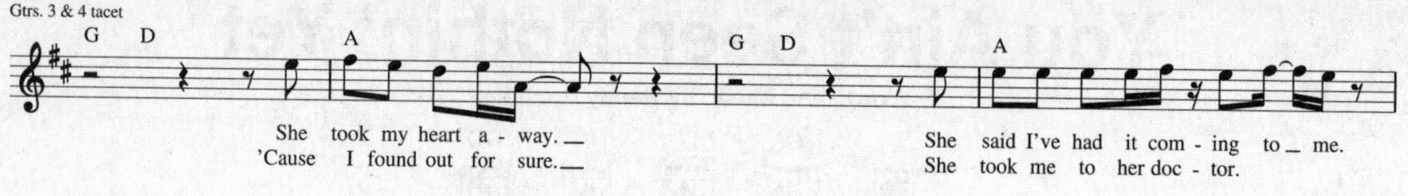
Gtrs. 3 & 4 tacet
G D A G D A
She took my heart a - way.
'Cause I found out for sure.
She said I've had it com - ing to me.
She took me to her doc - tor.

G D A G D
But I want-ed it that way.
And he told me I was cured.
I think that
He said that

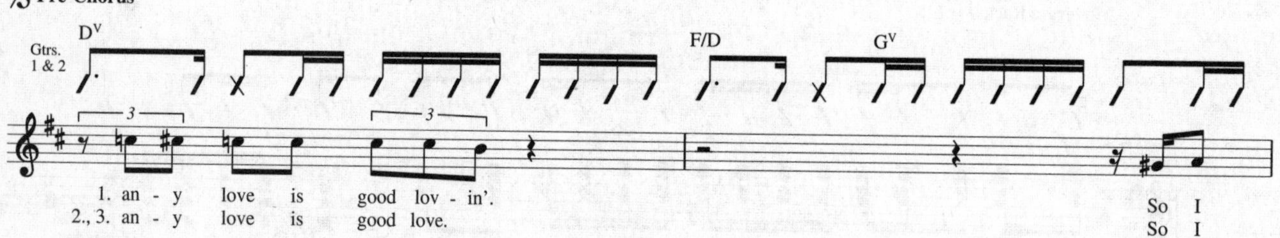
Pre-Chorus
Gtrs. 1 & 2
F/D
1. an - y love is good lov - in'.
2., 3. an - y love is good love.
So I
So I

C#m7 E/F# F#m7 E/F# F#m7
took what I could get.
took what I could get.
Mmm.
Yes I took what I could get.
Ooh.
And then
Ooh.
she

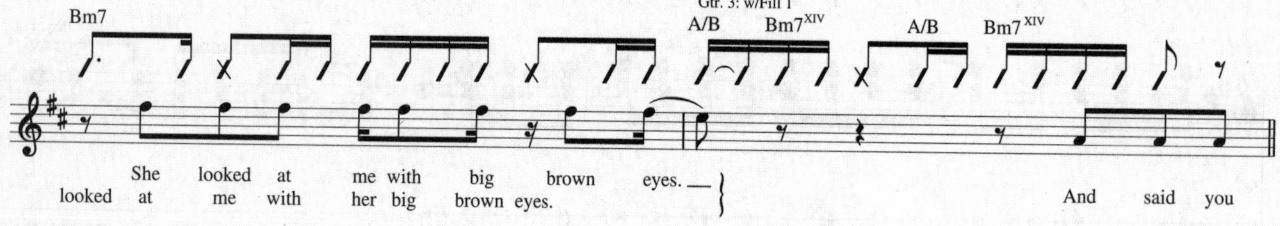
Bm7
Gtr. 3: w/Fill 1
A/B A/B
She looked at me with big brown eyes.
looked at me with her big brown eyes.
And said you

Chorus
Gtrs. 1 & 2 tacet
A5
Rhy. Fig. 2
Gtrs. 3 & 4
E5 D5
End Rhy. Fig. 2
f
ain't seen noth - ing yet.
B - B - B - Ba - by, you just ain't

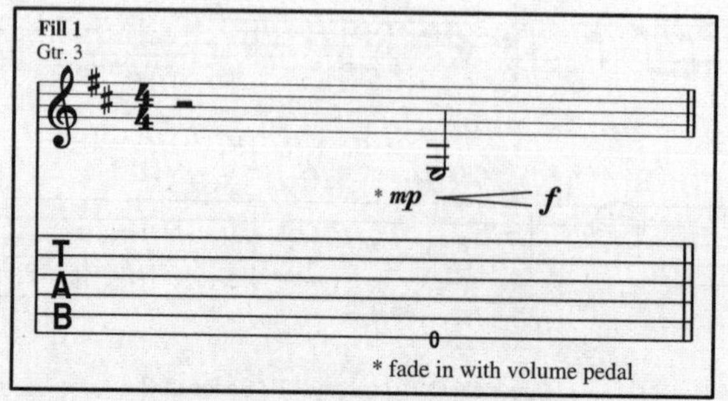
Fill 1
Gtr. 3
* mp f
T
A
B
0
* fade in with volume pedal

Gtrs. 3 & 4: w/Rhy. Fig. 2, 3 times
A5
E5
D5
seen - n - n noth - ing yet.
Here's some - thing that you're
A5
E5
D5
nev - er gon - na for - get.
B - B - B - Ba - by, you just ain't
To Coda
Gtr. 2: w/Rhy. Fill 1
A5
E5
D5
seen - n - n noth - ing yet.
Noth - ing yet, you ain't been a - round.
(2. Spoken: You need educating.)
1.
Interlude
Gtrs. 1 & 2: w/Rhy. Figs. 1 & 1A, 2 times
Gtrs. 3 & 4
A
G D
A
G D
mf
A
G
D
A
G
D
2. And
Rhy. Fill 1
Gtr. 2

2.
Guitar Solo
Gtrs. 1 & 2: w/Rhy. Figs. 1 & 1A, 4 times
A
G
D
Gtrs. 3 & 4
Spoken: Got-ta go to school.
slight vib.
full
8va
D.S. al Coda
Coda
Outro
Gtrs. 3 & 4: w/Rhy. Fig. 2, 8 times
Rhy. Fig. 3
End Rhy. Fig. 3
Gtrs. 1 & 2
E
Ain't seen noth-ing yet.
Spoken: That's what she told me.
She said I need-ed
Gtr. 5
loco
mf

Gtrs. 1 & 2: w/Rhy. Fig. 3, 7 times
A E D A E
ed - u - cat - ing. Go to school. I know I ain't seen noth-ing yet.
D A E D
I know I ain't seen noth-ing yet. Ooh, ooh, ooh.
slight vib.
A E D
Spoken: You got some-thing wait - ing for me when I get home.
slight vib.
A E D A E
It bet - ter be good. I've been eve - ry - where.
slight vib.
8va
D A E D
Fade Out
But I ain't seen noth - ing yet.
8va
slight vib.
slight vib.

You May Be Right

Words and Music by Billy Joel

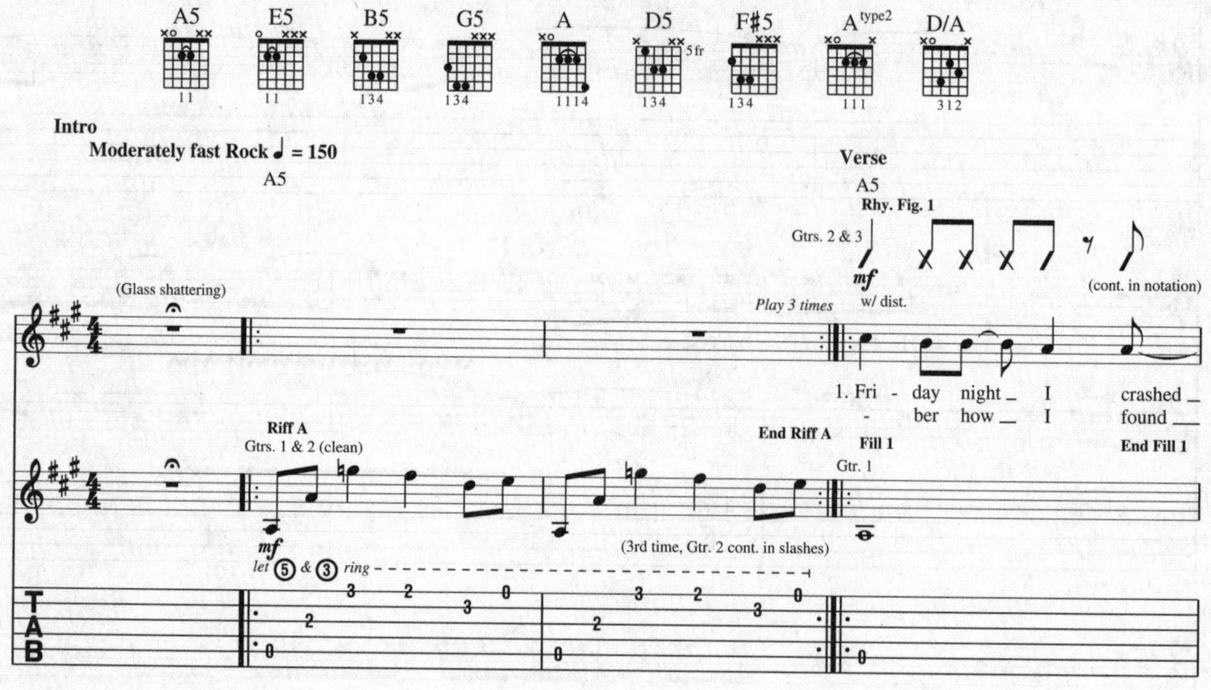

Gtr. 1 tacet

your par - ty, Sat - ur - day I said I'm sor - ry,
you there, a - lone in your e - lec - tric chair. I

Gtrs. 2 & 3

E5 E ⑥ open E5 E ⑥ open E5

Rhy. Fill 1 Gtr. 2 P.M. P.M. End Rhy. Fill 1

Sun - day came and trashed me out a - gain. I was on -
told you dirt - y jokes un - til you smiled. You were lone -

End Rhy. Fig. 1 Gtr. 3

(Gtr. 2 cont. in slashes)

B5
Rhy. Fig. 2
G5
- ly hav - ing fun, was - n't hurt - ing an - y - one,
- ly for a man, I said, "Take me as I am,
Rhy. Fig. 2A
G
3fr
F#
2fr
E
open
E5
E
open
E5
A
open
End Rhy. Fig. 2
P.M.
and we all en - joyed the week - end for a change.
'cause you might en - joy some mad - ness for a while."
End Rhy. Fig. 2A
let ring
Gtr. 1: w/ Riff A
A5
E
2fr
C#
4fr
E
2fr
Gtr. 1: w/ Fill 1
Gtr. 2: w/ Rhy. Fig. 1
A5
Asus4
I was strand - ed in the com - bat zone, I
Now, think of all the years you tried to find

Gtr. 3: w/ Rhy. Fig. 1 (last 4 meas.)
A5
walked through Bed - ford Stuy ___ a - lone, _ e - ven rode ___ my mo - tor - cy - cle in the rain. _
some - one ___ to sat - is - fy ___ you. I might be ___ as cra - zy as ___ you say. _

Gtr. 2: w/ Rhy. Fill 1
2nd time, Gtr. 3: w/ Fill 2
E5
Gtrs. 2 & 3: w/ Rhy. Figs. 2 & 2A
B5
And you told ___ me not ___ to drive ___ but I made _
If I'm cra - zy then _ it's true ___ that it's all ___
Gtr. 3
hold bend
1
11 12 12 11 (11) 9 4 4 2 0

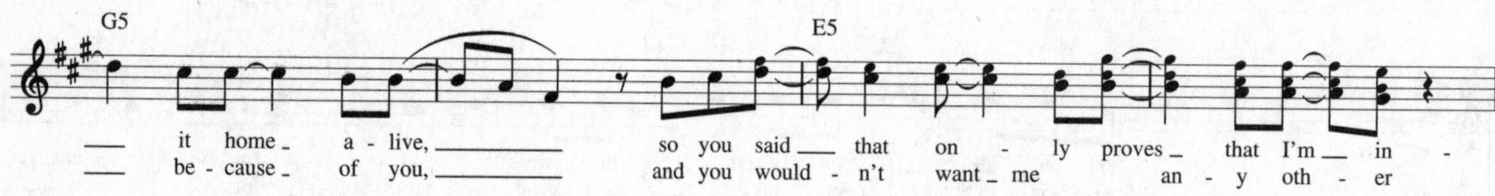
G5
E5
___ it home _ a - live, ___ so you said ___ that on - ly proves _ that I'm ___ in -
___ be - cause _ of you, ___ and you would - n't want _ me an - y oth - er

Chorus
3rd time, Gtr. 6 tacet
A5
A
E5
Gtr. 2
sane. ___
way. ___
You may _ be right, ___ I may _ be cra -
Gtr. 3
* Gtrs. 3 & 4
* Composite arrangement; Gtr. 4 (dist.) mf

Fill 2
Gtr. 3

A5
A
E5
D5
- zy.
1., 2. Oh!
3.Hey!
But it just may be a lu - na - tic you're
1/2
F#5
E
F#
A
6
6
5
open
2fr
open
A5
E5
look-ing for.
Turn out the light,
It's too late to fight,
Turn out the light,
don't try to save
it's too late to change
oh, don't try to save
* 2nd & 3rd times, this chord is omitted.
To Coda
A5
A
Rhy. Fig. 3
D5
1.
E5
End Rhy. Fig. 3
me.
me.
me.
You may be wrong for all I know, but you may be right.
Rhy. Fig. 3A
End Rhy. Fig. 3A
1/2

Interlude
Gtrs. 1 & 2: w/ Riff A (2 times)
Gtr. 4 tacet
A5
2.
E5
Well...
2. Re - mem - but you may be right..
Gtr. 3
Gtrs. 1 & 2: w/ Riff A
Gtr. 4 tacet
A5
Gtr. 3 tacet
Guitar Solo
Gtr. 1: w/ Fill 1
A type2
D/A
Gtr. 2
Gtr. 5 (dist.)
hold bend
A
E5
* Gtr. 6
Gtr. 5
divisi
* Sax arr. for gtr.
** Gtr. 6 to left of slash in tab.

Sax Solo
Gtr. 2: w/ Rhy. Fig. 2
Gtr. 5 tacet
Bm
G6
G5
Gtr. 6
Gtr. 3
D.S. al Coda
E
A type2
Gtr. 2
But you may be right,
hold bend
Coda
Gtrs. 2, 3 & 4: w/ Rhy. Figs. 3 & 3A
D5
E5
But you may be wrong for all I know, you may be right.
Outro
3rd time, w/ voc. ad lib (till end)
Gtrs. 1 & 2: w/ Riff A
Repeat and fade
Gtrs. 1 & 2: w/ Riff A
A5
A5
You may be wrong but you may be right.

You Really Got Me

Words and Music by Ray Davies

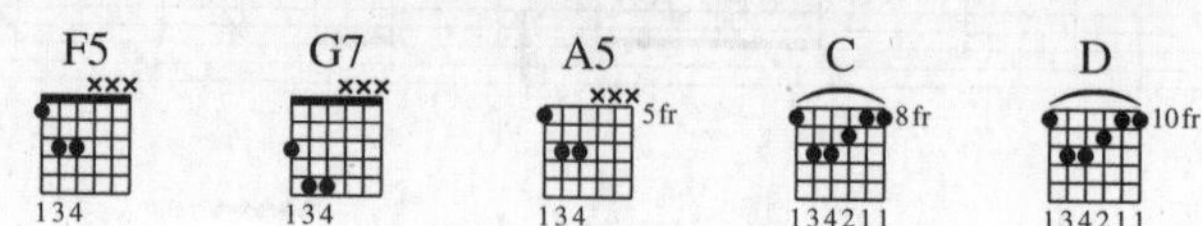

𝄋 Verse

Gtr. 2: w/ Rhy. Fig. 1, 3 1/2 times

G5 F5 G5 F5 G5 F5 G5 F5 G5 F5 G5 F5

1\. Girl, you real - ly got me go - in', you got me so I don't know what I'm do - in' __

2., 3. See, don't ev - er set me free, I al - ways wan - na be by your side. __

G5 F5 G5 F5 G5 F5 G5 F5 G5 F5 G5 F5

now. Yeah, __ you real - ly got me now, you got me

Girl, __ you real - ly got me now, you got me

Gtr. 1: w/ Rhy. Fill 1, 2nd time
Gtr. 1: w/ Rhy. Fill 3, 3rd time
G5 F5 G5 F5 G5 F5 G5 A5 G5 A5 G5
Gtr. 2
so I can't sleep at night.
so I can't sleep at night.
Yeah, you real - ly
(Yeah,
Gtr. 1: w/ Rhy. Fill 2, 2nd time
A5 G5 A5 G5 A5 G5 A5 G5 A5 G5 A5 C
got me now, you got me so I don't know what I'm do - in', ah. Oh
Rhy. Fill 1
Gtr. 1
Rhy. Fill 3
Gtr. 1
Rhy. Fill 2
Gtr. 1

D C D C D C D C D C D C
yeah, you real - ly got me now, you got me so I can't sleep at night. You
Yeah.)
To Coda
D C D C D C D C D C D
real - ly got me. You real - ly got me. You real - ly got me.
1.
C
2.
C
Oh, Lord.
full full full full full full 1/2
Guitar Solo
Gtr. 2: w/ Rhy. Fig. 1, 5 times
G5 F5 G5 F5 G5 F5 G5 F5 G5 F5 G5 F5
full full full full

G5
F5
G5
F5
G5
F5
G5
F5
full
1/2
1/2

G5
F5
G5
F5
G5
F5
G5
F5
let ring
1/2
1/2
1/2
1/2
1/2

D.S. al Coda
G5
F5
G5
F5
G5
F5
G5
F5
G5
F5
G5
F5
1/2
1/4

Coda
D
C
D
real - ly got me.

You're Only Lonely

Words and Music by John David Souther

A
F#m11
F#m
D
E
Gtr. 1
- ly.
Gtr. 2 (elec.)
mf
w/ clean tone
let ring
let ring

Verse

Gtr. 2 tacet
Gtr. 1: w/ Rhy. Fig. 1
A
F#m
2. When you need some - bod - y a - round on the nights that try you, re - mem - ber
Gtr. 2
let ring

D
Dmaj7
D6
Dmaj7
D
Dmaj7
I was there when you were a queen, and I'll be the

D6
Dmaj7
A
F#m
D
last one there be - side you.
So you can call out my name
Gtr. 2
let ring

Bkgd. Voc.: w/ Voc. Fig. 1
E
A
F#m
when you're on - ly lone - ly.
Now don't you ev - er be a -

Chorus
D
E7
A
Rhy. Fig. 2
Gtr. 1
Voc. Fig. 2
shamed;
you're on - ly lone - ly.
(You're on - ly lone - ly,
Gtr. 2
let ring

F#m
D
you're on - ly lone - ly,
you're on - ly lone - ly,
let ring
let ring

*When Voc. Fig. 2 is recalled, tie from E is omitted and slurs end in this meas.

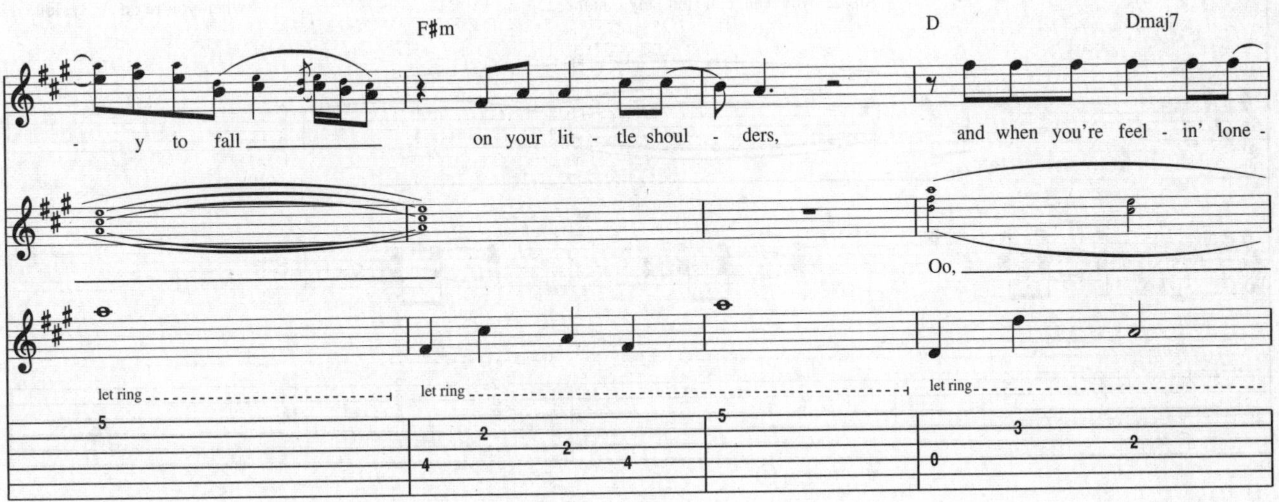

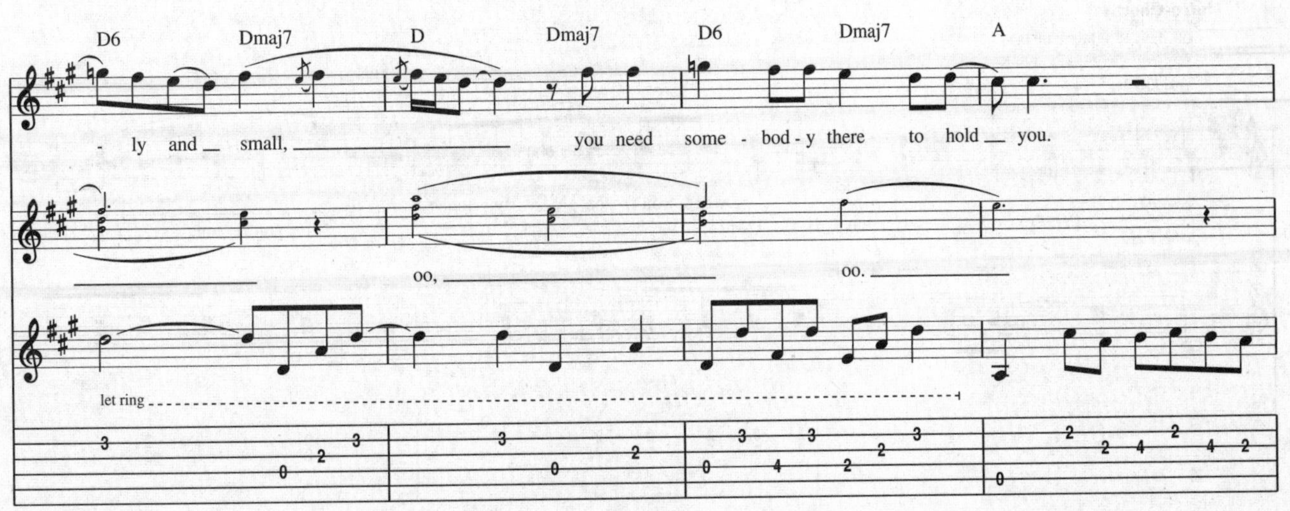

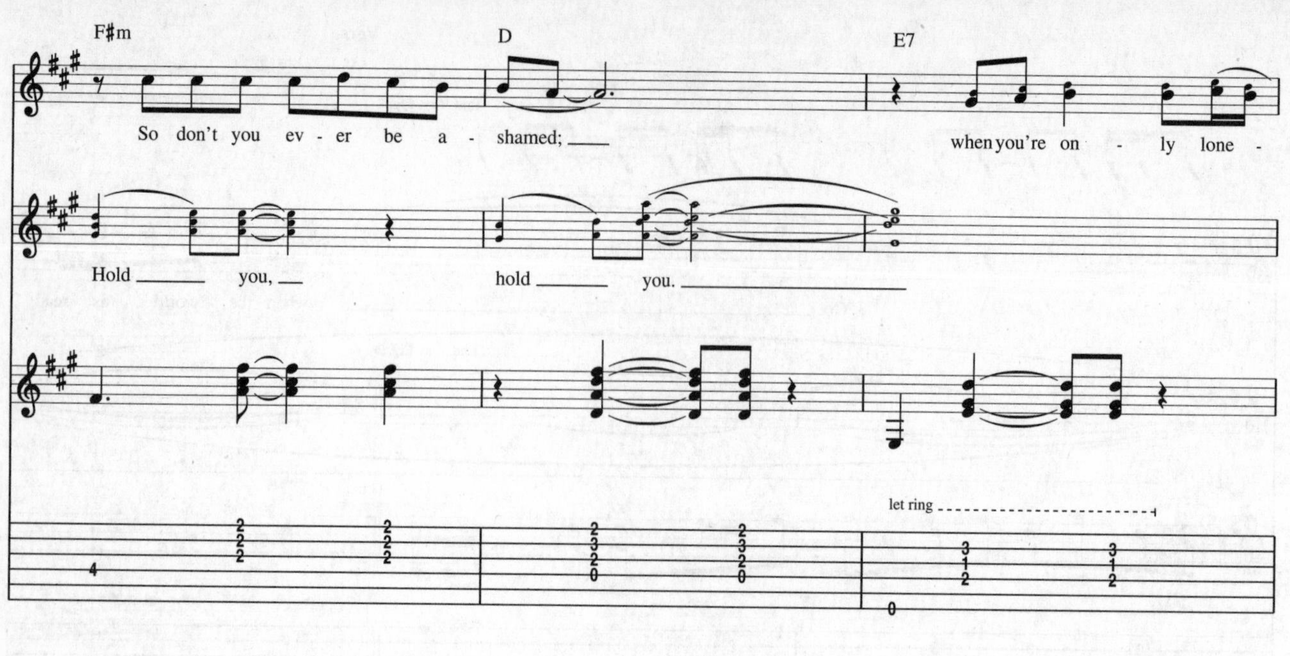

Outro-Chorus

Gtr. 1: w/ Rhy. Fig. 2, till fade

D
Oo, it's no crime,
- ly,
oo,
dar - lin', we've got lots of
oo.
E7
End Voc. Fig. 3
Bkgd. Voc.: w/ Voc. Fig. 3
A
time.
Whoa oh, whoa,
whoa oh, whoa, whoa
Rhy. Fig. 3
let ring
F♯m
oh, whoa.
D
No, there's noth - in' wrong with you,
let ring
E7
dar - lin', I get lone - ly too.
End Rhy. Fig. 3
let ring

Bkgd. Voc.: w/ Voc. Fig. 2, 2 times
Gtr. 2: w/ Rhy. Fig. 3, simile
A
F#m
So if you

D
E7
need me, all you've got-ta do is call me. Yeah, you're on-ly
Gtr. 2
let ring
let ring

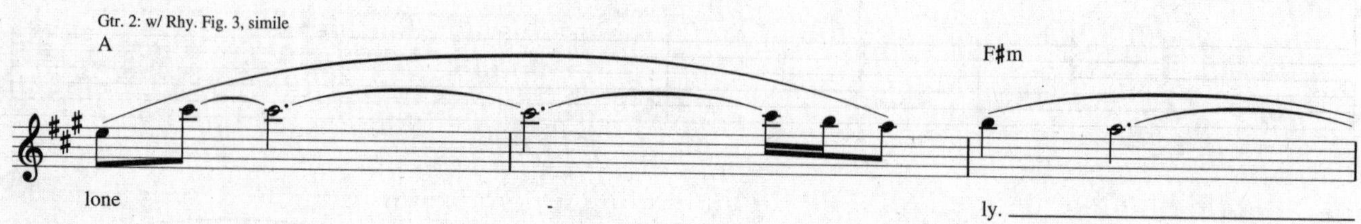
Gtr. 2: w/ Rhy. Fig. 3, simile
A
F#m
lone - ly.

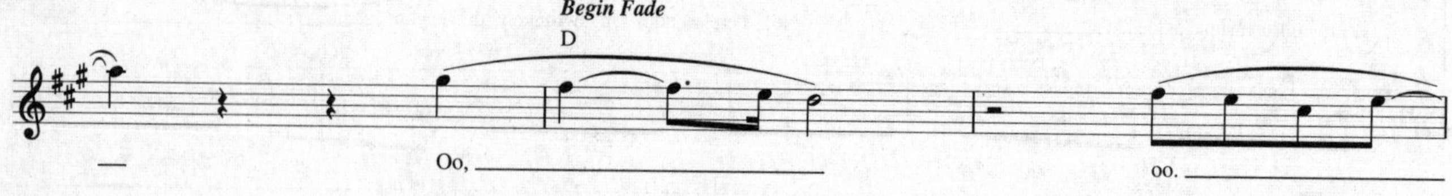
Begin Fade
D
Oo, oo.

Fade Out
E7
A
Oh, my, my, my, my, my, my.
Gtr. 2
let ring
let ring

You've Got Another Thing Comin'

Words and Music by Glenn Tipton, Rob Halford and K.K. Downing

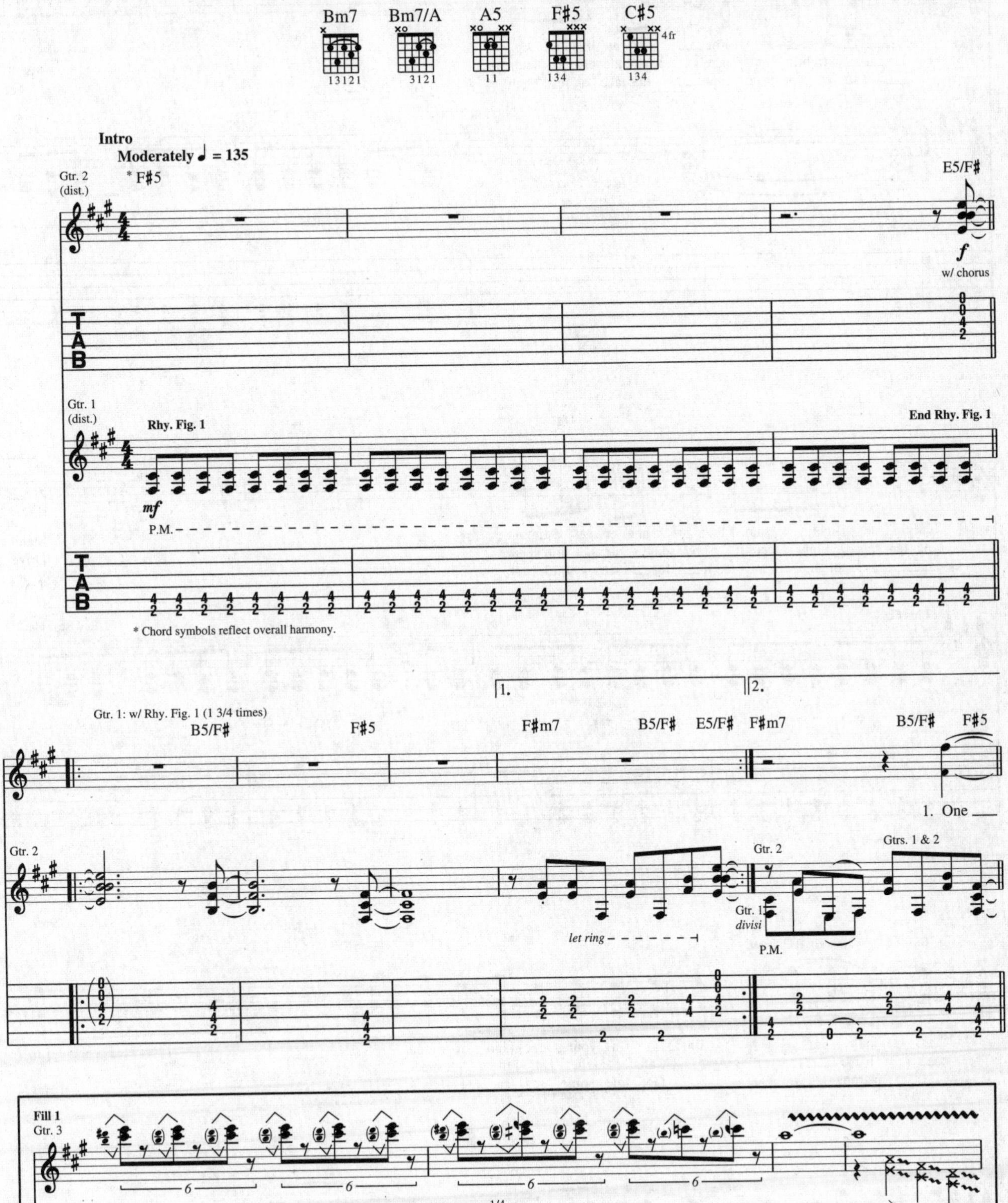

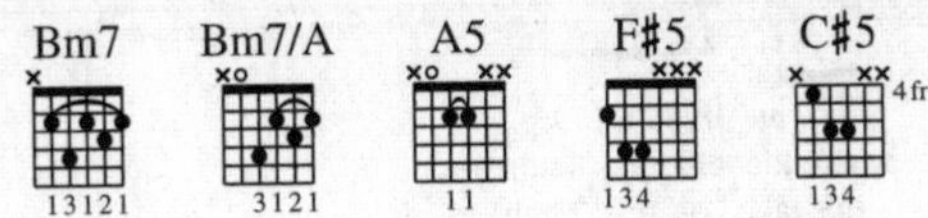

Intro

Moderately ♩ = 135

Gtr. 2 (dist.)

* F#5

E5/F#

f

w/ chorus

Gtr. 1 (dist.)

Rhy. Fig. 1

End Rhy. Fig. 1

mf

P.M.

* Chord symbols reflect overall harmony.

Gtr. 1: w/ Rhy. Fig. 1 (1 3/4 times)

B5/F# F#5 F#m7 B5/F# E5/F# F#m7 B5/F# F#5

1. 2.

1. One ___

Gtr. 2

Gtrs. 1 & 2

let ring

Gtr. 1 *divisi*

P.M.

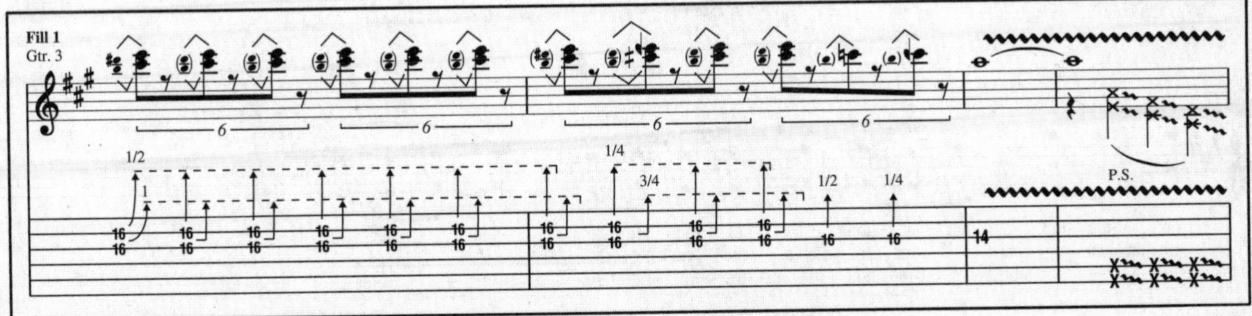

Verse
3rd time, Gtr. 3: w/ Fill 1
F#5
life, I'm gon-na live it up. I'm
right here's where the talk-ing ends. Well
so hot no time to take a rest, yeah. Act
P.M.
let ring
tak-in' flight, I said I'll nev-er get e-nough. Stand
lis-ten, this a night there'll be some ac-tion spent. Drive
tough, ain't room for sec-ond best. Real
Rhy. Fig. 2
End Rhy. Fig. 2
P.M.
P.M.
let ring
Gtrs. 1 & 2: w/ Rhy. Fig. 2 (2 times)
tall. I'm a young and kind of proud. I'm
hard. Call-in' all the shots. I
strong. Got me some se-cur-i-ty. Hey,
on the top, but as long as the mu-sic's loud.
got an ace card com-in' down the rocks.
I'm a big smash, I'm go-in' for in-fin-i-ty, yeah.

Pre-Chorus
F#5
D5
B5
F#5
1.,3. If you think I'll sit a - round as the world goes by, you're think - in' like a fool 'cause it's a case
2. If you think I'll sit a - round while you chip a - way my brain lis - ten I ain't fool - in' and you'd bet -
Rhy. Fig. 3
D5
B5
of do or die.
ter think a - gain.
Out there is a for - tune wait - ing to be had. If you
C#5
think I'll let it go you're mad. You've got a - no - ther thing com - in'.
1.
Chorus
F#m7
F#5
End Rhy. Fig. 3
P.M.
F#m7
B5/F#
F#m7
F#5
F#m7
B5/F#
F#5
You've got an - oth - er thing com - in'.
2. That's
P.M.
let ring

2.
F#m7
F#5
B5/F#
com - in'.
You've got an - oth - er thing com - in'.
Rhy. Fig. 4
End Rhy. Fig. 4
P.M.
Gtrs. 1 & 2: w/ Rhy. Fig. 4
To Coda
You've got an - oth - er thing com - in'.
Bridge
Bm7
Bm7/A
A5
Gtrs. 1 & 2
w/ clean tone
In this world we're liv - in' in we have our share of sor - row. An -
Gtr. 3 (dist.)
mf
C#5
- swer now is don't give in. Aim for a new to - mor - row.
fdbk.

Guitar Solo

Gtrs. 1 & 2: w/ Rhy. Fig. 4, 1st 2 meas. (4 times)
F#m7
F#5
B5/F#
8va
loco
Gtrs. 1 & 2: w/ Rhy. Fig. 3
D5
B5
C#5

D.S. al Coda
(take 2nd ending)
F#m7
B5/F#
F#5
3. Oh,
Gtr. 3
Gtrs. 1 & 2
Coda
Interlude
Gtr. 1: w/ Rhy. Fig. 4 (2 times)
F#m7
B5/F#
F#m7
F#5
F#m7
B5/F#
F#m7
F#5
You've got an - oth - er thing
ah.
F#m7
B5/F#
F#m7
F#5
F#m7
B5/F#
F#m7
F#5
F#m7
B5/F#
Com - in' on down!
Play 10 times and fade
Outro
w/ Voc. ad lib (till fade)
Gtr. 1: w/ Rhy. Fig. 4 (till fade)
E5/F#
B5/F#
F#5
You've got an - oth - er thing com - in'.

Your Disease

Words and Music by Josey Scott, Chris Dabaldo, Wayne Swinney, Dave Novotny and Paul Crosby

Verse
D5 F5 D5 F5 G5 Ab5 G5 Ab5 D5 F5 D5 F5 G5 Ab5 G5 Ab5
mo - ment I'm go - in' all the way. I make my po - et - ry ev - er - y - day. And I'm
bro - ken I'm go - in' up in smoke. If you breathe my toke I'm guar - an - tee - ing you choke. And I'm
Rhy. Fig. 1
End Rhy. Fig. 1
Gtr. 2: w/ Rhy. Fig. 1 (3 times)
D5 F5 D5 F5 G5 Ab5 G5 Ab5 D5 F5 D5 F5 G5 Ab5 G5 Ab5
fro - zen, com - in' right on time. I froze my mind with that ser - i - ous rhyme. And I'm
cho - sen to tes - ti - fy the mass - es, wear dark glass - es like the cops in Tex - as. All
D5 F5 D5 F5 G5 Ab5 G5 Ab5 D5 F5 D5 F5 G5 Ab5 G5 Ab5
o - pen, com - in' up in - side you know my mind has got a grand de - sign. And I'm
know - ing, it's not a pre - mo - ni - tion. Kill the com - pe - ti - tion like a man on a mis - sion. I'm
D5 F5 D5 F5 G5 Ab5 G5 Ab5 D5 F5 D5 F5 G5 Ab5 G5 Ab5
flow - in', go - in' all the way, I make my point to be ev - er - y - day, come on.
blow - in', com - in' up in - side. Like the Bee Gees cry, I'm just stay - in' a - live, come on.
Chorus
3rd time, w/ Voc. Fill 1
Dsus2 C
Rhy. Fig. 2A
Gtr. 3 (acous.)
mf
And I wan - na take you down, but your soul can - not be found.
Gtr. 2
Rhy. Fig. 2
Voc. Fill 1

Bb
C
End Rhy. Fig. 2A
It does-n't mat-ter much - you see, 'cause your dis-ease is kill-ing me.
End Rhy. Fig. 2
Gtrs. 2 & 3: w/ Rhy. Figs. 2 & 2A
Dsus2
C
And you know it's on - ly right, 'cause it feels like par - a - dise.
To Coda
Bb
C
I know noth-ing is for free, 'cause your dis-ease is kill-ing me.
1.
Gtr. 1: w/ Riff A
D5
Gtr. 3
2.
D5
Gtr. 3
2. My mind's
Gtr. 1
Gtr. 2

1/2
1/2
1/2
1/2
let ring
fdbk.
Bridge
G5
Rhy. Fig. 3
Gtr. 1 tacet
A
End Rhy. Fig. 3
So now I'm fin - 'ly go - in' down,
can I find my way back home?
Riff B
Gtr. 3: w/ Rhy. Fig. 3 (5 times)
G5
A
Now there's no one else a - round,
can I find my way back home?
Gtr. 2
End Riff B

Gtr. 2: w/ Riff B (2 times)
G5
A
Will I ev - er see __ the light __ e - ven though _ I'm fall -
G5
A
- in'? __
(Will there ev - er be __ an - y peace __ for me, __ an - y peace _ for me? __
E - ven though _ I'm fall -
G5
A
- ing. __
Will there ev - er be __ an - y peace __ for me, __ an - y peace _ for me? __
E - ven though _ I'm fall -
G5
A
D.S. al Coda
- ing. __
Will there ev - er be __ an - y peace __ for me, __ an - y peace _ for me?) __
Coda
Double time feel
Bkgd. Voc.: w/ Voc. Fig. 1 (2 times)
Gtrs. 2 & 3: w/ Rhy. Figs. 2 & 2A (2 times)
Dsus2
C
And I wan - na take __ you down, __ but your soul can - not __ be found. __
B♭
C
Dsus2
It does-n't mat-ter much _ you see, __ 'cause your dis - ease is kill-ing me. __ And you know it's on - ly right, __
C
B♭
C
rit.
'cause it feels like par - a - dise. __ I know noth-ing is __ for free, __ 'cause your dis-ease is kill-ing me. __
Free time
Dsus2
Gtr. 3
Gtr. 2
Voc. Fig. 1
(Yeah.
Yeah.) __

Your Mama Don't Dance

Words and Music by Jim Messina and Kenny Loggins

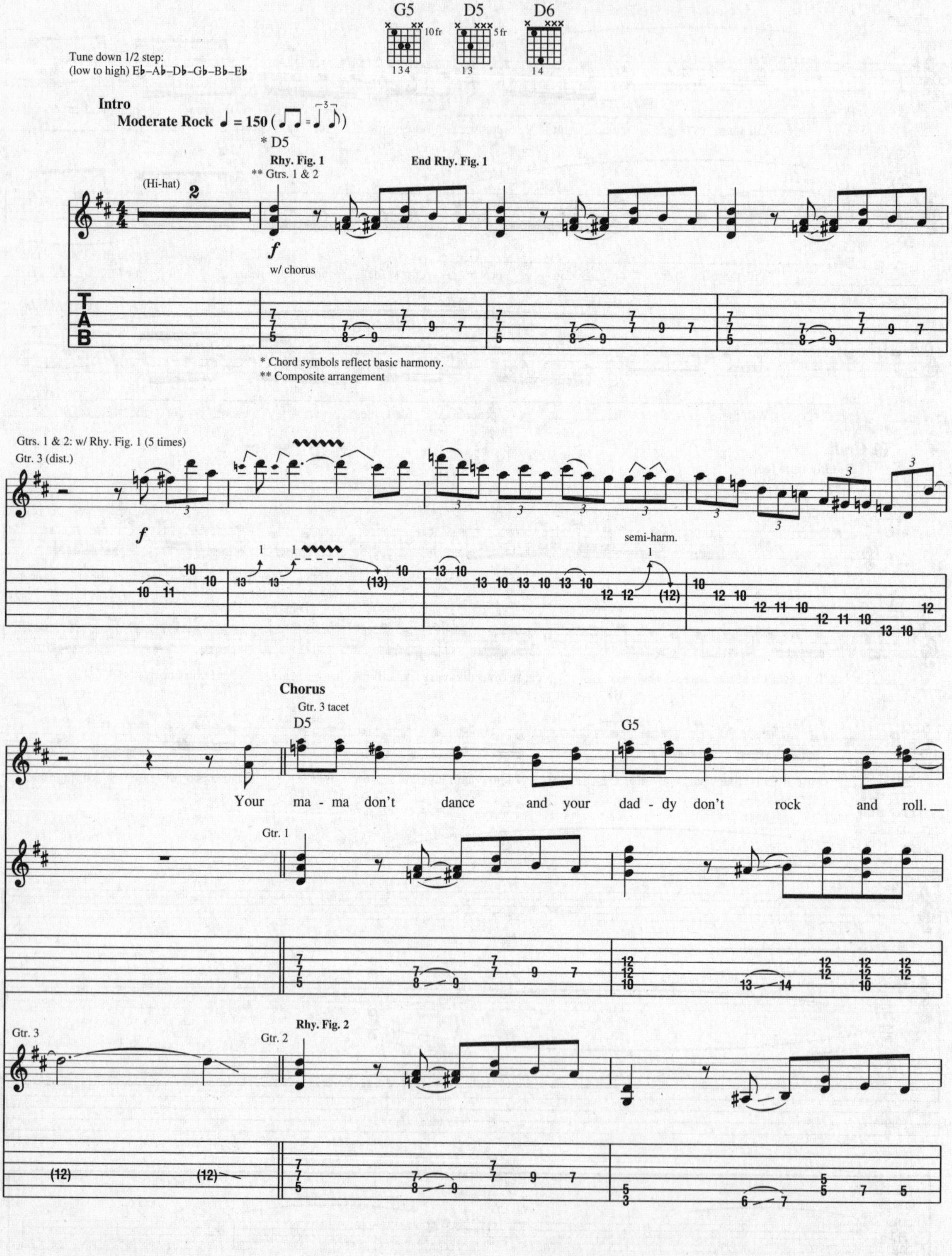

G5 D5 D6

10fr 5fr

134 13 14

Tune down 1/2 step:
(low to high) E♭–A♭–D♭–G♭–B♭–E♭

Intro

Moderate Rock ♩ = 150

* D5

Rhy. Fig. 1 **End Rhy. Fig. 1**

** Gtrs. 1 & 2

(Hi-hat)

f

w/ chorus

* Chord symbols reflect basic harmony.

** Composite arrangement

Gtrs. 1 & 2: w/ Rhy. Fig. 1 (5 times)

Gtr. 3 (dist.)

f

semi-harm.

D5
G5
Your ma - ma don't dance and your
dad - dy don't rock and roll.
D5
But when eve -
A5
G5
D5
- nin' rolls a - round and it's time to hit the town, where do you go?
You got - ta

Verse
Gtr. 2: w/ Rhy. Fig. 2
D5
G5
rock it!
The old folks say that you got-ta end your day by ten.
Gtr. 3
Gtrs. 1 & 2
End Rhy. Fig. 2
Gtr. 1
D5
G5
Mm, hm.
But if you're out on a date don't you
bring her home late 'cause it's a sin.
D5
You know

Gtr. 3 tacet
A5
G5
D5
there's no ex - cuse, you know you're gon - na lose you nev - er win,
I'll say it a -
Gtrs. 1 & 2
Chorus
D5
G5
gain.
(And it's all be - cause...)
Your ma - ma don't dance and your dad - dy don't rock and roll,
2nd time, Gtrs. 1, 2 & 3: w/ Fill 1
D5
G5
Your ma - ma don't dance and your
Gtr. 3
Gtrs. 1 & 2
Fill 1
D5
D6
D5
D6
D5
D6
D5
D6
Gtrs. 1 & 2
Gtr. 3

2nd time, Gtrs. 2 & 3: w/ Fill 2
D5
dad - dy don't rock and roll.
When

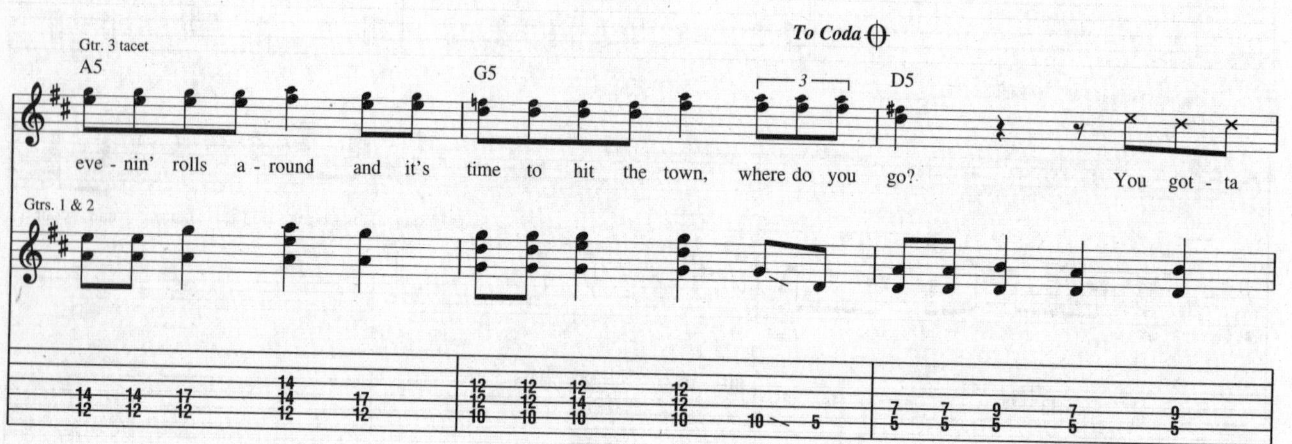
To Coda
Gtr. 3 tacet
A5
G5
D5
eve - nin' rolls a - round and it's time to hit the town, where do you go?
You got - ta
Gtrs. 1 & 2

Fill 2
Gtr. 3
Gtr. 2

Guitar Solo
D5
G5
Rock it!
Rock it!
Gtr. 3
Gtrs. 1 & 2
Rhy. Fig. 3
hold bend
8va
loco

A5
G5
D5
D5
Bridge
Gtr. 3 tacet
F#5
G5
F#5
Spoken: Yeah, I pull into a drive-in and I
End Rhy. Fig. 3
Rhy. Fig. 4
End Rhy. Fig. 4
Gtrs. 1 & 2: w/ Rhy. Fig. 4 (6 times)
G5
F#5
G5
F#5
G5
F#5
G5
F#5
found a place to park, we hopped into the back seat where it's always nice and dark. I'm just about to move thinkin' hmm
Gtr. 3

Outro

Gtr. 3 tacet

D5 G5

Your ma - ma don't dance and your dad - dy don't rock and roll. (Your

Gtr. 3

12 11 10 12 11 12 (12)

Gtrs. 1 & 2

7 5 7 5 9 5 7 5 7 5 7 5 9 5 7 5 7 7 5 5 5 3

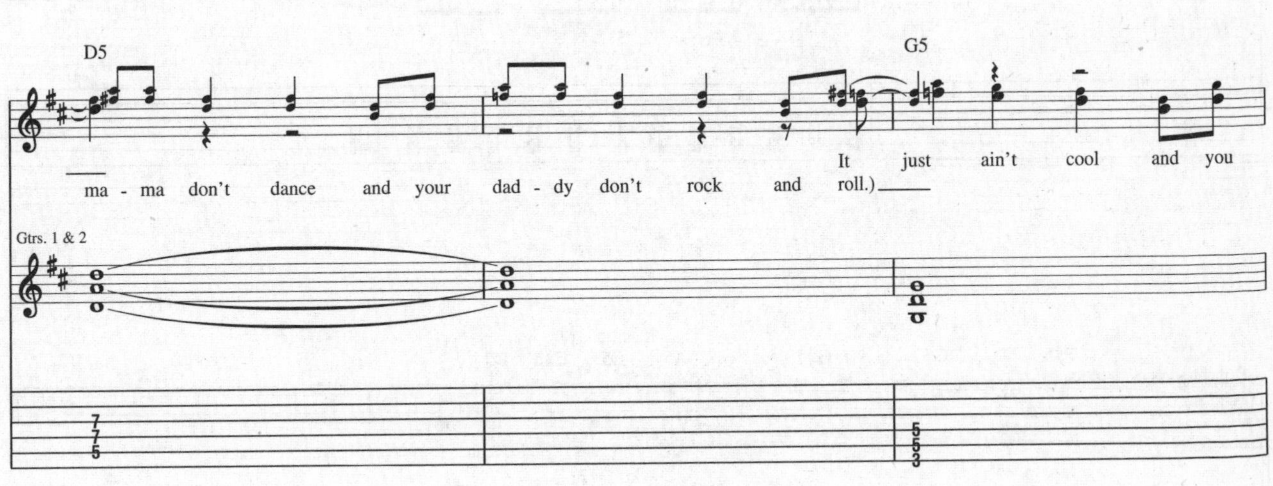

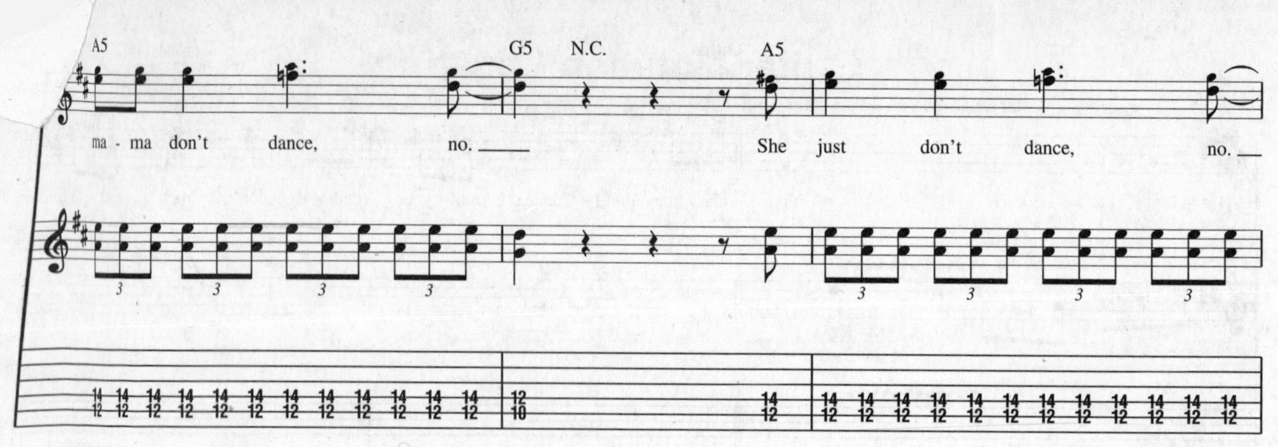
A5
G5
N.C.
A5
ma - ma don't
dance,
no.
She
just
don't
dance,
no.

G5
N.C.
A5
G5
N.C.
Your
ma - ma
don't
dance
and
your
dad - dy
don't
rock
and
roll.

D5
F#5
G5
G#5
A5
C5
C#5
D5
Ah,
yeah.
Gtr. 3
Gtrs. 1 & 2

Guitar Notation Legend

Guitar Music can be notated three different ways: on a *musical staff*, in *tablature*, and in *rhythm slashes.*

RHYTHM SLASHES are written above the staff. Strum chords in the rhythm indicated. Use the chord diagrams found at the top of the first page of the transcription for the appropriate chord voicings. Round noteheads indicate single notes.

THE MUSICAL STAFF shows pitches and rhythms and is divided by bar lines into measures. Pitches are named after the first seven letters of the alphabet.

TABLATURE graphically represents the guitar fingerboard. Each horizontal line represents a a string, and each number represents a fret.

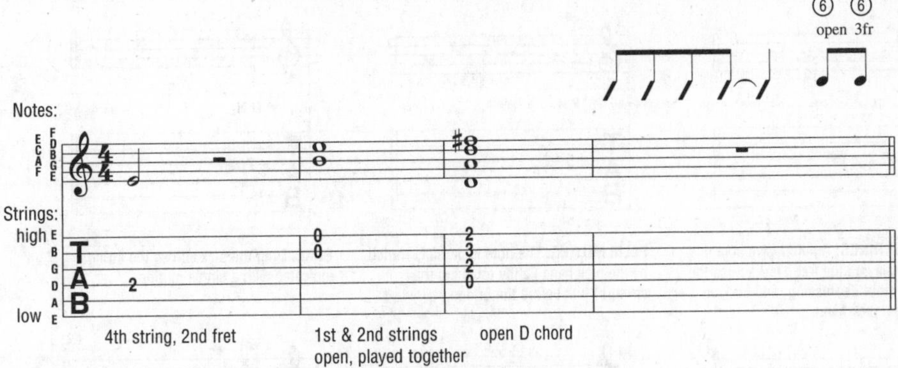

Definitions for Special Guitar Notation

HALF-STEP BEND: Strike the note and bend up 1/2 step.

WHOLE-STEP BEND: Strike the note and bend up one step.

GRACE NOTE BEND: Strike the note and immediately bend up as indicated.

SLIGHT (MICROTONE) BEND: Strike the note and bend up 1/4 step.

BEND AND RELEASE: Strike the note and bend up as indicated, then release back to the original note. Only the first note is struck.

PRE-BEND: Bend the note as indicated, then strike it.

PRE-BEND AND RELEASE: Bend the note as indicated. Strike it and release the bend back to the original note.

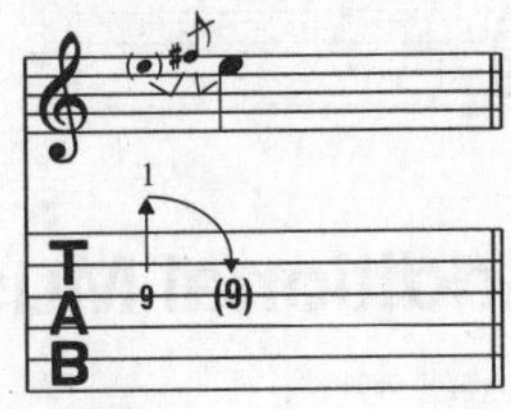

UNISON BEND: Strike the two notes simultaneously and bend the lower note up to the pitch of the higher.

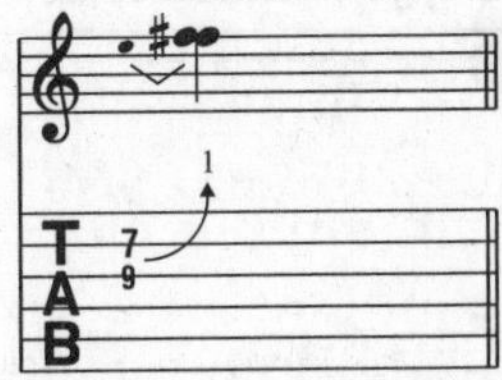

VIBRATO: The string is vibrated by rapidly bending and releasing the note with the fretting hand.

WIDE VIBRATO: The pitch is varied to a greater degree by vibrating with the fretting hand.

HAMMER-ON: Strike the first (lower) note with one finger, then sound the higher note (on the same string) with another finger by fretting it without picking.

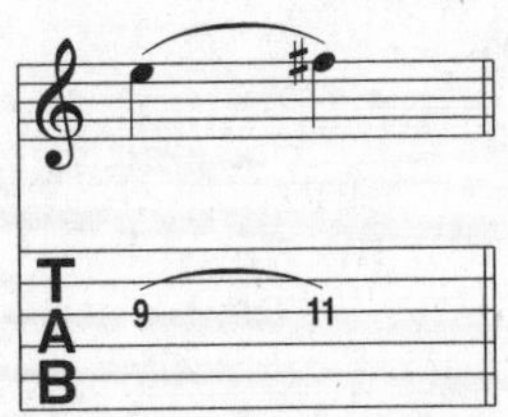

PULL-OFF: Place both fingers on the notes to be sounded. Strike the first note and without picking, pull the finger off to sound the second (lower) note.

LEGATO SLIDE: Strike the first note and then slide the same fret-hand finger up or down to the second note. The second note is not struck.

SHIFT SLIDE: Same as legato slide, except the second note is struck.

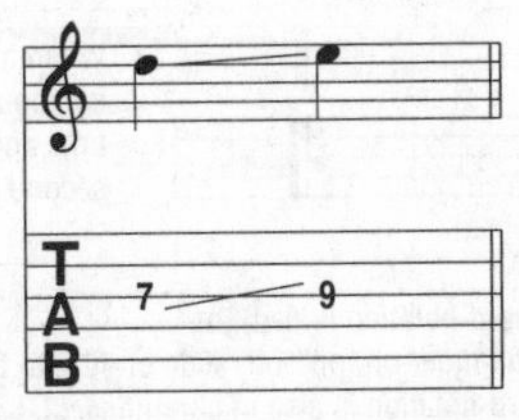

TRILL: Very rapidly alternate between the notes indicated by continuously hammering on and pulling off.

TAPPING: Hammer ("tap") the fret indicated with the pick-hand index or middle finger and pull off to the note fretted by the fret hand.

HARMONIC: Strike the note while ...and lightly touches the string ...ver the fret indicated.

PINCH HARMONIC: The note is fretted normally and a harmonic is produced by adding the edge of the thumb or the tip of the index finger of the pick hand to the normal pick attack.

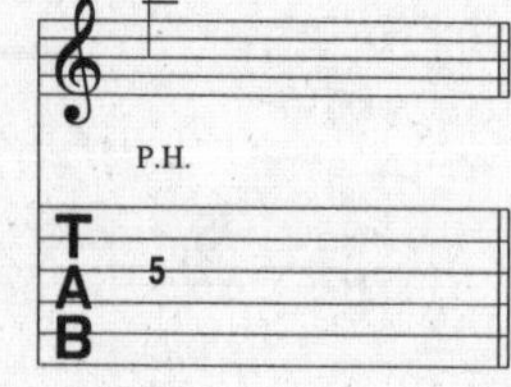

HARP HARMONIC: The note is fretted normally and a harmonic is produced by gently resting the pick hand's index finger directly above the indicated fret (in parentheses) while the pick hand's thumb or pick assists by plucking the appropriate string.

8va

H.H.

7(19)

PICK SCRAPE: The edge of the pick is rubbed down (or up) the string, producing a scratchy sound.

MUFFLED STRINGS: A percussive sound is produced by laying the fret hand across the string(s) without depressing, and striking them with the pick hand.

PALM MUTING: The note is partially muted by the pick hand lightly touching the string(s) just before the bridge.

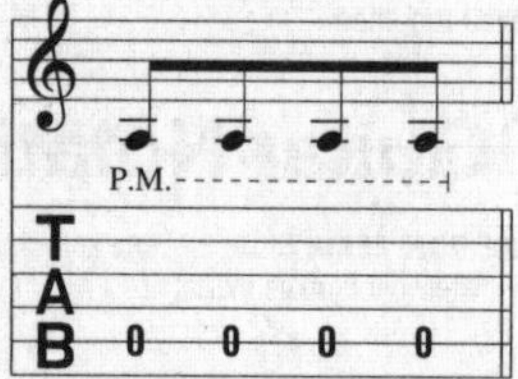

RAKE: Drag the pick across the strings indicated with a single motion.

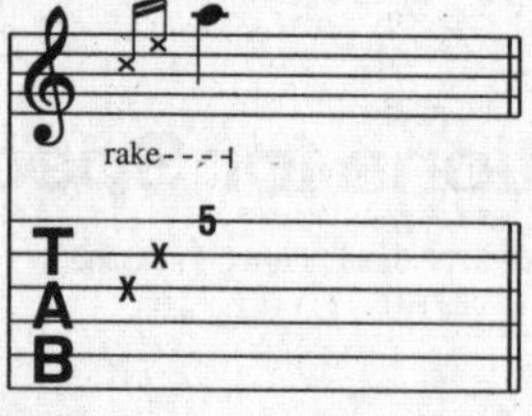

TREMOLO PICKING: The note is picked as rapidly and continuously as possible.

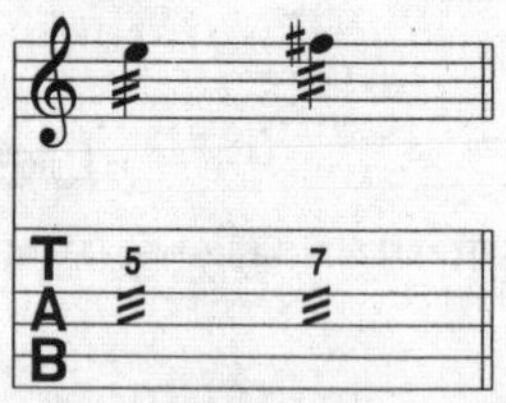

ARPEGGIATE: Play the notes of the chord indicated by quickly rolling them from bottom to top.

VIBRATO BAR DIVE AND RETURN: The pitch of the note or chord is dropped a specified number of steps (in rhythm) then returned to the original pitch.

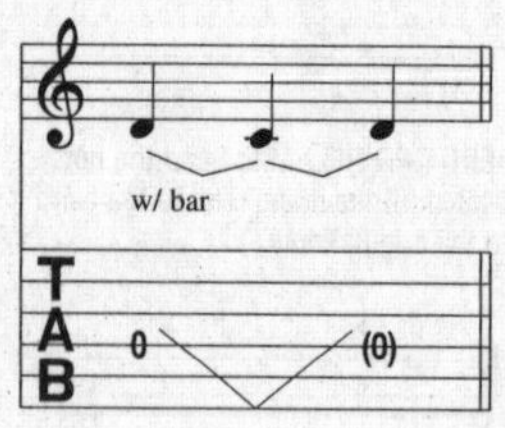

VIBRATO BAR SCOOP: Depress the bar just before striking the note, then quickly release the bar.

VIBRATO BAR DIP: Strike the note and then immediately drop a specified number of steps, then release back to the original pitch.

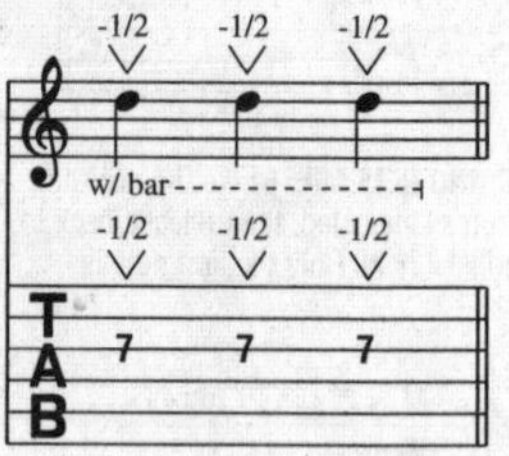

Additional Musical Definitions

(accent) • Accentuate note (play it louder)

(accent) • Accentuate note with great intensity

(staccato) • Play the note short

• Downstroke

V • Upstroke

D.S. al Coda • Go back to the sign (𝄋), then play until the measure marked "***To Coda***," then skip to the section labelled "**Coda**."

D.C. al Fine • Go back to the beginning of the song and play until the measure marked "***Fine***" (end).

Rhy. Fig. • Label used to recall a recurring accompaniment pattern (usually chordal).

Riff • Label used to recall composed, melodic lines (usually single notes) which recur.

Fill • Label used to identify a brief melodic figure which is to be inserted into the arrangement.

Rhy. Fill • A chordal version of a Fill.

tacet • Instrument is silent (drops out).

• Repeat measures between signs.

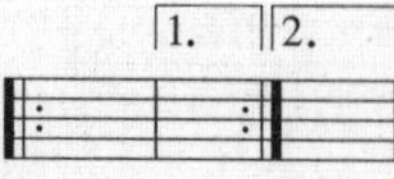

• When a repeated section has different endings, play the first ending only the first time and the second ending only the second time.

NOTE: Tablature numbers in parentheses mean:
1. The note is being sustained over a system (note in standard notation is tied), or
2. The note is sustained, but a new articulation (such as a hammer-on, pull-off, slide or vibrato begins), or
3. The note is a barely audible "ghost" note (note in standard notation is also in parentheses).